8X10

P9-DGZ-405

DISCARDED

Bastianich, Joseph.

Vino italiano.

$35.00

DATE			

BAKER & TAYLOR

Vino Italiano

The Regional Wines of Italy

Vino Italiano

THE REGIONAL WINES OF ITALY

JOSEPH BASTIANICH and DAVID LYNCH

Foreword by MARIO BATALI
Recipes by MARIO BATALI and LIDIA BASTIANICH
Photographs by ALESSANDRO PUCCINELLI

CLARKSON POTTER/PUBLISHERS
NEW YORK

For Deanna, Olivia, Miles, and Ethan. —J. V. B.

For Josie. —D. R. L.

Text copyright © 2002 by Joseph Bastianich and David Lynch
Photographs copyright © 2002 by Alessandro Puccinelli
Maps by Jeffrey Lindenmuth
Recipes by Mario Batali (pages 69–71, 254, 268, 286, 302, 318, 328, 342, 364, and 382) and Lidia Bastianich (pages 44, 92, 112, 126, 158, 172, 220, and 236) used by permission.

Portions of the chapters on Friuli, Tuscany, and Sicily first appeared in articles by David Lynch for *Wine & Spirits* magazine, and are used here by permission.

Published by Clarkson Potter/Publishers, New York, New York.
Member of the Crown Publishing Group, a division of Random House, Inc.
www.randomhouse.com

CLARKSON N. POTTER is a trademark and POTTER and colophon are registered trademarks of Random House, Inc.

Printed in the United States of America

Design by Memo Productions

Library of Congress Cataloging-in-Publication Data
Bastianich, Joseph
   Vino italiano : the regional wines of Italy/by Joseph Bastianich and David Lynch.—1st ed.
       p.   cm.
   Includes bibliographical references and index.
   1. Wine and wine making—Italy.   I. Lynch, David, 1967–   II. Title.
TP559.I8   B38   2002
641.2'2'0945—dc21 2001036456

ISBN 0-609-60848-7

10 9 8 7 6 5 4

First Edition

CONTENTS

The *Italian* Renaissance

MARIO BATALI

It's a great time to be an Italian restaurateur in America. Say what you want about Nuevo Latino, Pan-Asian, retro-*Brasserie,* or any of the other food trends of recent years: Italian cuisine is still considered the number one ethnic food in America, and is more exciting than ever as people grow more knowledgeable about its regional nuances. Our customers in New York City revel in the subtleties of Italian food—like the difference between San Daniele prosciutto from Friuli and Prosciutto di Parma from Emilia-Romagna, or how pasta prepared *all'amatriciana* compares to pasta *all'arrabbiata.* The term *Italian* continues to take on new and increasingly specific meanings.

This interest in authentic regional flavors has taken time to develop. One of the early pioneers was Lidia Bastianich, the celebrated chef, author, restaurateur, and television host, who tells some great stories about her early days in the business. She would walk through her first restaurant, Buonavia, in Queens, New York, handing out little samples of gnocchi with oxtails or *stinco di vitello* while her guests wanted to stick to their red-sauced pastas. This was in the late sixties, the checkered-tablecloth era. Change came slowly. These days, I enjoy a lot more creative freedom on the menus at Babbo, Lupa, and Esca, all of which I co-own with Lidia's son, Joe—one of the authors of this

book. But I'm not so sure I could have sold my Beef Cheek Ravioli even ten years ago. I can now, along with stinging nettles, eels, head cheese, and just about any other funky ingredient I dig up. Stop into Babbo some night and you'll see plates of calf's brains and lamb's tongue flying out of the kitchen. At Esca our specialty is *crudo,* Italian-style raw seafood. That's a long way from spaghetti and meatballs.

However, the Italian food renaissance hasn't yet expanded to include the full array of Italian wines. A certain clique of Brunellos, Barolos, Barbarescos, and "super-Tuscans" have become auction-house wines alongside Bordeaux. But beyond these, even the sophisticated drinkers at Babbo don't stray too far. For all the interest in regional Italian food, most people are content to stay with familiar names from Tuscany or Piedmont when it comes to wine. Maybe it's simple economics: a twenty-five-dollar plate of food is less of a risk than a fifty- or hundred-dollar bottle of wine. But it's more likely that people feel intimidated by the sheer breadth of Italian wine—and they're worried about getting something they won't enjoy.

I can't necessarily blame them. As great as some Italian wine is, there is still plenty of lip-puckering stuff that brings to mind the straw-covered flasks of the sixties and seventies. And Italian wine labeling can be confusing. Italy produces more wine than any nation in the world, from more than three hundred officially delimited wine zones (California, by contrast, has around eighty) and hundreds of different grape varieties. Getting to know Italian wine takes some doing.

I lived and worked in Italy for years, my restaurants have great Italian wine lists, and even I still feel I've only scratched the surface. Unless you're totally immersed in the topic, you need someone to boil it down to its essence and steer you in the right direction. That's what a good sommelier does, and that's what the authors do here: provide a base of knowledge in Italian wine, so you can make intelligent choices when dining out or entertaining at home. Like a good restaurant wine list, this book offers a representative sampling of the best Italy has to offer.

Italian wine is more exciting than it has ever been, so this kind of hands-on primer comes at a perfect time. Italy's winemaking technology and viticulture—historically a step or two behind the likes of France, Australia, and the United States—has become increasingly sophisticated. Throughout Italy, winemakers are making much better use of the country's unparalleled natural gifts.

Consider as one example the revolutionary changes in the Chianti Classico region of Tuscany, the latest of which went into effect in 1996. By refining their growing techniques and changing their production formula, the Tuscans turned what was once an insipid table wine into one of the great red wines of the world. Still, many people continue to dismiss Chianti as the flask wine of old. They don't know what they're missing!

The Italians, sometimes to their disadvantage, have traditionally created wines that are at their best with food. Yes, there are many super-ripe, oaked-up wines coming out of Italy these days (many of them made from international varieties like cabernet sauvignon, chardonnay, or merlot). But in general, Italian wine is still defined by a sense of proportion, a more moderate balance of fruit, acid, and tannin. It accentuates, rather than dominates, the food it's served with. And there's nothing quite like pairing a Roman dish with a Roman wine, or a Friulian dish with a Friulian wine. There's no substitute for that kind of elemental combination.

In our restaurants, we try to interpret the Italian food-and-wine culture in a way that's both authoritative and accessible. People are so eager to learn, and they're forever on the hunt for something new: a new cheese, a new salami, a new oil, and, more and more often, a new wine. Where's it from? How's it made? How do I get some? This is the part I love about my job, and it's what I love about Italian wine: There's always something new to discover, and the best is yet to come.

L'Ambiente del Vino

THE CULTURE OF WINE

When we started working on *Vino Italiano*, we saw ourselves as filling a void. There aren't many books available on the subject of Italian wine, which is surprising given the seemingly insatiable hunger of Americans for all things Italian. An up-to-date guide to the great wines of Italy seemed like a natural and necessary thing to do.

But we didn't really want to write a *guide*. A guide is a book that tells you what to buy, what to do, what to think. And we didn't want to talk about wine in a strictly literal sense, which would make for a fairly boring textbook. Instead, our goal was to communicate something essential about the Italian wine experience—or, rather, something about how to eat, drink, and live in the Italian style. So in addition to saying that such-and-such wine is made from such-and-such grapes, comes from such-and-such place, and costs so many dollars, it seemed equally useful to describe what the wines taste like, why they might taste the way they do (although no one ever knows that for sure), and perhaps most important, where they come from in a cultural sense.

The French have the concept of *terroir* to explain why wines taste the way they do. As defined in the *Oxford Companion to Wine*, *terroir* is the "total natural environment" of a vineyard.

First and foremost, this refers to the geology of the soil. But it also includes the topography of the vineyard, the climate of the surrounding area, the amount of sunlight the vineyard receives, and other natural factors.

One aim of this book is to remark on the *terroir* of Italian wines, and how that affects their personalities. But another objective is to tie in the elements of Italian lifestyle that enhance the enjoyment of the wines. Without Italian food and Italian culture to go along with it, Italian wine has no context. The same could be said of any wine from any part of the world, but it often seems as if very few wine drinkers—and wine publications—think this way. Most of the time, it's enough to tell (or be told) what's good, and leave it at that. But we assume that if you go to the trouble to buy a book about wine you'd want more than ratings and cold hard facts. You'd want a little context.

So in addition to who's who and what's good, this book attempts to describe the *ambiente* of Italian wine. The Italian word *ambiente* literally means "environment," or "habitat," but it also refers to ambience, the feel of a place. Applied to wine, *ambiente* is not just the geology, topography, and climate of a vineyard but the culture that surrounds it. The experience of drinking an Italian wine isn't complete without the food products that grow in the same soil, nor without some sense of the culture that created it. Italians truly thrive on personal contact, and they think very carefully about how everything at their table—the wine, the food, the people, the place—fits together.

The anecdotes, wine tastings, food talk, and recipes in these pages are not just meant to be descriptive, but to be actionable. It's always great to drink Italian wines in the places where they are made, but you can create *ambiente* in a walk-up apartment in New York, or in a subur-ban home. There's an art to making wine, and there's also an art to drinking it. These pages explore both.

It is important to know that nebbiolo is the grape in Barolo, and that the soils of the Barolo region are calcareous marls. But it is much more useful to understand what Barolo tastes like, and what regional foods the people who make Barolo like to drink it with. To know all that is to have a sense of *ambiente*, which is a lot more fun than rooting around in the *terroir*.

How to Use This Book

<hr>

Vino Italiano is divided into three parts. The first section covers the basics of Italian wine history, law, and labeling. It is intended as an overview, or orientation, particularly for newcomers to the subject. Much of the vocabulary of Italian wine is spelled out in these introductory sections.

The second part explores each of Italy's twenty-one regions, all of which produce wine. This regional tour begins in the extreme northeast of Italy in Friuli–Venezia Giulia, travels westward across the north, then ambles down the peninsula and finally out to the islands of Sicily and Sardinia. In two instances, two regions have been combined in one chapter: Trentino and Alto Adige, which were politically linked in 1948, are treated in a single chapter, though their differences are outlined. Abruzzo and Molise are also combined—mainly because Molise has little commercial wine production (too little to merit a chapter of its own). So although there are a total of twenty-one discrete regions of Italy, there are nineteen regional chapters here.

Each regional chapter begins with a short anecdote about the region, drawn from our personal experiences in Italy, as a means of introducing the place behind the wines. These anecdotes are followed by an overview of the region's wines, broken into as many as four style

categories: sparkling wines, white wines, red wines, and sweet wines. In those regions with significant sparkling-wine production, sparkling wines come first in the order. Otherwise, sparklers are combined with sweet wines at the end of the chapter. If a region does not produce any significant quantity of a particular category of wine, then the section is omitted entirely. This is not an Italian wine encyclopedia—we haven't mentioned every single insignificant wine. Rather, this is a survey of the most important wines and winemakers in each region.

The third section of the book is comprised of reference material. It includes a glossary of Italian wine terms that appear throughout the text. There's also an annotated listing of the hundreds of grape varieties grown in Italy, as well as a listing of Italy's more than three hundred official wine "appellations," known as *Denominazioni di Origine Controllata (e Garantita)*, or DOC(G)s. Finally, there's a producer directory that might be used as a shopping guide. Although some of the producers will be harder to find than others, all of those listed in the back of this book export at least some wine to the United States.

Within the regional chapters, the following elements merit brief explanation:

Wine, Grape, and Place Names

Throughout the text, the names of Italian wine production zones, or DOCs, are capitalized—for example, Chianti Classico. Grape names, such as sangiovese, are not capitalized, unless the grape name also happens to be a part of the DOC name, as it is in many cases (Verdicchio dei Castelli di Jesi, for instance). Additionally, countless Italian wines are labeled not only with grape or place names but also with vineyard designations or proprietary "fantasy" names, such as "Vigneto Cannubi" or "Cepparello." These proprietary names are set off in quotation marks, as they are here.

Maps

The maps in the regional chapters are obviously not designed to be used for traveling. They are included to help provide a sense of place, and to indicate approximately where the various wine production zones (DOCs) are located within the region in question.

Top Vintages

Wherever possible (or necessary), information is included in each chapter about exceptional vintages in the recent history of that region—from 1980 to 2000. This information was culled from the people who know best: the winemakers themselves.

La Strada del Vino
(Wine-Touring)

This book is not a travel guide (there are plenty of excellent books for that, many of which are included in the Bibliography). However, we have tried to point out a few wine-related destinations in each region, most especially regional and local *enoteche* (wine bars) where you can sample wines from that region. Generally speaking, Italian wineries are not well equipped with visitor facilities (as they are in California, for example), although in certain regions, such as Tuscany, Piedmont, and the Alto Adige, there are a significant number of wineries open to visitors. The travel tips in the regional chapters focus on restaurants, shops, tours, and other things to do in wine country.

Degustazioni
(Tastings)

Each regional chapter contains a series of wine flights, accompanied by some commentary about the wines. The intent of these tastings is for the reader to seek out the wines recommended and taste the wines side by side, using the notes as a reference point. The wines chosen for these tastings are all available in the United States and while it would be impossible to state their exact prices (which will vary from market to market and even store to store), we've indicated for each wine a price category in which it will fall, based on an educated estimate provided by the wine's importer: One dollar sign ($) means the wine costs less than $20 a bottle at retail; two dollar signs ($$) means the wine costs $20 to $40 dollars a bottle; and three dollar signs ($$$) means the wine costs more than $40 a bottle.

Wine Availability

Unless otherwise noted, all of the wines mentioned in these pages—and especially those included in the guided tastings—are available in the American market, albeit in varying quantities. As with any imported food product, the distribution of Italian wines is highly variable. Every effort has been made to suggest wines that are readily available nationally, but in some cases finding the wines herein might require a phone call to a trusted local retailer, or maybe a little time spent on the Internet.

La Cucina
(Food for the Wine)

What is Italian wine without Italian food to go with it? Each regional chapter contains a short commentary about the food culture of the region, followed by an original recipe by either Mario Batali or Lidia Bastianich. The premise of these recipes is to demonstrate how regional Italian wines are best showcased accompanying the regional food products that grow (or are made) alongside them.

PART I

THE BASICS

LE COSE FONDAMENTALI

La Storia

ITALIAN WINE THEN AND NOW

A lot of people think that the relevant history of Italian wine began ten years ago. Or maybe twenty. To some extent this is true: The last two decades have been a revolutionary period in Italian winemaking. Thanks to dramatic improvements in technology and viticulture, world-class wines can now be found all over Italy, not just in a handful of regions. In fact, when talking to producers, we hear over and over how 1990 was a watershed year for them—the year when the wine world really began to take Italy seriously.

What's so special about 1990? For one thing, it was one of the best vintages of the last century. But it was more than that. As many Italian winemakers explain it, '90 was great not only because of the weather but because of the changes they had been making in their cellars and vineyards.

It's not that there weren't great wines in Italy before 1990. You can trace legendary vintages of estate-bottled Italian wine almost as far back as you can Bordeaux: There's the 1928 Bertani "Acinatico" Amarone, '47 Giacomo Borgogno Barolo, '55 Biondi-Santi Brunello di Montalcino, '61 Gaja Barbaresco, '82 Giacosa "Santo Stefano" Barbaresco. These wines were so naturally blessed that they wouldn't necessarily have benefited from modern technology. But these historic bottlings were the exceptions, not the rule. As a source of reliable, high-quality wines at all price tiers, from every region, Italy didn't come into its own until very recently.

One reason for the recent developments is that the eighties and nineties marked a big generational shift in Italian winemaking. The post–World War II farmer or entrepreneur with limited training and a penchant for industrial-scale production gave way to a son or a daughter, often fresh out of enology school, who transformed the family property into more of a château. This shift wasn't just idealistic but economically necessary. The Italian government and the European Community invested heavily in new vineyards in the sixties and seventies, and although this helped revive Italy's flagging agricultural economy at the time, it also resulted in huge surpluses of wine. The EC then tried to reduce these surpluses by compelling vintners to send some of their grapes to huge industrial distilleries, or by paying growers to rip up vines and plant something else. Generally speaking, Italy was for a long time a welfare state for wine. Vintners continued to produce more than the market would bear, knowing that they'd get at least something for the extra; occasionally they just lived off the subsidies they got to let their land lay fallow, since planting other crops wasn't necessarily profitable.

The production excesses of the seventies and early eighties gave Italy a bad reputation among serious wine drinkers. But the profits from those excesses helped finance much of what has happened since then. Throughout Italy, it's a familiar story: The father had some vineyard land and made his living selling grapes to the local cooperative. But now his children are replanting those vineyards, building a cellar, buying new oak barrels for aging and vinification, and producing high-end wine under their own label.

Among the longer-established estates, vintners often pinpoint the year they switched from "old style" to new: the year they replaced their thirty-year-old, 50-hectoliter chestnut casks with new, 225-liter French oak barriques; the year they began "green harvesting" grapes in midsummer, so that their vines wouldn't over-produce; the year they bought their first "roto-fermenter," a space-age vessel that speeds up the process of extracting color and tannin from red grapes. These types of changes have been overwhelmingly recent—if not always welcome by Italian wine purists. On the whole, Italian winemakers are producing cleaner, more full-bodied, more oak-influenced wines than in the past, which has helped them in the international market—but has also caused some traditionalists to lament their loss of individuality.

The ancient history of Italian wine is much more romantic: the Etruscans training wild vines up trees, the Greeks bringing seeds across the Adriatic and more or less creating Italian viticulture. But as a modern-day consumer looking for a bottle of Italian wine in a shop or a restaurant, you need not look much further back than World War II. There was a thriving wine industry in Italy before then, but very few Italian producers sold wines as we know them

today—in bottles, with labels identifying who made them and where they came from.

When the merchants of Bordeaux created their famous 1855 classification—which ranked sixty established châteaus on the basis of price and quality—Italy wasn't yet a unified country. Italian winemaking at that time was defined by the *tenuta:* a vast farm estate, often controlled by a noble family, on which a number of *mezzadri* (sharecroppers) lived and worked. The *mezzadria* system, which prevailed throughout central and northern Italy up until the 1960s, was a culture in which the sharecropper made a little wine for himself and turned over the rest of his grapes (and portions of all his other produce) to the landowner as rent. The landlord vinified his sharecroppers' grapes in a central winery called a *fattoria* and typically sold it in bulk. In the south of Italy was the more oppressive *latifondo* system, in which peasants had no vested interests in the large landed estates.

After World War II, things began to change, and fast. Italy transformed itself from a monarchy to a republic, and its new government tried to redistribute Italy's land to the peasant population. Large estates in the south were broken up, and many landowners in the center and north were compelled to sell off parcels to their assorted *mezzadri*. But the Agrarian Reform, as it was called, didn't go far enough: Not only was the system of redistributing land hopelessly corrupt, the parcels the government eventually doled out were usually too small to do any one farmer much good.

Despite the Agrarian Reform—or perhaps because of it—rural Italians began leaving home in droves in the mid-fifties, emigrating to other countries or moving to one of the big cities of northern Italy (Turin and Milan especially) to find work. According to historian Paul Ginsborg, in his book *A History of Contemporary Italy: Society and Politics 1943–1988*, more than 9 million Italians were involved in "interregional migration" between 1951 and 1971.

A twentieth-century industrial revolution in Italy took hold incredibly fast. By the early sixties Italy was among the world's largest producers of washing machines, refrigerators, and cars, and only 30 percent of the population was still involved in agriculture; today that figure is less than 10 percent. Says Ginsborg: "In less than two decades Italy ceased to be a peasant country and became one of the major industrial nations of the West."

This "rural exodus" affected winemaking in a number of ways. For one, scores of wine farms were being sold or simply abandoned because there was no one left to work on them. This prompted a new class of entrepreneurs, most of them businesspeople and many of them foreigners, who snapped up these distressed or abandoned properties for weekend getaways. Eventually, these nonfarmers helped reshape the Italian wine business into a *real* business. Look at the current roster of *cantina* owners in Chianti Classico, for example, and you'll see not only a number of famous Italian industrialists but plenty of Swiss and British ones as well—not to mention doctors, lawyers, and advertising execs, all of whom turned their hobbies into enterprises.

In 1963, the Italian government drew up the *Denominazione di Origine Controllata* (DOC) laws, which created legally defined production zones and production formulas for what were once simple farmhouse wines. Modeled after French wine appellations (see "La Légge," on page 9), DOCs were seen as a first step in creating a commercial identity for Italian wines.

Concurrent with the DOC implementation, however, were the ongoing efforts of the Italian government and the EC to prop up the agricultural sector. The "Green Plans" of 1961 and 1966 financed massive plantings of various crops throughout Italy, although they tended to focus on the most fertile sites on the plains—not the best places for vines. To take pressure off small vine growers, cooperative wineries were set up throughout Italy, often run by local politicians. The main function of these wineries was to serve as a sponge for all of the grape juice people were producing. Even the wines classified as DOC, from private estates, tended to be mass-produced. Watery-tasting Soave, fizzy Lambrusco, and acrid Chianti became Italy's best-known wine exports.

Even now, people still talk about watery Soave and acrid Chianti—and, unfortunately, still drink them sometimes. And it is true that Italy is still a major producer of bulk wines and concentrated grape musts, particularly in Puglia and Sicily, which ship tanker loads of *vino da taglio* (cutting wine) to producers in northern Italy and beyond. But thanks to a number of circumstances—including changing consumer tastes and an EC ban on new vineyard plantings—Italian wine has been radically transformed.

Since 1988, the total vineyard area in Italy has declined by about 17 percent, and overall wine production by about the same amount. Of the 50 million hectoliters of wine now produced yearly in Italy (more than a billion gallons), nearly 25 percent of it is classified with a DOC designation, compared with just 5 percent in 1988. As we discuss on the following pages, a DOC is no guarantee of quality, but Italy has nevertheless reduced the amount of *vino da tavola* (table wine) it makes while increasing its production of "classified" wine. These days, the EC gives subsidies to vintners who restructure their existing vineyards to produce better-quality grapes, rather than simply buy everything and send the excess to a distillery. And many DOC production formulas—that is, the recipes vintners must follow in order to label their wines with a DOC designation—have been revised in recent times to reflect a greater emphasis on quality. The Chianti Classico DOC, which was extensively rewritten in both 1984 and 1996, is probably the most famous example.

Furthermore, the number of small- and medium-size Italian wineries seems to increase every day: countless wineries profiled in this book, for example, produced their first vintage in the nineties. No longer is great Italian wine found only in Piedmont and Tuscany. The whites of Friuli—Venezia Giulia—which, truth be told, have been great since the seventies—have become genuinely fashionable in the United States. In Sicily, still the undisputed champ of bulk-wine production, vintners have been ripping up big-production white grapes and planting the native red, nero d'avola, along with other reds like syrah and cabernet sauvignon. Often called the "Australia of Italy," the island once known for Marsala has become one of Italy's hottest sources for powerful dry reds.

In Puglia, the native primitivo grape has benefited from its proven paternity of American red zinfandel. The soft, plush reds from this grape are some of the best values to be found in Italy. There are also some excellent, well-priced reds to be found in the Marche (Rosso Cònero and scores of "super-red" blends), Umbria (the wines of Montefalco), and Abruzzo (Montepulciano d'Abruzzo). On the white side, the much-maligned Soave has been elevated by producers like Gini, Pieropan, Inama, and Anselmi, while farther north the winemakers of Trentino—Alto Adige are quietly turning out some of the best aromatic whites to be found anywhere in the world.

Without a doubt, the most exciting thing about Italian wine is its diversity. There are Italian sparklers, especially from Lombardy's Franciacorta region, that can stand toe-to-toe with Champagne. There are dessert wines, like Friuli's rare Picolit, that rival Sauternes. There are ethereal Barolos and Barbarescos that can take on the best of Burgundy. Cabernet blends from Tuscany to compare with Bordeaux. Friuli and Alto Adige whites that eclipse Alsace. Then there are countless Italian wines that defy comparison: Tuscany's reds from sangiovese, Friuli's whites from tocai, Basilicata's and Campania's reds from aglianico, and many others. The list goes on and on, as the following pages attest.

La Légge, Le Uve, e Il Viaggio del Vino

LAWS, GRAPES, AND IMPORTS

LA LÉGGE

Decoding Italian Wine Laws

Many wine drinkers are at least somewhat familiar with Italian wine laws and wine labeling. The basic idea is that Italian wines carry a place-name above all else, just like French wines: Chianti Classico is a place, and its specific boundaries are delimited by law, just like Bordeaux.

Yet in Italy, as in France, the particularity of these places makes reading a label feel like a geography test. Just where, exactly, is Salice Salentino? And what does that tell you, especially if you're an American who's accustomed to selecting wines by grape variety? The label doesn't say that the wine is a dry red from Puglia made from the negroamaro grape. Just "Salice Salentino." The rest is up to you, or the person selling it to you.

Not only is information often absent, there's also the occasional curveball. Sometimes Italians do throw grapes into their place names—like Montepulciano d'Abruzzo (the montepulciano grape of Abruzzo) or Ver-

mentino di Gallura (vermentino from Gallura, in northeastern Sardinia). Then there are wines branded with *nomi di fantasia* (fantasy names), such as "Sassicaia" or "Terre Alte." If you've never heard of these wines before, you'll need more information than just these names, either on the bottle (luckily, it's usually somewhere on the label) or on the wine list.

Thus, it helps to know Italy's wine laws, and by association its wine "zones"—an exhaustive field of study if there ever was one. The modern legislation governing Italian wine production was created in 1963, when the *Denominazione di Origine Controllata* (Denomination of Controlled Origin) was devised. Modeled after France's *appellation contrôlée* laws of the 1930s, the Italian version had the same goal: to classify and regulate the production of wines from specific geographic areas, not only to authenticate these wines but to help them develop commercial identities. Prior to the creation of DOCs, most Italian wine was sold in bulk as *Vino da Tavola* (table wine).

As overseen by Italy's minister of agriculture, there are now four official classifications of Italian wine: *Vino da Tavola*, or VdT (the most generic of the group); *Indicazione Geografica Tipica,* or IGT (Typical Geographic Indication, meant to be a step up from table wine, like French *vin du pays*); *Denominazione di Origine Controllata,* or DOC; and *Denominazione di Origine Controllata e Garantita,* or DOCG (Denomination of Controlled and Guaranteed Origin, reserved for a handful of wines considered of exceptional pedigree).

VdT

A wine labeled *Vino da Tavola* may come from anywhere in Italy, from any grape or combination of grapes. Most VdT wine is sold in bulk as *sfuso* (the stuff that's poured on tap in local restaurants) or blending wine, but there have been notable exceptions: Many excellent wines, sometimes the best in a producer's range, are labeled as VdT because they are made from grapes not allowed (because of either their type or their provenance) under DOC or IGT regulations. For example, most of the original "super-Tuscan" wines of the 1970s, including "Sassicaia," "Ornellaia," and "Tignanello," were labeled as VdT because they included cabernet sauvignon, a grape not included in any of the DOC prescriptions of the day. These wines were of exceptional quality and became some of the most famous Italian wines despite their bottom-of-the-barrel classification.

IGT

This classification was created in 1992, with most of the appellations drawn up in 1995, partly as a way of bringing Italy's wine industry in line with the rest of the European Community. It's a sort of middle ground between VdT and DOC, intended to create a larger population of "classified" wines and thus a greater level of confidence among consumers. An IGT designation does what its name implies: indicates that the wine is from a particular geographic area. That's all. Most IGT wines carry the name of the grape variety used, but production methods are not as closely prescribed as in DOCs.

DOC

The most important thing to remember about the DOC (and DOCG) designation is that it is both a place-name *and* a production formula: The designation "Collio," for example, refers not only to wine from the hills of Friuli–Venezia Giulia but to a specific set of things that must be done in order for the wine to carry the designation. A DOC *disciplinaria* (discipline) not only outlines where exactly the grapes are grown, but which grapes are to be used and how long some wines must be aged before release. Most DOCs further stipulate that a wine must be vinified in the same place where the grapes are grown, and most set limits on the production of grapes. Producers are required to send samples of each year's production to tasting committees so that the wines can be certified as DOC. There are more than three hundred DOC zones, each of which includes any number of different wine types. Although the DOC law was created in 1963, the first actual zone wasn't declared until 1966 (Vernaccia di San Gimignano, in Tuscany). Today, about 20 to 25 percent of all Italian wine produced is classified with a DOC designation. See Appendix III in the back of the book for a complete listing of DOC (and DOCG) zones, or see the map in each regional chapter for its zones.

DOCG

Though created along with the DOC in 1963, the first DOCG wasn't named until 1980 (Brunello di Montalcino, in Tuscany again). The wines that have been given the extra G (for *garantita*, or "guaranteed") include most of the more historic wines of Italy—wines that had delimited production zones well before 1963. Generally speaking, these are considered the most rigidly controlled of Italy's wines. There are now twenty-three zones (and hence wines) with DOCG status: Asti, Barbaresco, Barolo, Brachetto d'Acqui/Acqui, Gattinara, Gavi/Cortese di Gavi, and Ghemme, all in Piedmont; Franciacorta and Valtellina Superiore in Lombardy; Bardolino and Recioto di Soave in Veneto; Albana di Romagna in Emilia-Romagna; Ramandolo in Friuli; Brunello di Montalcino, Carmignano, Chianti, Chianti Classico, Vernaccia di San Gimignano, and Vino Nobile di Montepulciano in Tuscany; Montefalco Sagrantino and Torgiano Rosso Riserva in Umbria; Taurasi in Campania; and Vermentino di Gallura in Sardinia.

So, is a DOCG, DOC, or IGT designation an assurance of quality? Not really. Think of it first and foremost as a means of organizing the wines in your mind. For all of the refinements in Italian winemaking (and lawmaking) in the last decade, there are still no guarantees.

The Italian novelist Primo Levi, in his World War II novel *If Not Now, When?*, had this to say about Italians and laws:

> The Italians don't like laws: in fact, they like disobeying them: it's their game, like the Russians' game is chess . . . when someone cheats them, they think: look how smart he is, smarter than me. And they don't plan their vengeance, but at most another game, to get their own back.

So it is with Italy's winemakers. They have lots and lots of laws, which they delight in creating, revising, and most especially, debating. But obeying them is another story.

Take the case of the Soave DOC zone, in the region of Veneto. Originally defined in the 1930s, it consisted of a cluster of hills between the communes of Soave and Monteforte d'Alpone, east of Verona. In the years after the Soave DOC was created, the "official" production zone was expanded into the plains to the west and south, to accommodate giant industrial wineries. Today, only about 20 percent of all Soave produced is from the original "Classico" zone. If you pick up a bottle of Soave without any knowledge of the producer, you may get one of the mass-produced, insipid wines that gave the zone such a bad image in the past, or you may get an excellent, elegant white that you didn't think existed. The point is that you can't rely on the word *Soave* alone—something many vintners have lamented.

Although this has been the case in other DOC zones, and although there are any number of essentially useless DOCs all over Italy (created by local politicians to help winegrowers avoid the mandatory distillation rules of the EC), the designation does mean much more today than it once did. The Chianti Classico zone is one of many DOCs that has been revised for the better (see the Tuscany chapter for more on this). While there are no sure bets, a DOC designation most certainly improves your chances of getting a good bottle. When all is said and done, most of the best Italian wines you'll drink are apt to have one.

Reading an Italian Wine Label

1. Producer Name
2. Vintage
3. DOC Designation, as indicated by the term *Denominazione di Origine Controllata* (DOC). If the designation is an *Indicazione Geografica Tipica* (IGT), or a *Vino da Tavola* (VdT), it will say so.
4. Grape Variety. In this case, the DOC designation includes provisions for wines labeled by varietal. This is not always the case with DOC wines. In most instances only the DOC name is listed—leaving the consumer to figure out where the wine is from and what grapes it is made with.
5. Type of Wine. United States law requires that this be stated somewhere on the bottle.
6. Size and Alcohol Content. These must also be stated according to United States law.
7. Proprietary Name. Not an official designation.
8. Importer Name. Required by United States law. Usually found on the back label.
9. Sulfite and Government Warnings. Also required by United States law. This and the other warnings and specifications must be worded and positioned in a way that satisfies the U.S. Customs Service.
10. Producer Name. In most instances, it is the same as the name on the front label, but not always. The front label may carry a brand name, rather than an actual winery name, making this back label listing useful in determining exactly what the winery name is.

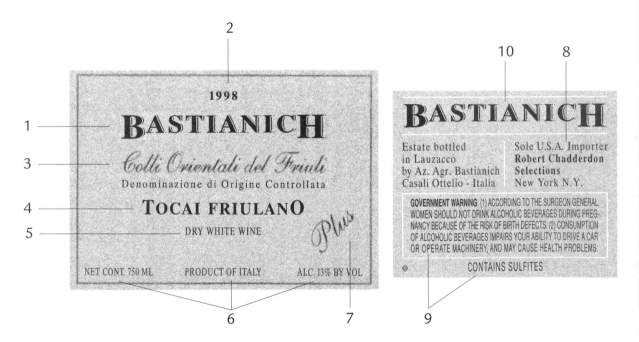

Le Uve

Key Grape Varieties

Trying to keep track of all the grape varieties in Italy is like driving in Naples—chaotic and exhausting. For those wine drinkers who think "grape first," Italian wines are a never-ending source of intrigue—or intimidation, depending on your outlook.

According to Attilio Scienza, a well-known professor of enology at the University of Milan, there are more than 800 distinct grape varieties to be found in Italy. Of these, 361 have been catalogued and "authorized" for planting by Italy's Ministry of Agriculture and Forestry (MIRAF). Naturally, the 500 or so that are not authorized are finding their way into some of the wines we drink, and may factor even more prominently in the future: Scienza has organized a consortium of producers to "adopt" certain varieties that are nearing extinction, as a means of preserving Italy's rich viticultural heritage.

Of course, it's not necessary to memorize all of Italy's grapes. Most of the best Italian wines come from a fairly narrow range of varieties. Among the reds, the wines of northern Italy are highlighted by the nebbiolo grape (Barolo, Barbaresco, and Lombardy's Valtellina), the center is dominated by sangiovese (Chianti, Brunello di Montalcino, Vino Nobile di Montepulciano), and the south is aglianico country (Taurasi, Aglianico del Vulture). Whites are tougher to pinpoint: The north tends to have a richer mix of indigenous grapes (tocai friulano in Friuli–Venezia Giulia, cortese in Piedmont, garganega in Veneto) and French/German imports (chardonnay, sauvignon blanc, gewürztraminer). But the center and south feature mostly neutral natives: trebbiano, the greco family, and inzolia (ansonica). On the map on the following page, we've highlighted the principal grape varieties of each region as a quick reference.

The chart on page 15 lists the dominant grape varieties in the vineyards of Italy, which now cover nearly 2 million acres in twenty-one regions. As evidenced by some of the most-planted varieties, there's still a tendency toward mass-production in much of the country. For example, cataratto, grown only on Sicily and used in Marsala, is also a favored grape for bulk wines and concentrated musts. The trebbiano family, if taken together, would easily rank first, even though the vast majority of trebbiano is anonymously blended. Merlot, the jewel of Pomerol in France, is typically more of a workhorse in Italy, helping vintners stretch production from the top to the toe of the boot.

But this is just an overview. And for every workhorse grape there's a distinctive, delicious one, like barbera or aglianico. Italy's daunting variety is its most dazzling asset. There are many Italian grapes that can't be found anywhere else in the world, and the wines they produce are unique expressions of Italian culture: teroldego from Trentino, tocai from Friuli, nero d'avola from Sicily . . . the list goes on. It may be overwhelming to keep tabs on them all, but that's a nice problem to have.

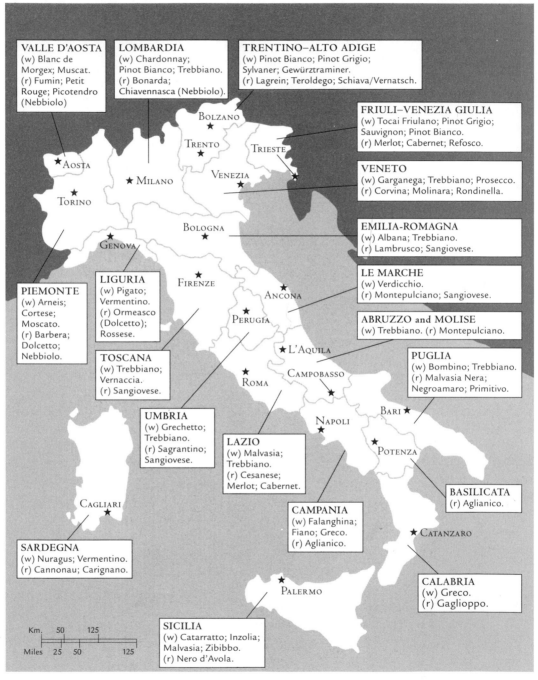

VALLE D'AOSTA
(w) Blanc de Morgex; Muscat.
(r) Fumin; Petit Rouge; Picotendro (Nebbiolo)

LOMBARDIA
(w) Chardonnay; Pinot Bianco; Trebbiano.
(r) Bonarda; Chiavennasca (Nebbiolo).

TRENTINO–ALTO ADIGE
(w) Pinot Bianco; Pinot Grigio; Sylvaner; Gewürztraminer.
(r) Lagrein; Teroldego; Schiava/Vernatsch.

FRIULI–VENEZIA GIULIA
(w) Tocai Friulano; Pinot Grigio; Sauvignon; Pinot Bianco.
(r) Merlot; Cabernet; Refosco.

VENETO
(w) Garganega; Trebbiano; Prosecco.
(r) Corvina; Molinara; Rondinella.

EMILIA-ROMAGNA
(w) Albana; Trebbiano.
(r) Lambrusco; Sangiovese.

LE MARCHE
(w) Verdicchio.
(r) Montepulciano; Sangiovese.

ABRUZZO and MOLISE
(w) Trebbiano. (r) Montepulciano.

PUGLIA
(w) Bombino; Trebbiano.
(r) Malvasia Nera; Negroamaro; Primitivo.

BASILICATA
(r) Aglianico.

CALABRIA
(w) Greco.
(r) Gaglioppo.

CAMPANIA
(w) Falanghina; Fiano; Greco.
(r) Aglianico.

LAZIO
(w) Malvasia; Trebbiano.
(r) Cesanese; Merlot; Cabernet.

UMBRIA
(w) Grechetto; Trebbiano.
(r) Sagrantino; Sangiovese.

TOSCANA
(w) Trebbiano; Vernaccia.
(r) Sangiovese.

PIEMONTE
(w) Arneis; Cortese; Moscato.
(r) Barbera; Dolcetto; Nebbiolo.

LIGURIA
(w) Pigato; Vermentino.
(r) Ormeasco (Dolcetto); Rossese.

SARDEGNA
(w) Nuragus; Vermentino.
(r) Cannonau; Carignano.

SICILIA
(w) Catarratto; Inzolia; Malvasia; Zibibbo.
(r) Nero d'Avola.

BOLZANO
TRENTO
TRIESTE
AOSTA
MILANO
VENEZIA
TORINO
BOLOGNA
GENOVA
FIRENZE
ANCONA
PERUGIA
L'AQUILA
ROMA
CAMPOBASSO
NAPOLI
BARI
POTENZA
CAGLIARI
CATANZARO
PALERMO

Km. 50 125
Miles 25 50 125

For each region, we've indicated the principal indigenous grape varieties, both white (w) and red (r).

THE 20 MOST PLANTED GRAPES IN ITALY

Rank	Variety	Type	Acres	% of Italy's Total
1.	Sangiovese	red	242,158	11.0%
2.	Catarratto Bianco Comune	white	148,260	7.0%
3.	Trebbiano Toscano	white	123,550	6.8%
4.	Barbera	red	98,840	5.0%
5.	Merlot	red	93,898	4.5%
6.	Negroamaro	red	86,485	4.0%
7.	Montepulciano	red	61,775	3.2%
8.	Trebbiano Romagnolo	white	43,242	2.0%
9.	Catarratto Bianco Lucido	white	43,242	2.0%
10.	Primitivo	red	43,242	2.0%
11.	Malvasia Lazio	white	42,000	2.0%
12.	Nero d'Avola	red	39,536	1.9%
13.	Garganega	white	29,650	1.4%
14.	Nerello Mascalese	red	29,650	1.4%
15.	Malvasia Bianca di Candia	white	28,416	1.3%
16.	Inzolia (Ansonica)	white	27,181	1.2%
17.	Dolcetto	red	23,474	1.1%
18.	Moscato Bianco	white	23,474	1.1%
19.	Aglianico	red	23,474	1.1%
20.	Nuragus	white	22,239	1.0%

*See Appendix II for descriptions of these varieties.

Source: Registro Nazionale delle Varietà Autorizzate e Raccomandate, *published by Italy's Ministry of Agriculture and Forestry (MIRAF), 1998.*

IL VIAGGIO DEL VINO
The Journey of the Wine

So you were in Florence on vacation, and you noticed that the bottle of Brunello di Montalcino you pay $100 for in the United States cost a third of that in the *trattoria* you ate in every night. This isn't just a function of favorable exchange rates. Italian restaurateurs, unlike most of their American counterparts, are allowed to buy wine directly from wineries (only in California do American restaurateurs have this luxury) instead of from distributors, who mark it up. Plus, Italian wine in Italy usually doesn't travel too far from winery to restaurant: If you're in Naples, the wine list will be mostly Campanian. If you're in Florence it'll be Tuscan. So it's only natural that Italian wines cost less in Italy.

Americans, of course, pay not only the pure shipping fees of getting a wine from Italy to the United States, but also the costs of the assorted people who make it happen. The first of these is the importer, who is licensed both federally and in the state in which he does business. A wine importer is essentially a facilitator: He locates an estate whose wines he thinks he can sell in the United States, cuts a deal with the winery to purchase some, then takes care of getting it here. The importer's two main tasks after finding and purchasing the wine are first to produce a label that meets requirements outlined by the U.S. Customs Service (which can be a nightmare of nitpicky bureaucratic editing), and second to consolidate the shipments of the wine, most of which leave Italy from the Tuscan port of Livorno. Naturally, the importer charges a fee for this service.

Once the wine lands on American shores, the law requires that a wholesale distributor take possession of it and oversee its sale to retail stores and/or restaurants. Some companies are both importers and distributors, in which case they must acquire distributor's licenses in each individual state. In most cases an importer is simply an importer, and therefore must form partnerships with various distributors across the country.

Before a retailer or restaurateur has a chance to buy a wine from a wholesale distributor, a variety of costs have been built into the wholesale price: shipping costs from Italy to America; the importer's fees; a variety of excise and other taxes; and the wholesaler's fees for storing the wine getting it from point A to B. After all that, the retailer or restaurateur takes a cut before the consumer price is set.

It works something like this: Let's say an American importer, who typically has exclusive rights to the products he brings to the States, pays an Italian winery $10 a bottle for a particular wine. Generally speaking, the costs of shipping, storing, and distributing the wine will likely double the price, to $20 wholesale in the States. A standard retail markup formula is 50 percent of cost, meaning that a wine bought at $20 wholesale will be marked up in a store by half of its cost ($10), putting the price to the consumer at $30. In a restaurant, where the standard markup has historically been three times cost, that same wine will be $60. As a general rule, if what you're paying in a restaurant is more than double what you pay at retail, you're being overcharged—although that's tough to say if the wine is very rare or an older vintage.

The above scenario is the most simple one. On occasion, an Italian winery may work with a consolidator, broker, or marketing concern when dealing with American importers, meaning that the importer can't buy directly from the winery and thus must absorb the costs of a middleman. And once the wine is here, its passage from importer to distributor to retailer or restaurateur is subject to lots of haggling. Finally, in the multitude of states known as "control" states, where the state government takes possession of wine before selling it to retailers and restaurants, prices will be higher still, because the state adds in its own layer of fees.

All of this can cause wide variations in price. It is far from safe to say that a wine that costs an importer $10 in Italy will cost $20 in the American wholesale market. Other than what the market will bear, there are no standards as to what importers and distributors charge. The same goes for restaurants and retail shops. Depending on their relationships with importers and distributors (i.e., how much wine they buy, how good they are at negotiating), they may be able to acquire a wine for less than the guys down the street, and thus offer a better price to you. In the case of restaurants in particular, the approach to markups is always evolving, with the traditional three-times-cost formula becoming increasingly antiquated. The best restaurants tend to scale their markups, so that the more expensive wines aren't priced out of the reach of customers. The lowest-priced wines are still often marked up three times, but higher-end bottlings are treated a little more gently: A popular formula is to double the cost and then add a set dollar figure, such as $10 or $15, across the board, so that wines at the very highest price tiers are marked up the least.

To market the incredible breadth of Italian wines, there is a vast array of Italian wine importers, large and small. Most of them in the United States are based on the East Coast, but not all have national distribution for the wines they import, whether because the wines aren't produced in sufficient quantity or because of the logistics of the importers forging partnerships with multiple distributors. Importers who are *not* also distributors face greater challenges: they must sell not only retailers and restaurateurs on their wines, but first must convince the distributors to carry their products.

Because there are so many players in the importing game, there are all sorts of names strewn across Italian wine bottles these days. One of them is Marc de Grazia, who is not an importer but a marketing agent of sorts for a large number of Italian wineries. He is based in Italy and acts as a broker and advisor to wineries, arranging to have his selections imported by the firm of Michael Skurnik Wines in New York, and others. A similar arrangement is shared by the U.S.–based Leonardo LoCascio and the national importing firm of Winebow, Inc. The list of noteworthy Italian wine importers is a long one, but some of the important names to remember are Robert Chadderdon Selections, Vias Imports, Vinifera Imports, Summa Vitis Inc., JK Imports, Lauber Imports, VinDivino, Artisan Wines, Vignaioli Inc., Panebianco LLC, Domaine Select Wine Estates, John Given Wines, Paterno Imports, and Palm Bay Imports.

Being a smart buyer of Italian wine means finding retailers and restaurateurs who are themselves smart buyers of Italian wine. Since all bottles carry the name of their importer on them, one approach is to see if a lot of different wines in a store are from the same importer. It could be a hint that the retailer has a good relationship with that importer and there's a chance it could be reflected in the price. Moreover, if you happen to notice a particular importer's name on a number of bottles you like, there's no harm in contacting the importer yourself. Explain that you are interested in his or her portfolio, and ask if there's a retail store in your area that carries a particularly broad selection of his or her wines. In many cases, importers will be willing to shuttle product through a local retailer for you, particularly if you're interested in a large quantity (by law, the importer cannot sell to consumers directly). Because of the relative ease of such a sale, both the importer and the retailer might

be inclined to shave their markups somewhat, since so little effort was required on their parts to make the sale.

As for Italian wine in restaurants, there's no surefire way to find values unless you're good at memorizing competitive prices. On most restaurant lists, you're likely to find good buys in the middle of the price scale (since the lowest-priced wines are usually marked up the most). And it never hurts to chat up the sommelier, maybe dropping a compliment or two about his or her selections; if you can find out what the wine people are genuinely excited about, you're in for something interesting.

PART II

THE REGIONS

LE REGIONI

Friuli–Venezia Giulia

A Clash of Cultures Creates
a Curious Harmony

Making the Scene at La Frasca

As we pull up two chairs on the patio of our friend Valter's *osteria*, a bearded giant named Paolo, who's seated at the head of a table of about twenty people, swings his bulky frame around to face us and throws out his arms in greeting. "Hey, American, up yours!" he barks, as his tablemates erupt in laughter. "Don't breaking my ball!"

Valter is harried as usual as he swoops in with two platters of prosciutto and a carafe of white wine. He catches Paolo's performance and smiles sheepishly, explaining that the group is his night-school English class, here to celebrate the last *lezione* of the semester. Gripping a wine glass in one hand and a forkload of prosciutto in another, Paolo delights his classmates with some more American profanity, as his mortified teacher protests her innocence.

Valter's restaurant, a popular roadside tavern called La Frasca, is filling up fast; there's a seat left for him at the English-class table, but he never does get back to it, other than to deliver plates of risotto with *bruscandoli* (hop shoots), gnocchi with *speck* (smoked bacon), *stinco*

(braised veal shanks), and of course more wine. When Paolo leads the class in song it passes by relatively unnoticed, as La Frasca is by then a smoky, plate-clanking cacophony of families with squealing children, young couples on their cell phones, and most characteristically, a large group of men in the bar area, many in coveralls with their names embroidered on them, engaging in the most Italian of dinner activities—the noisy, freewheeling, never-ending debate.

La Frasca is the center of what might be described as Valter's family compound. Surrounding it are his mother's house, his brother's house, his winery (where he makes his Scarbolo-labeled wines), and the small cinder-block shed where he raises about sixty pigs a year for prosciutto and salami. His vineyards spread out in a small plot set back from the road, with his own house behind them. There isn't a waking moment when Valter isn't working—in the restaurant, in the winery, and during the spring and fall, in the small *macelleria* (butchery) attached to the winery. He's like a nineteenth-century innkeeper transported to the modern day; but his customers, rather than hitch their horses to a post outside La Frasca, crowd the parking lot with Audis and Fiats instead.

Frasca is actually a generic term in Friuli denoting a casual restaurant often attached to a

The DOC Zones of Friuli–Venezia Giulia

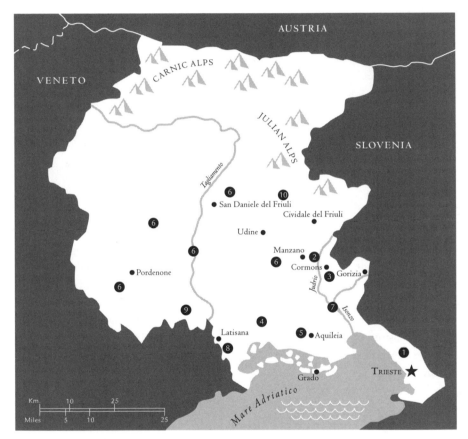

1 Carso
2 Colli Orientali del Friuli
3 Collio Goriziano/Collio
4 Friuli Annia
5 Friuli Aquileia
6 Friuli Grave
7 Friuli Isonzo
8 Friuli Latisana
9 Lison-Pramaggiore
10 Ramandolo DOCG*

*New in 2000–2001

winery; the word means "branch," or "bush," in reference to a traditional practice (apparently Austrian) of hanging a wreath of branches above the doorway of a farmhouse to signify that food and wine was for sale. The term is used somewhat interchangeably with *osteria* or *hosteria*, the latter describing a sit-down restaurant one step down the price-and-formality scale from a *trattoria*.

Situated on the main road between Palmanova and Udine, La Frasca is at an historic crossroads, about fifteen minutes from the Slovenian border and maybe forty from the Carnic Alps and Austria. The compound name, Friuli–Venezia Giulia, reflects the region's history of tangled allegiances and shifting borders. Friuli is named for the ancient Friulani who first inhabited the area, and includes the modern-day provinces of Pordenone and Udine, while "Venezia Giulia" (Julian Venice) takes in the more easterly provinces of Gorizia and Trieste, traditionally associated with the Venetian Republic. From about the tenth century onward, the region was tugged back and forth between the Venetians and the Hapsburgs, and it wasn't until 1954, when Trieste and a sliver of the Istrian peninsula were ceded to Italy in the postwar realignments of Europe, that Friuli–Venezia Giulia took its current geographic boundaries.

The faces and foods of La Frasca reflect this cultural mix: there are stews such as *jota* (beans, sauerkraut, potatoes, and sausage) vacuumed up under thick Slavic mustaches; Tyrolean touches such as poppy seeds, *speck*, and apple strudel; and even some Venetian specialties, although that influence is stronger in the Adriatic shore towns to the south, such as Grado or Muggia, the latter an evocative mini-Venice just south of Trieste.

Udine is prime salami and prosciutto country, headlined by the well-known prosciutto di San Daniele but including a raft of homemade variations. In Friuli, prosciutto-making is as much of an all-consuming, self-defining hobby as winemaking, and Valter is one of the best. A butcher's platter at La Frasca—which isn't so much a platter but a small cutting board with a handle on it—is spread with various types of *crudo* (raw) and *cotto* (cooked) salami and prosciutto, including *spalla*, a salt-cured pork loin and shoulder; *cotechino*, cooked pig's-skin sausage; and *ossocollo*, sort of a neck-cut prosciutto. Served with a carafe of *sfuso*—tap wine, usually the white tocai friulano—this is the quintessential Friulian appetizer.

For all of its Slavic and Germanic influences, however, the overall effect of La Frasca is unmistakably Italian. Restaurant dining in Italy is not theater, nor competitive sport, as it often is in the United States. The whole restaurant hierarchy as we know it is turned on its head: Although there are Michelin-starred restaurants all over the country, many of them are stiff and uncomfortable, and the food (a lot of it hyperstylized, eighties-retro kind of stuff) is often forgettable.

By contrast, for all the chaos of La Frasca—the restaurant seems chronically understaffed and overbooked—there's a fluidity and ease to the place, mainly because there are no grand expectations. It's an extension of Valter's home, literally and figuratively, and it feels like it. In the summertime, when he strings Christmas lights in the trees that frame the patio, eating there is like being at a wedding reception or a birthday party, even when the other faces are unfamiliar.

The hook, of course, is that most of the faces are familiar. Paolo, for one, had already been in at ten A.M. for a quick glass of *sfuso*, which he slugged down at the bar alongside four *carabinieri* (the Italian equivalent of state police), all decked out in their jackboots and white holsters. Then he came back at one-thirty for lunch, and back again for dinner. Although La Frasca does reserve tables, people tend to just show up and become absorbed into the mass. Valter, ever the amiable host as children dart past and the guys in the bar pepper him with good-natured abuse, doesn't stop working long enough to soak up the atmosphere he's created. By the time he sits down to his own dish of pasta, his whole English class—even Paolo—is long gone.

VINI BIANCHI
White Wines

Just as it takes cultural and culinary cues from neighboring Austria and Slovenia, Friuli–Venezia Giulia has a particularly international wine scene. Although it was among the regions most devastated by both World Wars, its economic recovery afterward (it's now the chair-making capital of Europe, among other things) and the development of its modern wine industry were especially swift. It is widely agreed that Friuli's winemakers, led in the late sixties and early seventies by local legend Mario Schiopetto, set the modern standards for making white wine in Italy.

How did they do it? On the surface it would seem they were just smarter, and worked harder, than most of their Italian peers. But the longtime domination of the Austrians had at least something to do with it: For centuries, Friuli was a getaway for Austrian nobles, as well as a major wine reservoir (mostly of red wine, as in the Alto Adige). So it might be said that a "quality" wine industry—one created to supply kings and their friends—developed early on in the region. Although the Friulians were among the first to capitalize on Italy's post–World War II industrial revolution, they were also in many instances culturally predisposed to think of their wines as something special.

The Austrian and French influences were especially strong in the vineyards. So-called "French" varieties such as chardonnay, sauvignon blanc, riesling, gewürztraminer, and "the pinots"—bianco (*blanc*) and grigio (*gris*)—have thrived in Friuli for centuries. These varieties complemented a better-than-average crop of native grapes, including tocai friulano, malvasia istriana, ribolla gialla, and picolit (once a Hapsburg favorite for the sweet, Sauternes-like wine it produces). Taken together, it's the most impressive roster of white grapes to be found in any Italian wine region, even when compared with other Austrian-influenced regions such as Alto Adige or the Veneto. As Burton Anderson writes in *The Wine Atlas of Italy*, "[There] are more than a few such havens for vines across the top of Italy, but nowhere else have winemakers shown the foresight, versatility and grit of Friulians in getting the most from them."

When people talk about Friulian wine, in fact, they often start with technique and move on to *terroir*. Before vintners such as Schiopetto came along, most Italians were fermenting white wines in the old farmhouse style: throwing their superripe grapes, skins and all, into open-topped wooden vats, where the fermentations would proceed naturally. The resultant wines were sweet, thick, high-alcohol, and heavily oxidized, drunk not as aperitifs but as fortification for an afternoon of farm work. But with the relatively mundane-sounding advent of the stainless-steel tank in the sixties—and the temperature control it permitted—everything changed. By most accounts, it was a change initiated first in Friuli.

The new-style wines of Schiopetto, Livio Felluga, and a handful of other sixties pioneers were designed to preserve the pure flavors of the grapes. They were made with only gently pressed juice (no skins), which was quickly sealed up in stainless steel so as not to become stale from oxidation. The lower-temperature fermentations in the refrigerated tanks created light-bodied, more aromatic wines that were bottled (and consumed) right away. There was no aging in oak barrels, and most of the time, no malo-lactic fermentation either ("malo" is a second fermentation whereby sharp-tasting malic acid in the wine is converted to softer lactic acid). The Friulian prototype was—and still is—a crisp, bright wine with pure varietal character.

This process is not easy. Even today, one of the best examples of Friulian precision is the Schiopetto winery in Capriva, in the Collio DOC zone. Cut into a vine-draped hillside like a secret bunker, the *cantina*, built in 1994, has the aseptic look of a NASA clean room. It has one primary function: to prevent, at each step of the winemaking process, the exposure of grapes to oxygen. The subterranean design allows for the fruit to be gravity-fed into the crushers (the minute a grape skin breaks, it begins to oxidize, so the gentler the handling the better), where the grapes are pressed and their juice centrifuged clean before it is transferred to the fermenters.

"By being so careful we are able to avoid sulfur in the winemaking process," says Giorgio Schiopetto, who with his twin brother, Carlo,

has taken over most of the winemaking responsibilities at Schiopetto. Anyone who's smelled an oversulfured wine (think of a boiled egg or a burned match) can appreciate his approach. While sulfur is a necessary antioxidant, the best winemakers minimize its use. "Because of how we handle our fruit, we don't have to use any sulfur before fermentation, and very little after," Schiopetto adds. "What we want is clean wines that speak of this place."

It helps, of course, that "this place" is well-positioned for white-grape growing. The Carnic and Julian Alps enclose the northern and eastern reaches of Friuli, walling it off from Austria and Slovenia, respectively. Yet in wine towns such as Cormòns, which sits in the pre-Alpine foothills, the Adriatic Sea is visible on a clear day. On the whole, only about eighty miles separate the ski slopes of Carnia from the lagoons of Grado, and the interplay of cool Alpine breezes and warm Adriatic currents is regarded as the secret to Friuli's white-wine supremacy: Although it's a northerly region, and is generally cooler than, say, Sicily, the key to Friuli is ventilation more so than temperature. Thanks to a kind of natural air-conditioning, say winemakers, grapes mature more slowly and evenly, retaining an elusive balance of rich fruit flavor, well-defined aromas, and an electric charge of acidity.

There are a total of ten DOC zones in Friuli–Venezia Giulia, stretching from its western border with Veneto to its eastern border with Slovenia. Much of wine-growing Friuli is based in the flatlands, including the alluvial high plains of Grave and Isonzo and the more fertile coastal plains of Latisana, Friuli Annia, and Aquilea. Although all of these lower-lying zones take advantage of the Alpine-Adriatic air-conditioning, they are considered somewhat less desirable in comparison to the hills that hug the Slovenian border, which are marked by the Carso, Collio, and Colli Orientali del Friuli DOCs. The Carso is actually more of a shelf of land running from the Isonzo River down to Trieste, but the heavy concentration of limestone in its soils gives it an advantage, since limestone preserves acidity in grapes. In the foothills of Collio and Colli Orientali, this limestone is mixed with marl and sandstone; combined with the higher elevations of the vineyards, this is considered the ideal.

"There are certain benefits to being on a hill," says Gianni Menotti, the thoughtful young winemaker at Villa Russiz, in the Collio DOC, which is well-known for crisp, aromatic varietal whites. "There's not a great deal of difference in temperature between here and the plain, but the quality of light in the hills, because of the angle the sun's rays hits the vines, is better. There's less humidity than in the plain, and better drainage. And the nights are cooler in the hills."

The varietal wines of Collio and Colli Orientali continue to set the standard in Friuli, although these days it is easier and easier to find distinctive whites from just about every DOC in the region. Plus, there's the added benefit of the wines being labeled by grape variety as well as denomination of origin, making it easier to know what it is you're drinking. And then there's the extraordinary variety of grapes to be discovered: pinot grigios that are fuller and more flavorful than any you've tasted before; minerally, spicy chardonnays that are a refreshing departure from the oak bombs of California; malvasias that hint at fresh-picked apricots; sauvignons as racy and clean as melted snow; tart, limey verduzzos; crisp, cidery ribollas; and

TALKING TOCAI

Nearly every meal in Friuli begins with an *affettato misto* of assorted *salumi* and *prosciutti*, not just from large producers in San Daniele but from local artisans such as Lorenzo d'Osvaldo, who makes a variety of *prosciutti affumicati* and *speck* (smoked prosciutto and bacon, respectively) at his farm in Cormòns. More often than not, the wine served with these meats is the local tocai friulano. There's something about the combination that seems preconceived, even if it isn't: The sweet-then-salty ham is matched by the fruity-then-minerally tocai, the fattiness of the prosciutto checked by the wine's brisk acidity.

What's unusual about tocai is that for all of its professed nobility, it is thought to be a mongrel variety. Some experts assert that tocai is related to the furmint grape of Hungary, which is used to make sweet wines in that country's Tokaji region. In Alsace, tokay is a synonym for pinot gris (grigio). Certainly Friuli has been influenced by both the French and the Austro-Hungarians, so what's the real story?

According to Giulio Columba of Italy's Slow Food organization, early (that is, nineteenth-century) editions of tocai friulano were most likely furmint. "Only in 1932 are there records of a new tocai, probably made from sauvignonasse, a minor French cultivar," says Columba. Other published sources confirm this.

While tocai could never be confused with the Tokaji wines of Hungary, the European Community has debated in recent years whether Friulians should drop the "tocai" from the name of their native grape. Although the matter was still under consideration at this writing, there are those who believe that the grape name "tocai friulano" may be a thing of the past.

STUDY GUIDE:
THE SUPER-WHITES

Friuli's multitude of blended white wines, incorporating a wide array of different grape varieties, are some of the most complex, full-bodied whites to be found anywhere in the world. But in looking at the bottles, the question arises: What are they, anyway? Often they carry only a *nome di fantasia* (fantasy name) on their labels, with nothing else to identify them. Some are rich and toasty from fermenting and aging in small oak barrels, others are crisper and lighter, fermented only in stainless steel. Based on the mix of grapes, the wine may be roundly fruity and full-bodied or exotically aromatic. But the only way to know what you're getting is through trial and error, or some advance research. A little of the latter is provided below.

Name	Producer	Blend	Notes
Vintage Tunina	Jermann	chardonnay, sauvignon, tocai, picolit	Considered the benchmark super-white. Cool, complex, plush, and aromatic, made without oak treatment.
Capo Martino	Jermann	tocai friulano, malvasia, pinot bianco	Round, creamy, barrel-aged white from native grapes. Big and rich.
Miani Bianco	Miani	chardonnay, malvasia istriana, riesling, pinot grigio	Fermented and aged in oak, an extremely rich, honeyed white from a boutique producer. A cult wine.
Vespa Bianco	Bastianich	chardonnay, sauvignon, picolit	Creamy and complex, with a powerful structure and a hint of apricot and dried flowers. (But we're biased, of course.)
Bianco della Castellada	La Castellada	tocai, pinot grigio, chardonnay, sauvignon	Smoky from time in oak, a rich and honeyed blend.
Flors di Uis	Vie di Romans	chardonnay, malvasia, riesling	Dewy and exotically aromatic from the use of malvasia and riesling. Steely and bright, no wood.
Prime Note	Venica	chardonnay, tocai friulano, sauvignon, ribolla gialla	Lots of citrus and peach fruit, very ripe and round.
Terre Alte	Livio Felluga	sauvignon, pinot bianco, tocai	Another benchmark. Clean and bright, with lots of sauvignon character.
Latimis Bianco	Ronco del Gelso	tocai, pinot bianco, riesling	Fermented all in steel, a cool, crisp, brightly aromatic white with surprising richness.
Tre Vigne	Zamò	chardonnay, tocai, sauvignon	Deep gold, smoky from time in oak, and almost a pineapple richness of fruit extract.
Blanc des Rosis	Schiopetto	tocai, pinot bianco, sauvignon, malvasia	In the aromatic, complex, unwooded camp. Luscious but firm.

spicy, aromatic rieslings and traminers. But above all else, there's tocai friulano, not only the everyday drink at the corner *osteria* but Friuli's signature contribution to the world of white wine (see "Talking Tocai," on the preceding page).

Although Friuli created a prototypical white wine that the rest of Italy tried to emulate—lean, crisp, aromatic—the region's winemakers have rarely been content to stand still. Continually refining their techniques and adopting new ones, the Friulians have built on the prototype in so many different ways that it is now very difficult to generalize about the Friulian "style." In the same way that they were pioneers of controlled-temperature fermentation, they were early proponents of a more "Burgundian" approach to white winemaking, as exemplified in the eighties by the rich, barrel-fermented white blends of Josko Gravner.

The shy, iconoclastic Gravner has since confounded the wine world by shifting to an essentially nineteenth-century approach to winemaking—his new style is a minimal-intervention, highly oxidative process in which the wines have a cloudy, cidery hue when bottled. But Gravner is credited with introducing French barriques and the process of barrel-fermentation to Friuli. His winery, located just steps from Slovenia in the hills of Oslavia, became the focal point for a movement that ran almost parallel to that of Mario Schiopetto's in the seventies and eighties. Along with a group of neighbors with similarly Slovenian roots—among them Stanislao Radikon and the Bensa brothers of the La Castellada estate—Gravner became known for a richer, oakier, more age-worthy style of white wine.

"After Schiopetto pioneered cold fermentation in this region, a lot of producers overdid it on the 'cold' part," says Alvaro Pecorari, who himself has experimented considerably with French oak at his Lis Neris estate in the Isonzo zone. "The result was a lot of wines that were stripped of any real character. Whereas in the past a lot of producers were fermenting their whites at sixteen degrees centigrade, now people have settled around eighteen to twenty-two, which allows for more development of flavor. Beyond that, we're learning how to use oak in a more effective way."

"In Friuli," adds Gianfranco Gallo, proprietor of the Vie di Romans estate, also in the Isonzo zone, "the mentality for many years was to make a technically perfect wine: clean, high acid. These days we're experimenting more."

This experimental bent has given rise to a highly variable collection of blended wines, usually labeled with fanciful names, that have come to be nicknamed the "super-whites." These blends began to emerge not long after the varietal wines of Schiopetto et. al., and in the eighties and nineties they became more widespread. In one sense they are truly modern, "international" wines, in that they are often fermented and aged in oak barrels, which lend a toasty, smoky, vanillin character that today's white-wine drinkers love. They are also often based on chardonnay, the world's trendiest white grape. But in another sense, the super-whites harken back to the old days in Friuli.

Such was the intention of Silvio Jermann, whose winery sits on a veritable island of hills near Farra d'Isonzo, an aberration on the otherwise flat Isonzo plain that is officially considered an adjunct of the Collio zone. Jermann has become one of the best-known winemakers in Friuli, having created the luxurious white blend called "Vintage Tunina" in 1975. It's a wine with a modern taste but a not-so-modern mind-set, a wine that bridges the gap between the Friuli of today and the Friuli of old.

Jermann created Vintage Tunina with his father and grandfather in mind; he wanted to pay tribute to the old-style Friulian "field blends" of his youth, where everything in the vineyard was tossed into a vat after a late harvest. Vintage Tunina is a blend of chardonnay and sauvignon blanc with the local tocai friulano and picolit, and incorporates a percentage of superripe, later-harvested fruit to give it more depth and complexity. At the same time, it's fermented in stainless steel, so while it gains a creamy richness from the late-harvested grapes, it also has bright acidity. Jermann similarly mixes the old and the new in his "Capo Martino," which incorporates mostly indigenous, normally harvested varieties (tocai, malvasia istriana, picolit, pinot bianco) that are fermented in large Slavonian oak barrels for a weightier, smokier profile.

As with super-Tuscan wines such as "Sassicaia" and "Ornellaia," the Friulian super-whites are often labeled as *Vino da Tavola* (VdT), or *Indicazione Geografica Tipica* (IGT), because they incorporate grapes or methods not allowed in the DOC provisions. And like the super-Tuscans, the super-whites have become luxury wines, breaking roughly into two main camps:

1. The brighter, more aromatic blends fermented only in stainless steel, among them Livio Felluga's "Terre Alte" (tocai/pinot bianco/sauvignon) and Vie di Romans' "Flor di Uis" (malvasia istriana/riesling renano/tocai friulano/chardonnay).
2. The richer, oak-fermented-and-aged blends, such as Le Vigne di Zamò's "Tre Vigne" (tocai/chardonnay/sauvignon, incorporating both late-harvest fruit and barrique fermen-

tation) and La Castellada's "Bianco" (tocai/ribolla gialla/pinot grigio/sauvignon).

There's such a dichotomy of wine styles in Friuli that winemakers often distinguish between *vini freschi* (fresh wines) and *vini barricati* (barrique wines) the way we would separate whites and reds. Whereas a straightforward varietal tocai or pinot grigio is the kind of lean, racy white to have with a simple *scampi alla buzzera* (breaded grilled shrimp) on the docks in Muggia, the super-whites can stand up to richer mountain foods—maybe a *raviolacci di sclopit* (an herb-filled ravioli) or *sarma* (cabbage stuffed with braised pork). Some super-whites can also be good with the local Montasio cheeses, especially the mozzarella-like *latteria fresca*, where the creamy flavors of both complement each other.

"This is still a young region, when you think about it," says Gianni Venica, one of the top producers in the Collio DOC. "In the last ten years there have been many new producers, and the styles of wine have evolved tremendously. What Friuli has done better than most is adapt to consumers' tastes and change accordingly."

VINI ROSSI
Red Wines

It's somewhat surprising to learn that more than 40 percent of Friuli's wine production is red, since the whites have traditionally received the lion's share of the attention. In fact, merlot is the most-planted variety of any type in the region, consuming nearly 20 percent of the vineyard area. Unfortunately, much of this is fairly innocuous, mass-produced merlot from the Grave plain.

Yet it is a mistake to think of Friuli as only a white-wine region. In recent years, many of the same winemakers who've become famous for whites have turned their attention to reds, finding that the vineyards that produce such balanced, flavorful tocai and chardonnay can also, if properly tended, turn out richly concentrated merlot and cabernet.

"In the past, Friulians vinified red wines in much the same way we vinified white wines," says Marco Felluga, who bottles wine under the Marco Felluga label as well as from his Russiz Superiore and Castello di Buttrio estates. Russiz Superiore, a spectacular château-style winery perched on a hilltop outside Capriva, is where Felluga has focused more on red-wine production, using cabernet sauvignon, cabernet franc, and merlot from Collio vineyards to create varietal reds as well as "Rosso Riserva Degli Orzoni," a Bordeaux-style blend. Felluga, like many Friulian vintners, believes that the *ronchi* (hills) of Collio and Colli Orientali, not to mention the alluvial vineyards of Isonzo and Grave (with their Bordeaux-like gravelly soils), can produce red wines of character.

"We are now looking at reds in a different way," says Felluga. "In the vineyard, we're taking lower yields per plant and planting more densely. In the winery, we're macerating the wines for longer periods and aging them in small oak barriques."

Walter Filiputti, who bottles his eponymous wines at the historic Abbazia di Rosazzo, an eleventh-century monastery overlooking the town of Corno di Rosazzo in Colli Orientali, adds: "One thing to remember is that most of the best vineyard sites in Friuli are planted to whites, because that's what we're famous for. But at the same time, we always made light reds, picking them when we picked the whites

and drinking them very young. So as a result, Friulian reds often taste green, not ripe and extracted like more famous reds."

There is a mantra, of sorts, repeated by any number of Friulian winemakers when the conversation turns to red wines. It pertains to three techniques that were long ago discovered elsewhere, yet are fairly recent innovations in Friuli. First, producers seeking higher-quality reds are pruning their vines more closely, and planting their vines more densely, so that each plant produces a smaller quantity of more concentrated, evenly ripe fruit. Second, vintners are leaving their fermenting wines to steep longer on their skins, creating more deeply extracted, powerful reds. And third, aging in oak has become a modern requirement, as the flavors, aromas, and tannins imparted by the barrels—and the controlled oxidation they facilitate—create a more luxurious and ageable red wine.

One of the best red-wine makers in Friuli is Girolamo Dorigo, whose vineyards are tucked into the hills near the tiny, fortress-like town of Buttrio, in the Colli Orientali zone. Those vineyards, including a plot called Montsclapade (which lends its name to a satiny cabernet-based blend), are prime examples of the kind of meticulous viticulture that's taken root throughout Italy. The vines are spaced very closely and they have a single, short cane jutting out from a thick, gnarled trunk. Only a minuscule amount of fruit can be produced from a vine this closely cropped. But while production is small, the quality of the fruit is exponentially better: The sun can get at the grape clusters, ripening them more evenly; and since the vine's nutrients are split among a smaller number of clusters, the grapes are more concentrated with flavor.

This premise of close-cropping holds true

whether the grape in question is merlot, cabernet sauvignon, or one of Friuli's indigenous red varieties, such as refosco or the scarcer but more intriguing pignolo and schioppettino. But then, how do you define indigenous? It's natural to think of Friuli's predominance of merlot and cabernet as a response to recent trends, but history shows that these grapes date back to the 1800s in the area. French count Theodore La Tour, for example, who built the Villa Russiz estate in 1869 with his Austrian wife, Elvine Richter, is considered one of many to have planted merlot and other "French" varieties long ago. And when the vine louse phylloxera destroyed most of Europe's vineyards at the end of the nineteenth century, the French varieties gained an even stronger foothold. To the locals' way of thinking, a Friulian merlot sounds every bit as natural as a French one. Nevertheless, shopping for merlot, cabernet, or Bordeaux-style blends from Friuli can be a dicey proposition. There are still plenty of overproduced, leafy-tasting merlots throughout Friuli (that "green" flavor thought to come from excessive vigor of the vine's canopy of leaves), so choosing the right producers is perhaps more critical for reds than when picking a Friulian white.

Generally speaking, the best merlots of Friuli are made in small quantities, often by smaller producers. Among the best are the powerful, barrique-aged wines of Radikon; the "Graf de la Tour" from Menotti at Villa Russiz; the luxuriously dense reds of Ronchi di Manzano, Edi Keber, and Ronco dei Tassi; and the elegant "Sossò" from one of Friuli's most distinguished elder statesmen, Livio Felluga. (Livio is the natty, more subdued older brother of the gregarious Marco, with whom he feuded and split long ago.)

As for Bordeaux-style blends, topping the list are the unctuous reds of Enzo Pontoni, whose tiny Miani winery in Colli Orientali ranks with Dorigo in producing both rich reds and slick whites. The Miani Rosso is a very rare, very expensive merlot-based blend that also includes some cabernet sauvignon; along with Dorigo's "Montsclapade" and Le Vigne di Zamò's "Ronco dei Roseti," it is a red that can compete with Bordeaux in depth and complexity.

As with the whites, the majority of the best Friulian reds are found in Collio and Colli Orientali, particularly from the hills near the Abbazia di Rosazzo. But in the Isonzo and Grave especially, the gravelly soils have yielded much more than just mass-produced merlot. Most of the Isonzo, as well as the northern and eastern reaches of the Grave, is cooler than the lower-lying plains along the Adriatic, and there are any number of producers in both regions whose wines rival those of their more celebrated neighbors.

For lovers of California wines especially, most of these merlots and blends from Friuli are an easy segue into the world of Italian reds. In fact, they can often taste quite a bit like Californian wines, all soft and supple from their time in oak, with ripe, juicy fruit flavors that are easy to enjoy. But for a challenge, check out the more ancient varieties of the region, especially refosco, pignolo, and schioppettino. These grapes speak volumes about Friuli's untapped potential as a red-wine zone.

In fact, for all of the popularity of merlot in Friuli, a number of star producers, including Enzo Pontoni at Miani, think refosco is Friuli's grape of the future. For the most part, refosco has been made as a simple, high-acid salami wine to be quaffed in a roadside *frasca;* at times, it can taste sort of light and grapey, like a Beaujolais. But when people apply the viticultural techniques described above to refosco, the results can be impressive.

"Refosco can be a big aging wine. We just haven't done the right things in the vineyards and the cellar to get it there," says Emilio Del Medico, an up-and-coming winemaker who consults not only to the Bastianich winery but for the well-regarded Zamò estate as well. "The problem with refosco is that it doesn't evolve over time. You put it in the barrel and it doesn't change."

Some vintners in Friuli are experimenting with refosco *appassimento,* whereby the grapes are dried and shriveled after harvest à la Amarone, creating an intense, off-dry red. There aren't any yet that will make people forget about Amarone, but there will be a day very soon when refosco is a more full-blooded red than it is now—*appassimento* or not. At the moment, refosco is extremely variable, ranging from light and tart to more robust and interesting: The better ones, like Venica's "Bottaz" and Valter Scarbolo's well-priced "Campo del Viotto" bottling, pair the stewed fruit flavor of a California zinfandel with the peppery spice of a Côtes-du-Rhône. Dorigo's refosco is chunkier and more powerful, thanks to low crop yields and a healthy dose of new-oak aging.

It's noteworthy that a number of California winemakers—who are already making good wines from Italian grapes such as sangiovese, barbera, and dolcetto—have begun to experiment with refosco. So keep your eyes open when you're in the wine shop: That little-noticed refosco on the shelf is likely to be a great value.

Two other ancient Friulian reds to seek out are pignolo and schioppettino, which are enjoying a comeback after being all but forgotten. Wines made from either grape are still quite rare, and only a few are exported to the United States. But these grapes can produce the kind of structured, ageworthy reds most people think are only found in Tuscany and Piedmont.

Schioppetino is the *nera,* or "black," version of ribolla gialla, and is best described as ornery. Its name means "gunshot," apparently because wines made from it crackle and pop when fermenting, and no doubt because a young schioppettino-based wine can be like a shotgun blast of tannin on the tongue. Only a handful of producers—among them Ronchi di Cialla, Girolamo Dorigo, Adriano Gigante, Zamò, and Livon—even bother with the grape anymore, because it is difficult to grow. "It is a very vigorous plant," explains Adriano Gigante, a winemaker in the Colli Orientali. "Schioppettino grows in very long bunches, so you have to go through the vineyard in May and do a green harvest, then go back in August and cut off the bottom third of the bunches, otherwise the grapes won't ripen."

When they do ripen, however, a schioppettino wine has a powerful core of spicy black fruit, like a good Rhône syrah. Taste some older schioppettinos from Girolamo Dorigo, for example, and there's no question that with time schioppettino smoothes out into a complex, smoky, silky red. When traveling in Friuli, especially if something fatty and rich like *stinco di vitello* (whole braised veal shank) is on the table, a schioppettino is well worth taking a chance on.

As for pignolo, the better ones have the black cherry flavors and tarry tannins of a good Brunello di Montalcino, but there are literally only a handful of pignolo-based wines in all of Friuli. The story of the grape's revival has some operatic Italian twists, in fact, with three protagonists: Walter Filiputti, he of the self-named winery at the Abbazia di Rosazzo; the Zamò family, Filiputti's neighbors (and former collaborators) in the hills of Rosazzo; and Girolamo Dorigo in Buttrio.

The three players tell the story differently, but here's how it breaks down: Filiputti, who was a journalist before going into winemaking, set out in the early eighties to revive winemaking at the Abbazia, where according to local legend pignolo was first propagated in the thirteenth century. A priest named Luigi Nadalutti helped Filiputti chart which grapes were in which of the abbey's run-down vineyards. As Filiputti began getting the winery up and running he took on some partners. Eventually the partnership included the Zamò family, well-known furniture manufacturers who own several different vineyards in the Colli Orientali zone.

"When I arrived at the abbey in seventy-eight, there were only two pignolo vines leaning against the south wall," says Filiputti. "Starting in seventy-nine we started to replant pignolo elsewhere using cuttings from those two plants."

The Dorigo family, meanwhile, claims to have gotten pignolo cuttings from Father Nadalutti in 1976. So for many years the two key pignolo makers were Dorigo and the Zamòs, for whom Filiputti was the winemaker. But in 1989 Filiputti resigned in a dispute—or was fired, depending on whom you ask. The Zamòs then called in well-known Tuscan consultant Franco Bernabei, who made the Abbazia wines between '89 and '96. At that point, the Zamòs' lease at the abbey expired. Through some maneuvering, Filiputti got the new lease and moved in, establishing the Walter Filiputti brand.

The Zamòs' stylish new *cantina*, along with one of their family residences, is just down the hill from Filiputti and the abbey. "We now make pignolo from other vineyards of ours in Rosazzo," says Pierluigi Zamò, who heads up his family's winemaking operations. "Basically, the pignolos and other wines from the abbey up through the '96 vintage have the Zamò name. After that they change."

Pignolo is one of those rare romance wines whose production is largely confined to three producers, although the ranks are growing. In recent years, a number of top Friulian producers, including Jermann, have begun experimenting with pignolo. Although there is not yet a lot of bottled evidence to support the assertion, the Friulians think pignolo will be their answer to the great reds of Tuscany and Piedmont. "I've often thought that pignolo was sangiovese grosso"—the grape clone used in Brunello—"but I can't prove it," says Pierluigi Zamò. "This I think is Friuli's biggest red."

Others disagree. "I think merlot is the premier red grape in Friuli," says Gianni Menotti of Villa Russiz. Adds Enzo Pontoni of Miani: "The future in Friulian reds is refosco." Regardless of whom you believe, there's an important point: The same factors that make Friuli a great white-wine zone will make it a great red-wine zone in time.

VINI SPUMANTI E DOLCI

Sparkling and Sweet Wines

Despite Friuli's relatively cool climate and its wealth of white grapes, there isn't a big sparkling-wine culture in the region. There are a handful of solid proseccos to be found, and a few sparklers made from varieties such as pinot bianco or ribolla gialla. But on the whole, Friuli is not a place to look for bubbly. Sweet wine, however, is another story.

The Friulian native picolit is made into a rich, honeyed sweet wine that was once admired by the royal courts of Europe. It's probably Friuli's most historic grape, having been a favorite of the sweet-toothed Hapsburgs. But these days it's a rather small-production specialty of a handful of producers, among them Livio Felluga, Dorigo, Ronco delle Bettule, and Rocca Bernarda, the historic estate in the town of Ipplis, in Colli Orientali, where many people believe picolit was first propagated. Although there are good picolits made elsewhere, Colli Orientali has long been the premier zone.

For all of its fame, picolit is also something of a "farmer's grape" in Friuli, long used to add sweetness and heft to dry whites and even some reds; it's still used to plump up some of the dry "super-whites," lending them an exotic edge. Picolit is difficult to grow, each vine typically yielding very little fruit. But what it does produce is turned into rich, floral, honeyed nectar with the heft of a Sauternes and the crisp acidity of a late-harvest German riesling. It is a silky dessert wine with the succulent aromas and flavors of apricots and peaches, a great wine to sip by itself or to pour over some fresh berries for a simple but decadent dessert. Yet picolit is not just a dessert wine: try it with some seared foie gras or paté. The rich, savory flavors of these foods, contrasted by the honeyed sweetness of the wine, is an incredible combination, a mouthwatering first plate that readies you for the next course.

The lesser-known grape used for sweet wines is the *giallo* (yellow) clone of verduzzo, also known as ramandolo. In contrast to the round, honeyed, almost petrol character of picolit, verduzzo is a little more citrusy, like an orange jelly candy. As with picolit, it's made only by a few vintners, including Ronchi di Cialla, Ronchi di Manzano, Giovanni Dri, and Livón, and in 2001 Verduzzo Ramandolo was elevated to DOCG status. Neither verduzzo nor picolit will make you give up Château d'Yquem, but at times they can come pretty close. And like just about everything else in Friuli, they're no longer a well-kept secret.

FAST FACTS:
FRIULI–VENEZIA GIULIA

PROVINCES	Pordenone (PN), Udine (UD), Gorizia (GO), Trieste (TS)
CAPITAL	Trieste
KEY WINE TOWNS	Buttrio, Capriva, Cormòns, Farra d'Isonzo, Oslavia, Rosazzo
TOTAL VINEYARD AREA*	18,704 hectares, or 46,218 acres. Rank: 14th
TOTAL WINE PRODUCTION*	1,018,000 hectoliters, or 26,895,640 gallons (13th); 52% white, 48% red
DOC WINE PRODUCED*	60.5% (2nd)
SPECIALTY FOODS	prosciutto di San Daniele; Montasio (cow's milk cheese); *prosciutto affumicato* (smoked prosciutto), bacon (*speck*), and *ricotta affumicata* cheese from the Carnic Alps.

*1997 figures. Rankings out of twenty regions total (Trentino-Alto–Adige counted as one). Source: Istituto Statistica Mercati Agro-Alimentari (ISMEA), Rome.

KEY GRAPE VARIETIES

WHITES

TOCAI FRIULANO	The signature Friulian white. Fleshy, with hints of peach, pear, and almonds, yet with a palate-cleansing zing of minerals and acid.
PINOT GRIGIO	Friuli's best are the best in Italy: fuller, rounder, nuttier, more expressive than the general run of bone-dry, insipid whites from the grape.
SAUVIGNON	Ranging from grassy and Loire-like to richer, peachier in character. One of the most interesting grapes in Friuli.

CHARDONNAY	Started to emerge in Friuli in the 1960s. The best suggest white Burgundy with their mineral flintiness and creamy textures. A key grape in super-white blends.
PINOT BIANCO	Faintly almondy, coppery, crisp, and light. Better as a blending grape, but produces some distinguished varietal bottlings.
OTHERS	PICOLIT, a native grape used for honeyed sweet wines; RIBOLLA GIALLA, also native, makes appley, fresh still wines and some *mèthode champenoise* sparklers; MALVASIA ISTRIANA, native, aromatic dry wines with hints of apricot and nuts; VERDUZZO, native, used for both lemony, bone-dry whites and sweet nectars; PROSECCO, for a few decent sparklers; also aromatic German/Alsace varieties MÜLLER-THURGAU, RIESLING (both "italico" and "renano" clones), and TRAMINER AROMATICO (similar to gewürztraminer).

REDS

MERLOT	Has been in Friuli since at least the 1800s. Most are simple, fruity, often leafy-tasting. The standouts are dense, concentrated, flashy reds.
CABERNET FRANC	Herbal, earthy, cherry-scented red; some nice individual wines but more often used in Bordeaux-style blends.
CABERNET SAUVIGNON	Some wines taste Californian, some like Bordeaux, but usually with distinctly tarry, smoky Italian character.
REFOSCO	The most-planted "native" grape, but few exceptional wines. Often light, purple and Beaujolais-like; a tart picnic wine. Most producers believe it could be ageworthy with better viticulture and winemaking. Best clone is refosco dal pedunculo rosso, or "refosco with the red stalks."
CABERNET	Cross of franc/sauvignon. Generally a blending variety.
OTHERS	PIGNOLO, a rare but resurgent native that makes some of the densest, most ageworthy reds in Friuli, reminiscent of Brunello; SCHIOPPETTINO, also a rare native that's hard to grow, syrah-like in its spiciness, and tannic, powerful, and ageworthy; TAZZELENGHE, a tart-tasting native whose name means "tongue cutter"; and TERRANO, a refosco clone used in the Carso.

TOP VINTAGES IN FRIULI—VENEZIA GIULIA, 1980—2000

Most of Friuli's white wines, especially the single-varietal wines made without oak treatment or malolactic fermentation, are meant to be drunk young. As in right away. One to two years' aging is more than enough for Friuli's varietal whites. The larger-scale white blends can go longer, so look for older vintages from good producers as well as newer releases. On the red side, Friuli's cooler climate is reminiscent of Burgundy's, in that a great vintage can make a great wine; in general, the highs are high and the lows are low. With the better red blends, and with wines made from the pignolo and schioppettino grapes, aging between five and ten years is recommended. Top Years: 1982, '85, '89, '90, '93, '95, '97, '99, 2000.

LA STRADA DEL VINO
WINE TOURING IN FRIULI—VENEZIA GIULIA

It's a little off the wine path, but one excursion worth making is a trip to a *prosciuttificio* (prosciutto factory) in the little town of San Daniele, northwest of Udine. San Daniele hams are among the "Big Three" of Italian *prosciutti,* and after touring one of the production facilities there are a number of small, rustic *osterie* in San Daniele where you can sample a wood paddle–full of *prosciutto a mano* (cut by hand), washed down with a carafe of tocai friulano. Contact the Consorzio del Prosciutto di San Daniele (tel: 0432-95-7 5-15; Via Odberto 1, 34, San Daniele) for more information.

Another great spot for tasting wines and soaking up the *ambiente* of the Friulian hills is the Enoteca di Cormòns, where a wide variety of Friulian wines and foods can be sampled (and bought) in a homey *osteria* with a sunny patio on the Cormòns town square. Just outside of Cormòns is one of Friuli's great country restaurants, La Subida (0481-60531), which serves hearty Friulian mountain food and has an extensive Friulian wine list. And by all means go see our friend Valter Scarbolo at La Frasca (Viale Grado 10, Pavia di Udine; 0432-87-51-50).

Other authentic restaurants include Al Capello in Udine (Via P. Sarpi 2; 0432-50-11-86) and Da Giovanni in Trieste (Via San Lazzaro 14; 040-63-93-96). A great place to stay amid the vineyards of Buttrio is the Agriturismo Scacciapensieri (0432-67-49-07).

DEGUSTAZIONI
TASTINGS

TOCAI FRIULANO

Schiopetto Collio
Tocai Friulano, $$

Ronco del Gnemiz COF
Tocai Friulano, $

Le Vigne di Zamò COF
Tocai Friulano "Vigne
Cinquant'Anni," $$

Selecting just three tocais is a difficult task: Friuli has a wealth of cool, clean varietal wines, and the native tocai grape tops the list. In these wines you'll get a good sense of the flavor and body spectrum of the wine, which can range from appley, minerally, and spicy (Schiopetto), to more creamy, peachy, and round (Zamò). One of the intriguing flavors typical to tocai is a hint of brown spice, such as nutmeg or mace. Other grace notes include scents of pear and apricot, but regardless of how round and fruity the wine gets, it typically finishes with a minerally savor. These are the ultimate prosciutto wines, but you'll find them versatile with a wide variety of foods.

Other good tocais for substitutes: Russiz Superiore, Ronco dei Tassi, Borgo del Tiglio, Ronco delle Betulle.

PINOT GRIGIO

Aldo Polencic Collio
Pinot Grigio, $

Volpe Pasini COF
Pinot Grigio "Zuc di
Volpe," $$

Lis Neris-Pecorari Isonzo
Pinot Grigio "Gris," $$

Although most consumers regard pinot grigio as a light, watery wine for a plate of fried calamari, Friulian vintners are among those who insist that the grape can make a rich and full-bodied wine if treated with care. These wines demonstrate that. They are creamy and round, not assertively aromatic, but with a certain weight on the palate that makes them immensely satisfying. In the Lis Neris wine in particular, you'll also note a toasty flavor from fermentation in small oak barrels. These wines are somewhat reminiscent of chardonnay in their plump fruitiness, and can well stand up to heartier dishes such as pasta with speck or the Friulian classic *gnocchi di susine* (gnocchi stuffed with fresh plums, then finished in a butter-cinnamon sauce).

Villa Russiz Collio
Sauvignon "Graf de la
Tour," $$

Venica e Venica Collio
Sauvignon "Ronco delle
Mele," $$

Livio Felluga
"Terre Alte," $$

Vie di Romans
"Flor di Uis," $$

Jermann
"Vintage Tunina," $$$

Marco Felluga
"Molamatta," $

Bastianich
"Vespa Bianco," $$

La Castellada
"Bianco della
Castellada," $$$

SAUVIGNON

Intensely aromatic, brightly acidic, these wines represent some of the best of Friuli sauvignon. The Villa Russiz wine has some grassy, herbal notes reminiscent of the sauvignon of the Loire, but the intensity of the flavors is a little headier than your average Sancerre. The Venica wine shows off a more citrusy side to the grape, with aromas of white grapefruit and flavors reminiscent of mandarin oranges. They are exotic, powerful whites that leap out of the glass, for assertively flavored dishes.

SUPER-WHITES 1—UNWOODED BLENDS

Part of the fun of tasting super-whites is trying to detect which varieties you can recognize in the blend. In these wines, which are all fermented only in stainless steel, the appeal is a pure chord of complex fruit flavor. In "Terre Alte" the sauvignon in the blend pokes its head out a little more than the others, while "Flor di Uis" takes on a hint of apricot from the malvasia and riesling in its mix. The fullest and most tropically fruity of the three is the "Vintage Tunina," but, like the other two, it delivers its clear flavors on a raft of cleansing acidity. Try these with mineral-tinged seafoods such as whole *branzino* (sea bass) baked in a crust of salt.

SUPER-WHITES 2—RICHER, BARREL-AGED BLENDS

The common denominator here is a creaminess and richness imparted through fermenting at least a part of the wine in small oak barrels. The lightest of the three is the "Molamatta," which is a blend of ribolla gialla, tocai, and pinot bianco, with only the pinot bianco fermented in wood. The other two wines include substantial percentages of chardonnay and more wood treatment, so they come off thicker and richer—especially the Castellada wine, which has a smokiness imparted by the barrels. The cool, fleshy, grapey personality of "Molamatta" makes it great for sipping on its own or with hors d'oeuvres, while the tightly coiled power of the "Vespa" demands food, maybe a hearty risotto. The La Castellada wine, with its pineapple fruitiness and smoky complexity, can take on fuller-flavored dishes as well, or even a hunk of the local Montasio cheese.

Vistorta Friuli Grave
Merlot, $

Ronchi di Manzano
COF
Merlot
"Ronc di Subule," $$$

Russiz Superiore
Collio Rosso
"Riserva degli Orzoni," $$

Scarbolo Grave Refosco
"Campo del Viotto," $

Walter Filiputti COF
Picolit, $$$

Livio Felluga COF
Picolit Riserva, $$$

VARIETAL REDS AND BLENDS

Here's a panorama of Friulian reds, starting with two of the better-regarded merlots in the zone. Whereas many Friulian merlots are light, clipped, and somewhat vegetal on the palate, these wines offer a depth of fruit concentration suggestive of a vineyard zone farther south. Both the Vistorta and the Ronchi di Manzano wines are a deep ruby color, with flavors of cherries, plums, and tar, hemmed in by slightly drying tannins. In the Russiz Superiore wine, a Bordeaux-style blend, the earthy, vegetal flavors of cabernet franc show through, giving the wine a push-pull of sweet and savory flavors. The refosco is distinct from the others, with a hint of exotic spice and fruit flavors that are more "black" than "red." What you'll notice in all these wines, however, is a certain restraint; they aren't quite as big and blowsy as the reds made farther south in Italy, but with a slight hint of bell pepper or mint showing through, especially in the merlot wines. They typically need food to show their best.

PICOLIT

These are the dessert nectars of Friuli, made from late-harvested fruit and infused with a whiff of botrytis smokiness. Honeyed, citrusy, and luscious, they start out coating the palate, then clean up on the finish with a zing of acidity. Traditional accompaniments for picolit include simple *biscotti* or dry, nut-filled cakes.

La Cucina

FOOD FOR THE WINE

RECIPE BY LIDIA BASTIANICH

There is so much diversity to Friulian cuisine that it is difficult to pinpoint a single dish that embodies the region's cooking. There is no more elemental Friulian combination than prosciutto di San Daniele and tocai friulano, of course; the Friulians are considered among the best pork butchers in the world. A trip to the region is a journey to prosciutto and salami heaven, with any number of different artisanal products served in paper-thin slices on thick wooden cutting boards in the local *osterie*.

Although there are scores of delicate seafood preparations found all over Friuli's arc of Adriatic coast, the foods that really evoke the region are the foods of the mountains: *stinco di vitello* (braised veal shank), *brovada* (turnips marinated in grape pomace), and lots of rich gnocchi dishes are staples of the hills of Collio and Colli Orientali, where the Austro-Hungarian and especially Slavic aspects of the cuisine really come to the fore.

The recipe that follows has become well-known to Americans, and it incorporates one of Friuli's signature food products: Montasio cheese, a buttery cow's-milk variety that's great for eating on its own but becomes something better still when transformed into a *frico*. This is a classic Friulian nosh, and a great partner for full-bodied white wines as well as reds.

Frico Friulano
FRIULIAN MONTASIO CHEESE TART

1 cup ARBORIO RICE
2 medium IDAHO POTATOES
¼ cup plus 2 tablespoons EXTRA-VIRGIN OLIVE OIL
2 medium SPANISH ONIONS, peeled and sliced into thin rounds (use a mandolin if possible)
½ teaspoon SALT, plus more to taste
2 tablespoons BALSAMIC VINEGAR
4 medium GREEN PEPERONCINI (in vinegar), diced fine
1 pound MONTASIO CHEESE, shredded on the coarse side of a box grater
2 bunches ARUGULA
Juice of 1 LEMON

MAKES TWO 8-INCH ROUNDS;
SERVES 6 TO 8 AS AN APPETIZER

In a large pot, bring 1 quart of salted water to a boil. Add the rice and cook until al dente, about 15 minutes. Drain the rice in a colander and spread it out on a sheet pan to cool.

Meanwhile, in another large pot, bring another 2 quarts of salted water to a boil. Add the potatoes and cook for 30 minutes, or until soft when pricked with a fork. Drain, allow to cool, then peel and slice into rounds about ⅛-inch thick.

Heat ¼ cup of the olive oil over medium flame in a large sauté pan. Add the onions and ½ teaspoon salt, and sauté for about 10 minutes, until the onions are slightly wilted. Add the balsamic vinegar, mix well, and remove from heat. Let the onions cool and absorb the vinegar, so that they turn brown.

In a large bowl, mix the cooled, cooked rice and the shredded Montasio. Heat a 9-inch nonstick pan over medium flame until hot, about 2 to 3 minutes. Take a quarter of the rice-cheese mixture and cover the bottom of the hot pan evenly. The cheese will immediately begin to form a crust on the bottom. Add half of the sliced potatoes in an even layer, half of the balsamic onions, and half of the minced peperoncini. Top with another quarter of the cheese-rice mixture. Cook for about 2 minutes, so that the bottom is golden brown, then flip over, like an omelette, and cook the other side for 3 to 4 minutes, or until golden brown. The cooked *frico* should look like a golden-brown pizza. Repeat this process to make a second *frico*.

Slice the *fricos* in quarters, as if cutting a pizza. In a bowl, combine the remaining 2 tablespoons of olive oil, the lemon juice, and salt and pepper to taste. Toss with the arugula to coat. Top with the *frico* wedges and serve.

WINE RECOMMENDATION: A rich Friulian super-white, such as the Bastianich "Vespa," La Castellada "Bianco," or Jermann's "Capo Martino." These whites will match the creaminess of the cheese with a creaminess of their own. Alternately, try a spicy, peppery refosco to take on the fried-cheese fattiness with a little tannin.

Veneto

Balancing Quantity and Quality

—⟨⟩—

They Eat Horses, Don't They?

The plate lands with a thud on a table that's as bulky as a fallen tree. At first glance it doesn't look so bad: a neat pile of shredded, cured meat on a bed of arugula, with a few lemon wedges to squeeze on top. But this is horse meat. Even a die-hard carnivore might draw the line at horse, although no one in this particular *osteria*—a medieval-looking tavern in Verona called Al Carro Armato—is giving it a second thought. Listed on the blackboard are a variety of horse dishes: the aforementioned *sfilacci* ("strands," which are dried and sometimes smoked); *bistecca di cavallo* (horse steak); and a rich braise called *pastisada*. This is standard fare all over Verona, but the rustic confines of Al Carro Armato definitely enhance the horse-eating experience; it looks like a place where someone might walk in any minute with a hind leg of something slung over his shoulder.

Still, it seems odd that Italians would eat horse. It's hardly a delicacy, and throughout Italian history horses held relatively exalted positions among animals. The Etruscans were reputedly great horse trainers, and the ancient Veneti were, too. The Greeks wrote the first treatises on horse breeding. Roman emperors treated their chariot horses better than they did most people.

But in times of need, even the Romans may have eaten horses. The Roman army was nearly all cavalry in its later incarnations, the better to match up against the mounted armies of the Longobards and Attila the Hun. So it's not hard to imagine a felled horse being used for food amid the ravages of war. Most Italians, however, pin the horse-eating tradition on the Longobards, or Lombards, who ruled what is now the Veneto, Lombardy, and much of north-central Italy from the sixth to the eighth centuries.

These days, *cavallo* and sometimes *asino* (donkey) are specialties in a number of mostly northern Italian cities, including Brescia, Milan, Verona, and Trieste. There are butchers who specialize in horse (*macellerie equine*), and their cuts have an eerily familiar ring to them: flank steak, rump roast, and so on.

Horse cookery has become most readily associated with Verona, although it's hard to say exactly why that is. If it was the Longobards who bequeathed the tradition, it would seem that the area near Milan would be the epicenter—the town of Monza, near Milan, was the historic Longobard capital. There are, in fact, several large horse butchers in Milan. But it's

THE DOC ZONES OF VENETO

DOCG

1 Recioto di Soave

3 Bardolino

DOCs

2 Bagnoli di Sopra/Bagnoli

4 Bianco di Custoza

5 Breganze

6 Colli Berici

7 Colli di Conegliano

8 Colli Euganei

9 Gambellara

10 Garda/Garda Classico

11 Lessini Durello

12 Lison-Pramaggiore

13 Lugana

14 Montello e Colli Asolani

15 Prosecco di Conegliano
    Valdobbiadene

16 S. Martino della Battaglia

17 Soave

18 Valdadige/Etschtaler

19 Valpolicella/Recioto della
    Valpolicella

20 Vini del Piave/Piave

21 Arcole*

22 Merlara*

23 Vicenza*

*New in 2000–2001

much easier to find horse on a menu in Verona or Vicenza; maybe this is because Verona was such an important market town in ancient times, thanks to its strategic positioning on the Adige River.

Whatever the reasons, the communal table at Al Carro Armato is now loaded with horse, as a group of young men at the other end start in on their own plates of *sfilacci*. Of the various ways in which horse is served, this is probably the best way for the uninitiated to get started: Flavor-wise, *sfilacci* is like a cross between bacon and beef jerky, savory and chewy and a little bit smoky.

In steak form, horse can be a jaw-buster. For an entrée, it's better to go with preparations like *pastisada*, which involves several hours of slow cooking in liquid (usually wine) to soften up the sometimes stringy meat. It is decidedly gamier than beef. Ultimately it is not an especially great addition to the Italian table; its role seems more symbolic than anything else, a reminder of how Italian cuisine was so often born out of desperation.

As exemplified by horse steaks, there's a weightiness to Veronese cooking that belies the city's elegant façade. Verona's main contribution to Italian cuisine is the humble *bollito misto* (mixed boiled meats), served with a bone-marrow-and-bread-crumb sauce called *pearà*. In Venice, too, the food is simple—rice and peas, liver and onions—but there's much more style and variety to the cooking there. It's not just the added dimension of seafood, which Verona sees very little of, but the Venetian attitude that makes the difference. As Waverly Root described eating in Venice in *The Food of Italy,* "Nowhere else has liver with onions become so refined, nowhere else has rice been treated with

such subtlety . . . nowhere else has polenta been made with such fine grain."

This Venetian sense of style—its "fascination with the façade," as Root put it—is what defines the Veneto region in most visitors' minds. Where Verona is tidy and statuesque, Venice is chaotic and ornate, fancily dressed but with a shirttail always hanging out. Where Verona is the industrious winemaker, Venice is the charismatic rabble-rouser and sometime salesman. Where Verona is Veneto's principal source of wine, Venice is its principal source of wine style.

Sometimes, style has won out over substance in the Veneto—with mixed results. By mastering the process of semi-drying grapes, the region's winemakers took a ho-hum blend of local varieties and created Amarone, one of the most unique red wines in the world. On the other hand, the Veneto has become one of Italy's biggest mass-marketers, creating wines that are simple, consistent, and well-priced, if rarely memorable.

Plenty of other wine regions have a similar mix of industrial and artisan producers. But in the Veneto, the contrasts may be the most dramatic. The region is home to most of the largest commercial producers in Italy, including Bolla, Santa Margherita, Zonin, and Gruppo Italiano Vini (GIV). The latter, in fact, is the largest wine company in Italy, turning out 60 million bottles a year from a number of estates, including the Folonari, Lamberti, and Santi properties in the Veneto. It's not that these wines are bad (in fact, some are very good), but like any mass-market products they've fixed a certain image in the collective consciousness. When someone says "Soave" or "Valpolicella" to you, what comes to mind?

The Veneto ranks third in Italy in the quantity of wine produced, trailing only Sicily and Puglia. The difference is that the vast majority of Sicily's and Puglia's wines leave in tanker trucks, not in bottles. And yet the Veneto isn't just bargain-rack wine. Soave can be a rich, aromatic, mouth-filling white. Valpolicella can be a luscious, ageworthy red. Even Prosecco, the wine for carefree nights in Venice, can be a serious sparkler. And Amarone, of course, is Amarone: There's nothing quite like it.

"This region has such incredible potential," says Stefano Inama, an outspoken producer of high-end Soave and of cabernet sauvignon from the Colli Berici DOC zone. "The problem is, we're not oriented toward high quality. The province of Verona is the most productive winemaking province in all of Europe. I suppose there are some people who are happy about that, but not me."

VINI SPUMANTI
Sparkling Wines

Prosecco may be the best example of a classic Veneto wine: simple and refreshing, a great wine to sip absentmindedly on a Venetian terrace with some *tramezzini* (finger sandwiches) on the side. Although there are a handful of proseccos with the power and structure of more serious sparklers, the hallmark style is light and easy.

The prosecco grape, historically a late-ripening variety, is thought to be a native of neighboring Friuli, where there is a town called Prosecco not far from Trieste. Before the advent of modern technology, prosecco wines, like most farmhouse whites, were at least lightly fizzy: the often overripe grapes, picked very late in the growing season, would stop fermenting in the cold winter months but then recommence in the spring, creating carbon dioxide bubbles in the wine. Often the wines had some residual sugar left in them because of the fits and starts of these natural fermentations, and for generations this became the prevailing style in the area.

The modern era of prosecco began with chemist/enologist Antonio Carpenè, who founded his Carpenè Malvolti firm in 1868 and an enology school at Conegliano in 1873 (the school is still one of Italy's best). Carpenè was the first in Italy to develop the "tank method" of making sparkling wine, in which the secondary fermentation that gives the wine bubbles is done in a large pressure tank, rather than in individual bottles. This method, called Charmat after its French inventor, was the foundation on which the prosecco industry was built. In typical Veneto fashion, this industry has ballooned into a giant: More than 250 million bottles of wine were produced in the Prosecco di Conegliano-Valdobbiadene DOC zone in 1997.

This industrial-scale production tends to obscure the fact that the Colli Trevigiani, as the hills between the communes of Valdobbiadene and Conegliano are called, are not only beautiful and tourist-friendly but well-suited to the making of sparkling wine: The often steep slopes are well-drained and within striking distance of the Alps. An interplay of cool Alpine breezes sweeping down from Belluno and warmer air blowing off the Adriatic creates a similar environment to that in neighboring Friuli, which is ideal for preserving acidity and aromas in the grapes.

The principal difference is that prosecco is a little less giving than many of the classic Friuli grapes; it's late-ripening and not especially aromatic. The better prosecco wines have a peachy softness, which is a little more pronounced in the lower-lying vineyards near Conegliano and checked with more minerality and acidity in the higher reaches of Valdobbiadene. Some of the better examples of the Conegliano style are made by Carpenè Malvotti and Zardetto, while on the Valdobbiadene side look for Nino Franco, Ruggeri & C., Desiderio Bisol, Mionetto, and Col Vetoraz.

Of the massive amounts of prosecco produced every year, roughly 8 million bottles are labeled with the denomination Cartizze, meant to indicate a wine from a select cluster of vineyards just north and east of Valdobbiadene. Extremely steep and low-yielding, the Cartizze vineyards—which total only about 250 acres—are considered the top crus of the DOC, and there are a number of wines from the zone that show off the firmer, broader, more powerful side of the prosecco grape.

On balance, however, prosecco is best as a light apéritif, whether it's from Conegliano, Valdobbiadene, or Cartizze. Although a number of producers are striving for more, these are still celebration wines, wines of the moment—usually the kind of moment you don't want to spoil by thinking too much.

VINI BIANCHI
White Wines

The Veneto is the largest producer of DOC wine in Italy, which is not to say that it makes the highest percentage of DOC relative to its total: That distinction goes to Trentino–Alto Adige, and there are five other regions ahead of the Veneto on that front. But the Veneto does produce the most *total* bottles of DOC wine. That's what's called a dubious achievement.

There are twenty-three DOCs in the Veneto, yet almost 30 percent of the region's classified wine comes from just one zone: Soave. Without exaggeration, this is the most maligned, misunderstood, and polarized wine district in Italy. Everything about the Soave production discipline has been debated and adjusted so much—from where the vineyards can be planted and how much production is allowed to what grapes can be used in the blend—that the Soave designation has lost much of whatever prestige it may have started with.

"Soave could be the Chablis of Italy," says Stefano Inama with a sigh. "But this is a zone where cooperatives handle the majority of production. Everything about this region is geared toward mass production."

The Soave zone was originally mapped out in 1927, and consisted of a narrow band of hills between the communes of Soave and Monteforte d'Alpone, due east of Verona. The Soave hills include remnants of ancient volcanoes, with elevations ranging from 500 to 1,100 feet. Although the soils vary, the basic profile is mineral-rich basaltic rock mixed with calcareous clays. In this poor but well-drained mixture, vines send down deep roots in search of nutrients—an ideal situation for growing flavorful, well-balanced wine grapes.

Not long after the Soave DOC was created, in 1968, there was pressure from large producers to make the zone bigger. The success of the Bolla family in the U.S. market inspired a raft of imitators, and the DOC zone was dramatically expanded: Vineyards spread into the more fertile plains south and west of Soave, adding more than 10,000 acres of vines to the zone.

Moreover, many producers looked to cash in on the Soave boom by planting vineyards in the *tendone* style, in which the vines were trained onto high, flat trellises: This not only facilitated mechanical harvesting but pushed production as far as it could go in the richer alluvial soils of the plains.

Then some producers started toying with the ingredients. The classic recipe for Soave called for a predominance of garganega, a fleshy, fruity variety, and trebbiano di Soave, an aromatic local variant of the ubiquitous trebbiano. Over time, however, the DOC formula has been adjusted to include the more productive (and less interesting) trebbiano toscano, and as much as 30 percent chardonnay. While it's true that chardonnay is one of the world's great white grapes, it's also very productive and easy to grow. It serves a valuable role around the world as filler, and this is mostly how it has been used in the Veneto.

In the seventies, Soave became more of a brand than a distinctive style of wine. This is a familiar story in many parts of Italy, but in Soave there's one fundamental difference: Nothing much has changed. Of the nearly 6 million bottles of Soave produced each year, fewer than a quarter are produced in the original zone, which is now known as the "Classico." The number of producers making genuinely interesting wines is very small, but they are out there, and they're worth looking for.

"Garganega can be something special if you treat it with care," says Claudio Gini, who runs the highly regarded Gini winery with his brother, Sandro. The family's vineyard holdings include parcels on Monte Froscà and Monte Foscarino, two of the best-known hillside sites in the Classico zone, and the Gini wines have power and flavor not typically associated with Soave. "On Foscarino, which has more volcanic material, we get good structure. On Froscà, which has more clay and limestone, we get more finesse and aroma. But the important thing is that garganega is the right grape for this area."

Indeed, what Gini and other producers note is that garganega, like so many other native Italian grapes, matures later in the season. The elevations in Soave are far from dizzying, and despite being in northern Italy, the climate is quite hot. "It is too low and too hot here for good chardonnay, even in the Classico," Gini asserts. "We have vineyards at higher elevations that do well with chardonnay, but in general it's not a good grape for the Soave area."

In actuality, there are some strong similarities between garganega and chardonnay, as grapes if not as wines. Both are durable, vigorous, semiaromatic varieties, and both are highly variable in their expression. The garganega most people know is flinty, lightly appley, and high in acid—not unlike, say, a midlevel Chablis. But when crop levels are held back and the grape is allowed to fully ripen, it balloons into a juicier, more tropical-tasting wine, with ripe flavors of green melon and pear. In fact, what a well-made Soave offers that a lot of Italian whites don't is good weight on the palate, which American drinkers in particular have come to expect in their whites.

When garganega is blended with trebbiano di Soave, rather than trebbiano toscano, Soave is more invitingly aromatic, with aromas of white flowers and even a touch of pine on top of the clean, melony fruit. A number of producers are now experimenting with fermenting their wines in oak barrels, including Gini and especially Inama, although the results are mixed. Garganega can be very deeply flavored and even juicy in texture, but it doesn't have the stuffing to stand up to a lot of oak.

The difficulty, then, is finding the good Soave in a sea of mediocrity. "The DOC just doesn't mean anything anymore," says the excitable Roberto Anselmi, who in 1999 abandoned the Soave DOC altogether, choosing instead to label his well-known wines with an IGT designation. As one of the best-known vintners in the area, his exit was high Italian drama, punctuated by a fiery Dear John letter to the Soave zone, which he published in a variety of trade journals.

Anselmi's main beef is with the *tendone* system of viticulture, which he says is incapable of producing quality grapes. He prefers a cordon-spur, or guyot, system, where the vines are trained lower to the ground, planted more densely, and closely pruned, so that the juicier side of garganega can come out. He also laments the gradual disappearance of trebbiano di Soave from the zone, and says that the Recioto di Soave designation, a DOCG reserved for sweet wines (see below), is "a joke" because it allows for the production of sparkling versions of the wine. In his open letter to the industry—a heartfelt, occasionally comic rant against politicians, cooperative wineries, and everyone else he held responsible for the destruction of Soave—he likened his exit to a "divorce" from a longtime love.

"You are not 'suave' as your name implies, you are uncontrollable, untameable, unfaithful," Anselmi wrote. "So that's it. I'm going. I'm leaving you, and this letter tells you why . . . It is easy to understand that hillside viniculture is potentially very different indeed from the viniculture of the plains. Unfortunately, the market mistakes one for the other: The bad vine chases the good vine away!"

A lot of wine drinkers have given up on Soave for that very reason, but this means missing out on Anselmi's fat and fruity whites, especially his single-vineyard "Capitel Foscarino." It also means missing out on the elegant, floral whites of Leonildo Pieropan, one of the best small producers in the zone, and of Gini and Inama, whose Soaves show off the plump, mouth-filling character of ripe garganega. Artisan producers such as Graziano Pra, Ca' Rugate, Tamellini, and Suavia are all turning out good wine. And even among the larger houses, there are some eye-openers, among them Bolla's "Tufaie" Soave Classico and Bertani's Soave Classico Superiore. The problem, in the minds of winemakers like Anselmi, is that people consider good Soave a surprise.

At this writing, Italy's national DOC committee is considering elevating Soave to DOCG status, but without any significant changes in production methods. This, in fact, is what caused the apoplectic Anselmi to flee. "There are no limitations on yields in the vineyards, and because so many big wineries take grapes from both the Classico area and the plains, there's no distinction being made by the consumer between the two," he says. "Who on earth explains to the consumer that the Classico is better? No one!" For him, the only solution now is to create an entirely new DOC for the Classico vineyards, but these days he stands on the DOC periphery rather than getting into the fray.

Veneto white wine does not begin and end with Soave. But while there are some other noteworthy white-wine DOCs and a smattering of varietal wines from selected producers, none of them coalesce into a broad "category" like Soave. Probably the two most interesting non-Soave DOCs are Lugana (the majority of which is in Lombardy, on the southern shores of Lake Garda) and Gambellara (abutting Soave to the east), which showcase the local duo of garganega and trebbiano di Soave to sometimes great effect.

In the case of Lugana, trebbiano di Soave is the grape on display, and in some of the better bottlings the aromatic qualities of the variety really show through. Ca' dei Frati of Sirmione in Lombardy is widely regarded as the top Lugana producer, although the Zenato winery of nearby Peschiera (in Veneto) gives them a run for their money, especially with their "San Benedetto" bottling.

In Gambellara, which is anchored by Zonin but includes notable smaller producers such as La Biancara and Dal Maso, it could be argued that the wines are purer expressions of garganega than those of neighboring Soave. The Gambellara production formula is less diffuse than that of Soave, calling for a minimum of 80 percent garganega and allowing only 20 percent of other varieties in the blend. Although still regarded as "little brothers" of Soave, there are some solid Gambellara wines to be found: La Biancara's "Sassaia" and "I Masieri" versions are great examples, although Zonin's Gambellaras will likely be easier to find in the United States.

Aside from that, Veneto white wine tends to be highly variable. The ubiquitous Santa Margherita Pinot Grigio, well-known to American consumers, comes from a winery based near Verona but carries the Valdadige DOC designation, meaning that the grapes can be sourced from Trentino–Alto Adige as well as Veneto. There's also an ocean of easy-drinking varietal wines, such as those from Folonari, which hail mostly from the eastern plains of Veneto and carry either the Piave DOC or the Veneto or Delle Venezie IGT designations. Although there are some good wines to be found in these easterly reaches (including some interesting dry prosecco), as a general rule it's safer to stick with some of the more central DOCs, such as Breganze and Colli Euganei.

VINI ROSSI
Red Wines

The red-wine scene in the Veneto, like the white, is rooted in Verona. Although there are a number of excellent reds farther afield (headlined by the cabernets and merlots of Fausto Maculan in Breganze), the Veneto, for better or worse, is defined by Valpolicella. Although less so than Soave, Valpolicella is saddled with a long-standing bad reputation. But an attentive buyer can now find a tremendous amount of interesting wine in the zone. In fact, if Soave is the most discredited DOC in Italy, Valpolicella may be its most underrated.

The Valpolicella zone is often described as an open hand, whose "fingers" start in the Monte Lessini range north of Verona and spread southward. The long, vine-covered ridges flank a series of mountain streams, which amble down past Verona in search of the Adige River. Like Soave, Valpolicella has a more historic "Classico" zone, reaching from the commune of Sant'Ambrogio in the west to Negrar in the east. But unlike Soave, the areas outside the Valpolicella Classico—the Valpantena, Squaranto, Mezzane, and Illasi valleys, all to the east—are natural extensions of the zone. They were part of the original DOC when it was created in 1968, and today there are as many important producers outside the Classico as there are inside.

Because the name Valpolicella has become a mass-market brand in its own right, a lot of modern wine drinkers overlook what is one of the most evocative wine regions in Italy. In Verona, a place with more Roman ruins than any other Italian city outside of Rome, many of the narrow streets are paved with the reddish *rosso veronese* marble mined in the Valpolicella hills. Just off the broad Piazza Brà, the well-preserved Roman arena is the site of a summerlong opera festival. It's a genteel, clean, manageable city. And for all of the heavy braises and grilled meats on menus, there are also some incredible food products on display in the market on the Piazza delle Erbe: delicately perfumed olive oils from the shores of Lake Garda and the hills of Valpolicella; Asiago and the more pungent Monte Veronese cheese, the latter an aged cow's-milk variety from the Monti Lessini; peaches and especially cherries from communes such as Garganago and Cazzano, also in the Valpolicella hills. Biting into one of those cherries when they're picked in June is a taste preview of the harvest season yet to come: It's like there's an inch of cherry flesh between the skin and the pit, the juice tart and spicy and sweet all at once, a perfect evocation of the wines from the neighboring vineyards.

Valpolicella, which means "valley of many cellars," is home to a series of red grapes, most of which have unclear origins and are rarely found elsewhere in Italy. Corvina, a dark-berried, thick-skinned variety, is the principal grape in red Valpolicella wines, forming the backbone of the blend with its firm tannins and rich, smoky, red-cherry scent (there's also a bigger-berried version of corvina called corvi-none, which some people think is a sub-variety, like brunello is a sub-variety of sangiovese). The other key grape is rondinella, also deeply colored but considered more aromatic than corvina. After those two, which comprise a minimum of 60 percent of the blend and usually much more, the roster of ingredients is highly variable: There's molinara, the high-acid third banana in Valpolicella, which is increasingly being phased out; local rarities such as croatina, negrara, and dindarella, often used as light seasoning in Valpolicella blends; and "international" varieties such as merlot and cabernet sauvignon.

What can be difficult to understand about Valpolicella wines, aside from what's in them, is the hierarchy of styles. Crisp, cherry-red Valpolicella, and its lighter counterpart from Bardolino, are the wines people most readily associate with the zone (also worth a mention is the Bardolino rosé called *chiaretto*, which can be a great quaffer in the summer). But these lighter wines are more recent creations. They were preceded in history by the sweet Recioto della Valpolicella and its unusual dry counterpart, Amarone. By most accounts, Recioto came into fashion during Roman times, when wines were made sweet and alcoholic to withstand the rigors of travel. The Romans are said to have developed the process of *appassimento*, in which grapes were either left to dry on the vines or on straw mats to concentrate their sugars; since yeast typically stops working when wines approach 20 percent alcohol, traditional Reciotos had a considerable amount of residual sugar left over.

Recioto, whose name is thought to be a derivate of either *recia* (dialect for "ear," purportedly in reference to the shapes of the drying grape clusters) or the Latin *racemus* (meaning a grape cluster that has been cut and left to dry), is still one of the great wines of Verona, an Italian answer to Port. But the wine regarded as Verona's greatest achievement is Amarone, which may have been discovered by accident.

The conventional wisdom is that Amarone was created when someone left a barrel of Recioto unattended, and somehow the yeasts in the barrel continued to work and the wine fermented to dryness. The style came to be known as Recioto Amaro (*amaro* meaning "bitter," in reference to the more tart, almondy, dried-fruit flavors of the wine), and later as Recioto della Valpolicella Amarone. Known today as Amarone della Valpolicella, it's a wine that still confounds people with its vinous split personality: Densely concentrated and deeply colored, often almost syrupy in texture, it behaves like a sweet wine without technically being sweet. Amarone is the big palate tease, letting all its luscious, sappy fruit flavor hang out before covering up with a savory robe of alcohol, acidity, and tannin.

As a wine in a bottle on sale in a store, Amarone is a very recent phenomenon: Bolla first commercialized Amarone in the fifties, and was quickly followed into the market by Masi and Bertani. A mass of producers didn't develop until much later. Because Amarone isn't produced in very large quantities, there isn't a lot of old wine to be found, but the opportunity to drink an Amarone from a vintage such as 1967 or 1983 should not be missed. The aromas of these wines—a melding of cherry syrup, coffee, leather, almonds, tar, spice, and so much else—are matched only by older Barolos and Barbarescos from similarly great years. The difference comes in the texture: In an older Amarone the glycerine richness created by *appassimento* continues to show through,

coating the palate like a nectar. As Sandro Boscaini, technical director of Masi, puts it: "No other wine is so positively affected by the hand of man."

The most simple description of Amarone comes from one of the Valpolicella zone's most famous boutique producers, Romano Dal Forno, who likens the process of *appassimento* to "leaving a peach on the counter to ripen." And while there are some who view *appassimento* as cheating, as a way of extracting personality from boring grapes, Dal Forno insists that "*appassimento* is only as good as the material you're starting with."

Typically, corvina, rondinella, and the other Valpolicella grapes are harvested in early October, after which they are spread out to dry on straw mats called *graticci*. The drying process usually lasts until January, with the grapes losing between 30 to 40 percent of their weight before they are pressed and vinified (grapes for Recioto are dried longer). And while a number of producers, including Tedeschi and Allegrini, have created temperature- and humidity-controlled drying rooms in which to carry out the *appassimento*, most still cling to the natural method of drying the grapes in open lofts or barns. The relatively mild winter climate in Valpolicella, moderated by nearby Lake Garda, is generally credited as the secret to Verona's success with *appassimento*. But this is not to say that success is guaranteed: too much humidity and the grapes could rot. So in addition to simply opening the windows, most producers are using at least some kind of fan or dehumidifier system to hedge their bets.

What, exactly, happens during *appassimento*? "There's a dramatic increase in sugars without a corresponding increase in acidity," says Sandro Boscaini. "Essentially, the water evaporates out of the grapes, leaving a purer, more concentrated fruit extract inside." This, he says, is what many people mistake for sweetness when tasting Amarone; it's not sugar that's coating your mouth, but fruit extract. This makes Amarone the ultimate "reduction wine" for braises and stews, but of course it's much more than that.

In tasting through a series of Amarone wines, a clear style spectrum emerges: Some are juicier, more syrupy, more colorful, even hinting at Port-like sweetness, while others have more dried fruit flavors, even a tarry, resiny quality, and less color. While this has at least something to do with the ripeness of the corvina and other grapes going in, much of the variation in Amarone style can be explained in technical terms. In general, Amarone style is defined by the following factors:

- *Grapes and Blending:* Naturally, some producers grow fuller-bodied corvina than others. Beyond that, what is their blending formula? If they're still using a good percentage of molinara, for example, the wine will likely be higher in acid, less deeply colored, and lighter-bodied.
- *Length and Type of* Appassimento: Boscaini contends that grapes dried at higher elevations will produce more powerful, fruity, tannic wines, while those dried in lower, more humid locations are more likely to be attacked by the noble rot called *Botrytis cinerea,* which essentially consumes tartaric acid to create glycerol. Wine affected by botrytis, he says, has a telltale glycerine richness. As for the length of *appassimento,* the effect is obvious: "The longer the drying, the more concentration," Boscaini says.
- *Method of Aging:* One of the key changes in Amarone in recent years has been the type of barrels used for aging and the length of time the wines are aged. In the past, when fermentation was carried out naturally, it may have taken a year or more for the wine to ferment to dryness. This caused the wine to become oxidized, even Madeira-like, during the process, losing color and developing secondary aromas of nuts and dried fruits. Although most wines are now fermented in stainless steel using yeasts specially developed to work more quickly, the practice of long-aging in large, old barrels is still used—creating a more lightly colored, spicy, mature-tasting Amarone. By contrast, some producers are using new oak barriques to age their wines, and are leaving the wine in wood for a shorter time, since the surface area of the wine in contact with the wood is much greater. The faster influx of oxygen in the smaller barrique stabilizes the wine's color, while the tannins in the newer wood are absorbed by the wine. The result is a denser, more youthful style of Amarone.

"Today, the new imperative is to achieve as much extraction as possible with minimal oxidation," says Boscaini. "A lot of this is accomplished with select yeasts that are able to work at higher alcohol levels. We don't leave the wine to macerate on its skins as long as we once did, which reduces the amount of bitter tannin in the wine and helps us preserve color." Indeed, as is often noted by winemakers, all of the color in a red wine is extracted in the first twenty-four to thirty-six hours of maceration; after that, it won't get any deeper, but may in fact begin to break down as the chemical reactions of fermentation proceed.

Then there's the question of botrytis. Is it noble rot that gives Amarone wines their syrupy texture, or is that just the weight of the extract playing tricks on winemakers' minds? It's a hotly debated topic in Valpolicella, with both sides holding firm. "Certainly there's a smoky element to the aroma of Amarone that indicates botrytis," says Riccardo Tedeschi, winemaker at the Tedeschi estate. "The softness and richness of Amarone is in direct relation to the degree the grapes are attacked. For us, we usually see about 30 percent of botrytis-affected fruit."

"In our case, anyway, botrytis is not something we want," counters Marilisa Allegrini, whose family winery in Fumane produces some of the most potent Amarone and Valpolicella in the zone. "It breaks down the skins of the grapes, which in turn destroys the structure of the wine. Botrytis may make the wine sweeter and rounder, but it breaks down acid and tannins, both of which we want to give the wine a long life."

Given all the variables influencing Amarone style, it's not surprising that people have trouble deciding when to drink it—and whose to drink. Will it be a rich, syrupy style for a traditional pairing with stinky cheese? (The local Monte Veronese is great with a richer-style Amarone, but even better with Recioto.) Or is it a more balanced, spicy, dried-cherry expression of Amarone better suited to game birds or lamb? Most people are content to sip Amarone on its own or with the cheese course, but it's a mistake to think of the wines only in this context.

Although it's difficult to generalize, some of the traditional producers of Amarone include Bertani, Tommasi, Speri, Le Ragose, Le Salette, Bolla, and Accordini, all of whom make wines in a more approachable, spicy, medium-bodied style that is readily compatible with food. For fuller, richer, more extracted wines better suited to cheeses, look to Masi (particularly the single-vineyard "Mazzano"), Corte Sant'Alda, Allegrini, Tedeschi, Tenuta Sant'Antonio, Tommaso Bussola, and Dal Forno Romano. Of the latter two, expect a raw power to rival that of vintage Port.

Somewhere on their own plane, occupying a middle ground between the resiny maturity of the traditional and the juicy extract of the modern, are the wines of Giuseppe Quintarelli. His estate in the heights of Negrar, home not only to vines but to cherry orchards and a wide variety of vegetables, has been the benchmark in Valpolicella for decades. Quintarelli only makes Amarone in exceptional vintages, and ages his wines for more than six years in large Slavonian oak casks before they are released. Yet even after long aging, Quintarelli wines, like the octogenerian winemaker himself, hold on to their youthful energy: It's rare to find a red wine from anywhere in the world that combines power and complexity the way a Quintarelli Amarone does. It's a wine that keeps you guessing, grasping for descriptors, wondering how all those seemingly divergent flavors found their way into one bottle.

More so than in the past, in fact, the magical properties of Amarone are coloring the other dry reds of the zone, especially Valpolicella. While the pizza-parlor Valpolicella of the seventies was made only with freshly harvested grapes, most producers today are either blending in a percentage of Amarone-style wine or employing a process called *ripasso*, in which a Valpolicella vinified in the fall is poured over the wine-drenched skins and pulp left over from an Amarone fermentation. This "repassing" incites a secondary fermentation, infusing the wine with a hint of the tarry, spicy, glycerol kick of Amarone.

Although most producers indicate on the label when a wine is a *ripasso*, there is often no telling exactly what's in the bottle of Valpolicella or Valpolicella Classico these days. When made with only "fresh" grapes (a good example F.illi Zeni's "Vigne Alte"), the smoky cherry flavor of corvina is checked by a tart acidity, making it a great choice for tomato-sauced pastas. In *ripasso* Valpolicella, that buoyant cherry is fleshed out with a resiny, toffee-ish richness. In still other Valpolicellas, most notably those of Dal Forno Romano and Marion, the use of a percentage of *appassimento* wine pushes them in the direction of Amarone. In this respect, Valpolicella is a work in progress, and as more producers refine their growing techniques for corvina, the "fresh" style of Valpolicella may come back into vogue, albeit with a new look. Even the light and easy Bardolino is getting a face-lift, as producers such as Le Fraghe and Masi plump it up, ever so slightly, to suit modern tastes. Bardolino, in fact, was made a DOCG in 2001.

"It's very hard to explain to consumers the changes that have occurred in Valpolicella," says Riccardo Tedeschi. "Today we're producing important wines, and the younger producers are unanimous in the belief that corvina can produce world-class reds without the use of *appassimento*."

Other Veneto Reds

As the Veronese try to figure out what they want Valpolicella to be, winemakers in other parts of the Veneto have stolen some of their thunder, often with Bordeaux-style blends of cabernet sauvignon, cabernet franc, and merlot. Chief among them has been Fausto Maculan, who in 1972 began making wines in the rela-

tively far-flung commune of Breganze, north of Vicenza. His wines, including a luxurious, barrique-aged cabernet sauvignon called "Fratta" and a single-vineyard merlot called "Marchesante," have become the cult wines of the Veneto, a region where cabernet and merlot are widely grown but rarely interesting.

Maculan's success has inspired other producers outside of Verona to experiment with Bordeaux-style wines, particularly in the volcanic soils of the Colli Berici and Colli Euganei DOC zones. Stefano Inama, whose flinty, complex "Bradisismo" cabernet sauvignon is made in the Colli Berici DOC, says that the zone was the first in Italy to feature cabernet sauvignon. "Although they're only now getting attention, the Colli Berici and Colli Euganei are traditional zones for cabernet and merlot," Inama says. "The whole northeast of Italy has been a traditional place for these grapes, since the days of the Austrian domination, if not before. The string of volcanoes here in the Veneto is the only volcanic terrain in the north of Italy, and it's perfect for cabernet."

Only now is the wine scene in these zones beginning to develop. In Breganze, both Maculan and Vigneto due Santi have become sought-after names, while in Colli Berici, practically unheard of just a few years ago, producers such as Inama, Dal Maso, Domenico Cavazza, and Conte Alessandro Piovene are putting the zone on the map. Colli Euganei is headlined by the smoky, cabernet-based blends of Vignalta, which are beginning to see wider distribution in the United States.

It may seem unfair to ignore the mass of red wine being made in Piave and Lison-Pramaggiore, in the eastern Veneto. But with so much inexpensive and higher quality merlot and cabernet sauvignon being made in Chile,

Argentina, and Australia, it's difficult to find a place for inexpensive—and not-so-high-quality—merlot and cabernet from Veneto's plains. Plus, there isn't much of this wine to be found anyway, unless you're drinking red wine on tap in a Venetian *osteria*. Lison-Pramaggiore has almost as much vineyard area as the Valpolicella Classico, but you'll be hard-pressed to find the DOC name on much bottled wine, and the same goes for Piave: There are lots of vineyards, more than any other Veneto DOC zone, in fact, but hardly any producers bottling wine under the Piave designation.

VINI DOLCI
Sweet Wines

Unjustly lost in the shuffle, as so many sweet wines are these days, are the Recioto wines of Soave and Valpolicella, the Veneto's answer to Sauternes and Port, respectively. In Recioto di Soave, a DOCG-designated wine, the vibrant acidity of garganega and trebbiano helps keep the rich glycerol sweetness of the *appassimento* in check, so that the wines are sweet without being cloying. Most of the better Soave pro-

ducers make good Reciotos as well, including Pieropan, Gini, and Anselmi, although Anselmi has taken the DOCG designation off his luscious, golden-hued "I Capitelli." Also well worth seeking out are the trio of sweet wines from Maculan, especially his "Torcolato," made from the local vespaiolo grape.

Like Sauternes, these wines often have a smoky tint to their honeyed, melony fruit flavors, making them compatible with savory foods as well as sweet ones. Because so many restaurants prefer to serve sweet whites such as Recioto with sweet desserts, the complex flavors of the wine can get lost in a clash of sugar-on-sugar. Try them with aged cheeses instead.

The same goes for Recioto della Valpolicella, the ultimate match for a hunk of Gorgonzola or Robiola, two of Italy's more potent cheeses. Unlike Amarone, Recioto is made by arresting the fermentation of the wine (sometimes by chilling down the must) so that some residual sugar remains. With all that sugar, the extract, and the alcohol, a Recioto can be almost overwhelming in its intensity, with fruit aromas as head-spinning as gasoline vapors and a weight on the palate that makes it a meal in itself.

FAST FACTS: $\mathcal{V}$ENETO

PROVINCES	Belluno (BL), Padova (PD), Rovigo (RO), Treviso (TV), Venezia (VE), Verona (VR), Vicenza (VI)
CAPITAL	Venice
KEY WINE TOWNS	Bardolino, Breganze, Negrar, Soave, Valdobbiadene, Verona
TOTAL VINEYARD AREA*	75,314 hectares, or 186,101 acres. Rank: 3rd
TOTAL WINE PRODUCTION*	6,785,000 hectoliters, or 179,260,237 gallons (3rd); 55.4% white, 44.6% red
DOC WINE PRODUCED*	29.1% (7th)
SPECIALTY FOODS	Asiago (cow's milk cheese); Grana Padano (cow's milk cheese); Monte Veronese (cow's milk cheese); Ubriaco (cow's-milk cheese soaked in grape pomace; *ubriaco* means "drunk."); radicchio trevisano (red radicchio from Treviso); cherries and peaches from Valpolicella.

*1997 figures. Rankings out of twenty regions total (Trentino–Alto Adige counted as one). Source: Istituto Statistica Mercati Agro-Alimentari (ISMEA), Rome.

KEY GRAPE VARIETIES

WHITES

GARGANEGA	A semiaromatic white thought by some to be related to the greco or grecanico of southern Italy. As the principal grape in Soave, its personality is highly variable. It can be juicy and mouth-filling, with distinctive apple and pear scents, or watery and light, depending on how it is grown.
TREBBIANO	Two types thrive in the region: the aromatic trebbiano di Soave, used as a blending variety in Soave and Lugana whites

	(and thought to be related to the verdicchio of the Marche), and the workhorse trebbiano toscano, know more for its productivity than any particular flavor or aroma.
PROSECCO	Late-ripening white that gives the sparkling wines of northeastern Veneto their characteristic peachy softness.
OTHERS	CHARDONNAY; TOCAI FRIULANO; RIESLING; INCROCIO MANZONI; PINOT BIANCO; VESPAIOLA, a tart, lemony native used mainly in the Breganze DOC.

REDS

CORVINA	Considered native to the Valpolicella region, this dark-skinned, richly flavorful variety is the basis for Valpolicella and Amarone. Meaty, tannic, and aromatic. Increasingly popular is the larger-berried CORVINONE, which some producers say is a clone and others say is a distinct variety.
RONDINELLA	Local native used for color and body in Valpolicella/Amarone blends.
MOLINARA	Local native that traditionally added acidity to Valpolicella/Amarone blends, but that is becoming increasingly scarce.
CABERNET	Cabernet sauvignon, cabernet franc, and a mix of the two known simply as "cabernet" are all found in abundance here, as in most of northeast Italy. Although the family has a long history in the region, the majority of wines made from these grapes have a nagging green-bell-pepper flavor that arises when grapes are not fully mature.
OTHERS	RABOSO (dark and tannic native found mainly in the Piave plain); MERLOT.

TOP VINTAGES IN THE VENETO, 1980—2000

Amarone is the Veneto's principal collector's wine, and it is built to last: Because of its high alcohol content, thick tannins, and deep concentration, it is a wine typically aged from three to six years before it is released. It is a unique wine in that it is approachable when young but can also spend twenty to thirty years or more in bottle and still be rich and satisfying when opened. Legendary older vintages include 1967 and 1976. More recent top years: '83, '85, '88, '90, '93, '95, '97, '98, '99.

LA STRADA DEL VINO
WINE TOURING IN THE VENETO

A rite of passage for many American wine professionals is a trip to Verona for the annual VinItaly wine fair, which is held every April at the city's exposition center, called Veronafiera (see www.vinitalyonline.com for more information). Verona is definitely the Veneto's principal wine town, and whether or not you're there for VinItaly it's worth making a trip to the Antica Bottega del Vino (Via Scudo di Francia 3; 045-800-45-35), a worn-at-the-edges wine bar not far from the city's main square, the Piazza Brà. The selection of Veneto wines is encyclopedic, most of them listed on a large blackboard, but just about every region of Italy is well-represented. It's a fun place with a solid *osteria*-style menu. Also noteworthy is the nearby Valpolicella region, just ten to fifteen minutes outside of the city, where you'll find a host of excellent country restaurants set amid beautiful vineyards. Set yourself up in a Verona hotel, preferably during early July through early September, during the Verona opera season, so you can check out the opera in Verona's Roman Arena. Then take day trips into the Valpolicella hills and eat like a king in places such as Al Covolo (Sant'Ambrogio; 045-773-23-50); Trattoria Dalla Rosa Alda (San Giorgio; 045-680-04-11); and Trattoria Alla Coà (Ospedaletto; 045-676-74-02). There's also a regional Valpolicella *enoteca* in the town of Fumane (045-683-914-67) that serves light fare and a broad array of the region's wines. Also worth a visit is the Serègo Alighieri estate in Gargagnago, a villa where the poet Dante once lived. It is the site of some prized vineyards now used by the Masi firm to produce wine, oil, and condiments. Tours are available and there is a shop that sells the various food products, including the great Serègo Alighieri Amarones (045-770-36-22; www.seregoalighieri.it). Another good contact is the Consorzio Tutela Vino Valpolicella in San Floriano (045-770-31-94; www.valpolicella.it). And finally, there's Venice, a great wine town even if no grapes are grown there. Check out the enoteca-pizzeria All'Aciughetta (Campo

San Filippo e Giacomo 4357; 041-522-42-92), or for more serious diners, Al Covo (Campiello della Pescaria 3968; 041-522-38-12) and Da Fiore (Calle del Scaleter 2202/A; 041-72-13-08).

DEGUSTAZIONI
TASTINGS

PROSECCO

Mionetto
Prosecco di Valdobbiadene "Casada," $

Zardetto
Prosecco di Conegliano Brut, $

Ruggeri
Prosecco di Valdobbiadene Cartizze, $

Starting with the Mionetto wine and finishing with the Ruggeri, you'll get a good sense of the style spectrum of sparkling prosecco: from light and faintly peach-scented to richer and more firmly structured. Even in the Ruggeri wine, however, there's a delicacy and softness of texture that makes it best-suited to sipping as a light apéritif, maybe with some smoked salmon or *tramezzine* sandwiches (see recipes that follow). Other reliable prosecco producers: Carpenè Malvotti, Nino Franco, Bellenda, Collalbrigo.

SOAVE

Leonildo Pieropan
Soave Classico Superiore "Vigneto La Rocca," $

Roberto Anselmi
"San Vicenzo," $

Gini Soave Classico Superiore "La Froscà," $

This, too, is a climb up the ladder in terms of mouthfeel: Pieropan's wines are known for their delicacy and balance, and you'll likely find the "Vigneto La Rocca" to be the most crisp and aromatic of these three wines. Anselmi's "San Vicenzo," while no longer called a Soave, is a benchmark, known for its appley, mouth-filling fruit. It shows off the juicy texture of the garganega grape. Gini's "La Froscà" includes a percentage of barrel-fermented garganega, so it tacks on a layer of creamy richness. These wines all have a cool, soothing feel on the palate; rather than being tartly acidic, they have a smooth, dewy quality that might remind you of cantaloupe or honeydew melon, as opposed to citrus. Other notable names in Soave: Inama, for a more wood-aged style; Graziano Pra; and La Cappuccina, also for more wood-aged styles.

CLASSIC VALPOLICELLA

F.illi Zeni Valpolicella Classico Superiore "Vigne Alte," $

A basic, dry Valpolicella—one that has not been put through the *ripasso* process or blended with a percentage of Amarone to pump it up—is becoming harder and harder to find these days.

Le Ragose Valpolicella Classico, $

Speri Valpolicella Classico Superiore "La Roverina," $

Boscaini Valpolicella Ripasso, "Santo Stefano,"$

Bertani Valpolicella Valpantena, "Secco Bertani," $

Giuseppe Quintarelli Valpolicella Classico, $$

Bolla Amarone della Valpolicella, $$$

Masi Amarone della Valpolicella, $$$

Allegrini Amarone della Valpolicella, $$$

In these three wines you get the crisp acidity and spicy cherry flavors of corvina, the principal grape in the Valpolicella blend. These are lighter-styled wines for red-sauced pastas, pizza, or barbecued foods: Their brambly red-cherry and wild-berry flavors have a sharp, rustic edge. Consider giving them a slight chill to mute the acidity somewhat.

VALPOLICELLA *RIPASSO* AND *APPASSIMENTO*

In these three wines the naturally light and fruity Valpolicella is given a super-charge, either by being passed over the lees of just-fermented Amarone (*ripasso*) or by the inclusion of a small amount of Amarone-type wine to the blend. These wines have a "blacker" fruit quality than a traditional "fresh" Valpolicella, tacking on some extra weight from their time in contact (or in concert) with Amarone. In the "Secco Bertani" bottling in particular, flavors of red raspberries and dried cherries are intertwined with a coffee-toffee character that is a typical result of *ripasso*. The Quintarelli wine, meanwhile, has a hint of glycerine-like sweetness thanks to the presence of a small percentage of Amarone in the blend. Not just bigger and fleshier but more aromatically complex, these Valpolicellas have the stuff to take on richer dishes, especially heartier stews and braises.

AMARONE

Another rich, richer, and richest lineup, this trio represents three benchmark Amarones at three distinct price points. Technically, they are not sweet wines, but when you smell and taste them you may be inclined to think they are: On the nose there are inviting scents of bitter chocolate, coffee, stewed cherries, blackberry jam, resin, leather, even cinnamon, and on the palate the rich, even syrupy concentration of the wine may lead to the perception of sweetness. The principal distinction among these wines is the level of weight, or viscosity, in the mouth. As you get to know the style spectrum of Amarone, you'll know to reserve more medium-bodied wines such as the Bolla and Masi for *osso buco* or maybe a steak, while setting aside the Allegrini for the cheese course. For other medium-weight styles look to Tedeschi, Bertani, Le Ragose, Cesari, and Le Salette. For more powerful, sappy styles go with Tommaso Bussola or Dal Forno Romano. For a wonderfully complex mixture of both, look for the long-aged Amarone of Giuseppe Quintarelli.

SWEET WHITES

Anselmi "I Capitelli," $$

Maculan "Torcolato," $$

At one time not long ago, "I Capitelli" was the best-known example available of Recioto di Soave, the Veneto's DOCG sweet wine. The Anselmi winery no longer uses a DOCG designation on the wine, but it remains a luscious example of what the garganega grape becomes when it is made in an *appassimento* style: rich and honeyed, with hints of banana, mango, and citrus, with a whiff of exotic spice and smoke, all cleaned up with a refreshing wave of acidity. Not to be outdone, Fausto Maculan of Breganze gives the *appassimento* treatment to his local vespaiolo grape, creating a Sauternes-like dessert sipper with a similarly sweet-yet-crisp personality. These are nectars to be sipped on their own or paired with desserts such as a *torta di mandorla* (almond torte) or *pan d'oro* (golden bread, a vanilla cake that is a specialty of Verona). And don't hesitate to try them with cheeses, including aged versions of the Veneto's star, Asiago, or milder local cheeses such as Montasio.

The Venetian Cocktail Party

RECIPES BY MARIO BATALI

Although Verona is the Veneto's wine-making center, Venice is both the political and stylistic capital of the region. Venetian cuisine is a fusion of land and sea, with a list of famous dishes that runs the gamut: liver and onions; risotto *di seppie* (cuttlefish-ink risotto) and myriad other seafood risotti; sardines *in saòr* (sardines marinated in vinegar, onions, raisins, and pine nuts); grilled *seppie* (cuttlefish); and lots of polenta. Like any true trading capital, Venice has a certain exoticism that's hard to match in the areas farther inland.

To enjoy the greatest wine of Verona —Amarone—is fairly simple. Prepare a plate of full-flavored cheeses: Start with some Grana Padano and Monte Veronese from the Veneto, then borrow a few from neighboring Lombardy (Gorgonzola, Robiola). Pop the cork and savor the combination of salty, earthy, pungent cheeses and luscious red wine.

But what about light whites such as Soave and the Veneto's signature sparkler, prosecco? Here's where a little Venetian style is in order. Think of yourself as a wealthy Venetian spice trader in the twelfth century, watching your fleet return to the Grand Canal after a successful run to the Far East. This sense of noblesse oblige still infuses every aspect of Venetian cooking and entertaining.

The best way to get into the spirit of the Veneto is to re-create the flavors and the atmosphere of a Venetian *palazzo*, maybe on some balmy summer night when you feel like having some friends over for cocktails. Start with an *aperitivo* (apéritif) incorporating prosecco or simply sip some Soave as you munch on finger foods such as the *tramezzini* below.

Aperitivo: The Merchant of Venice

½ teaspoon fresh POMEGRANATE JUICE
   or POMEGRANATE SYRUP
Pinch CINNAMON
Prosecco SPARKLING WINE

MAKES 1 DRINK

In a Champagne flute, add the pomegranate juice or syrup. Fill the remainder of the glass with prosecco, then add a pinch of cinnamon. If you are making a bunch of drinks, it's best to pour the prosecco into a pitcher and keep the pitcher on ice. This will diminish the amount of foaming when you pour the drinks.

Finger Foods: Venetian-Style Crostini

Grappa Cured Salmon Crostini

Make ahead note: The curing process for this dish takes 3 days.

2 cups KOSHER SALT
1 cup SUGAR
2 tablespoons DRIED THYME
1 teaspoon RED CHILI FLAKES
1 tablespoon coarsely ground BLACK
   PEPPER
1 side high-quality fatty Scottish or
   Norwegian SALMON (about 2 to
   3 pounds), filleted
1 cup clear, unflavored GRAPPA
1 18-inch BAGUETTE
4 stalks fresh DILL
1 tablespoon extra-virgin OLIVE OIL

SERVES 8

In a large bowl, mix together the salt, sugar, thyme, chili flakes, and pepper. Place the side of salmon on a grate within a baking sheet and coat the fish thoroughly on both sides with the salt mixture. Place the salmon in the refrigerator, uncovered, for 48 hours.

After the second day there should be a substantial amount of liquid in the bottom of the pan. Remove the salt crust from the salmon slab, and clean out the baking pan. In the same grate and pan, use a kitchen brush to coat both sides of the slab with the cup of grappa until you create a glaze (be sure to do this while the salmon is still cold, to create a shiny finish).

Return the salmon to the refrigerator. Repeat the process of coating it with the grappa 3 more times every 3 hours, for a total of 4 times. Allow the salmon to rest another day, then cut it into thin slices with a very sharp serrated knife.

Slice the baguette into ½-inch rounds and toast the slices by placing them under a broiler or in a toaster oven. Place the salmon slices across the toasts and top each toast with a small sprig of dill and a drop or two of olive oil.

NOTE: It does not make sense to cure a smaller quantity of salmon, so there will be a substantial amount of salmon left over from this recipe. It can be wrapped up and stored safely in the refrigerator for several weeks, to be used for another occasion.

Chicken Liver Crostini

½ cup extra-virgin OLIVE OIL
2 pounds fresh CHICKEN LIVERS
1 teaspoon SALT, plus more to taste
2 medium RED ONIONS, minced to yield
   2 cups
½ cup dry SALTED CAPERS (not capers
   from a jar), soaked 6 hours and
   minced
¼ cup BRANDY
1 cup RED WINE
⅛ cup chopped ITALIAN PARSLEY
1 teaspoon PEPPER
1 18-inch BAGUETTE

SERVES 8

In a large sauté pan, heat ¼ cup of the olive oil over a medium-high flame until shimmering. Add the chicken livers and salt, and sauté until they are well done, about 10–15 minutes, or when the livers are crumbling apart.

With a slotted spoon, remove the livers from the pan. To the same pan, add the other ¼ cup oil and sauté the chopped red onions until they are wilted. When the onions are wilted and translucent, add the minced capers, and sauté for 2 to 3 minutes more.

Add the brandy to the onion-caper mixture, allowing it to flame. When the flame dies out, add the red wine. Bring to a boil, then return the cooked chicken livers to the pan. Reduce heat to medium low and simmer for another 5 minutes, using a potato masher or wooden spoon to crush the livers and create a thick paste.

Remove the mixture from the sauté pan, let it cool, then purée in a food processor. Add extra virgin olive oil if necessary to create a consistency similar to peanut butter. Blend in the chopped parsley, salt to taste, and the pepper.

Slice the baguette into ½-inch rounds and toast the slices by placing them under a broiler or in a toaster oven. Spread the liver mixture generously on each toast, about 1 tablespoon per toast, and serve.

Egg, Asparagus, and Red Onion Crostini

2 bundles large ASPARAGUS (about
   2 pounds)
4 large EGGS
1 large RED ONION, diced
¼ cup extra-virgin OLIVE OIL
2 tablespoons RED WINE VINEGAR
1 tablespoon DIJON MUSTARD
SALT and PEPPER to taste
1 18-inch BAGUETTE

SERVES 8

To prepare asparagus, peel the stalks using a potato peeler, from midway down the stalk to the base. Cut off the bottom inch of each stalk.

In a large pot or steamer, boil or steam the asparagus until tender. Drain. Refresh in an ice bath until cool, then drain again. Slice on the bias into ½-inch pieces. Set aside.

Boil the eggs until they are extra hard, about 15 minutes. Cool, peel, and chop the eggs and place in a large mixing bowl. Add in the sliced asparagus, the chopped red onion, the oil, vinegar, and mustard and mix well. Add salt and pepper to taste. The mixture should have the consistency of a deli-style potato salad.

Slice the baguette into ½-inch rounds and toast the slices by placing them under a broiler or in a toaster oven. Using a large spoon, scoop the egg-onion-asparagus mixture atop each baguette slice.

Trentino–Alto Adige

An Unsung Source of World-Class Whites

—⊙⋙⊙—

Fire on the Mountain

Unless you're a skier, the start of summer is the perfect time to be in the Alto Adige. Along the serpentine road from Chiusa to Cortina d'Ampezzo, gondolas that would be packed in wintertime carry relatively light loads of hikers, most of whom head for the high country of St. Ulrich or Wolkenstein. Dressed in shorts and T-shirts, they scatter like mice across the broad meadows and disappear into the glades, shading their eyes as the sun bounces off the snow in the Dolomites. The thin mountain air lends resonance to every little sound: the clank of a cowbell, a distant laugh, the whine of a remote-controlled airplane as it buzzes the blooming wildflowers.

It's July 2, a crisply sunny afternoon in the hills of St. Ulrich. We've climbed to more than ten thousand feet, well above the thick tufts of humidity that clog the valley below. The stripped-down ski runs, strewn with boulders and thick with tall grass, are tantalizingly empty. This has been a four-hour trek along a high ridge and then back down to town, followed by a bowl of giant *canederli* (bread and flour dumplings), which are flecked with

chunks of smoked bacon and swimming in broth. By the end of dinner the blindingly bright day turns black and thick as tar, making the drive out of St. Ulrich feel like a ride through a mineshaft.

But once on the autostrada, which follows the Isarco River down to Bolzano, everything is ablaze: Huge fires are burning in the hills that flank the Isarco and Adige river valleys, continuing on past Bolzano like a string of Christmas lights. Many of them are built in the shapes of hearts and crosses, casting a glow over vineyards that cling to the steep mountain slopes. In Caldaro (Kaltern), a wine town on the *strada del vino* southwest of Bolzano, people sit in the cafés with plates of *bresaola* (air-cured beef) and pitchers of wine, staring up at the blazes as if there were a movie playing.

The occasion for the fires is the *Festa di Sacro Cuore* (Day of the Sacred Heart), typically held two Sundays after the better-known Corpus Domini celebrations in late June. Fires in the mountains have long been a summertime ritual in the Alto Adige, first as pagan offerings to the sun gods and later as Christian tributes to Saint John, whose saint's day coincided with the summer solstice. It wasn't until the nineteenth century that they evolved into the *Fuochi di Sacro Cuore*, commemorating Christ's protection of the Alto Adige—then known only as

THE DOC ZONES OF TRENTINO–ALTO ADIGE

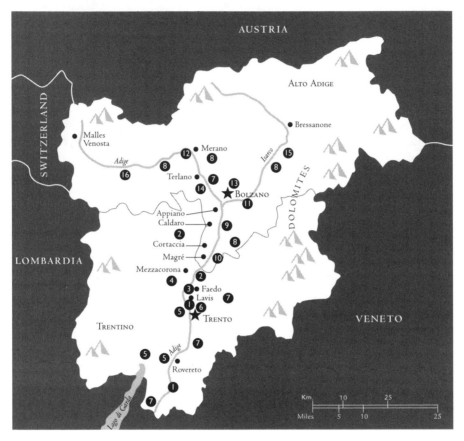

TRENTINO

1 Casteller
2 Lago di Caldaro/Caldaro *(shared with Alto Adige)*
3 Sorní *(subzone)*
4 Teroldego Rotaliano
5 Trentino
6 Trento
7 Valdadige/Etschtaler *(shared with Alto Adige and Veneto)*

ALTO ADIGE

8 Alto Adige/Südtirol
9 Lago di Caldaro/Südtirol Kalterersee *(shared with Trentino)*

10 Valdadige/Etschtaler *(shared with Trentino and Veneto)*
11 Alto Adige Colli di Bolzano/Bozner Leiten *(subzone)*
12 Alto Adige Meranese/Südtirol Meraner *(subzone)*
13 Alto Adige Santa Maddalena/Südtirol St. Magdalener *(subzone)*
14 Alto Adige Terlano/Südtirol Terlaner *(subzone)*
15 Alto Adige Valle Isarco/Südtirol Eisacktaler *(subzone)*
16 Alto Adige Valle Venosta/Südtirol Vinschgau *(subzone)*

the *Südtirol*, or South Tyrol—during the Napoleonic Wars.

In essence, the *fuochi* are symbolic "signal" fires, built to herald an invasion that never happened. Legend has it that Napoleon, after arriving in Milan in May of 1796, had planned to pass through the southern Tyrol en route to Innsbruck, where he would meet up with one of his generals and then march on to Vienna. On hearing this, religious leaders in the region convened a special council at the Duomo in Bolzano. They made a solemn oath in front of the altar of the Sacred Heart, praying that Christ would ward off the advancing French troops.

Napoleon got as far as Trento, but decided against continuing on through the Brenner Pass and instead headed east to Belluno, attacking Vienna by way of Friuli–Venezia Giulia. He wound up annexing the Alto Adige anyway, but that miraculous right turn out of Trento was given its own place in the religious mythology of the region. It might be considered just another *festa* in a country that seems to have one every day, but *Sacro Cuore* is unique in that it is markedly un-Italian—even the neighboring Trentino, to which Alto Adige is attached as a political entity, doesn't celebrate it. The mesmerizing *fuochi* are not just religious offerings but almost a gesture of defiance, a uniquely Tyrolean tradition in a place that in some ways still considers itself a part of Austria.

Sometimes the Trentino–Alto Adige union feels natural, other times forced. The two regions share a physical similarity and a good amount of history, but the more northerly Alto Adige remains aloof not just from Trentino but from Italy as a whole. Both regions were under Austrian rule from the start of the nineteenth century to the end of World War I, when they were annexed to Italy as "Venezia Tridentina" in 1919. The difference is that the Alto Adige, consisting of the province of Bolzano, had been the southern part of Austria's Tyrol state since the Middle Ages. Trentino, the province of Trento, had been more of an occupied territory, ruled for centuries by prince-bishops. It was only officially annexed to the Tyrol in the 1800s.

The common denominator is the Adige River, which cuts a celadon-green course from the Swiss Alps through Bolzano, Trento, and Verona on its way to the Adriatic. It's the thread that binds the "Tre Venezie," and it may well have been the point of entry for many of the region's indigenous grape varieties. Some experts believe that Trentino's marzemino grape, among others, came from Greece by way of the Adriatic and then the Adige. It may well have been planted by ancient Veneti tribes, who some think were refugees from Troy.

In this context, Trentino–Alto Adige doesn't seem quite as Germanic as it does on the surface. Confounded as we may be by its German street signs and Austrian Jügendstil architecture, the argument could be made that the region is as Italian as anyplace else on the peninsula. Maybe it's easier to imagine Greeks and Romans in the south, but they left their mark up here as well.

Trentino–Alto Adige's wine culture has much more in common with that of Austria or Germany than with southern Italy. The signature wines of the region are crisp, aromatic whites from Germanic grapes—gewürztraminer, müller-thurgau, sylvaner, riesling—grown in an environment best-suited to mountaineers, not gondoliers. At their best, these wines taste like they bubbled up from a mountain spring. But on the whole, they don't get the recognition they deserve.

Within Italy, Trentino–Alto Adige has been eclipsed by Friuli–Venezia Giulia, while in the United States, where aromatic whites are a tough sell to begin with, the whims of fashion have favored just about every other notable white-wine zone in the world: the Loire, Alsace, Germany, and more recently, Friuli, New Zealand, and Austria.

This may be because, despite all the evidence to the contrary, Trentino–Alto Adige is viewed as a low-quality producer. As much as 90 percent of Trentino's production is confined to large, industrial co-ops, among them MezzaCorona and Ca' Vit, two well-known brands. The Alto Adige also sees about 70 percent of its annual harvest go to co-ops, although theirs are a different breed: Unlike the majority of co-op wineries in Italy, which were created in the fifties and sixties and often run by provincial politicians, many Alto Adige co-ops were already producing wine in the nineteenth century, with the impetus for their creation having come from local farmers, not the government. Some of these collectives— the *cantine sociali,* or *kellerei,* of San Michele Appiano (St. Michael Eppan), Santa Maddalena (St. Magdalener), and Colterenzio (Schreckbichl)—are ranked among the best wineries in Italy. They are not well-known in the United States, because their traditional focus was on tart, light-bodied reds for export north. But as their attentions have shifted to whites, the wines from these co-ops are increasingly sought-after.

When you get past an ocean of pinot grigio and lightweight *spumante,* you'll find in Trentino and Alto Adige some of the most perfumed, well-structured whites in the world (and occasionally some powerful reds). Throughout the Adige Valley, vines occupy high-altitude sites in mostly gravel soils, amid the interplay of cool breezes from the Alps and warm, drying air off Lake Garda. It's a similar dynamic to that in Friuli–Venezia Giulia, where breezes off the Adriatic mingle with Alpine currents. But the conditions in Trentino–Alto Adige are more extreme: cooler, higher, and rockier.

Yet as much as Trentino and Alto Adige are physically similar, there are enough cultural (and viticultural) distinctions to merit treating them separately. Magré, home to the Alto Adige's best-known wine producer, Alois Lageder, is the southernmost German-speaking village in Europe. Roveré della Luna, not ten miles down the road, marks not only the start of the Trentino region but the linguistic shift to Italian. The two provinces share a number of DOC zones and a variety of grapes— including the light red schiava and the omnipresent chardonnay and pinot grigio—but the best wines from each are specialties of their respective areas.

VINI SPUMANTI
Sparkling Wines

Among the regional specialties are the dry sparklers of Trentino, which, despite being turned out in mass quantities, are made in the classic *mèthode champenoise.* The category is divided between industrial giants, such as Ca' Vit, MezzaCorona, and Ferrari, and tiny estates like Balter and Dorigati. They all work with the traditional Champagne grapes, chardonnay and pinot noir, along with smaller percentages of pinot bianco. The Trento DOC zone (not to be confused with the Trentino denomination) was created in 1993 to classify these sparkling wines, which have become one of Trentino's most important exports.

Despite their commercial success, Trentino sparklers tend to occupy a distant third place behind the dry *spumanti* of Franciacorta in Lombardy and those of Valdobbiadene in Veneto. The large co-ops dominate the market, and while their gleaming facilities are some of the most technically advanced in Italy, their tendency is to make light, well-priced wines for reliable apéritifs. But they won't make anyone forget Champagne.

The standout is Ferrari, a privately owned estate that produces 4.5 million bottles a year, making it one of top ten sparkling-wine firms in the world (by way of comparison, the Spanish *cava* makers Codorníu and Freixenet are much bigger, as is the Champagne house Moët et Chandon). Based in Ravina in an immense, corporate-looking facility overlooking the A22 autostrada, the Ferrari winery is a technical marvel: inside are some twelve million bottles at varying stages of maturation, and most of the *rémuage*—the process of rotating the bottles so that the spent yeasts from the second fermentation collect in the neck and are disgorged —is carried out in stainless-steel cages called *gyropalettes,* each of which holds five hundred bottles.

Ferrari was the pioneering producer of sparkling-wine in the Trentino, whose success inspired the Trentino *spumante* boom of the 1970s. Since the region's grape choices were long informed by the Austrians, there was plenty of chardonnay and pinot noir to work with when Giulio Ferrari founded his company in 1902. But no one had yet thought to emulate Champagne, at least not on a commer-

cial scale. Ferrari, who had no children, sold out to the Lunelli family years later, but his name lives on in Ferrari's top wine, a vintage-dated, all-chardonnay sparkler aged a minimum of eight years before it's release. Finely tuned and delicately aromatic, it's a minerally, earthy sparkler that rivals some Champagnes in its complexity.

Among the smaller Trentino producers to look for are the aforementioned Balter and Dorigati, both of which build a firm, fine structure into their best wines. They focus mainly on chardonnay, which in the Adige Valley retains its crisp, appley fruit character, rather than becoming blowsy and tropical as it does in warmer regions. The sparklers made from their chardonnays tend to be brisk, palate-cleansing wines.

As for the Alto Adige, *spumante* production is much more limited, and those wineries choosing to make some don't always export it. If you happen across an Alto Adige *spumante,* chances are it will be well worth a try; otherwise you'll have to head for the Alto Adige's well-traveled *strada del vino* (*Weinstrasse*), where the wines will taste even better with some *speck* (Tyrolean smoked bacon) and fresh apples.

VINI BIANCHI
White Wines

Apple orchards are almost as common as vines in the Adige Valley, turning the area a spectacular shade of green in summer. The river surges down the middle of the valleys, with orchards and vineyards spreading out on either side and climbing up mountain walls carved long ago by receding glaciers. The orchards often look a lot like vineyards: The tightly spaced trees are pruned very close and supported by canes, each tree devoting its energy to a small quantity of fruit.

When a similar approach is taken in the vineyards, the resulting white wines can taste like biting into a ripe green apple. There's a burst of tooth-chattering acidity at first, followed by a ripe, cool mouthful of flavor—everything in harmonious balance. The wildcard is aroma, which ranges from clean and flinty to exotically fruity and spicy, since the Adige Valley is home to an unruly array of grapes—from the more subdued pinot grigio, pinot bianco, and chardonnay to the Teutonic temptresses gewürztraminer, müller-thurgau, and sylvaner. Luckily, the labels almost always state the grape variety under the regional heading, one of the great features of the Trentino–Alto Adige DOC system.

Trentino Whites

The blanket Trentino DOC classification covers nineteen "varietal" wines, ten of which are dry whites. Part of this diversity is cultural, and part is topographical. "One reason we have so many grapes is because we have so many microclimates," notes Nicola Balter, who not only makes *spumante* at his farm in Rovereto but also excellent gewürztraminer and sauvignon. "We have vineyards from the valley floor to one thousand meters elevation, so there are a lot of things you can plant."

Chardonnay, pinot grigio, and to a lesser extent pinot bianco dominate at the lower elevations, since all are durable enough to handle the sometimes intense heat and humidity of the valley floor. Of the three, chardonnay is probably the most interesting, if only because

its personality here differs from the rich, alcoholic chardonnay of Australia or California. Though many Trentino producers ferment and age chardonnay in small oak barriques, the majority strive for a fresher, fruitier style of wine, emphasizing its acidity. The better ones have a refreshing minerality, not unlike young Chablis.

But the more interesting Trentino whites are the aromatic varieties: sauvignon blanc (usually called simply sauvignon), which is increasingly popular in both Trentino and Alto Adige; nosiola, Trentino's one true native white; and müller-thurgau, which, while much more famous in Germany, can be exceptional in both Trentino and Alto Adige.

Sauvignon is planted in a wide range of terrains all over the world, and it often reacts dramatically to changes of scenery. In the Loire Valley of France, it's described as grassy, flinty, and redolent of "cat's pee," whereas in New Zealand it can have an almost petrol-like intensity. Friuli–Venezia Giulia sauvignon takes on a peachy, citrusy character, often leaning toward the potency of New Zealand. In Trentino–Alto Adige, sauvignon is generally more restrained than its Friulian counterparts. The gravel and limestone soils of the Adige Valley are the ideal composition for the grape, and the cooler climate lends balance—something that's often missing from warm-weather sauvignons, which tend to turn hot from an overdose of alcohol.

Nosiola, grown principally in the Valle dei Laghi just north of Lake Garda, is one of those tart Italian whites that gets more respect in a sweet version—in this case a rare but excellent Vin Santo (see below). But as a dry wine, nosiola is better than average: generally supertart and light-bodied, it has an appealing lemon-apple flavor and a refreshing mineral finish that in certain situations is just what you need. But since American tastes run to fuller, wood-aged whites, and since nosiola is made in small quantities, it's not easy to find in the United States. Like falanghina in Campania or vermentino in Liguria, nosiola is a grape that grows in stature when it's drunk in the place where it's made. After a day in the Dolomites, and with a *bresaola* salad drizzled with lemon juice, you'll think it's the best white you've ever tasted.

Müller-thurgau, meanwhile, takes things in a more exotic direction. The grape is one of the most widely planted in Germany, and has gotten a measure of fame in the United States thanks to the Oregon winery Sokol Blosser. But Trentino may be its ideal habitat. Of all the varieties growing in the Tyrol, müller-thurgau is the one that thrives at the highest altitudes (five hundred meters and up), and is often harvested later than many red varieties. It is at its best in Trentino's Val di Cembra, a band of hills that runs north of the Avisio River. The most impressive example may be the müller-thurgau made by Pojer & Sandri, a wine that packs so many unusual aromas into one glass that it's impossible to characterize.

Yet what Pojer & Sandri and other top Trentino müllers share is balance and brightness. Müller-thurgau, like some of the other Germanic whites, can turn oily on the palate when it is very ripe, making it a little tiring to drink. In the upper reaches of Trentino, though, the grapes hold on to their freshness, giving an already aromatic wine a sort of nervous spiciness. Instead of seeming sweet, as many müller-thurgaus do, the Trentino versions retain those exotic aromas—dried apricots, white flowers, wild herbs—without being too heavy.

"Our philosophy is to make wines that are above all aromatic, with a slightly lower grade of alcohol than you might find in other areas," says Pojer & Sandri's Fiorentino Sandri, whose winery and distillery look down over the Adige Valley from the heights of Faedo. "We're not focused on making big, fat, alcoholic whites, one of the reasons being that we can't. We're up too high, it's too cool . . . our style is dictated in large part by our surroundings."

Alto Adige Whites

The Alto Adige, also, is home to a dizzying array of white grapes grown at often dizzying heights. As in the Trentino, there is an all-encompassing Alto Adige DOC that includes eleven varietal white wines, among them the aforementioned müller-thurgau, chardonnay, sauvignon, and the pinots bianco and grigio. The main differences are which grapes the Alto Adige's producers choose to focus on, and the more pervasive use of the German language on labels—Alto Adige becomes Südtirol, pinot bianco becomes Weissburgunder, *rosato* becomes *Kretzer*, and so on. Sometimes labels mix the two languages, adding to the fun of figuring out just what it is you're drinking.

It's hard to know where to start in describing Alto Adige whites. There are innumerable chardonnays, some fermented only in stainless steel and sold young, some fermented or aged in oak to add that telltale layer of vanilla and smoke. Sauvignon, too, may be wood-aged or not, but for the most part producers seem to prefer the latter. The most appealing (and typical) Alto Adige sauvignons are the bright, acidic ones, the ones that shimmer in the glass and tingle in your mouth.

In fact, if your preference is for crisp, clean

whites, a good rule of thumb is to look for the most inexpensive bottling from a solid producer—say Alois Lageder, Colterenzio, San Michele Appiano, or Tiefenbrunner—rather than a wine with a vineyard designation or proprietary name attached (the suffix *-hof* typically refers to a single vineyard, as in Lageder's "Haberlehof" pinot bianco). Alto Adige producers make a lot of different wines, usually starting with simple, unaged varietals and progressing on to single-vineyard *cru* wines and special blends, which often employ more oak and are weightier on the palate.

Pinot bianco may be most dramatically affected by this phenomenon. Widely planted in the Alto Adige, it can be a fairly nondescript wine when produced in large quantities. In the past, growers in the region confused it with chardonnay, and at its simplest pinot bianco will be crisp, appley, faintly nutty on the finish, but nothing to write home about. When allowed to ripen fully in a low-yielding vineyard, however, that nutty flavor expands and the wine becomes much richer. Like chardonnay, it responds well to fermenting and aging in oak—the wood flavors complement rather than obscure the natural flavors of the grape.

"Pinot Bianco is the most important white grape in the South Tyrol," says Hans Terzer, winemaker at the striking Cantina Produttori San Michele Appiano (St. Michael Eppan), one of the region's most esteemed co-op wineries. "This is partly because it gives a good crop every year, but it's also because of it's versatility. The only wines we age in wood are pinot bianco, pinot grigio, and chardonnay, because they are the only ones that can handle it."

For all of the interest in pinot bianco, however, the spicy gewürztraminer is the more overt symbol of Alto Adige wine culture. It is widely believed that the Alto Adige town of Termeno (Tramin) is the original home of the grape, which is also known by the names traminer and traminer aromatico. Anyone who's ever tried a gewürztraminer from Alsace knows that it's an acquired taste. But its pungent aromas and flavors can be great for heavy mountain foods like *gnocchi alle erbe* (gnocchi with wild herbs) or smoked sausages. The heavy use of cinnamon in Alto Adige cooking seems tailor-made for gewürztraminer, which itself gives off a distinctive aroma of cinnamon—along with rose petals, lychee nuts, and drippingly ripe peaches.

What distinguishes Alto Adige gewürztraminer is the same thing that distinguishes Trentino müller-thurgau: freshness. Producers seem intent on preserving as much of the grape's natural acid as they can, since without it the sugar-rich gewürztraminer can be fat, syrupy, and overalcoholic.

Also worth seeking out is the steely sylvaner of the Isarco Valley (look for the Val d'Isarco/Eisacktaler DOC designation), of which the tiny Kuen Hof estate and the scenic Abbazia di Novacella are two of the best producers. Less weighty than gewürztraminer but with a similar aromatic kick, sylvaner is yet another shimmering, aromatic white in a place that's overflowing with them. For a white-wine drinker looking for something different, there's probably no better place to experiment than the Alto Adige.

"Fifteen, twenty years ago, there weren't many restaurants in Italy or elsewhere that were willing to pay much for Italian white wines," says Hans Terzer, reflecting on why Alto Adige whites are just now being discovered. "As that has changed, so have we. There has been a dramatic shift in the types of wines we're making."

Vini Rossi
Red Wines

It comes as a surprise to many people that, even now, there is more red wine than white produced in Trentino–Alto Adige. In the Alto Adige, more than 50 percent of the vineyards are planted to the light red schiava (vernatsch in German), while in Trentino schiava is mixed with another mass-market red, lambrusco. The light, tart wines made from these grapes are not without appeal, but they are a remnant of a bygone era—namely, the days when Trentino–Alto Adige wasn't northern Italy, but southern Austria. It isn't necessarily that the region is incapable of producing more full-bodied wines, but that old-time farmers weren't looking for them. The *contadini* of the past wanted rustic reds that could be consumed all day long, not for pleasure as much as nourishment.

In fact, it is not at all implausible to think of Trentino–Alto Adige as a red-wine zone. Producers in the Alto Adige are quick to point out that Bolzano, which sits at the convergence of the Isarco (Eisack) and Adige (Etsch) Rivers, is consistently one of the hottest cities in Italy during the summer. "The Adige Valley is all about is topography," says Alois Lageder, whose ultramodern winery is in the picture-book village of Magré. "The valley floor can actually get very hot and humid, as exemplified by Bolzano, which is like a bowl that collects heat. Once you get up in the hills on either side, the climate changes dramatically."

What's most fascinating about the Trentino–Alto Adige winegrowing environment is a phenomenon known as the *ora*—a warm, drying breeze that originates on Lake Garda and travels up the Adige Valley to Bolzano. Whereas nighttime in the Adige Valley brings cool air from the Alps, the *ora* is a moderating influence during the day. "It arrives every afternoon like clockwork," says Nicola Balter, who notes that Riva del Garda, at the tip of Lake Garda in southern Trentino, is warm enough to grow olives (it is, in fact, the northernmost limit of olive production in Italy, and a source of incredibly delicate, perfumed oils).

In recent years, Trentino–Alto Adige vintners have significantly scaled back on schiava and lambrusco in favor of pinot nero (pinot noir), merlot, and especially cabernets sauvignon and franc. These international varieties tend to overshadow native reds such as teroldego (Trentino), marzemino (Trentino), and lagrein (predominantly Alto Adige), which is too bad: The native grapes are often more interesting.

Trentino Reds

In a nod to the past, the DOC classifications Casteller (which covers most of the province of Trento) and Lago di Caldaro (shared with the Alto Adige) are given to light reds based on schiava and/or lambruscos—simple wines that are for the most part consumed locally. Lago di Caldaro reds are more substantial than lambruscos, and are often a great accompaniment to doughy mountain dishes like *canederli* (*knödel* in German). Light and refreshing, they cut through heavy dishes and are also great reds to drink slightly chilled during warm weather.

But the preference these days is for denser, weightier reds, and merlot and cabernet—not just cabernet sauvignon and cabernet franc but a cross of the two called simply cabernet—have become increasingly popular. And although merlot and cabernet have a long history in both the Trentino and Alto Adige, interest in them is, for all intents and purposes, a fairly recent phenomenon.

In both the Trentino and the Alto Adige, the dominant system of vine training is called *pergola trentina*, in which the vines are trained onto high canopies supported by wooden arms. Harvesters can walk under these canopies without ducking. In the past the benefit of the *pergola* was that it produced massive quantities of grapes (on the valley floor, their height also helped combat humidity, because breezes could pass underneath). A *pergola* vine's principal advantage, other than productivity, is that its dense canopy of leaves shades the fruit so that it can ripen more slowly. But with red grapes this isn't always a benefit. When the vines are not pruned carefully and the crop size is not reduced, red grapes—especially the late-maturing cabernet family—struggle to ripen in the cool climate of Trentino–Alto Adige.

Although there are notable exceptions, a vast number of Trentino–Alto Adige cabernets and merlots have a vegetal aroma and flavor reminiscent of green bell peppers. Producers often say that this is the character of cabernet as grown in the region. But in reality it's the character of grapes that aren't fully mature. Many producers have begun to plant vineyards with the Bordeaux *guyot* system, where the vines are trained closer to the ground, to take advantage of the earth's heat, and planted very densely, so that the vines produce fewer grapes. Yet for all of the publicity Trentino–Alto Adige cabernets and Bordeaux-style blends have gotten in the press, a majority of them still have a nagging greenness that turns off lots of drinkers. For anyone accustomed to the rich, cassis-scented cabernet sauvignon of the Napa Valley (or Tuscany, for that matter), the more clipped versions from Trentino–Alto Adige can be a letdown.

Producers say that this will change as the region's viticultural practices evolve. "The problem with cabernet here is not temperature," explains Roberto Cesconi, a young Trentino vintner whose small family farm in Lavis produces a rich cabernet sauvignon and a richer merlot. "It's hot enough here. The problem is rain during harvest time. We are almost assured of getting rain at the end of September or beginning of October, so lots of times producers just pick early to avoid it. Unfortunately, unless it's a really advanced year, the fruit isn't likely fully mature by the end of September."

In Trentino, the best-known cabernet sauvignon producer is Marchese Carlo Guerrieri Gonzaga, whose aristocratic Tenuta San Leonardo is at the southern end of the region, in Avio. His San Leonardo Rosso—a Bordeaux-style blend of cabernet sauvignon, cabernet franc, and merlot—debuted in 1982 and has become the benchmark for Trentino (and Alto Adige) cabernets. Gonzaga, a cousin of Mario Incisa della Rocchetta of Tuscany's Tenuta San Guido, studied enology in France and has tried to bring a French château concept to the Trentino—in spite of the odds.

"It is not easy to grow cabernet and merlot up here," he says. "In 1989 we lost almost all of our production to rain. We did not produce San Leonardo in '92 or '98, either. But when the weather cooperates and the vines are in balance, the cabernet and merlot we have here is elegant and fragrant, and the wines can have a structure to compete with Bordeaux."

Farther north in Trentino, the region's most interesting native red, teroldego, is attracting as much attention as the Bordeaux blends—partly because its rarity has made it fashionable. Thought to be a relative of the still rarer marzemino, a grape of Greek origin, teroldego has been famous in the Trentino since the fifteenth century. At present it is more or less confined to the towns of Mezzacorona and Mezzolombardo, an area known as the Campo Rotaliano, which comprises the Teroldego Rotaliano DOC zone.

In the sandy, gravelly, limestone-rich soils of the Noce River basin, teroldego plumps up in the intense heat and, despite its thin skins, produces a deeply colored red with a distinctly tarry, savory, crushed-berry flavor. "It has beautiful color and rich fruit, but sometimes the tannins can be a little drying," says Elisabetta Foradori, whose family estate in Mezzolombardo is considered the leading producer of Teroldego. "You need to hold on to it for a while or pair it with gamey foods, but the flavor is unique. And you can't find it anywhere else in the world but here."

Foradori's barrique-aged teroldego, and their longer-aged, teroldego-based blend called "Granato" show off the grape at its most dense and fragrant: Deep purple in color, with scents and flavors of crushed blackberries and savory notes of coffee and bitter chocolate. Teroldego has a unique push-pull of sweet and savory flavors with a distinctive tarriness on the finish. (This is much more appealing than it sounds.) Look also for teroldegos by Dorigati, Gaierhof, Roberto Zeni, and Barone de Cles.

Alto Adige Reds

Although schiava remains a dominant component of the Alto Adige's vineyards, most Americans wanting to try it will have to head to Bolzano. American importers avoid schiava-based reds, which include those with the DOC names Lago di Caldaro/Kalterersee, Santa Maddalena/St. Magdalener, Colli di Bolzano/Bozner Leiten and Meranese di Collina/Meraner Hugel. Sipping a bottle of Kalterersee or St. Magdalener with a plate of Wiener schnitzel in an Alto Adige *Gasthaus* is a perfectly natural thing to do, and on occasion the wines can be reminiscent of light, fragrant pinot noirs. But on the whole, schiava-based wines remain resolutely local.

More available are the Alto Adige's cabernet sauvignons and merlots, especially those of Castello Schwanburg, Peter Dipoli, Baron Widmann, Alois Lageder, and most of the top co-ops, including Colterenzio, San Michele Appiano, and Cornaiano/Girlan. Yet despite the unprecedented popularity of these wines, the "international" grape that seems best-suited to the region is pinot nero (pinot noir). The more delicate pinot nero grape is better adapted to the altitudes and climate of the Adige Valley, and many of the above-named producers have had success with the variety—in vineyards on the east side of the river in particular. The steep, terraced slopes to the right of the Adige capture only the afternoon sun, allowing the heat-sensitive pinot nero to develop slowly and evenly.

"More so than cabernet or merlot, pinot nero is right for this area," says Hans Terzer of Cantina San Michele Appiano, whose "Sanct Valentin" Alto Adige pinot nero is one of the best pinot noirs available in Italy. "Everything that pinot nero likes, we have: high-altitude vineyards, good exposure to the sun, and, most especially, good fluctuations in temperature between the day and the night. This last part is critical because it helps preserve the aroma of pinot nero, which is its best feature."

Among the native grapes, the Alto Adige has its own dark red that thrives in the sandy soils of the plains: lagrein, which is made not only as a dark, dry red (called *scuro* or *Dunkel*) but also as a spicy, fragrant, deeply flavorful rosé (called *rosato* or *Kretzer*). The durable lagrein grape needs intense heat to mature, making it a perfect choice for the alluvial Bolzano basin. It is considered at its best from vineyards near the village of Gries, where the winery at the Benedictine monastery Muri-Gries is one of the best lagrein producers.

Like the Trentino's teroldego, Alto Adige lagrein is dense and dark to look at, and is generally deeply flavored—if a little spicy and clipped on the finish. More so than teroldego, though, lagrein can be rough around the edges: It's a light but wintry red to drink with aged mountain cheeses or a bowl of *gulasch,* and is readily available in the United States from a wide array of producers.

Vini Dolci
Sweet Wines

As in so many regions, sweet wines in Trentino–Alto Adige tend to be afterthoughts and are generally produced in small quantities. Yet like so many dessert wines, they can be total revelations.

In the Adige Valley, there are three very interesting options: the gold-amber Vin Santo from the Valle dei Laghi region in Trentino, which is made from nosiola grapes; late-harvest moscato giallo or goldmuskateller from both provinces; and the rarer but delicious moscato rosa, or rosenmuskateller, also from both provinces.

The term *vino santo* (holy wine) prompts most wine drinkers to think of Tuscany. But the northern tip of Lake Garda is home to a small community of artisan Vin Santo producers. The Valle dei Laghi, running north from Riva del Garda toward Trento, takes best advantage of the warming *ora* breezes. Like Tuscan Vin Santo, the Trentino version is made using grapes that are hung to dry for three to six months, after which they are fermented and aged in small wood barrels for a minimum of three years. In essence, the Valle dei Laghi is the only part of Trentino–Alto Adige that's dry enough in the winter months for the *appassimento* to proceed without the grapes rotting. Only a handful of Trentino producers still make Vin Santo, including the tiny producers F.illi Pisoni and Gino Pedrotti and the large co-ops of Ca'Vit and Pravis, but even the latter don't travel too far away from home.

From the deeply colored moscato giallo, which can also be made into a refreshing, cidery dry wine, producers make honeyed sweet wines, by either leaving the grapes on the vine to become superripe (*vendemmia tardiva*) or by picking and then drying them to concentrate their sugars (*appassimento,* or *passito*). Both giallo and rosa are members of the same moscato family, one of the largest and most widespread in Italy. In Trentino–Alto Adige, the *giallo* makes a yellow-gold sweet wine with sappy, peachy flavors reminiscent of German *auslesen,* while the *rosa* becomes an exotic, spicy pink wine with aromas and flavors of rosewater and cinnamon. Good luck finding either on an American restaurant's wine list, but if you do, try it—especially if *panna cotta* is on the dessert menu.

TRENTINO—ALTO ADIGE

PROVINCES	*Trentino:* Trento (TN). *Alto Adige:* Bolzano (BZ)
CAPITALS	*Trentino:* Trento. *Alto Adige:* Bolzano
KEY WINE TOWNS	*Trentino:* Avio, Faedo, Lavis, Mezzacorona, Mezzolombardo, Rovereto, Trento. *Alto Adige*: Appiano (Eppan), Bolzano (Bozen), Bressanone (Brixen), Caldaro (Kaltern), Cornaiano (Girlan), Magrè (Margreid), Termeno (Tramin)
TOTAL VINEYARD AREA*	Combined: 12,810 hectares, or 31,653 acres. Rank: 16th.
TOTAL WINE PRODUCTION*	Combined: 953,000 hectoliters, or 25,178,335 gallons (14th); 45% white, 55% red
DOC WINE PRODUCED*	Combined: 79.1% (1st)
SPECIALTY FOODS	*speck* (Tyrolean smoked bacon); *bresaola* (air-dried beef); rennet apples; Asiago cheese; *strangaolopreti* ("priest-choker" gnocchi of Trentino); *canederli,* or *Knödel* (bread-and-flour dumplings of Alto Adige, often mixed with chopped *speck* or other meats, cheeses, and herbs).
	*1997 figures. Rankings out of twenty regions total (Trentino–Alto Adige counted as one). Source: Istituto Statistica Mercati Agro-Alimentari (ISMEA), Rome.

KEY GRAPE VARIETIES

WHITES

GEWÜRZTRAMINER	May have originated in the Alto Adige town of Termeno (Tramin). Goes by the names traminer and traminer aromatico and is grown in both the Trentino and Alto Adige.
PINOT BIANCO	Called pinot blanc in French, and of French origin, this grape is widely planted in Italy, though in the past it was confused

	with chardonnay. An especially important variety in Alto Adige.
CHARDONNAY	Trentino's *spumante* boom in the sixties and seventies led to more widespread planting; it is now one of Trentino–Alto Adige's (and Italy's) most diffuse.
SYLVANER	Most dense in the Isarco Valley of the Alto Adige, where it probably arrived by way of Germany.
MÜLLER-THURGAU	A cross of riesling and sylvaner, born at Germany's Geisenheim Research Institute and now fairly widespread in northern Italy. Trentino's Val di Cembra is a favored position for the grape, which thrives at high altitudes.
PINOT GRIGIO	The French pinot gris (so named for the grayish color of ripe grapes). When fully ripe it can be rich and potent, but most producers opt for thin, high-acid versions.
OTHER NOTEWORTHY WHITES	NOSIOLA, a tart native of Trentino; SAUVIGNON, the French sauvignon blanc, increasingly popular in northern Italy; MOSCATO GIALLO, part of one of the world's largest grape families, but a distinct and distinctive sub-variety of the Trentino–Alto Adige.

REDS

SCHIAVA (VERNATSCH)	Still the most widely planted grape of any type in Trentino–Alto Adige. Thought to be of Slavic or German origin. A light red favored in Austria and southern Germany.
LAGREIN	One theory is that it originated along the Lagarina River of Trentino, thus the name; now thrives in the sandy, alluvial soils around Bolzano. Tannic and spicy, it is also grown in Trentino's Campo Rotaliano plain, near Mezzacorona.
TEROLDEGO	Possibly a relative of marzemino, but better regarded, it is mostly confined to the Campo Rotaliano plain of northern Trentino, at the confluence of the Noce and Adige rivers.
MARZEMINO	A specialty of the Trentino, particularly the area around Isera, where it produces grapey, plump wines. Thought by some to have been brought by the Greeks via Venice and the Adige River.
PINOT NERO (PINOT NOIR)	Increasingly popular French variety thrives at higher altitudes and can produce fruity, perfumed reds.

CABERNET SAUVIGNON	Also cabernet franc, and "cabernet" cross of franc-sauvignon. Thought to have arrived in Italy in the early 1800s, and widely planted both before and especially after phylloxera hit at the turn of the last century.
MERLOT	Easy-to-grow Bordeaux native now one of the most-planted reds in Italy.
OTHER NOTABLES	MOSCATO ROSA, a native variety used in interesting sweet rosés.

TOP VINTAGES IN TRENTINO— ALTO ADIGE, 1980–2000

Because of their high natural acidity, the region's whites will hold up to some time in the bottle, but generally speaking, these are wines to drink between one and three years from the vintage date. It would certainly be worth trying some whites from the mid- to late-nineties vintages cited on the following pages, but these citations are more useful for Trentino–Alto Adige reds. Given the cool climate and extreme conditions of the South Tyrol, reds tend to be very vintage-sensitive. You'll find, however, that a top-quality teroldego or lagrein from a good vintage can be very distinctive. Top recent years for whites include 1997 and '99; for reds, '96, '97, '99, and 2000. Years to avoid for reds include '92 and '98, when many producers didn't even make their reds.

LA STRADA DEL VINO
WINE TOURING IN TRENTINO—ALTO ADIGE

Both Trentino and Alto Adige are relatively unexplored by American wine wanderers, despite the fact that the wineries in the region are especially well equipped for tourism. In the Alto Adige especially, there is a well-marked *strada del vino* (*Weinstrasse* in German) that runs from Salorno all the way to Bolzano, through the picturesque wine villages of Magré, Tramin, Caldaro, and Appiano, to name a few. Small *agriturismo* (agro-tourism) lodges are found throughout both the Trentino and the Alto Adige, and many of the wineries have shops and restaurants attached where you can sample the wines and purchase products. The nearby Dolomites provide plenty of hiking and skiing options, but for the true wine hound there are a number of well-marked trails along the *strada del vino* that take you right through some of the region's top vineyards, with stops along the way at wineries for a quick snack or tour. For those who love both the outdoors and wine, Trentino–Alto Adige is hard to beat. Contact the Bolzano Chamber of Commerce for more information on touring the Alto Adige (0471-94-55-11; fax: 0471-94-56-20). In Trentino, contact Vino e Turismo in Lavis (0461-24-63-15; fax: 0461-24-23-40).

DEGUSTAZIONI
TASTINGS

TRENTO DOC SPARKLERS

MezzaCorona Trento Rotari Brut "Arte Italiana," $

Ferrari "Giulio Ferrari," $$

Here are two sparkling wines to file under the category of Pleasant Surprises. Lean, firm, and fine, they are both lightweight but well-structured sparklers made in the Champagne method, excellent as apéritifs but with enough acid and minerality to stand up to food. In the "Giulio Ferrari" in particular, you'll find a depth of flavor and firmness of structure to rival that of a good Champagne. Relatively speaking, these wines are a steal.

ALTO ADIGE PINOT BIANCO (WEISSBURGUNDER)

CP San Michele Appiano (St. Michael Eppan) Alto Adige Pinot Bianco "Schulthauser," $

Elena Walch Alto Adige Pinot Bianco "Kastelaz," $

Although both of these wines are high in natural acidity, they have a creaminess of texture and slightly nutty flavors to identify them as pinot biancos. Aromas of white flowers and green melon are followed by flavors of minerals and raw almonds, with an aftertaste reminiscent of green apple skin. Although they are generally lighter-bodied than pinot grigios, pinot biancos tend to be more aromatic and spicy. You might play up the almondy notes in the wine by pairing it with an amandine-style fish preparation.

Ca' Vit Pinot Grigio, $

Franz Haas "Kris" Alto Adige Pinot Grigio, $

Elena Walch Alto Adige Pinot Grigio "Castel Ringberg," $

TRENTINO AND ALTO ADIGE PINOT GRIGIO

Pinot grigio is one of the most highly variable grapes in Italy, as these three wines demonstrate. Starting with the Ca' Vit and finishing with Elena Walch's "Castel Ringberg," you'll see that the style spectrum runs from delicately aromatic and chalky on the palate to more round, pear-appley, and unctuous. As with pinot bianco, there's a flinty minerality to pinot grigio that tickles the palate and gets the salivary glands working. But in the Franz Haas and Elena Walch wines in particular, there's also a plump layer of fruit flavor that coats the tongue. Pinot grigio is not assertively aromatic, but rather a wine that expresses itself *in bocca* (in the mouth), and in the case of these Alto Adige versions, there's a cool, dewy, spring-water quality to each that evokes the mountain valleys from which they come. With a salad of rennet apples, cubed cheese, and maybe a little speck or bresaola, dressed with lemon juice and oil, there's no more elemental choice.

Tiefenbrunner Alto Adige Gewürztraminer, $

Colterenzio Alto Adige Gewürztraminer "Cornell," $$

ALTO ADIGE GEWÜRZTRAMINER

Exotic aromas of peach, mandarin orange, white flowers, lychee, and cinnamon leap from the glass when sampling these wines, leading the taster to believe that the wines will be sweet. Yet a distinguishing feature of Alto Adige gewürz is that while it is round and unctuous across the palate (as evidenced especially by the "Cornell" wine), it finishes with a drying tingle of acidity. Sometimes gewürztraminer can be a little oily and cloying, but these wines have a sense of balance and proportion. Exotic, yes. Cloying, no. They are great with gnocchi or filled pastas in slightly sweet sauces incorporating cinnamon or cumin.

Graziano Fontana Müller-Thurgau di Faedo, $

Pojer & Sandri Trentino Müller-Thurgau, $

TRENTINO MÜLLER-THURGAU

Müller-thurgau bears some aromatic similarity to gewürztraminer, although it tends to exhibit more herbal notes. These wines give off scents of apricot and peach, but then there are also hints of sage and thyme. Where gewürztraminer is floral and fruity, müller-thurgau is slightly more spicy and savory, a little bigger and brassier and, generally speaking, a little oilier and richer on the palate. Try these crisp, forceful whites with a classic *gnocchi alle erbe* (gnocchi with mountain herbs) for a true taste of the hills of Trentino.

Foradori Teroldego
Rotaliano, $

Roberto Zeni Teroldego
Rotaliano, $$

TRENTINO TEROLDEGO

Deeply colorful—almost black, in fact—and deeply flavorful, teroldego is something of an anomaly in a region known mostly for lighter-style reds. The thick skins of the teroldego grape gives its wines their deep purple hues, and the flavors, too, might be described as "purple": think of Welch's grape jelly, only with a good dose of road tar and coffee grounds (that may not sound too appetizing, but it is). If there's a knock on these full-flavored wines is that they are a little "short"—their flavors don't persist very long after you've swallowed the wine, but rather seem abbreviated by a somewhat drying blast of tannin. They need a good piece of mountain cheese or maybe some *gulasch* to absorb this tannic bite.

CP Santa Maddalena
Alto Adige Lagrein
"Perlhof," $–$$

Muri-Gries
Alto Adige Lagrein, $$

Franz Gojer
Alto Adige Lagrein
Riserva, $$

ALTO ADIGE LAGREIN

One thing that these reds share is a savory, spicy, herbal flavor reminiscent of tobacco leaves. They vary in their amounts of red fruit extract on the palate, but there's an earthiness to each that distinguishes them. This push-pull of sweet and savory lends the wines a singular personality. Though not for everyone, these funky reds are great accompaniments to hearty mountain stews and braises.

CP San Michele Appiano
(St. Michael Eppan)
Alto Adige Pinot Nero
"Sanct Valentin," $

Hofstätter
 Alto Adige Pinot Nero
"St. Urbano," $$$

ALTO ADIGE PINOT NERO

Good pinot noir—that is, pinot noir that tastes like pinot noir—is not easy to find in Italy. But as these two wines demonstrate, there are areas of Italy with an aptitude for this notoriously difficult variety. In the "Sanct Valentin" wine, the classic pinot noir aroma of red cherries and a touch of woodsy smoke wafts up from the glass like a perfume. The Hofstätter has a similarly foresty, wild-berry aroma, but with a little more density of fruit concentration. These reds are extremely versatile with food, with heady aromas and flavors balanced by bright acidity and soft tannins. When you're in the mood for a more delicate, aromatic red, these are great choices.

La Cucina

FOOD FOR THE WINE

RECIPE BY LIDIA BASTIANICH

The heavily German and Austrian influences in both Trento and Bolzano (and especially Bolzano) make for some hearty eating: big, doughy *canederli*, or *knödel* (dumplings) are made from a combination of stale bread and flour and are often served with chunks of Tyrolean smoked bacon (*speck*) in hot consomme. Gnocchi of all types, usually served in browned butter with mountain herbs or spinach, are big in the Trentino. Naturally, hearty stews and *gulasch* are popular winter warmers, as are wine-based soups. At the same time, the food of the Adige Valley doesn't need to be heavy: One great salad of the region combines chopped green apples (widely grown in the valley) with slices of air-dried beef (*bresaola*), tossed with olive oil (from Lake Garda), lemon juice, and poppy seeds. It's fantastic with one of the region's many aromatic white wines.

The recipe below is inspired by Alto Adige *canederli* but made in the (smaller) size of gnocchi. *Canederli* is a peasant dish, in that it likely incorporated old, hard bread in the past (reconstituted in water or milk) as a means of saving flour.

Gnocchi Tirolese

FOR THE DOUGH

1 loaf (about 12 ounces) DARK BREAD, cubed (look for a dark seedless rye or a light pumpernickel with no nuts or raisins)
1¼ cups MILK
2 large EGGS
¼ cup grated GRANA PADANO CHEESE (Parmigiano-Reggiano may be substituted)
SALT and PEPPER to taste
¾ cup FLOUR

FOR THE SAUCE

2 tablespoons OLIVE OIL
½ pound SPECK (or pancetta), medium dice
2 tablespoons BUTTER
SALT and PEPPER to taste
2 tablespoons chopped fresh MARJORAM

SERVES 4 AS A MAIN COURSE
OR 8 AS AN APPETIZER

To make the dough, soak the cubed or chunked bread in 1 cup of the milk until it falls apart, about 2 hours. Work the soaked bread with your hands to break it up thoroughly. In a separate bowl, beat the eggs. Add them to the bread and milk, and stir to combine. Mix in the grated cheese and season with salt and pepper. Fold the flour into this mixture, adding more milk if it's too sticky or more flour if it's too wet. Let the dough rest for 15 minutes.

Bring a large pot of salted water to a boil. Meanwhile, on a lightly floured surface, make the quenelle-shaped gnocchi by scooping out the dough with a tablespoon and scraping it off onto the floured surface with another spoon. Roll the quenelles gently in the flour to lightly cover them. After you've made all the gnocchi, add them to the boiling water in batches and cook for about 3 to 5 minutes, or until they float to the surface.

Drain and reserve in a colander set over paper towels. Also reserve ¼ cup of the cooking water.

To make the sauce, heat the oil in a medium to large sauté pan over medium-high flame. Add the speck or pancetta and sauté until the fat is rendered, about 5 to 7 minutes. Add the butter and cook until the froth subsides and becomes a chestnut color, but not brown. Add the reserved pasta water to arrest the cooking process. Reduce the heat to low, gently add gnocchi, and toss to coat. Season with salt and pepper. Add the marjoram at the last minute.

WINE RECOMMENDATION: Either a white or a red will work here; if you're feeling adventurous, try a gewürztraminer or müller-thurgau to pick up the aromatics of the marjoram. Alternatively, go with a crisp lagrein to counter the doughiness of the dish.

Lombardia

ARTISAN WINES IN THE CAPITAL OF INDUSTRY

———— ◦⁂◦ ————

SELLING THE SPARKLE

Brother Pietro is a fairly contemporary-looking monk, preferring blue jeans, a band-collared shirt, and Birkenstock sandals to the more traditional vestments. He is the head man at the Convento dell'Annunciata, a sixteenth-century abbey in the commune of Rovato, in the gently rolling hills between Bergamo and Brescia in central Lombardy. Rovato lies within the Franciacorta wine zone, and the Convento dell' Annunciata is one of a number of historic monasteries in the region. Brother Pietro and the handful of others who live in the cloister spend their days studying and praying among Romanino frescoes, or gazing out from their perch atop Monte Orfano at the broad expanse of the Padana plain to the south. Their principal source of income, other than church donations, comes from the vineyards that tumble down the hillside below the abbey. They don't cultivate the vines themselves but instead lease them to the Bellavista winery in nearby Erbusco, which is owned by construction titan Vittorio Moretti.

"There have been vineyards here for centuries," says Brother Pietro, his voice a smoke-cured growl. On a tour of the abbey, he pads softly and slowly through the labyrinthine halls, leading the way down to the old wine cellar, first excavated in the sixteenth century. "After the fall of the Roman Empire, it was the monasteries that kept the culture of the vine alive," he continues. These days, though, he and his monastic brethren are nonfactors in a wine economy that has changed dramatically.

Brother Pietro and Vittorio Moretti are an unlikely pair, one that embodies the melding of Old and New Worlds in Italian wine country. When touring the verdant vineyards of Italy, it's easy to forget that the owner of the big *tenuta* on the hill might well be a dentist from Switzerland, or that the proprietor of the little *podere* around the corner is a cement contractor, not a sharecropper. And perhaps nowhere does the reality of Italian wine collide with the fantasy of Italian wine quite like in Franciacorta, where the rural idyll has been transformed into suburban bliss. Or resort-town chic.

It's not that Franciacorta doesn't have history. The name is said to have first appeared in 1277, in the statutes of the municipality of Brescia. It was spelled Franzacurta (from the Latin *franchae curtes*) and denoted a district of monasteries that was exempt from taxation. The Convento dell'Annunziata and the many other abbeys in the zone harken back to this

The DOC Zones of Lombardia

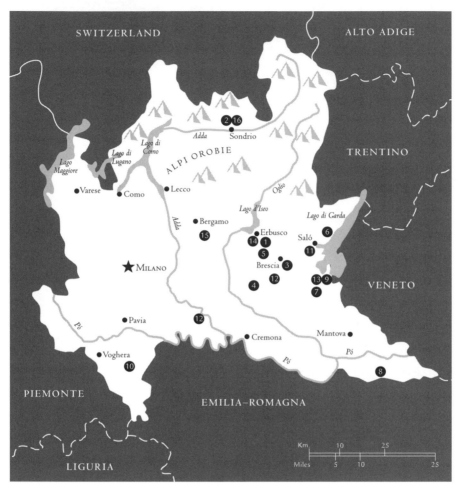

SWITZERLAND

ALTO ADIGE

TRENTINO

VENETO

Adda

Sondrio

Lago di Como

Lago di Lugano

Lago Maggiore

ALPI OROBIE

Oglio

Lago d'Iseo

Lago di Garda

Varese

Como

Lecco

Adda

Bergamo

Erbusco

Saló

Brescia

MILANO

Pavia

Cremona

Mantova

Pò

Pò

Pò

Voghera

PIEMONTE

EMILIA–ROMAGNA

LIGURIA

Km

Miles

DOCG

1 Franciacorta
2 Valtellina Superiore

DOC

3 Botticino
4 Capriano del Colle
5 Cellatica
6 Garda
7 Garda Colli Mantovani
8 Lambrusco Mantovano

9 Lugana
10 Oltrepò Pavese
11 Riviera del Garda Bresciano/
   Garda Bresciano
12 San Colombano al Lambro/
   San Colombano
13 S. Martino della Battaglia
14 Terre di Franciacorta
15 Valcalepio
16 Valtellina

time, but they're surrounded by ultramodern, conference-style hotels, a golf course, and well-manicured lake towns such as Sárnico and Iseo, which seem custom-designed for tourism. A few miles east of the Convento, in the commune of Castegnato, is a shopping mall built to resemble a medieval castle. Its parking lot stretches for acres.

"There isn't anything like Franciacorta anywhere in Italy," says Mattia Vezzola, the long-time enologist at Bellavista. As he says this, he leans intently over the mahogany bar in the Bellavista tasting room, which is lavishly decorated with leather couches and modern art. "Franciacorta as we know it today is a very recent phenomenon."

The Franciacorta of today is a wine zone famed for its *méthode champenoise* sparkling wines, made mostly from chardonnay and pinot noir in some of the biggest, sleekest, and most expensively appointed wineries in Italy. A good number of the producers are wealthy industrialists like Moretti, many of whom are from nearby Brescia. But what's most notable is how fast they built their properties: Nearly all of them arrived in the last two decades, turning what was once a sleepy collection of farmhouses and weekend getaways into a coterie of commercial wine powerhouses.

Although it is likely that the old-time monks of Franciacorta experimented with sparkling wines, in the past the region was really known only for rustic reds. It wasn't until the sixties that *spumante* production began in earnest, when a local enologist named Franco Ziliani, while working for the Guido Berlucchi estate (one of maybe five commercial wineries in the zone at the time), decided to try his hand at Champagne-style sparklers from some of Berlucchi's pinot noir grapes.

"Ziliani had a laboratory in Brescia, and he felt that there was potential for sparkling wine in this zone," Vezzola explains. "From there it skyrocketed, because the seventies were a time of explosive economic growth in this region, especially Brescia. And it so happened that right when Ziliani made his discovery, there was plenty of money here to fuel more experiments."

Not only did the Berlucchi winery grow into a 5-million-bottle-a-year operation, but new *cantine* started popping up on every corner. This included Moretti's Bellavista and Maurizio Zanella's Ca' del Bosco, which he started as a well-financed teenager right out of enology school (Zanella's father was one of Italy's largest auto-parts manufacturers). "There's a real entrepreneurial force here in Lombardia," says Vezzola. "The people of this region have always been great business people. And that has shaped the wine culture in a profound way."

Brescia was once known principally for metallurgy and arms manufacturing—Beretta firearms are made just outside the city. But these days, the area also has a swanky string of sparkling wine estates, complete with Relais & Châteaux Hotels (Moretti's L'Albereta, which also houses a Michelin two-star restaurant) and all the other creature comforts. At times Franciacorta feels like an exclusive gated community, which to a certain extent it is.

"To make sparkling wine, you need money, plain and simple," Vezzola says, citing the need for more expensive equipment and more space in a sparkling-wine *cantina* than in an average winery. "If you want to be making sparklers you need more room to store the bottles, because they must be rotated and therefore you need to be able to get at them. You also have much more money tied up in inventory than most wineries. It's an incredible investment."

This is the reality of modern Italian wine, however much we might like to believe otherwise. The rural idyll is more or less a thing of the past, which, in wine terms, is probably a good thing.

Lombardia has always been the center of big business in Italy, be it silk and textile manufacturing in the Lake Como area, banking in Milan, or mining and metallurgy in Brescia. But its richness is not merely financial. The Padana plain spreads across the bottom third of the region, fed not only by the Po but by a tangle of its tributaries, which flow down from the Alpine lakes. The lowlands of the Padana produce a wealth of rice for risotto and offer one of the largest stretches of pasture in Italy. In fact, few other Italian regions can rival Lombardia's assortment of cheese, most of which are from cow's milk: There's the salty, nutty Grana Padano, the more widely produced sibling of Parmigiano-Reggiano; the pungent, veiny Gorgonzola, named for a small town east of Milan; the soft, funky Robiola; and the sharp, runny Taleggio, a specialty of Alpine towns such as Bergamo and Lecco.

Despite being Italy's biggest and most populous region, and despite boasting the country's most high-tech (and most productive) farming industry, Lombardia is not a prodigious wine producer. Only the Oltrepò Pavese, in the southwestern corner of the region, is a significant source of wine, with an annual output that places it among Italy's most productive DOCs. Traditionally, Oltrepò Pavese has been Milan's wine reservoir, turning out a mass of light reds and sparkling wines to be vacuumed up in the city's restaurants. Other than those from the Oltrepò Pavese, Lombard wines are specialty items: For all of the success of Franciacorta sparklers, for example, they still only amount to about one-sixth of the amount of Prosecco produced in Conegliano-Valdobbiadene, in neighboring Veneto.

Stylistically speaking, Lombardia has everything: serious Franciacorta sparklers that most agree are the best in Italy; crisp, aromatic still whites from Lake Garda, which at a minimum stand up to the best of Soave; powerful, aromatic nebbiolo reds on the terraces of the Valtellina, which can rival Barolo in depth and complexity; and a new generation of plump bonardas, fragrant pinot noirs, and *méthode champenoise* sparklers from the once-unheralded Oltrepò Pavese. Not only is Lombardia rich in natural and financial resources, it makes the most of them.

VINI SPUMANTI
Sparkling Wines

In one sense, Franciacorta is the Silicon Valley of Italian wine: It's not only the birthplace of a revolutionary product but of a culture of entrepreneurs. Yet for all of the resources of Franciacorta's wine producers, there's something less tangible about the southern shores of Lake Iseo that distinguishes the wines that are made there.

Monte Orfano, where the Convento dell'Annunciata sits, is one of the first points at which the Padana plain, which is nourished by the Po, begins to give way to the Orobie Alps. In fact, the swath of hills that includes Orfano—essentially the southern flank of the Franciacorta DOC—looks almost like a giant bunker when viewed from the south.

"Orfano means orphan in English," explains

Martino De Rosa, the son-in-law of Vittorio Moretti, who helps run both Bellavista and the family's newer Contadi Castaldi winery. "It's believed that the Orfano hills were formed by tectonic rather than glacial movement, whereas the area of Franciacorta is a glacial basin. Monte Orfano is like a wall separating Franciacorta from the Padana plain. There's a different climate and different soils on either side."

Whereas the soils of the Padana are richer and more fertile mixtures of heavy clays and alluvial deposits, the Franciacorta hills are a silty, pebbly glacial moraine, which DeRosa says helps slow the ripening of grapes. Add to this the moderating effect of Lake Iseo, which makes the winters in Franciacorta slightly warmer and provides cooling breezes in the summer, and the normally fast-ripening chardonnay and pinot noir can slow down a bit—giving them a chance to develop complex aromas and flavors while maintaining acidity. It's not that simple, of course, but it's no exaggeration to say Franciacorta has a distinctly cooler climate than much of the area that immediately surrounds it, sitting in its natural amphitheater that looks across the lake to the Alps.

Franciacorta's sparklers are made from varying percentages of chardonnay, pinot nero (pinot noir), and pinot bianco (blanc), although chardonnay has become the dominant variety in the zone, covering more than two-thirds of the 3,500 acres now planted there. No one in Franciacorta can say for sure when these and other French grapes first arrived in the area, but it is possible that they were introduced by Napoleon, who made Milan the capital of the Cisalpine Republic in 1797; they may well have been there even earlier, possibly in the vineyards of the region's many monasteries. The point is that while the sparkling wines of Franciacorta may be a recent phenomenon, the grapes they're made from are not.

"At the end of the nineteenth century, phylloxera destroyed the vineyards of Franciacorta," says Giovanni Cavalleri, whose eponymous winery in Erbusco is typically mentioned in the same breath as top dogs like Ca' del Bosco and Bellavista. "Throughout the north, many French varieties were introduced at that time as the vineyards were replanted." If you look at it that way, then, the so-called French varieties have been here for at least a hundred years.

As for the style of Franciacorta sparklers, they are patterned very closely after their counterparts in France. Franciacorta wines are made only in the traditional Champagne method, in which the secondary fermentation of the wine is carried out in bottle. And Franciacorta producers favor French terminology on their labels—they tend to use *rosé* instead of *rosato*, for example, and the designations indicating the residual sugar level in the wines are the same as in France: Extra Brut (the dryest, with less than 6 grams per liter of residual sugar); Brut (less than 15); Extra Dry (12 to 20); Sec (17 to 35); and Demi-Sec (33 to 50). The sweetest designation for French sparklers, Rich or Doux, is not included in the Franciacorta DOCG discipline.

Many producers also have wines labeled as Satèn, indicating that it is made only from white grapes in a *crémant* style—meaning that the wine has a slightly lower atmospheric pressure than a traditional *méthode champenoise* sparkler. Another popular style in Franciacorta is Pas Dosé or Pas Operé, which indicates a wine that has not been given a *dosage* before bottling. *Dosage* is the mixture of wine and sugar syrup typically added to sparkling wines to balance out their often intense acidity, and is typically a major determinant of sparkling-wine style; Pas Dosé wines are therefore the most bone-dry of the Franciacorta lot.

Yet for whatever reason, wine experts are reluctant to allow Franciacorta wines into the rarefied company of Champagne—there always seems to be some disclaimer attached to any praise of Italian sparklers, however effusive that praise may be. Not only are they made from essentially the same grapes, and produced by the same methods, but Franciacorta wines can be every bit as firmly structured, aromatic, and balanced as anything from France. As even the most expert sommelier will tell you, evaluating sparkling wines is the most difficult tasting exercise of them all, but in the better wines of Ca' del Bosco, Bellavista, Cavalleri and others, it's not so much a specific flavor but a *feel* that links them to Champagne: Rather than plod across your palate, these wines stand on their tiptoes, tense and nervous, always maintaining their sinewy posture.

Whether Franciacorta's firm, minerally, aromatic sparklers are ultimately a product of a charmed location or simply a triumph of winemaking technology is the subject of some debate. Either way, the wines are what some would call "correct." Among many other things, the producers of Franciacorta are extremely well organized, having not only created one of the most tourist-friendly wine zones in Italy but one of the more clear-cut DOCG disciplines. A basic nonvintage cuvée spends at least eighteen months aging in the bottle before release, while a vintage wine spends a minimum of thirty. Grape yields are carefully limited. What can be said on the label is strictly controlled—they don't, for example, allow the word *spumante*, which evidently is too suggestive of cheap, off-dry sparklers to be attached to a Franciacorta wine. There's no escaping a sense that Franciacorta is a planned community, a country club with very strict bylaws.

"In 1968, there was nothing here," says the magnanimous Maurizio Zanella, the unofficial ambassador of Franciacorta, referring not only to the hill where his giant winery now sits but to Franciacorta as a whole. In his younger days, Zanella flew to the annual VinItaly wine fair in a helicopter (despite the fact that the fair, in Verona, is about forty minutes by car), and he bubbles with the same nervous energy as his wines. A few financial setbacks have tamed him somewhat, and he sold a significant stake in Ca' del Bosco to the giant Santa Margherita group several years ago. Nevertheless, Zanella exudes the easy confidence of an empire builder, a guy who gets things done. As much as any aspect of the Franciacorta *terroir*, this attitude goes a long way in explaining why Franciacorta wines are the way they are.

"If you compare us to many other regions of Italy, we don't really have any tradition to speak of," Zanella says. "But that was a good thing. Without tradition weighing us down, we were able to make decisions based on what works, not on what came before."

The pinot noir-based sparkling wines of the Oltrepò Pavese, in Lombardia's southwestern corner, merit a mention, even though they have been on the wane as dry reds have grown in popularity. Situated at the foot of the Apennines, the hills of the Oltrepò Pavese have attracted increasing interest among Italian wine buffs. Although the zone is one of those wide-ranging DOCs in which everything from sweet, *frizzante* reds to dry white sparklers are made (there are a total of twenty styles allowed), it is widely believed that the cool, limestone-rich slopes are suited to more than just mass-produced quaffers. The DOC includes provisions for a *spumante* made from a minimum of 70 percent pinot noir, made in the *méthode champenoise*. Among the top producers of Oltrepò Pavese *spumante* is the Tenuta Il Bosco estate, owned by the Veneto-based Zonin Group, and there are number of other *cantine* making *spumante*, although much of it is destined for the local market.

Vini Bianchi
White Wines

Of the sixteen DOC zones scattered throughout the vast Lombardia region, nine include provisions for some kind of dry white wine, and most of these are clustered along the western and southern shores of Lake Garda. From the steeper slopes along the west bank down to the richer, heavier clays of the plains above Mantova, a fairly random assortment of grapes is headlined by the well-traveled trebbiano and the star of Soave, garganega, which factor into a handful of Garda-area DOC blends. The only instance in which either is given a prominent role is in the wines of the Lugana DOC, where the reputedly superior subvariety known as trebbiano di Lugana (or trebbiano di Soave) creates fragrant, minerally whites that are a cut above the majority of other trebbiano-based wines in Italy.

Lugana from top producers such as Ca' dei Frati, which is headquartered in the lakeside resort town of Sirmione, shows off a more floral, spicy, and forwardly fruity side to the trebbiano grape. Most experts chalk this up to the trebbiano di Lugana variety itself (which some scientists say is genetically related to the more aromatic verdicchio of the Marche), as opposed to any aspects of *terroir* that might contribute. The Lugana zone is in fact hot and flat, with heavy, fertile soils. But rather than become flabby, the better wines of Lugana retain a shimmer of acidity that lends them a kinship to the mountain wines of the Alto Adige. Along with Ca' dei Frati's benchmark "I Frati" bottling, other Luganas worth looking for include the Veneto-based Zenato winery's Lugana "San Benedetto," and a number of selections from the Provenza estate (which is also known for the spicy rosé known as Chiaretto, made from a local mix of grapes that includes sangiovese, marzemino, barbera, and groppello).

In Franciacorta, meanwhile, producers are opting for rounder, plusher white wines based principally on the local chardonnay, again looking to France for inspiration. But while the sparklers emulate their counterparts in Champagne, the whites under the DOC heading Terre di Franciacorta tend to resemble something more Californian than Burgundian.

At one time sparkling and still wines were grouped together under the Franciacorta DOC, but the local producers petitioned for and got a DOCG designation for the sparklers in 1995, their goal being to associate the name "Franciacorta" solely with sparkling wine, à la Champagne. With Franciacorta elevated to DOCG, a new DOC was created for still wines called Terre di Franciacorta, whose production discipline includes provisions for a Bianco from chardonnay, pinot bianco and/or pinot nero (vinified as a white), and a Rosso from a mix of cabernets sauvignon and franc, merlot, barbera, and nebbiolo. Generally speaking, the Terre di Franciacorta whites have been solid, many of them given a toasty roundness through fermentation and aging in French oak barrels. Ca' del

Bosco's Terre di Franciacorta Chardonnay is typical of the style, as is the Terre di Franciacorta "Uccellanda" (100 percent chardonnay) from Bellavista. Also worth mentioning is Bellavista's Terre di Franciacorta Bianco from its vineyards at the Convento dell'Annunciata, which combines chardonnay and pinot bianco to create an extremely rich, fruity wine.

Finally, there's the Oltrepò Pavese, which, as some producers have found, has the altitudes, soils, and mountain-cooled climate to produce more than just light sipping whites. In the calcareous clays of these often steep slopes, Oltrepò Pavese producers such as Martilde, Ca' di Frara, and Bruno Verdi are continuing to impress with wines from riesling, particularly the riesling renano subvariety. Although they are lighter-styled wines, the Oltrepò Pavese rieslings are redolent of ripe peaches and white flowers, and like the rieslings of Friuli–Venezia Giulia, they finish crisp and dry. Although many producers are also having success with chardonnay and pinot grigio in the zone, the more aromatic riesling is emerging as the most interesting white from the area. Although they are more difficult to find in the United States, the rieslings of the Oltrepò Pavese are examples of the Italian take on Germanic varieties—they're fragrant and full of flavor, but made in a more bone-dry style than most of their more northerly counterparts.

VINI ROSSI
Red Wines

Although red wines are made throughout Lombardia, the two principal centers of production are the Oltrepò Pavese, in the south-west, and the Valtellina, one of the most northerly wine zones in all of Italy. And though a number of Bordeaux-style blends are being released to much hype in Franciacorta, the wines have yet to make any serious impact on the market. Probably the best known of the Franciacorta reds is the "Maurizio Zanella" bottling from Ca' del Bosco, a luxurious barrique-aged blend of cabernet sauvignon, cabernet franc, and merlot (more interesting is Ca' del Bosco's pinot noir called "Pinero"). Otherwise, the Terre di Franciacorta reds tend to be earthy, spicy, simple blends, many of which have a distinctly vegetal note from cabernet franc. Again, that leafy, bell-pepper flavor is often viewed as a flaw, a telltale sign of cabernet (especially franc, but also sauvignon) that isn't fully mature. Throughout the northern regions of Italy, from Lombardy to Veneto to Alto Adige, producers argue over whether that greenness is in fact a fault or is just the way the cabernet family expresses itself in cooler climates. But either way, it's a taste that takes some getting used to.

Yet while Franciacorta remains more committed to its sparkling wines, the Oltrepò Pavese, still a huge producer of both its own *spumanti* and base wines for sparklers produced outside of the zone, is seeing a surge of interest in its reds. It has often been noted that the Oltrepò Pavese was one of the first regions in Italy—if not *the* first—in which pinot noir was planted. Traditionally, most of the grapes and wines made from pinot noir in the zone were sold off in bulk, especially to large Piedmontese *spumante* producers such as Cinzano and Gancia. But in recent years, the dry, still, and often barrel-aged pinot noir of the Oltrepò Pavese has become almost trendy in wine circles. Add to this a wider range of solid reds from both barbera and the local bonarda (a synonym for croatina), and the zone has become one of Italy's new frontiers.

These days, a savvy red-wine drinker who doesn't want to spend a lot of money has a variety of lesser-known regions to explore for serious but relatively inexpensive wines: there's Rosso Cònero in the Marche, Castel del Monte in Puglia, the entire island of Sicily, and, increasingly, the Oltrepò Pavese. The name of the zone means "on the other side of the Po from Pavia" and refers to the small chunk of Lombardia wedged between southeastern Piedmont and northwestern Emilia-Romagna, where the Ligurian Apennines begin to make their southward turn.

Oltrepò Pavese is an interesting case. On the one hand, the zone is still a mass-producer of wines, whether they're base wines for Piedmontese *spumanti* or bulk wines drunk as *sfuso* (tap wine) in Milan. Somewhat surprisingly, the Oltrepò Pavese zone turns out more wine per year than the famously profligate Soave DOC in Veneto. But as in so many other wine zones throughout the peninsula, a growing number of producers are changing their mindset and trying to more fully exploit the favorable natural conditions in the area.

Where most barberas from the zone were once lean and harsh in comparison to the majority of their Piedmontese counterparts, they are increasingly fuller-bodied and lush in the hands of producers such as Martilde and Bruno Verdi. And while most producers were content to make light, semisweet *frizzante* from bonarda, a growing number are making full, round, well-structured dry reds from the grape. Admittedly, the use of the name bonarda is confusing—the real bonarda is Piedmontese, and nearly extinct at that, whereas in Lombardia the name bonarda is simply a synonym for croatina. But the wines themselves are developing a very clear-cut personality: a plush core of ripe red-berry fruit, with soft tannins and an almost sweet fruitiness on the palate, a personality not unlike the montepulciano of Abruzzo. They are reds that can be consumed young, with the better varietal bottlings coming from Vercesi del Castellazzo, Martilde, Bruno Verdi, Le Fracce, and Zonin's Tenuta Il Bosco.

Some experts suggest that the best wines of the zone are more traditional blends, most of which are based on a combination of the acidic, aromatic barbera and the plump, generous bonarda. There are two official subzones of the Oltrepò Pavese DOC: Buttafuoco (whose name means "sparks") and Sangue di Giuda ("blood of Judas"). Both combine barbera and croatina with the local uva rara, ughetta, and occasionally pinot noir. Although both Buttafuoco and Sangue di Giuda can be dry, semisweet, sweet, and often *frizzante*, the dry, still versions are gaining in popularity. They are fruity, aromatic wines with good acidity for tomato-sauced pastas or light salads with some shaved Grana Padano on top.

And then there's pinot noir—or pinot nero in Italian—the grape that some say is the future of the Oltrepò Pavese. With altitudes reaching to four hundred meters and higher, and the Apennines a stone's throw away, the climate in the zone is a cool, continental one, which is a key to maintaining balance in the notoriously delicate pinot noir grape. Many of the above-named Oltrepò producers are showing an increasingly deft touch with the variety, which hasn't as yet had much success in Italy, mainly because the majority of the wine world still views Italy as simply too hot for the fickle grape. Places like the Oltrepò Pavese, along with a few other pockets across northern Italy, may one day prove the wine world wrong.

Although quality still varies widely, shopping for wine in the Oltrepò Pavese is a little like going to a thrift store: If you're patient, and you look around a bit, you are bound to find something interesting. And relatively cheap.

More established as a source of distinctive reds is the mountainous zone of Valtellina, a forty-kilometer stretch of spectacular terraced vineyards along the north bank of the Adda River, near Lombardia's border with Switzerland. This area was historically part of the Swiss canton of Grigioni, its wines drunk by noble families in the court of the Hapsburgs. Even today, the Swiss market is the most important one for the small community of Valtellina winemakers, whose grape of choice is the hard-to-ripen nebbiolo. It's called chiavennasca here, and is planted in steep, rocky, terraced vineyards at altitudes reaching to a two thousand feet.

Valtellina has a lot in common with the Valle d'Aosta, not only in its striking mountain scenery but in the orientation of its vineyards, which run east-to-west along the contours of the Adda. Driving along the river basin through Alpine towns such as Sondrio and Tirano, the leafy terraces are like knife slices in the mountain wall, punctuated by the pointy church steeples in the tiny hillside settlements. Everything looks as if it could all come tumbling down in a good rain (which it sometimes does).

As in places such as the Alto Adige and the Valle d'Aosta, the Valtellina is its own distinct culture, essentially walled off from its neighbors save for a few mountain passes, many of them ancient trade routes originating in Venice. The people of the Valtellina have been toughened by their rugged surroundings, and their food is hearty mountain fare: aromatic cheeses such as Bitto (a mix of cow's and goat's milk) and Casera (cow) are a specialty, as is the air-dried beef known as *bresaola*, all of it chased down with the tart, complex, intensely perfumed nebbiolos (or chiavennascas) of the region.

Simply put, the Valtellina is one of the most fascinating and unique red-wine zones in Italy. When or how the nebbiolo grape arrived in these parts is anyone's guess, but it is widely believed that the vineyard terraces, which climb the valley walls in giant steps, were built by the ancient Liguri, who used sand, clay, and rocks hauled up by hand from the valley floor. Even today the angle of the slopes makes any mechanization impossible, and the mere thought of having to harvest grapes in this place is enough to make your thighs burn.

Commercial winemaking in the Valtellina dates back more than a century. One of the first producers in the region was a horse trader and innkeeper named Nino Negri, who married a Swiss noblewoman whose castle, in the village of Chiuso near Sondrio, is still the home of the winery. Negri created his *azienda agricola* (agricultural firm) in 1897, which makes it one of the oldest commercial wineries in Italy. His son Carlo, who ran the winery well into the 1970s, became one of the first formally trained enologists in the country. Yet even after it became a part of unified Italy, the region's leanings have always been toward Switzerland.

In fact, the Valtellina was traditionally a wine lake for the Swiss, viewed as the red wine–producing south in the same way that the Alto

Adige was the "warm" southerly flank of Austria. According to Casimiro Maule, who has been the winemaker at Nino Negri since 1971, the Swiss market has historically been both boon and bane to Valtellina wine producers.

"In the past, Swiss importers were required to buy a certain quantity of Valtellina wine," he begins. "There was a trade accord between the Swiss and Italian governments. In the early eighties, we were sending 4.5 million liters of *vino sfuso* alone to Switzerland. But about eight years ago the accord was eliminated, and that export total has gone way down. In some ways, though, this was good: Instead of just blindly shipping off wine, people have reduced production and raised their standards."

According to the Valtellina producers' *consorzio*, there are only twenty-one actual bottlers of Valtellina wines, many of whom buy grapes from the hundreds of tiny growers still tending plots in the region. Only a handful of producers make enough wine to be known outside of their home region, but those who do—Nino Negri, Triacca, Sertoli Salis, Sandro Fay, and Rainoldi, to name the biggest—are turning out nebbiolos to rival Barolo. They do not typically have the depth of concentration of their Piedmontese cousins, but their often ethereal aromas of tea and tar and tobacco lend them a certain grace and style that places them in their own distinct category.

Despite the high altitudes of the vineyards and the northerly latitude of the Valtellina, the zone boasts a unique combination of geography and climate that even the reticent nebbiolo can adapt to. Much in the same way that the cool climate in the Alto Adige is moderated by warm, dry breezes off Lake Garda, the Valtellina vineyards are similarly affected by the *breva* winds that whisk up through the Adda Valley from Lake Como. Additionally, the east-west orientation of the vineyards, all of which are planted on the north bank of the river (and thus face south), places the vines in the direct path of the sun all day long. "The intensity of sunlight here is similar to that of Pantelleria in Sicily," says Carlo Alberto Panont, who runs the *consorzio* of Valtellina wine producers, which is based in Sondrio. "What's incredible is that there are tropical plants like *fichi d'india* [prickly pears] growing in the terraces, despite the latitude here." The terraces, he adds, are like a giant solar panel, collecting the sun's rays all day long and storing some of that heat in the rocks and pebbles in the soil.

Still, the nebbiolo of the Valtellina is a leaner, finer, more feminine style than that grown farther to the south. Although some wines from specific vineyard sites can approach Barolo in concentration, producers have traditionally turned to *appassimento* (drying grapes) as a means of adding concentration. The term *sfursat*, or *sforsato*, is used in the Valtellina to describe their tarry, glycerine-rich dried-grape wines from nebbiolo, which are reminiscent of Amarone but with a more savory, spicy aromatic profile.

"Compared to Barolo, Valtellina wines are more nervous," says Casimiro Maule. "To arrive at the concentration of a Barolo we have to dry the grapes. I remember Carlo Negri used to say that the wines of Valtellina were like the people of Valtellina: They're tough at first. You really need to get to know them, to give them time."

Among the non-*sforsato* reds, the best are said to hail from a string of four officially delimited vineyards, which occupy a twenty-kilometer stretch from Sondrio to Teglio. These are what might be called the grand crus of

Valtellina, and the wines made from their grapes are labeled with the Valtellina Superiore DOCG. Each of the four vineyard sites is named for a church or castle in the subzone they inhabit, and each offers a slightly different expression of nebbiolo based on its exposure and aspect.

SASSELLA

Just west of Sondrio, the Sassella vineyard covers a total of 368 acres, making it the second-largest after Valgella. It is considered the rockiest of the four Valtellina Superiore *crus* (thus the name, derived from the Italian word *sasso*, for stone), and is also extremely steep. The grapes here often wither in the intense summer heat that collects in the rocky soils. Sassella reds are among the easier vineyard-designated Valtellina wines to find, and are usually among the more powerful and concentrated. Negri, Triacca, and Rainoldi, all of which export to the States, make Sassella wines.

GRUMELLO

Just east of Sondrio, the slopes in Grumello are less steep, with larger terraces and more soil, generally producing more immediately giving, fruit-forward wines. Nino Negri produces one of the few commercially available examples.

INFERNO

Farther east of Sondrio, Inferno is the smallest, rockiest, and steepest of the four *crus*. Casimiro Maule of Nino Negri says that the rocks absorb the sun and cause the vineyard to be "an inferno to work in" during the summer months. Because of its favorable aspect, it pulls in the sun all day and generally produces the most deeply colored, powerful wines of the four Valtellina Superiore vineyards. Both Rain-

oldi and Negri are producing wines from among the 150 acres of Inferno vines.

VALGELLA

The easternmost and highest-altitude subzone, Valgella is also the largest vineyard zone of the four. Valgella's vines are the latest to mature, as much as two weeks behind Sassella. Generally speaking, the Valgella wines are the most delicate and perfumed of the lot. The leading producer in the zone is Sandro Fay.

Aside from questions of *terroir*, however, Casimiro Maule says that the producers of the Valtellina are focused on making their often angular, hard-edged reds more lush and immediately pleasurable. The goal is to tack on a layer of ripe cherry fruit and maybe some toasty oak without losing the leathery aromatics so unique to the grape as grown in the region. Among the modern leaders in the region are Domenico Triacca, who has conducted extensive experiments with vine-training systems to bring out more concentration in chiavennasca, while Maule has set his sights on new techniques in the winery.

"One of the big changes here is similar to that of Barolo," Maule explains. "When we ferment chiavennasca now, we don't let it sit on its skins as long as we once did. Generally speaking, you extract all the color you need from the skins in the first forty-eight hours of maceration; after that it's a question of the quality of tannins you're looking for. In the past we would leave the wine to macerate longer, sometimes forty days or more, and this not only extracts bitter tannins from the skins but also seed tannins, which are unpleasant. What we're aiming for is a more accessible style."

Either way, there will always be a spicy, tannic bite to Valtellina reds, but that is part of their charm. While *sforsato* versions satisfy drinkers who want a bigger, rounder, more fruit-forward style, the more straightforward Superiore wines are for those who prefer a sensation of earthiness along with the fruit. For a taste of Alpine Lombardy, cut a few rounds of dark-grained bread, melt some Gorgonzola over the top, and chase it down with an angular, aromatic Inferno or Sassella. As the tannin and acid of the wine slices through the fatty cheese like a knife, you realize this is what red wine is all about.

VINI DOLCI
Sweet Wines

It isn't entirely true to say that Lombardia is the wine region that has everything. Save for a handful of *passito* moscatos and *frizzante* malvasias made in the Oltrepò Pavese, and a bunch of semisweet Lambruscos made in the plains south of Mantova, sweet wine is relatively scarce in Lombardia. In a place famed for cheese, butter, cream and risotto, it may be that no one has any room for dessert.

FAST FACTS: $\mathcal{L}$OMBARDIA

PROVINCES	Bergamo (BG), Brescia (BS), Como (CO), Cremona (CR), Mantova (MN), Milano (MI), Pavia (PV), Sondrio (SO), Varese (VA)
CAPITAL	Milano
KEY WINE TOWNS	Erbusco (Franciacorta), Pavia (Oltrepò Pavese), Sirmione (Garda), Sondrio (Valtellina)
TOTAL VINEYARD AREA*	26,951 hectares, or 66,596 acres. Rank: 11th
TOTAL WINE PRODUCTION*	1,665,000 hectoliters, or 43,989,432 gallons (11th); 38% white, 62% red
DOC WINE PRODUCED*	47.3% of total (5th)
SPECIALTY FOODS	*bresaola* (air-cured beef); butter; Bitto (cow's-and-goat's milk cheese from Valtellina); Grana Padano (declassified parmigiano-style cow's-milk cheese); Gorgonzola (blue-veined cow's-milk cheese); mostarda (whole fruit pickled with mustard seeds); Robiola (red-rinsed cow's-milk cheese from Bergamo); Taleggio (washed-rind cow's-milk cheese); rice; *speck* (smoked bacon).

*1997 figures. Rankings out of twenty regions total (Trentino-Alto–Adige counted as one). Source: Istituto Statistica Mercati Agro-Alimentari (ISMEA), Rome.

KEY GRAPE VARIETIES

WHITES

CHARDONNAY	The dominant variety in the Franciacorta zone, used in both *méthode champenoise* sparklers and still whites. Also grown in the Oltrepò Pavese and in certain zones near Lake Garda.

GARGANEGA	More famous in Soave, in neighboring Veneto; it is used in some white blends in the Garda area.
PINOT BIANCO	The second white grape of Franciacorta.
TREBBIANO DI LUGANA	Also called trebbiano di Soave, a purportedly superior sub-variety of the large trebbiano family. Thought to be related to the verdicchio of the Marche. At its best in the wines of the Lugana DOC, on the southern shores of Lake Garda.
RIESLING RENANO/ RIESLING ITALICO	Two distinct subvarieties found in both Oltrepò Pavese and the western shores of Garda. Renano is considered the superior of the two, producing dry whites with distinctly peachy, flowery aromas.

REDS

BARBERA	Found throughout the Oltrepò Pavese, this import from Piemonte tends to be a little gruff in comparison to Barberas from Alba or Asti.
BONARDA	The name used for croatina in Lombardia. Produces plump, berryish reds on its own and is also combined with barbera in Oltrepò Pavese blends.
CHIAVENNASCA (NEBBIOLO)	A local subvariety of nebbiolo of unclear origins; it produces wines of great perfume and finesse in the high mountain terraces above Sondrio.
LAMBRUSCO	Found also in Emilia-Romagna, it is grown on a swath of Lombardy's plains south of Mantova.
PINOT NOIR	Growing in popularity for fragrant dry reds in the Oltrepò Pavese, and also used in Franciacorta's sparkling and still wines.
UVA RARA	Literally, "rare grape." Used in Oltrepò Pavese blends.

TOP VINTAGES IN LOMBARDIA, 1980—2000

Since the vintners of Franciacorta tend to release vintage-dated wines only in years they deem appropriate, much of the worry of "which" vintage is taken out of the equation when shopping for sparklers. And while the reds of the Oltrepò Pavese are on the rise, there hasn't yet been a critical mass of wines that would merit long aging: most are plump bonardas and fine, fragrant pinot noirs that will be at their best two to three years from the vintage. Valtellina wines, however, have the kind of sharp acidity and biting tannins that demand a few years' cellaring. In speaking with a variety of Valtellina producers, these are the vintages that stand out in their memories: 1985, '88, '89, '90, '95, '97, '98 (both 1999 and 2000 were considered above average, if not outstanding).

LA STRADA DEL VINO
WINE TOURING IN LOMBARDIA

Although the tourist-friendly shores of Lake Garda are no slouch, the serious wine drinker is more apt to visit either Franciacorta, with its network of luxury hotels, restaurants, and eighteen-hole golf course; or Sondrio, where red-wine-and-cheese tasting might follow a day of skiing or hiking. In Franciacorta, don't miss the Bellavista (030-776-20-00) or Ca'del Bosco (030-776-61-11) wineries, both of which are open to visitors. In Valtellina, the regional wine *consorzio* provides maps of hikes that take you through the terraced vineyards. For more information on both zones, contact the Consorzio per la Tutela del Franciacorta (030-776-04-77; www.franciacorta.net) and the Consorzio Vini Valtellina (0342-52-72-47; www.valtellinavini.com).

DEGUSTAZIONI
TASTINGS

LUGANA

Zenato
Lugana "San Benedetto," $

Ca' dei Frati
Lugana "I Frati," $

Here are two light yet flavorful whites that show off a more aromatic side to the much-maligned trebbiano grape. Firmly acidic and redolent of sour apples, both wines have a cool, dewy, almost grassy quality. Although some producers are experimenting with barrel fermentation (such as Ca' dei Frati with its "Il Brolettino" bottling), the appeal of these whites is their freshness. Try them with grilled whole fish stuffed with herbs to highlight the similarly herbal qualities of the wines.

FRANCIACORTA

Bellavista Franciacorta Brut, $$

Ca' del Bosco Franciacorta Satèn, $$$

Cavalleri Franciacorta "Collezione Rosé," $$

Both the Cavalleri and Ca' del Bosco wines will carry vintage dates, but don't be concerned if you can't find the same year of each. The purpose of this tasting is to check out the style spectrum of Franciacorta: from a dry, minerally, apple-scented nonvintage brut to a creamier Satèn (made in a *crémant* style, only from white grapes) to a spicier, cherry-scented rosé. The Satèn is the softest on the palate, the rosé the fullest, the nonvintage brut the crispest. Not just apéritifs, these wines can stand up to a wide variety of food: Try them with rich dishes such as a creamy polenta or a risotto, and let their scrubbing bubbles go to work.

VALTELLINA

Aldo Rainoldi Valtellina Superiore Sassella Riserva, $

Nino Negri Valtellina Sfursat "5 Stelle," $$$

The contrast here is between a firm, fine Valtellina Superiore and a plusher *sforsato,* or *sfursat,* a wine made from semidried grapes. What distinguishes these wines is their aromatic complexity. Start with the Sassella, with its scents of leather and tobacco and powerful structure, then move to the *sfursat,* which builds on the characteristically savory aromas of chiavennasca (nebbiolo) by adding a dollop of sappy red-berry fruit. The process of drying the grapes for *sfursat* helps soften the tannins of the wine, making it more accessible when young. For even sappier, Amarone-like *sfursat,* check out the wines of Triacca as well as Rainoldi's "Ca' Rizzieri." Negri's powerfully built Inferno, meanwhile, is a good example of the more angular Valtellina Superiore style.

OLTREPÒ PAVESE

Martilde Oltrepò Pavese Bonarda "Zaffo," $$

Vercesi del Castellazzo Oltrepò Pavese Bonarda, $$

Though a little harder to find, these are two round, plump reds with pronounced flavors of "black" fruits: think of blackberries, black cherries, black currants. At the same time, there's considerable weight of fruit extract in both bottlings—these are wines of some substance, excellent choices for one of the rich beef- or pork-filled pastas of the Po plain.

La Cucina
FOOD FOR THE WINE

RECIPE BY LIDIA BASTIANICH

The word *heavy* is often used to describe Lombardia's food, which, thanks to one of the largest pastures in Italy, is indeed rich in butter, cream, and especially cheese. Risotto, most notably the saffron-tinged *risotto alla Milanese*, is another specialty of the region. But the ultimate Lombardian meal might well be a loaf of crusty bread and a wooden wheel filled with hunks of the local cheeses: Taleggio, Gorgonzola, Robiola, and Grana Padano leap immediately to mind, but there are also a number of mountain cheeses from the Valtellina to be added to the list. With a rich, aromatic Valtellina red to accompany all that cheese, it would be hard to find anything more evocative of the region.

That said, the recipe below explores the lighter side of Lombardia, while also combining a product of the mountains (*bresaola*, or air-cured beef) with a product of the plains (Grana Padano, Parmigiano-Reggiano's first cousin). It's a simple, elemental combination, one that is enhanced immeasurably by a glass of Franciacorta sparkling wine. If you don't think sparklers have a place at the table,

make the salad below and pour yourself a glass: The acidity of the wine offsets that of the lemon, while the wine's mineral edge points up a similarly earthy, minerally note in the cheese. This is the kind of combination you might enjoy in a café on Lake Como, while staring out at the Alps in the distance. What says Lombardia better than that?

Insalata di Bresaola e Grana
SALAD OF BRESAOLA AND GRANA PADANO

1 pound ARUGULA, washed, hard stems removed
Juice of 2 LEMONS (about ¼ cup)
¼ cup OLIVE OIL
SEA SALT and freshly ground BLACK PEPPER to taste
¼ pound GRANA PADANO (substitute Parmigiano-Reggiano)
½ pound BRESAOLA, sliced paper thin

SERVES 6 TO 8

In a large mixing bowl, toss the arugula and toss it with the lemon juice and olive oil. Season with salt and pepper. Toss again to combine and slightly wilt the greens.

Portion the tossed greens onto six (or more) plates, forming a tight mound.

Arrange 2 to 3 slices of bresaola on each. Using a potato peeler, shave the cheese in 3- to 4-inch slivers over the top, or to each person's preference. Top with a drizzle of olive oil and cracked black pepper.

WINE RECOMMENDATION: Any good nonvintage Franciacorta Brut.

Valle d'Aosta
THE FORGOTTEN CORNER

PARADISE FOUND

Like a true aficionado, Costantino Charrère chose his favorite mountain in the Valle d'Aosta based on quality, not quantity. From his hometown in Aymavilles, a few miles west of Aosta, he can see the most famous peaks of the Alps just by turning in place: the massive Monte Bianco (Mont Blanc) to the west; Gran Paradiso, the highest peak within Italy's borders, to the south; and Cervino (the Matterhorn) to the northeast. But none of them compares—in Charrère's mind, anyway—to the softly contoured Monte Grívola, a twelve-thousand-foot crest dividing the villages of Cogne and Valsavarenche. Standing shin-deep in wildflowers on a hiking trail in the Parco Nazionale del Gran Paradiso, he stops and frames Grívola like a film director blocking a scene.

"It's got perfect proportions," he says, although it's difficult to see those proportions through the comet's tail of snow shrouding the summit. "When the afternoon sun hits it, there is nothing like it in the world."

Even in mid-August, the snow in the Alps makes the Valle d'Aosta look like a giant merengue pie, sliced to reveal its lush, green filling: Looking down from the heights of the *Parco*, the banks of the Dora Baltea river swell with wine grapes, rennet apples and Martin Sec pears, all of them fed by ancient Roman irrigation canals that crisscross the valley floor. As Charrère charges ahead, we pass cows grazing in a meadow and imagine the creamy, piquant cheese that will be made from their milk. The woods below are filled with chestnuts and wild mushrooms. In fact, for all the barren expanses of its upper reaches, the Valle d'Aosta seems as flush with produce as the Po plain or the Amalfi coast.

Charrère, who is not only the Valle d'Aosta's best-known wine producer but a sometime ski instructor and hiking guide, is one of those tall, wiry mountain men who seem to weather rather than age. With his long, crooked nose and intense, deep-set eyes, he looks like a bird of prey when he stops suddenly and points out an ibex mountain goat off in the distance, its big rack of horns barely detectable against the boulder-strewn backdrop. When he greets a friend on the trail in his French-inflected Valle d'Aosta *patois*, it's yet another example of the indefinable, imprecise nature of "Italian" culture.

We stop at a *rifugio* (mountain cabin) for a sandwich stuffed with *mocetta* (a local prosciutto made from ibex and/or chamois) and some icy mountain water. That's followed with a few slices of the Valle d'Aosta's trademark

The DOC Zones of Valle d'Aosta

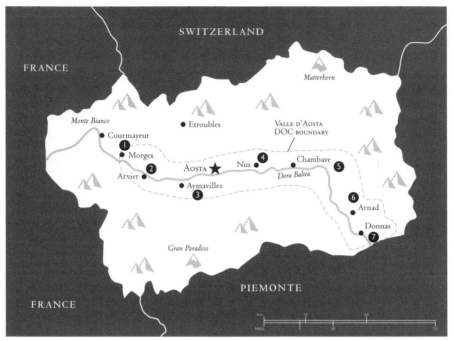

VALLE D'AOSTA
Covers the entire province, and includes thirteen styles of wine, most of them identified by grape name. Twelve other styles carry the Valle d'Aosta designation plus of one of the following seven subzone designations.

1 Blanc de Morgex et de La Salle
2 Enfer d'Arvier
3 Torrette
4 Nus
5 Chambave
6 Arnad-Montjovet
7 Donnas/Donnaz

fontina cheese, as the blinding mountain rays bake the sunbathers who've spread out on the deck. After an uphill climb of some two hours, the food has the effect of an intravenous transfusion; it's hard to remember a more satisfying sandwich, more fortifying cheese, more quenching, mineral-tinged water.

Off in one direction is Monte Bianco, walling us off from France, while behind us is the Gran Paradiso, shutting us off from the rest of Italy. Like any frontier, Valle d'Aosta doesn't feel like a part of anywhere in particular, but rather like some kind of hybrid mininâtion whose borders can't be clearly defined. It's the mountain in a chain that no one notices, until someone with a good eye points it out.

On the way back down to Aymavilles, Charrère points to a grassy hillside on which the outlines of ancient terraces can still be made out. "Those all used to be vineyards," he says, explaining how viticulture all but disappeared in the region during (and especially after) the two World Wars. "At the end of the 1800s there were more than three thousand hectares of vines in the Valle d'Aosta. Now there are less than eight hundred, although viticulture is making a comeback."

It is, however, a very small-scale revolution. Considering not only the physical contours of the Valle d'Aosta but the tiny population of the region, its wine production is an occasionally interesting footnote to Italy's overall output. There are single estates elsewhere in Italy that produce more wine annually than the entire region of Valle d'Aosta, which has only 385 acres of vineyards registered under its all-encompassing DOC. These vineyards are divided among thousands of different growers, so many of them are not much bigger than

family vegetable gardens. The commercial wine industry in the region consists of about a dozen private estates (of which Charrère has become the unofficial ambassador) and five regional co-ops, among them the local enology school, the Istitut Agricole Régional, which produces some excellent wines.

Aosta was once a Roman colony, and perhaps the best place to try the full range of Valle d'Aosta wines is at the Ad Forum *enoteca*, a regional wine-promotion center built on ancient Roman walls in the center of the city. In fact, for an American—for any non-valdostano, really—the only way to truly learn about the wines is to go there. Given the minuscule quantities of wine and the substantial number of tourists coming in to hike and ski (Courmayeur and Cervino are the two most famous ski areas), very little Valle d'Aosta wine makes it out of the region, never mind overseas.

But if there were ever a wine region that merited a field trip, Valle d'Aosta is it. The valley often feels like a land that time forgot, with a string of Medieval castles set on dramatic hillside perches and terraced vineyards where tractors would fear to tread. As in nearby Liguria and the Valtellina region of Lombardy, viticulture here seems more like an endurance sport than a way to make a living. At the western end of the zone, in Morgex, vineyards are cultivated at twelve hundred meters and up, making them some of the highest in Europe.

Once a colony of Piedmont, when the region was ruled by the House of Savoy, the Valle d'Aosta consists of a single province bisected by the A5 autostrada. The soils in the vineyards are predominantly glacial moraine (a rocky, gritty, semifertile mixture), so grape choices and wine styles are primarily determined by altitude. Vineyards climb from about three hundred meters in Donnas and Arnad to a median of about eight hundred in Aosta, and then up again to the heights of Morgex and La Salle, where the flowery, superacidic blanc de Morgex grape manages to become a wine.

Not surprisingly, Valle d'Aosta is a hodgepodge of Italian, French, and Swiss grape varieties. The headliner is the local version of nebbiolo, called picotendro, which gives the wines of Donnas and Arnad a vague resemblance to Barolo. Moscato bianco, here called muscat chambave, is made into exotically fruity dry and sweet wines, as is pinot grigio, which is confusingly referred to in Chambave as malvoisie. French varieties such as chardonnay, gamay, grenache, pinot noir, and syrah give some wines a familiar ring, but on the whole the viticulture of Valle d'Aosta is as singular as its dialect: The Institut Agricole Régional has cataloged thirteen "indigenous" grapes of the region, which factor into the majority of DOC-labeled wines here. The most diffuse of these are petit rouge, a tart, spicy red found throughout the central Aosta valley; and fumin, a meatier, syrah-like red that Charrère and others say will be the native red of the future.

Because of the mix of grape and place names on Valle d'Aosta wine labels (not to mention the mix of French and Italian), figuring out just what's in the bottle can be a little confusing. The region has a single overarching Valle d'Aosta DOC, much like that of Alto Adige. But the twenty-five styles of wine that fall under the DOC classification are both varietal wines (chardonnay or pinot noir) and geographically designated wines (Donnas or Torrette). There are seven subzones of Valle d'Aosta, in which twelve distinct wines are made, along with ten varietal wines and three wines best described as catchall styles. Since it can be tough to remember which is a grape and which is a place (and because Valle d'Aosta wine is such a limited universe), we've listed all twenty-five styles below.

VINI SPUMANTI
Sparkling Wines

BLANC DE MORGEX
ET DE LA SALLE SPUMANTE

This is one of those combination grape/place names. The blanc found primarily in the communes of Morgex and La Salle is known also as prié blanc, although blanc de Morgex et de La Salle is more widely used. The rare, steely sparklers made from the grape are made in the *metodo classico* (Champagne method), although like most Valle d'Aosta wines they're rarely found outside their home base. The local co-op, Cave du Vin Blanc de Morgex et de La Salle, makes a version you might sip after a day's worth of runs at Courmayeur.

VINI BIANCHI
White Wines

BLANC DE MORGEX ET DE LA SALLE

The easy comparison is to mountain spring water—maybe mountain spring water that flows through a meadow of wildflowers. Light and piercingly acidic, this bone-dry white is one of the more densely planted varieties in Valle d'Aosta, with all of fifty-four acres registered as DOC plots in Morgex and La Salle. Aside from the Cave du Vin Blanc, producers include Albert Vevey, Marziano Vevey, and Carlo Celegato.

Chambave Muscat

As a dry wine, this local version of moscato bianco is very exotic, almost cidery in taste. It's another place/grape combination, in that it refers to moscato (muscat) grown in and around the commune of Chambave, about ten miles east of Aosta. The co-op La Crotta di Vegneron and the private estate of Ezio Voyat are the two key producers.

Nus Malvoisie

A clone of pinot grigio (gris) grown in and around the commune of Nus, the curiously named malvoisie (it has no relation to malvasia) is a little more fragrant than your typical pinot grigio. La Crotta di Vegneron is the principal producer.

Valle d'Aosta Chardonnay

Costantino Charrère's Les Crêtes winery has become famous for its barrel-fermented and -aged chardonnay called "Cuvée Bois," a luxuriously smoky wine that may bring to mind a midlevel Burgundy. But his unoaked chardonnay, "Cuvée Frissonière," may be the more consistently interesting wine of the two: It's a chardonnay that tastes like what the chardonnay grape tastes like. In the cool heights of Aymavilles, Charrère coaxes the fruit and perfume out of a typically creamy and unaromatic grape. While critics (and Charrère) may disagree, Frissonière seems to better express what the Valle d'Aosta is about than the Cuvée Bois. Other chardonnay makers in the zone include Renato Anselmet.

Valle d'Aosta Müller-Thurgau

This German variety is widely planted in the region. Both the Institut Agricole Régional and La Crotta di Vegneron have solid versions.

Valle d'Aosta Petit Arvine

Better known in the Swiss Valais, this variety makes a light, flinty wine with hints of grapefruit and mandarin orange. Les Crêtes, the Institut Agricole Régional and the tiny Grosjean estate, the latter headquartered in Quart, just east of Aosta, are the key producers. The Grosjeans also make a sweet *vendemmia tardiva* version.

Valle d'Aosta Pinot Gris/Pinot Grigio

Sparsely planted, it turns up here and there, but it takes a back seat to some of the other more unique locals.

Valle d'Aosta Pinot Noir Blanc/Bianco

This is pinot noir vinified *in bianco,* or as a dry white wine, by gently separating the juice from the skins, as is done in Champagne. It's practically impossible to find.

Vini Rosati
Rosé Wines

Valle d'Aosta Prëmetta

The prëmetta grape is referred to as a *rosato naturale,* in that its skins are so thin and light that all it is capable of making is a pinkish wine. But it can be a great rosé—strawberry scented and brightly fruity, with a spicy cinnamon kick. Costantino Charrère makes one at his second winery, which bears his name, but those wines are not yet exported to the United States.

Valle d'Aosta Rosato

A catchall denomination for rosé wines made from any combination of approved local grapes.

VINI ROSSI
Red Wines

As in other northern-Italian wine zones, it's surprising to learn that a greater percentage of Valle d'Aosta wine is red rather than white—in this case a whopping 90 percent is red, the vast majority of it light, fruity, Beaujolais-like wine made from local varieties such as petit rouge (the most widely planted) and fumin. What's also surprising is how good these simple wines can be sometimes, especially when paired with some of the heavier mountain foods of the region. A red such as Torrette (based on petit rouge) is a light, acidic counterbalance to a rich fondue or one of the region's many cheese-based soups; alternately, it's a great type of red to serve slightly chilled at a summer picnic.

Aside from the DOC wines listed below, one grape on the rise in the region is syrah, which both Costantino Charrère (in his "Coteau La Tour" bottling) and the Institut Agricole ("Trésor du Caveau") have employed to great effect. Given that the Valle d'Aosta sits at nearly the exact latitude as the heart of the Côtes-du-Rhône, it's not surprising that producers are having success with the grape, although, as Charrère admits, red wine is never easy in the heights of Aosta. "We have wonderful light here, but once we get to late September the temperatures really start to drop," he explains. "Around the end of September we have to cut foliage off the vines so that the grapes get the maximum exposure to the sun. But our red wines don't have deep concentration. What we lack in density we make up for in bright, clear fruit."

ARNAD-MONTJOVET
Along with Donnas, this easterly subzone is home to the picotendro (nebbiolo) grape, a minimum of 70 percent of which must be used in wines labeled Arnad-Montjovet. Sometimes compared to the nebbiolo-based wines of Carema in neighboring Piedmont, they are aromatic reds with firm tannins. The co-op La Kiuva and the tiny estate of Dino Bonin are the key producers.

CHAMBAVE ROUGE
A petit rouge–based blend (minimum 60 percent) from Chambave and a few surrounding communes. The best example is Ezio Voyat's Rosso "Le Muraglie," although it doesn't carry the DOC designation.

DONNAS/DONNAZ
Once a discrete DOC, it was folded into the regional Valle d'Aosta appellation and is now treated as a subzone. The occasional Donnas wine sneaks into the United States, usually by way of the auction houses, where committed nebbiolo fiends snap it up as a curiosity. The principal producer is a co-op, Caves Cooperatives de Donnas.

ENFER D'ARVIER
This, too, was a discrete DOC at one time. The wine is based on petit rouge, a light and pleasant red for sipping after a summer hike with some *mocetta* or *bresaola*.

NUS ROUGE
A practically extinct local grape called *vien de Nus* is the base of this rare red blend, which can also contain petit rouge, pinot noir, and a variety of other red grapes.

TORRETTE

One of the better known DOC wines of the region, it is based on petit rouge (70 percent) and can include pinot noir, gamay, fumin, vien de Nus, and other red varieties. Spicy and juicy like a Beaujolais, it's a great red wine for summer—or for winter, if *fonduta* or something similarly weighty is on the table. There's a Les Crête and a Costantino Charrère version, as well as a good version from F.illi Grosjean. Try it chilled.

VALLE D'AOSTA FUMIN

With a little more stuffing and color than petit rouge, fumin is a native grape on the rise, vaguely reminiscent of a Côtes-du-Rhône syrah in its pepperiness. Again, look to Les Crêtes as well as La Crotta di Vegneron for bottles.

VALLE D'AOSTA GAMAY

The grape of Beaujolais aptly pops up here, although it's more commonly used in blends than on its own.

VALLE D'AOSTA PETIT ROUGE

The varietal version of petit rouge, not dramatically different in style from Torrette, Chambave, or Enfer d'Arvier.

VALLE D'AOSTA PINOT NOIR

A number of producers are experimenting with the grape, although Valle d'Aosta vintners haven't been able to capture the concentration of Burgundy despite being at a more southerly latitude.

VALLE D'AOSTA NOUVEAU/NOVELLO

A catchall designation for *nouveau*, or *novello*, red wines.

VALLE D'AOSTA ROUGE/ROSSO

A catchall designation for red blends that is rarely used.

VINI DOLCI
Sweet Wines

CHAMBAVE MUSCAT FLÉTRI

Flétri is the French equivalent of *passito*, and this exotically perfumed sweet wine from moscato bianco is definitely worth seeking out in a cheese-rich region such as Valle d'Aosta. It makes an interesting partner for a salty, buttery hunk of *Fontina* or a more pungent *Toma* or *Robiola* from neighboring Piedmont.

NUS MALVOISIE FLÉTRI

La Crotta di Vegneron keeps this all-but-extinct style of wine alive. It's pinot grigio like you've never tasted before, a late-harvest wine with aromas of peaches and wildflowers checked with firm acidity. It's the ultimate local oddity in a region full of them.

It bears repeating that, aside from Les Crêtes, hardly any of the above wines can be found in the United States. So we have not included a tasting section in this chapter, although we do recommend the Les Crêtes wines should you come across them in your area. But like any wines, they are immeasurably improved when consumed in the place where they're made. After a day of hiking with Charrère in the Parco Nazionale del Gran Paradiso, he took us to a small mountain restaurant where we drank a dry Chambave Muscat from La Crotta di Vegneron with an appetizer of lard and boiled chestnuts, and then his Les Crêtes Fumin with *zuppa alla veca,* a rich soup of melted fontina cut with broth, orzo, and mountain herbs. Both were the kinds of inimitable combinations that make eating and drinking in Italy such an unpredictable experience.

Nevertheless, the Valle d'Aosta is not a place for the wine collector. It's a place for the wine adventurer, the person in search of culture rather than commodities. Wines like Blanc de Morgex or Donnas aren't world-class, but then again, there's nothing else in the world to compare them with.

FAST FACTS: VALLE D'AOSTA

PROVINCES	Aosta (AO)
CAPITAL	Aosta
KEY WINE TOWNS	Aosta, Aymavilles, Donnas, Morgex
TOTAL VINEYARD AREA*	635 hectares, or 1,569 acres. Rank: 20th
TOTAL WINE PRODUCTION*	22,000 hectoliters, or 581,241 gallons (20th); 10% white, 90% red
DOC WINE PRODUCED*	22.8% (8th)
SPECIALTY FOODS	Fontina cheese; rennet apples; Martin Sec pears; *boudin* (blood sausage); *lardo di Arnad* (lard with mountain herbs); *mocetta* (local prosciutto, often made from chamois or ibex); porcini mushrooms; chestnuts.

*1997 figures. Rankings out of twenty regions total (Trentino–Alto Adige counted as one). Source: Istituto Statistica Mercati Agro-Alimentari (ISMEA), Rome.

KEY GRAPE VARIETIES

WHITES

BLANC DE MORGEX (PRIÉ BLANC)	Tartly acidic white grown in the westerly communes of Morgex and La Salle, in the shadow of Mont Blanc. Vines reach altitudes of twelve hundred meters and more, making them some of the highest in Europe.
MUSCAT/MOSCATO	Dry and sweet wines are made in Chambave from the local clone of moscato bianco, otherwise known as muscat blanc à petits grains.
PETITE ARVINE	Light, citrusy variety better known in wines of the Swiss Valais.

CHARDONNAY	Burgundy's star can be interesting in the heights of Valle d'Aosta.
OTHERS	MÜLLER-THURGAU; PINOT GRIS/GRIGIO.
	REDS
PETIT ROUGE	The most widely planted native red. Used in Enfer d'Arvier (85%), Torrette (70%), Chambave Rouge (60%), Nus Rouge (30 percent), and varietal wines.
PICOTENDRO	Local synonym for nebbiolo; used in wines in the Donnas (minimum 85%) and Arnad-Monjovet (minimum 70%) subzones.
PREMETTA	A lightly colored native red used to make a spicy rosé.
FUMIN	Ascendant local variety that bears a slight resemblance to syrah in the jammy, peppery wines it produces.
OTHERS	GAMAY; PINOT NOIR; GRENACHE; SYRAH.

TOP VINTAGES IN VALLE D'AOSTA, 1980–2000

Most of Valle d'Aosta's whites and reds are meant to be drunk within a few years of release, although their naturally high acids will certainly preserve them for a few years or more. The reds of Donnas and Arnad-Montjovet, based on the nebbiolo grape, can certainly stand up to five or even ten years' aging; occasionally some Donnas wine turns up in American auctions, and in good years it can bring to mind a lighter-styled Barolo. Top years: 1985, '88, '90, '95, '96, '97, '99.

LA STRADA DEL VINO
WINE TOURING IN THE VALLE D'AOSTA

The most difficult question is: Do you go to the Valle d'Aosta in the winter or summer? Do you hike in the Parco Nazionale del Gran Paradiso or do you ski at Courmayeur? This is a place of incredible natural and culinary diversity. Base yourself in

Aosta, and get a grounding in the local wines at the rustic
Enoteca Ad Forum (0165-400-11), which has just about every
wine made in the region available for sampling. Alternately,
choose a mountain lodge within the Parco Nazionale, perhaps
in Villeneuve or Aymavilles. There are a number of excellent
guides published by the Azienda di Promozione Turistica Grand
Paradis (Loc. Champagne 18, Villeneuve; 0165-950-55;
www.granparadiso.org).

La Cucina
FOOD FOR THE WINE

RECIPE BY LIDIA BASTIANICH

You can't think of the Valle d'Aosta without thinking of fontina, the milky, buttery, soft cheese made in every corner of the region. There's the classic *fonduta*, in which vegetables or hunks of bread are dipped in hot melted fontina and other cheeses. The Valle d'Aosta is also big on cheese-based soups, in which some melted Fontina is cut with beef or chicken stock and mixed with a wide range of ingredients, including toasted bread or another starchy ingredient such as orzo, shredded cabbage, and herbs such as thyme and marjoram. As in the Alto Adige and other mountain regions, the Valle d'Aosta offers a predominance of light, acidic, fruity red wines, which aren't exactly in fashion these days but are natural accompaniments to heavier food preparations. Instead of matching heavy with heavy, we've suggested a lighter-styled red for the dish below, one you're likely to see during a visit to the Valle d'Aosta.

Cotoletta alla Valdostana
VEAL (OR PORK) CUTLET, VALLE D'AOSTA STYLE

2 pounds VEAL or PORK CUTLETS, pounded to about ¼-inch thickness and cut into 4-by-2-inch medallions
½ cup all-purpose FLOUR
4 large EGGS, beaten
6 cups BREAD CRUMBS
4 tablespoons BUTTER
¼ cup OLIVE OIL
¼ pound PROSCIUTTO, thinly sliced
¼ pound FONTINA CHEESE, thinly sliced

SERVES 6

Preheat the broiler.

After pounding the cutlets, bread them by dusting first with flour, then dipping in the beaten eggs followed by the bread crumbs.

In a medium nonstick skillet, heat the butter and olive oil over a medium-high flame until the foam subsides. Add the cutlets in one layer and sauté in batches until golden brown on both sides, approximately 3 minutes per side. Add more butter and oil if necessary.

Top each cutlet with a slice or two of prosciutto followed by a slice or two of fontina. Place the cutlets in a baking tray and broil for 1 to 2 minutes, or until the fontina melts. Be careful not to scorch the cheese by placing the rack too close to the flame. Sautéed bitter greens such as broccoli rabe or escarole make a great side dish.

WINE RECOMMENDATION: Les Crêtes Valle d'Aosta Fumin. If you can't find the Les Crêtes try a Barbera d'Alba from Piedmont or maybe one of Piedmont's more northerly nebbiolo-based wines, such as Ghemme or Gattinara.

Piemonte
The Wine Mecca

———⟨⁘⟩———

The Guns of Barbaresco

As wine towns go, Neviglie is not one of the main stops on a tour of Piedmont. But it should be, if only for the view: It sits just outside the Barbaresco DOCG zone, at an elevation of around fifteen hundred feet, looking out over the Barbaresco vineyards of Treiso to the west and Neive to the north. Farther south are the wine towns of Barolo, poking through shrouds of mist from their hilltop perches. And farther still are the Maritime Alps that shut Piedmont off from France, the rumpled ridges shimmering white with snow even in the dead of summer.

This is the panorama from Walter Bera's small *cantina* in Neviglie, where he makes a little bit of everything; plump, fruity reds from dolcetto and barbera, plus a great Asti *spumante*, are among the wines we're sipping in his cool cellar. He's not a famous producer, but instead one of thousands of small-scale vintners who work the hills around the towns of Alba and Asti, making wines that would get far more critical attention if they were made in a less populous region. His winery is just up the hill from his home, and after a half-hour or so of

tasting we head back toward the house for some of his homemade sausage.

But there's a problem. When we went into the cellar it was bright and sunny, albeit very humid. Yet as we come back outside, a mass of clouds is moving in over Treiso like a giant brushstroke. It's as if the sky has been divided in half, one side white and one black. *"O dio,"* Walter says. "That doesn't look good at all."

Hail is always a looming threat in wine zones such as Barolo and Barbaresco, which sit in the Langhe hills of southeastern Piedmont. It's a region shaped by rivers such as the Tanaro and Belbo, which flow down from the Maritime Alps separating Piedmont and Liguria. The particular positioning of the Langhe hills leaves them vulnerable to wet weather throughout the summer and fall.

Standing quietly in Walter's driveway, looking out at the patchwork of vineyards blanketing the soft contours of Treiso, we hear the first reports from what might be called the guns of Barbaresco: a series of air cannons that shoot sound waves into the clouds. Wine lore is full of nineteenth-century *vignerons* pointing their old, creaky cannons to the skies, blasting at the clouds to try and shatter the stones inside. Evidently, this seemingly superstitious practice lives on in a new, high-tech incarnation. Walter says that wine producers through-

THE DOC ZONES OF PIEMONTE

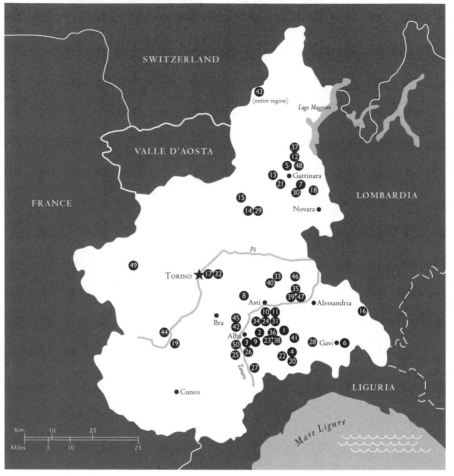

out the Barbaresco zone chipped in to buy the cannons, which are now thundering away at regular intervals. Each blast is followed by a warbling, whistling sound, like the strange music a saw blade makes when it is shaken. The booming of the cannons echoes through the hills. With all the gray clouds hovering overhead, the Langhe looks and sounds like some fiery battlefield.

"The idea, I guess, is that the waves not only break up the hail but move the clouds along," Walter explains. From our lofty perch we can see the storm moving toward us, and soon the hail is pockmarking the earth at our feet. We take cover in the winery and listen to the stones battering the roof. "They don't sound big," Walter says, trying to remain good-humored as the storm hovers overhead, threatening his livelihood.

Luckily, it is a brief hit. We take a quick walk through the vineyards to survey the damage, and it looks fairly minor: some shredded leaves, some ruptured grapes, but nothing too bad, although a few of the bunches will probably rot now that their skins have burst. The cannons are still booming and whistling away as the roiling sea of Langhe vineyards—probably the densest concentration of vines anywhere in Italy—begins to glisten in the shafts of sunlight now piercing the clouds.

Walter picks up a nugget of hail and examines it, almost bemusedly. It's no exaggeration to say that five minutes of hail could have wiped out the whole year's production. Maybe those shock waves did break it up on its way down. It seems highly unlikely. But in a place like the Langhe, where wine is everything, hail calls for drastic measures. If the big guns are what it takes to win the war, so be it.

Piedmont, more so than even Tuscany, is the wine-lover's mecca. It is often referred to as Italy's answer to Burgundy—still a farmstead wine culture compared to more developed wine regions such as Tuscany. What sets Piemontese towns such as Alba and Asti apart is that people go there almost exclusively for the wine and food. Their scents alone are enough to draw you in, like some cartoon character being pulled along by the vapors of a pie warming on the windowsill. In the Langhe hills it's the aromas—of truffles, mushrooms, hazelnuts, coffee, and above all else, Barolo and Barbaresco wine—that sweep people off their feet.

Although there are a number of noteworthy vineyards in the Alpine foothills of northern Piedmont, the main concentration of wine activity is in the Langhe and Monferrato hills to the southeast, which spill through the towns of Alba, Asti, and Alessandria en route to the plains flanking the Po River. Alba and Asti are set among hills so densely planted to vines, in parcels so fragmented, that it's hard to imagine any other commercial activity in the region other than viticulture. In fact, Alba's only real industry is a small textile factory and the Ferrera chocolate plant, makers of Nutella. Other than that, it's all about wine.

"When you go into a bar around here, chances are the people aren't talking about politics or the football game," says Alberto Chiarlo, export director for the well-known Michele Chiarlo estate. "They are talking about wine. There is an *enoteca* around every corner in the Langhe."

The concentration of vineyards and wineries in Piedmont is remarkable. The entire surface area of the village of Barbaresco, one of three adjacent communes that comprise the

Barbaresco DOCG, is about seventeen hundred acres, of which roughly twelve hundred are planted to vineyards. There are more than eight hundred bottlers of Barolo and Barbaresco wine in Piedmont, each of them squeezing a relatively tiny amount of wine from their (mostly small) vineyards. Based on figures compiled by Italy's Ministry of Agriculture, the average size of a Barolo/Barbaresco vineyard is about five acres, with an average annual production of about ten thousand bottles. That is minuscule by today's standards. There are scores of individual wineries throughout Italy that produce more than the Barolo and Barbaresco zones combined, and then some.

Piedmont has more DOC zones (fifty) than any other Italian region, and more history and nuance to its wines than could possibly be summed up easily. It really has to be seen to be believed, and must be experienced to be appreciated. What follows is a thumbnail sketch to get you started on what may become—as it has for many Italophiles—a lifelong obsession.

VINI SPUMANTI
Sparkling Wines

For all of the prestige and mystique of dry red Barolo and Barbaresco, the wines that have long driven the Piedmontese wine economy are sweet, white *spumanti* and *frizzanti,* made from moscato bianco grapes in the hills southeast of Asti. Even today, with sweet sparklers seemingly out of fashion, the DOCG of Asti is the most productive single wine zone in Italy. In 1997, production of sparkling Asti Spumante and semisparkling, or *frizzante,* Moscato d'Asti

topped 650,000 hectoliters (about 17 million gallons). And this despite an entire generation of wine snobs turning up their noses at these fun, fruity, and often surprisingly complex wines. (Since Asti Spumante and Moscato d'Asti often toe a fine line between dry and sweet, they are discussed here instead of in the Sweet Wines section below.)

Like the lambrusco grape of nearby Emilia-Romagna, the moscato of Asti has become, to some extent, a victim of its own success. People remember the cheesy television ads for Martini & Rossi Asti Spumante—a perfectly pleasurable, if mass-produced, wine—and think of themselves as uncool if they deign to drink such things. While it is true that the wines of Asti can be cloyingly sweet, the category shouldn't be written off altogether.

In fact, there may be no more direct link to the winemaking traditions of centuries past than a *frizzante* wine. At one time, farmer-winemakers simply tossed super-ripe grapes into open-topped wooden vats and let the grapes ferment naturally, creating wines that were sweet, syrupy, oxidized, and often fizzy. It was not uncommon for fermentations to stop during the cold winter months and then start up again as ambient temperatures rose during the springtime, which naturally created bubbles in the wine. In many cases, farmers would try to bottle these wines, only to have them explode as the secondary fermentations caused carbon dioxide pressure to build in the bottle.

The production of fizzy wines is more controlled these days. Producers of modern *frizzante* arrest the fermentation, usually by rapidly chilling the fermenting juice so that the yeast stops working. This is how the wine retains its balance of natural bubbles and residual sugar.

The main difference between a *frizzante* and a full-on *spumante* is that the fermentation of a *frizzante* is arrested earlier, usually at an alcohol content of between 4 and 6 percent. At this level the fermentation has not yet gotten to a full boil, so the carbonation is gentler and the wine richer in sugar. Conversely, a *spumante* is allowed to reach alcohol levels of up to about 9 percent before it is chilled down, creating a wine higher in alcohol, with more effervescence and less residual sugar. Technically speaking, an Asti Spumante should be crisper and more aromatic and a Moscato d'Asti softer, plumper, and sweeter. But it doesn't always work out that way. As with any wine, the best Asti Spumante and Moscato d'Asti are marked by balance—in this case, a balance of peach-and-apricot sweetness with a cleansing surge of acidity.

Like the off-dry Prosecco of the Veneto, Asti Spumante—some of which is made in the classic Champagne method, where the wine undergoes its secondary fermentation in bottle—can be a mouthwatering apéritif. The typically fuller, fruitier Moscato d'Asti is more often reserved for desserts, especially dryer cakes such as panettone, where the delicate peachy sweetness of the wine isn't drowned out in a clash with an equally sweet dish. The lower alcohol levels of both Asti wines make them easier to place within a multicourse meal, whether as apéritifs or accompaniments to desserts. They aren't as overwhelming as fortified wines (such as port) can be at the end (or beginning) of a long dinner.

Although many of the wines of giant *spumante* houses such as Gancia, Cinzano, and Martini & Rossi are perfectly serviceable, the more interesting wines are to be found on a slightly (or much) smaller scale. The American-owned Villa Banfi winery in Piedmont—no slouch itself when it comes to pumping out bottles—makes solid, crisp Asti Spumante, as does the Giuseppe Contratto estate in Canelli (Contratto also makes dry, Champagne-style sparklers from chardonnay and pinot noir). The Fontanafredda winery in Serralunga d'Alba, better know for Barolo, also dabbles in *spumanti*. In the high altitudes of the classic moscato vineyards southeast of Asti, in tiny communes such as Neviglie, Canelli, and Santo Stefano Belbo, the moscato grapes are not only high in natural sugars but high in acidity as well, and the better *spumanti* are evidence of this: They have an almost spicy, citrusy character to complement their sweetness.

Although large houses dominate production, there are a multitude of smaller artisanal producers of both Asti and Moscato d'Asti. They include Walter Bera, Cascina Fonda, and Paolo Saracco, all of whom make the more softly contoured Moscato d'Asti as well. Other great Moscato d'Asti wines are made by Michele Chiarlo, whose "Nivole" bottling is one of the best, and the Forteto della Luja estate in Loazzolo, which bottles the full array of Piedmontese *spumanti e dolci* (see page 149 for more on sweet wines).

With its relatively cool continental climate, Piedmont is able to produce good dry sparkling wines, many of them based on pinot noir and chardonnay (as is Champagne). The limestone-rich soils and high altitudes of the Langhe hills have inspired many Barolo and Barbaresco makers to plant chardonnay for both dry and sparkling wines; the grape often takes on a crisp, minerally character reminiscent of the chardonnay of Burgundy. But given the high labor and equipment costs of making sparkling wines, *spumante* is not a widespread product. Nevertheless, there are some *méthode champenoise* sparklers from the Langhe well worth checking out. One of the best is "Brut Zero," made at the Rocche dei Manzoni estate, a well-known Barolo producer, in Monforte d'Alba.

Lesser-known but equally interesting are the handful of *spumanti* made in the far-flung white-wine DOCs of Gavi, in the southeastern corner of Piedmont, and Caluso, in the north, near the border with Valle d'Aosta. The erbaluce grape of Caluso has the requisite sharp acidity to make fine, fragrant sparklers, as does the cortese grape of Gavi. In each zone, *spumante* takes a backseat to still wines made from these grapes, but the sparklers of producers such as Ferrando in Caluso and La Scolca in Gavi are surprisingly good and relatively affordable.

VINI BIANCHI
White Wines

The name Piedmont means "foot of the mountain," yet despite its northerly positioning and mountainous borders (ringed by the Alps and Apennines) it is still oriented much more to red wines than whites. Like many of Italy's other northern regions, Piedmont's wine traditions challenge conventional wisdom. It would seem given Piedmont's position in the shadow of the Alps, and its relatively cool, often damp climate, that it might be better suited to white wine production. Nevertheless, 70 percent of all Piedmontese wine is red.

It's often noted that the Piedmontese town of Alba sits at a latitude similar to the city of Bordeaux, but you can't really compare zones such as Barbaresco and Barolo with, for exam-

ple, St. Emilión. Only the white-wine zone of Gavi, in Piedmont's extreme southeast corner, receives any kind of Bordeaux-like maritime influence, from Mediterranean breezes blowing up through Liguria. Otherwise, viticultural Piedmont has a classic continental climate, which means that temperatures drop quickly in autumn, making things dicey for later-ripening red grapes.

It's more accurate to compare Piedmont to Burgundy. The relatively cool climate may be more naturally suited to making white wine, but certain red grapes, planted in the right spots, can do amazing things. Piedmont's focus on reds has historically been greater than Burgundy's, but in recent times a handful of white grapes, including Burgundy's chardonnay, have attracted their own fans.

ERBALUCE
Even in Piedmont's northerly DOC zones—the ones that run along the border with Valle d'Aosta and follow the contours of the Alps toward Lake Maggiore—white wines get short shrift. There are more than a dozen wine zones in these Alpine foothills, and yet only one of them—Caluso, north of Turin—is dedicated to white wines. In a glacial basin around the towns of Caluso and Canavese, the erbaluce grape is made by a handful of producers into a chalky, searingly acidic dry white, as well as *spumante* and some excellent *passito* sweet wines (see page 149). A number of these wines are exported, including dry whites from the Ferrando and Orsolani estates, which are marked by delicate floral aromas and the sharp, minerally tingle of mountain spring water. Generally speaking, the *passiti* from Erbaluce are more sought-after, but the dry whites are refreshing at a minimum, and well suited to a plate of

prosciutto or *bresaola* drizzled with olive oil. Some experts compare Erbaluce to France's chenin blanc, noting how it retains its refreshing acidity even when it is vinified sweet.

ROERO ARNEIS

As lilting and floral as erbaluce, but more substantially fruity on the palate, the arneis grape has risen from relative obscurity to become what some people consider the most interesting white in Piedmont. Its principal area of production is the thickly forested Roero zone west of Alba, where it was traditionally interspersed with the more prevalent red nebbiolo. Sometimes it was blended with red grapes to soften them, but more often it was used to keep birds and bees away from the reds. Only in the late seventies and early eighties did vintners start making significant amounts of wine from arneis, following the lead of pioneers such as Ceretto (whose Blangé estate in Roero is still a top arneis producer) and Bruno Giacosa. While the grape is now popping up in other parts of the Langhe, the sandier soils of the Roero seem to be its preferred habitat—in fact, from 1989 to 1998, production of Roero Arneis DOC wine has more than quadrupled, with vineyard plantings surging from three hundred acres to more than one thousand.

The aromas of arneis are generally more fruit-driven than those of the herbal erbaluce, with scents of white grapefruit and sour apple mingling with those of white flowers. There's also a smokiness to arneis that brings to mind the fiano of Campania, but arneis is more fruity than savory, and is more full-flavored. It's also a good value. In addition to Ceretto's "Blangé," which is still a benchmark, look for arneis from Cascina Ca' Rossa, Matteo Correggia, Monchiero Carbone, and Vietti, among

many others. They are easy to find and great for light pastas and salads.

CORTESE DI GAVI

One of the anchor towns of the Gavi DOCG zone (also called Cortese di Gavi) is the commune of Novi Ligure, which suggests an allegiance to somewhere other than Piedmont. In fact, the territory now known as Gavi was once a part of the city-state of Genoa, and is still profoundly influenced by neighboring Liguria. As noted above, the climate in the Gavi zone is nearly Mediterranean, but the chosen local grape, cortese, isn't designed to take advantage of these more temperate conditions. It is one of a number of Italian whites that ripens stubbornly and unevenly, and its aromas are fairly mild, like those of garganega in Soave or trebbiano in Tuscany.

The soils in the Gavi zone, which includes the commune of Gavi itself almost smack in the center, are limestone-rich clays, generally whiter and chalkier-looking than the similarly limestone-rich soils of Langhe to the west. The classic style of Gavi, as popularized by producers such as Banfi Vini (with their "Principessa Gavia") and La Scolca, directly reflects the wine's origins: There's a chalky minerality on the palate that some producers say is similar to some white Burgundy. That is a bit of a stretch, but then there tend to be very wide ranges in the style and quality of Gavi. Like Soave, to which it might be better compared, it is a light, refreshing white that became extremely popular in export markets (especially Germany and the United States), which in turn spurred the rise of large-scale, industrial producers and lots of watery wine.

For all of its commercial success, the Gavi region—like Soave again—isn't a place people can readily conjure in their minds. There is very little tourism in the zone, leaving its multitude of smaller producers to eke out a living on the fringes. But there are many good wineries coaxing more concentrated apple and peach flavors out of the reticent cortese grape, including Broglia, Castelari Bergaglio, Castello di Tassarolo, and Michele Chiarlo. But the one producer really trying to make Gavi hot again is Villa Sparina, whose wild-man proprietor, Stefano Moccagatta, has been turning a part of his family's estate into a Relais & Château hotel and restaurant. The Villa Sparina Gavis are more rich and extracted than most of their peers'—leading to speculation about what grapes aside from cortese might be blended in —and Moccagatta's winemaker, Beppe Caviola, has experimented with fermenting and aging cortese in wood. But while the barrel-fermented Villa Sparina Gavi "Monterotondo" gets a lot of press, it is very tropical, fat, and somewhat atypical. Gavi is usually a wine of freshness and simplicity, which may not be fashionable but is often pleasurable. For some reason, *simple* has become a dirty word in Italian wine, even as the simplicity of Italian cooking is praised up and down. Maybe when people come around, so too will the fortunes of Gavi.

Chardonnay

Of course, a region that likes to compare itself to Burgundy would not be complete without chardonnay. To its credit, Piedmont typically produces what might be called a Burgundian style of chardonnay. Most of the region's chardonnay vineyards are located in the Langhe DOC zone, which includes within its boundaries both the Barbaresco and Barolo DOCGs, plus a broader swath of hills east and west of the Tanaro River. Created in 1994, the Langhe appellation is a catchall for producers in Barolo, Barbaresco, and beyond, enabling them to make wines from nebbiolo, for example, under less restrictive guidelines than those of Barolo or Barbaresco. The Langhe DOC includes provisions for a number of varietal wines, white and red, but the one that sticks out is chardonnay—mainly because it is the only non-native variety on the list.

In the calcareous clays of the Langhe hills, often on slopes not suitable for nebbiolo, chardonnay retains its acidity and minerality, whereas in many other areas farther south its sweeter, tropical-fruit side comes through. The same producers who looked to France for inspiration for their Barolos are doing the same with chardonnays, fermenting them in barriques to lend them a smoky, creamy complexity. To name just a few of a growing group, the Langhe chardonnays of Pio Cesare ("Piodilei"), Angelo Gaja ("Gaia & Rey"), Aldo Conterno ("Bussiador"), and Paolo Saracco ("Bianch del Luv") have carved their own niches in a wine market inundated with the variety. In fact, Langhe Chardonnay may now be the biggest white-wine category in Piedmont, with countless producers making rich, complex, well-structured versions. Trendy as they may sound, these wines are not gimmicky: The better ones reflect where they come from in a very direct way.

VINI ROSSI
Red Wines

Pio Boffa, the affable, fourth-generation proprietor of the Pio Cesare winery in Alba, says that confronting the intricacies of Piedmontese reds requires not just patience but humility. "Socrates said that the first step to knowledge is to admit that we don't know anything," Boffa says. Nowhere in Italian winemaking is this more apropos than in Piedmont. In the zones of Barbaresco and Barolo in particular, where the wavy landscape is portioned and parceled according to each slope's particular relationship to the sun, the wines have been discussed and debated so thoroughly that it is hard to know where to begin. Most people tend to wax poetic, remarking on the ethereal aromas of a well-aged Barolo as if they were describing a religious experience, while others are all about science: the soil compositions of the myriad vineyard sites, their relative exposures to the sun, and of course the tricks of the trade used in the winery. The discussion and debate is ongoing, leading to subtle (and not-so-subtle) changes in the wines with each new vintage.

Looking at the big picture, Piedmontese reds don't seem overly complicated. In the DOC zones north of the Po, there's an almost unbroken chain of wines made principally from the nebbiolo grape—Carema, Canavese, Gattinara, and Ghemme, among others. Typically, these wines tame the high acidity and occasionally ragged tannins of northern-limits nebbiolo (here called spanna) with softer, fruitier local varieties such as bonarda and vespolina, which comprise 40 percent (or more) of certain DOC blends. Among this group, the purest expressions of nebbiolo are Gattinara and Ghemme—two of Piedmont's seven DOCG zones—which at times can be as powerful, concentrated, and aromatic as the Barolos and Barbarescos made farther south.

South of the Po, nebbiolo shares the Langhe and Monferrato hills with the plump and purple dolcetto grape and the super-prolific bar-

bera, along with a smattering of lesser-known varieties such as freisa, grignolino, and ruché. That sounds easy enough, too, until you consider the tangle of DOCs in the southeast. There are three "grape-specific" DOCs for barbera and a whopping seven for dolcetto, even though few people aside from the producers themselves could hope to sort out the differences between Dolcetto d'Acqui, for example, and Dolcetto d'Asti.

And yet, for all of the different choices, there's a logic to Piedmont's reds that contrasts with the often scattergun approach to wine in many other Italian regions. However much they might vary in character within their respective families, the three principal red grapes— barbera, dolcetto, and nebbiolo—are distinct entities. Together they fit together like pieces in a puzzle: barbera and dolcetto make the more readily accessible, "fun" wines, the ones to drink while the more brooding nebbiolo ages. And each of the three has characteristics that the other two lack, allowing for a variety of balanced and intriguing blends. In dolcetto, you get soft tannins and plump, grapey fruit. In barbera, you get bright acidity and a more sour, spicy red fruit character. And in nebbiolo, you get tar and leather and spice. Where dolcetto and barbera are ripe and ready, nebbiolo is more about complexities revealed over time. That's Piedmont in a nutshell: so many wines, so little time.

BARBERA

Thought to be native to the Monferrato hills, near Asti and Alessandria, barbera is equally at home on the slopes of the Langhe, near Alba. Aside from the DOCs of Barbera d'Asti, Barbera d'Alba, and Barbera del Monferrato, the grape factors into other lesser-known appellations, such as the Rubino, Gabiano, and Colli Tortonesi wines of the extreme southeast. Barbera is the most heavily planted red grape in Piedmont, accounting for more than 50 percent of DOC red wine production in the region. Without a doubt, it is the most adaptable and vigorous of Piedmont's three main red grapes, a fact that has led to an almost impossibly broad range of styles. Even within its specific DOC zones, barbera tends to vary widely, from bright and cherry-scented, firmly acidic, and a little rustic to more rich, robust, and silky smooth. A lot of this depends on where its growers choose to plant it, but it is also the product of changing winemaking practices. Of course, this is true of any wine, and barbera is an interesting case study in how a wine grape reacts to different soils, climates, and techniques.

Barbera's constants are a high level of natural acidity and a relatively low level of tannin, although the grape generally produces wines of a deep ruby color. The variables are the levels of fruit extraction in the wine, and the degrees to which tannins have been added through aging in oak barrels. "If you taste a tannic barbera," says Bruno Ceretto, coproprietor of the Ceretto estate in Alba, "it's because the winemaker has either used a lot of new oak or is blending it with some other more tannic variety. Barbera on its own gets a bite from acidity, but it doesn't have tannin."

Among the first producers to address this was the late, legendary Giacomo Bologna. His estate in the Asti DOC zone, called Braida, was among the first to create barbera wines that had not only been planted in choice vineyard sites —to increase their concentration of red-cherry flavor—but had been aged in French oak barriques, which lent the wood's tannins to the wine. When Bologna's "Bricco dell'Uccellone"

Barbera was released in the early eighties, its then-uncommon richness and seeming ageability sparked a wave of experimentation with the grape that continues today.

In the past, especially in the hills of the Langhe, the durable and easy-to-grow barbera was often used used as "filler" in vineyard sites incapable of maturing the more stubborn, weaker, and later-ripening nebbiolo. So it was often only natural that barbera wines were relatively light, acidic, and even a little rough around the edges. These days, the average barbera is considerably more colorful and plush, its character leaning more toward red fruits (cherries, currants, raspberries), at least when it hasn't seen a lot of time in oak barrels. But since there is such a wide variety of barbera produced, it is extremely difficult to generalize about the category. Beyond that, it's a question of scale, and, as might be expected, the hottest-selling barberas these days are the larger-scale versions.

One way to sort through the barbera style spectrum is to start with what might be called "baseline" bottlings—namely, those that say simply Barbera d'Alba, Barbera d'Asti, or Barbera del Monferrato. These are likely to be the simpler, leaner, more acidic styles emphasizing fresh red-fruit flavors, as most producers typically offer a *vino fresco* (fresh wine, one that is bottled soon after the vintage, for immediate sale). As an introduction to barbera, pick up a simple Barbera d'Alba or d'Asti from a benchmark Barolo or Barbaresco house such as Pio Cesare, Bovio, Bartolo Mascarello, Vietti, or Renato Ratti (to name a few among the hundreds). You'll find these wines to be slightly rustic, with a sharp tingle of acidity that needs a little food to tame it. The flavors are likely to be more reminiscent of dried cherries, with a touch of earthiness, whereas those wines carrying a vineyard designation (like "Bricco dell'Uccellone") or a *nome di fantasia* (fantasy name) will be more densely fruity and, most especially, toasty and rich from time spent in oak barrels. For examples of a denser, more extracted style of barbera, look to producers such as Hilberg Pasquero, Aldo Conterno, Prunotto, and Michele Chiarlo, whose "La Court" is a good example of the depth barbera takes on when it is aged in barrique.

Probably the most notable feature of "modern" barbera is the weight of fruit extract it exhibits on the palate. Whereas barbera was little more than filler in the past, vintners have found that it grows into a densely concentrated wine when grown in choice south-facing sites. As a general rule, today's barbera is much bigger than the barbera of the past.

Of the three main barbera DOCs, those of Alba and Asti are expansive, with Monferrato bringing up the rear. In Monferrato, which is situated to the east of Asti, producers to look for include Villa Sparina (which makes some dense, superextracted reds to go with its Gavis), Giulio Accornero, Scrimaglio, and Vicara. But in Alba and Asti, the list of noteworthy names is almost as long as that for Barolo and Barbaresco, near which the Barbera of d'Alba and Barbera d'Asti DOCs are situated. Most Barolo and Barbaresco producers make at least one version of Barbera d'Alba and/or Asti and often several, many of which are single-vineyard wines with the structure (and price tags) to stand up to some Barolo.

DOLCETTO

Like barbera, the dolcetto grape, whose name means "little sweet one," is highly permeable. As the earliest-ripening of the three main Piedmontese reds, it is often planted in sites where even barbera might not become fully ripe. It distinguishes itself from both barbera and nebbiolo with its deep purple-violet color, its low acidity (making it a good blending partner for both of the others), and its full yet sweet tannins. Dolcetto is the most gregarious, forwardly fruity wine of the bunch, and is usually drunk young. But many producers see it as something more.

Dolcetto wines are produced under seven different DOC classifications, among them d'Alba, d'Asti, di Diano d'Alba, d'Acqui, and delle Langhe Monregalesi. There are excellent wines from each of these areas, of course, but all of these DOCs overlap with several others, from Moscato d'Asti to Brachetto d'Acqui. When you see Dolcetto d'Alba, it's not as if dolcetto is the only grape planted there— rather, the grape shares space with a host of others, including barbera. Two zones considered more specialized in dolcetto are the Dolcetto di Ovada DOC (in the extreme southeast near Gavi) and the Dolcetto di Dogliani DOC (south of Alba). The dolcetto grape is believed to have been discovered in the commune of Dogliani, where references to the grape can be traced back to the fifteenth century. Modern-day producers in Dogliani believe that theirs is not only the original dolcetto, but also the richest and most flavorful, and there is considerable experimentation being done with the grape in that zone to turn it into a full-blown international red. Equally interesting is Ovada, another historic territory for the grape, where dolcetto takes on a more rustic, full-bodied character than in many of the other zones.

With aromas of violets and black fruits, and usually a tinge of licorice and even coffee on the palate, dolcetto might best be described as part of a vinous color scheme. Barbera and nebbiolo tend to produce more "red" red wines—with flavors of fresh and dried cherries, red raspberries, and then a variety of earthy, spicy, leathery notes. But the dolcetto grape is more a purple or black wine, as evidenced not only by its deep color (something nebbiolo in particular lacks) but its black-fruit flavors. It is the juiciest and fruitiest of the Piedmont reds; the more full-bodied, barrel-aged versions taste like a spread of blackberry jam on toast.

Depending on the level of extraction a producer goes for in his dolcetto—a function not only of viticulture but the length of time the wine spends on its skins during fermentation—the wine may be light, soft, and almost Beaujolais-like in character, or plumper, rounder, with silty-sweet tannins and a sappiness reminiscent of California merlot. Given the success of wines styled in the latter fashion—such as those of Beppe Caviola in Alba, or of the tight-knit crew of wineries in Dogliani (including Abbona, Pecchenino, Quinto Chionetti, and San Romano)—dolcetto is being held up as the new-generation wine of Piedmont.

"Because of the low acids, it is accessible when it is young," says Tino Colla, owner of the Poderi Colla estate in Alba. "But dolcetto is very sneaky. Its tannins are sweet, but they are abundant. When you tack on some time in oak barrels, you have a wine with the ability to be aged. But of course the overwhelming preference of the market today is for wines that can be drunk in their youth. Dolcetto is our answer to that."

Colla makes a Langhe DOC–classified blend called "Bricco del Drago," combining 85 percent dolcetto and 15 percent nebbiolo, a wine that distinctively demonstrates how Piedmont's reds complement and contrast one an-

other. Whether on its own or as part of a blend, dolcetto is a generous variety. "Dolcetto has incredible roundness, but it doesn't really have focus," Colla explains. "Nebbiolo, of course, has focus."

BARBARESCO, BAROLO, AND LANGHE NEBBIOLO

The nebbiolo grape, and the wines made from it in the zones of Barbaresco and Barolo, have been subjected to more scrutiny than any other wines in Italy. This is partly the fault of the producers, who are not only numerous but generally a contemplative lot. Centuries ago, farmer-winemakers examined the rolling hills to see where the winter snow melted first, deducing that these were the sites that received the most sunlight and therefore the most appropriate places to plant vines. Viticulture in the Langhe is all about subtle variations in altitude, exposure to the sun, and soil composition, and it seems as if every ripple in the earth around Alba and Asti has been studied and charted. Often, vintners own chunks of more than one slope, and when it comes time to bottle their wines they have distinct brands determined not by the whim of the winemaker but by the whims of nature.

This is the romantic view, of course. But what is wine without a little romance? For someone who loves wine, there may be no more heady experience than winding through the hills of Barolo and Barbaresco, through medieval villages such as Neive (in Barbaresco) and Castiglione Falletto (in Barolo), marveling at the rows of vineyards snaking like braids over every available slope. At every curve in the road is a sign for a wine estate, ranging in size from garage to sprawling compound. Restaurants are filled with the pungent scents of truffles or wild mushroom risottos, golden Toma cheeses, all sorts of chestnut and hazelnut *torte*. The rich food of Piedmont is best described as *forestale* (foresty), and in Barolo and Barbaresco they have wines to match, with assertive scents of cedar and wild mushrooms and earth.

The land of nebbiolo south of the Po is a broad swath of hills around the Tanaro River, which runs through the towns of Alba and Asti before hooking up with the Po near Alessandria. The key DOC zones along this route are Barolo, southwest of Alba; Roero, on the left bank of the Tanaro west of Alba; and Barbaresco, northeast of Alba. In this relatively small space are a wide array of producers, without a doubt the densest concentration of winemaking activity in Italy.

Nebbiolo is often described as one of Italy's noble varieties. It is known first and foremost for being fiercely tannic, and yet those gripping tannins are extracted from very thin skins that don't hold a lot of coloring pigments. Many Barolos and Barbarescos, especially those that have begun to take on a characteristically orangey cast with age, look in the glass to be relatively light wines. But even well-aged ones grab the tongue with those tannins, and explode across the palate with an array of flavors that taxes the imaginations of even the most flowery wine writers. Because of their tannic grip and fairly high levels of alcohol, Barolos and Barbarescos are often described as heavy wines. And they certainly can be. But the mark of a good Barolo is not its weight on the palate but the penetrating, perfumy aromas of the nebbiolo grape. Like sangiovese in Tuscany and aglianico in Campania and Basilicata, nebbiolo is one of those grapes with fairly precise aromatic indicators: The fruit component is of dried cherries and other dried red fruits, with

other scents ranging from wild roses to truffles to cinnamon, lending the wine complexity. These aren't fruity, jammy wines. They are wines with a balance of sweet, savory, and spicy elements that tingle on the palate, their aromas like vapors that waft up into your brain and lodge themselves in your memory forever.

Is that a little too much? Well, probably. But this is what nebbiolo does to people. Although it's difficult to grow and extremely late-ripening, its producers are willing to wait until late October and November to harvest it, despite the ever-looming threat of rain after September. The variety is said to be derived from the word *nebbia*, Italian for "fog," presumably in reference to the dense blankets of the stuff that roll into the Langhe every fall, cooling the vines with their mists and allowing the grapes to hang on the vine that much longer to develop more complex aromas and flavors.

Nebbiolo drinkers, too, are willing to wait. It was traditionally said that both Barolo and Barbaresco needed to age some two decades before being "ready to drink." According to the production disciplines of their DOCGs, Barbaresco and Barolo must be aged several years before they are even released. In Barbaresco, where the slightly cooler climate is said to produce slightly finer versions of nebbiolo, the minimum aging is two years (one of which must be spent in oak or chestnut barrels); in Barolo, the minimum aging is three years, two of them in barrels. And for *riserva* wines, the totals go up to four and five years of total aging, respectively. Usually, these aging periods start at the beginning of the year following the vintage, meaning that a vintage 2000 Barolo, for example, will not be released until three years after 2001, or 2004. Wines made under the Nebbiolo d'Alba and Langhe DOC classifications are subject to less stringent geographic and technical requirements, which allows producers to make softer, more readily accessible nebbiolos and blends (usually with barbera and/or dolcetto) to complement their more burly Barolos or Barbarescos.

Although wine has been made in Piedmont since ancient times, viticulture in the region was heavily influenced by the French, when Piedmont was part of the House of Savoy, from the early eighteenth century to the time of the Italian unification in 1861. Barolo in particular is referred to as the "king of wines and the wine of kings," since the earliest dry red wines from the Barolo area were developed by noble families from Turin and the ruling Savoyards. Most sources attribute the creation of Barolo to Giulietta Falletti, the marchioness of the village of Barolo, who in the early 1800s developed a Bordeaux-style wine from nebbiolo with the help of French enologist Louis Oudart. Oudart had been summoned to the Alba area in the first place by Camillo Benso di Cavour, a local count who not only became the prime minister of Piedmont but one of the leaders of the movement for Italian unification. Another noteworthy noble who helped shape the Barolo zone was Vittorio Emanuele II, the first king of unified Italy, whose son Emanuele (borne by a royal mistress named Rosa Vercellana) planted vines around a family refuge called Fontanafredda, near Serralunga d'Alba. (Fontanafredda is still one of the best-known names in the Barolo DOCG, and one of its largest contiguous properties).

Although they were not known for Barolo or Barbaresco, large commercial wine houses such as Martini & Rossi and Gancia were formed in the late nineteenth century, to be followed by numerous others at the turn of the twentieth. More so than other regions, Piedmont was not just a culture of myriad individual *contadini* (farmers) but actually had a wine "industry" to speak of well before the First World War. Although it went through much of the same upheaval as the rest of Italy during the fifties and sixties, with families abandoning the countryside in search of work in the cities, winemaking remained firmly rooted in places like Alba and Asti. Today there are a number of wine houses—including Barolo makers such as Prunotto and Pio Cesare—whose strings of vintages date back more than a hundred years, interrupted only by the two World Wars.

Barolo and Barbaresco offer a lifetime's worth of study for those wine drinkers obsessed with comparison and contrast. Although the soils in both zones are predominantly limestone-rich marls (marl is a cool, crumbly clay that helps to slow ripening and to build acidity), and the altitudes in the zones relatively uniform (usually between four hundred and twelve hundred feet), the subtle differences imparted by these and other natural factors are what Barolo and Barbaresco are all about. Strange-sounding names such as "Sorì San Lorenzo," "Rabajà," "Cannubi," and "Brunate" are emblazoned across the labels, inviting the curiosity of the uninitiated. They are vineyard names, carrying with them all sorts of cryptic information: If you know that Cannubi, for example, is a low-lying slope just outside the town of Barolo, with a southeastern exposure that gives it full access to the morning sun (which is said to impart to the wines a certain power but a less aromatic personality), then "Cannubi" might mean something to you. But to get to that point is to reach the pinnacle of wine geekdom—a point at which you've thrown over nearly everything else in your life in order to search for subtle differences that are usually obscured by the varying techniques winemakers use once they get their Cannubi or Brunate grapes into the cellar. For more on the highly variable personality of the great wines of Barolo and Barbaresco, see the preceding boxes on vineyard designations and style. But be warned: This is only the beginning of what can easily become an all-consuming and expensive hobby.

NORTHERN
NEBBIOLO

Reaching toward the lake district of northern Lombardy, with Milan not far to the east, the nebbiolo DOCs of northern Piedmont are home to some hidden gems. These regions have generally poorer, grittier soils of glacial moraine, and breezes from the Alps sweep through from the north. Here in Carema, Gattinara, Ghemme, and other north-of-the-Po DOCs, nebbiolo struggles even more mightily than it does elsewhere to get fully ripe. So these wines are typically more delicate and higher in acid than their Langhe counterparts, and only in exceptionally hot and dry vintage years ('97 was an especially good one, as was '99) will they approach the power of Barolo or Barbaresco.

Because nebbiolo here is higher in acidity and occasionally gruffer in personality than even Barolo, it requires a little blend. Yet there are some incredible finds within these DOCs, most of them wines that showcase the perfumy side of the nebbiolo grape. From Carema, look for the wines of Luigi Ferrando and the local co-op, Cantina Produttori Nebbiolo, for an especially aromatic take on nebbiolo. From Gattinara, a little farther east, producers such as Nervi, Travaglini, Dessilani, and Antoniolo are making brawny, funky nebbiolo to compete with Barolo. Gattinara, a DOCG, represents the purest expression of nebbiolo of the northern zones. And in Ghemme, the wines of the Cantalupo estate strike a balance between delicate and dense.

OTHER
PIEDMONT REDS

After all that dolcetto, barbera, and nebbiolo, Piedmont is loaded with a wide variety of other oddities, many of which are surprisingly likely to turn up on American wine lists or in shops. The rarest is a light red called grignolino, produced in small quantities in the Monferrato hills, which produces very light, almost *rosato* wines with a spicy tang and orangey color. Another local red is freisa d'Asti, a uniquely flavorful variety that is made in both dry, sweet, and *frizzante* styles, sort of Piedmont's answer to Lambrusco. The same goes for ruché, another curiosity with a distinctive berryish aroma, whose main claim to fame is that it will grow in spots where even barbera won't mature. These wines are easily classified as "farmhouse" reds, the wines to drink when winding through the hills of Piedmont on a tour of the vineyards. Take a break from serious Barolo sniffing to sip a lightly chilled freisa or ruché alongside a plate of prosciutto: You may be surprised how much you like it.

BAROLO AND BARBARESCO: THE VINEYARDS

The vineyards of the Barolo and Barbaresco DOCG zones are not extensive, but they are the most carefully charted stands of vines anywhere in Italy. Both zones are originally delimited in the 1890s, but it wasn't until the 1960s that the concept of demarcating individual vineyard sites truly caught on in Piemont.

The early days of commercial Barolo and Barbaresco production were dominated by large, *négociant*-style producers who blended wines from a variety of different vineyard sites in the respective zones. But in more recent times, the single-vineyard, or "cru," wine has been the gold standard in Barolo and Barbaresco. This is not to say that cru vineyards are a recent phenomenon; the prized exposures, or *sorì*, many of which were chosen based on where the winter snow melted first, have undoubtedly existed in the oral traditions of the area for centuries. But it wasn't until local visionaries such as Renato Ratti, who meticulously mapped the Barolo zone in the sixties, did the concept of cru get put down on paper.

In the seventies, eighties, and nineties, the crus of Barolo and Barbaresco became boutique brand names unto themselves. This has created some consumer confusion, since any number of producers may bottle wines from a particular cru vineyard, with varying results. Unlike the cru vineyards of Burgundy, to which they are often compared, the crus of Barolo are not ranked in any specific way.

Nevertheless, Barolo and Barbaresco enthusiasts pore over the subtle differences in the wines imparted by vineyard location. With all the experimentation going on in the wineries these days (see "Barolo and Barbaresco Style . . ."), the distinctions of individual *terroirs* are increasingly obscured, but it still helps to understand the lay of the land when trying to get a handle on the complex flavors of a Barolo or Barbaresco.

BAROLO

In the Barolo DOCG, the surface area of vineyards is about 3,100 acres, planted in all or part of eleven communes south of the city of Alba: Barolo, Castiglione Falletto, Serralunga d'Alba, Diano d'Alba, Grinzane Cavour, Monforte d'Alba, Novello, Cherasco, La Morra, Roddi, and Verduno. All of these communes lay in the undulating hills east of the River Tanaro, and are traversed by a number of small tributaries. Of the above 11 communes, those with the key vineyards are La Morra and Barolo in the western half of the zone, and Monforte, Castiglione, and Serralunga in the eastern half.

The conventional wisdom on Barolo wines was that those wines sourced from the western half of the zone around La Morra and Barolo— where the soils are more fertile calcareous marls—were softer, more delicate. Meanwhile, those wines from the easterly communes of Castiglione Falletto, Monforte, and especially Serralunga—where the soils are a slightly poorer mix of calcareous marls and sandstone—were denser, deeper. You may find this to be true in comparing and contrasting different Barolos— say, a characteristically fine and fragrant La Morra Barolo from Elio Altare against a chunkier, more muscular Monforte Barolo from Aldo Conterno. But such a comparison of *terroirs* assumes that everything else is held constant, namely how the wines are treated in the cellar. Of course, each estate makes its wines in its own way, making it difficult to generalize about the effect of *terroir* on Barolo.

That said, it is nevertheless intriguing to seek out the distinctive traits of individual crus. This is what Barolo (and Barbaresco) drinking is all about for the hard-core enthusiast: How, for example, does Aldo Conterno's "Bussia Soprana," which is sourced from a variety of sites on Monforte's prized Bussia cru, compare with his "Vigna Colonello," which is also from Bussia, but from a single high-altitude plot.

Below is a list of the key cru sites in each of the five major towns of the Barolo DOCG, with a very brief note on the types of wines to expect from those vineyards:

- *La Morra*. In the northwestern sector of the Barolo DOCG, this commune includes, among others, the Arborina, Marcenasco, Monfalletto, Cerequio, and Brunate vineyards (the latter two are shared with the commune of Barolo). These vineyards typically produce especially aromatic, perfumed Barolos, as evidenced by the wines of Elio Altare (whose most famous Barolo is from the Arborina cru), Renato Ratti (Marcenasco), Gianfranco Bovio (Arborina), Marcarini (Brunate), and Michele Chiarlo (Cerequio). Probably the most famous La Morra producer these days in Roberto Voerzio, who is one of the more outspoken modernists in the zone, and whose wines tend to be especially powerful. His wine from the Brunate cru is the best evidence of this—although Brunate is a directly south-facing site, and one from which many other producers are making denser-than-average wines.

- *Barolo*. Some of the broadest, most open vineyard sites are located within the commune of Barolo, resulting in some of the broadest, most open, and most youthful Barolos available. The best-known cru in the commune is Cannubi, known for plush and warm Barolos from producers including Luciano Sandrone, Paolo Scavino, Marchesi di Barolo, and Prunotto. Other choice sites in Barolo include Sarmassa and the Barolo part of Brunate.

- *Castiglione Falletto*. Although it is technically on the eastern side of the Barolo zone, the commune of Castiglione lies near the geographic center of the appellation. Stylistically, the wines occupy a middle ground between the ethereal, perfumed wines of La Morra to the west and the dense, tannic wines of Serralunga and Monforte to the southeast. Prized vineyards in Castiglione include Rocche (top producers from this site include Vietti and Aurelio Settimo), Momprivato or Monprivato (Brovia, Giuseppe Mascarello), and Villero (Bruno Giacosa, Vietti, Brovia, Giuseppe Mascarello).

- *Serralunga d'Alba*. Here at the eastern edge of the Barolo DOCG the wines gain added depth and concentration from soils which are richer in sandstone, creating more deeply extracted and tannic Barolos. Key vineyard sites include Lazzarito (Fontanafredda), Vigna Rionda (Giacosa, Oddero), Prapò (Mauro Sebaste), Ornato (Pio Cesare), and Monfortino (the famed vineyard of Monforte legend Giacomo Conterno, who produces one of the longest-lived Barolo wines ever made).

- *Monforte d'Alba*. The vineyards that lie between the town of Monforte d'Alba and its neighbor due north, Castiglione Falletto, may be the best in all Barolo. Many of the most celebrated Barolo producers are located here, and they may be so celebrated because of the vineyard sites that also lie within the commune. Big and bold, dark and rich, Monforte Barolos are characterized by crus such as Bussia (Aldo Conterno is the most famous interpreter, but there's also Armando Parusso, Prunotto, Poderi Colla, and many others), Ginestra (Domenico Clerico, Elio Grasso), and Santo Stefano di Perno (Rocche dei Manzoni).

(continued on next page)

BARBARESCO

Where Barolo is situated in the south and west of Alba, the Barbaresco DOCG lies to the north and east. Barbaresco is fairly tiny, comprising about 1,200 acres of vines planted in the communes of Barbaresco, Treiso, Neive, and part of San Rocco Seno d'Elvio. Traditionally, Barbaresco was thought of as finer and more feminine than Barolo, the "queen" to Barolo's "king." The nebbiolo grape typically ripens earlier in Barbaresco than in Barolo, and the calcareous soils of the zone favor a gentler style of wine, but these days there's no way to pigeonhole Barbaresco strictly into the "queen" category. Some Barbarescos are every bit as macho as Barolos, some even more so.

Although there are fewer cru sites in the Barbaresco DOCG than in Barolo, there are three in particular that are especially famous: Sorì Tildin, Sorì San Lorenzo, and Costa Russi, all owned by Angelo Gaja. These three tiny vineyards lie within a larger cru site, the Secondine vineyard, which occupies the southern slopes of the village of Barbaresco. Until recently, when Gaja abandoned the Barbaresco DOCG for his cru wines (they are now Langhe DOC), the wines from these vineyards represented the benchmarks in single-vineyard Barbaresco. Sorì San Lorenzo, a site that faces directly south, is the source of Gaja's most forceful, densely concentrated cru wines. Sorì Tildin, although it also faces predominantly south, produces a wine with more *equilibrio* (balance). Costa Russi, which faces southwest (and is therefore not in the direct path of the sun all day), typically produces more delicate wines.

Of course, Barbaresco does not begin and end with Gaja. Of the myriad cru sites in the zone, here are some of the best, commune by commune:

- *Barbaresco:* Most of the better-known Barbaresco crus lie within the commune of Barbaresco itself, especially along a south-southwest-facing ridge that runs along the road from Barbaresco south toward Treiso. This ridge includes the aforementioned Secondine cru, along with Pajé (whose best-known producer is Roagna-I Paglieri), Asili (Ceretto most famously, but also Michele Chiarlo and Ca' del Baio), Martinenga (Marchese di Gresy), and Rabajà (Bruno Rocca, Cascina Luisin). Due east of the village of Barbaresco is the south-facing Montestefano cru, made famous by the legendary co-op Produttori del Barbaresco. As always, it is difficult to generalize, but Barbarescos of the commune of Barbaresco tend to be among the fruitiest and most generous, especially wines from crus such as Asili and its neighbor to the west, Faset, which face directly south, thereby taking in the sun all day long.

- *Neive:* The northeastern chunk of the Barbaresco DOCG is characterized by a typically leaner, more austere style of wine. The village of Neive sits at the highest altitude of any of the Barbaresco communes and its higher-altitude vineyards tend to produce more perfumed grapes with firmer tannic structures. Key Neive vineyard sites include Basarin (Moccagatta makes the best-known wine from the site), Gallina (the supercharged bottling from La Spinetta is the most famous, if a little atypical), Starderi (also La Spinetta), and Serraboella (Cigliutti).

- *Treiso:* At the southern end of Barbaresco, Treiso's crus are probably the least known, but there are some excellent wines. Probably the best-known, Treiso Barbaresco, is Pio Cesare's firm and fine "Il Bricco," sourced from the Treiso cru of the same name. Other key sites include Bernardot (Ceretto-Bricco Asili), and Nervo (Elvio Pertinace).

BAROLO AND BARBARESCO STYLE, THEN AND NOW

Maybe it was a sommelier at your favorite Italian restaurant. Maybe it was a colleague with a serious Barolo jones. Maybe you saw it in a magazine. But somewhere along the line, if you drink Barolo and Barbaresco, you've heard mention of so-called modern wines and so-called traditional wines. In reality, these monikers can be very helpful in selecting a Barolo or Barbaresco that's right for you. But what do they mean, exactly?

A traditional Barolo or Barbaresco—the kind of wine that dominated production in both zones well into the 1980s—was (and in some cases is) made by fermenting nebbiolo grapes in large wooden *botti* (casks), many of them made of chestnut and having a capacity of 50 hectoliters or more. The fermentation and subsequent maceration of the wine on the skins of the grapes lasted as long as two months, as producers felt it was necessary to extract as much tannin from the grape skins as possible to ensure the wines a long life. These fermentations in the large wood casks were typically carried out without temperature control (which made the wine susceptible to bacterial infections). When the wine was left in similarly large wood casks to age, typically for extended periods, the usually old, creaky barrels allowed for a fair amount of oxidation, creating wines that were typically brickish or even orange in color. A well-made traditional Barolo had (and has) a mix of sweet and savory flavors, with notes of dried cherry interspersed with the likes of rose petal, leather, tar, and earth. However, a poorly made traditional Barolo tended to showcase all the flaws inherent in the old-fashioned winemaking process—it may have tasted dirty (thanks to dirty old barrels), or oxidized, or downright funky from bacterial infection.

In the 1960s, pioneering producers such as Renato Ratti, Angelo Gaja, and Elio Altare began challenging the conventional wisdom on Barolo and Barbaresco production. The first modern-era overhaul was the introduction of controlled-temperature fermentation, which enabled producers to make more balanced, less volatile wines, wines less susceptible to infections and more expressive of their fruit character (when a fermentation gets too hot, many flavor compounds simply burn off, leading to a cooked taste, which many old-time Barolos had).

The big mark of the modernist was the purchase of new French oak barrels of a much smaller capacity. Angelo Gaja is widely credited as being the first to experiment with these 225-liter French oak barriques, contending that their sweet wood tannins would offset the often harsh tannins of the nebbiolo grape. It was also believed that the use of smaller wood barrels would help stabilize the color of the wine, and that the wine would mature more quickly in the smaller barrels, leading to a richer, fruitier product in the bottle.

"The skin of nebbiolo is very thin, like pinot noir, and doesn't give a lot of color," says Bruno Rocca, a producer of sleek, modern Barbarescos. "The toast on the inside of the barriques helps me add color. But I don't believe in this whole modern versus traditional debate. Up until about twenty years ago, ninety percent of the wines were defective, oxidized. So that's tradition?"

In addition to employing barriques, modernist producers in Barolo and Barbaresco also began shortening fermentation and maceration times. Their belief, which has largely been borne out, was that all of the color available in a grape's skin can be extracted within the first day or two of maceration. The longer the maceration, the modernists said, the more the color of the wine would destabilize through oxidation, and the more the bitter tannins would be extracted. The contention among the modernists was that tannin was not the end-all be-all of Barolo.

Such is the view of Elio Altare, one of the living legends of Barolo: "To anyone who tells me a Barolo can't age without tannin, I respond with a question," he says. "How is it, then, that the best white Burgundies can age for forty years? It is balance that allows a wine to age, and the goal of my experimentation with shorter fermentations and barriques was to create a wine that had enough fruit to stand up to all that tannin."

Many of the most technologically advanced producers in Barolo and Barbaresco are fermenting their wines in roto-fermenters, space-age devices that continually mix the skins with the fermenting juice. In many cases, what was once a fermentation/maceration of forty days has been cut to four. The result, say the modernists, is a more forwardly fruity, readily accessible style of wine with fewer bitter tannins and a more appealing deep ruby color. Often there's also a creamy, toasty sheen lent by aging in new oak barrels, although many producers take this too far.

These days, there remains an older guard of producers who adhere to a traditional style, among them legendary houses such as Giacomo Conterno, Bartolo Mascarello, Gianfranco Bovio, and Francesco Rinaldi in Barolo, and Roagna in Barbaresco. But even they have made concessions to modern times, whether in the vineyard or in the cellar. While there's still lots of leathery traditional Barolo out there, it is typically a cleaner, riper wine than in the past.

"The term traditional has come to mean defective—and that's very, very wrong," says Roberto Conterno, who, along with his father, Giovanni, runs the Giacomo Conterno winery in Monforte d'Alba. "What we've tried to do is blend the traditional with the modern. We still believe in long macerations, but maybe not so long as in the past. We control the temperature of our fermentations. We still use large oak casks for aging, but they are newer, cleaner casks, and we're more careful about not exposing the wines to too much oxygen throughout the process."

And yet the real revolution, producers say, has come not in the wineries but in the vineyards. "It's got a lot more to do with whether or not you use barriques," says Riccardo Seghesio, of the Seghesio winery in the Barolo village of Monforte. "In the last ten years there has been a big evolution in how we work in the vineyards—not only with green harvests but by making more careful clonal selections." Indeed, while twenty years ago it was unheard of to cut off excess grape bunches and plant vines more densely to generate more concentrated fruit, these days it is a guiding principle. Says Seghesio: "Until just a few years ago, Barolo was a difficult wine to drink. Our vinification methods changed and it's now a wine that can be drunk sooner. Tannins aren't what enable a wine to age. Acidity and balance are what enable a wine to age. Barbera has very little tannin but in a good ripe year it can age for ten years. Because it has good natural acid."

Elio Altare agrees, noting that while there are any number of techniques in the cellar that have contributed to the plumping up of modern Barolo, there's no substitute for ripe fruit. "I remember visiting Château Margaux, and the manager, Paul Pontallier, told me something I will never forget," says Altare. "He said, 'You don't make the barrique for the wine, you make the wine for the barrique.' Think about that for a second, and it starts to make a lot of sense."

Vini Dolci

Sweet Wines

Because most (but not all) of Piedmont's sweet wines are sparkling, and most (but not all) of its sparkling wines are sweet, it's difficult to decide how to classify them. Asti is without a doubt a sweet wine, but it tends to be grouped among *spumanti* nonetheless. Meanwhile, the red Brachetto d'Aqui, which is most often made as a sparkling wine, is usually grouped among the *dolci*. Brachetto, another of Piedmont's dry-or-sweet reds, has managed to climb all the way to DOCG status, in fact, at least in part because of the wine's natural affinity with the great chocolate of Piedmont. Rose-scented, with delicate hints of strawberry on the palate, a good sweet brachetto—either still or sparkling—is a unique sweet-wine experience. Rather than being weighty or sappy on the palate, these wines have an appealing brightness that won't weigh you down at the end of a meal. For a great example of a sweet-yet-still version, check out the brachetto from Forteto della Luja, an estate in Canelli known for a variety of dessert wines from both brachetto and moscato. The other noteworthy nectars of Piedmont are the passito wines made from the erbaluce grape in Caluso, best exemplified by the wines of Ferrando.

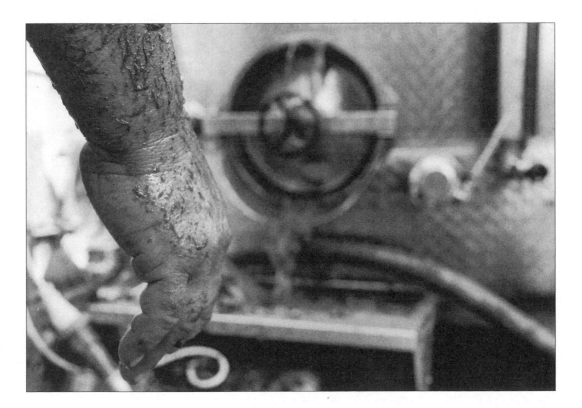

FAST FACTS: $\mathcal{P}$IEMONTE

PROVINCES	Alessandria (AL), Asti (AT), Biella (BI), Cuneo (CN), Novara (NO), Vercelli (VC)
CAPITAL	Torino
KEY WINE TOWNS	Alba, Asti, Barbaresco, Barolo, Castiglione Falletto, Gavi, La Morra, Monforte d'Alba, Neive, Serralunga d'Alba
TOTAL VINEYARD AREA*	57,487 hectares, or 142,050 acres. Rank: 6th
TOTAL WINE PRODUCTION*	3,405,000 hectoliters, or 89,960,369 gallons (6th); 70% red, 30% white
DOC WINE PRODUCED*	55.8% (3rd)
SPECIALTY FOODS	hazelnuts; chestnuts; truffles; *carne cruda* (raw meat, usually veal, topped with oil, lemon, and often truffles); *agnolotti del plin* (small meat-filled pasta, often served with a brothlike sauce in Alba); *bollito misto* (mixed boiled meats, usually served with savory red and green dipping sauces); Bra (cow's- and goat's-milk cheese, often sharp); Toma (wide-ranging family of mostly cow's-milk cheeses).

*1997 figures. Rankings out of 20 regions total (Trentino–Alto Adige counted as one). Source: Istituto Statistica Mercati Agro-Alimentari (ISMEA), Rome.

KEY GRAPE VARIETIES

WHITES

ARNEIS	Records of this grape date back to the 1400s in the Roero hills. It was traditionally used as a blending grape to soften red nebbiolo wines, but recent years have seen a surge in plantings. It produces fine, floral, citrusy whites.

CORTESE	Grapier, plumper, and less aromatic than arneis, it is the base of Gavi DOCG wines. Considered a native to the Monferrato hills.
ERBALUCE	Herbal, piercingly acidic variety grown in the northerly reaches of Piedmont near Valle d'Aosta, particularly the town of Caluso north of Turin. Makes crisp dry whites and sharp, fragrant sparklers, as well as passito sweet wines.
MOSCATO	The Piedmontese use the superior moscato bianco (*muscat à petits grains* in French), which has come to be known as moscato canelli, after the town of Canelli, not far from Asti. Used in the famed *frizzante* and *spumante* whites of the Asti DOCG.
OTHERS	CHARDONNAY, increasingly popular in the Langhe hills.

REDS

BARBERA	Piedmont's most-planted red, considered a native of the Monferrato hills. Durable and extremely productive, it grows just about anywhere and is thus planted in just about every conceivable place—leading to wide variations in style.
BRACHETTO	A native red used for sweet wines, both still and sparkling.
DOLCETTO	The name means "little sweet one," in reference to its sweet taste when ripe. Deeply colored but with soft tannins, the variety ripens early and produces soft, fruity, accessible reds with plush black fruit flavors. Increasingly, producers are creating denser wines from the variety by aging their wines in small oak barrels.
NEBBIOLO	Purportedly named for *la nebbia* (fog) that descends on the hills of Barolo and Barbaresco every fall, this is Italy's answer to pinot noir. Considered native to Piedmont, records of its cultivation date back to the 1300s. Late-ripening and sensitive to adverse vintage conditions, it nevertheless produces Italy's most uniquely perfumed and powerful red. Its skins are surprisingly thin for a grape known for its biting tannins, making it susceptible to breakage, and typically the color of Barolo leans more toward light ruby, even as a young wine.
OTHERS	FREISA and RUCHÉ, used in light, fruity reds; GRIGNOLINO, used to make rosé-style wines.

TOP VINTAGES IN PIEMONTE, 1980–2000

Every vintage year is a nail-biter in Piedmont, where the late-ripening nebbiolo races with the weather each October and November on its journey to ripeness. Autumn in the hills of the Langhe is reliably damp and foggy, so not only is a hot, dry summer essential for full maturation of the grapes, but the autumn rains must hold off long enough for producers to pick grapes at the optimal level of maturity. Whereas the early-ripening dolcetto and the durable barbera are fairly consistent wines from vintage to vintage (both of these softly tannic varieties are meant to be consumed young, for the most part), the nebbiolo-based wines of Barolo and Barbaresco are another story. In cool or excessively damp years the wines are likely to be thin and harshly tannic, whereas a favorable vintage brings out incomparable flavors, textures, and aromas in nebbiolo. Recent years have been very good to Piedmont, with 1995 through 1999 all producing excellent wines (it's too early to comment on 2000 and '01); "For me, '96 and '98 were the best expressions of Piedmont," says Domenico Clerico, a leading Barolo producer, who says that the years '96 through '99 were one of the most glorious runs Barolo has ever enjoyed. As in other parts of Italy, '97 and '99 were exceptionally hot, dry years, producing wines with more power and extract; '96 and '98, according to Clerico, were more climatically even, creating wines that were powerful in their own right but more aromatically expressive and balanced. Here's a list of the best of the last two decades in Barolo and Barberesco: 1982, '85, '88, '89, '90, '96, '97, '98, '99, 2000.

LA STRADA DEL VINO
WINE TOURING IN PIEMONTE

The undulating hills around Alba and Asti are Mecca for the serious wine enthusiast. In fact, there isn't much else to do in Alba and Asti but eat and drink. Of the two towns, Alba is more quaint and probably better as a base of operations for visiting the vineyards of Barolo and Barbaresco. Go in September or October, as the nebbiolo vines are reaching their full maturity and the weather is starting to turn cool, and just amble (by car or, if you're in shape, bike) through one of the most striking stands of vineyards anywhere in the world. There's an enoteca seemingly around every corner in the villages of the Barolo and Barbaresco DOCs, the best known being the Enoteca Regionale del Vino Barolo in—you guessed it—the medieval village of Barolo (Piazza Falletti; 0173-562-77). The Barbaresco zone has its own Enoteca Regionale in its own namesake village, and it, too, is an ideal place to sample local wines. As for restaurants, Piedmont is the place to go for rich, wintry fare, highlighted by the region's famously fragrant white truffles. In the heart of Alba is a known winemaker hangout called Osteria dell'Arco (Piazza Savona 5; 0173-36-39-74), while in the village of Barolo the Locanda nel Borgo Antico (Piazza Municipio 2; 0173-563-55) offers a similar sense of being one with the wine crowd. In La Morra, winemaker Gianfranco Bovio's Belvedere (Piazza Castello 5; 0173-501-90) is one of the benchmark restaurants of the Barolo area; in Neive, in the heart of the Barbaresco DOCG, the landmark restaurant is La Contea (Piazza Cocito; 0173-671-26).

DEGUSTAZIONI
TASTINGS

DOLCETTO

Bartolo Mascarello
Dolcetto d'Alba, $-$$

Ca' Viola
Dolcetto d'Alba, $$

Chionetti
Dolcetto di Dogliani
"Briccolero," $-$$

Here's a good look at the style spectrum of dolcetto, from the earthier, more traditional wine of Bartolo Mascarello, with its brambly, spicy blackberry tones, to the plump and chunky wines of Chionetti and Ca' Viola, two producers who strive for a greater level of extraction in their wines—the better to stand up to their aging in small oak barriques. While long thought of as Italy's answer to Beaujolais, dolcetto has become a considerably more powerful, extracted red, as illustrated by the Ca' Viola wine in particular. What's noteworthy about all of these wines is how soft and accessible they are, and how deeply colorful. These are plump, "purple" wines for sipping with sausages, prosciutto, and other snacks, always ready to go on release. Other good dolcettos to seek out: Villa Sparina's Dolcetto d'Acqui "D'Giusep"; the Dolcetto di Doglianis of Marzieno and Enrico Abbona; and the Dolcetto d'Alba of top

Barolo and Barbaresco producers such as Luciano Sandrone, Roberto Voerzio, Paolo Scavino, Ceretto, and Giacomo Conterno—usually these wines tend to mirror the style of their respective house's Barolo (i.e., if the Barolo is rich, extracted, and oak-influenced, chances are the dolcetto will be too, albeit at a much more agreeable price).

BARBERA

Vietti Barbera d'Alba "Tre Vigne," $

Prunotto Barbera d'Alba "Pian Romualdo," $$

Braida di Giacomo Bologna
Barbera d'Asti "Bricco dell' Uccellone," $$$

Here are three benchmark barberas that demonstrate how variable the character of the grape (and the wine) can be. The Vietti wine, widely available and consistent from vintage to vintage, is a good place to start: Its aromas and flavors of red cherries are carried along on a wave of bright acidity, giving the wine a liveliness that is typical of more fresh (i.e., little or no wood aging) barberas. The Prunotto wine, also easy to find, is a little more deeply extracted than the Vietti, with slightly "blacker" fruit flavors, and there's also a distinctly oakier note that lends the wine a deeper, more somber tone. And then there's "Bricco dell' Uccellone," a legendary (and therefore rare and expensive) wine that should be tasted by anyone looking to gain a deeper understanding of barbera. The brightness and red fruit flavors of the Vietti wine are found in this bottling as well, as are the smoky, creamy oak notes of the Prunotto. Yet the hallmark of "Bricco dell' Uccellone" is how well integrated those seemingly diverse elements are. This is a wine of serious structure that nevertheless retains a certain youthful exuberance. Like the others, it's very versatile with food—try it with game birds or some of the lighter Piedmontese cheeses.

"SUPER-PIEMONTE" BLENDS

Poderi Colla "Bricco del Drago," $$

Rocche dei Manzoni "Bricco Manzoni," $$

Conterno Fantino "Monprà," $$$

This flight is all about the interplay of Piedmont's "big three" of red grapes: nebbiolo, barbera, and dolcetto. The Poderi Colla wine was one of the first commercial blends of dolcetto and nebbiolo, and in tasting the wine you get a clear sense of what each grape brings to the table: The inky color and jammy fruit come from the dolcetto, while the firm structure and hint of dried-fruit aroma come from the nebbiolo. In Rocche dei Manzoni's "Bricco Manzoni" it's barbera, rather than dolcetto, that's used as the softening agent for the angular, aromatic nebbiolo. This wine has a slightly more savory profile, with notes of woodsy red cherry and a hint of cinnamon, essentially a Barolo flavor profile but a barbera "feel" on the palate.

Finally, there's "Monprà," which combines nebbiolo, barbera, and cabernet sauvignon. This is the densest and most extracted of the group, layering the ripe, sweet fruit flavors of barbera and cabernet over a tannic, savory base of nebbiolo. It's a deep, rich wine for steaks or stews.

NEBBIOLO 1: BARBARESCO

Produttori del Barbaresco Barbaresco Torre, $$

Moccagatta Barbaresco, $$$

Gaja Barbaresco, $$$

It's often said that Barolo is the king of wines, and Barbaresco the queen. In tasting through these base-level bottlings from three famous producers, you may detect a certain femininity in the wines: They all have heady perfumes of dried cherries, tea leaves, cinnamon, and other elements both sweet and savory, while on the palate they are full-flavored and tannic yet fine and focused. Barbaresco is rarely a sappy, juicy wine: It is firm, angular, and tightly coiled, particularly as a young wine (we assume you'll be comparing current vintages of these). Barbaresco seems almost nervous on the palate, and as a young wine needs some weighty, fatty food to counter its tannic bite and bring out the fruit flavor. Of these three wines, you'll likely find the Produttori del Barbaresco wine the most rustic and earthy, the Gaja wine silkier and sweetly fruity (although there are trademark notes of cinnamon and rose petals amid all that fruit). The Moccagatta wine has a great balance of sweet and savory elements, and is, of the three, probably the most readily drinkable—its tannins don't have quite the bite of the other two.

NEBBIOLO 2: BAROLO

Bartolo Mascarello Barolo, $$$

Pio Cesare Barolo, $$$

Aldo Conterno Barolo, $$$

As compared with the Barbaresco flight above, you'll likely find these wines to be deeper, darker, and earthier, with scents of tar, cedar, and tobacco intermingled with the dried cherry-berry scents of nebbiolo. They are rich and tannic wines, to be sure, but there's a perfumy quality that makes them more readily comparable to pinot noir than to "bigger" reds from cabernet sauvignon or syrah. Start this flight with the Mascarello wine, the most traditional in style, then move into the Pio Cesare and Aldo Conterno bottlings. The Mascarello wine is probably the most fruit-driven, with bright and expressive aromas and a certain delicacy on the palate. The Pio Cesare is a little more extracted, with a touch more black fruit character, as is the Aldo Conterno. The Conterno is aged in newer, smaller oak barrels, lending it more toastiness and preserving its inky color; the Mascarello wine is aged in traditional, larger casks, giving it a more oxidative, resiny aroma and a lighter color; the Pio Cesare finds a balance between the two.

GAVI

La Scolca Gavi, $

Villa Sparina Gavi di Gavi "La Villa," $$

Cool, clean, and crisp: that's Gavi. In this comparison, you'll likely find the La Scolca has a more pronounced minerality, a chalkiness on the palate. The Villa Sparina is a bit fatter, dewier. Both wines are delicately aromatic, offering a whiff of green apples and green melon, and they clean up on the finish with a whisk of acidity. With a salad or maybe a pasta sauced with a pesto from nearby Liguria, this type of wine is at its best.

ARNEIS

Ceretto Arneis "Blangé," $

Cascina Ca' Rossa Roero Arneis "Merica," $

F.illi Brovia Roero Arneis, $

More assertively aromatic than Gavi's cortese, Roero's arneis is a bright, tingly white tailor-made not only for pastas seasoned with mountain herbs but for grilled and roasted seafood of all stripes. There's a smoky quality to the aroma of arneis, along with hints of white flowers and white grapefruit. The distinctions to be made among these three wines are fairly subtle: the Ca' Rossa is probably the fullest-bodied, although all three are characterized by a citrusy acidity and lilting aromas that distinguish them from a mass of more neutral, bland-tasting Italian whites.

MOSCATO D'ASTI

Michele Chiarlo Moscato d'Asti "Nivole," $$

Paolo Saracco Moscato d'Asti, $$

The peachy sweetness of moscato is checked with a dose of bracing acidity in these two popular bottlings, two of the best examples around of Moscato d'Asti. Made in the *frizzante* (semi-sparkling) style, they are sweet without being cloying, with moderate alcohol levels for after-dinner sipping. Try them alongside some *biscotti* or a bowl of fresh berries; if you're feeling decadent, pour a little of the wine in the bowl with the berries and toss it around. The sweet, peachy, floral flavors of the wine lend an exotic edge to the fruit.

La Cucina

FOOD FOR THE WINE

RECIPE BY LIDIA BASTIANICH

As in other landlocked regions, Piedmont draws its flavor from the earth. There is no more signature Piedmontese image than that of the *trifolau piemontese* (truffle hunter) and his nervy dog, rooting around the hills for white truffles, wrapping them lovingly in folds of canvas, and selling them furtively on the streets of Alba.

The lush, foggy hills of Alba and Asti are rich not only in vines but in hazelnuts, chestnuts, root vegetables, and mushrooms, all of which find their way into the hearty risottos that characterize the region's wintry cooking. Well-supplied with rice from paddies in Vercelli and Novara north of the Po, the cooks of Alba infuse their dishes with the same kinds of earthy flavors found in the wines. An Albese specialty is *agnolotti del plin*, little folds of pasta filled with shredded meat and topped with butter and truffles, a dish improved immeasurably when countered with the tannic, acidic bite of a good Barolo.

Piedmont is not for the meek, and it's not for vegans: Go to Alba and you'll eat enough beef and lamb tartare (often topped with truffle shavings) to last you a lifetime. And the same goes for risotto, Italy's ultimate comfort food. The preparation below evokes the image of a weathered old *contadino* (farmer) returning from a day of vine-pruning in the raw chill of December, warming himself with a creamy bowl of risotto spiked with some of his wine. Put in a good day's work yourself before you tackle this hearty dish: It will taste all the better.

Risotto al Barolo

8 large CARROTS, peeled and quartered
2 fresh BAY LEAVES
Pinch SALT
Pinch freshly ground black PEPPER
1 bottle BAROLO WINE (OR OTHER HEARTY, DRY RED)
½ cup OLIVE OIL
4 medium SHALLOTS, diced fine
1 pound ARBORIO RICE
5 tablespoons BUTTER
1 cup PARMIGIANO REGGIANO CHEESE, grated

SERVES 4

FOR THE STOCK

In a large stockpot, bring 4 quarts of water to a boil. Add the medium-size carrots and bay leaves, and simmer for 1½ hours. Remove the carrots and bay leaves, place them in a bowl, and mash them up to create a purée with about 1 tablespoon of butter and a pinch of salt and pepper. Meanwhile, in a sauté pan, bring half of the wine to a boil, and allow the alcohol to burn off (literally flambé the wine). After the wine has boiled for five minutes, add it to the stockpot containing the carrots and water. Continue to boil the mixture until it reduces down to about 1½ quarts of liquid. Cover and keep at a bare simmer while you start the rice.

FOR THE RICE

In a heavy-bottomed skillet, heat ½ cup of olive oil over low flame until the oil begins to shimmer. Add the chopped shallots and salt, and sauté until the shallots wilt, about 2 to 3 minutes.

Adjust the heat to medium-high and add the rice. Mix vigorously with a wooden spoon, to keep the rice from sticking to the bottom of the pan and to lightly toast it. After 3 minutes, add 1 cup of the remaining Barolo. Stir vigorously.

Lower the heat to medium. Begin adding the simmering carrot stock to the rice 2 tablespoons at a time, maintaining the mixture at a consistency between slightly watery to creamy. Continue adding the stock until the rice cooked but is al dente. The entire process should take 18 to 20 minutes.

When the risotto is done, take it off the burner. Continue to stir vigorously while adding the remaining 4 tablespoons of butter and the grated Parmigiano cheese. Try to whip up the mixture to make it as creamy as possible. Spread some of the hot carrot purée on a hot plate and top with the risotto.

WINE RECOMMENDATION: Barolo is a natural, but any nebbiolo-based wine—Barbaresco, Gattinara, Ghemme, or a simple Nebbiolo d'Alba—will do.

Liguria

Coaxing Wine from Stubborn Seaside Slopes

— ❧ —

THE FRY GUYS

It's coming up on noon as we near the old port of Genoa, and the streets are filled with the unmistakable aroma of hot olive oil. The sailor's quarter, as this area is called, is a tangle of narrow alleys and hulking *palazzi*, and on nearly every corner the tiny fry shops known as *friggitorie* are coming to life. Cast-iron pots hiss and sputter with calamari (squid), *gamberetti* (shrimp), *sarago* (bream), and pinky-size anchovy spawn called *bianchetti*, which come out of the oil looking like French fries with eyes. The cooks are bouncing off one another in their cramped kitchens, energized by the crowds at their take-out windows, like pizza-makers who toss the dough a little higher when they know they're being watched.

We stop at a weathered-looking *friggitoria* not far from Genoa's aquarium, as a cook tosses some just-fried calamari in a big black colander, aerating the glistening rings before dumping them in a heap on the counter. The minuscule kitchen is outfitted in white tile and fronted by a marble slab that looks as if it was installed at the beginning of time. Assorted *fritti* are piled high across the counter, and there's an old counter-weighted scale to measure out the portions, but the mustachioed fry man who

takes our order doesn't bother with it: He just plunges his hand into the mound of calamari, wraps up the take in the trademark pink newsprint of the *Gazzetto dello Sport*, and shoves it across the counter with a curt *"Prego,"* already off to his next task.

But he doesn't disappoint. His *calamari fritti* are a far cry from the rubbery, soggy stuff found in so many restaurants. In fact, aspiring restaurant cooks should be sent to Genoa to study with this guy: The coating is crispy and just slightly moist, the squid tender and juicy, neither of which is a small feat. Hardly any grease bleeds through the newsprint, and it is just as good cold as hot.

We hang around a bit and press the cook for details on his technique, but he's too busy to be much help. The heat of the oil is obviously critical, and the way he's tossing and spreading the *fritti* on the counter seems to play a role, too. But there's something else going on in there that keeps people coming back, something they can't replicate at home—namely, the fact that the calamari at the *friggitorie* are cooked in olive oil, something that's very expensive for a home cook to do, but indispensable in creating that light texture.

We continue on through the maze of old-town Genoa, methodically emptying the newspaper cone of calamari, checking out the bustle

THE DOC ZONES OF LIGURIA

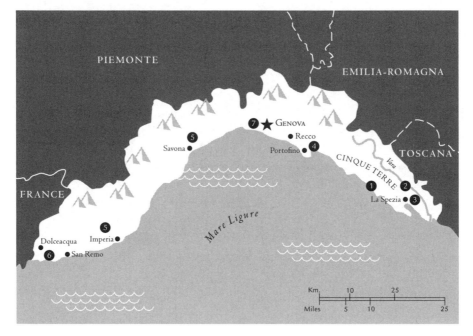

1 Cinque Terre/Cinque Terre Sciacchetrà
2 Colli di Luni
3 Colline di Levanto
4 Golfo del Tigullio
5 Riviera Ligure di Ponente
6 Rossese di Dolceacqua/Dolceacqua
7 Val Polcevera

of the port and winding our way through the meandering streets. Some of the *friggitorie* are not so much storefronts as tiny caves chipped out of ancient stone walls, but nearly all are doing a brisk business; it's obvious that the fritto misto (mixed fry) is not just an occasional snack but a staple of the Genovese diet. For all of the people eating fried fish like ice cream on the street, there are others who bundle up their *fritti* and take them home, to spread on top of a salad or serve cold with a drizzle of olive oil and lemon juice.

It's an addiction, and a tough one to kick: Just when you think you've got your fritto misto intake under control, you're back down at the docks, ducking furtively down dark alleys. The fry men are always there, always well-supplied, luring you back in spite of yourself.

As good as fritto misto may be, however, Genoa is not defined by it. The city may be one of the most underrated food towns in Italy, since most tourists see it only as a jumping-off point for Portofino or Cinque Terre. True, Genoa is a major commercial port—Italy's largest in fact. But as the capital and geographic heart of Liguria, it is more than just an industrial center. Like its old maritime rival, Venice, it's not just a city but a culture unto itself.

In many regions of Italy, the foods of the coast and the foods of the interior uplands are so dramatically different they seem like separate cuisines. In Liguria, the mountains and the coast are often one and the same, and their produce comes together on the tables of Genoa. Although the city is right on the water, Genoa is most famous for pesto, a sauce that speaks not of the sea but of the Apennines and

Alps farther inland. The Genovese practice of tossing olives into *ciuppin* (fish stew) is another example of this land-sea fusion.

And Liguria is nothing if not dramatic. Its coastal villages don't so much sit on the sea as pull themselves out of it, clawing a little way up the rocky slopes and then holding on for dear life. Some, like the fishing hamlets of the Cinque Terre, are best approached by boat. The inland towns are tossed like rafts on a stormy sea of olive groves and umbrella pines, accessed by roads that zigzag up sharp inclines. The few vineyards to be seen, most of them planted on steep terraces, are striking examples of the lengths to which some people will go to make a little wine.

But these scattered vineyards don't add up to much: Within Italy, only the Valle d'Aosta, which is similarly inhospitable to vines, has less vineyard area (and produces less wine) than Liguria. Olive groves outnumber vineyards in Liguria five-to-one, and many former vintners have turned to the more profitable business of flower-growing, a big industry around the western port of Imperia. For a region so rich in food products—sweet olives and their delicate oils, giant artichokes, wild mushrooms, fragrant herbs—Liguria just can't support a mass of vineyards, despite having an ideal mix of hot, dry weather and poor soils. According to Filippo Rondelli, whose Terre Bianche estate is in the western Ligurian village of Dolceacqua, "the only problem with Ligurian wines is the work."

In total, Liguria turns out a little over 2 million bottles of DOC-classified wine per year, every ounce wrested from unforgiving slopes. Given their high cost of production, Ligurian wines can be pricey, which makes them a tough sell in the American market. The conventional wisdom on Liguria is that it makes light wines for sipping at the beach, leaving importers to wonder why they would pit them against fuller-bodied, less expensive bottles from the New World. This is perfectly logical, and it says a lot about the handful of Ligurian wines that do make it to America: Someone (presumably someone with other sources of income) likes them enough to bring them in anyway.

VINI BIANCHI
White Wines

For many wine drinkers, the main reference point for Ligurian wine is the network of vineyard terraces above Cinque Terre, carved from the rock thousands of years ago by the Liguri tribes that gave the region its name. The Liguri, contemporaries of the Etruscans, were the great terrace-builders of ancient Italy, reaching as far as the Valtellina region on Lombardy's border with Switzerland. But while we can marvel at their accomplishments when hiking the footpaths of Cinque Terre, it's hard to say much about the modern-day wines. Although there are a handful of producers who are striving for more (notably Walter De Battè in Riomaggiore, who relies on fanatically low yields and a touch of oak aging to extract more flavor from the bosco grape), Cinque Terre remains first and foremost a light vacation white, and not one to write home about at that.

Liguria's experience is yet another example of Italy's mostly forgettable recent history with white wine: For all of the interesting white grapes out there, the last three decades have

been dominated by what might be called tourist wines: Cinque Terre in Liguria, Frascati in Rome, Galestro in Tuscany, and so on. As elsewhere, only now are consumers discovering what Liguria is really capable of.

Save for a few notable exceptions, Liguria is white-wine country, and the wines to look for above all others are those made from vermentino. As in Sardinia and coastal Tuscany, where the grape also thrives, vermentino not only weathers the intense heat and dryness of the Ligurian hills but seems to assume some of the herbal aromas that so distinguish Ligurian cooking. Thought to have been brought to the Italian Mediterranean by the Spaniards (via Corsica), vermentino is emerging as one of Italy's truly distinguished native whites.

Generally speaking, the vermentino-based wines of Liguria are a little more delicate and perfumed than their counterparts from elsewhere in the grape's Mediterranean triangle: Sardinia, in particular, is known for fuller-bodied versions. In eastern Liguria, known as the Levante, it is used in varietal wines in the Colli di Luni and Golfo del Tigullio DOC zones, and plays a supporting role in the Cinque Terre and Colline di Levanto blends. In western Liguria, known as the Ponente, it reaches perhaps its greatest heights in the wide-ranging Riviera Ligure di Ponente zone, which ranges from the outskirts of Genoa to the French border. The main difference is that most Ponente wines are pure varietals, while the Levante wines tend to be blends.

The prime vermentino country in the Ponente is a network of mostly inland villages near Imperia, which, incidentally, is Liguria's principal olive oil–production zone. In the dusty, scrubby heights of Diano Castello,

Ranzo Borgo, Pieve di Teco, and Dolceacqua, vines battle for space with some of Italy's most beautiful olive groves. It's impossible not to taste these surroundings in the better Riviera Ligure di Ponente vermentinos: They are distinguished not only by scents of wild fennel and herbs, but by an almost briny quality on the palate. Vermentino is structured enough to stand up to fermentation and aging in small oak barrels, which lends a sheen of creaminess to the otherwise savory flavors. Above all, vermentino is an appetite-whetting wine: It gets you salivating for a bite of calamari, a bowl of garlicky fish soup, maybe some pesto-drenched pasta, each sip and each bite evoking not only the sea but the dewy, piney mountain forests that separate Liguria from Piedmont.

The acknowledged leader in vermentino these days is the Colle dei Bardellini farm in the hills above Imperia, owned by Genovese restaurateurs Pino and Luigi Sola. They make two vermentinos under the Ligure di Ponente DOC, including the single-vineyard "Vigna U Munte," which shows off not just the aromatic qualities of the grape but a juicy, mouth-filling character more readily associated with Gallura in Sardegna. Another reliable Ligurian name is Terre Bianche, which, like Colli dei Bardellini, is among the few Ligurian brands imported to the United States.

Other producers to keep an out for are Enoteca Bisson, whose "Vigna Erta" vermentino is one of the best in the Levante; Maria Donata Bianchi, from Diano Castello in the Ponente; Tenuta Giuncheo, from Camporosso, also in the Ponente; and Ottaviano Lambruschi, from the eastern end of Liguria in the Colli di Luni. As vermentino grows in popularity, especially in restaurants, it's worth remembering these producers and DOCs for future reference, as their presence in the American market is sure to grow.

Liguria's other white-wine star, pigato, may be even longer-established than vermentino, although its origins are unclear. Believed to be an ancient Greek export, pigato is not always easily distinguished from vermentino, even by those who make it. "As vines, they are very similar," says Filippo Rondelli of Terre Bianche. "In fact, they look like practically the same plant."

Vermentino and pigato do share some of the same herbal, scrub-brushy qualities and a similarly salty kick on the palate. But pigato is generally considered the more intense wine of the two. "Pigato tends to be more perfumed, and a little more biting on the finish," says Pino Sola of Colle dei Bardellini. "Vermentino is a little rounder and softer, maybe a little fruitier."

In addition to both Colle dei Bardellini and Terre Bianche, some great pigato is being made by Loredana Faraldi at her A Maccia farm in Ranzo Borgo, a tiny amount of which makes it to the States. There's also the *cantina* of Tommaso and Angelo Lupi in Pieve di Teco, but despite being one of Liguria's largest private estates, their generally excellent whites (and reds) have had an inconsistent presence in the United States. Among Italians, the big names in pigato also include Riccardo Bruna and Feipu dei Massaretti in Albenga, the latter one of the more historic wineries in western Liguria. If the chance presents itself, these are wines worth checking out. In a market dominated by sweet, oaky, often overly alcoholic whites, pigato and vermentino are like refreshing sea breezes, wines that speak very clearly of where they come from.

Vini Rossi
Red Wines

The idea that a wine—by way of its aroma or flavor—can transport you to a different place has a lot to do with how a Ligurian red wine finds its way onto a restaurant wine list. Since only about a third of Liguria's already small production is devoted to reds, and since many of Liguria's best-known reds—Rossese di Dolceacqua in particular—can be a little strange, a restaurant list is probably the only place you're likely to find them. Aside from the desire to look smart, a sommelier probably selects a Ligurian red precisely because it is a little strange. The overwhelming preference these days is for sweet, densely concentrated, well-oaked reds, and at times it seems as though all the reds of the world are veering toward the same style, regardless of grape variety. There doesn't seem to be any danger of that happening in Liguria.

As with white wines, there are fairly clear divisions among the red wines of the western region of Ponente and the eastern region of Levante. The Ponente is dominated by two grapes: rossese, which has its own DOC zone in Dolceacqua, and ormeasco, the local name for dolcetto, which pops up as a varietal wine. In the Levante, the wines are highly variable blends, often incorporating grapes more readily associated with Tuscany, such as sangiovese, canaiolo, and ciliegiolo. In either case, expect a foresty, earthy, mushroomy quality to these reds, particularly those from the Ponente, which seems to take its stylistic cues from neighboring Provence.

Rossese di Dolceaqua and ormeasco from Riviera Ligure di Ponente tend to be lighter-styled reds, with lots of *frutti di bosco* flavors, red and black raspberries in particular. Many of the above-named producers of whites (Lupi, Terre Bianche, A Maccia) are also producing noteworthy reds, but drinkers should be warned: these are decidedly savory wines. Like their white counterparts, they seem to absorb the scents and flavors of the thick Mediteranean scrub, giving the very fresh, berried flavors of the fruit a resiny, herbal tang. This is less pronounced in ormeasco than rossese, but on the whole the Ligurian version of dolcetto is not easily confused with the rounder, plumper Piedmontese version.

On the eastern Riviera, the reds from the Colli di Luni DOC may remind some people of small-scale Chiantis (La Colombiera makes a good one), and the rare varietal ciliegiolo (red or rosé) from the Golfo del Tigullio DOC is worth reaching for if you happen to see some in a Portofino café (Enoteca Bisson, which uses the Golfo del Tigullio DOC, exports a small quantity of ormeasco- and ciliegiolo-based reds and rosés). Overall, Rossese di Dolceacqua remains the definitive Ligurian red. And as more Ligurian producers modernize what are generally considered some of the more technologically stunted wineries in Italy, there is reason to believe that Rossese, among others, could be a richer, more full-bodied red in the future.

It would certainly seem that Liguria, for all its physical difficulties, is capable of more. With its mix of Alps and Apennines blocking off moisture from the west, it is an exceptionally dry region, and its soils—mostly poor, calcareous sands on very steep, well-drained slopes—are a red winemaker's dream. It all comes down, once again, to logistics: In a sleepy region that seems to have all but left wine behind, the conversation is still more about potential than results.

VINI SPUMANTI E DOLCI
Sparkling and Sweet Wines

Although a handful of Liguria's seven DOC zones allow for the production of sparkling wines, there are barely any to be found. Sweet wines, too, are mostly local oddities, the most noteworthy being the sweet version of Cinque Terre called Sciacchetrà. Its commercial production is more or less limited to Walter De Battè, but since a little of his wine is exported, it merits a mention. Redolent of honey, dried fruits, and nutmeg, the principal attraction of this *passito* is its cleansing acidity; like all great sweet wines, it presents its rich flavors without being cloying. If you're up for a little detective work, it's worth a look.

FAST FACTS: $\mathcal{L}$IGURIA

PROVINCES	Genova (GE), Imperia (IM), La Spezia (SP), Savona (SV)
CAPITAL	Genova
KEY WINE TOWNS	Albenga, Dolceacqua, La Spezia, Ranzo Borgo
TOTAL VINEYARD AREA*	4,837 hectares, or 11,952 acres. Rank: 19th
TOTAL WINE PRODUCTION*	165,000 hectoliters, or 4,359,313 gallons (19th); 66% white; 34% red
DOC WINE PRODUCED*	13.9% (13th)
SPECIALTY FOODS	olives and olive oil; artichokes; pesto (sauce of fresh basil, garlic, pine nuts, olive oil, and grated Parmigiano cheese); *ciuppin* or *burrida* (fish stew, often flavored with olives); focaccia (salty, olive oil–flavored bread); wild mushrooms.

*1997 figures. Rankings out of twenty regions total (Trentino–Alto Adige counted as one). Source: Istituto Statistica Mercati Agro-Alimentari (ISMEA), Rome.

KEY GRAPE VARIETIES

WHITES

BOSCO	Fairly light white found principally in the terraces of Cinque Terre.
PIGATO	Thought to be of Greek origin, it is largely confined to the western Riviera, most densely planted around Albenga. Sharp, herbal, and distinctive.
VERMENTINO	Found in both eastern and western Liguria, this dewy white of Spanish origin best captures the wild, rugged nature of the region. Exotically aromatic, with an almost salty tang on the palate.

	REDS
ORMEASCO	The Ligurian name for dolcetto. Primarily found in the western end of the region, particularly around Pieve di Teco and Ranzo Borgo.
ROSSESE	Liguria's most distinctive red, thought to have come from neighboring Provence. Makes savory, woodsy reds.
SANGIOVESE	The base of most blends in the eastern Riviera, including the Colli di Luni, a DOC zone that is shared with Tuscany. Often blended with other Tuscan grapes such as ciliegiolo and canaiolo to create bright, berried reds.
CILIEGIOLO	Found also in Tuscany, this cherry-scented red makes light reds and rosés.

TOP VINTAGES IN LIGURIA, 1980–2000

As with so many of Italy's whites, Liguria's wines are best consumed within a few years of the vintage. Most of the reds, too, are made in a lighter style and are not meant for long aging. However, as in much of Italy, the last six vintages (1995 to 2000) have generally been kind to the region's vintners.

LA STRADA DEL VINO
WINE TOURING IN LIGURIA

A great spot for wine lovers in Genova is the Sola Enoteca (Via Barabino 120 R.; 010-594-513), owned by Pino and Luigi Sola, the proprietors of the Colle dei Bardellini wine estate in nearby Imperia. They offer not only their own wines but a panorama of the rest of Liguria as well. In the hills above the well-traveled village of Dolceacqua, not far from the French border, the Terre Bianche winery has a small *agriturismo* and restaurant that are well worth the treacherous drive to get to (0183-314-26). East of Genoa, a not-to-miss food town is the little village of Recco, where the foccacia alone is worth the trip. And in the coastal town of Chiavari, check out the Enoteca Bisson (0185-31-44-62), which is both a winery and wine shop.

DEGUSTAZIONI
TASTINGS

VERMENTINO AND PIGATO

Enoteca Bisson Golfo del Tigullio Vermentino "Vigna Erta," $–$$

Colle dei Bardellini Riviera Ligure di Ponente Vermentino "U Munte," $–$$

Terre Bianche Riviera Ligure di Ponente Pigato, $$

Limited availability of wines makes a Ligurian tasting a bit difficult. The above producers each offer both pigato and vermentino, so feel free to use either depending on availability. Bisson's "Vigna Erta" is textbook vermentino, with a trademark herbal tang reminiscent of the Mediterranean scrub. The Colle dei Bardellini vermentino has a rounder, more juicy quality offset by a mineral-edged, almost salty sensation on the finish. The flavors may remind you of wild herbs: fennel, sage, mint, and so on. You'll find similar aromas in the pigato, with a slightly sharper, finer edge to them. These are great whites for fragrant fish soups, salty fish fries, or pesto-topped pastas. Other vermentino and pigato producers from western Liguria to look for include Lupi, A Maccia, and Tenuta Giuncheo, while from eastern Liguria keep your eyes out for whites from the Colli di Luni DOC.

LIGURIAN REDS

La Columbiera "Terrizo" Colli di Luni Rosso, $

Terre Bianche Rossese di Dolceacqua, $

The Rossese in particular is likely to remind you of a light-styled Côtes-du-Rhône or some of the more savory reds of Provence: Its fresh berry flavors have an earthy, savory edge, a little more so than the brighter, fruitier Colli di Luni wine. Both are crisp, lighter-styled reds for dishes with a little tang: think of sauces such as *puttanesca* (spiked with capers and anchovies) or maybe classic Ligurian stuffed peppers. Other producers of Rossese include Lupi (who also makes ormeasco) and Tenuta Giuncheo. Note: All of these wines are produced in very small quantities, although they are exported.

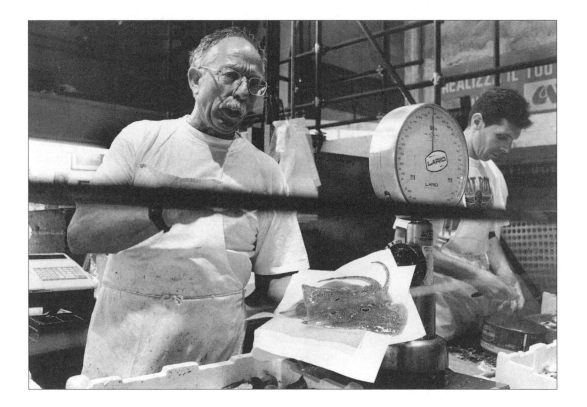

La Cucina

FOOD FOR THE WINE

RECIPE BY LIDIA BASTIANICH

In Liguria, a relatively sparse wine culture struggles to do justice to a richly diverse cuisine. Since Liguria is a mere sliver of seacoast, the classic Italian contrast of land and sea is much more dramatic. In beach towns such as Alassio and Albenga, on the western Riviera (the Ponente), the focus is on *pesce*. But not twenty minutes inland, in Ranzo Borgo or Pieve di Teco, fish all but disappears from the menu. Suddenly you're eating a rosemary-scented saddle of rabbit and the ocean is a distant memory, completely walled off from view.

The herbal qualities of Ligurian white wines in particular make them great accompaniments to a classic Genovese pesto sauce, while the almost salty tang of the wines makes them perfect partners for fritto misto. Deep-frying is a tricky thing to do at home, given the difficulty of getting oil hot enough, but it is possible to replicate the *calamari fritti* of the great Genovese *friggitorie*. It's a balancing act of interior and exterior moisture, and while it seems like a waste, it requires a lot of oil to get the job done right. Follow the directions below, open up a bottle of well-chilled Ligurian vermentino, and imagine yourself on a sailboat off the coast of Portofino, dangling your feet in the water and toasting your good fortune.

Perfect Fried Calamari

3 pounds medium CALAMARI, cleaned and sliced (see instructions below)
2 cups all-purpose FLOUR (or for a grainier, crunchier texture, mix 1 cup flour with 1 cup finely ground cornmeal)
1½ cups good-quality VEGETABLE OIL (or canola oil)
1½ cups extra-virgin OLIVE OIL
1 teaspoon coarse SEA SALT

SERVES 4

TO CLEAN CALAMARI

When buying the squid, be sure that its outer membrane is intact and its eyes are glossy and black, rather than murky gray. To clean, gently pull the head from the body, extracting the internal organs. Cut the tentacles just below the eyes and set aside. Peel the skin from the body, remove the clear backbone from inside, and wash the tentacles and body well with cold water. Detach the fins from the body and cut in ¼ inch rings, discarding the very tip of the body. Wash the pieces well in a colander and drain thoroughly.

PREPARATION

Spread the rings and tentacles on a large cutting board and pat down with a dry cotton kitchen towel. The squid should be as dry as you can get it, although it will by nature remain somewhat slimy.

Place a large piece of newspaper or wax paper on a countertop and spread with all the flour. Take one-third of the calamari pieces, toss them in the flour to coat lightly, and shake off the excess in a colander. Only flour as much of the squid as you are going to fry at that time; with the above quantities, it is advisable to fry it in thirds. Make sure the pieces are not sticking to one another and that they are coated evenly.

Heat the combined oils over a medium flame until very hot, shimmering but not smoking. Use a small fleck of flour to test: If it turns immediately brown in the oil when tossed in, the oil is properly heated. When the oil is ready, gently place the calamari in the oil, dropping them in piece by piece so they don't stick together and tilting the skillet as necessary to cover all the pieces with oil. Fry until golden brown, 3 to 4 minutes. Remove with a slotted spoon or tongs and spread out on paper towels to dry. Salt immediately, using ⅓ teaspoon or to taste.

Repeat with the second and third batches. Salt each batch immediately as it is removed from the oil. Let cool for a few minutes and serve.

WINE RECOMMENDATION: Ligurian vermentino or pigato is a no-brainer choice here. Good producers include Colle dei Bardellini, Giuncheo, A Maccia, and Enoteca Bisson.

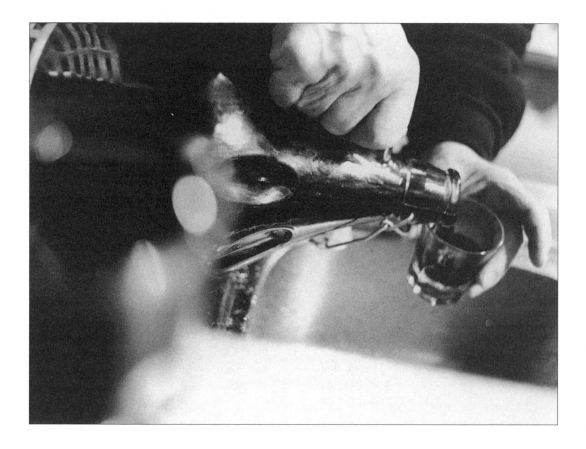

Emilia-Romagna

ITALY'S HEARTLAND

THE WAITING GAME

With his lumbering gait and deliberate, soft-spoken manner, Marco Picci seems the perfect personality type to produce Aceto Balsamico Tradizionale. True aged balsamic vinegars, such as those made at his family's small *acetaia* near Reggio Emilia, are the province of the patient. More impetuous sorts are advised to stick with winemaking, which, relatively speaking, offers a much faster return on your investment and effort.

Reggio Emilia is one of the famous food towns on the ancient Roman trade route known as the Via Emilia, which runs from Piacenza, near the border with Lombardy, all the way down to the Adriatic resort of Rimini. Reggio is better known as the home of Parmigiano-Reggiano cheese, and Reggio's vinegar production is eclipsed by that of Modena to the east. But Reggio has a small community of commercial *aceto* producers who make about twenty thousand three-ounce bottles of *tradizionale* per year. Most of these bottles will be sold locally; only about six of Reggio's producers, Picci among them, are large enough to consider exporting.

"This is something that everyone here does," Marco says, as he plods up the stairs to the Picci *acetaia*, which occupies the second and third floors of a family home. What was once the kitchen is outfitted with three stainless-steel fermenters, each of which holds about a hundred gallons, and some laboratory equipment set on the countertop. Two adjacent rooms—what were once a living and dining area—are filled with rows of weathered wood barrels, arranged in *batterie* (batteries) of five. Another loft in the attic houses more barrels, all of which are sealed with a square of canvas fixed in place with a wooden stopper. The walls are decorated with old tools and the windows are draped with lacy farmhouse-style curtains, making the place look a little like a museum. It's not yet harvest time for the trebbiano grapes growing in the backyard, so there isn't much to do other than gawk at the tidy rows of barrels and breathe in the heady smell. Marco flashes a world-weary grin and says, "As you can see, this is a very exciting business."

But to call this a business is a bit of a stretch. While some of Picci's elaborate, wax-sealed cruets of *aceto* make it as far as Williams-Sonoma, this is more a hobby than an enterprise. Touring the Picci *acetaia* is like being in your grandfather's workshop, where it looks as if not one thing has moved for several decades.

The DOC Zones of Emilia-Romagna

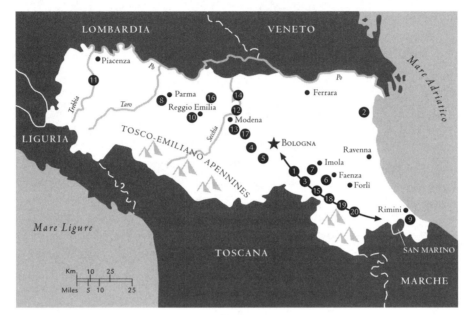

DOCG

1 Albana di Romagna

DOC

2 Bosco Eliceo
3 Cagnina di Romagna
4 Colli Bolognesi
5 Colli Bolognese Classico Pignoletto
6 Colli di Faenza
7 Colli di Imola
8 Colli di Parma
9 Colli di Rimini
10 Colli di Scandiano e di Canossa
11 Colli Piacentini
12 Lambrusco di Sorbara
13 Lambrusco Grasparossa di Castelvetro
14 Lambrusco Salamino di Santa Croce
15 Pagadebit di Romagna
16 Reggiano
17 Reno
18 Romagna Albana Spumante
19 Sangiovese di Romagna
20 Trebbiano di Romagna

Marco's father started the business more than twenty-five years ago, but some of the liquid in these barrels is older than that.

"There are maybe eighty commercial producers in Reggio," Marco offers. "But that doesn't include all the people who make their own and circulate it within their families." The Piccis are restaurateurs, giving them a place to showcase their *aceti*, and they are of course proud of their preciously packaged creations. But Marco doesn't describe the *acetaia* like he's the proprietor of a business: There is no talk of expanding production, and the sense is that his American importers found him, not the other way around. "In Modena there are large firms, but they aren't making *aceto tradizionale*. Even in Modena the *tradizionale* producers don't add up to much, maybe twice as much as in Reggio."

The only time the laconic Marco gets animated, in fact, is when he's describing the differences between an *aceto artigianale* (artisan vinegar) and an *aceto industriale* (mass-produced vinegar). Most balsamic vinegars, he says, carry the name Aceto Balsamico di Modena, which means only that they are wine vinegars produced in the area of Modena; usually, these are standard wine vinegars thickened with *saba*, cooked grape must, and colored with caramel, with no aging requirements. Another member of the balsamic family is a product called Condimento Alimentario, made in both Reggio and Modena, which is not an actual *aceto* but rather cooked grape must aged for a minimum of four years in wood. "Condimento is basically like *saba*, except aged," he notes. "It is used mostly in cooking."

Aceto Tradizionale di Reggio (or di Modena) is covered by a *Denominazione di Origine Controllata* (DOC) like those used for wines. It is subject to regulations on its production and on the origins of the wines used to make it. An *aceto tradizionale* starts as grape must, of course; most producers in Modena use the red lambrusco, while those in Reggio prefer the higher-acid white trebbiano. But before the grape musts for *aceto tradizionale* are fermented, they are first heated for forty hours, a process that reduces them to sugar-rich syrups. The cooked musts are then left to ferment throughout the winter, reaching an alcohol content of about 4 to 5 percent, after which they are transferred to barrels for aging. "We are starting with a superconcentrated wine, which becomes more concentrated and complex as it ages," Marco says. "The other way, you're just adding sugar."

A typical *batteria* is set up like a Sherry *solera*, and functions in much the same way. The barrels are arranged in groups of five that become progressively smaller, with the largest one holding about twenty-five gallons of liquid and the smallest ones often no bigger than a football. Long since sapped of their tannins and seasoned from repeated use, the old barrels enable the liquid inside to breathe through their creaky staves, so that the oxygen in the air turns the wine into vinegar by converting alcohol to acetic acid. The barrels are never filled to the top, so every year a portion of each is lost to evaporation. This requires that they all be "topped up" with vinegar from the barrel next in line, with newly produced wine going into the largest barrel at the end of the row. "You start a *batteria* by filling the smallest one first, then moving progressively up the line for four more years," Marco explains. "Then you start the topping up after that. When we bottle, we are taking from the smallest barrel, since it obviously contains the oldest liquid."

The different-size barrels have different effects on the *aceti* aging inside them: The smaller ones accelerate the aging process by putting more of the liquid's surface area in contact with wood—intensifying not only the flavoring from the wood but aiding the process of oxidation. Different types of wood are used to make the barrels, including oak ("more neutral, good for long aging," says Marco), chestnut ("good for color"), and more exotic varieties such as cherry and juniper ("good for perfume"). In all, the Aceto Balsamico Tradizionale DOC requires a minimum of twelve years' aging, and twenty-four for products labeled *extra vecchio*.

As Marco notes, "It takes a hundred liters of grape must to make two liters of *aceto tradizionale*." So even at a hundred dollars an ounce, this stuff is not very profitable. This in turn begs the question: Why bother?

Marco has taken a seat at a table among the *batterie*, methodically chunking Parmigiano while explaining the vinegar-making process. He drizzles some twelve-year-old *tradizionale* over the cheese and slides the plate across the table. The salty, nutty cheese and the sweet, almost chocolatey *aceto* clash at first, throwing off sparks of contrasting flavor. But then they fuse into an intense, creamy whole. Marco is matter-of-fact about the whole thing, devoid of the bluster that makes a lot of *artigiani* difficult to be around. His "business" seems a happy byproduct of something that he would have done anyway, so the question of why just hangs in the air with the vapors. In a place where you can collaterize a bank loan with wheels of Parmigiano, what's so unusual about waiting a few decades for something to pour on top?

The Via Emilia, known less poetically as the SS9, not only runs the length of Emilia-Romagna but effectively divides it in two. To the north, the humid Padana plain ambles toward the Po River, which forms most of the border between Emilia-Romagna and its northern neighbors, Lombardy and Veneto. To the south are the Apennines, of which Emilia-Romagna has a longer stretch than any other Italian region. It is surprising, in fact, to see how mountainous Emilia-Romagna actually is, given how closely the region is associated with the Po and its incredibly fertile flatlands.

As its hyphenated name suggests, Emilia-Romagna was once two regions. Historically, the eastern half, which runs from Bologna to the Adriatic, was fully integrated into the Roman Empire (thus the name Romagna); the western half was only colonized by the Romans, and was later a loose conglomeration of city-states. What pulled the two pieces together were the Via Emilia (named for the Roman Emperor who built it) and the Po, and all of the trade those two arteries supported.

Emilia-Romagna is often referred to as the most abundant of Italy's regions—the fount of the best *prosciutti*, *salumi* (cold cuts), and *salsicce* (sausages), the best cheeses, the best wheat for bread and pasta, and so many fruits and vegetables that it truly wants for nothing. What aren't mentioned as often, or at least not in the same breath as the foods, are the wines. They are a scattered, highly variable lot, many of them sweet or fizzy, and however good they may in fact be with a plate of prosciutto or a hunk of Parmigiano, they have long since been passed over by "serious" wine drinkers. Although Emilia-Romagna produces a substantial percentage of DOC-classified wines, its wines fall overwhelmingly in the light-and-quaffable category. In fact, the region may be the best example of all of the shortcomings of the DOC system.

Put simply, Emilia-Romagna is Italy's farm-stead, and its best-known wine—Lambrusco—is Italy's farmstead wine (in theory, at least). Lambrusco, like the fizzy moscato of Asti, is a remnant of the winemaking of centuries past, when wine fermented naturally. Depending on the whims of the winter weather, Lambrusco may have fermented all the way to dryness, or stopped with some residual sugar still in solution, and when it warmed up in the spring it may well have started bubbling again in the bottle. Modern-day *frizzante* is obviously produced in a more controlled manner, in industrial-scale quantities, but the fundamental style of the wine is the same.

Visit a *caseificio* (cheese factory) in Reggio and you'll learn that one of the things that distinguishes Parmigiano-Reggiano is that it is *alive:* The enzymes used to coagulate the milk continue to work even after the cheese is a solid round, lending complexity to the cheese as it ages. Lambrusco is alive, too, along with most of Emilia-Romagna's other whites and reds: Nearly all of the region's twenty DOCs include provisions to make wine *vivace* (literally "lively," in this case meaning slightly fizzy, or *frizzante*). The sweet, bubbly Riunite Lambrusco, far and away the dominant Italian wine brand of the seventies and early eighties (and still no slouch), may not be a great wine but it is not a marketing gimmick, either (well, at least the traditional Lambrusco isn't). Lambrusco, in fact, is believed to be one of Italy's oldest grape varieties, an ancient *vitis silvestris* (wild vine) that was likely domesticated by the Etruscans.

Nevertheless, Lambrusco—especially the sweeter styles—may be a piece of vinous history you'd just as soon forget. Fair enough. Even the locals will admit that the wines of Emilia's plains are meant to be fun and functional, their bubbles not only festive but helpful in the digestion of an exceptionally rich cuisine. Only recently have some wines taken on the *artigianale* cachet of a Parmigiano-Reggiano or an *aceto tradizionale.* Although Emilia's heartland is still a river of fizz, a trickle of serious still wine is springing from the Apennine foothills along the southern border. As with everything else, the region has choice hillside vineyards in abundance; all it needs, it seems, is more time to better exploit them.

VINI SPUMANTI E DOLCI
Sparkling and Sweet Wines

Without question, the most unique feature of Emilia-Romagna's wine is how much of it is either *frizzante* (semisparkling), *spumante* (sparkling), *amabile* (semisweet), *dolce* (sweet), or some combination of all of the above. Although Lambrusco *amabile* has roots in antiquity, it wasn't until Americans and Germans went crazy for it in the seventies that it took on any commercial significance. Made by an array of mostly large-scale co-ops—including Riunite, which is not just a co-op but a consortium of several co-ops—the sweet and fizzy style of Lambrusco has obscured the more appealing (and more locally favored) dry version, particularly the type made in the traditional way, with a secondary fermentation carried out in the bottle. The subtle dried-cherry flavors and crisp acidity of a Lambrusco *secco* is a perfect partner to a plate of thinly sliced prosciutto, whereas the sappy, sodalike quality of the sweet stuff makes it more of a confection than a wine. Neither style of Lambrusco is a wine for aging, but when placed alongside a huge plate of fresh pasta, even an *amabile* has its place.

The rules governing Lambrusco production are wide-ranging. There are currently four Lambrusco DOCs in Emilia-Romagna, whose production disciplines allow for both red and *rosato* (rosé) versions of the wines, which in turn can be either *secco, amabile,* or *dolce,* but always *frizzante.* Further, some Lambrusco is vinified *in bianco* ("as a white," meaning without skin contact) to produce Lambrusco Bianco Spumante, a dry, fully sparkling white.

The vineyards that produce these wines are concentrated in the broad Emilian plains north of Reggio and Modena, where myriad subvarieties of the lambrusco grape grow in the rich, alluvial soils. Among these are lambrusco sorbara, named for the commune north of Modena of the same name; lambrusco grasparossa ("red stalks"), found mostly to the south of Modena; and lambrusco salamino, so named for its salami-shaped grape bunches. Each of these three varieties has its own DOC production zone, with Lambrusco Grasparosso di Castelvetro thought to produce the most full-bodied wines and the Lambrusco di Sorbara DOC noted for more elegant styles. Of the four Lambrusco DOCs, however, the quantity leader is Lambrusco Reggiano, propelled by Riunite and its *amabile.* For better or worse, this is what most consumers know Lambrusco to be.

It's probably worse for small private producers in Reggio such as Ermete Medici, whose "Concerto" Lambrusco Reggiano is an example of how refreshing and flavorful a good dry version of the wine can be, and Vittorio Graziano, whose rustic Lambrusco di Grasparossa is one of the classic examples of a dry yet full-bodied style. Also worth look-

ing for are the wines of larger houses such as Cavicchioli, known for dry Lambrusco di Sorbara and Grasparossa, and Rinaldini, which specializes in *bianco spumante* made in the classic Champagne method.

And Lambrusco is not the only wine in Emilia-Romagna that bubbles. Many producers, including Medici, create interesting *frizzanti* and *spumanti* from the malvasia grape as well. In the Colli Piacentini, the broad swath of Apennine foothills south of Piacenza, the steep slopes of the Tidone, Trebbia, Arda, and Nure river valleys are becoming known for delicate *méthode champenoise* sparklers made from pinot noir and chardonnay. Dry and sweet *spumanti* are also made from the trebbiano and albana grapes of Romagna.

In fact, one thing sure to elicit at least a snicker and usually a sneer from wine producers is the mention of Albana di Romagna's elevation to DOCG status in 1987. Seen mainly as a political response to pressure from Romagna's wine producers, the Albana di Romagna DOCG is much maligned, mainly because the albana grape in its pure state is not especially interesting. As a dry wine it is sour and chalky, good for some shellfish after a day on the beach in Rimini. Only a handful of producers even bother with *secco* versions of the wine, leaving others to lament the dilution of DOCG's impact.

On the other hand, the high natural acidity of albana serves it well when it is put through the process of drying, or *appassimento,* to concentrate its flavors. Where Albana di Romagna Secco is a simple, faintly fragrant white, Albana di Romagna Passito fairly explodes with flavors of quince, citrus fruits, and apricots, with a bracing dose of acid on the finish to lift up the flavors and keep the wine from going flabby.

Along with some of the *passiti* made from malvasia in the Colli Piacentini, Albana Passito has the benefit of being both sweet and refreshing, especially as interpreted by producers such as Fattoria Zerbina in Faenza, Fattoria Paradiso in Bertinoro, and Umberto Cesari in Castel San Pietro Terme. Check out Zerbina's "Scacco Matto," or Paradiso's "Gradisco" Albana di Romagna Passito for a taste of a grape transformed for the better by the hand of man.

VINI BIANCHI
White Wines

The dry whites of Emilia-Romagna—or the majority of them, anyway—fall into an anonymous mass of light, slightly sour sippers from semiaromatic grapes. Dry whites are produced within thirteen of the region's twenty DOC zones, some of them in great quantities, and yet the amount of bottled white wine seems relatively scarce.

In Romagna's half of the region, vineyards planted with trebbiano, albana, and pagadebit grapes spill down from the Apennine foothills and spread out onto the plains north of the Via Emilia. Based on the scarce availability of even trebbiano di Romagna, the most-planted variety in the region, it's clear that most of these grapes, especially those on the hot, fertile plain, are being turned into light, innocuous bulk wine to be drunk on tap along the nearby Adriatic. There are some three and a half million gallons of Trebbiano di Romagna produced each year, but even the most extensive wine guides list only a handful of producers who actually bottle wine from the variety. At present the standards in Trebbiano di Romagna

are set by producers such as Umberto Cesari (not to be confused with the Cesari winery in neighboring Veneto) and Tre Monti, although they tend to be fairly simple standards.

Ditto for the wines from the other special gapes of Romagna: pagadebit (the local name for bombino bianco, which is also found in Puglia) and albana. The supervigorous pagadebit, which prefers the more calcareous clays of the hills around Bertinoro and other places south of the Via Emilia, has a piercing acidity and a mouthwatering chalkiness that makes it a good wine for the *zuppe di pesce* (fish soups) of the nearby Adriatic. As for Albana di Romagna, there are some palatable versions of *secco* being made by Tre Monti, Leone Conti, Celli, and Stefano Ferrucci, but, unlike the *passito* versions, they tend not to be worth searching too hard for.

To the west, in Emilia's hills, the dry white scene is even more of a hodgepodge. In the high-altitude vineyards of the Colli Bolognesi, producers are having some success with both chardonnay and sauvignon blanc, which seem to be edging out the tart, limey local variety called pignoletto. The cool slopes of the Colli Piacentini are also proving hospitable to chardonnay and sauvignon, as Apennine mountain currents sweep through the vineyards to refresh the vines and keep the withering heat of the nearby plains in check. Sauvignon in particular shows its fruity side in the calcareous clays of the Colli Piacentini, as does the equally aromatic malvasia bianca, which is used in both dry and sweet wines. As in the neighboring Oltrepò Pavese region of Lombardy, to which it is often compared, the Colli Piacentini DOC is emerging as a zone especially well-suited to aromatic varieties—white and red—because of its interplay of hot and cool. The whites of the

La Stoppa and La Tosa estates are some of the better examples of the area's potential, although there are many others.

VINI ROSSI
Red Wines

It is possible, according to some researchers, that the beloved sangiovese grape of Tuscany actually cropped up first somewhere in Romagna. Academics such as Attilio Scienza, an enology professor at the University of Milan, are fairly certain that sangiovese, like lambrusco, was a *vitis silvestris* native to the Italian peninsula, rather than one of the many varieties brought as seed by the ancient Greeks. The question is, where was it discovered first? There's now little doubt that the Tosco-Emiliano Apennines are the original territory of the vine, but what was the pattern of its migration? The Romagnoli contend that it started on their side, the Tuscans the opposite.

Some theories on the origins of the name sangiovese contend that it was derived from *sangue dai gioghetti* ("blood of the ridges"), in reference to a blood-red wine grown on a rounded peak or ridge (or *giògo*, a word derived from the Romagnan word *jugum*). Another theory says that sangiovese means "blood of Jove," in reference to rural holy days sacred to Jove. But it seems just as plausible that it could mean "blood of Giove," in reference to Monte Giove near Rimini in Romagna.

The thing to take from all this is that sangiovese has a long history in Romagna's hills, its prime territory being south of the Via Emilia, from Bologna to the Adriatic. Yet sangiovese di Romagna lags behind the other sangioveses of Italy in recognition. Generally speaking, the Romagnan sangiovese is a plumper, rounder, juicier one, with a solid core of black-cherry fruit but generally softer tannins and acidity than its counterparts across the Apennines. This may owe to the more pronounced maritime influence in key Sangiovese di Romagna towns such as Bertinoro, which are within eyeshot of the Adriatic. Or it may simply be the character of the sangiovese di Romagna clone, which most producers contend is distinct from Tuscany's prugnolos, brunellos, and so forth. In any case, the Sangiovese di Romagna DOC has been the region's best shot so far at something more than just fizzy and fun.

"From where we are, it's only twenty kilometers to the border of Tuscany," explains Claudio Fiore, the young manager of the Castelluccio winery in Modigliana, one of the top producers of sangiovese in Romagna (but not all of Castelluccio's wines carry the DOC designation). At a perch of more than fourteen hundred feet, looking north to Faenza and south to the bulk of the Apennines, the Castelluccio estate epitomizes the Emilia-Romagnan winemaking culture south of the Via Emilia, where the altitudes are every bit as high (if not higher) than Chianti, and the scenery every bit as foresty. A single two-lane road crisscrosses the hills that tumble down from Modigliana to Faenza and Forlì, where the landscape abruptly flattens out and the humidity settles like cake frosting.

"On any given day, there are five to six degrees of temperature difference between here and Faenza, which is only a few kilometers away," explains Fiore, who is the son of Vittorio Fiore, a well-traveled winemaking consultant. Vittorio had originally purchased Castelluccio with a partner, a journalist and film director named Gianvittorio Baldi. But the Fiore family bought a majority stake in the winery in 1991, since Vittorio—who has consulted to a wide variety of top Tuscan sangiovese producers—felt that something special could be done with the sangiovese variety in Modigliana.

In the hills that run inland from Cesena, which sits less than twenty kilometers from the Adriatic, sangiovese changes with the landscape. The lower-lying, more marine-influenced sites tend to produce broader, more diffuse, more fruit-forward styles; as you climb up and in they take on a bigger, more brooding tannic structure. Castelluccio's wines, from twelve hectares of steep-sloping vineyards above Modigliana, have more in common with Chianti Classico than they do with their Romagnan counterparts in the plains, with perfumy scents of black cherry and tar and a gripping sensation on the palate. Over in the slightly lower-lying Bertinoro, the Fattoria Paradiso estate extracts a little more fruit richness from its Sangiovese di Romagna "Vigna delle Lepri." Down in Faenza, the Fattoria Zerbina has won fans with a sappy sangiovese–cabernet sauvignon blend called "Marzieno."

"People think of Romagna's viticulture as the viticulture of the plains. But the reality is that we probably couldn't get cabernet sauvignon ripe up here," says Carlo Fiore. "But they can as close by as Faenza. This area has a diversity of soils and microclimates that we're only now beginning to utilize properly."

Indeed, in tasting through a series of Sangiovese di Romagna wines, you're likely to find wide variations in style. But there's a clear movement toward greater concentration in the wines. As more producers experiment with grapes such as cabernet sauvignon and syrah, Romagna is becoming a source of some super-charged, "new world" style reds. One of the best known is "Magnificat," a pure cabernet made by the Tenuta La Palazza in Forlì. And there are a growing number of other reds from Romagna that remain relatively unknown—and well-priced as a result. The Castelluccio wines head the list, but other names to look out for include Tre Monti, Poderi del Nespoli, Stefano Ferrucci, and Umberto Cesari.

The other two hot spots for red winemaking in Emilia-Romagna lie along the Apennine spine farther inland: the Colli Bolognesi, centered on the communes of Sasso Marconi and Monte San Pietro southwest of Bologna; and the Colli Piacentini, the broad band of western hills that gives way to Lombardy's Oltrepò Pavese. And more so than in Romagna, producers have turned largely to nontraditional grape varieties to capture the consumer's attention.

In the Colli Bolognesi, producers such as Tenuta Bonzara and Vallona have made a name for Emilia-Romagna's cabernet sauvignon. In the more continental climate of Bologna's hills, the grape enjoys a long growing season in mostly calcareous clay soils, with harvest often pushed back until November. Cabernet in cooler, damper vintages can take on a slightly herbaceous character in the Colli Bolognesi, not unlike many of the cabernet wines grown farther north in the Veneto and Alto Adige. At altitudes topping fifteen hundred feet, estates such as Bonzara—whose "Bonzarone" Cabernet Sauvignon may be the best-known Colli Bolognesi red—actually struggle to get cabernet ripe, since temperatures never get very high. The fertility so prized in the plains is unheard of up here, which in a warm, dry vintage works to the benefit of the wines. They do not have the depth and concentration of some of their better-known Tuscan counterparts, but the cabernets of the Colli Bolognesi, like the white sauvignon, have a more aromatic, balanced quality that makes them food-friendly. They are serious wines, but they also have that Emilian sense of fun.

In the Colli Piacentini, the traditional preference for reds from bonarda (a local synonym for croatina) and barbera mirrors that of the neighboring Oltrepò Pavese of Lombardia. In both regions, the shift in recent years has been toward pinot noir and cabernet sauvignon. The same cool breezes that cure the hams of nearby Parma are at work in the Colli Piacentini vineyards. So even in the traditional local DOC red, Gutturnio (a barbera-bonarda blend),

there's a depth of concentration and color that's difficult to accomplish in the vineyards of the plains, where the grapes ripen much faster, resulting in jammy and soft wines. As Colli Piacentini producers such as La Stoppa and La Tosa continue to experiment successfully with both cabernet sauvignon and pinot noir, there is more and more seriously fun red wine coming out of the region. You can debate whether a full-bodied cabernet or a fizzy Lambrusco *secco* is the right choice for a hearty *ragù bolognese*, but it might not be a fair fight: Even the *Emiliani* might agree that it's time to move on to the bigger red, of which there are more and more available.

FAST FACTS: $\mathcal{E}$MILIA-$\mathcal{R}$OMAGNA

PROVINCES	Bologna (BO), Ferrara (FE), Forlì (FO), Modena (MO), Parma (PR), Piacenza (PC), Ravenna (RA), Reggio Emilia (RE)
CAPITAL	Bologna
KEY WINE TOWNS	Bertinoro, Bologna, Forlì, Modena, Piacenza, Reggio Emilia.
TOTAL VINEYARD AREA*	58,237 hectares, or 143,904 acres. Rank: 5th
TOTAL WINE PRODUCTION*	4,733,000 hectoliters, or 125,046,235 gallons (4th); 43% white; 57% red
DOC WINE PRODUCED*	21.4% (9th)
SPECIALTY FOODS	Parmigiano-Reggiano; Prosciutto di Parma; Aceto Balsamico Tradizionale di Modena/Reggio; dried and fresh pastas; strawberries; breads.

*1997 figures. Rankings out of twenty regions total (Trentino–Alto Adige counted as one). Source: Istituto Statistica Mercati Agro-Alimentari (ISMEA), Rome.

KEY GRAPE VARIETIES

WHITES:

ALBANA	A light-bodied, high-acid white native to Romagna. Simple and light when vinified as a dry wine, it takes on rich notes of apricot and honey when dried and made into Albana Passito.
MALVASIA	Aromatic white found throughout Italy, here used in still, sparkling, and sweet whites in the hills of Piacenza and Parma.
PIGNOLETTO	Limey, tart white grape found principally in the Colli Bolognesi, southwest of Bologna, as well as in other DOCs in both Emilia (Reno) and Romagna (Colli d'Imola and Colli di Rimini).

TREBBIANO	The most-planted white grape of Romagna, used in light, soft dry whites and in a variety of *frizzante, spumante,* and *dolce* variations.
OTHER WHITES	CHARDONNAY; ORTRUGO, native to Colli Piacentini; SAUVIGNON BLANC.
	REDS
SANGIOVESE	Possibly of Romagnan origin, it is more famous in Tuscany but makes distinctive wines throughout the Apennine foothills from Bologna to Rimini.
BONARDA	Name used for the croatina grape in the Colli Piacentini and in the Oltrepò Pavese zone in neighboring Lombardy. The true bonarda is said to be from Piedmont. Makes plump, deeply colored reds.
BARBERA	Often blended with bonarda in the Colli Piacentini, or used on its own to make a hearty red.
CABERNET SAUVIGNON	Gaining in popularity all along Emilia-Romagna's Apennine spine, from the Colli Piacentini and Colli Bolognesi to the hills of Romagna. The elongated growing seasons in these hills build good concentration into the grapes.

TOP VINTAGES IN EMILIA-ROMAGNA, 1980 TO 2000

Only in recent years have Emilia-Romagna's vintners turned out red wines that merit more than a few years' aging. When picking up a top-level Sangiovese di Romagna, Colli Bolognesi Cabernet, or maybe one of the region's IGT or VdT bottlings (such as Tenuta La Palazza's "Magnificat" Cabernet Sauvignon), the years 1995 through '99 are all worth a look ('97 in particular).

LA STRADA DEL VINO
WINE TOURING IN EMILIA-ROMAGNA

One of Emilia-Romagna's claims to fame is the organization of its wine routes. The various *consorzi* of wine producers in the different regions are known for being especially tourist-friendly, and there are a number of regional *enoteche* in which to sample the local wines. The king of them all is the Enoteca Regionale Emilia-Romagna in the hilltop town of Dozza, about a half-hour east of Bologna on the Via Emilia. Here you can sample just about any wine from Emilia-Romagna you can think of (although the emphasis in on the Romagna's producers) in the basement of a medieval castle. In Bologna check out the tiny Drogheria Della Rosa (Via Cartoleria 10; tel: 051-22-25-29), a former drugstore that now houses a small restaurant with one of the better wine lists in the city.

Bologna, of course, is one of the great food towns in a country loaded with great food towns, but two other excellent restaurants to try are Battibecco (Via Battibecco 4; 051-22-32-98), a fine interpreter of *la cucina emiliana* right in the city center, and La Pernice e La Gallina (Via dell'Abbadia 4; 051-26-99-22), known for its selection of regional pork products. For the prosciutto-phile, Bologna's great *gastronomia* (specialty food shop) called Tamburini (Via Caprarie 1; 051-23-47-26) is a day trip in itself, while in Modena the mecca of pork is the Salumeria Giusti (Vicolo Squallore 46; 059-22-25-33). One non-food related excursion would be a trip to Stefano Branchini's *calzoleria* (shoe store) on the Via Castiglione in Bologna. Branchini custom-makes shoes and clothes in an ultra-modern Italian style. The shoes—big, bold, hand-stiched styles with thick, angular soles—are definitely not for everyone, but at a minimum the well-appointed shop is worth a look.

DEGUSTAZIONI
TASTINGS

LAMBRUSCO

Riunite Lambrusco, $

Ermete Medici "Concerto" Lambrusco Reggiano Secco, $

Where the first wine is concerned, don't knock it till you've tried it: Though the off-dry taste and sappy fruit may be a little cloying for some, it's not hard to imagine enjoying the Riunite wine with a slight chill alongside a plate of Prosciutto di Parma. Still, the more appealing wine of the two is the Medici, which is not only a dry style but a well-balanced, savory one at that. The dried-cherry flavor, crisp acidity, and slight fizz whet the appetite for a bite of cheese, a nibble of ham, a forkload of pasta, something. With a light chill at a summer picnic, neither would be a bad choice—be the first on your block to make Lambrusco trendy again.

ALBANA PASSITO

Fattoria Paradiso Albana Passito "Gradisca," $$

Fattoria Zerbina Albana Passito "Scacco Matto," $$

With their scents of apricots, wild honey, and nuts, these wines have unctuous flavors and textures that are cleaned up by a whisk of acidity on the finish. Of the two, you'll probably find the "Gradisca" to be more concentrated. Their nectarlike qualities make them a natural accompaniment to biscotti and chestnut tortes, but don't hesitate to contrast sweet with savory by pairing these wines with a hunk of salty cheese.

SANGIOVESE DI ROMAGNA

Castelluccio Sangiovese "Ronco delle Ginestre," $$

Tre Monti Sangiovese di Romagna "Thea," $

Here are two smoky, savory examples of Romagna's sangiovese, the Castelluccio a little more angular and perfumed, the Tre Monti a little chunkier and jammy. This may be a function of the relative positioning of the wineries in Romagna's hills (Castelluccio lies at a much higher altitude), or it may be a simple divergence in winemaking style. Either way, these reds exhibit the classic black cherry aromas and foresty flavors of sangiovese, and present them in an accessible package. Try them with hearty pastas such as *pappardelle bolognese,* where the crisp acidity of the wines will stand up to the fatty, meaty ragù.

La Stoppa Colli Piacentini Cabernet Sauvignon "Stoppa," $$

Tenuta Bonzara Colli Bolognesi Cabernet Sauvignon "Bonzarone," $$

Drei Donà Tenuta La Palazza Cabernet Sauvignon "Magnificat," $$$

CABERNETS OF THE COLLI

Cabernet's sweet, cassis-scented fruitiness is on display in all three of these wines, which are arranged from lightest-bodied to fullest. The La Stoppa wine has a certain pepperiness typical of many northern-Italian cabernets, while the Bonzara wine has a similarly savory note under a richer layer of blackberry fruit. The Tenuta La Palazza wine is a cabernet to take on some of the "super-Tuscans," with its inky density of color and flavor. The tannins of all three wines are fairly soft, making them approachable as young wines. Also worth looking for is the sangiovese-cabernet blend called "Marzieno" from Fattoria Zerbina, a wine with a dense, inky personality of its own. Hearty baked pastas and braised meats are the way to go here.

La Cucina
FOOD FOR THE WINE

Preparing a recipe is one thing. Understanding technique is another. Both are critical to the Italian food experience, especially in places such as Emilia-Romagna, where artisanal foods are held to such rarefied standards that there are very specific ways to treat (and eat) them.

Emilia-Romagna's specialties, such as Parmigiano-Reggiano, Prosciutto di Parma, and Aceto Balsamico Tradizionale are products of national pride. But often the "right product," *il prodotto giusto,* can be ruined by poor technique. It's not enough to have the right goods. You must have the proper tools and technique. This means that Parmigiano must be chunked with a special Parmigiano knife, which looks a little like a martial-arts weapon. Prosciutto must be sliced paper-thin on an antique slicer or surgically sliced *a mano* (by hand) with the proper knife. Once you've mastered the technique, it's the details that separate the men from the boys. Are you serving spring- or fall-milk parmigiano? Is your prosciutto eighteen, twenty-four, or thirty-six months old? As with wine, the nuances of different food products are dissected and debated to the point of distraction.

The specialty foods of Emilia-Romagna don't need to be incorporated into recipes. They have enough flavor and complexity to stand on their own. But there is an art (and, to some degree, a science) to presenting these products that goes well beyond opening a plastic deli bag and spreading the stuff on a plate. What follows is not a recipe, per se, but rather a stylized *presentation* of Emilia-Romagnan delicacies. No self-respecting wine sophisticate would eat these foods any other way.

Antipasto Emiliano-Romagnolo

½ pound thinly sliced PROSCIUTTO DI PARMA

1 package ITALIAN GRISSINI BREADSTICKS

1½-inch round imported ITALIAN MORTADELLA

1 piece fresh HORSERADISH

2- to 3-pound wedge PARMIGIANO-REGGIANO

1 bottle of the oldest ACETO BALSAMICO TRADIZIONALE your budget will permit

FOR THE PROSCIUTTO

A simple enough concept: Go to a good deli, Italian specialty store, or gourmet retailer. Speak to the man at the deli counter. Ask him for the name of the producer of Prosciutto di Parma he carries. Prosciutto di Parma is a consortium of different producers that maintains certain standards and quality guidelines. The quality among various producers within the consortium may vary. One of the best producers is Galloni, whose hams can be found fairly easily in the States

If the shop does not have a manual slicer, ask the deli man to cut the prosciutto extra thin and to lay it evenly on wax paper. The key is to buy it as close as you can to the time that you will be serving it. Prosciutto di Parma should be rose-red in color with a solid band of fat about an inch thick surrounding each piece of meat. Some people remove the fat. This is wrong. Those who do should be severely scolded and perhaps given a backhand across the head. The balance of the sweet meat and the luscious texture of the salty fat is the magic of Prosciutto di Parma. Simply wrap the slices of prosciutto around the edge of the grissini, covering about the last two inches of the breadstick. Fan them out on a plate and serve.

GRILLED MORTADELLA WITH FRESH HORSERADISH

Mortadella is way of life. Once you are hooked, there is no turning back: You begin to research every conceivable way of enjoying this Emilian specialty of slowly cooked pork meat, salt, and fat. Mortadellas come in all conceivable sizes, yet always have a cylindrical, zeppelin-like shape. For large festivals and momentous occasions, mortadellas can be made up to eight feet long and resemble pink nuclear warheads. The mortadella sandwiches at the Vinitaly wine fair in Verona are mythical, and many a wine geek in training has proclaimed on his first visit to the mecca of Italian wine that these sobering morsels are worth the trip over.

Approach your deli man again and ask him if his mortadella is imported from Italy. Imports have only been allowed recently, and many people may not be aware of current developments in Italian pork-product importation. Once you're pretty sure you're getting the real McCoy, ask the deli man to cut you a ring about an inch and a half thick. This will eventually yield about 35 or so 1-inch to inch-and-a-half cubes.

When you are ready to prepare, remove the outside skin from around the edge of the mortadella and place the round on a hot grill. (If you don't have a grill, a stovetop cast-iron skillet will do.) Cook on each side for about 4 minutes or until you achieve some nice grill marks and caramelization. The concept here is not to cook the mortadella through, but to create a contrast between the traditional mortadella flavor in the interior and the new flavor created by cooking the outside.

Once cooked, place the round of mortadella on a cutting board, and with a chef's knife proceed to cut it first vertically, and then horizontally in 1-inch increments. Place the cut warm cubes on a plate, stick some toothpicks into them, then generously grate fresh horseradish over them using the coarsest side of your box grater.

PARMIGIANO-REGGIANO WITH ACETO BALSAMICO TRADIZIONALE

Parmigiano-Reggiano is the king of all cheese. These fifty-pound forms are made from the milk of selected cows grazing in selected pastures during selected times of year. The most intriguing aspect of Parmigiano-Reggiano is the subtle variation within the product. Although all wheels must age a minimum of 18 to 20 months, some people prefer to eat them in their youth while others store different vintages of Parmigiano in their cheese caves like bottles of the finest Barolo and refer to particular aspects of a vintage as they would a wine. Some aficionados favor Parmigiano-Reggiano made with spring milk, noting the presence of clover and wildflowers in the aroma and flavor; others prefer fall-milk versions for a more lactic and luscious flavor.

If your cheese merchant is serious, he should also sell cheese knives. Ask for a medium-size Parmigiano chunking knife (it's not 100 percent essential, but your friends will be impressed when they see you chunking away). The technique is easy. From the side of the wedge, pry off pieces of cheese about the radius of a half dollar and about a half-inch in thickness. Don't chunk more than you will immediately consume. It's easier and more fun to keep the chunking going through the night, and makes for a tastier, creamier cheese. Place the remainder of the wedge and the pieces of Parmigiano on a cutting board with your knife proudly displayed. In a small, shallow glass bowl, pour out ½-teaspoon of your Aceto Tradizionale. Instruct your guests to dip a small corner of a piece of Parmigiano into the aceto. The complexity of these two powerful products consumed together is astounding.

There are 649 producers of Parmigiano in five official production zones. Zanetti is a top producer whose cheese is widely available in the States. If you're in New York City, visit DiPalo's Specialty Foods on Grand Street in Little Italy for the ultimate Parmigiano experience.

WINE RECOMMENDATION: For an authentic Emilian experience, consider a dry Lambrusco from an artisanal producer such as Ermete Medici. With the prosciutto in particular, the light dried-cherry flavors and slight sparkle of the wine are a perfect complement. Otherwise, a big sangiovese from Romagna will be a crowd pleaser.

Toscana

The Center of the Italian Wine Universe

—⁂—

Bushwacking in Bolgheri

Daniele is chewing on the remains of a cigar as he tramps through the Bolgheri woods, a battalion of hunters in fatigues trailing behind him. He is a gamekeeper at the Tenuta San Guido, and every Sunday from November through January he runs the *caccia al cinghiale*, or wild-boar hunt, at the estate. Tenuta San Guido is known to wine lovers as the home of Italy's first super-Tuscan wine, "Sassicaia." But only 150 of its 6,200 acres of land are vineyards; the rest is a vast nature preserve around Bolgheri, which Daniele and two partners are charged with maintaining.

Bolgheri is about a half-hour south of Livorno on Tuscany's Mediterranean coast, part of a band of maritime hills that stretches down past Grosseto. This area, known as the Maremma, may be Italy's most densely populated with *cinghiale*. They take refuge in the thick Mediterranean scrub, called *macchia*, or in the woods farther inland in Chianti and Montalcino, usually coming out only at night. Omnivorous and stealthy, they are known to like ripe wine grapes—in fact, vintners often lament that boars are true grape connoisseurs, choos-

ing only the best-quality fruit when they raid a vineyard. And of course their looks don't win them any sympathy: With those prehistoric faces, they're like mythic beasts come to destroy the village, even though all they really want is to be left alone.

Still, boar are mean when provoked and armed with those fearsome tusks, which can slice a dog from stem to stern. The *caccia al cinghiale* is often described as a war, and Daniele, with his three-day beard and Clint Eastwood stogie, fits his role perfectly: Like a grizzled sergeant heading into a firefight, he positions his hunters about twenty yards apart along a hillside trail. There are nearly thirty riflemen (*fucilieri*) in all—most of them older men, huffing and puffing as they try to keep up—lining up across the ridge like a firing squad. With his hawk's eyes Daniele glares at the new guys, explaining in no uncertain terms where they can and cannot shoot (should someone track a boar too far to his right or left, he could shoot the neighboring rifleman—not uncommon in the loosely regulated world of Italian boar-hunting).

On the other side of the crest, Daniele's friend Loris struggles through the thicket with six dogs, all of them howling and straining at their leashes. Loris is the head of the *bracchieri*, a group of about ten dog handlers whose job it

THE DOC ZONES OF TOSCANA

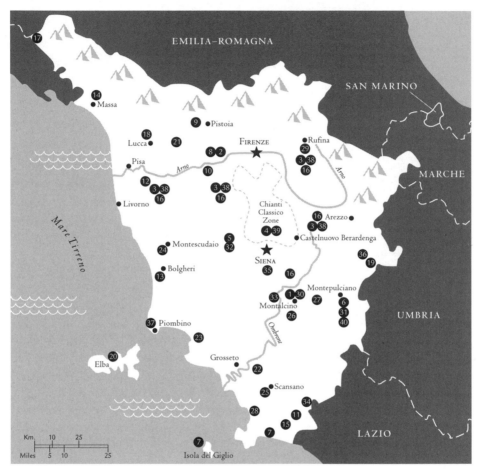

DOCG

1 Brunello di Montalcino
2 Carmignano
3 Chianti
4 Chianti Classico
5 Vernaccia di San Gimignano
6 Vino Nobile di Montepulciano

DOC

7 Ansonica Costa dell'Argentario
8 Barco Reale di Carmignano / Carmignano
9 Bianco della Valdinievole
10 Bianco dell'Empolese
11 Bianco di Pitigliano
12 Bianco Pisano di San Torpé
13 Bolgheri / Bolgheri Sassicaia
14 Candia di Colli Apuani
15 Capalbio
16 Colli dell'Etruria Centrale
17 Colli di Luni
18 Colline Lucchesi
19 Cortona
20 Elba
21 Montecarlo
22 Montecucco
23 Monteregio di Massa Marittima
24 Montescudaio
25 Morellino di Scansano
26 Moscadello di Montalcino
27 Orcia
28 Parrina
29 Pomino
30 Rosso di Montalcino
31 Rosso di Montepulciano
32 San Gimignano
33 Sant'Antimo
34 Sovana
35 Val d'Arbia
36 Valdichiana
37 Val di Cornia (also Val di Cornia Suvereto)
38 Vin Santo del Chianti
39 Vin Santo del Chianti Classico
40 Vin Santo di Montepulciano

is to flush the *cinghiale* in the direction of the firing squad. Stumbling along with a rifle on his back, walkie-talkie in one hand and dogs in the other, Loris curses and yanks hard on the leashes as he and his crew get into position.

When he's finally ready, Loris barks to Daniele over the speaker. At the sound of Daniele's horn from the other side, the *bracchieri* begin unchaining the dogs one by one. Loris exhorts each mutt like a boxing trainer, shouting *"Avanti!"* and *"Vai!"* and *"Attenti alla strada!"* and shooting birdshot into the air. The crazed dogs fan out in search of *cinghiali*, and for a moment the ridge becomes strangely calm.

Meanwhile, Marcello, the white-haired manager of the Sassicaia estate and one of the *fucilieri*, sits on a camp stool, his rifle in his lap. Surrounded by the fragrant *macchia*—a mix of holm and cork oaks, evergreens, juniper bushes, wild herbs—he listens to the commotion of the dogs off in the distance. At first the howls are diffuse, disorganized, but soon they concentrate, and then the roar is on the move and getting closer. Marcello hops up, aiming his rifle at a tiny clearing a few yards away, the racket of the dogs now right in front of him. He readies his gun, lowers it, then readies and lowers it again, in concert with the crescendos.

Twenty yards up the ridge, there's a rifle blast. Then another one. The barking subsides and the panting dogs squirt out of the brush, one of them bloodied from a tusk to the chest. After only about fifteen minutes of action, it's all over—and this is the last of three passes before lunch—so Marcello packs up and trudges up the path. Everyone assembles in a small clearing where the two dead *cinghiali* have been dragged, and it's at this point that the one-sidedness of the battle becomes clear: There are more than forty men and as many dogs, all

for two boar of about 120 pounds each. The only one who still looks like much of a warrior is Daniele, who hoists the bloodied boar into a small pickup truck.

At lunch, the hunters settle into a happy Tuscan domesticity, breaking out their packed pasta lunches and bottles of homemade wine. There are steaks on the grill, and hunks of pecorino sliced with big hunting knives. One of the *fucilieri*, a chain-smoker named Bacci, pulls back the tinfoil on his wife's "famous" chestnut torte, making his way around the tables like Martha Stewart. Of all the hunters' picnics in all the world, only an Italian one includes a five-minute debate on the type of flour used in a *castagnaccio*.

A hired hand begins to field-dress the two boar, both of which are males. He starts by disemboweling them, rather casually tossing their testicles into the bushes. "Aw, they shouldn't throw those away," remarks Alfio, one of the older men in the group—and also the most dapper in his corduroy car coat, green wool pants, and matching fedora. Only a few nod in agreement when Alfio refers to the testicles as *"molto delicati."*

The head, heart, and liver of a *cinghiale*, all of which are considered delicacies, are given to the hunter who shoots it. Alfio hooks the arm of one of the successful shooters—a tall, younger guy dressed head to toe in camouflage—and begins to explain the finer points of boar-head cookery: "It's not very big, so use a little more oil. Wash it good, and on the last wash use some red wine vinegar." The young guy seems only mildly interested.

"Bring it to my house and my wife'll do it," Alfio blurts. The camouflaged one laughs at this left-handed invitation. "You know what? Bring the liver, too."

Most people are content to have some spicy *cinghiale* salami or a *ragù di cinghiale* over polenta and forget about those grizzled snouts staring at them from the butcher-shop walls. But they certainly lend atmosphere to a region that has become the tourism capital of Italy. People these days would rather shop for porcini mushrooms in the hills of Chianti than walk through a *duomo,* or so it seems by the sounds of all those English and German voices in the wine-country restaurants.

No doubt part of the appeal is Tuscany's importance as a wine region. Some people rank the wines of Piedmont higher, but from a commercial standpoint, there's no comparison—Tuscany's brand recognition is far greater. Tuscany is Italy's Bordeaux, Piedmont its Burgundy: One is worldly and market-minded, the other more insular and scholarly. And both seem to like it that way.

Only Piedmont, in fact, outdoes Tuscany in enological complexity, with a whopping fifty DOC(G) zones to Tuscany's forty. Yet when you factor in the vast array of super-Tuscan wines with only a *nome di fantasia* (fantasy name) to identify them, Tuscany may ultimately take the prize as Most Confusing Region. In both cases, though, appearances can be deceiving.

As freighted as Tuscany is with history, geographic diversity, and an encyclopedic array of great wines, the region is nevertheless dominated by two grapes: the white trebbiano and the red sangiovese. They are the two most-planted varieties not just in Tuscany but in Italy as a whole, and they share a number of similarities: Both are believed to have been native wild vines that were domesticated by the Etruscans; both are large families of varieties and clones that cover a broad area (trebbiano is also diffuse in France, where it is known as

ugni blanc); and both can be used, in varying percentages, in thirty-one of Tuscany's forty DOC(G)-classified wines.

VINI BIANCHI
White Wines

Whereas sangiovese has become one of the world's great reds, trebbiano has mostly been an anonymous role player. Trebbiano-based wines are the ones sipped absentmindedly in Florentine *trattorie,* from the light table wine called *Galestro* to relatively unknown DOC whites like Montescudaio or Montecarlo. Italy's history as a pumping station for light white wines made trebbiano a favorite in the vineyard; it is incredibly productive, disease-resistant, and naturally high in acidity, giving the other fairly neutral whites a thirst-quenching crispness.

There are some good wines based on trebbiano—from the Montescudaio and Montecarlo DOCs in particular—though it is principally a blending grape. It offers little in the way of aroma or fruit extract and is generally eclipsed by more assertive varieties such as vermentino, sauvignon, and chardonnay. Trebbiano's best claim to legitimacy is its part in Vin Santo (see page 212), but even there it's regarded as an acidic second banana to malvasia.

Of course, Tuscan whites don't begin and end with trebbiano. The vernaccia of San Gimignano is another native grape with more star power, although that may have more to do with San Gimignano itself, a medieval village whose hilltop locale and lofty towers are a big tourist draw—there's also a museum devoted to medieval instruments of torture. The vernaccia grape (the name comes from the Latin word for "indigenous," which is why it is attached to unrelated grapes elsewhere in Italy) is more aromatic and structured than trebbiano, but it too falls on the lighter side of the white-wine spectrum.

Vernaccia is one of Tuscany's most historic wines, first cited in San Gimignano town records in the thirteenth century. It was also celebrated in literature, including poems by Dante and Francesco Redi, whose *Bacco in Toscana* (1685) lavished particular praise on it. The weight of all this history may have factored into Vernaccia di San Gimignano becoming Italy's first DOC in 1966, and to its subsequent elevation to DOCG in 1993—the latter despite the wine having become a fairly insipid, mass-produced product by the 1980s. At its best, vernaccia can be a floral, crisp white with a note of bitter almond on the finish. But for American drinkers it's hardly the big mouthful of fruit that a California chardonnay is. Most producers these days, including local giant Teruzzi & Puthod, add body and complexity by including chardonnay and vermentino in the mix; both play a big role in Teruzzi & Puthod's well-known "Terre di Tufi," although that wine is labeled as an IGT, not DOCG (the DOCG regulations permit only 10 percent of grapes other than vernaccia).

There are a number of other noteworthy vernaccia producers, including Mormoraia, Vincenzo Cesani, Giovanni Panizzi, and Melini. Most of them use "international" techniques—for example, adding chardonnay or aging their wines in barriques—to contemporize the old dowager that is Vernaccia di San Gimignano. Yet while San Gimignano's high altitudes and calcareous, often chalky soils seem well-suited to producing structured, aromatic whites, it may be that vernaccia lacks the stuff-

ing to go it alone. The main problem is aroma: There isn't much, and while many of the newer barrique-aged wines are bigger and rounder than in the past, they often feel like wines on steroids, pumped up past their natural limits. These days many producers are focusing more on chardonnay or, more recently, on red wines from sangiovese (Vincenzo Cesani makes a particularly good one called "Luenzo").

As with just about every other region, Tuscany has a smattering of big-name chardonnays (Querciabella's "Batàr" or Ruffino's "Cabreo La Pietra") and sauvignons (Ornellaia's "Poggio alle Gazze"). And while chardonnay in particular is showing some interesting results in the high altitudes of the Chianti Classico zone, the white grape of the future may be vermentino, more typically associated with Liguria but with a long history in Tuscany. With all of the investment pouring into the Maremma these days, vermentino is a white to watch.

At present there are eleven mostly coastal DOCs in Tuscany—notably Bolgheri, Val di Cornia, and Colli di Luni, the latter shared with Liguria—that incorporate vermentino in some way. And while there isn't yet a mass of wines from which to sample, the grape thrives in the maritime climate. "Vermentino is built for heat, because it is extremely durable and very late ripening," says Piermario Meletti Cavallari, whose Grattamacco estate in Bolgheri makes one of the best vermentino-based wines in Italy. Grattamacco Bianco, like the better-known vermentinos of Liguria and Sardinia, seems to capture its origins in a bottle: It's like a refreshing sea breeze, carrying scents of wild fennel and pine and finishing with a salty kick. People don't immediately think of the Mediterranean when they think of Tuscany, but vermentino, while tough to find, could become the most characteristic Tuscan white of them all. (Antinori's Tenuta Belvedere in Bolgheri makes a good one, as does the Martelli-Busdraghi estate in Suvereto, and there are some good Colli di Luni vermentinos.) It's got the muscle to stand up to strongly flavored fish soups, which are found all along Tuscany's coast. Liguria may be more famous for those, too, but Tuscany more than holds its own.

VINI ROSSI
Red Wines

Even now, coastal Tuscany is a frontier, both for winemakers and tourists; much of the southern Maremma, in fact, was malarial marshland until Mussolini drained it in the 1930s. While the islands of Giglio and Elba and a handful of towns along the southern coast have their share of visitors, most of the action (and this goes for wine, too) is centered in the thickly forested hills around Florence and Siena.

Wines notwithstanding, it's hard to compete with some of the images: like winding along the Strada del Chianti (SS 222) in Chianti Classico, cresting the hill at Panzano and descending through the Conca D'oro (golden bowl), a sun-splashed arc of vineyards that seems to open onto the entire south of Italy; or approaching the bulky mass of Montalcino, which sits like an island in an undulating sea of wheat fields and pasture; or peering over the east wall of Montepulciano and taking in nearly all of the Vino Nobile DOCG zone in one shot. These three areas are the "big three" of Tuscan red wine, showcasing the many faces of the sangiovese grape—the most diffuse, most intensely studied, and along with the neb-

biolo of Piedmont, most important native red of Italy.

Though sangiovese was likely a native wild vine, no one is 100 percent sure. The origins of the name are debated as well. As noted in the Emilia-Romagna chapter, one theory is that sangiovese derives from *sangue di Giove* ("blood of Jove") or *di Giovanni* (Saint John), while another suggests *sangue da giogo/gioghetti* ("blood of a crest, or ridge"); the latter ostensibly refers to the Apennines between Tuscany and Emilia-Romagna, where the variety is thought to have originated. In any case, an author named Soderini, in a 1590 book on viticulture, describes a "Sangiogheto," the first known written reference to the grape.

In spreading throughout Tuscany and elsewhere, the grape picked up different names in different places—prugnolo gentile in Montepulciano, brunello in Montalcino, and morellino near Grosseto, all of which are said to be individual strains of sangiovese. Generally speaking, though, these subvarieties fall within two basic categories of sangiovese: one with large berries (sangiovese *grosso,* which includes prugnolo and brunello) and another with small ones, sangioveto, Chianti's version.

Is this really important? Well, some say that sangiovese *grosso's* thicker skins are what give brunello a more tannic bite and thus a greater capacity to age. Others say that the idea of a distinct, widely propagated clone such as brunello or prugnolo is nonsense—that the varying personalities of the wines come from planting the same grape in different places. What everyone can agree on is the unique character of the variety: In sangiovese you get not only a telltale aroma and flavor of black cherry but a distinctive savor that roots the wine in Tuscany. A good Chianti, or Brunello di Montalcino, or Vino Nobile di Montepulciano, has a foresty, smoky quality; drinking it is like eating berries in the woods, the spicy scents of the underbrush mingling with the sweetness of the fruit.

Sangiovese is very vigorous (meaning that it has to be closely pruned to produce concentrated fruit), sensitive to its environment, and difficult to get fully ripe, which is one of the reasons old-style Chiantis had such an acidic kick. The variety also tends to be low in anthocyanins, the natural phenolics in the skins that give a wine color (brunello seems to be an exception). This is why lesser-known grapes, such as canaiolo and colorino, found their way into Chianti blends in the past—and it's why cabernet sauvignon and merlot have become nearly as important as sangiovese in Tuscany over the last thirty years. In looking at the current red-wine scene in Tuscany, it's these last three—perfumed sangiovese, powerful cabernet, and plump merlot, either alone or in combination—that have come to define the region.

Chianti and Chianti Classico

Since the Middle Ages, when Florence was probably the most powerful of the city-states, the hills south of the city have been the epicenter of commercial winemaking in Italy. Although there are other wine zones that are equally if not more historic (including San Gimignano and Montepulciano), Chianti was the first real "delimited" wine zone as we know it today.

The Florentine Republic identified the hills between Florence and Siena as "Chianti" in the fourteenth century. Years later, in 1716, the Grand Duke Cosimo III de' Medici created what is considered the first "legislation" governing wine production. He identified the communes of Greve, Radda, Gaiole, and Castellina as a discrete production zone. Later still, in the 1870s, Gaiole nobleman Bettino Ricasoli (the second president of unified Italy and an ancestor of present-day Castello di Brolio scion Francesco Ricasoli) devised what became a "formula" for Chianti-area reds: a base of sangiovese, with a touch of the softening canaiolo and a significant dose of white grapes for those who wanted fresher wines (or, later, for those who wanted to stretch their production).

In the twentieth century, three bad things happened to Chianti. First, the original zone, now referred to as the Classico, was expanded to include a huge swath of central Tuscany, as the government envisioned Chianti as a "brand" more than as a site-specific wine. Second, the Ricasoli recipe became doctrine in Chianti, and when the DOC production formula was created in 1967 it allowed for up to 30 percent white grapes in the blend. And third, as elsewhere in Italy, there was a mass exodus from the Tuscan countryside in the fifties, which in turn prompted the Italian government and the European Community to finance large-scale replantings of Tuscany's vineyards in the sixties—all geared toward mass production.

At present, the Chianti DOCG zone takes in more than forty-two thousand acres, of which seventeen thousand are the original Classico. There are now seven Chianti subzones: Colli Aretini, near Arezzo; Colli Fiorentini, south of Florence, north of the Classico; Colli Senesi, all around Siena to the north and south; Colline Pisane, south of Pisa; Montalbano, west of Florence; Rufina, east of Florence; and Montispertoli, also west of Florence.

So then, what were you drinking if you drank Chianti in the seventies and eighties?

Probably a mouth-puckering, browning-at-the-edges red in a straw-covered *fiasco*—the cheap pizza-parlor wine that became world-famous, enticing producers to crank out even more. There's still a good amount of it around today, and the down-market image of the *fiasco* with a candle melting over its edges still haunts the industry.

"For so long, our wine culture was based on quantity, not quality," says Marchese Piero Antinori, head of one of the many noble families that have anchored the Tuscan wine scene. Antinori was one who bucked the trends in the seventies, chafing at what he and others saw as shortsighted Chianti DOC regulations. He followed the lead of his uncle, Marchese Mario Incisa della Rocchetta of Sassicaia (see page 208), and in 1971 introduced "Tignanello," a blend of 80 percent sangiovese and 20 percent cabernet sauvignon aged in French oak barriques. Because cabernet sauvignon and barrique aging were not allowed in the DOC regulations of the day, he labeled Tignanello as a *vino da tavola*. Along with "Sassicaia" and a raft of other nontraditional reds, it came to be known as one of the super-Tuscans—most of which were either 100 percent sangiovese (which also wasn't allowed in the Chianti discipline), or a mix of sangiovese with international varieties like cabernet or merlot.

"In the past, Italy produced mass quantities of wine because we were an agricultural economy and people used wine to quench thirst," says Antinori. "After the Second World War, consumption went way down as we became more industrialized. But our mentality toward winemaking did not change: Even now I'd say a high percentage of the vineyards in Chianti Classico are the old-style, high-production vineyards of the sixties."

That may well be true, but Chianti—and Chianti Classico especially—is not the wine it once was. In fact, it has undergone a more profound change in the last twenty years than practically any other wine in Italy. The Chianti Classico zone is now a source of world-class reds, bottles you should stick in your cellar for a few years, not stick candles into.

It started in 1984, when Chianti and Chianti Classico were upgraded to DOCG, which adjusted the blending formula to include a minimum of only 2 percent white grapes and allowed "foreign" varieties such as cabernet and merlot to be included in percentages up to 10 percent (in 1996 it changed again, eliminating the minimum for white grapes and upping the amount of "foreign" grapes to 15 percent). Further, the DOCG placed tighter restrictions on yields in the vineyards, essentially forcing people to cut excess fruit in the summer to produce more concentrated grapes.

In the cellars, winemakers not only benefited from the enriching effects of merlot and cabernet, but more and more of them adopted controlled-temperature fermentation in stainless steel (to preserve aromas) and aging in smaller, newer oak barrels instead of big, musty *botti* made of chestnut (stabilizing the wine's color and adding richness and tannin). People began striving for more power in their wines, employing longer contact with the skins of the grapes during fermentation to extract more color and tannin.

But the biggest change has come in the vineyards. Since 1989, the Chianti Classico *consorzio*—a producers association whose symbol is the *gallo nero*, or black rooster—has overseen a viticultural research project known as "Chianti Classico 2000." Originally headed by Carlo Ferrini, now the most famous winemaking consultant in Tuscany, the project centered on a series of experimental vineyards planted at the estates of *consorzio* member-producers. The principal aim was to identify new clones of sangiovese that had thicker skins, higher anthocyanins, and sparser grape bunches (sangiovese grows in a notoriously tight bunch, which prevents light from entering and ripening all the grapes evenly).

Parallel to the Chianti Classico 2000 project, any number of producers were making their own clonal selections and also replanting their vineyards more densely so that each vine could be more closely cropped to produce less. The basic idea behind planting vines more densely, which is discussed elsewhere in this book, is that the vines are not only producing a smaller quantity of fruit per vine, but that they are competing with one another for nutrients in the soil. In theory, these struggling vines will produce fruit that is more deeply flavorful, since all of the plant's energy is being directed toward a carefully controlled number of grape bunches.

So, concurrent with the Chianti Classico 2000 research, noble estates such as Antinori, Badia a Coltibuono, Fonterutoli, and Castello di Brolio, along with smaller producers such as Fontodi and Isole e Olena, ignited a mini-revolution in the Chianti Classico vineyards, aggressively re-planting their properties with the intent of transforming sangiovese. Rather than have a vineyard with about two thousand vines per hectare, producing four or five kilos (or more) of grapes per plant, they were upping the number to five thousand vines or more, but with only one to two kilos per plant as an ideal. And with new clones at that. The quality implications are pretty obvious.

As some Italian-wine fans are aware, the vintages 1997 through 2000 were great years in Chianti Classico—especially '97, which was hailed as the vintage of the decade. Many producers say that this was not just the luck of weather, but a refinement of the raw ingredients. "One reason '97 was great was because it was a point of convergence—of good weather and years of improvements in the vineyards," says Roberto Stucchi, winemaker-proprietor of Badia a Coltibuono in Gaiole. "That was probably the first year when a good number of the vineyards replanted in the late-eighties and early nineties were coming into production."

Stefano Porcinai, the current in-house enologist at the Chianti Classico *consorzio*, is a little more conservative in his estimates of the effects of replanting in the nineties. The results of the Chianti Classico 2000 project, for one, are just concluded: Actual seedlings of the four new clones the *consorzio* isolated were only put on the market in 2001. As for the re-plantings carried out privately, Porcinai says that maybe 20 percent of the Classico's seventeen thousand acres have been replaced in the last decade. The best is yet to come.

"Super-Tuscans were very important for gaining world recognition of Italian wines, but they also created some anarchy in the marketplace," Porcinai explains. "With the changes in the laws, Chianti is technically a super-Tuscan. But if the progress with sangiovese continues, you'll probably see more Chianti wines that are 100 percent sangiovese instead of being blended with other grapes."

So then, what are you drinking if you drink Chianti Classico in the twenty-first century? From the heights of Gaiole, Greve, Castellina, Radda, and Panzano, where the crumbly, schist-like soil called *galestro* dominates, you get a wine that captures not only the perfume of sangiovese but also its power. Often the wines have a sheen of new oak, and are sweetened with merlot and cabernet. They're denser, darker, more ageworthy reds, but in comparison to other wines of the world they're still angular and firm rather than fat or musclebound. The best Chianti Classicos are about grace, which doesn't fade with age.

Brunello di Montalcino

Not far from the southern reaches of Chianti Classico, the commune of Montalcino towers over the surrounding area, one of those trademark Tuscan towns that seems to perch on a ledge. It's only about twenty-five miles south of Siena, but in that short span the climate shifts from the damper, cooler continental climate of the Chianti Classico to a dryer, hotter, more Mediterranean environment. While Montalcino's altitudes are similar to those in Chianti (vineyards are usually found from three hundred to five hundred meters), the soils are different, generally containing more limestone and sand than the soils farther north.

It's these differences, along with the purported superiority of the brunello clone, that make Brunello di Montalcino the most powerful sangiovese around. Not only is the climate hotter—Montalcino is always the first of the "big three" to start the harvest in the fall—but the soils are, too: Where cooler clays and marls tend to slow down ripening, sandier soils speed it up. Potentially disastrous October rains, always a concern in Chianti Classico, aren't much of a problem in Montalcino, since the harvest typically finishes in mid- to late-September. Along with Barolo and Barbaresco from Piedmont, Brunello di Montalcino has become one of the handful of DOC wines hunted by wine collectors, because its depth of flavor and tongue-curling tannins give it the potential to age for decades. The lighter-styled Rosso di Montalcino, sort of a younger, "declassified" Brunello (and usually a great value), was created so people could drink a more immediately accessible Montalcino wine while they waited for their Brunellos to age; DOCG law requires a minimum of four years before Brunello can go on the market.

Most experts credit the discovery of brunello to Clemente Santi, who is said to have isolated the clone in the 1840s. When his grandson Ferruccio Biondi returned to the family farm in Montalcino after fighting in the Risorgimento (the movement for Italian unification), he planted the vineyards with Brunello and created the Biondi-Santi brand in 1888. It wasn't until the 1950s that Fattoria dei Barbi, Costanti, and a handful of other estates joined Biondi-Santi on the scene, and in general Montalcino was relatively unknown well into the seventies. According to the Brunello di Montalcino *consorzio*, there were some 800,000 bottles of wine made in the zone in 1975, from about 25 producers; in 1995, that number had ballooned to 3.5 million bottles, from more than 120 estates.

In fact, where Chianti Classico was already well-developed in the 1970s, Montalcino was still the boondocks—sort of like the way Grosseto is today. The exodus of the area's farmers in the fifties and sixties left Montalcino landowners holding the bag, and many were content to unload property inexpensively. Among the early investors in the zone were the vermouth-making Cinzanos of Piedmont, who bought the Col d'Orcia estate in 1973, and the American wine importers John and Harry Mariani, who started acquiring property for their Banfi estate in 1978.

Although they're regarded by some as interlopers, there's no measuring the impact the Marianis had on Montalcino. Having made their fortune importing Riunite Lambrusco, they did things in Montalcino on a big, international scale—building one of the most high-tech wineries in Italy, planting a California-sized tract of vineyards, and making the whole place tourist-friendly. Banfi's compound may be an example of American excess, but the buzz it created spurred new investments in the area. The Frescobaldi clan of Chianti Rúfina fame bought the Castel Giocondo estate in 1989, and both Piero Antinori (Pian delle Vigne) and Barbaresco legend Angelo Gaja (Pieve di Santa Restituta) arrived in the nineties. Along with these bigger players came a raft of newer, more boutique estates, including Siro Pacenti, Uccelliera, Le Machioche, and Salvioni, and once-quiet Montalcino grew thick with high-end wineries.

Generally speaking, Brunellos are described as bigger, "blacker" wines than Chiantis or Vino Nobiles. But Giacomo Neri, winemaker-proprietor at the well-regarded Casanova di Neri estate, puts a finer point on Brunello style. He, like many of his peers, believes there are differences between the wines grown in vineyards north of Montalcino and those from vineyards to the south. The Montalcino commune, which takes in smaller villages such as Torrenieri (northeast of Montalcino) and Castelnuovo dell'Abate (southeast), is like a big circle, with Montalcino in the center. The vineyards that fan out to the north, characterized by cooler calcareous clays and a slightly cooler microclimate, produce, in Neri's view, more perfumed, elegant wines. In vineyards facing south, such as in Castelnuovo dell'Abate and Sant'Angelo in Colle, the soils are significantly sandier and the climate more full-on Mediterranean. This, says Neri, creates denser, fuller-bodied wines with less acidity.

"When you cross over Montalcino and start heading south toward Castelnuovo, it's like going into a different world," says Neri. "The vegetation actually changes. On the north side, it's more like the Chianti forests, with lots of oaks and pines. On the south side it turns into the màcchia, more scrub brush. Go in October—on the south side of Montalcino the olives are turning black; on the north side they're still green."

To put Neri's hypothesis to the test, you might try a side-by-side comparison of a Brunello from the northern part of the zone (like Tenuta Caparzo, Biondi-Santi, Silvio Nardi, or Altesino) with one from the south (maybe Mastrojanni, Banfi, Col d'Orcia, or Casanova di Neri). Given the wide array of techniques being applied these days (types of wood aging, lengths of macerations) it may be difficult to sort out the intricacies of *terroir*, but it sure would be fun trying. Most important of all is this: While the Chianti, Vino Nobile, and Carmignano DOCGs all allow for other grapes to be blended in with sangiovese, Brunello is the grape unadorned. For a thick *cinghiale* or rabbit *ragù*, a classic pasta topping of the Tuscan hills, there may be nothing better.

Vino Nobile di Montepulciano

Somewhere in the middle of Chianti Classico and Brunello di Montalcino, literally and figuratively, lies Vino Nobile di Montepulciano. It is the smallest of the "big three" DOCGs, with about twenty-five hundred acres under vine.

And despite having a history at least as illustrious as Chianti's, it tends to be the forgotten middle child in the group.

Montepulciano itself is like a mini-Florence, and for that reason alone it's worth a visit. But some would argue that this is the only reason. Like Chianti and Brunello, the modern Vino Nobile industry developed in the 1920s and '30s (Fanetti and Contucci are two estates from that era still making wines). And, like Chianti, the establishment of the Vino Nobile DOC in the sixties led to a dramatic surge in vineyard plantings and wine production. The main difference is that in the seventies the largely mediocre Vino Nobile wines didn't become famous in spite of themselves, as Chianti wines did. As Burton Anderson writes in the *Wine Atlas of Italy:* "Even when enjoyable, [Vino Nobile] tended to vary so radically from one vintage—or even one bottle—to the next that it was hard to determine a Vino Nobile personality or define any one house's style."

It wasn't until the beginning of the eighties that Montepulciano began to gain momentum, thanks in large measure to the Avignonesi and Poliziano estates, both dynamic marketers as well as forward-looking producers. Avignonesi, run by brothers Ettore and Alberto Falvo (the name and the original property in Montepulciano comes from Ettore's ex-wife, Adriana Avignonesi), began as a small-scale producer of Vin Santo but eventually grew into a force. The Falvos, whose family was in the hotel business, not only invested heavily in the area—their properties in Montepulciano and neighboring Cortona now include 375 acres of vineyards—but created a more international array of wines. Ettore Falvo, a passionate viticulturist, focused on getting the most out of his sangiovese (prugnolo), introducing his first Vino Nobile

in 1978. But he wasn't shy about planting cabernet, merlot, and other "international" varieties, particularly in Cortona. His cabernet-prugnolo blend "Grifi" (discontinued after the '96 vintage) and the merlot-cabernet "Toro Desiderio" weren't Vino Nobile wines, but they did what Tignanello did for Chianti a decade earlier: show what the zone was capable of.

In the case of Poliziano, which was founded in 1960, it was a question of shifting focus. Poliziano was a big producer of fairly mundane Chianti Colli Senesi until Federico Carletti, son of the founder, got a degree in agronomy and began directing the estate in 1980. His vineyard holdings have ballooned to about 300 acres in Montepulciano and Torrita di Siena (for Chianti, which he still makes). And with the help of consultant Carlo Ferrini, he has created probably the slickest Vino Nobiles on the market. He uses traditional varieties but adds a substantial amount of new barrique for aging. He also makes a super-Tuscan, "Le Stanze," a supercharged cabernet-merlot blend.

Since the early eighties, Montepulciano's development has been similar to Montalcino's, albeit on a smaller scale. Big-name investors came in, including the Marche's Fazi-Battaglia winery (their estate in Montepulciano is called Fassati); the SAI insurance company (Fattoria del Cerro); the Ruffino wine house (Lodola Nuova); and Antinori (La Braccesca). There's also a new generation of smaller producers, many of them as yet undiscovered: Valdipiatta, La Ciarliana, Salcheto, and Il Macchione, to name a few. Relatively speaking, there are some great values to be found among this group.

Still, the style of Vino Nobile remains stubbornly difficult to pinpoint. One reason for this may be the DOCG discipline for Vino Nobile, which even now isn't as closely prescribed as

Brunello's or Chianti Classico's when it comes to the grape mix. Although a Vino Nobile di Montepulciano can now be 100 percent sangiovese (thanks to changes in the law in 1999), the official formula still allows for up to 20 percent canaiolo and/or up to 20 percent other grapes, including a maximum of 10 percent white varieties. Another development has been a liberalizing of the aging requirements for Vino Nobile, in that producers are no longer required to age their wines a minimum of two years in wood. Depending on the producers' choices, you'll find some Vino Nobiles that are more resiny, spicy and herbal, and some that are more forwardly fruity and rich—although that could be said about Chianti Classico, too.

If there's any broad, sweeping generalization to be made, it's that Vino Nobiles have softer tannins than Brunellos and broader, less acidic profiles than Chianti Classicos—while maintaining the appealing aromas of sangiovese. The slopes of Montepulciano are more open and gently rolling than the tight, steep pitches of Chianti Classico or Montalcino (allowing in more sunlight), and the soils are generally sandier and more alluvial than either of the others (advancing ripening), yet the elevations are the same. Like most middle children, Vino Nobile strikes a balance between its more extreme siblings, and is often the more interesting because of it.

Carmignano and Rúfina

If Vino Nobile is the neglected middle child of Tuscany's DOCG wines, then Carmignano, a small zone west of Florence, and Rúfina, to the east, are the favorite cousins from north of the Arno River. Florence and Siena being historic rivals, it's interesting to note that Carmignano and Chianti Rúfina are truly Florentine wines, while most Chianti Classicos and all Brunellos and Vino Nobiles are *Senesi*.

Carmignano, situated on the eastern slopes of Monte Albano at the convergence of the Ombrone and Arno rivers, was one of Cosimo III de' Medici's four original production zones in his decree of 1716. There are only about 300 hectares of vineyards registered under the DOCG, and production is dominated by three producers—Capezzana, Artimino, and Fattoria Ambra—who make some of the more exotic-tasting wines of the sangiovese family. One reason is that the blending formula for Carmignano is more far-flung, incorporating a minimum of only 50 percent sangiovese, along with up to 20 percent canaiolo nero, 10 to 20 percent of cabernets francs and/or sauvignons, 10 percent of white grapes, and 10 percent of other grapes. Side by side with a Chianti Classico, Carmignano—along with its younger, fresher sibling, Barco Reale—is likely to be even more nervous with acidity and perhaps more assertively fragrant. The vineyards of Carmignano are lower-lying than those of Chianti Classico, and are almost all east-facing, giving them the ripening benefits of the morning sun. But this is still a northerly latitude for the fickle sangiovese.

Rúfina, probably the best-regarded of the seven non-Classico Chianti zones, is also at a northern limit for sangiovese, and is dominated by just two producers—Frescobaldi and Selvapiana. Situated in hills not far from Tuscany's border with Emilia-Romagna, the calcareous soils of Rúfina turn out firm, angular Chiantis, with aromas that seem to leap out of the glass. Like Carmignano, Rúfina showcases the elegance and aroma gained from cooler vineyard sites. For the Chianti lover, there may be no better values on the market than Frescobaldi's "Castello di Nipozzano" and "Montesodi" Chiantis from Rúfina, two affordable wines that feature sangiovese at its most aromatic.

The Maremma

"Until ten years ago, Tuscany was thought of only as Chianti," says Piermario Meletti Cavallari of Grattamacco, one of the earliest arrivals in the now-famous hills of Bolgheri. "But now it's the Maremma that everyone is talking about." Whereas central Italy is a bastion of tradition (at least on the surface), the coast has always been more free-wheeling. Cavallari's late neighbor, Mario Incisa della Rocchetta, was the first to spark serious interest in the Bordeaux-type varieties, which then spread inland and down into the Grosseto area.

Even now, as more and more development comes to Tuscany's coast, the area around Bolgheri still feels like an oasis. The maritime hills, blanketed by the thick *màcchia,* spill down into marshes and dunes near the sea, the whole thing bisected by the ancient Via Aurelia, which hugs the coast all the way down to Rome. Giant umbrella pines sway in the salty air and the open spaces seem more vast and unpopulated. Yet tucked away in those seemingly uninhabited hills are some of the best red-wine vineyards in the world.

When Mario Incisa della Rocchetta, who was originally from Piedmont, married Clarice della Gherardesca, part of a Tuscan noble family, the Della Gherardesca's Tenuta San Guido in Bolgheri became Mario Incisa's hobby farm, for horse breeding, primarily, but also for viticulture. Taking a cue from a friend—Duke Francesco Salviati, who planted cabernet at his

property near Pisa before the Second World War—Mario Incisa planted his first vineyard in 1944, intending to make some Bordeaux-style wine for his own consumption. Eventually, the wine he called "Sassicaia" (meaning "place with a lot of rocks," in reference to the vineyard near Castagneto Carducci) became a commercial venture; he released the first wines for sale in 1968, and the phenomenon of the super-Tuscans was born.

Meletti Cavallari of Grattamacco, a former management consultant and wine-shop owner from Bergamo, arrived in 1977, originally purchasing his house and land in Bolgheri as a fishing getaway. Then Lodovico Antinori, brother of Piero and nephew of Mario Incisa, started his Ornellaia estate on some of the other family land. Antinori believed that cabernet and merlot would thrive in the maritime climate and sandy-clay soils of Bolgheri. Following the cabernet-dominated Sassicaia into the market were "Grattamacco Rosso" (a blend of cabernet sauvignon, merlot, and sangiovese, first released in 1982) and "Ornellaia" (cabernet-merlot; first vintage 1985).

Piero Antinori was not to be left out, releasing in 1990 a wine called "Guado al Tasso" (cabernet-merlot-syrah), made at a Bolgheri estate called Tenuta Belvedere, which also belonged to the family. (Piero and Lodovico Antinori's mother was the sister of Clarice Della Gherardesca. Both the Ornellaia and Tenuta Belvedere properties were once a part of a vast della Gherardesca holding that included what is now Sassicaia as well.) The great irony of the early super-Tuscans was that they were considered the best Tuscan reds around but were labeled with the seemingly lowly *vino da tavola* designation. Then, as now, they proved that DOC designations were no guarantees of quality. But a Bolgheri DOC was created in 1984 to bring them into the fold.

In the last decade, the Bolgheri area has exploded with winemaking activity. It is now almost an exclusive seaside club full of boutique wine producers, including Michele Satta (who makes "Piastraia," a blend of cabernet, merlot, syrah, and sangiovese, among other wines); Le Macchiole (producers of the acclaimed "Paleo" and the all-merlot "Messorio"); and newcomer Angelo Gaja of Piedmont, whose 150-acre Ca' Marcanda estate is just now releasing its first wines, "Magari" and "Camarcanda" (both cabernet-merlot blends).

Although merlot thrives just about anywhere, the relatively late-ripening cabernet sauvignon is not always easy to mature in inland zones such as Chianti Classico. On the coast near Bolgheri, however, the maritime influence moderates the climate, so that day-night temperature fluctuations are not too dramatic and the intense heat is checked by cooling breezes. "It tends to be a little too hot and dry here for sangiovese," says Meletti Cavallari of Grattamacco, who continues to diminish the amount of sangiovese in Grattamacco Rosso, saying that the grape loses its trademark aromatics when it is "super-mature."

The rise of Bolgheri is often viewed as the first example of cabernet and merlot arriving in Italy, but this is far from being the case. By the early 1800s it was prominent throughout northern Italy, particularly in French- and Austrian-dominated zones such as Piedmont and Friuli–Venezia Giulia. It gained momentum after phylloxera destroyed most of Europe's vineyards at the turn of the century, and vintners throughout Italy were exposed to a wealth of new plant material as they set about replanting their vineyards. To view either caber-

net or merlot as foreign varieties seems strange given their long history in the country, but purists still refer to them as such.

What Bolgheri did was validate the potential of cabernet and merlot in Italy, and especially Tuscany (Friuli and Trentino–Alto Adige, two other cabernet/merlot strongholds, haven't yet made as convincing a case). As the super-Tuscan craze has spread, cabernet and merlot—and, increasingly, syrah—have become integral parts of the Tuscan landscape. Most important, the wines don't taste like cabernet sauvignons, merlots, and syrahs from everywhere else in the world; they take on tarry, woodsy notes that brand them as Tuscan.

And what Bolgheri was to the Tuscany of the seventies and eighties, the more southerly reaches of the Maremma are to the Tuscany of the twenty-first century. Centered around the town of Scansano, home to the Morellino di Scansano DOC, the desertlike *bassa* (lower) Maremma is the new winemaking frontier. Often referred to as "the California of Italy," the southernmost chunk of Tuscany has been the hottest piece of real estate around.

Pioneering estates such as Moris Farms, Erik Banti, and Fattoria Le Pupille were the first to put Morellino di Scansano on the map, and since then the roster of producers investing in land in and around Scansano has been like a who's who of Tuscan wine: the Mazzei family of Castello di Fonterutoli in Chianti, who launched their Tenuta Belguardo wines in 1997; Federico Carletti of Poliziano, whose newish, twenty-hectare Lohsa estate in Magliano produces a well-priced Morellino di Scansano; the Biondi-Santi estate of Montalcino, whose Cantina Montepo is in Scansano; the Widmer family of La Brancaia in Chianti Classico, with their seventy-acre Poggio al

THE -*AIAS* HAVE IT:
A Super-Tuscan Quick Reference

In his book *Bacchus & Me,* Jay McInerney put it most succinctly: "If it ends in -*aia,* it's bound to be very good, indeed." The suffix -*aia* is a modifier, generally attached to a word the way the letter y is in English (for example, a place with a lot of *sassi,* or stones, is *sassicaia,* just like a place with a lot of sand is sandy). Though not all super-Tuscan wines end in -aia, they do share an annoying coyness, in that their fanciful names reveal nothing about what's in the bottle. Here's a list of twenty top super-Tuscans and a brief thumbnail on each.

Name	Producer
Sassicaia	Tenuta San Guido, Bolgheri
Grattamacco Rosso	Podere Grattamacco, Bolgheri
Ornellaia	Tenuta Ornellaia, Bolgheri
Tignanello	Antinori Santa Cristina, Mercatale Val di Pesa
Solaia	Antinori Santa Cristina, Mercatale Val di Pesa
Guado al Tasso	Antinori Tenuta Belvedere, Bolgheri
Lupicaia	Tenuta del Terriccio, Castellina Marittima
La Brancaia	Podere Brancaia, Radda
Paleo Rosso	Le Macchiole, Bolgheri
Cepparello	Isole e Olena, Barberino Val d'Elsa
Sassello	Castello di Verrazzano, Greve
Casalferro	Castello di Brolio, Gaiole
Camartina	Querciabella, Greve
Saffredi	Le Pupille, Scansano
Fontalloro	Fattoria di Felsina, Castelnuovo Berardenga
Felciaia	Villa La Selva, Bucine
Olmaia	Col d'Orcia, Montalcino
Luce	Mondavi-Frescobaldi, Montalcino
Summus	Castello Banfi, Montalcino

Blend	Notes
cabernet sauvignon 80% or more; cabernet franc remainder	The one that started it all, still the most elegant of the super-Tuscans.
cabernet sauvignon 50%; merlot 25%; sangiovese 25%	Piermario Meletti Cavallari was early on the scene in Bolgheri, and continues to produce this sexy, savory red with the help of Tuscan legend Maurizio Castelli. One of the best values in the group.
cabernet sauvignon; merlot; cabernet franc	Lodovico Antinori's landmark estate now has Mondavi as a majority partner. Look not only for Ornellaia but the 100% Merlot "Masseto," a pricey but delicious rarity.
sangiovese 80%; cabernet sauvignon 15%; cabernet franc 15%	The first to follow in Sassicaia's footsteps, though it is made in Chianti Classico at Antinori's Santa Cristina estate.
80% cabernet sauvignon; 20% sangiovese	The reverse of Tignanello, also from vineyards at the Santa Cristina estate.
cabernet sauvignon 60%; merlot 30%; syrah 10%	Rich, plush, luxurious blend from Bolgheri. Usually the earliest-drinking of Antinori's 3 super-Tuscans.
cabernet sauvignon; merlot	Off-the-beaten-track producer with a long history of smooth Bordeaux-style wines. Also "Tassinaia," which adds some Sangiovese to the Merlot-Cabernet base.
sangiovese 60%; merlot 35%; cabernet sauvignon 5%	Swiss-owned firm has long collaborated with consultant Carlo Ferrini on this sweet, smooth, easy-to-drink red.
merlot; cabernet sauvignon	Tiny-production boutique wine adored by critics and snapped up by collectors and restaurants before it hits the docks. Be ready to pay up for it.
sangiovese 100%	Powerhouse pure Sangiovese, very rare and much in demand.
sangiovese 100%	Smooth, elegant, pure Sangiovese from a top Chianti house.
sangiovese 100%	Created back when Chianti Classico could not contain 100% Sangiovese; a brawny, black wine that's closer to Brunello in style than Chianti, despite its origins.
sangiovese 60%; cabernet 30%; merlot 10%	High-toned and fragrant, in the house style, but with some muscle.
sangiovese; syrah; alicante	A fruit-bomb red from the top producer in the *bassa* Maremma.
sangiovese 100%	Another pure expression of Chianti Classico terroir—just without the Chianti Classico label.
sangiovese 100%	With the help of young consultant Stefano Chioccioli, this well-known Chianti estate showcases Sangiovese on its own, and with some Cabernet in "Selvamaggio."
cabernet sauvignon 100%	A luxurious diversion for this top maker of Brunello.
sangiovese; merlot	Italo-American joint production; soft, plush and, relatively speaking, affordable.
sangiovese; syrah; cabernet sauvignon	American-owned Banfi scores with this well-priced beauty and its sibling, "Excelsus."

Sasso estate; and any number of other well-heeled investors who see the *bassa* Maremma as a place to make affordable yet powerful wines. The ingredients range from sangiovese (morellino) to merlot, cabernet sauvignon, syrah, and alicante (grenache), which is widely planted in the area. Some producers are also experimenting with tempranillo, Spain's famous red, and others are reviving the local ciliegiolo, whose bright, cherry-red color and flavor is reflected in its name (*ciliegi* means "cherry" in Italian).

As more and more wines from Grosseto come on the market—as *vini da tavola*, IGT, or DOC—there's a temptation to group them with the wines of Bolgheri. But the two zones are different, with the significantly hotter, more inland *bassa* Maremma producing soft, rich wines that are plusher and more immediately enjoyable. "Bolgheri wines should have more finesse and structure," says Nicolò Incisa della Rochetta, son of Mario (who died in 1983) and current head of Tenuta San Guido. "In the *bassa* Maremma you get sheer power. Up here I think you get more balance."

Noteworthy Newcomers

Finally, after tasting through all of the above, are there any new frontiers to be found? Absolutely. For one, there's the recently created Cortona DOC, not far from the Umbrian border and just north of the Vino Nobile di Montepulciano zone. Known for the watery DOC white called Bianco Vergine della Valdichiana, the low, hot, and fairly fertile slopes south of Arezzo have proved hospitable to syrah and merlot. Right now the Cortona DOC is anchored by the Tenimenti D'Alessandro, whose "Il Bosco" syrah is considered one of the best in Italy. But with large estates like Avignonesi,

Ruffino, and Antinori beginning to make reds there, the Cortona DOC is one to look out for on a label.

VINI DOLCI
Sweet Wines

The best thing about a true Italian meal is its balance: of food groups, of portion sizes, of flavors. And while many Americans haven't yet figured it out, Italians find that the best match for a sweet wine is a "dry" dessert, like a *castagnaccio* or a panettone. This is exemplified by the well-known practice of dunking almond *biscotti* in Vin Santo, which seems to bring out the best in both. Rather than explode with a blast of sugar, as most sweet-on-sweet combinations do, the Vin Santo–*biscotto* combo is an intuitive melding of opposites: The wine sweetens and softens the dry cookie, while the cookie cushions the blow of the intense, even spiritous wine.

There are wide variations in Vin Santo's quality—those producers who make good ones tell ominous tales of others cutting their wines with spirits to bring them up to the required alcohol level, adding caramel for color and flavor, and so forth. But Vin Santo is a unique experience, almost like a cross between a wine and a whiskey. Usually getting up to about 16 to 18 percent alcohol and taking on a deep, amber color from the small chestnut or oak casks in which it is aged, Vin Santo is more robust than most other dessert wines made from white grapes. Although it is produced in other regions of Italy, it is a Tuscan signature, the kind of wine most Tuscan vintners make at least a little bit of for special occasions.

The basic formula for Vin Santo incorporates the white grapes trebbiano, malvasia, and occasionally grechetto, which are dried after harvest anywhere from three to six months (most DOC regulations call for the wine to begin vinification the March after the harvest). This *appassimento* is the same process as that for Amarone in Veneto, although Vin Santo producers tend to hang strung-together bunches from hooks rather than lay the grapes on mats to dry.

Once the dried grapes are pressed, the juice is vinified in small casks of chestnut or oak, which vary in size but are not usually larger than five hundred liters. The fermentation literally takes years, and no new wine is added during the fermentation and maturation, meaning that over the course of the three-plus years a Vin Santo is required to age, there is some evaporation. The resultant wines are usually a burnished amber, except for the rare, rose-colored *occhio di pernice* (eye of the partridge) versions, which are usually made with two-thirds red grapes and one-third white. Depending on the sugar levels of the raw material, Vin Santos can be dry, semisweet, or sweet. Usually, yeast stops working at around 18 percent alcohol. So if there are still significant amounts of sugar in the must—a function not only of the ripeness of the grapes but the length of time they were dried—the wine will be more unctuous. If not, it will be drier, even Sherry-like, in character.

Because of the high production costs involved, good Vin Santo wines are tough to come by in a store. Avignonesi, whose tiny-production version is matured in fifty-liter casks for more than six years, is a cult favorite among wine lovers. And scattered throughout Chianti Classico, Carmignano, Montepulciano, and elsewhere in Tuscany are some great Vin Santos to snap up—among the best are those from Isole e Olena in Chianti Classico, Cappezzana in Carmignano, and Selvapiana in Rúfina. With these, you can forget the *biscotti;* they're desserts in themselves.

FAST FACTS: TOSCANA

PROVINCES	Arezzo (AR), Firenze (FI), Grosseto (GR), Livorno (LI), Lucca (LU), Massa Carrara (MS), Pisa (PI), Pistoia (PT), Siena (SI)
CAPITAL	Firenze
KEY WINE TOWNS	Bolgheri, Carmignano, Gaiole in Chianti, Montalcino, Montepulciano, Panzano, Radda in Chianti, Rúfina, San Gimignano, Scansano
TOTAL VINEYARD AREA*	63,633 hectares, or 157,237 acres. Rank: 4th
TOTAL WINE PRODUCTION*	2,156,000 hectoliters, or 56,961,690 gallons (8th); 30% white, 70% red/rosé
DOC WINE PRODUCED*	55.5% (4th)
SPECIALTY FOODS	*fagioli* (white beans); *bistecca alla fiorentina* (beef steaks from Chianina cattle); game meats (wild boar, duck, rabbit, partridge, pigeon); *pecorino toscano* (sheep's-milk cheese).

*1997 figures. Rankings out of twenty regions total (Trentino–Alto Adige counted as one). Source: Istituto Statistica Mercati Agro-Alimentari (ISMEA), Rome.

KEY GRAPE VARIETIES

WHITES

TREBBIANO	The most planted white variety in Italy, it goes by trebbiano toscano in Tuscany, factoring into a wide variety of crisp, somewhat neutral DOC whites, as well as in the table wine Galestro.
VERMENTINO	Probably brought by the Spaniards by way of Sardinia. A durable coastal white with a cool, dewy, green-melon flavor

	and a salty finish. Best from the Bolgheri, Val di Cornia, and Colli di Luni DOCs.
VERNACCIA	A light, fragrant white, it is more or less limited to the area around San Gimignano.
OTHERS	MALVASIA, used in Vin Santo blends; GRECHETTO, also used in Vin Santo; SAUVIGNON BLANC.

REDS

SANGIOVESE	Italy's most noble and most diffuse red grape, the base of Chianti Classico, Vino Nobile di Montepulciano (where it is called prugnolo), Brunello di Montalcino (where it is called brunello), and Morellino di Scansano (morellino). Naturally high in acid and aroma.
CANAIOLO	A native grape typically used as a softening complement to sangiovese in the blends of Chianti Classico and Vino Nobile.
CABERNET SAUVIGNON	It's difficult to pinpoint when it arrived in Tuscany, but this "French" grape has been in Italy since the early nineteenth century, if not before. While tough to ripen farther north, it matures beautifully in Tuscany, producing wines with a luscious combination of sweet cassis fruit and firm tannins. The base of many "super-Tuscans."
MERLOT	Ubiquitous, but in the Tuscan hills it seems to ripen more slowly and develop a more powerful, woodsy structure. Usually more of a blending ingredient than a star, though it shines in Ornellaia's "Masseto."
OTHERS	SYRAH; ALICANTE (grenache); CILIEGIOLO.

TOP VINTAGES IN TUSCANY: 1980–2000

• Chianti Classico: '85, '88, '90, '97, '98, '99, 2000

• Brunello di Montalcino: '80, '82, '85, '88, '90, '95, '96, '97, '99, 2000

• Vino Nobile di Montepulciano: '85, '88, '90, '93, '95, '97, '99

• Bolgheri: '82, '85, '88, '89, '90, '95, '97; '99

The last four years of the twentieth century were charmed ones throughout Italy, and especially Tuscany. The 1997 vintage, in particular, was hailed by some as the "vintage of the century" in Chianti Classico, though many believe 1999 was better—it was a very even year in terms of weather, allowing for slow, even flavor development, whereas 1997 was marred by a rare frost in the spring and an exceptionally hot summer that favored superpowerful wines.

LA STRADA DEL VINO
WINE TOURING IN TUSCANY

For most Italian wine lovers, the first trip to "the source" is to Tuscany. This is without a doubt Italy's best-equipped region for wine tourism, with more attractions—*enoteche,* shops, restaurants, museums, or wineries themselves—than could possibly be listed here. Certainly there's no more elemental introduction to Italian wine country than a drive down Superstrada 222 from Florence to Siena, known as the Strada del Chianti. Passing through the Chianti Classico towns of Greve, Gaiole, Castellina, and others, there are any number of wineries to be visited, among them the striking Castello di Brolio (0577-7301) and Badia a Coltibuono (0577-74-94-98) estates, both of which are in Gaiole and both of which boast excellent country restaurants onsite.

While in Chianti country, you should definitely pay a visit to celebrity butcher Dario Checchini, whose Macelleria Checchini in Panzano (Via XX Luglio 11; 055-85-20-20) has become something of a cult favorite among foodies, thanks in large part to the theatrics of Dario himself. One restaurant worth a detour into the Chianti zone is out-of-the-way Vicolo del Contento in Castelfranco di Sopra, which sits outside the Chianti Classico zone to the east, in the direction of Arezzo (Ponte a Mandri 38, Castelfranco di Sopra; 055-914-02-77). Another out-of-the-way gem is the Osteria di Rendola in Montevarchi (Loc. Rendola, 76/81; 055-970-74-90), a great place to sample Tuscan specialties such as *piccione* (wild pigeon) and *cinghiale* (boar).

For the hard-core wine taster, Siena is a must-see. It is the home, of course, of one of the most extensive regional *enoteche* in Italy—the Enoteca Italiana (Piazza Matteotti 30; 0577-21-75-94), where wines not just from Tuscany but from all over Italy are available in a library-like setting. Another great place to sit and sip in Siena is the Enoteca I Terzi (Via di Termini 7; 0577-443-29). Ask for Michele.

In Florence, where authentic restaurants are harder to find than you might think, check out Da Delfina (Via della Chiesa 1; 055-87-18-07) for dining, while for drinking you might stop for a *panino* (sandwich) and some wine at one of two beautiful wine bars run by two well-known Chianti estates: the Cantinetta dei Verrazzano (Via dei Tavolini 18/20R; 055-26-85-90), and the Cantinetta Antinori (Palazzo Antinori; 055-29-22-34). The selection in these places is limited to wines from the Castello di Verrazzano and the Marchesi Antinori, respectively, but the food and atmosphere make them worth checking out.

DEGUSTAZIONI
TASTINGS

SANGIOVESE 1: CHIANTI CLASSICO AND RISERVA

The first two wines are simpler *annata* Chiantis, meaning that they are only required to be aged for a year before being sold. The second two are *riserve,* meaning that they're aged for two years, with a minimum of three months in the bottle. Taste the first two first and you'll get a feel for classic sangiovese from the Chianti zone: bright, crisp, redolent of Bing cherries and roses, firm, and spicy. In the *riserva* bottlings, you'll feel the effects of wood (including small oak barriques) and a little more time in the bottle: a good *riserva,* as both of the above are, is more resiny, earthy, and viscous, with richer tannins, more extraction, and a flavor expression leaning more toward black cherry. These days, styles of Chianti are all over the map, and good producers are everywhere, so you'll need to experiment to find a producer and style that suits you. (See the Producer Directory for more suggestions.)

Querciabella Chianti Classico, $$

Isole e Olena Chianti Classico, $$

Tenute Marchese Antinori Chianti Classico Riserva, $$–$$$

Fontodi Chianti Classico Riserva, $$

Mastrojanni Brunello di Montalcino, $$$

Col d'Orcia Brunello di Montalcino, $$–$$$

Fattoria dei Barbi Brunello di Montalcino, $$$

SANGIOVESE 2: BRUNELLO DI MONTALCINO

Power is the first word that comes to mind when drinking Brunello, typically a more full-bodied, "blacker," and muscular wine than Chianti Classico—yet elegant and aromatic at the same time. These are three classic Montalcino reds, the Barbi probably the most rustic of the three, the Mastrojanni the most softened from aging in new oak. The Col d'Orcia strikes a balance between these two, finding that elusive combination of power and finesse. What's great about Brunello is how it offers rich fruit concentration without being sweet or flabby. With a big hunk of *bistecca alla Fiorentina,* there really isn't any better choice. (For other more classic, rustic Brunellos, try the wines of Casse Basse, Biondi-Santi, and Costanti; for oak-kissed, softer styles go with Caparzo, Casanova di Neri, and Banfi.)

Boscarelli Vino Nobile di Montepulciano, $

Avignonesi Vino Nobile di Montepulciano, $$

Poliziano Vino Nobile di Montepulciano, $$

SANGIOVESE 3: VINO NOBILE DI MONTEPULCIANO

It is probably more difficult to generalize about Vino Nobile than Chianti, and that's saying something. In the Boscarelli wine you get a classic sangiovese nose of cherry, tea leaves, and spice, a more *terroir*-driven wine than the slicker Avignonesi and Poliziano bottlings. In the latter two you'll find a deeper, richer expression of sangiovese, falling somewhere between a big Chianti Classico Riserva and a lighter-styled Brunello. Although the style is perhaps the most variable of the Tuscan "big three," Vino Nobile is a once-dormant category that's loaded with good, young estates.

Le Pupille Morellino di Scansano, $

Cecchi-Villa Cerna Morellino di Scansano "Val delle Rose," $

Moris Farms Morellino di Scansano, $

SANGIOVESE 4: MORELLINO DI SCANSANO

In the last ten years, as Chianti Classico prices shot up dramatically, Morellino di Scansano stepped into the void with fruity, accessible, affordable Sangiovese-based wines. The markedly hotter climate in the Scansano area tends to plump up the normally high-acid sangiovese, toning down its spicy bite and emphasizing more sappy, berried fruit. Think fresh raspberries right off the bush and you've got a feel for Morellino, as evidenced by these three wines, all of which have a certain richness of warm, jammy fruit flavor.

Tenuta San Guido
"Sassicaia," $$$

Tenuta dell'Ornellaia
"Ornellaia," $$$

BOLGHERI BORDEAUX BLENDS

You'll have to pay up to do this tasting, but chances are it will be worth it: Here are the two super-Tuscans that started a craze, both of which remain at the top of an ever-growing heap. The Sassicaia wine is typically leaner and more angular than Ornellaia, thanks in some part to a telltale dose of cabernet franc that lends the aroma a slightly peppery quality. Ornellaia, by contrast, is a cabernet-merlot blend, and the plumper and plusher for it. In both wines the sweet cassis-scented fruit of cabernet sauvignon is wrapped in a wooly blanket of tannin, each wine like a tightly coiled spring not yet ready to release its potential energy. As young wines these tight, tannic beauties need a steak or a braise to open them up, although the better course of action is to lay them down and let the secondary aromas of dried cherry, roses, and saddle leather come to the fore.

Fattoria Selvapiana Vin
Santo della Rúfina, $$

Capezzana Vin Santo di
Carmignano, $$

VIN SANTO

Halfway between wine and whiskey, these almondy, caramelized sweet wines are some of the most distinctive after-dinner wines found in Italy. Note how these two wines balance their unctuousness with spicy notes of cinnamon and nutmeg, which, like their luxurious golden-amber hues, are picked up during long aging in small wooden casks. These are classic *vini da meditazioni* (meditation wines), to be sipped slowly on their own or paired with delicately flavored cakes and *biscotti,* particularly those incorporating nuts and candied fruits.

LA CUCINA
FOOD FOR THE WINE
RECIPE BY LIDIA BASTIANICH

Feathered and furred game are staples of the Tuscan diet, as Tuscany is the most thickly wooded of Italy's regions. Visit Siena or Montalcino or Grosseto in October and you'll be serenaded by the distant pops of shotguns in the woods. The *ragù* (of duck, rabbit, partridge or wild boar) is a fundamental component of Tuscan cooking, a favorite in the local *osterie* ladled over grilled polenta or wide-ribbon noodles such as *pappardelle*. The richness of a *ragù di cinghiale*, for one, is perfectly checked by a crisply acidic Chianti Classico or a Brunello di Montalcino, the latter's powerful tannins cutting through the fat and matching the *cinghiale*'s robust flavor. Should you not be game for hunting down a *cinghiale* on your own, there are a number of specialty food purveyors who can get it for you, with no tusks to slow you down.

The recipe below is very versatile. If you like, you can slice the braised boar meat and serve it over creamy polenta as an entrée, or shred the meat into the sauce to create a hearty *ragù* for pasta, especially a thick dried pasta such as rigatoni, or a broad-ribbon fresh pasta such as *pappardelle*.

Cinghiale in Umido
BRAISED WILD BOAR

3½ pounds boneless BOAR ROAST
   (or 6-pound bone-in shoulder roast)
SALT and PEPPER to taste, plus
   ½ teaspoon of each
½ cup all-purpose FLOUR
½ cup OLIVE OIL
6 ounces PANCETTA or bacon, cut into
   1-inch cubes (1¼ cups)
1 large yellow ONION, diced (1½ cups)
2 large CARROTS, shredded (1½ cups)
4 stalks CELERY, diced (1½ cups)
6 whole CLOVES
2 sprigs fresh ROSEMARY, chopped
   (or 1 teaspoon dried)
1 bottle CHIANTI or other hearty red wine
1 28-ounce can peeled Italian whole
   plum TOMATOES (preferably San
   Marzano)
2 cups CHICKEN STOCK

SERVES 8

Preheat the oven to 350°.

To prepare the roast, dry the meat and season well with salt and pepper. Place the flour in a large, shallow plate, and turn the meat in the flour to coat lightly, shaking off the excess.

In a large, heavy-bottomed stockpot or Dutch oven, heat ¼ cup of the olive oil (enough to fully cover the base of the pot) over medium-high flame until the oil is shimmering but not not yet smoking. Add the meat and brown deeply on all sides, allowing the pieces to sit on each side long enough to develop a thick brown crust. There will be considerable splattering of oil during this process, so use caution. The total browning time should be about 15 minutes.

Meanwhile, heat the other ¼ cup of the olive oil in a heavy-bottomed skillet or sauté pan over medium-low flame. Add the diced pancetta or bacon and sauté about 7 minutes, or until golden brown. Remove with a slotted spoon and reserve. Add the onion, carrot, celery, cloves, rosemary, and ½ teaspoon each of salt and pepper to the pot, increase the heat to medium-high, and sauté about 10 minutes, or until the onions are translucent and the other vegetables are soft and almost mushy. Remove the mixture from the pot and set it aside.

When the meat has finished browning, begin to add the wine one cup at a time.

It will splatter and hiss, which is good—you want the alcohol to burn off. Bring the wine to a full boil around the browning meat. Boil for five minutes, then add the sautéed vegetables and the reserved pancetta. Pour in the can of tomatoes, the 2 cups of stock, and 2 cups of water.

Remove the stockpot from the stovetop, cover it with aluminum foil, and place it on the middle rack of the preheated oven. Simmer for 3 hours, until the liquid has reduced and the meat is literally falling off the bone. The mixture should be thick and gelatinous.

Remove from the oven and carefully remove the meat, using two large spoons or spatulas. Take the remaining liquids and solids in the pot and press them through a fine sieve using the back of a wooden spoon, collecting the liquid in a large bowl. Skim the fat from the surface of the strained liquid. At this point, you may either slice the meat and serve it topped with the liquid, or shred the meat with a knife or by hand and combine it with the liquid to create a thick pasta sauce.

NOTE: If you can't find boar meat, you may substitute pork shoulder, which is easily found at most butcher shops.

WINE RECOMMENDATION: Brunello di Montalcino, Vino Nobile di Montepulciano, or Chianti Classico—any hearty sangiovese-based red will do.

Umbria

The Sleeper

———— ⁂ ————

ALL IN THE FAMILY

The village of Torgiano, located just outside Perugia, is one of the many meticulously preserved medieval towns that dot the landscape in Umbria. It is a quaint cluster of buildings on a gentle slope, looking west to the crater lake of Trasimeno and east to the Apennines that separate Umbria from Le Marche. At times it feels more like a movie set than an actual place where people live and work, but it is in fact the latter. The chief employer seems to be the Lungarotti family, whose winery, hotel, restaurant, wine shop, and assorted museums have turned a town that can be traversed in five minutes (on foot) into the nerve center of winemaking Umbria.

True, the town of Orvieto—with its giant Gothic duomo and historical significance as a summer retreat for the Papacy—is more famous. So is Assisi, home of Umbria's favorite son, Saint Francis. But Torgiano, thanks to the Lungarottis, has become the repository of Umbrian wine culture. The white wines of Orvieto may have been sipped as far back as the Middle Ages, but it was the red wines of Lungarotti— first produced in the early 1960s—that gave

Umbrian wine a real commercial identity. Yet when founder Giorgio Lungarotti died in 1999, he didn't just leave behind a successful brand name and some casks of wine. He left an entire town devoted to the cult of the vine.

There's a commercial side, of course: Adjacent to the wine museum that the Lungarottis built in 1974—which contains amphorae and other artifacts dating back to 3000 B.C.—is a luxury hotel–restaurant–conference center called Le Tre Vaselle, where the Lungarotti wines and olive oils are on prominent display. There's also a Lungarotti-owned *enoteca* and a Lungarotti-run *agriturismo* (bed-and-breakfast) just outside of town. In one sense, Torgiano is a vinous answer to Niketown. But the wine museum, which contains one of the best collections of its type in Italy, is another story. And so is a new museum devoted completely to olive oil, which opened in May 2000. Both are the creations of Giorgio Lungarotti's wife, Maria Grazia, and both have a seriousness of purpose that make them more than just a tourist draw.

The new oil museum's centerpiece is a huge, nineteenth-century wooden *frantoio* (olive-oil press) in a building once used for oil production. The exhibits spread across ten rooms, with murals and dioramas detailing the botanical characteristics of olive trees, the most com-

The DOC Zones of Umbria

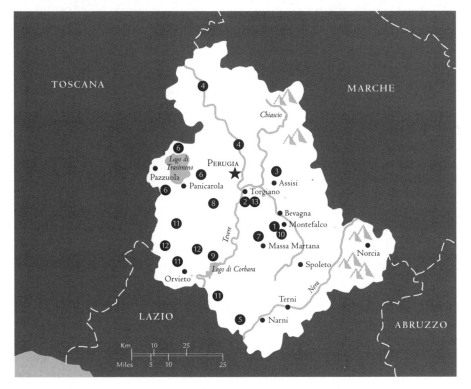

DOCG
1 Montefalco Sagrantino
2 Torgiano Rosso Riserva

DOC
3 Assisi
4 Colli Altotiberini
5 Colli Amerini
6 Colli del Trasimeno / Trasimeno
7 Colli Martani
8 Colli Perugini
9 Lago di Corbara
10 Montefalco
11 Orvieto
12 Rosso Orvietano / Orvietano Rosso
13 Torgiano

mon varieties of olive in Umbria, and the principal methods of olive-oil production. For anyone other than the hard-core foodie, this wouldn't seem to be a big draw. But the Lungarottis built it anyway—as much for themselves, it would seem, as for anyone else.

Touring the museum with Teresa Severini, the daughter of Maria Grazia and the winemaker at the Lungarotti estate (she was one of Italy's first well-known female winemakers), the sense is that the Lungarottis are not only out to preserve history but to make a case for their native Umbria. "Many people don't know it, but Umbria produces the highest percentage of extra-virgin olive oil in Italy," Teresa says, leading the way into an exhibit entitled "Oil as Light," a display of olive-oil lamps from the pre-Roman age up through the nineteenth century. A number of the votive-style lamps are lit, giving the room a soft glow. Their wicks are set in disks of cork that float on the gold-green oil, a simple but ingenious design.

"Olives are a larger part of the Umbrian agricultural economy than grapes," Teresa notes. "But we're not as well-known for our olive oils as we should be."

In fact, Umbria has any number of delicacies for which it isn't well-enough known. The region's fruity, full-bodied olive oils are eclipsed in the marketplace by those of neighboring Tuscany. Its black truffles, found in abundance in the densely forested hills of Norcia and Spoleto, are overshadowed by those of Alba in Piedmont. And the Umbrian wines, well, they've barely managed to register. Other than Lungarotti, the most famous wine name in Umbria is a Tuscan one—Antinori, whose Castello della Sala in Orvieto makes the only Orvieto wines readily recognized by foreign consumers.

Umbria's dense concentration of medieval villages brings swarms of tourists to places such as Orvieto, Gubbio, and Assisi, and many American expats, priced out of Tuscany, have bought their dream fixer-uppers here instead. The annual arts festival held in Spoleto has also become a major international draw. And yet Umbria still feels like undiscovered, uncharted territory. It's often said that the people of Umbria identify closely with Saint Francis, the patron saint of ecologists, who preached the importance of communing with nature. In this context, opening an olive oil museum seems like a very Umbrian thing to do.

"We feel an obligation to preserve the history of our craft," says Teresa. Despite all the very modern conveniences of Torgiano, there's still an old-world sensibility to the place. The same goes for Umbria as a whole. This may change as more latter-day Lungarottis invest in the burgeoning local wine scene, but for now the region is more museum than mall. If Torgiano is any indication, maybe they can keep it that way.

Despite its proximity to Tuscany, and all the spillover traffic this proximity has generated, Umbria's commercial wine history is a relatively short one. Twelfth-century popes who summered at Lake Corbara drank what was then a thick, sweet white from Orvieto. But aside from that, Umbrian wine remained a very localized "farmhouse" phenomenon well into the 1970s. Today, Umbria ranks an impressive sixth among Italian regions in the percentage of DOC-classified wine it produces, and yet DOC barely existed here just twenty years ago. Of the thirteen DOC zones now in the region, eight were created after 1980. It's not that Umbria isn't well-suited to wine. It's more that

Umbrians—pre-Lungarotti, anyway—weren't inclined toward the wine business.

There's also the question of size. Umbria is Italy's fourth-smallest region, and wine has always taken a back seat not only to olive oil but to other agricultural products (particularly grains for pasta and bread). That said, the region has all the tools to make great wine. It is essentially an extension of Tuscany, walled in on three sides by the Apennines but traversed by numerous rivers and streams, including the great Tiber River that bisects the region before heading down to Rome. It's hard to believe that landlocked Umbria can feel the moderating effects of the sea, but the Tiber is in fact a funnel of sorts that carries warming currents up from the Mediterranean. Offset this with cool breezes from the Apennines and you've got that classic push-pull of air so critical to the even ripening of grapes.

Along the western edge of the region in particular, where lakes Corbara and Trasimeno are remnants of ancient volcanoes, the vines are forced to bear down through clay and limestone into a hard, mineral-rich volcanic *tufa*, another factor that would seemingly enhance the quality of the wines. Yet for all of these favorable natural conditions for growing grapes, there is still a relatively small selection of Umbrian wines from which to choose.

Orvieto remains the anchor of the Umbrian wine scene, producing a good 70 percent of all the region's DOC-classified wine. And then there's Lungarotti in Torgiano, which now turns out a staggering two and a half million bottles per year. Their ever-expanding product line runs the gamut from barrique-aged chardonnay to Vin Santo, but their wines essentially stand alone, with nothing to compare them to. There are other much smaller producers in the Torgiano DOC, but not many.

One area of increasing interest is Montefalco, a town not far from Torgiano, where a small community of winemakers makes one of Italy's cult classics: the rich, spicy, full-bodied Sagrantino di Montefalco. And here there are enough wines—and enough *good* wines—to constitute a critical mass. The same could be said for a somewhat looser collective of new-wave producers, among them La Fiorita–Lamborghini (yes, *that* Lamborghini), Palazzone, and Antinori's Castello della Sala, who are experimenting with slick, modern blends incorporating cabernet sauvignon, merlot, chardonnay, and other international grapes.

There is a winemaking movement afoot in Umbria. It is still coming in somewhere under the radar, but it is happening. A region once thought of as Tuscany's satellite state has begun to assert itself, something Giorgio Lungarotti might well have responded to thusly: It's about time.

VINI BIANCHI
White Wines

As with the wines of San Gimignano in Tuscany, the wines of Orvieto tend to incite more commentary about the place they come from than about what's in the glass. On the one hand, Orvieto is a quintessential Italian white: cool and clean, with hints of green melon and green apple and a crisp, minerally finish. On the other hand, it is a quintessential Italian white: It's often too light to excite palates tuned to a heavier, oakier, more alcoholic frequency.

The Orvieto zone hugs the western edge of this tiny region, spilling over slightly into Lazio to the south. Most of the vineyards designated as the *classico* zone huddle around the commune of Orvieto itself, then spread north and east to take in the area around Lake Corbara, a Tiber-fed reservoir. The soils in the Classico—which comprises about 65 percent of the total vineyard area in the zone—are especially chalky, which is often reflected in wines with a tactile, mineral edge and naturally high acidity.

What makes Orvieto style difficult to pinpoint is the highly variable grape mix prescribed by the DOC. The formula calls for 40 to 60 percent trebbiano (the ultra-vigorous trebbiano toscano clone is widely used), 15 to 25 percent verdello (a light local variety), and a mix of grapes including grechetto, canaiolo bianco (here called drupeggio), malvasia toscana, and others. Naturally, this allows for wide variations in the wines' personalities.

As such, Orvieto wine tends to be divided into two camps: estates whose wines are yet another addition to the sea of neutral Italian trebbiano; and those who take advantage of the liberal DOC blending policy and use as much of the other, more interesting grapes as possible. The two varieties gaining prominence are grechetto, a distinctive local variety, and chardonnay.

The most dramatic example of this is the wine called "Cervaro della Sala," a blend of 80 percent chardonnay and 20 percent grechetto made by Antinori's Castello della Sala estate. Introduced with the 1985 vintage, the wine is easily the most recognized label in Orvieto—although it isn't an Orvieto DOC wine. Originally a *vino da tavola* and now labeled with an Umbria IGT designation, Castello della Sala is in one sense emblematic of the difficulties that the more traditional Italian whites have had in the market recently. In another sense, "Cervaro della Sala" opened the eyes of producers in Orvieto to what was possible in the zone: In the cool, chalky heights, chardonnay retains the minerally class it exhibits more readily in Burgundy, while the local grechetto adds not only a firmness of structure but an assertively aromatic note reminiscent of rennet apples.

Antinori literature describes grechetto as a "small, dark-yellow, thick-skinned, highly acidic, low-yielding, notably tannic Umbrian grape that produces creamy wines with unique spicy, herbal, freshly mown hay flavors, good structure, good aging potential, and elegance." That's a mouthful, to be sure, but there's no question that grechetto has emerged as the premier native grape in Umbria. Although it is believed to be related in some way to the greco of Campania, there's really no confusing the two: Where greco is faintly aromatic, grechetto is assertively so; where greco is generally crisp yet creamy, grechetto checks its juiciness with an almost tannic grip.

Increasingly, Orvieto producers are upping the amount of grechetto in their blends to the maximum the DOC law will allow, lending the wines more penetrating aromas than the notoriously faint trebbiano can give them. Chardonnay, meanwhile, is increasingly used to add some fat to the often thin Orvieto frame.

Beyond tinkering with their blending formulas, Orvieto producers are also doing more with what they've got in both the vineyards and the cellar. Some are experimenting with barrel-fermented versions of their wines—examples include "Velico" from the Le Velette estate. Others are identifying their top vineyard sites and making cru wines from them, such as La Carraia with its "Poggio Calvelli" bottling and Bigi with its "Tenuta di Corbara." In fact, when compared to some of Italy's other classic white-wine DOCs, Orvieto may well be the most dynamic. The liberal blending formula gives producers a broader palette to work with, and as evidenced by the Orvieto wines from top producers such as Palazzone, Decugnano Barbi, Barberani, and those mentioned above, each vintage is a slight remodeling of the classic Orvieto structure. In the same way that Gavi or Soave shouldn't be dismissed out of hand because of what they *once* were, Orvieto merits another look for what it is—and for what it's becoming.

Outside of Orvieto, meanwhile, Umbrian white wine is a hodgepodge. Trebbiano and grechetto are the ruling grape varieties, although generally speaking the latter is the one to look for. Not only are many Orvieto producers making "varietal" grechettos (Bigi and Barberani among them), but some excellent grechetto-based whites can be found farther inland, in the Colli Martani DOC zone.

The Colli Martani spreads across a broad swath of central Umbria, taking in the commune of Montefalco, which is more famous for its red, Sagrantino. But many of the producers who are famed for sagrantino-based reds are making grechettos in the Colli Martani DOC, including Arnaldo Caprai, Antonelli, and Rocca di Fabbri; others are making blends or IGT grechettos à la Antinori. Other good places to look for good grechetto are the Colli del Trasimeno zone, surrounding the giant Lake Trasimeno near the border with Tuscany, and the newish Assisi DOC, which includes provisions for a varietal grechetto.

And then there are whites that don't fit into any category at all, such as the varietal chardonnays made at Lungarotti, among many other estates. Without a doubt, these chardonnays are often excellent wines (also worth checking out

are those of Rio Grande and of course Castello della Sala), but as is so often the case in the diversified world of Italian wine, how do you find the time to drink it when there's so much else out there?

VINI ROSSI
Red Wines

On the red side, there are some interesting parallels to be drawn between Umbria and its sometime overlord, Tuscany. For one, sangiovese remains the most-planted grape variety, used most famously in the Torgiano Rosso DOCG blends of Lungarotti but found throughout the region. For another, the Bordeaux varieties have staged a bona-fide invasion of Umbria, with the result being a new crop of "super-Umbro" reds modeled after their more famous Tuscan neighbors. Right now, Umbria is a clash of the traditional earthy, foresty sangiovese-based blends of Lungarotti (and the bigger, blacker sagrantino reds from Montefalco) versus the modern—a growing population of wines from cabernet, merlot, and other international varieties, made toastier and richer by way of barrique aging.

It all still starts with Lungarotti, whose classic sangiovese-canaiolo blend, "Rubesco," remains the benchmark Umbrian red. Warm and spicy, the wine is a traditional style in that it is aged not in small barriques but in large casks, or *botte,* that hold more than a thousand gallons. Whereas a wine aged in barrique retains more color and forward fruitiness (along with a decided toastiness from the wood), a wine aged in a larger cask has more surface area exposed to oxygen, which naturally sneaks through the staves in the barrel. Like any *botte*-aged wine,

Rubesco tends toward a brickish-ruby color and has a more mature aromatic profile, even as a young wine: Layered on top of its core of black-cherry fruitiness are notes of cinnamon, saddle leather, and tar, savory aromas that don't necessarily jibe with the "fruit bomb" model so popular today.

"The secret to our wines is not a long time spent in wood but a long time spent in bottle," says Teresa Severini of Lungarotti, noting that most of her top reds—including the Rubesco cru "Vigna Monticchio" and the sangiovese-cabernet blend "San Giorgio"—are held for a minimum of five years in bottle before they are released for sale. "You don't see many wineries holding wines for that long anymore."

Indeed, you don't. And as such the Lungarotti wines continue to stand alone—not because there aren't any other reds on the market, but because there still really aren't any reds to compare them to. Whereas the trend in Umbria today is toward blacker, richer, sweeter reds, the Lungarotti wines remain resolutely savory. In a sense, they've been pre-aged before they hit the store shelf.

Bridging the gap somewhat between traditional and modern are the wines of the Montefalco DOC zone, which takes in five towns in a broad basin of vineyards southeast of Torgiano. Created only in 1979, the Montefalco DOC is nevertheless a historic one, and its native grape—the mysterious sagrantino—belongs only to the locals.

"Sagrantino doesn't exist anywhere else," asserts Marco Caprai, the young owner of the Arnaldo Caprai estate in Montefalco, probably the best-known in the area. The theories on sagrantino's origins abound—some say it's of Greek heritage, others say it was brought to the area from France by the Franciscan friars. And while it is not produced in great quantities it has become the red grape most readily identified with Umbria.

Montefalco wine is broken in two. The basic Montefalco DOC *rosso* is actually comprised primarily of sangiovese (60 to 70 percent), with a minimum of 10 percent sagrantino and the remainder filled with other grapes of the maker's choosing. The varietal Sagrantino di Montefalco, comprised of 100 percent sagrantino, has always been given its own DOC designation. In 1992, Sagrantino di Montefalco was elevated to DOCG status, a move that made official what most producers already knew: That the dense, dark, sappy reds made from sagrantino are like nothing else in Italy.

The sagrantino vineyards of Montefalco and its surrounding communes sit in a basin enveloped by the Apennines, in fairly rich clay soils interspersed with varying percentages of sand and limestone. Although the heat in the area can get intense during the summertime, the interplay of mountain and Mediterranean currents brought up via the Tiber help moderate the climate somewhat, lengthening the growing season. In this environment, sagrantino grows into a burly, brambly red with aromas ranging from blackberry jam to pine tar, the overall effect being a contrast of savory and sweet flavors, wrapped in a powerful package.

"Sagrantino is exceptionally rich in the polyphenols that give a wine color, and is considerably more tannic than sangiovese," says Caprai. "This is a wine with incredible aging potential, but the tannins are sweet rather than sharp, which makes it drinkable when it's young."

The only thing holding sagrantino back is that there isn't that much of it. Only about 250 acres of sagrantino vines are in existence, making the wines difficult to locate (Lungarotti alone produces more wine than the entire Sagrantino di Montefalco DOC). But they are out there, and they are definitely worth looking for. Along with Caprai, the noteworthy names include Colpetrone, Milziade Antano, Fratelli Adanti, Rocca di Fabbri, Antonelli, and the great Paolo Bea, whose earthy wines bring to mind some of the inkiest Australian shiraz.

Beyond the Torgiano-Montefalco hills, meanwhile, anything goes when it comes to reds. The two most interesting areas at the moment are the hills of Lake Trasimeno, where producers take advantage of a very liberal blending formula in the Colli del Trasimeno DOC to craft rich, international-style blends; and Orvieto, where a growing number of producers are making eye-opening reds to complement their oft-overlooked whites.

Bordeaux-style blends are the order of the day in these zones, particularly in Orvieto, where the recently created Rosso Orvietano DOC is especially broad-based in its prescriptions for which grapes can be used. (Of course, this tends to be academic since many of the better-known super-Umbro wines are made outside the parameters of DOC.) And it merits mentioning that the mastermind behind an alarming number of these wines is a consultant named Riccardo Cotarella. Although Cotarella works with a wide array of wineries all over Italy, his consultancy is based in the southern-Umbrian city of Terni, and as such he has his fingers in the fermenters of an exceptionally high number of Umbrian estates. At this writing, he works with: the Pieve del Vescovo property near Lake Trasimeno, whose "Lucciaio" Rosso is a unique blend of merlot, sangiovese, canaiolo, and gamay; La Carraia in Orvieto,

whose well-regarded "Fobiano" is 90 percent merlot and 10 percent cabernet; Palazzone in Orvieto, whose "Armaleo" is a blend of cabernets sauvignon and franc, aged for a year in barriques; and Rio Grande in Penna, which makes a Bordeaux blend called "Casa Pastore." And those are just the biggest names on his roster.

Cotarella is known for being unabashedly modern in his winemaking approach, creating reds that are as extracted as possible, with a creamy sheen of new oak. His touch is definitely evident in the above-mentioned wines, which have become some of Umbria's most critically acclaimed: They are reds that are both powerful and immediately accessible, with a luxurious, almost sweet fruitiness. Some purists see these blends as a standardization of Umbrian wine, but then again, Cotarella has seized the moment in a region with little red-wine tradition to speak of. Although a wine such as La Palazzola's rich and extracted merlot (not made by Cotarella) may not strike the traditionalist as an authentic Umbrian wine, there's no clear indication—other than sagrantino—of what an authentic Umbrian wine is. In the spirit of Giorgio Lungarotti, the region's producers are looking forward, not back, and the results are increasingly interesting.

Vini Spumanti e Dolci
Sparkling and Sweet Wines

As in other regions of Italy, Umbria has a few DOC zones in which a handful of *spumanti* are produced—or allowed to be produced, anyway. But they are generally more localized products.

On the other hand, Umbria is quietly turning out some of the best sweet wines in Italy. In their late-harvest wines, the producers of Orvieto transform an often ho-hum white into a golden nectar tinged with the smoky complexity of botrytis bunch rot, while in Montefalco the sagrantino grape is made into a sweet *passito* so powerful it brings to mind a vintage Port.

The sweet wines of Orvieto have been heralded for centuries. In the past, the wines were thick and sweet because that was all the winemaking technology of the day would allow. But the wines—however accidental—became the favored tipple of the popes who summered at Orvieto's Lake Corbara. These days, vintners allow their grapes to hang on the vine until they are superconcentrated, then allow the cool autumn fog that descends on the vineyards of Orvieto to work its magic and create the "noble rot" (*muffa nobile*) called botrytis. As discussed elsewhere, the effect of botrytis is to create a glycerine-rich wine with a hint of smokiness, and there are a number of excellent Orvieto sweet wines available in the market: Castello della Sala's luscious "Muffato della Sala" tops the list, but nearly all of the best Orvieto producers make a late-harvest version, including Barberani (theirs is called "Calcaia") and Decugnano dei Barbi ("Pourriture Nobile").

Even more intense are the sweet reds of Montefalco, made by drying the grapes on straw mats to concentrate their sugars, à la Recioto della Valpolicella. The *appassimento*, or *passito*, process transforms an already dense red wine into an evocation of liquid milk chocolate and blackberry preserves, so inky and rich it is a dessert in itself. Among the better versions are the knockout *passito* made by Paolo Bea, as well as the *passiti* of Antonelli, Caprai, and Adanti. If you do nothing else in your explorations of Umbria, find these wines.

FAST FACTS: # UMBRIA

PROVINCES	Perugia (PG), Terni (TR)
CAPITAL	Perugia
KEY WINE TOWNS	Montefalco, Orvieto, Torgiano
TOTAL VINEYARD AREA*	16,503 hectares, or 40,779 acres. Rank: 15th
TOTAL WINE PRODUCTION*	740,000 hectoliters, or 19,550,858 gallons (16th); 58% white, 42% red
DOC WINE PRODUCED*	30.5% (6th)
SPECIALTY FOODS	olive oil; black truffles from Norcia and Spoleto; lentils from Castelluccio; *Chiuscolo* (a soft, spreadable sausage from Norcia); dried pasta; chocolates (most famously those of Perugina).

*1997 figures. Rankings out of 20 regions total (Trentino–Alto Adige counted as one). Source: Istituto Statistica Mercati Agro–Alimentari (ISMEA), Rome.

KEY GRAPE VARIETIES

WHITES

GRECHETTO	Thought to be a sub-variety of greco, it has emerged as the best native white vine in the region. Many producers are vinifying it on its own or increasing its role in their Orvieto blends at the expense of blander varieties such as trebbiano.
TREBBIANO	This highly mutable family is widespread in Umbria, the most popular sub-variety being the prolific trebbiano toscano. There's also a distinct subvariety called trebbiano Spoletino (named for the town of Spoleto).

CHARDONNAY	Made famous in these parts by Castello della Sala's "Cervaro della Sala," which combines chardonnay with grechetto to create a rich yet crisp white.
OTHERS	VERDELLO, used in Orvieto, Torgiano, and Colli Trasimeno blends; DRUPEGGIO, the Umbrian name for CANAIOLO BIANCO, a blending variety also found in Tuscany.

REDS

SANGIOVESE	Considered a Tuscan import, it is the dominant red variety in the region, and found in the majority of the region's DOC-classified reds.
SAGRANTINO	Found only in Umbria, it's origins are unclear, and only about 250 acres of vineyards are planted with the variety. A deep, dark, tannic grape whose wines have an exotic spiciness.
GAMAY	Although more readily associated with Beaujolais, this variety turns up throughout Italy, and plays a significant role in Umbria's Colli Trasimeno DOC, where it is sometimes vinified as a varietal wine.
OTHERS	CABERNET SAUVIGNON, used increasingly in IGT and VdT blends; MERLOT, also popular in new-generation blends; CANAIOLO, a Tuscan native used in Torgiano and elsewhere.

TOP VINTAGES IN UMBRIA, 1980–2000

For most of its modern history, Umbria had but a handful of red wines capable of aging for any significant period—the sangiovese-based reds of Lungarotti in Torgiano and the Montefalco Sagrantino wines made a few communes over. Not much has changed, although the last decade has seen a host of powerful, barrique-aged reds come into the market from a variety of far-flung places, including Orvieto, which was previously known only for whites. Benchmark years for the Lungarotti wines include 1990, 1995, and 1997. For Montefalco Sagrantino, the last decade in particular was especially kind: Look for wines from 1995 and 1997 to 2000. All were exceptional years for this powerhouse red.

LA STRADA DEL VINO
WINE TOURING IN UMBRIA

There may be no more harmonious melding of wine and history than Orvieto, a striking medieval town in southwestern Umbria, steps from the border with Lazio. Aside from the renowned duomo and other historic attractions, wine lovers can check out the dramatic Castello della Sala, owned by Tuscany's Antinori family, which can be visited by appointment (076-38-60-51). Those in search of the ultimate mountain food should make an excursion to the upland town of Norcia in Umbria's Apennine foothills, a town which is famous for a variety of pork products as well as truffles. And those who prefer one-stop shopping might choose to base themselves in Torgiano, at the Lungarotti family's famed Le Tre Vaselle (Corso Garibaldi 48, 075-988-04-47; www.lungarotti.it), where you can eat well and visit both a wine and olive-oil museum in the course of about two blocks. Torgiano is also a good base from which to visit Assisi, Spoleto, and Montefalco.

DEGUSTAZIONI
TASTINGS

ORVIETO CLASSICO

Poggio del Lupo
Orvieto Classico, $

Castello della Sala
Orvieto Classico
Superiore, $

Palazzone
Orvieto Classico
 "Terre di Vineate," $

Cool, clean, dewy, delicately aromatic: These descriptors could be applied to any number of light Italian whites. And so it is with Orvieto, another delicate white based on trebbiano but, in this case, including a wider array of "supporting" varieties. These wines share certain characteristics—aromas of green apple and fresh-cut hay, and crisp acidity—but they differ in weight on the palate. The Poggio del Lupo wine is perhaps the most straightforward and clean of the three. The Castello della Sala wine includes a substantial percentage of chardonnay in its blend, which may account for its rounder, fleshier character. And the Palazzone is probably the most succulent, an example of the peachier, creamier flavors that can be extracted by leaving the grapes on the vine longer and fermenting their juice (or at least a portion of it) in oak barrels. Still, these are lighter-styled whites that offer a crisply acidic contrast to truffle- and butter-drenched pastas.

Lungarotti Torgiano
Rosso "Rubesco Riserva
Vigna Monticchio," $

La Fiorita-Lamborghini
Rosso dell'Umbria
"Campoleone," $

SANGIOVESE-BASED REDS

These two bottles mark a generational shift in Umbrian winemaking: On the one hand is the Lungarotti wine, made from a
more traditional mix of sangiovese and canaiolo, aged in
mostly large oak barrels and held in bottle for more than five
years before release. The wine is spicy and savory, with the
black-cherry and forest-floor aromas typical of sangiovese, but
its structure is fine, even delicate, with a good dose of acidity.
The Lamborghini wine is a little more supercharged, not just
with a softening dose of merlot in the blend but with time
spent in small oak barriques. It is a more youthful, chunky,
deeply colorful wine, with more toasty oak influence layered
over the core of fruit; plump and oaky, it is emblematic of the
direction many modern Italian wines are going. On the other
hand, the Lungarotti wine, aromatic and earthy—if not quite as
thick and juicy—is what might be called a traditional style. Is
one better than the other? That's the debate raging in Italy
these days.

Fattoria Milziade Antano
Sagrantino di Montefalco,
$$

Paolo Bea
Sagrantino di Montefalco,
$$$

Arnaldo Caprai
Sagrantino di Montefalco,
$$$

SAGRANTINO DI MONTEFALCO

Make an effort to locate these three reds, because they are
some of the true sleepers in the world of Italian red wine (the
first two will be tougher to locate than the third, but all three
are available in the States). All are warm, rich, weighty reds, the
kinds of wines that bring to mind a hearty, spicy stew. The
Antano wine is probably the most restrained of the three,
although it is not short on flavor: think of blackberries and
wintry spices such as mace and nutmeg. The Bea wine is earth-
ier, funkier, with a personality not unlike that of a burly Aussie
shiraz. And the Caprai is black as night and slick as dark
chocolate, a melding of the black fruit flavors of the sagrantino
grape and the toasty aromas and texture that comes from
barrique aging. Try these rich yet spicy reds with birds such
as pheasant and squab (both Umbrian favorites) and other
game meats.

La Cucina

FOOD FOR THE WINE

RECIPE BY LIDIA BASTIANICH

As noted earlier in this chapter, Umbria doesn't always get the recognition it deserves for its rich array of local specialties: lentils from the mountain town of Castelluccio; truffles and pork sausages from nearby Norcia; plush and aromatic olive oils from groves around Spoleto, Montefalco, and Assisi. Umbria's is a robust cuisine of the earth, since it is one of the few regions of Italy not touched by the sea. The only well-known fish dish in the region is made from eels from the giant Lake Trasimeno, which sits in western Umbria near the border with Tuscany.

When you think of Umbria, think of game birds, think of roast suckling pig, and think of truffles. Most of northern, eastern, and southern Umbria is defined by the Apennines, whose foothills spill down toward the broad basin of olive groves and vineyards in the center of the region. Traversed by countless rivers and streams, including the Tiber that flows down past Rome, Umbria is lushly green all year round. Its dense upland forests are prime truffle-hunting territory.

When it comes to truffles, people typically think first of Alba in Piedmont, where the truffle hunts are mythical and the prices astronomical. But Umbria, too, is a major source of these odoriferous delicacies. The town of Norcia is the best-known source, with a "hunting" season that begins shortly after Christmas and reaches its peak in March. The easy-to-execute recipe below is a contrast of powerful primal flavors: an example of how a dish can be both simple and complex.

Spaghetti alla Norcina

½ pound fresh BLACK TRUFFLES, grated (or substitute canned French black truffles in truffle juice, a 140 gm size, and reserve the liquid the truffles are packed in)

1 pound thin SPAGHETTI

¼ cup extra-virgin OLIVE OIL

4 cloves fresh GARLIC, crushed with the side of a knife

4 canned ANCHOVY FILLETS, chopped fine

SALT to taste

SERVES 4

Prepare fresh black truffles for grating by cleaning and brushing them under cold running water. Pat dry thoroughly with a towel, then grate them with a box grater. (If using canned presliced black truffles, remove them from the can, strain out the oil, and set aside. These truffles generally come sliced, so chop the sliced truffles into a fine mince and measure out an amount equaling one cup. A grater will also work fine.)

In a large stockpot, bring 6 cups of salted water to a boil. Add the pasta, and begin preparing the sauce as the pasta is cooking.

Heat the olive oil in a medium sauté pan over medium-high flame. When the oil is shimmering, add the garlic and sauté until lightly golden, about 3 minutes. Add the chopped anchovies and sauté until they disintegrate, about 3 to 4 minutes, stirring to break them up. Stir in all but 1 teaspoon of the grated truffles, coating them well with the oil, reduce the heat to medium-low, and add 2 tablespoons of the pasta's cooking water, or, if you are using canned truffles, 2 tablespoons (or more) or the reserved truffle juice. If you are using canned truffles, stop cooking here. If you are using fresh truffles, cook for about 10 minutes, adding water 2 tablespoons at a time, until the mixture reaches the consistency of a loose pesto. Remove from the heat and set aside.

When the pasta is finished, drain and add it directly to the pan containing the sauce. Mix until the pasta is evenly coated, and may even take on a black color from the truffle (especially if you are using fresh black truffles). Divide among 4 plates, and top each with the remaining teaspoon of grated truffle, but no cheese.

WINE RECOMMENDATION: There are many ways to go with wine here: Either offset the earthy intensity of the dish with a clean, simple white from Orvieto, or go with a richer red Sagrantino di Montefalco to meet the truffle flavor head on.

Le Marche

A Region on the Rise

A Raw Deal

The road to Portonovo is like a waterslide, corkscrewing its way down a steep, thickly wooded slope and emptying out into the Adriatic. Portonovo is one of a handful of tiny resort towns tucked into the crevices of the Monte Cònero massif, which juts into the sea to create the little nook in which Ancona, the capital of Le Marche, sits. The name Ancona is from the Greek *ankon*, meaning elbow, in reference to the way it angles out onto the water. Ancona is not at the top of many tourists' lists, or at least the town proper isn't: It's a big, rambling port, thick with cars and trucks waiting for incoming ferries and commercial freighters. Portonovo, maybe fifteen minutes to the south, is another story. It sits on a stretch of coast to rival anything in Amalfi, or Liguria, or anywhere else there's a *riviera*. But relatively few people know about it.

Crisp and salty from a day of bobbing in the Adriatic, we're clambering over the rocky sliver of earth that passes for a beach in Portonovo, gazing up at the cliffs rising abruptly from the water. The destination is a tiny beachside restaurant called Al Clandestino, which, as its name would suggest, is said to be a well-kept secret among the locals. But of course it's not a well-kept secret. The chef, a wild-eyed, somewhat blissed-out character named Moreno, is well known for another fancier restaurant he owns up the coast in Senegallia. Al Clandestino is his summertime lark. It is little more than a shack not ten yards from the water, with umbrella-topped tables spread across a small patch of sand, everything sheltered by tall maritime pines. It's the toughest reservation around.

Moreno's specialty is *crudo*, or Italian-style raw seafood, and he plays it to the hilt; he bills his menu as *sushi italiano* and sports a white headband with a big red dot in the middle. He has a Japanese chef behind the small counter carving up the Adriatic catch, which ranges from gleaming purple hunks of *tonno* (tuna) to spiny *ricci* (sea urchins) and big, silvery *alici* (anchovies). Moreno, who looks like a young Michael Keaton, busies himself with the hipster crowd, most of which is lolling around in bikini tops and bare feet.

But this is no clambake. From the humble little shack come small rectangular plates of delicate raw fish in architectural presentations, drizzled with olive oil and/or balsamic vinegar where a soy sauce might otherwise have been. A piece of *pesce spada* (swordfish) is like a cooling breeze on the tongue, the more pungent *ricci* like a taste of the ocean floor. A couple of

THE DOC ZONES OF LE MARCHE

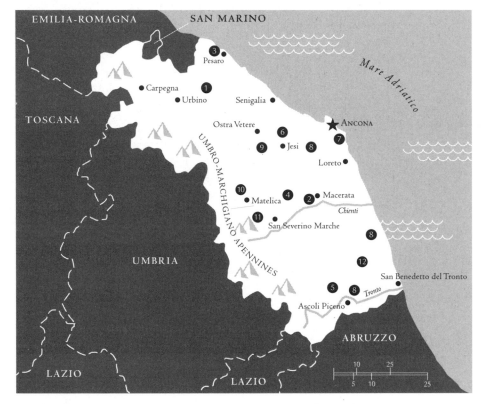

1 Bianchello del Metauro
2 Colli Maceratesi
3 Colli Pesaresi
4 Esino
5 Falerio dei Colli Ascolani
6 Lacrima di Morro/Lacrima di Morro d'Alba
7 Rosso Cònero
8 Rosso Piceno
9 Verdicchio dei Castelli di Jesi
10 Verdicchio di Matelica
11 Vernaccia di Serrapetrona
12 Offida*

*New in 2000–2001

shrimp swim in a marinade of oil and orange juice, everything an electrifying tingle of acidity and minerality. To drink we've got a local Verdicchio dei Castelli di Jesi, which is electric in its own right. Its scents of pignoli nuts and Bosc pears are lifted by its acidity, which sears into the *crudo* like a branding iron. Maybe it's all that sun, but this may be the perfect restaurant experience.

The Marche is actually more famous for cooked fish—namely *brodetto,* or fish soup, bequeathed by the Greeks who founded Ancona and now available in so many incarnations that no one agrees on the real recipe. But *crudo* is just as pervasive. Moreno, whom we've befriended over the course of several visits, clearly relishes his role as the zen master of raw seafood. His Japanese chef has a piece of *branzino* (sea bass) on the counter, and is about to fillet it as Moreno leans his bandannaed head over the counter and puts his hand to his ear. "You know you're doing it right when you hear the click of the knife on each vertebrae of the fish," he says, his bug eyes widening at the resonance of this little revelation. "Every time he misses a click, it costs me money, because that means we're not cleaning it off the bone properly."

Crudo is found all over the Italian coast, and particularly the Adriatic, where—if you buy into such theories—the seafood takes on inimitable flavors from the exceptionally high salt and mineral contents of the water. And there's something nebulous about *crudo* preparation that lends it an air of mystery. "All you need is a sharp knife and some good oil" to make it, according to Moreno, but few lay cooks would ever dare, even if they could pull a fish straight from the sea and cut it up right there. The ability to recognize a fresh fish and then serve it

raw is a step up the culinary skills ladder that most people would rather someone else take.

Talk to someone like Moreno about the "hows" of *crudo* preparation and you'll get some of those standard answers that always sound simple enough in cookbooks or on television but seem difficult to put into practice: Look for glassy eyes, he says, and a wet, slimy texture (well, yes, it does seem obvious not to buy a dried-out fish), and most notably, rigor mortis. "The stiffer the fish, the better," he says.

But we can leave it to him to worry about all that. The sky is going black and the cliffs of Cònero are looming somehow larger in the darkness, a rising moon glinting off the water. Al Clandestino is like a burning ember on the deserted slice of beach, populated with a bunch of happy castaways eating raw fish in the sand. It doesn't get any simpler than this, and yet it would be impossible to replicate.

The Marche's long Adriatic coastline is offset by a spine of Apennines that runs the length of the region, with the area in the middle diced up by a series of river valleys that run east to the sea. The region is equally famous for mountain foods, whether the prosciutto of the northern hamlet of Carpegna or the stuffed suckling pig called *porchetta* found throughout the interior regions, but ultimately it's the Adriatic that wins out. The climate from the tip to the toe of the Marche is fairly uniform, thanks to sea breezes that temper the weather in the markedly gentle river valleys. Only when you go very deep into the Umbro-Marchigiano Apennines does the landscape get rugged; everywhere else is softly contoured, lending the Marche a reputation of being a very easygoing place.

Historically, Le Marche (as it is called in Italian) was a frontier, a buffer zone of sorts between the Papal States of Rome and their various enemies farther north. As a wine zone, too, it seems caught in the middle, with one eye on the fragrant white wines of the north and the other on the plump reds of the south. It is a difficult region to characterize, despite being the source of one of the more enduring images in Italian wine: the fish-shaped bottles of the Fazi-Battaglia winery, whose Verdicchio dei Castelli di Jesi was (and is) the Marche's mass-market answer to the Soave of Veneto.

VINI BIANCHI
White Wines

Marche white wine can be summed up in one word: verdicchio. There are a handful of DOC whites produced throughout the region that don't feature the grape. But these wines—including Bianchello del Metauro (made on the north coast near Pesaro from the rare biancame variety) and Bianco di Colli Maceratesi (made near Macerata, south of Ancona, from the equally obscure maceratino grape)—don't add up to much. The Marche is the land of verdicchio, as expressed not only in the gentle hills west of Jesi but in the more rugged Apennine basin farther inland in Matelica.

Verdicchio is often described as one of Italy's "most interesting" native white grapes, which is often intended as a backhanded compliment; given the reputation of Italian whites such as trebbiano and greco, the implication is that verdicchio is the king of the also-rans. But with each new vintage, the wines of Jesi and Matelica develop a more definable and durable personality. In the past, most Verdicchio dei Castelli di Jesi has been of the type sold

in amphora- and fish-shaped bottles—light, chalky, almost mouth-puckeringly acidic. But many producers, Fazi-Battaglia among them, are now building more flavors and aromas into a wine that is still somewhat fragile but undoubtedly unique.

Of all the DOC-classified wine produced in the Marche, more than half is Verdicchio dei Castelli di Jesi, an appellation that refers to the verdicchio grape grown on either side of the Esino River west of Jesi, a striking medieval hill town. Jesi isn't actually part of the DOC zone but is more of a gateway to it, looking out over rolling hills comprised mainly of crumbly limestone- and mineral-rich clay—a good soil for both whites and reds, but especially good for whites because it delays ripening and helps preserve acidity. Most of the vineyards in the zone are within twenty miles of the Adriatic, which moderates the climate. The positioning of Jesi's vineyards is not unlike that of some of the vineyards of Friuli–Venezia Giulia, which also sit at a midpoint between mountains and sea.

The verdicchio grape is considered native to the Marche, although most experts believe that it is somehow related to the greco of Campania and in turn the trebbiano of Tuscany and elsewhere. (As noted in the Campania chapter, greco may well be the grandaddy of nearly all of Italy's indigenous white grapes.) Genetic studies have more specifically linked the verdicchio of Marche to the trebbiano of Lugana (Lombardy) and Soave (Veneto); if you placed inexpensive versions of Verdicchio dei Castelli di Jesi, Lugana, and Soave side by side, they might well be difficult to tell apart. Chances are, though, that the verdicchio would stand out. Although it is not typically a full-bodied white, it has a distinctive aroma and flavor. It has what vintners call varietal character, in that you can tell what it is when you smell and taste it, even if you can't precisely define what those smells and tastes are. The same cannot be said of trebbiano, which is more often than not light to the point of neutrality.

What are the smells and tastes of verdicchio? Like the fiano and greco of Campania, verdicchio often has a distinctly piney, resiny flavor, along with suggestions of sour apple, bosc pear, and green herbs. It's a "green" grape flavor, and the variety is also known for its naturally high acidity. Verdicchio wines are both savory and fruity. Although it is always dangerous to generalize about such things, most verdicchio makers would agree that the varietal stamp of their grape is somewhere in the above ballpark.

Ampelio Bucci, the proprietor of the Fratelli Bucci estate in the Castelli di Jesi zone, describes verdicchio thusly: "It has a sour fruit character on the nose and palate, like sour apples and quince, even lime. But then on the finish there's an almond-skin bitterness that is very typical of the grape. I don't know where that nutty finish comes from, but for me it's something that defines verdicchio."

What producers emphasize is that, like many other Italian whites, it wasn't so much the grape as the mentality of the producers that kept verdicchio from getting more widespread critical acclaim. In reality, the temperate and very dry climate of the Jesi hills is an excellent environment for a hardy, vigorous vine like verdicchio. Jesi's natural advantage is a long and mostly dry growing season, which, when producers control their crop yields, brings out the fuller, fruitier side of variety.

In fact, Verdicchio dei Castelli di Jesi is one of many wines in Italy today that exemplifies the evolution of Italian white wine over the past several decades. Before the advent of controlled-temperature fermentations in the early seventies, Marche verdicchio was no doubt like much of the rest of the farmhouse white wine found throughout the country: coppery in color from a fermentation that included the skins of the grapes in the mix, and rich and slightly oxidative in taste because those fermentations proceeded naturally, at ambient temperatures. As also noted in the Friuli chapter, the advent of stainless steel fermenters and the ability to ferment grape juice at cooler temperatures created a whole new prototype for Italian whites: clean, delicately aromatic, and brightly acidic.

But of course verdicchio, like so many other Italian whites, became a mass-market item in the seventies. And when a producer is trying to grow as many grapes as he can, to make as many bottles as he can, the goal is not a balance of extract and acidity in the grapes but a basic minimum level of sugar and that's it. While perfectly pleasant with seafood, verdicchio became one of a number of Italian whites that was stripped of its personality in a production process that favored "clean" over character. The especially high acidity of verdicchio made it a tarter quaffer than most, and only recently has the grape been shown to be capable of more. What producers emphasize is that light, tart, anonymous verdicchio was a choice, not a reflection of the grape's true personality.

"Verdicchio is one of those grapes that ripens very late," explains Giancarlo Soverchia, a winemaking consultant who works with dozens of Marche estates. "It is very important that you trim excess grapes during the summer because verdicchio is also very productive. It sounds so simple, but reducing yields is a very recent thing in the Marche. That is one of the big differences between old verdicchio and new verdicchio: more careful work in the vineyards."

This refrain is heard a lot in Italy, but it is essentially true. In many respects, verdicchio and many other Italian whites have come full circle: In the old days they were thick, often sweet, and deeply flavorful. Then they became crisp and delicate—sometimes too much so. And now the better ones are settling into a place somewhere in the middle, with more fruit extract and aroma, but still that cleanliness that comes with more sophisticated technology. It may not be as easy to pin down as, say, sauvignon blanc, but verdicchio has character. Now the question is, how best to showcase it?

Today, the style spectrum of Verdicchio dei Castelli di Jesi is quite broad, as producers experiment not only with single-vineyard bottlings but, increasingly, with fermentation in wood barrels. Although some feel that the flavors of verdicchio are still too delicate for wood, a wide variety of Jesi vintners have had success with fermenting at least a portion of their wines in barrels. Among the more noteworthy examples of Jesi verdicchios incorporating at least some wood are Bucci's "Villa Bucci," Zaccagnini's "Salmàgina," Umani Ronchi's "Casal di Serra," Sartarelli's "Balciana," Fattoria Coroncino's "Gaiospino," and Fazi Battaglia's "San Sisto," to name a few.

In the end, however, the push toward barrel fermentation may be a little more than the delicate verdicchio can handle. Rather than ferment their wines 100 percent in oak, most producers —including those noted above—are instead using only a portion of barrel-fermented wine, as a way of enriching, rather than obscuring, the natural flavors of the grape. And many of the most interesting Jesi wines are the ones made without any oak influence whatsoever, such as Vallerosa Bonci's "San Michele," Sartarelli's "Tralivio," Tavignano's "Misco," and Bucci's basic Verdicchio dei Castelli di Jesi Classico. These wines have enough depth and clarity of flavor to forego that extra kick from oak. They are wines for a delicate slice of *crudo* with a drizzle of olive oil, or maybe a whole roasted fish stuffed with fresh herbs.

Even more seafood-ready are the wines of the Verdicchio di Matelica DOC, which lies farther inland than Jesi. Located in a high mountain basin to the southwest of Jesi (not far from the spring from which the Esino River originates), the commune of Matelica is the center of production for a firmer, more aromatic, and slightly more powerful version of verdicchio. Situated at considerably higher altitudes than their counterparts in Jesi, in a basin cooled by mountain air from the west, producers such as Bisci and La Monacesca are known for a more aromatic, nervous style of verdicchio in comparison to the broader, increasingly plush styles being turned out in Jesi. What's interesting is to compare wines from both zones side by side; while they share certain telltale aromas of green fruits and herbs, the Matelica wines tend to be more muscular and firmly structured.

"The difference is that we are twenty kilometers from Umbria, and the producers of Jesi are twenty kilometers from the sea," says Giuseppe Bisci, the proprietor of the Bisci winery in Matelica. The implications are intended to be obvious: Matelica's more continental climate is cooler, its altitudes higher, creating an environment in which the grapes mature that much more slowly than their counterparts near Jesi. "They harvest verdicchio ten days earlier than us," Bisci says, again assuming he is stating the obvious—that those extra ten days on the vine lend an extra degree of concentration and aroma. "The verdicchio here is more structured," Bisci contends. "It's a white with the structure of a red."

Other than the wines of Jesi and Matelica, meanwhile, the Marche offers fairly slim pickings for white wine. Down at the southern end of the region, near the city of Ascoli Piceno, there's a significant production of a crisp, trebbiano-based white called Falerio dei Colli Ascolani, of which Saladini Pilastri, Ercole Velenosi, and Cocci Grifoni make the best examples. The ever-popular chardonnay is also popping up here and there, most notably in the big, blowsy, barrique-aged "Villa Angela" from Ercole Velenosi and a range of chardonnays and chardonnay-based blends from Boccadigabbia and Oasi degli Angeli, two up-and-coming estates located along the Adriatic coast south of Ancona. Some critics dismiss their new-generation whites as show wines, but it's hard to ignore the sheer pleasure they offer. Even verdicchio stalwarts such as La Monacesca in Matelica have gotten on the chardonnay bandwagon, although La Monacesca's well-regarded "Mirum" (a verdicchio plumped up with a touch of chardonnay) could not be confused with the rich chardonnays made farther south.

VINI ROSSI
Red Wines

Although the white verdicchio keeps getting better, the red wine of the Marche has been capturing more critical praise. The combination of a dry maritime climate and limestone-rich soils in places such as Monte Cònero is, as noted above, just as favorable for reds as whites, and in the last decade or so the DOC of Rosso Cònero has become known as an up-and-coming appellation.

The story of Marche red wines follows a similar arc to that of the whites: Although there are a wide range of red grapes grown in the region, there is a single dominant variety (montepulciano) and two DOC wines made from that variety (Rosso Cònero, Rosso Piceno) that more or less define what the region is all about. Although the dominant variety in question has become more famous in neighboring Abruzzo (where the Marche version appears to have originated), the red winemakers of Le Marche have adopted the variety as their own.

The Rosso Cònero DOC follows the contours of the Cònero massif as it wraps around Ancona, covering a fairly small area: In total, the vineyards of the zone amount to less than a thousand acres, or about one-tenth of the vineyard area covered by the more expansive Rosso Piceno DOC, which wraps around the Cònero zone to the north and west and spreads to the border with Abruzzo. Rosso Piceno is considered more of a catchall appellation, as evidenced not only by its geographic breadth but by its production formula. Rosso Piceno wines are made from a combination of 30 to 50 percent montepulciano, 30 to 50 percent sangiovese, and 15 percent of other red grapes, to be left to the producer's discretion. Rosso Cònero reds are made from a required minimum of 85 percent montepulciano, and a maximum of 15 percent sangiovese—and nothing else. As such, the wines of Rosso Cònero have a more precise identity than those of Rosso Piceno: Generally speaking, the Rosso Piceno wines taste more of sangiovese, with aromas and flavors that suggest a softer version of Chianti; the Cònero wines taste more of montepulciano, suggesting a more firmly tannic version of Montepulciano d'Abruzzo. The wildcard in both wines is sangiovese, which is much more firmly rooted across the Apennines in Umbria and Tuscany, and even to the north in Emilia-Romagna. In the Marche there is some debate as to how much sangiovese should be used in the local blends, even among producers of Rosso Piceno, who are required by the DOC discipline to use it.

A good example of this is offered by the Saladini Pilastri winery near Ascoli Piceno, one of the leading producers of Rosso Piceno. According to enologist Domenico D'Angelo, the sangiovese vine is considerably more productive than that of montepulciano, and many producers in the Marche have treated the grape more as a workhorse than as the noble variety it can be. Unlike the Tuscans, who have studied sangiovese intently to come up with appropriate clones of the grape for different sites (brunello in Montalcino, prugnolo in Montepulciano), the *marchigiani* have traditionally valued it more for its vigor. At Saladini Pilastri, the winery's lowest-priced, most basic Rosso Piceno is a blend of 70 percent sangiovese and 30 percent montepulciano, whereas its pricier, more limited-production Rosso Piceno, "Vigna Montetinello," essentially reverses those proportions. The basic Rosso is a solid wine, with some of the savory, earthy, foresty notes of a good sangiovese, while the "Vigna Montetinello" is considerably bigger, blacker, and plusher, with a more sweetly tannic personality.

Comparisons could be made between the Rosso Piceno and Cònero zones and the wine regions of the Tuscan coast, where sangiovese thrives. But D'Angelo is among those who believe sangiovese does better on the other side of the Apennines. "Sangiovese is an important variety, and we can make good sangiovese here, but there is more interest now in what we can do with montepulciano," he says.

Based largely on their experiences with mass-produced *abruzzese* reds, wine critics have tended to regard montepulciano as a second-tier red grape. But producers of both Rosso Piceno and Rosso Cònero (not to mention their neighbors in Abruzzo) think otherwise. "Montepulciano is a grape with some of the highest levels of anthocyanins in Italy," says D'Angelo, referring to color pigments. "It has very high tannins, but they are sweet tannins, and it offers very generous amounts of extract. So you have this wine that is very colorful, sweet, and fruity, but it is also deceivingly able to age."

The Rosso Piceno DOC discipline was changed in recent years to allow for a greater percentage of montepulciano in the blend—up to 70 percent montepulciano can now be used, as opposed to a maximum of 40 percent in the past. But even now the style of Rosso Piceno wine varies widely from producer to producer. Considering that some of the big names in Rosso Piceno are located farther north near Jesi and Macerata (Bucci, Garofoli, Bonci) while others are clustered around Ascoli Piceno (Saladini Pilastri, Ercole Velenosi, Cocci Grifoni), it is impossible to generalize about the wines—other than to say that they can be some of the best values around.

The purer expressions of montepulciano—and some of Italy's greatest red-wine values—are found in the Rosso Cònero zone. "We are the only area on the whole Adriatic coast that is both hilly and near the sea," says Antonio Terni, the owner of Fattoria Le Terrazze in

Numana, one of the leading producers of Rosso Cònero. He is among a growing number of people who believe that the conditions of Cònero are better suited to montepulciano. "It's just a little too hot and dry here for good sangiovese," he says.

Terni's "Sassi Neri" Rosso Cònero and his limited-production "super-Marchigiano" wine called "Visions of J" (for a Bob Dylan song) are two potential examples of the power and concentration of montepulciano. Both wines are given a healthy dose of barrique aging, which infuses the normally sweet and fruity montepulciano with a savory edge, not to mention a more grippingly tannic bite. The same could be said of the Rosso Cònero wines made by Alessandro Moroder in Montacuto, whose "Dorico" Rosso Cònero rivals Sassi Neri in color and concentration of flavor. These wines, along with a host of others from producers such as Lanari (check out his "Fibbio"), Umani Ronchi (their "Cùmaro" was one of the first Rosso Còneros to gain worldwide critical attention), and Garofoli ("Piancarda") are some of the best values in Italian wine.

"You could compare some of the better Rosso Cònero wines to some of the new wines of the south," says Terni, "but I think Rosso Cònero offers more structure." Cònero, he says, offers a unique combination of intense heat; light, poor soils; low humidity; and cool evenings on steep, well-ventilated slopes. The wines develop more slowly than in points farther south, and in so doing develop more complexity. Most of the best Rosso Cònero wines are 100 percent montepulciano, as are many of the better "super-Marchigiano" wines, including the "Kurni" montepulciano made by the Oasi Degli Angeli winery.

At this writing, Antonio Terni is pushing for a DOCG designation for the Cònero zone, one in which the montepulciano grape would be given what he feels is its proper due. "The way I see it, the wine would be 100 percent montepulciano and say simply 'Cònero.' It would be something like Montalcino: The Cònero wine would be the top wine, made from a single variety, and Rosso Cònero would be the simpler, lighter, blended wine." Whether or not he gets his wish, wine drinkers are already able to sample montepulciano *in purezza* (pure) from any number of the above-mentioned estates. For red wines with lots of flavor and power at everyday prices, it is very hard to beat the slopes of Cònero.

As with white wines, the Marche offers a fairly limited selection of reds outside of the Rossos Piceno and Cònero. An interesting native red called Lacrima di Morro d'Alba, produced by a handful of estates in an area just west of Ancona, is a soft, dolcetto-like red that some locals think could be an important wine in the future, but it's too soon to tell. A smattering of pure sangioveses are made farther north in the region, most notably in the Colli Pesaresi DOC zone, but they too are mostly local products.

More noteworthy is the growing crop of "super-Marchigiano" reds, usually bottled with an IGT designation and incorporating grapes such as cabernet sauvignon, syrah, and merlot. Probably the most famous of these is the "Akronte" cabernet made by Boccadigabbia, but there is a grocery list of others, including Umani Ronchi's "Pélago" (cabernet-montepulciano-merlot), La Monacesca's "Camerte" (sangiovese-merlot), and Le Terrazze's "Chaos" (montepulciano-syrah-merlot). These wines are as big and lush as anything from the other side of the Apennines, but without the eye-popping price tags. Yet. As these wines find a wider audience, they may well start costing as much as "super-Tuscans." But they will probably be worth it.

VINI SPUMANTI E DOLCI
Sparkling and Sweet Wines

Many producers in the Jesi and Matelica zones note that the verdicchio of the Marche was one of the first spumanti made in Italy, with a history dating back to the nineteenth century. A number of top verdicchio producers continue to make sparkling versions of their wines, including some made in the *mèthode champenoise*, but they are fringe items in the American market. More interesting are the handful of late-harvest sweet wines made from the verdicchio grape, including Fazi-Battaglia's luscious "Arkezia" and Zaccagnini's "Cesolano," both of which take on the smoky complexity of botrytis bunch rot. These are especially exotic sweet wines, in that they are intensely flavored yet extremely light and crisp at the same time. Verdicchio's high natural acidity is there, even in the superripe grapes, lifting the flavors and giving the wine a brightness that all the great sweet wines of the world share.

FAST FACTS: $\mathcal{L}$E $\mathcal{M}$ARCHE

PROVINCES	Ancona (AN), Ascoli Piceno (AP), Macerata (MC), Pesaro (PS)
CAPITAL	Ancona
KEY WINE TOWNS	Ancona, Ascoli Piceno, Cupramontana, Matelica, Numana
TOTAL VINEYARD AREA*	24,590 hectares, or 60,762 acres. Rank: 12th
TOTAL WINE PRODUCTION*	1,815,000 hectoliters, or 47,952,443 gallons (10th); 62% white, 38% red
DOC WINE PRODUCED*	19.6% (10th)
SPECIALTY FOODS	*formaggio di fossa* (pecorino cheese aged in caves); *brodetto* (fish stew); *porchetta* (suckling pig stuffed with herbs); *prosciutto di Carpegna*; *olive ascolane* (stuffed olives, breaded and fried).

*1997 figures. Rankings out of 20 regions total (Trentino–Alto Adige counted as one). Source: Istituto Statistica Mercati Agro-Alimentari (ISMEA), Rome.

KEY GRAPE VARIETIES

WHITES

VERDICCHIO	Thought to be a part of the vast greco-trebbiano family, it has been genetically linked to subvarieties such as the trebbianos of Lugana and Soave. The grape has a distinctive aroma of green fruits and a trademark almondy finish, and very high natural acidity.
TREBBIANO	Usually the trebbiano toscano subvariety, it is found in a variety of Marche DOC whites, most notably the light, crisp Falerio dei Colli Ascolani.

OTHERS	BIANCAME, a rare local grape used in the Bianchello del Metauro DOC; MACERATINO, also a rare local with its own DOC; CHARDONNAY; SAUVIGNON BLANC.
	REDS
LACRIMA	The name means "tears," in reference to the grape's tendency to rupture easily and spill tears of juice on the bunch. It is grown in a small area west of Ancona and makes distinctively fruity, Beaujolais-like reds.
MONTEPULCIANO	Apparently borrowed from neighboring Abruzzo, it may reach its greatest heights of expression in Rosso Cònero.
SANGIOVESE	Tuscany's star variety is used here in both Rosso Cònero and Rosso Piceno blends; it factors more prominently in the latter.
OTHERS	CABERNET SAUVIGNON; SYRAH; MERLOT.

TOP VINTAGES IN LE MARCHE, 1980—2000

Don't be fooled by the soft, sweet tannins of Montepulciano: This is a wine that can age, as evidenced by some of the better bottlings of Rosso Cònero. Older vintages of these wines are not likely to be in great supply—this isn't Barbaresco. But a survey of Rosso Cònero producers yields the following list of top vintages: 1985, '88, '90, '93, '97, '98 (considered the best of the decade in Rosso Cònero). Stay away from '95 and '96. Both '99 and 2000 look extremely promising, especially '99.

LA STRADA DEL VINO
WINE TOURING IN LE MARCHE

Americans don't often make it over the Apennines to Le Marche, preferring to remain in the medieval villages of Umbria and Tuscany. But the Marche should not be overlooked. Ascoli Piceno, in the south, and Urbino, in the north, are two beautiful medieval towns in their own right, but the real appeal of Marche is its relatively unspoiled coast. Unlike Emilia-

Romagna's Rimini, the beach resort towns south of Ancona are true getaways, particularly those in the Parco Regionale del Monte Cònero—which is also the home of Le Marche's best red wines. After a day on the beach at Portonovo, head up to the Moroder wine estate on the outskirts of Ancona, whose restaurant, Aión (071-89-82-32), has a beautiful outdoor patio overlooking the vineyards. For more information on visiting the Cònero area, contact the Parco Regionale offices at 071-933-03-76. Useful websites include www.regione.marche.it and www.le-marche.com.

DEGUSTAZIONI
TASTINGS

VERDICCHIO DEI CASTELLI DI JESI

Sartarelli Verdicchio dei Castelli di Jesi "Tralivio," $

Umani Ronchi Verdicchio dei Castelli di Jesi "Casal di Serra," $

Bucci Verdicchio dei Castelli di Jesi Classico "Villa Bucci," $–$$

This flight begins with a fresh but full-bodied verdicchio redolent of sour apple, pear and green herbs, all cleaned up with a refreshing blast of acidity and that trademark bitter-almond finish. Many of the same flavor components are found in the Umani Ronchi wine, but, through the addition of a percentage of wine fermented in oak, there's more roundness and creaminess. Even the Villa Bucci, which is fermented and aged in large oak barrels, retains the piney, herbal aromatics of the grape while it tacks on more weight from its time in the barrels. All three wines will age well for several years and become more expressive of citrus fruits with time, but they are great to drink young with simple grilled seafoods.

VERDICCHIO DI MATELICA

La Monacesca Verdicchio di Matelica, $

Bisci Verdicchio di Matelica "Vigneto Fogliano," $

Expect more penetrating aromas and a firmer, finer structure in these wines as compared to those of Jesi. Here the floral, minerally side of verdicchio really comes to the fore, and it helps to tame the penetrating acidity of these wines with a little food. Some nice, plump scampi should do the job, maybe with some char marks from the grill and a good drizzle of olive oil.

Moroder Rosso Cònero
"Dorico," $

Fattoria Le Terrazze Rosso
Cònero "Sassi Neri," $

Lanari Rosso Cònero
"Fibbio," $

ROSSO CÒNERO

Here are three of the top reds of the Marche, all of them based on montepulciano, as evidenced by their inky colors. All have the juicy blackberry fruit and sweet tannins characteristic of well-made montepulciano: They are dense, dark wines, each with a sheen of new oak layered over flavors of black currants, black raspberries, and black cherries. In the Moroder wine, you get a slightly more smoky edge from a longer period of aging in oak before release, while in the Le Terrazze and Lanari wines the juiciness of the fruit leaps to the fore. What's especially appealing is how soft and accessible they are as young wines. These are tongue-staining reds to go alongside a hearty *porchetta* (stuffed suckling pig) or maybe a steak.

La Cucina

FOOD FOR THE WINE

RECIPE BY MARIO BATALI

With one of the longest stretches of coastline in Italy, the Marche is a seafood lover's heaven. Recipes for the famed *brodetto di pesce marchigiano* (fish stew) are said to vary significantly from port to port. But the most important concept we can learn about the seaside food culture of the Marche is simplicity. Whether it's eating the daily catch raw, marinated in olive oil and seasoned with local sea salt, or a famed northern Adriatic *branzino* (sea bass) roasted and served whole, only the freshest fish will do.

The recipe below isn't *marchigiano* per se, but more an evocation of the Adriatic in general. To pull it off, it will be important to have a good working relationship with your local fishmonger. European *branzino*, or sea bass, is now widely available in the United States and is probably the best type of fish to use for whole roasting, because of its delicate white flesh and easiness to clean.

The most important element of this dish is that the fish is as fresh as possible. By cooking the fish whole, you are effectively poaching the flesh within the original body of the fish. The "whole" concepts translates into more flavor by allowing the fish to stay intact through the cooking process and until you are ready to eat.

Branzino Arrosto
ROASTED WHOLE SEA BASS

1 BULB FENNEL, with lots of greens
1 ORANGE
2 LEMONS
½ cup plus 2 tablespoons extra-virgin OLIVE OIL
½ cup CALAMATA OLIVES, pitted
2 sprigs each SAGE, THYME, and ROSEMARY (¼ teaspoon each if dried)
SALT and PEPPER to taste
1 two-to-three-pound BRANZINO (European sea bass), cleaned and scaled but with head and tail on, or other firm, white-fleshed fish, such as striped bass, red snapper, porgy, or pompano

SERVES 2

Preheat the oven to 350°F.

Remove the leafy green fronds from the fennel and place them in a large mixing bowl. Cut the fennel bulb in half and slice it as thin as possible across the grain with a knife (or even better, on a slicer or a mandolin) and add to the tops. Zest the orange and one of the lemons and combine with the fennel. Juice the zested fruits and set the juice aside. Add ¼ cup of the olive oil, the olives, sage, thyme, and rosemary, and season with salt and pepper. Toss the mixture to dress it like a salad.

Coat the entire fish with the other ¼ cup of olive oil. Salt and pepper the fish aggressively, especially inside. Stuff the cavity with the fennel mixture and set the fish on a baking sheet. Cut the second lemon into rounds about ⅛ inch thick and set them on top of the fish.

Place the baking sheet on the middle rack of the preheated oven and roast the fish for 20 minutes per pound, or about 40 to 50 minutes total, depending on the size of the fish. A meat thermometer inserted where the head ends and the body starts should register 135°F. The skin should begin to blister and separate from the flesh. Remove the fish, allow to cool for 5 minutes, and fillet.

In a small bowl, combine the reserved lemon-orange juice, the remaining 2 tablespoons of olive oil, and the chopped parsley to create a zippy sauce to drizzle on top of the fish fillets. Season the sauce with salt and pepper and serve on the side.

WINE RECOMMENDATION: Verdicchio dei Castelli di Jesi or Verdicchio di Matelica. Many producers of Verdicchio dei Castelli di Jesi at one time played up the affinity of their whites for fish by packaging the wines in fish-shaped bottles, and while it may have been kitschy, it did make a point. The crisp acidity and herbal tang of a good verdicchio, from either Jesi or Matelica, will point up all the delicate flavors of the *branzino*.

Lazio

IN THE LONG SHADOW OF ROME

DERBY DAY

The twice-yearly meeting of Rome's two Division I soccer teams, AS Roma and SS Lazio, is the Italian equivalent of a Subway Series. In fact, you could say that New York's Yankees and Mets have similar geographic and cultural distinctions to those of Roma and Lazio: The Yankees are primarily the inner-city team, like Roma, while the Mets' fans are mostly suburbanites, like Lazio's. But in the end it really isn't the same. Roma and Lazio share not only the same city but the same home stadium, and nearly a century of bitter competitive history.

Italy's *Serie A* (Division I) season runs a marathon thirty-four weeks, from late September to early June. American baseball, World Series and all, is about thirty. When Lazio-Roma matches are on, the city practically closes down. Yes, there are still the pilgrims marching over to St. Peter's Square in their yellow neckerchiefs, and the tourist cafés on the Piazza Navona are still brimming. But the locals retreat to either their homes or to the eighty-five-thousand-seat *Stadio Olimpico*, in the northern neighborhood of Montemario, to witness a battle that has raged since the 1920s. An eerie calm falls over the abandoned streets during gametime, broken only by announcers' voices in

passing taxis or the occasional roar from behind closed doors.

With the help of a friend, Corrado (a lifelong Roma fan), we've scored tickets for the first derby of the 2000–'01 season—they actually use the English word *derby*, for whatever reason, to describe the Roma-Lazio matches. On this particular Sunday, a cool December afternoon, Lazio is the home team, meaning that we are outnumbered by Lazio fans ten to one. Yet neither Corrado nor his friends seem very concerned as they strut into the stadium in their bright red-and-yellow Roma scarves.

Once inside and ensconced in the *curva sud*—the hardest-core fans for each side establish themselves at the curved ends of the stadium, with Roma always assigned the southern end (*sud*) and Lazio the northern—the mood grows more bloodthirsty. Banners and flags are unfurled at either end, and at one point a group of Lazio fans, all in bright white T-shirts, creates a huge formation that spells *Roma merda!* (Roma is shit!) across the whole of the *curva nord*. This prompts a predictably angry response from the *sud* crew, which counters with shouts of *Mortacci tua!* (Death to yours!) and other epithets.

Things are heating up.

"That's just stupid," Corrado says of the obscene formation. "The big thing when you

The DOC Zones of Lazio

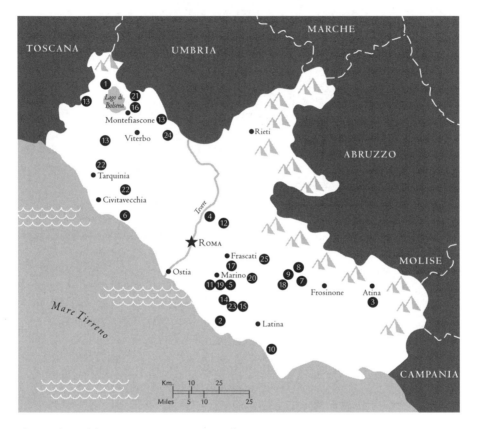

1 Aleatico di Gradoli
2 Aprilia
3 Atina
4 Bianco Capena
5 Castelli Romani
6 Cerveteri
7 Cesanese del Piglio
8 Cesanese di Affile/Affile
9 Cesanese di Olevano Romano
10 Circeo
11 Colli Albani
12 Colli della Sabina
13 Colli Etruschi Viterbesi

14 Colli Lanuvini
15 Cori
16 Est! Est!! Est!!! di Montefiascone
17 Frascati
18 Genazzano
19 Marino
20 Montecompatri-Colonna/
   Montecompatri/Colonna
21 Orvieto
22 Tarquinia
23 Velletri
24 Vignanello
25 Zagarolo

sit in the *curva* is you try to make it more beautiful than the other side's *curva*." He explains how, when they aren't spelling out nasty words, the fans hold up placards of different colors to compose giant Italian flags or other more palatable messages. But of course things can get ugly: At one point a banner is raised in the *curva sud* that translates to "We're number one, you're dopers!" (in reference both to Roma's first-place position and to the recent suspension of a Lazio player for blood doping).

"Usually there's not too much fighting or bad signs like that. But the Lazio fans definitely think they are superior," Corrado continues. "Their team was founded first, in 1900. Roma was founded in '24. Also, the Lazio team was founded by noble families in the northern part of Rome, whereas the Roma team was always more the team of the *popolino*. Roma's team was founded in Testaccio, which is the more working-class, southern part of the city. So like everything else in Italy, the rivalry is politicized. Unfortunately, Lazio has been the better team lately, but this year . . ."

He interrupts himself to watch a Roma midfielder named Batistuta, known for having a cannon of a right leg, line up a free kick. The game has been an American's nightmare up to this point, mostly played at midfield, with few scoring opportunities for either team. But as Batistuta approaches the ball, there's a great surge of energy in the *curva sud*. Then an agonizing group roar shakes the bleachers as Batistuta's shot, a rocket from thirty yards out, is batted away by the Lazio goalkeeper.

Almost immediately afterward, the *curva sud* bursts into song: A good shot on goal, apparently, is as good a reason as any. In fact, if there's one thing that unequivocally distinguishes an Italian soccer match from an American sporting event, it's not the fanaticism and it's not the sporadic violence—we've got plenty of both—it's the singing. While Corrado and his friends are more subdued sorts, nearly everyone around us in the *curva* is a singing and dancing machine. They are perpetually hopping up and down, arm in arm, belting out their verses so that their crescendos drown out those of the *curva nord* at the other end. And where we Americans have "*Take Me Out to the Ball Game,*" the Italian fans have a songbook so extensive and poetic it's like a mini-*concerto*.

Maybe, we volunteer to Corrado, there's so much singing because the fans need something to do in the absence of any scoring. "Ah, typical American," he says with a laugh. "Everything is scoring with you!"

We cross the seventy-minute mark in the game, still tied 0–0, and things are getting increasingly tense. The *curva sud* surges again as a Roma attacker makes a run and launches a high-arching cross. One of Roma's players emerges from a cluster in the penalty box and gets off a header on goal, but Lazio's goalie makes a great diving save. As the ball dribbles out in front of the goal mouth, one of Lazio's stars, a midfielder named Alessandro Nesta, winds up to belt the ball out of trouble, only to hit one of his teammates in the back with it and have it bounce back into the Lazio goal. The *curva sud* erupts in wild celebration as those smug Lazio fans (hey, we're Roma guys now) cope not only with the prospect of losing but with the particular humiliation of an "own goal."

And despite some furious attacks at both ends of the field, that's how it ends, with the Roma supporters singing all the way out the stadium doors. With Corrado's help, we join in on the main chorus:

Roma Roma Roma, t'ho dipinta io
(Roma, Roma, Roma, I have drawn you)
gialla come il sole e rossa come il core mio!
(yellow as the sun and red as my heart!)
Can you imagine a Yankee fan singing *that*?

Although the name of the team is Lazio, it is really Rome that its players represent, albeit a particular part of Rome. Lazio the region remains a somewhat indefinable entity. Even those who have visited Rome don't always know that Lazio is the region in which Rome sits. And as many writers and historians have noted, Lazio's borders are geographically and historically arbitrary. Its northern reaches were originally Etruscan territory, and even later, when the region came under the sway of the Pope, it has traditionally been thought of as a place whose pieces don't fit together.

Rome's size and political importance make it an entity unto itself, to the point where Rome and Lazio feel like distinct places. Whereas Florence manages to nestle seamlessly into the cypress-studded hills of Tuscany, Rome at times feels like an island on land—that much more urban, that much bigger, and ringed by an outer beltway that cuts it off, like a moat, from the verdant hills just fifteen minutes outside of town. It is striking to look out over Rome from the vineyards of the nearby Castelli Romani and feel at once very close to and very far from the city. This is a handicap for the beautiful but lightly regarded wine towns of Frascati, Marino, and the rest of the Castelli Romani villages, because they ultimately feel more like suburbia than the ancient land of wine. The shadow of the city looms large.

Rome has been both a blessing and a curse to Lazio winemaking. On the one hand, the city's tourists drink everything the wineries produce, and the wineries produce a lot—Lazio is the sixth most productive wine region in Italy. On the other hand, those Roman legions usually don't think too much about what they're drinking, and don't remember it afterward. This has led to a wine culture in which 85 percent of total production is white, and most of that is very light and nearly clear, to be sipped by the carafe in Roman *osterie*.

There are twenty-five DOC zones in Lazio, and yet there are very few distinctions to be made among them. Aside from the easy-to-pronounce Frascati and the creatively titled Est! Est!! Est!!! di Montefiascone, the DOCs of Lazio are all but interchangeable, some might say arbitrary. There's no single grape variety on the rise, no one zone with a cadre of up-and-coming producers, no unifying force whatsoever on the Lazio wine scene. That leaves consumers with nothing to go on but trial and error, and leaves wine writers with little to do but wax rhapsodic about Rome and handpick the best of a scattered lot.

VINI BIANCHI
White Wines

It's such a defining moment to sit in the open air on some narrow lane in Trastevere, twirl some *spaghetti alla carbonara* on your fork, and sip from a dewy *caraffa* of *vino bianco* while soaking up the sun, that it seems pretty silly to critique said *vino bianco*. But then again, this is a wine book.

In Lazio, the white-wine landscape is neatly summarized: Of the twenty-five DOC zones in the region, twenty include provisions for the production of white wine—and all of those twenty call for the use of trebbiano and/or malvasia in some percentage. There are numerous officially documented clones of both grapes, with no fewer than three trebbianos in widespread use: trebbiano giallo, thought to be related to greco; trebbiano verde, thought to be of Umbrian origin; and trebbiano toscano, the best known and most widely planted. Yet regardless of which clones are used, the wines made from them tend to suffer from an age-old Italian problem: neutrality.

Although the whites of the Frascati DOC, in the northern reaches of the Alban Hills south of Rome, have had international success, it has been at the low end of the market. Unlike the wines of, say, Soave in Veneto or Chianti in Tuscany, Frascati hasn't made its triumphant return to fashionability. It remains mostly in those dewy carafes, anonymous, since most Frascati producers are content to keep it that way.

What a lot of wine experts bemoan is how much more could be done in Lazio, particularly in the Alban Hills. These hills were once a summer refuge for Roman nobles, who built their villas, or *castelli*, in their heights to escape the heat of Rome. Towns such as Frascati, Montecompatri, Marino, and Velletri sit at a range of altitudes (two hundred to a thousand feet) on well drained, well ventilated volcanic soils, flanking the crater lakes of Albano and Nemi. These former volcanic masses are ideal soils for winemaking, porous and rich in potassium, particularly in more northern reaches such as Frascati, where the Mediterranean influence isn't felt as acutely as in Marino or Velletri. In all there are nine DOC zones clustered in the Alban Hills, forming a sort of half-moon around the crater lakes. Yet while they are geographically distinct, their blending formulas—and wines—are quite similar.

At their highest levels, the wines of Frascati and, say, Marino are in fact distinguishable—the Frascati will likely be more high-toned and fragrant, the Marino a little fleshier, since the latter is grown at slightly lower altitudes in a slightly warmer microclimate. But most of the wine of the Alban Hills is part of an amorphous, industrial-scale mass. Taken as a whole, the nine Castelli Romani DOCs (Colli Albani, Colli Lanuvini, Cori, Frascati, Marino, Montecompatri, Velletri, Zagarolo, and the all-encompassing Castelli Romani) account for more than 80 percent of *all* DOC-classified wine in Lazio.

"The biggest problem with Frascati is Rome," says Fabrizio Santarelli of Castel de Paolis. Santarelli's newish winery in Grottaferrata breaks the established Frascati mold, not just by extracting more flavor from the traditional malvasia and trebbiano but by throwing in "foreign" grapes as far-flung as viognier. "When you have a market twenty minutes away that will swallow up everything you make regardless of its quality, what path are you going to choose? Everyone here grows as much as they can and produces as much as they can."

Of course, it's not fair to dismiss the whites of Castelli Romani out of hand. Although trebbiano is a very mild grape even in the best of circumstances, malvasia can have a floral aroma, often reminiscent of orange blossoms, and a distinctive, tropical-fruit character that many producers are showcasing. The well-known Fontana Candida winery, in addition to making some of the more flavorful Frascatis available, makes a Malvasia del Lazio that highlights the full-bodied fruitiness of the grape. So does the Conte Zandotti winery, whose Malvasia del Lazio "Rumon" is honeyed and rich on the palate yet has plenty of acidity to balance it. And in Frascati wines such as Castel de Paolis's "Vigna Adriana," Villa Simone's "Vigna Filonardi," and Fontana Candida's "Santa Teresa," the fuller flavors of malvasia are on display.

Under the Frascati production discipline, it is possible for a producer to use as much as 100 percent malvasia in a wine, or 100 percent trebbiano. Additionally, as much as 10 percent of the wine can be of "other" white varieties (read: chardonnay, sauvignon, viognier). This makes for wide variations in style. For example, Villa Simone's Frascatis tend to be finer, firmer, and more perfumed, while the wines of Castel de Paolis tack on a little more fruity extract, approaching California whites in style. Which is the "true" Frascati?

"There is no such thing anymore," says Santarelli of Castel de Paolis. "What we need to do is make good wine and not worry about 'typicity.' Because what is typical, at least recently, is not very good."

Outside of the Frascati DOC, the Castelli Romani is not producing much wine for export. In Marino, Paola DiMauro and her son, Armando, are making very crisp, aromatic whites from their tiny Colle Picchioni Estate, most notably the Marino Bianco "Selezione Oro," a blend incorporating malvasia and trebbiano with a splash each of sémillon and vermentino. It is the kind of clean, citrusy, full-flavored white that would be widely praised if it were made in Friuli, but it remains overlooked by wine drinkers with bad memories of insipid Roman wines. It is a great value, a well-balanced wine with personality. Should Lazio whites ever come back into fashion, Colle Picchioni will be hailed as one of the pioneers.

Maybe—and it's a big maybe—the same will be said of northern Lazio's Falesco winery, and its down-but-not-out DOC, Est! Est!! Est!!! di Montefiascone. Based more on trebbiano (a minimum of 65 percent) than the Castelli Romani whites, Est! Est!! Est!!! is one of those wines—like Vernaccia di San Gimignano in Tuscany—whose history is more compelling than what's currently in the glass. Its name is believed to have been invented when a twelfth-century German bishop, on his way to the Vatican, sent a scout ahead of him to find inns that served especially good wine (the bishop was quite the gastronome). When the scout found a good place he wrote *Est* ("It is" in Latin) on the door. Apparently, after tasting the wines at one *osteria* in Montefiascone, a village on the southern shores of Lake Bolsena, the scout scrawled *Est! Est!! Est!!!* on the door in a fit of exuberance. These days, the Est! Est!! Est!! DOC is dominated by the Falesco estate, owned by the well-known winemaking consultant Riccardo Cotarella. But even he doesn't go for anything mythical in his versions of the wine: Falesco's Est! Est!! Est!!! is appley, brightly acidic, and delicately aromatic, as trebbiano usually is. It makes a good accompaniment to Roman specialties such as fritto misto (a mixed fry of meats and vegetables) or *carciofi alla giudea* (deep-fried artichokes). The Est! Est!! Est!!! wines of Italo Mazziotti are similarly delicate and aromatic, and are considered, along with Falesco's whites, to be the best in the region.

Outside the realm of DOC, another Lazio

white worth mentioning is a sauvignon-sémillon blend called "Somigliò," made by Giovanni Palombo at his winery in Atina, not far from the border with Campania. Creamy and rich on the palate thanks to the sémillon, with citrusy fruit and bright acidity from the sauvignon, it has drawn renewed attention to the overlooked winemaking territory around Frosinone, where the milder climates, higher altitudes, and calcareous soils allow for a longer, more balanced growing season. Although the Frosinone area has traditionally been known for reds (such as the traditional Cesanese del Piglio—see below), Palombo's wines illustrate what's possible with whites as well.

VINI ROSSI
Red Wines

Although the overwhelming majority of Lazio wine is still white, many of the region's winemakers believe that the region's true talent is for reds. Yet other than the indigenous cesanese grape, which is still found in a few DOC wines in the hills between Rome and Frosinone, Lazio has no red varieties to call its own.

The best-known and best-regarded red wines from Lazio these days are the merlots and cabernets made by Riccardo Cotarella at Falesco, on the volcanic slopes of Lake Bolsena. As in parts of the Castelli Romani, the tufa underneath the topsoil is rock-hard, forcing the vines to work harder to put down roots; it is porous at the same time, keeping the vines water-stressed so that they don't overproduce. Using superconcentrated grapes and a healthy dose of barrel aging, Cotarella's "Montiano"

(his top wine, made from merlot) and "Vitiano" (made mostly from cabernet and aged in oak for less time) are plump and deeply colorful reds, almost chocolatey with extract and oak. They are criticized by some Italian wine purists as being blatantly "international" wines, but in a region with so little red-wine tradition, it is really difficult to level such a criticism.

There are still some good cesanese wines to be found—namely Cesanese del Piglio, of which there is significant commercial production. But Lazio's vineyards are increasingly populated with red varieties that are more readily associated with other regions: Tuscany's sangiovese, Abruzzo's montepulciano, Campania's aglianico, and the world's cabernet sauvignon and merlot. Yet given all the physical similarities that Lazio shares with its neighbors (especially Campania, also known for volcanic terrain), why not showcase these grapes?

"The cabernets in particular do very well here," says Paola DiMauro of Colle Picchioni, whose "Vigna del Vassallo" (a blend of cabernet sauvignon, cabernet franc, and merlot) is a savory, cedary, tobacco-scented red that has been compared by some wine critics to great Bordeaux. DiMauro says the layer of tufa under the thin topsoil of Marino is so hard it is impossible for her to excavate a proper wine cellar. It is quite similar, in fact, to the soil of the Loire Valley in France. And there are indeed comparisons to be made between the Colle Picchioni reds and the deep, spicy, cabernet franc–based wines of Chinon in the Loire (perhaps more so than Bordeaux).

Giovanni Palombo in Atina is also making notable wines from the cabernets and merlot, including "Colle della Torre" (merlot–cabernet sauvignon) and "Rosso delle Chiaie" (all cabernet sauvignon). As with the Colle Picchioni reds, the Palombo reds are not just plump and fruity but have structure—enough that you might consider aging them for a few years to see how they develop.

More experimental is Castel de Paolis in Frascati, and the giant Casale del Giglio estate in Borgo Montello, the latter set on reclaimed marshland known as the Pontine lowlands. At Castel de Paolis, Fabrizio Santarelli uses not just cabernet and merlot but touches of syrah and petit verdot in a plush red blend called "I Quattro Mori," a wine that rivals the luxuriousness of Falesco's Montiano. At Casale del Giglio, the soils of the Pontine flats are a heavier, more fertile mixture of sand and clay mixed with volcanic residue, so winemaker Antonio Santarelli (no relation to Fabrizio) has turned to syrah. He says that syrah, a vine which not only weathers intense heat but doesn't overproduce in more fertile soils, is the grape of the future along the southern Lazio coast.

"Particularly here south of Rome, there is really no red-wine tradition at all. No wine tradition, period," Santarelli says. "I don't look at that as a bad thing. I look at it as a license to do whatever I want. This area has a very 'New World' feel: hot climate, fertile soils, plenty of water. An early-ripening variety like merlot matures too fast here, but cabernet? Syrah? Petit verdot? They are perfect. We are in a position to compete with Chilean wines, Australian wines, American wines, and that's what we want to do."

VINI SPUMANTI E DOLCI
Sparkling and Sweet Wines

For all of the white-wine grapes in Lazio, there are really no sparkling wines to speak of in the region, save for *frizzante* (slightly fizzy) versions of some wines. Although a handful of the region's DOC disciplines include provisions for *spumante*, it doesn't seem to be of much interest to producers, who've been successful enough with simpler dry wines.

Sweet wines, too, are fairly scarce in the zone. Along with the occasional *spumante*, there are some *amabile* (semisweet) or *dolce* (sweet) versions of certain DOC whites—although they too are rare. Most notable is the Frascati Cannellino of Villa Simone, a late-harvest wine touched with the smoky, glycerine richness of botrytis bunch rot.

The sweet red Aleatico di Gradoli, made from the aleatico grape in a small zone on the northern shores of Lake Bolsena, has all but faded from existence, not unlike the aleatico wines of Puglia. Only a tiny patch of aleatico vineyards is still registered under the Gradoli DOC, and only one producer—a cooperative known as Cantine Sociale di Gradoli—makes any significant quantity of the wine. For the most part, it's an oddity that might turn up in a wine bar in Rome, but it is worth trying if the opportunity arises.

FAST FACTS:

PROVINCES	Frosinone (FR), Latina (LT), Rieti (RI), Roma (RM)
CAPITAL	Roma
KEY WINE TOWNS	Frascati, Montefiascone, Marino, Roma
TOTAL VINEYARD AREA*	47,884 hectares, or 118,321 acres. Rank: 7th
TOTAL WINE PRODUCTION*	2,940,000 hectoliters, or 77,675,033 gallons (7th); 84% white, 16% red
DOC WINE PRODUCED*	6.5% (14th)
SPECIALTY FOODS	artichokes; asparagus; peas; pecorino (sharp, hard sheep's-milk cheese); Caciocavallo (hard cow's-milk cheese).
	*1997 figures. Rankings out of twenty regions total (Trentino–Alto Adige counted as one). Source: Istituto Statistica Mercati Agro-Alimentari (ISMEA), Rome.

KEY GRAPE VARIETIES

WHITES

MALVASIA	Several different subvarieties exist, including malvasia bianca di candia and malvasia del lazio. Though the malvasia family is typically associated with sweet wines, it makes dry, citrusy whites in Lazio.
TREBBIANO	Widely planted, delicately flavored white, also with a number of subvarieties, including trebbiano giallo (yellow, thought to be related to greco), trebbiano verde (green), and trebbiano toscano. Used with malvasia in all of the region's whites.
OTHERS	SAUVIGNON BLANC; CHARDONNAY; VIOGNIER.

FAST FACTS

265

	REDS
CABERNET SAUVIGNON/FRANC	Many Lazio producers have had success with these varieties, which have taken well to the region's predominantly volcanic terrain.
MERLOT	A highly adaptable variety given its own measure of Lazio celebrity thanks to Falesco's "Montiano."
CESANESE	Known in the past to make plump, deeply fruity reds in hill zones between Rome and Frosinone, it's a variety on the wane.
OTHERS	SYRAH; PETIT VERDOT; SANGIOVESE; MONTEPULCIANO.

TOP VINTAGES IN LAZIO, 1980-2000

As with most Italian whites, the white wines of Lazio are predominantly made in a light, fresh style and are intended to be drunk young. Wines such as Frascati, Marino Bianco, and Est! Est!! Est!!! di Montefiascone are best consumed the summer (or, given the time they take to cross the Atlantic, fall) following the vintage. Red wines, meanwhile—or at least ageworthy red wines—have a relatively short history in the region, but there have been a few noteworthy recent vintages from which some interesting Lazio reds will still be available. Look for reds from '95, '97, '98, '99 and 2000.

LA STRADA DEL VINO
WINE TOURING IN LAZIO

On the one hand, the Castelli Romani zone south of Rome is an ideal destination for the wine wanderer, because of its close proximity to the city. On the other hand, there aren't many wineries in the zone equipped to receive visitors. Of course the sights of the Castelli Romani are interesting in themselves—the Pope's summer palace at Castelgandolfo, the crater lakes of Albano and Nemi—and the views of Rome are incredible from the heights of wine towns like Frascati or Grottaferrata.

Rome is a great wine town, and is loaded with *enoteche* (wine bars/shops) in which to sample different wines—

although they're likely to have more wines from other regions than from Lazio. Some good *enoteche* to try include Il Goccetto (Via dei Banchi Vecchi 14; 06-686-42-68) and L'Angolo Divino (Via dei Balestrari, 12; 06-686-44-13), the latter right off the Campo dei Fiori market. A restaurant that shouldn't be missed is Checchino (Via Monte Testaccio 30; 06-574-63-18), particularly if you have a taste for old-school Roman dishes such as *pajata* (slow-cooked lamb's intestine, usually served in a tomato sauce over rigatoni) and *coda alla vaccinara* (oxtail stew).

DEGUSTAZIONI
TASTINGS

FRASCATI

Villa Simone Frascati Superiore "Vigneto Filonardi," $

Fontana Candida Frascati Superiore "Santa Teresa," $

Castel de Paolis Frascati Superiore "Vigna Adriana," $

Like many of the tastings in this book, this flight is arranged in ascending order based on body. While all three are examples of fuller and more-flavorful-than-average Frascatis, the Castel de Paolis wine is probably the plumpest and most tropically fruity of the three, thanks to a dollop of viognier in the blend. Both the Villa Simone and Fontana Candida wines showcase the bright, floral, slightly citrusy aromatics typical of good Frascati, as well as the refreshing acidity. Any of the three will shine alongside a good *carbonara* or *cacio e pepe* preparation (see recipes), where their lively acidity will be put to good use in cutting through the fat of butter and cheese.

LAZIO REDS

Colle Picchioni "Vigna del Vassallo," $$

Giovanni Palombo "Rosso delle Chiaie," $$

Falesco "Montiano," $$$

The first two wines, based on cabernet sauvignon, share a decided tarry, cigar-box character, a trait also found in many Bordeaux and Loire cabernets. They are the kinds of full-bodied, savory reds that will complement a hearty Roman dish such as *coda alla vaccinara*. In the Montiano, a varietal merlot, there's a plumper, rounder, slightly sweeter personality, and a toastiness that comes from aging in small oak barrels. It is probably the most luxurious, extracted wine of the three, and has attracted a cult following in the United States as a result. (Also worth a look is Palombo's higher-end "Duca Cantelmi" cabernet sauvignon, although both it and the "Rosso delle Chiaie" are the hardest to find of the above group.)

La Cucina

FOOD FOR THE WINE

RECIPES BY MARIO BATALI

The suffix *alla romana* is so common that it is impossible to choose a single dish that exemplifies Lazio—or, more specifically, Roman—cuisine. The Romans are great vegetable eaters, among other things, and one of the most common starters in the average *osteria romana* is a mixed fry (fritto misto) of fresh vegetables. Another incredible fried dish is *carciofi alla giudea* (artichokes Jewish-style), in which fresh artichokes are flattened and fried in hot oil, coming out looking like golden flowers.

Yet as diverse as the Roman kitchen is today, it wasn't always that way. Before the Romans showed up, Lazio was predominantly a region of shepherds. Even today, for all of the urban sprawl of the eternal city, Lazio continues to be a huge cheese producer. *Pecorino Romano* is well known to American palates—sharp, hard, and slightly salty, great for grating or eating on its own or with fruit. Another Lazio specialty, *caciocavallo*—horse's cheese, so named for its bulbous shape, which allows it to be tied with rope and slung over a saddle—is becoming more widely known as the simple pasta *cacio e pepe* starts to catch on here.

Below are three of the simplest yet most frequently botched pasta preparations in Italy. All are rich and decadent, unmistakably Roman, and all of them share an affinity for the light, bright whites of the region. Think of crisp, well-chilled Frascati as a counterbalance to a weighty *alfredo* or *carbonara*. Although a tannic red is another way to take on butter and cheese, a Frascati or Marino bianco will cleanse the palate more thoroughly and won't weigh you down.

A note on the preparations: Lazio, like neighboring Abruzzo, is a major producer of dried pastas, particularly in the Ciociaria hills southeast of Rome. All three sauces below are meant to be used with dried pastas, primarily because of the textural interplay they offer. With a fresh pasta, you're looking to absorb the flavor of the sauce—say a hearty lamb or boar *ragù*. But with dried pasta, cooked al dente, the sauce and the pasta don't so much fuse but play off each other. The creamy richness of an *alfredo* or *carbonara* is best contrasted with a chewy noodle. And again, a light, fragrant white will refresh your taste buds after several butter-drenched bites.

The Cheese Sauces of Rome

For each of the following sauces, a pound of pasta is recommended. Use spaghetti for the *carbonara,* fettuccine for the *alfredo,* and *bavette* or *bucatini* (thick, tubular spaghetti) for the *cacio e pepe.*

Carbonara

2 tablespoons SALT
1 pound GUANCIALE, or pancetta, or
    good-quality slab bacon, cut into
    1 inch matchsticks
1 large RED ONION, cut into ½-inch dice
4 jumbo EGGS, whites and yolks
    separated, with the yolks placed into
    individual small bowls
½ cup freshly grated PECORINO
    ROMANO CHEESE, plus ¼ cup for
    garnish
2 tablespoons freshly ground BLACK
    PEPPER

SERVES 4

Place 6 quarts of water to boil in a large pot with 2 tablespoons salt.

Place the guanciale and the onion into a cold 12- to 14-inch sauté pan over medium heat. Cook until the guanciale and the onion are very soft and most of the fat has been rendered from the meat, about 10 minutes. Remove the pan from the heat, drain all but 4 tablespoons of the fat and reserve.

Cook the spaghetti about 1 minute less than the package instructions and drain, reserving 1 cup of the cooking water. Toss the spaghetti into the pan with the guanciale mixture and the reserved pasta cooking water. Set over medium heat and cook until the pasta is dressed like a salad, about 1 minute, then remove the pan from the heat. In a small bowl, beat the egg whites together with the ½ cup pecorino and the black pepper, and pour into the pan with the pasta. Toss or stir until well combined, about 30 seconds. Divide among 4 plates and place one egg yolk on the top of each serving (don't worry, the heat of the pasta will lightly cook the egg; if you're worried about raw eggs, either omit this step or blend the yolk into the hot pasta so that it cooks more thoroughly). Sprinkle with the remaining cheese and serve immediately.

Alfredo

6 tablespoons BUTTER
1 cup HEAVY CREAM
¼ cup PASTA COOKING WATER
½ cup grated PARMIGIANO-REGGIANO
    CHEESE

SERVES 4

In a medium-large sauté pan, melt the butter over low heat. When the foam subsides, increase the heat to high, add the cream, and bring the mixture to a boil, stirring occasionally.

Reduce the heat to a simmer. When the pasta is almost done cooking, add ¼ cup of the pasta water to the butter-cream mixture to thin slightly.

Add the cooked pasta, stir to coat with sauce, then mix in ¼ cup of the Parmigiano. Sprinkle the remaining cheese on each of the four portions before serving.

Cacio e Pepe

1 tablespoon crushed BLACK PEPPER
¼ cup PASTA WATER
2 tablespoons BUTTER
1 cup CACCIOCAVALLO CHEESE, grated
    (Pecorino Romano can be
    substituted)

SERVES 4

Crush the peppercorns by wrapping them in a kitchen towel and beating the bundle with a mallet or the bottom of a cast-iron skillet. (You can use a grinder, but will get more intense pepper flavor by crushing it.) Set aside.

As the pasta is finishing cooking, set aside 1 cup of its cooking water. Drain the pasta, and in the same pot it was cooked in, add back ¼ cup of the pasta water and the butter. Stir to melt the butter. Add the cooked pasta, toss to coat, and sprinkle evenly with the cheese and pepper. (If the mixture is too dry, add a little pasta water.)

Abruzzo and Molise

EMERGING FROM ANONYMITY

HIGHER GROUND

The last leg in the ascent of the Corno Grande, the highest peak in Italy's Apennine chain, requires that you do some "scrambling"—that is, crawling on all fours over loose clods of shale, each step unleashing a mini-avalanche of rock and dust. It's not that tough, to be truthful, and on a clear day the reward for reaching the summit is a view of both the Mediterranean and Adriatic seas. Unfortunately, today is not a clear day.

It's late August, and what was a sticky and humid morning at lower elevations is a windy, cold, and cloudy afternoon on the Corno Grande. This ten-thousand-foot hunk of limestone is the centerpiece of the Gran Sasso d'Italia, or "great rock of Italy," the cluster of mountains that dominates northwestern Abruzzo. While the verdant meadows of the Alto Adige or Valle d'Aosta might bring to mind a scene from *The Sound of Music,* the uplands of Abruzzo (and neighboring Molise) are more barren, drained of color, giving the area around the Gran Sasso the look of a lunar surface. Things might be different on a brighter day, but standing atop the Corno Grande today prompts mixed emotions. Even with all of the chatty fellow climbers sprawled out on the rocks around us, we're feeling kind of dreary, dissociated. Maybe we're just out of shape.

Still, there's something very lonely about this place. True, it is a destination for hikers, climbers, and skiers from all over the world, but the Gran Sasso is hardly a bustling resort. In fact, it is starkly unpopulated. At Campo Imperatore, which is less a town than a point on a map, there is a single mountain hotel, creatively named the Albergo Campo Imperatore. It sits at about seven thousand feet, at the top of a chairlift that originates in the tiny village of Assergi down below, and is famous for being the hotel in which the deposed Mussolini was held prisoner for a time toward the end of World War II. Besides the chairlift, all that connects the hotel to civilization below is a two-lane road that snakes across a plateau of sawgrass and strewn boulders, populated only by wild horses and the occasional wolf. Aspen this is definitely not.

Albergo Campo Imperatore and its handful of satellite buildings (which house things like a ranger station and a small bar) are the only evidence of development in Campo Imperatore. The hulking, vaguely Alpine-looking *albergo* isn't as populated in the summer as it must be in winter, and it's hard not to walk through it without thinking of the hotel that Jack Nichol-

THE DOC ZONES OF
ABRUZZO AND MOLISE

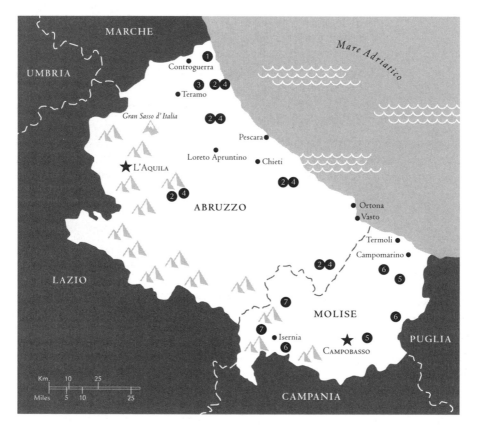

ABRUZZO
1 Controguerra
2 Montepulciano d'Abruzzo
3 Montepulciano d'Abruzzo Colline Teramane
4 Trebbiano d'Abruzzo

MOLISE
5 Biferno
6 Molise/del Molise
7 Pentro di Isernia

son bloodied up in *The Shining*. Outside, there's the parking lot, a smattering of ski lifts, and a vast stretch of nothing. The Gran Sasso is called "the roof of Italy," and with good reason: The mountains are ruggedly beautiful, of course, but all of the things that make Italy *Italian*—the glinting canals of Venice, St. Peter's Square in Rome, a tiny *osteria* in Florence, whatever—are a world away.

This made the Albergo Campo Imperatore a good spot in which to hide Mussolini after he was double-crossed by King Vittorio Emmanuele III and arrested, in July 1943, as the Allies began to gain the upper hand in World War II. The Germans saw the rescue of Mussolini as their only way to maintain a foothold in Italy against advancing Allied troops—their thinking was that Italians loyal to Mussolini would stay on the German side. So upon learning of his confinement at the *albergo*, the Germans organized an aerial attack on Campo Imperatore. To maintain an element of surprise, they descended on the hotel in gliders, most of which crash-landed in the rocky meadow in front of the hotel; other soldiers came up via the chairlift. The Italian troops guarding Mussolini offered no resistance, enabling the Germans to spirit him away in the one plane they managed to land correctly on the plateau. It was a big propaganda coup, if little else, for the Germans, and there are numerous pictures to be found of *Il Duce*, looking like a Mafia don in his black overcoat and black fedora, being whisked to a waiting SS plane.

After scrambling up and down the Corno Grande, we warm up in the Campo Imperatore with some *caffè*, take a look at Mussolini's old room, and try to shrug off the *Shining* vibe of the whole place. On the drive back down to Assergi, a limpid afternoon sun peeks through the clouds on a few occasions. As if on cue, a group of about a dozen wild horses bolts across the broad expanse ahead. There's still no sight of the Adriatic, but more of the green, inhabited Abruzzo comes into view. With the mountain winds whipping through the open car windows, it's as if we're flying, like old Benito being carried off more than half a century ago. Soon we're in Assergi, with a tour bus advancing from the south, and the (self-imposed) exile comes to a not-so-glorious end.

The Apennines define Abruzzo and neighboring Molise, which were regarded as one entity until Molise was granted regional status in 1963. Nearly all of Italy's regions have both a coastal stretch and a mountainous interior—and all of the cultural contrasts that come with that. But in Abruzzo and to a lesser extent Molise, the physical distances between mountains and sea are especially short. Although *brodetto* (fish stew) is a classic dish along Abruzzo's hundred-mile coastline, the region is known more for meat-based mountain fare: the food of the shepherds, cattle ranchers, and other rugged types who inhabit the craggy interior.

As in Calabria to the south, Abruzzo and Molise are cut off from their neighbors by a forbidding Apennine wall, which in some ways dilutes their identities as regions. There are plenty of things that are uniquely *Abruzzese*—like saffron, a specialty of the interior uplands, or DeCecco pasta, made in the town of Fara San Martino. But there aren't many well-known destinations in either Abruzzo or Molise to root them in foreigners' memories. Unless you're a rock climber, skier, or naturalist (the *Parco Nazionale d'Abruzzo*, south of the Gran Sasso, is one of Italy's biggest national parks and the only place in the country where bears are found), chances are the Abruzzo and Molise are not on your Italy hit list, despite their proximity to Rome.

As wine zones, too, they tend to be overlooked, and yet the Abruzzo is the fifth-most productive region in the country. Its annual wine output is almost double that of Tuscany's, even though Tuscany has nearly twice as much vineyard area. And this is the story in a nutshell: Although the *Abruzzesi* have proved better than many of their neighbors in creating branded, bottled wines, theirs has still been a culture of mass production. The local industry is dominated by giant cooperative wineries such as Cantina Tollo, Casal Thaulero, Casal Bordino, and Citra (the favored screw-top wine on Alitalia flights), which account for 80 to 90 percent of the region's commercial wine production.

Abruzzo's only real star among private vintners is the reclusive Edoardo Valentini, whose estate is considered one of Italy's best—but whose wines are not only hard to find but difficult to comprehend. And in Molise, there is essentially one producer from whom an American consumer can buy wine: Alessio Di Majo Norante, whose property in Campomarino, not far from Molise's Adriatic coast, is a source of some excellent full-bodied reds and fragrant whites. There are a number of other notable names, but they're generally drowned under the tidal wave of *Abruzzese* wine. For most international consumers, the Abruzzo is a "wine lake": a place for cheap, plush, and (despite their brand names) anonymous supermarket wines.

If this whole story sounds familiar, it's because the entire Italian south is going through something similar: the evolution from bulk-wine producer to boutique-wine producer—or, more accurately, from a strictly industrial wine culture to one in which an artisanal product can have commercial success. Wine critics, even Italian ones, take on a condescending tone when talking about the wines of the *Mezzogiorno,* treating the southern Italians like hyperactive children who need a little structure and discipline in their lives before they can do great things. What goes without saying is that many better-regarded French (and northern Italian) wines are in reality a good part *Abruzzese,* since so much Abruzzo bulk wine is still shipped north for blending. Is a great wine one that moves you on some physical or emotional level, or is it a wine that is consistent from year to year? Like so many of their southern-Italian peers, the *Abruzzesi* can have it both ways.

VINI BIANCHI ABRUZZESI
White Wines of Abruzzo

The pre-autostrada isolation of the Abruzzo, and the somewhat depressed economy it engendered, is one reason why the local wine culture has been so dominated by large co-ops. Historically, small landowners in the Abruzzo had little choice but to band together in order to survive, and the *Abruzzesi* co-ops were more successful than most in creating branded wines, however generic they may have tasted. Trebbiano d'Abruzzo and Montepulciano d'Abruzzo have consistently been two of the most exported DOC wines in Italy, which has been good for the hard-working vintners of the region but not so good for the image of Italian wines abroad.

Abruzzo has all of the requisite elements for making great wine: rolling foothills that spill down toward the sea, a desirable mix of mountain and maritime air, and a relatively dry climate—particularly when weather patterns originate in the west by way of the Apennines. (When the opposite happens and storms approach from the east, as in 1996 and 1999, the mountains trap the moisture, resulting in a subpar vintage.) Most of the Abruzzo's vineyards are situated along a series of river valleys that run from the Apennines to the Adriatic, and the west-east orientation of these vineyards allows for all-day exposure to the sun. Some locales, including the Abruzzo's largest mass of vineyards south of Chieti, can suffer from excesses of humidity, soil fertility, and heat. But the north—particularly along the border with the Marche, where the Apennines reach especially close to the sea—boasts altitudes, soil conditions, and microclimates comparable to those of the Marche, Umbria, and even Tuscany.

What has held Abruzzo back, critically speaking, is its chosen raw materials. For reasons that seem largely economic, the favored white grape of the Abruzzo is trebbiano, the most productive (and therefore most planted) white variety in Italy. Known as ugni blanc in France (and thought of first and foremost as a grape for brandy, not wine), trebbiano is the grape most foreign consumers consider the benchmark Italian white: high in acid, low in natural extract, producing chalky, faintly aromatic wines just about everywhere it is planted. In certain instances, a well-chilled, lightly floral trebbiano is just the thing to offset the heat of a *brodetto abruzzese* (fish stew, typically more heav-

ily spiced in Abruzzo than elsewhere along the Adriatic). But these days, white-wine drinkers want power. Occasionally, Trebbiano d'Abruzzo can give a little bit more, but it is still a white that walks softly—albeit with a big, acidic stick.

Up until 1996, when the Controguerra DOC was created in the northern reaches of Abruzzo, Trebbiano d'Abruzzo was the region's only classified white wine. Created in 1972, the Trebbiano d'Abruzzo DOC zone covers most of the region. This naturally allows for wide variations in style, but generally speaking Trebbiano d'Abruzzo doesn't deviate too widely: It is light and crisp, with faint hints of apple and wildflower in the aroma and a pronounced acidity on the palate.

Some texts say that Trebbiano d'Abruzzo is not made from trebbiano at all but from the lesser-known bombino bianco, a variety also found in Puglia; in the Trebbiano d'Abruzzo DOC discipline, in fact, bombino is listed as a synonym for trebbiano. Regardless of which variety it actually is, however, the end results have tended to be less than memorable. As a result, many *Abruzzese* producers are doing the predictable (and commercially prudent) thing and combining trebbiano with more forceful varieties. Chardonnay is one of the favored blending partners, and in some cases winemakers are throwing over trebbiano altogether—some of the most popular Abruzzo whites these days are in fact chardonnays. These include the "Marina Cvetic" bottling from the Masciarelli winery near Chieti; "Cenalba" chardonnay from Dino Illuminati in Controguerra; and "Roccesco" chardonnay from the Orlandi Contucci Ponno estate in Roseto degli Abruzzi, where young proprietor Marina Orlandi Contucci has invested heavily in the French duo of chardonnay and cabernet sauvignon.

Most of these producers stick with trebbiano for well-priced base bottlings, but the one winemaker who seems to really believe in the variety is Edoardo Valentini. His small estate is in Loreto Apruntino, west of Pescara in central Abruzzo, and he has developed the reputation as something of a mad scientist. Considered in wine circles to be the dean of *Abruzzese* winemakers and an innovator on a par with Italian giants such as Angelo Gaja, Valentini has found a way to get more from trebbiano (or bombino, depending on whom you ask) than anyone else in Italy.

Valentini uses what many producers consider an outmoded system of vine training: the *tendone*, in which the vines are draped over high trellises to form canopies. The word *tendone* has become a dirty one in Italian viticultural circles, because it is most readily associated with giant flatland vineyards in the Veneto and Emilia-Romagna, where the large trellises allow for mass-production of grapes. Critics of the *tendone* say that it encourages overproduction and that its canopy of leaves excessively shades the grapes, inhibiting the ripening process. Valentini combats this with meticulous pruning and extremely close-cropping, so that each plant produces a meager amount of fruit.

Having achieved a level of uncommon ripeness in his trebbiano, Valentini then ferments and ages his wines in large oak vats, resulting in a yeasty, creamy richness that adds complexity to trebbiano's notoriously faint perfume. In one sense, it is difficult to taste Valentini trebbianos because there is really nothing to compare them to: Rich and round, with oxidative notes of caramel and nuts overlapping their plush apple-and-pear fruitiness, the Valentini whites are known to age well for years. He typically delays releasing them for several years after the vintage, having found a way to maintain the life-preserving acidity of the trebbiano grape while also extracting more flavor from it.

Other *Abruzzese* producers with an eye toward the international market have experimented with barrel fermentation for their trebbianos, but the result is often a wine that is bigger and oakier but not necessarily better. Among those who are getting more than average from the grape are Masciarelli (whose "Marina Cvetic" trebbiano has gotten a fair amount of press), Illuminati, and the Cataldi Madonna winery in the high plains of Ofena. On the whole, however, the best thing to do with Trebbiano d'Abruzzo is not complicate it too much: Chill it well and crack it open when you're grilling whole fish. One thing you can say for certain about it is that the price is usually right.

VINI ROSATI
ABRUZZESI
Rosé Wines of Abruzzo

As mentioned elsewhere, rosé wine has gotten a bad rap in the United States thanks to white zinfandel, prompting many American importers to pass over the *rosati* of their Italian clients. This is a big mistake. Throughout southern Italy, and particularly in the coastal areas, a good dry *rosato* is a prized bottle of wine.

Abruzzo's classic DOC red, Montepulciano d'Abruzzo, becomes known as Cerasuolo when it is vinified in a rosé style. (The word *cerasuolo* means cherry-red, an apt descriptor for the deeply colorful *rosati* produced from the montepulciano grape.) Montepulciano d'Abruzzo Cerasuolo is produced by employing a short maceration of the juice with the skins of the grapes, after which the lightly colored juice is separated and vinified much like a white wine, with minimal exposure to oxygen. Because the montepulciano grape is high in natural coloring pigments, Cerasuolo rosés tend to go well beyond pink in color and well beyond pink in flavor; they are some of the heartiest *rosati* to be found in Italy, with hints of strawberry, dried cherry, and exotic spices such as orange peel and cinnamon.

Most of the top producers in Abruzzo make a Cerasuolo, and thankfully some of them are exported. As a general rule, it's best to look for recent vintages of these wines, because their relative lack of tannins makes them, like all rosés, subject to more rapid oxidation. Italians typically drink their *rosati* during the summer following the vintage, the better to preserve the wines' bright fruit flavors and crisp acidity.

At a minimum it's nice to have some *rosato* around for summertime apéritifs, but the versatility of rosé with food is often overlooked. The *Abruzzesi*, for example, are known for their liberal use of *peperoncini* (chili peppers) in the kitchen, in preparations such as *maccheroni alla chitarra* (pasta "guitar style," named for the way the sheets of pasta are cut by pressing them through steel wires), which is dressed with a simple but spicy tomato-*peperoncino* mixture. Although the soft red Montepulciano d'Abruzzo is a good "pillow" for that chili heat, a Cerasuolo not only cools it down but points up the *peperoncino* flavor with a little spiciness of its own. The same goes for mouth-tingling

Abruzzese seafood specialties such as *polpi in purgatorio*—octopus cooked in oil, garlic, tomato, and lots of red pepper—for which a Cerasuolo is a cool-but-hardy complement. Check out the *rosati* of producers such as Masciarelli, Cataldi Madonna, Illuminati, Spinelli (their brand is called "Terre d'Aligi"), and if you can find it, Valentini, and see for yourself.

VINI ROSSI
ABRUZZESI
Red Wines of Abruzzo

The red wines of Abruzzo are a little puzzling: Most of the time, they are as soft and generous as their surroundings are rugged and ungiving. Such is the character of the montepulciano grape, the dominant variety both here and in the neighboring Marche, where it is used in Rosso Cònero.

As with Trebbiano d'Abruzzo, the Montepulciano d'Abruzzo DOC zone, outlined in 1968, covers most of the region. Unlike Trebbiano d'Abruzzo though, efforts have been made to identify superior growing areas through more specific appellations.

Generally speaking, the best montepulcianos come from northern Abruzzo, where the Apennines reach closer to the sea. In the foothills around Teramo, the soils are a poorer mix of ferrous clay and limestone, and the vineyard elevations and microclimates are higher and cooler, when compared to those of the broad, rolling river valleys of the southerly Chieti province. Many of the larger cooperatives are based in the hotter, more fertile southern end of Abruzzo, while most of the smaller private wineries are huddled in the north, along the border with the Marche. Of the half million hectoliters of Montepulciano d'Abruzzo produced each year, two-thirds is produced in the province of Chieti.

In recent years, two new appellations have been created to help distinguish the montepulcianos of the north from those of the south. Producers who source their montepulciano grapes from within a defined area near Teramo can use the subzone designation Colline Teramane (created in 1995), while those within a much smaller area around the commune of Controguerra may opt out of the Montepulciano d'Abruzzo DOC altogether and use the Controguerra DOC instead. At the moment, the only well-known producers to embrace the Controguerra DOC (established in 1996) are Dino Illuminati and Camillo Montori, both of whom continue to make Montepulciano and Trebbiano d'Abruzzo as well.

The existence of these new DOCs represents an effort on the part of the *Abruzzesi* to make more than just mass-produced airplane wine. "The viticulture of the Abruzzo has changed dramatically," says Camillo Montori, whose "Fonte Cupa" Montepulciano d'Abruzzo and "Leneo Moro" Controguerra Rosso are two of Abruzzo's better-regarded reds. "Only in the last four to five years have we really started to concentrate on red wine. Before that we were making a majority of *bianchi*."

Beyond that, Montori echoes the quantity-versus-quality refrain heard so often in the Italian south. "On the one hand, Montepulciano d'Abruzzo has long been the most-exported DOC wine from Italy," he says. "But we really only made 'house' wines. We communicated badly, and we remained backward in our methods. I think the first year I ever did a green harvest"—the practice of trimming excess grape bunches in summertime to ensure fuller ripening—"was in 1997. But we're learning that if you grow and vinify montepulciano correctly, you can make a very big wine."

Unlike the lightly regarded trebbiano, montepulciano offers quite a bit to the winemaker: It's deeply colored, with naturally sweet tannins and low acidity, giving the wines that are made from it a fruity softness that makes them accessible when young. "Montepulciano is very interesting," says Montori. "It is the only wine that is drinkable immediately and also ten years down the line."

Indeed, montepulciano is like a forgotten little brother among the big boys, taking a back seat to sangiovese and aglianico in central and southern Italy the way dolcetto and barbera take a back seat to nebbiolo in Piedmont. Like the Rosso Cònero of neighboring Marche (which is often, but not always, buttressed with sangiovese), Montepulciano d'Abruzzo can be a wine of great depth and durability. If it lacks anything it's the tannic structure and the evocative, sometimes ethereal aromas that distinguish the big three of sangiovese, nebbiolo, and aglianico. At their best, montepulciano wines are inky-purple in color and almost syrupy in texture, with scents of black berries and a touch of earthy funk. But they can be one-note wonders—all ripe, juicy fruit and not a lot else.

The montepulciano grape is plump and generous where sangiovese and nebbiolo are leaner and more reticent. Yet, as some *Abruzzese* producers assert, the youthful exuberance of montepulciano doesn't fade with age. "The funny thing about montepulciano is that you put it in wood for years and years and it doesn't change," says Stefano Illuminati, the current head of the historic Illuminati winery in Controguerra. "That's both a good and a bad thing. On one hand, you open a well-aged montepulciano and it's still fresh and full bodied. On the other hand, you don't always get the more complex secondary aromas that develop with age. It tends to stay somewhat static."

With the help of small oak barriques, longer macerations, and more careful selections in the vineyards, the *Abruzzesi* are looking beyond "house reds" to something burlier, more substantial. In its "Villa Gemma" and "Marina Cvetic" Montepulciano d'Abruzzos, the Masciarelli winery has two deep and satisfying reds to compete with the best of the north, while Illuminati's "Zanna" and "Lumen" montepulcianos further exemplify how potent the grape's black-berry flavors can be. There are a number of other producers to seek out when exploring the flavors of montepulciano, among them Valentini and Emidio Pepe, whose earthy, long-aged wines have had spotty distribution in the United States; Farnese, for their top-end "Opis;" and Cataldi Madonna, whose "Toní," sourced from some of the highest-elevation vineyards in Abruzzo, has not only the full fruitiness of montepulciano but a firm structure born of a longer growing season.

Even the giants like Citra and Casal Thaulero turn out solid montepulcianos. In fact, the screw-top Montepulciano d'Abruzzo on Alitalia is not bad at all. The generosity of the grape makes it difficult to foul up, and we can only imagine what montepulciano will be like after a few more years of experimentation.

VINI MOLISANI
The Wines of Molise

Touched by Abruzzo, Lazio, Campania, and Puglia, the tiny chunk of mountains and alluvial plains known as the Molise is the lost world of Italian wine. In the densely wooded heights around Isernia and Campobasso, there are more than a few havens for wine grapes, especially red ones. There is a fair amount of prospecting underway in the mountainous interior—Enzo Ercolino of the Feudi San Gregorio estate in neighboring Campania is said to be planting vineyards near Isernia. But as of yet we've got no *Molisano* mountain wine to sample in the United States.

There are three DOC zones in Molise: Pentro d'Isernia, based around the town of Isernia near the Campanian border; Biferno, based around Campobasso, the regional capital; and Molise or Del Molise, which takes in the entire zone. All three DOCs include *bianchi, rosati,* and *rossi* based on trebbiano and montepulciano as in the Abruzzo, but here the influence of Campania is felt a little more strongly. The white falaghina and the red aglianico are both widely planted in Molise, whose distinctive aromas benefit the local wines. But these are wines that are, for the most part, truly local—as in go to someone's house and drink them locally.

The lone wolf of the Molise is Alessio Di Majo Norante, whose family estate in Campomarino has produced bottled wines since 1968. Di Majo Norante's wines take their cues from Campania more so than the Abruzzo: He has a greco, fiano, and falangina in his lineup, along with varietal aglianico, sangiovese, and a red blend called "Ramitello," which combines the soft montepulciano and the sharp aglianico to great effect. Most recently, he introduced a wine called "Don Luigi," made from 100 percent montepulciano, that stands right alongside the best of the Abruzzo.

But it is more intriguing to think of what might be possible farther inland, where the poorer soils and higher elevations around Iser-nia and Campobasso lengthen the growing season and add perfume and structure to the wines. Molise's history of poverty is such that the investment is likely to come from the outside, whether it's deep-pocketed Campanians such as Ercolino or other entrepreneurs from farther north. In an area full of new winemaking frontiers, this is one of the newest.

FAST FACTS:

ABRUZZO AND MOLISE

PROVINCES	*Abruzzo:* L'Aquila (AQ), Chieti (CH). Pescara (PE), Teramo (TE). *Molise:* Campobasso (CB), Isernia (IS)
CAPITALS	*Abruzzo:* L'Aquila. *Molise:* Campobasso.
KEY WINE TOWNS	*Abruzzo:* Controguerrra, Loreto Apruntino. *Molise:* Campomarino
TOTAL VINEYARD AREA*	*Abruzzo:* 33,252 hectares, or 82,166 acres. Rank: 10th. *Molise:* 7,650 hectares, or 18,903 acres (18th)
TOTAL WINE PRODUCTION*	*Abruzzo:* 4,184,000 hectoliters, or 110,541,611 gallons (5th); *Molise:* 360,000 hectoliters, or 9,511,228 gallons (18th)
DOC WINE PRODUCED*	*Abruzzo:* 17.6% (11th); *Molise:* 3.9% (16th)
SPECIALTY FOODS	Mortadella; salsiccia di fegato (pork liver sausage); dried pasta; saffron; Scamorza (soft, mild, pear-shaped sheep's-milk cheese); lamb.
	*1997 figures. Rankings out of twenty regions total (Trentino–Alto Adige counted as one). Source: Istituto Statistica Mercati Agro-Alimentari (ISMEA), Rome.

KEY GRAPE VARIETIES

WHITES

TREBBIANO	Found throughout Italy, the local version is thought by some to be the bombino bianco also found in Puglia. Either way, it is known for light, crisp, somewhat neutral wines from the vast Trebbiano d'Abruzzo zone.

MONTEPULCIANO

REDS

Not to be confused with the Tuscan town of the same name, this deeply colorful, sweetly tannic variety was thought in the past to be a distant relative of sangiovese. Not anymore. But while it is unique to Abruzzo and a few of the region's neighbors, no one knows for sure where it originated. No matter: It is showing increasing class in deeply colorful Abruzzo wines.

TOP VINTAGES IN ABRUZZO AND MOLISE, 1980–2000

A special dispensation is given here to the white wines of Edoardo Valentini, whose Trebbiano d'Abruzzo is among the few southern-Italian whites that can (and should) be drunk after significant periods of aging. The vintages that follow are cited by the Abruzzo's top montepulciano producers as the best recent years for their reds, but they might also be applied to Valentini trebbianos: 1985, '88, '90, '94, '95, '97, '98.

LA STRADA DEL VINO
WINE TOURING IN ABRUZZO AND MOLISE

It's not often that an American tourist makes a trip specifically to the Abruzzo, despite the fact that its regional capital, L'Aquila, is in close proximity to Rome. In fact, L'Aquila is well worth a day trip from the Eternal City. Take a hike in the heights of Campo Imperatore and then return to L'Aquila for an overnight stay: It's a quiet, isolated city high in the mountains, with lots of hearty food. Check out the Ristorante Ernesto (Piazza Palazzo 22; 0862-210-94) and its sister *enoteca* across town (Via Cavour 60; 0862-612-74) for a sophisticated take on *Abruzzese* mountain food and a panorama of the region's wines. Or, if you're making your way down the Adriatic coast, stop off in Pescara at the Cantina di Jozz (Via della Cascine 61; 085-69-03-83), one of the most highly regarded restaurants in the region.

DEGUSTAZIONI
TASTINGS

TREBBIANO D'ABRUZZO

Casal Thaulero
Trebbiano d'Abruzzo, $

Cataldi Madonna
Trebbiano d'Abruzzo, $

Edoardo Valentini
Trebbiano d'Abruzzo, $$$

Here's a fairly broad panorama of trebbiano from Abruzzo, starting with a very light, very chalky white that will be best with a good chill, and finishing with a creamy, minerally, full-bodied white that will show its complexity best closer to room temperature. All three wines share cool flavors of pear and apple on the palate, but the scale of each wine is markedly different. The Valentini wine, which won't be a cinch to get, is best viewed as an abberration: The Trebbiano d'Abruzzo style is better reflected in the clean, light, simple wines of Casal Thaulero and Cataldi Madonna.

MONTEPULCIANO D'ABRUZZO

Cantina Tollo
Montepulciano d'Abruzzo
"Villa Diana," $

Masciarelli
Montepulciano d'Abruzzo
"Marina Cvetic," $

Illuminati Montepulciano
d'Abruzzo "Zanna," $$

Always soft and generous, with a heaping helping of black berry fruit, montepulciano grows into a more brooding, coffee-scented powerhouse when it is grown and vinified with a more exacting eye—as is the case with "Zanna," a single-vineyard montepulciano of exceptional concentration. All three of these wines might be described as "jammy," with a certain syrupy texture and sweetness of fruit flavor that makes them immediately pleasurable. But underneath each is a whiff of earthiness, a touch of funk, that places them with hearty Abruzzese foods such as sausages or lamb stew. Under all that generous fruit extract is a solid structure that will allow the wines to age well for years. They're not as simple and straightforward as they may seem on the surface.

La Cucina

FOOD FOR THE WINE

RECIPE BY MARIO BATALI

The Abruzzi—as Abruzzo and Molise were once collectively named—are especially well known for pork products, including the Abruzzo's own version of mortadella sausage, which is spicier and more garlicky than the Bologna version. But another specialty of this mountain region is lamb (and also kid). The high-altitude provincial capitals of Teramo, L'Aquila, Isernia, and Campobasso are still the domain of countless shepherds, and lamb dishes are a specialty in both regions.

As in the nearby regions of Basilicata and Puglia, *peperoncino* finds its way into many Abruzzese preparations, which suits Montepulciano d'Abruzzo just fine. Whereas more aggressively tannic reds would clash with the following recipe (tannins tend to exaggerate spice), a soft montepulciano is a perfect pairing. No doubt the wool traders of the Abruzzo highlands ate a dish like the one below (albeit roasted on a spit instead of cut into dainty chunks), and they likely washed it down with the local red.

Abbacchio al Diavolo

SPICY ROASTED LAMB

FOR THE LAMB

5 pounds bone-in or 3 pounds boneless
  BABY LAMB (leg or shoulder), cut into
  2-inch cubes (it is better to have some
  bone-in pieces)
¼ cup plus 2 tablespoons extra-virgin
  OLIVE OIL
1 teaspoon SALT
1 teaspoon ground BLACK PEPPER
1 PARSNIP, scraped and cut into 1-inch
  half moons
4 stalks CELERY, cut into 1-inch pieces
2 large CARROTS, cut into 1-inch pieces
2 large WHITE ONIONS, peeled and
  chopped into 1-inch chunks
1 cup CHICKEN STOCK

FOR THE CONDIMENT:

6 ANCHOVY FILLETS
¼ cup extra-virgin OLIVE OIL
4 SAGE LEAVES (or 1 teaspoon dried sage)
1 teaspoon RED CHILI FLAKES
2 tablespoons MUSTARD OIL
3 tablespoons RED WINE VINEGAR

SERVES 6

Preheat the oven to 500°F.

In a large mixing bowl, combine the lamb chunks with ¼ cup of the olive oil and the salt and pepper. Add the parsnip, celery, carrot, and onion. Mix well.

Heat a heavy-duty roasting pan for 20 minutes in the preheated oven, remove, and add 2 tablespoons of the olive oil to coat the inside of the pan. Add the contents of the mixing bowl, return to the oven, and roast for 20 minutes, so the meat develops a crust.

Lower the temperature to 425°F. Add ¼ cup of the stock to the pan, and with a spatula scrape the bottom of the pan to deglaze. Repeat this process with a new ¼ cup of stock every 5 minutes for the next 15 minutes, for a total of 4 deglazings, or 1 cup of stock. Cook until the meat is well browned and the carrots and vegetables are tender, about 5 to 10 minutes more.

Total cooking time with high-heat roasting and deglazing should be about 50 minutes.

Remove the lamb from the oven and let cool for 10 minutes. Meanwhile, prepare the condiments. Place the anchovies, the ¼ cup of olive oil, sage leaves, chili flakes, mustard oil, and vinegar in a mortar and pestle. Muddle together to create a paste.

Place the cooked lamb and vegetables in a mixing bowl, add the condiment, and toss everything together as if it were a salad. Serve with roasted fingerling potatoes and a radicchio *insalata*.

WINE RECOMMENDATION: Montepulciano d'Abruzzo: Its soft tannins won't clash with the spice, making the wine a fruity pillow for the fiery dish. Look for wines from Masciarelli, Illuminati, or if you feel like splurging, Edoardo Valentini.

Campania
Recapturing Past Glory

La Sartorìa Napoletana

Naples is scorching, and the shopkeepers are starting to lock their doors as *pranzo* (lunch) approaches. The midday hordes are spilling out of the *palazzi* and onto the sticky, cobbled streets near the Piazza del Plebiscito. And if there's one thing that jumps out right away, it's how well turned out most everyone is. The men in particular are impossibly composed in the wilting heat: With their thick-knotted neckties bulging out of high-rising spread collars, they may as well be wearing scarves. Most of their suits are slim-cut three- and four-button numbers, side-vented, the top two buttons fastened so the tie pops out a little bit, those outrageously big knots always just slightly askew, studiously raffish. The dandier dressers offset their dark suits with light brown shoes, usually big, hand-stitched split-toes with thick, angular leather soles. Even the dumpy guys manage to look good—their pants break properly, their shirt cuffs peek out from under their jacket sleeves. They *flow*, regardless of body type.

If Milan is Italy's center of high fashion, Naples is the capital of high style. There is a difference. Ask any well-dressed Italian man where the best men's clothes are made, and he'll say the *sartorie* (custom tailors) of Naples. *La sartoria napoletana* survived decades of decay in a city that has only recently cleaned itself up. And as it reclaims some of the glory it enjoyed in the past as the capital of the Kingdom of the South, the *sartorie* are there to keep the restless nobles, their courtiers, and the average Giuseppe flowing.

The big names in Naples tailoring include Attolini and Kiton, known mostly for suits; Borelli, a shirtmaker; and Marinella, whose necktie shop on the Riviera del Chiaia is a river of silk. For all of its persistent poverty, petty crime, and overcrowding, Naples still harkens back to the days of royal *ateliers* on every corner.

We're on our way to a shop off the Via Chiaia owned by a small, stooped, chain-smoking suitmaker named Carlo, a friend of a friend, to see *la sartoria napoletana* firsthand. His studio is on the third floor of an old Baroque *palazzo*, where the thick marble stairs wrap around the open elevator shaft. Our footsteps bounce loudly off the marble as the lift purrs by with just the slightest rattle of its chains. We enter the studio to a blast of cigarette smoke, hanging in the tight space like a cloud, and are greeted by Carlo with a wink over the top of his bifocals. As it happens, he's got a client on the dais, stripped to his underwear.

THE DOC ZONES OF CAMPANIA

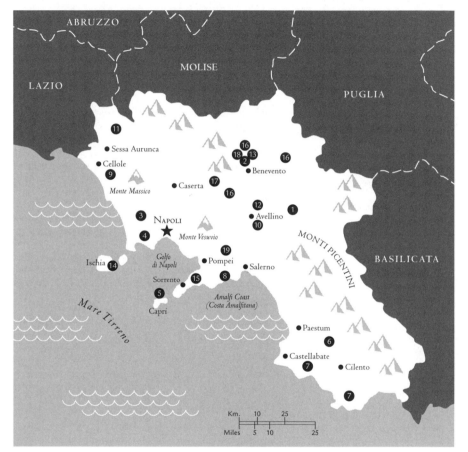

DOCG		9	Falerno del Massico
1	Taurasi	10	Fiano di Avellino
		11	Galluccio
DOC		12	Greco di Tufo
2	Aglianico del Taburno/Taburno	13	Guardia Sanframondi/Guardiolo
3	Aversa	14	Ischia
4	Campi Flegrei	15	Penisola Sorrentina
5	Capri	16	Sannio
6	Castel San Lorenzo	17	Sant'Agata dei Goti
7	Cilento	18	Solopaca
8	Costa d'Amalfi	19	Vesuvio

Carlo's is a two-man operation, although the second man doesn't do much other than sit in a thick mahogany chair and shoot the breeze with Carlo as he takes the man's measurements. Carlo remarks on the customer's features to the man in the mahogany chair as if the customer weren't there. "He's like that guy from the other day," Carlo says, to the customer's mild amusement. "Big shoulders, short arms."

As Carlo pulls down bolts of fabric for the customer to look at, he rubs the fabric lightly between thumb and forefinger. That's his way of telling what grade of wool it is—the term is "the hand" of the fabric. As they survey different swatches, it's clear that the customer is going to get what Carlo tells him to get. "This is the right color for you," Carlo says, holding up a bolt of navy blue fabric with a tight pinstripe. "This'll slim you down a little bit." The customer just nods and makes his way back to the changing room.

"A good suit is in the details," Carlo explains, pulling a finished jacket out of a cubby hole behind the counter. "The button holes on the sleeves actually button. The lapels are hand-sewn." "The lining," he continues, turning the jacket inside-out, "is canvas, hand-stitched. When you buy a suit like this, you buy it for life."

Feeling a little full of himself in the presence of an audience, and knowing that we're wine guys, he says that fabric is subject to the whims of *terroir*. "Different sheep eating different kinds of grass in different places produce different wool," he explains. "There's no question about it: I can tell by the hand where the wool comes from, and probably also where it's been milled."

It would certainly be nice to live like some Neapolitan nobleman, buying shirts with mother-of-pearl buttons, suits that mold to your body like a second skin, shoes cut to match the contours of your feet. And it wouldn't hurt to know exactly what it is that creates the *crema* on top of a well-made espresso, or when a tomato is perfectly ripe. Italians, and especially Neapolitans, tend to focus intently on such details. It's not a choice between looking good and feeling good—both are necessities in Naples, for princes and paupers alike.

It might be said that the wines of Campania have a lot in common with the city of Naples: They've faded over the years, but they still have a certain nobility. In his *Wine Atlas of Italy*, published in 1990, Burton Anderson was particularly hard on Campania, bluntly stating that the region's noteworthy winemakers could be "counted on one's fingers."

But the last decade has been a dynamic one in Campania, with new and notable wine estates popping up all over the region, especially in the Taurasi DOCG zone. Feudi di San Gregorio, for example, is a rapidly expanding estate that makes a wide array of whites and reds, most notably one of the more concentrated Taurasis available; its first commercial vintage was 1991. Antonio Caggiano, an architect and grape grower in the Taurasi DOCG, began bottling his own wines in 1994, and has become one of the better-regarded producers in the area. And the Terredora estate, the product of an acrimonious split between brothers Antonio and Walter Mastroberardino (Antonio got the brand name, Walter the family vineyards), started bottling Taurasi and other wines in 1994.

But it doesn't stop in Taurasi. Campania is also the home of two of Italy's most sought-after "boutique" reds, both of which debuted in 1994: "Terra di Lavoro," a powerful, aglianico-based wine made by Fontana Galardi, in the northern Campania village of Sessa Aurunca; and "Montevetrano," an aglianico-merlot-cabernet blend made at a small estate in the southerly Cilento region. Other nineties newcomers included Bruno DeConciliis and Luigi Maffini, both known for potent reds (and whites) from the arid hills south of Salerno.

Yet for all of the new boldfaced names, Campania still has a long way to go. The region produces a tremendous amount of wine, but less than 3 percent of it is classified as DOC, the third-lowest percentage in Italy (only Basilicata and Sicilia produce less DOC wine as a percentage of their total output). Perhaps this is because Campania has been celebrated since antiquity for its agricultural productivity: Along the flatlands south of Salerno, surrounding the ancient Greek city of Paestum, there are as many as four harvests a year in the rich soils, of everything from artichokes to strawberries. Along the rocky Amalfi coast and up onto the volcanic slopes of Mount Vesuvius, citrus groves (especially lemons) flourish, while the cool hills of Avellino are thick with chestnut and hazelnut trees. Benevento, farther north, is one of the world's largest suppliers of tobacco. In the midst of this productivity, wine grapes have mostly been viewed as just another commodity to be consumed hungrily by one of Italy's densest populations.

In modern times, Campanian wines have been known for fancy names (like Lacryma Christi, or "tears of Christ") and historic pedigrees, but not much else. Yet just as Naples has begun to turn itself around after decades of decay, so too are the region's wines beginning to live up to their past.

VINI BIANCHI
White Wines

Campania is the main repository for the viticultural history of the Italian south—a history tied almost exclusively to the original migrations to Italy by the Greeks. The islands of Ischia and Capri are thought to have been the first two Greek colonies in Italy, followed closely by Naples (the Greek Neapolis), Herculaneum, Pompeii (originally Greek), and Paestum, to name a few. The most obvious remnant of Greek viticulture is the greco family of white grapes, found throughout the southern Mediterranean and as far off as Umbria (where it has mutated into a subvariety called grechetto) and Sicily (where it known as grecanico). As some historians and scientists tell it, greco may well have been the progenitor of most of the white varieties grown in Italy, including trebbiano, verdicchio, and the garganega of Soave in the Veneto.

While the Greeks introduced systemized viticulture to their southern-Italian colonies, it was the Romans, a few centuries later, who documented it all. Campania, particularly the coast between Naples and what is now Lazio, was not only the summer playground of rich Romans but also an agricultural heartland. Viticulture in northern Campania—the name is derived from the Latin *campania felix*, or "fortunate country," a testament to its legendary fertility—was described in great detail by writers such as Pliny the Elder, Columella, and Virgil.

More so than any other region of Italy, Campania is like an archaeological dig of ancient grapevines. Among the whites, there's falanghina, whose name is thought to derive from the Latin word *phalanga*, meaning stake or pole, in reference to the early Greek method of training vines to poles in the low *alberello* (bush) method. It's further believed that *vinum phalanghinum* evolved into *vinum phalernum* and became not only the description of a wine but of a specific geographic zone on Campania's north coast, thus giving rise to one of the most famous wines of ancient Rome, Falernum (now Falerno del Massico). There's also the spicy white grape fiano, known as *vitis apiana* by the Romans because its juice attracted bees (*apis* in Latin), and coda di volpe or *cauda vulpium* (tail of the fox), so named by Pliny to describe the elongated shape of the grape clusters. And there's asprinio, a native wild vine domesticated by the Etruscans, still used in sparkling and dry wines from the Aversa DOC north of Naples.

All of these Campanian whites share traits that make it easy to imagine them originating from the same parent. They're all lightly colored, delicately aromatic, brightly (and sometimes sharply) acidic, and somewhat fragile, prone to relatively rapid oxidation. As most of its best producers will admit, wines such as Greco di Tufo and Fiano di Avellino are best consumed young. Tasting these wines side by side is often challenging, because they can resemble one another so closely, but there are subtle differences to be discerned.

GRECO

This may sound ridiculous, or like a cop-out, but greco makes *grapey* wine. The Greco di Tufo zone is named for the village of Tufo itself in the hills near Avellino, while Tufo is named for the solid base of tufaceous rock that lies under a mix of clay and sand. Bisected by the Sabato

River, Tufo lies in the path of ancient volcanoes that run all the way from Basilicata up through Lazio and beyond, and these soils can lend a minerally finish to a white that otherwise tastes like a ripe, green table grape. When young, Greco di Tufo has a clean, refreshing flavor and bright acidity, with a touch of grape-skin bitterness. It's a simple white, and the knock on it is that it tends to oxidize quickly, giving it a somewhat caramelized aftertaste that detracts from the freshness of the fruit.

"Greco is not a long ager," says Roberto DiMeo, who makes both Greco di Tufo and the red Taurasi at his family estate in Salza Irpinia. "It is really at its best one or two years from the vintage."

Like trebbiano, greco's mild-mannered, aromatic personality makes it a very difficult grape to pin down. At times it can be downright juicy and tropical, as in wines such as Feudi di San Gregorio's "Cutizzi," a Greco di Tufo made with a percentage of more sugar-rich, late-harvested fruit. More often, greco starts out fleshy and then turns chalky and minerally, as in the wines of DiMeo, Terredora, and Mastroberardino. Terredora's "Loggia della Serra" and Mastroberardino's "Vignadangelo" Greco di Tufos are consistently accurate expressions of the grape—they don't bowl you over with extract, but there's a purity to these wines that makes them natural partners to the delicate seafoods of Naples and Amalfi, especially *polpo* (octopus) and *seppia* (cuttlefish).

FIANO

Probably the most assertive and interesting white grape in Campania is fiano, whose flavor is often strongly reminiscent of pine nuts and herbs, almost a pesto in a bottle. Although it is grown in coastal areas (such as the Cilento DOC zone south of Salerno), fiano is at its best in the densely wooded hills of Avellino, where vineyards reach elevations of eighteen hundred feet and higher.

Indeed, one of the most dramatic features of Campania is how quickly the landscape changes. Whereas the coastal areas near Vesuvius and Cilento have full-on Mediterranean climates reminiscent of Sicily or Calabria, the inland regions around Avellino and Benevento are more readily comparable to Piedmont. The tightly packed, pre-Apennine hills of the interior begin to rise west and south of Avellino, almost walling the region off from Naples. Approaching from the south on the *superstrada* from Salento, there's a short tunnel that acts almost as a gateway to the vineyards of Taurasi and Tufo. At the south entrance to that tunnel, say locals, the temperature is consistently ten degrees lower than at the northern entrance— only about a quarter-mile away.

Avellino and most of the surrounding towns in the region—known as Irpinia—were destroyed in a devastating earthquake in 1980. So today the wine towns of the zone have a more modern, almost suburban feel in comparison to the quaint medieval wine towns of, for example, Tuscany. The often soaring heights are blanketed with chestnut trees, whose produce fall to the ground inside prickly casings of tennis-ball green. The vineyards, despite the modernization of the area, remain planted predominantly to fiano and its sometime blending partner, coda di volpe.

Fiano di Avellino is not a full-bodied wine, but it is very aromatic, a direct reflection of the dewy, piney hills in which it grows. A slight suggestion of hazelnut, another big Irpinia crop, is often detected in Fiano di Avellino. But the predominant aromas and flavors are sour and herbal, with scents of pine needles and cider apples, infused with an almost peaty smokiness. "There's a *selvático* [savage] quality to fiano that sets it apart," says Enzo Ercolino, proprietor of Feudi di San Gregorio, one of the better producers of Fiano di Avellino. As with his "Cutizzi" Greco di Tufo, Ercolino uses a proportion of late-harvested fruit in a Fiano di Avellino called "Pietracalda," a wine that has attracted a lot of attention for its atypically fat, plump texture.

Yet a wine like Pietracalda seems more market-driven than typical of the grape. Fiano is by its nature a lighter-styled, more aromatic white. But as producers experiment with barrel fermentation and late harvesting—both designed to add body to fiano's thin frame—they often lose something in the translation. Fiano will always be better as a young, fresh, palate-cleansing wine, however much its producers try to pump it up.

For great examples of classic Fiano di Avellino, check out the "Radici" bottling of Mastroberardino, and the single-vineyard "Terre di Dora" from Terredora. A more modern, riper, but not overblown style of fiano is being made by the two young newcomers in the Cilento— Bruno De Conciliis and Luigi Maffini—whose "Perella" and "Kràtos" bottlings, respectively, have a roundness not found in most Avellino fianos.

FALANGHINA

Occupying a sort of middle ground between greco and fiano, literally and figuratively, is falanghina. It borrows some of the piney fragrance of fiano and some of the juiciness of greco to create a refreshing, mostly coastal white, a wine to be sipped in a café in Positano or Capri, with a classic *caprese* salad of tomatoes, mozzarella, and basil.

The prime territory for falanghina runs mostly along the coast, from the Falerno del Massico DOC zone in the north, where it is thought to have originated, down past Naples and onto the rugged *costa amalfitana*. Unlike fiano and greco, falanghina is not usually showcased on its own, but rather blended with a variety of other local grapes. On the slopes of Vesuvius, it's thrown in with verdeca, coda di volpe, and greco; on the Sorrentine peninsula (taking in the Penisola Sorrentina and Costa d'Amalfi DOCs) it is combined with biancolella and/or greco, as it is on the island of Capri. On the Amalfi Costa in particular, the grape takes on a decidedly floral aroma, with notes of citrus blossoms, in the wines of producers such as Marisa Cuomo. Cuomo's "Ravello" (so named for a town on the Amalfi coast) and "Fiorduva" falanghinas are probably the best wines from the grape available today, although a number of producers throughout Campania—including Feudi di San Gregorio in Avellino and Ocone in Benevento—are producing interesting varietal bottlings.

OTHER WHITES

Coda di volpe is another grape that finds its way into a variety of DOC wines, as well as in varietal bottlings on its own. Enzo Ercolino of Feudi di San Gregorio describes it as a wine with *vinosità*—vinousness—in reference to its sour, almost vinegary acidity. And the rarer biancolella remains in circulation largely thanks to the D'Ambra winery on the island of Ischia, whose wines from the grape are great seafood whites for a hot day in Naples—or New York, for that matter. Like the rest of Campania's white-wine brigade, these wines are not high-alcohol cocktails of fruit and oak: In a region full of extroverted people, the wines are marked by delicacy and finesse, most of them content to blend in among the swelling masses of Napoli.

VINI ROSSI
Red Wines

For all of the different white-wine grapes in Campania, the region still produces more red wine than white, the vast majority of it made from either piedirosso (found mostly along the coast) or aglianico (found mostly inland, particularly near Avellino). In aglianico in particular the region's vintners have found a variety with which to distinguish themselves, and indeed the realm of Campanian aglianico has spread well beyond its traditional confines in Taurasi.

Actually, it is not entirely accurate to say that aglianico was confined to Taurasi—it's more accurate to say that the wines worth drinking from aglianico were confined to Taurasi. In fact, up until a decade ago they were mostly confined to a single winery: Mastroberardino, whose rich, complex "Radici" Taurasi essentially started the red-wine revolution of the Italian south. Without the success of Mastroberardino, there's no telling where Campanian winemaking may have gone.

As discussed later in the Basilicata chapter, the origins of aglianico are the subject of some debate. The most popular theory is that it landed on Campania's north coast with the Greeks, to be later dubbed *ellenico* (Hellenic) by the Romans and later still aglianico as the word permutated over time. It is interesting to trace aglianico's modern-day path, from the slopes of the dormant Monte Massico volcano, on Campania's north coast, inland to Benevento and Avellino and then onward to the slopes of Monte Vulture, in northern Basilicata. All of these zones sit atop ancient volcanoes, like a long, winding archipelago on land. And the question remains today: From which direction did the grape come?

Within the confines of Campania, the various DOC reds that feature aglianico offer different expressions of the grape. On the coast, the more purely volcanic, ashy soils of the Falerno del Massico zone produce densely concentrated but slightly less tannic versions of aglianico than zones such as Taburno and Taurasi, where the almost aggressively tannic personality of the grape is on display. Down south on the relatively new frontiers of Salerno and Cilento, producers such as Silvia Imparato (Montevetrano), Luigi Maffini, and Bruno De Conciliis may have the fruitiest, sappiest aglianicos of them all, albeit with the tarry spiciness that characterizes the grape.

But it all began—commercially speaking, anyway—in Taurasi, a zone that flanks the Calore River east of Avellino, where vineyards spill down slopes that reach to elevations of twenty-one hundred feet and higher. The soils are a mix of volcanic deposits and calcareous marls, and the high limestone content in the soil is often said to lend the reds of Taurasi their tannic bite. The Taurasi production discipline calls for a minimum of three years' aging (with at least one year in oak barrels) to soften its rough edges, but even on release most Taurasi is brawny stuff: Mastroberardino's early wines were called the "Barolos of the south." But while the aglianico of Campania (and Basilicata) is tarry and tannic, its aromatics

aren't directly comparable to those of nebbiolo in Piedmont. It's true that both Taurasi and Barolo have earthy notes reminiscent of saddle leather, tea leaves, and cigar boxes, but in aglianico the fruit flavors lean more toward blackberries and other black fruits, while nebbiolo wines are more reminiscent of red fruits and are typically more uplifted and ethereal than aglianicos. Both are big, brooding wines, but on balance aglianico tends to brood just a little bit longer.

Like the nebbiolo of Barolo, the aglianico of Taurasi is not harvested until late October or early November, as the climate in Irpinia is a far cry from the four-harvests-a-year heat of places like Cilento. "In a good year, the altitudes and cooler temperatures help preserve the aromas in the grapes," says Antonio Caggiano, whose "Macchia dei Goti" Taurasi captures all of the woodsy, earthy flavor of Irpinia. "In more difficult years, the wine can have bitter tannins. It is very difficult, regardless, to have a pure aglianico wine because of the tannins."

In the hills of Taburno, too, which are even more northerly than Irpinia's, aglianico has a fierce character that can only be tamed with age. The wines of the Aglianico del Taburno DOC have a raw power, with deep fruit flavors laced with the scents of the tobacco leaves that grow nearby. While lesser-known than those of Taurasi, the Taburno wines can be just as impressive, as evidenced by the reds of Domenico Ocone, in Ponte, and the Cantina del Taburno, in Foglianese.

"Maybe when you look at Campania on a map it looks like the south, and so you view it as uniformly hot and dry," says Domenico Ocone, one of the best-known producers in the Taburno zone. "But the wines of Taburno and Taurasi are mountain wines. We sometimes have to pick grapes in the snow, and that long growing season gives the wines structure and aroma you can't get on the coast."

Salvatore Avallone, proprietor of the Villa Matilde in Cellole, in the Falerno del Massico zone, might disagree. In his "Vigna Camarato" aglianico, produced in (but not labeled with) the Falerno del Massico DOC, he covers the biting tannins of the grape with a layer of almost sappy, blackberry extract. It's a trait shared by another north-coast aglianico, the sought-after "Terra di Lavoro" from Fontana Galardi, an estate set on a spectacular hillside in Sessa Aurunca, overlooking the Mediterranean. Although both "Vigna Camarato" and "Terra di Lavoro" are built to age, they have an immediate pleasurability that not all Taurasi can match. Along with the wines of De Conciliis, Maffini, and Montevetrano farther south, they've become the kinds of reds that are snapped up by collectors before they even hit store shelves—the "cult" reds of southern Italy.

Lighter-bodied than aglianico but similarly *selvatico* in its wild-berry flavor is piedirosso, a grape used both in combination with aglianico and on its own. It lends a distinctive savor and bright acidity to the DOC reds of Capri, Vesuvio, and Ischia, while factoring into blends in zones as far-flung as Taurasi and Cilento. Piedirosso's relatively soft tannins and berryish flavors are kicked up with a spicy note of cinnamon and dried cherry, and many producers—including Luigi Maffini, Feudi di San Gregorio, and Ocone—make stand-alone wines from the grape. The Mastroberardino estate, which has been dedicated in recent years to research-ing the multitude of indigenous grapes of the region, recently released an aglianico-piedirosso blend called "Historia," a wine that is both approachable and deeply concentrated. "The piedirosso adds a fruity sweetness to the wine that aglianico definitely lacks," says Carlo Mastroberardino of the Mastroberardino winery. A similar push-pull can be found in the potent "Serpico" of Feudi di San Gregorio, a blend of aglianico, piedirosso, and sangiovese.

For the most part, producers in Campania seem content to stick with native varieties. Although cabernet sauvignon and merlot are spreading throughout the region—the Montevetrano wine, for one, incorporates both varieties with aglianico—the Campanians have refashioned their traditional reds, as opposed to reinventing them.

VINI DOLCI
Sweet Wines

For all of the comparisons the Campanian coast draws to the coasts of Sicily or Calabria, there are very few sweet wines produced here. Other than some sparkling versions of Lacryma Christi, Greco di Tufo, and a handful of other DOC whites (most of which are decidedly local and, more notably, not worth drinking), there's no tradition of *spumante* in Campania. The same could be said of *vino dolce*, of which there is very little, save for the occasional *amabile* (semisweet) red. But with so many good new dry reds to drink from the region, who has time for dessert?

FAST FACTS: *C*AMPANIA

PROVINCES	Avellino (AV), Benevento (BN), Caserta (CE), Napoli (NA), Salerno (SA)
CAPITAL	Naples
KEY WINE TOWNS	Avellino, Benevento, Ravello, Taurasi
TOTAL VINEYARD AREA*	41,129 hectares, or 101,630 acres. Rank: 9th
TOTAL WINE PRODUCTION*	1,971,000 hectoliters, or 52,073,976 gallons (9th); 36% white, 64% red
DOC WINE PRODUCED*	2.8% (18th)
SPECIALTY FOODS	mozzarella di bufala; San Marzano tomatoes; pizza; lemons and oranges; eggplant; chestnuts; hazelnuts; almonds.

*1997 figures. Rankings out of twenty regions total (Trentino–Alto Adige counted as one). Source: Istituto Statistica Mercati Agro-Alimentari (ISMEA), Rome.

KEY GRAPE VARIETIES

WHITES

FALANGHINA	Thought to have been brought by the ancient Greeks, it may have gotten its name from the Latin word *phalanga,* meaning stake or pole, in reference to the early Greek method of training vines to poles. While found throughout the region, it is most interesting on the Amalfi coast.
FIANO	Spicy, smoky, and crisp, it is probably the most assertively aromatic and fullest-bodied of Campania's white grapes.
GRECO	Brought by the ancient Greeks and possibly the progenitor of any number of Italian white varieties. It makes fleshy, grapey whites in high-altitude vineyards around Avellino.

CODA DI VOLPE	Named "tail of the fox" by Pliny because of the shape of its grape clusters. It is used in Vesuvio DOC blends (among others) and in varietal bottlings.
	REDS
AGLÍANICO	Campania vies with Basilicata for ownership rights to this variety. Most experts believe it was brought by the Greeks, its name a mutation of the Italian word for Greek, *ellenico*. Found primarily in the hills of Irpinia (Taurasi DOC) and Benevento (Taburno DOC), but is also on the rise on the north coast (Falerno del Massico).
PIEDIROSSO	Found in a variety of Campania's DOC wines, this light red (so named for its "red feet," or red stalks) is mostly used as a blending ingredient.

TOP VINTAGES IN CAMPANIA, 1980–2000

As a rule, the dense, tannic reds of Taurasi are aged a minimum of three years before they are released for sale, à la Barolo. And like Barolo, the wines from the often steep, cool slopes of the Taurasi zone are made from a late-ripening grape that is sensitive to the whims of vintage. In a good year these can be some of the most powerful and complex reds in Italy, and they can take ten years in the bottle or more. Top years in Taurasi include 1985, '88, '90, '93, '97, '98, '99.

LA STRADA DEL VINO
WINE TOURING IN CAMPANIA

There may not be a more scenic, relaxing wine town in all of Italy than Ravello, a tiny village on the precipitous Amalfi coast. Ravello lends its name to an official subzone within the Costa d'Amalfi DOC zone (Marisa Cuomo is the most famous producer), but more than any direct link to wine Ravello is a link to another time. It's almost like a play town, with a handful of excellent restaurants, all of which have outdoor cafés in which you can sit with a sweaty glass of falanghina and contemplate life.

DEGUSTAZIONI
TASTINGS

GRECO

Vega-D'Antiche Terre
Greco di Tufo, $

Cantine Grotta del Sole
Greco di Tufo, $

A tasting of these wines can easily devolve into a gulping, be-cause they are so simple, straightforward, and easy to drink. Not especially complex but grapey and fresh on the palate, these two wines are textbook greco: very delicate aromas, a juicy richness at first, and then a gripping mineral finish. For Neapolitan *insalata di mare* (seafood salad) these are the whites to chill down and crack open.

FIANO

Feudi di San Gregorio
Fiano di Avellino, $

Terredora Fiano di
Avellino "Terre di Dora," $

More complex and structured than the light, loose greco, fiano takes on a smoky, woodsy, foresty quality that evokes its ori-gins in the thickly wooded hills of Irpinia, near the town of Avellino. The Terredora wine has an almost peaty quality to its aroma, layered over a crisp blast of apple-pear flavor. The Feudi di San Gregorio wine is similarly smoky, with fresh fruit flavors and piercing acidity. These wines are best showcased with dishes incorporating fresh herbs, such as a classic *insalata caprese,* where the wine's own herbal qualities get a chance to shine.

AGLIANICO

Villa Matilde Falerno del
Massico Rosso, $

Antonio Caggiano Taurasi
"Macchia dei Goti," $$

Mastroberardino Taurasi
"Radici," $$

Here are three faces of aglianico. The first (Villa Matilde) is a little softer and more velvety, owing perhaps to a more temper-ate seaside growing region: Its black-berry flavors are inter-twined with savory notes of coffee grounds and tobacco, but the overall impression is a fruity one. The Caggiano Taurasi has a more savory bite, showing off the earthy side to the aglianico grape, with hints of Earl Grey tea and wild mushrooms in the aroma. Then there's the legendary Mastroberardino "Radici," one of the best-known reds of the Italian south, which seems to combine elements of the other two: There's that trademark aglianico nose of cigar boxes and leather, offset by an almost sweet taste of black cherries and black currants. These are big, brooding wines for baked pastas, or, if you're feeling extrava-gant, a big, sausage-topped pizza.

La Cucina
FOOD FOR THE WINE
RECIPE BY MARIO BATALI

Without a doubt, the relatively small clump of mostly volcanic soil between Naples and Salerno may be one of the most gastronomically important pieces of land in Italy. This is where San Marzano tomatoes are grown and where water buffaloes are raised to make the milk for mozzarella di bufala. Each of these products is great on its own. But as anyone knows who has been to Naples, they're even better in tandem—be it on one of Naples' incomparable *pizze,* in an *insalata caprese,* or in the recipe below, a favorite along the Sorrentine peninsula that juts out into the Mediterranean toward Capri.

Campania's cuisine is all about what the Italians call *materia prima*—the raw materials, the ingredients themselves. It's about taking an exceptional tomato and presenting it with a minimum of adornments. The most striking example of this is the pizza of Naples, one of the best examples there is of a dish that is simple and complex at the same time.

Gnocchi alla Sorrentina
GNOCCHI SORRENTO-STYLE

FOR THE GNOCCHI DOUGH

3 pounds russet POTATOES
2 cups all-purpose FLOUR
1 large EGG
1 teaspoon SALT

FOR THE SAUCE

¼ cup extra-virgin OLIVE OIL
1 medium ONION, chopped into ½-inch dice
2 cloves GARLIC, crushed
1 28-ounce can San Marzano ITALIAN PLUM TOMATOES, crushed by hand, juice reserved
2 tablespoons SALT
1 pound fresh MOZZARELLA, cut into ¼-inch cubes
12 fresh BASIL LEAVES, cut into thin strips

SERVES 6 AS A MAIN COURSE
OR 12 AS AN APPETIZER

FOR THE GNOCCHI

Place the whole potatoes in a saucepan with warm water to cover. Bring to a boil and cook at a low boil until they are soft, about 45 minutes. Cool slightly and while still warm, peel the potatoes and pass them through a vegetable mill onto a clean pasta board.

Make a well in the center of the potatoes and sprinkle all over with the flour. Break the egg into the center of the well, add the salt, and using a fork, stir into the flour and potatoes as if you were making pasta. Once the egg is mixed in, bring the dough together, kneading gently until a ball is formed. Continue kneading gently for another 4 minutes, or until the ball is dry to the touch.

Divide the dough into 6 large balls. Roll each ball into 3/4-inch-diameter cylinders and cut the cylinders into 1-inch pieces. Flick the pieces off of a fork or along the concave side of a cheese grater to score the sides.

FOR THE SAUCE AND SERVING

Place the olive oil in a 10- to 12-inch in sauté pan over a medium flame and heat until the oil is just smoking. Add the onion and cook until light golden brown and softened, about 7 to 8 minutes. Add the garlic and cook two minutes more.

Add the crushed tomatoes and the juices and bring to a boil. Lower the heat to a high simmer and cook until the mixture takes on the texture of oatmeal, about 15 to 20 minutes. Remove pan from heat and set aside.

Meanwhile, bring 6 quarts of water to a boil and add the salt. Drop the gnocchi in and cook until they float aggressively, bobbing at the top of the water. Remove the gnocchi with a slotted spoon and place immediately into the pan with the tomato sauce. Return the pan to medium heat and simmer until the gnocchi have absorbed some of the sauce and the dish is dressed like a salad, about 2 to 3 minutes. Add the mozzarella cubes and remove the pan from the heat. Stir gently and quickly divide the gnocchi and sauce among four plates. Sprinkle equal proportions of the shredded basil leaves over each plate and serve immediately.

WINE RECOMMENDATION: With all this cheese, dough, and tomato, a tart, somewhat tannic red wine is probably in order. Go with a Taurasi if you want something fuller-bodied, or a red from Vesuvio if you'd rather something lighter.

Puglia

The South's Unlimited Potential

—◦※◦—

More Than
Words Can Say

It's often noted that people in southern Italy use more hand gestures than people in the north. On the surface, there doesn't seem to be a big difference. But most southern Italians do acknowledge their more demonstrative tendencies, usually with joking references to hot blood or humble upbringings. Whatever the reasons, hands really start flying as you go farther and farther south of Rome.

It would take a sociologist to say for sure why this is. Since the "true" Italian language is said to be Florentine Tuscan, it may be that southerners were slower to pick up the speech patterns of unified Italy. Given how Italy has developed in more recent times, with a tremendous amount of migration toward the industrial centers of the north, it's only natural that the clash of regional dialects necessitated some sign language. Much of it has become universal, although in places like Naples, Palermo, and Bari it's used with a little more gusto.

The enduring classic is the gesture in which you turn your palm skyward, press your four fingers to your thumb and shake your hand at chest height. This carries a wide range of

meanings, from *What the hell are you talking about?* to *Get a load of this guy* and *Watch it, pal.* It's usually accompanied by an amused, sarcastic, or disgusted purse of the lips, depending on usage.

Then there's the one where you press your hands together as if you were praying, then shake them up and down, usually with a roll of the eyes (or other exasperated facial expression). This is the *Why don't you listen to me?* or *You're going to be the death of me* gesture, a favorite among Italian mothers.

Another classic, though lesser-known, is what might be called the *esatto* (exactly), a dramatic flourish used to say *You are exactly right* or *This is perfect.* It is done by making a sideways okay sign with thumb and index finger (so the *o* faces up), then drawing your hand across your chest in a fluid motion. Some people use a vertical motion instead, going from neck to waist as if they were unzipping an invisible jacket.

But this is only the beginning. As we learn firsthand during a visit to the Taurino winery in Guagnano, Puglia, the sign language of southern Italy merits its own illustrated dictionary.

Pino, a longtime vineyard worker at Taurino, is the man who introduces us not only to the Taurino estate but to the nuances of the unspoken word. Dressed in standard Puglian vineyard worker attire—cut-offs, mesh tank top, Dr. Scholl's–style wood-soled sandals—he

THE DOC ZONES OF PUGLIA

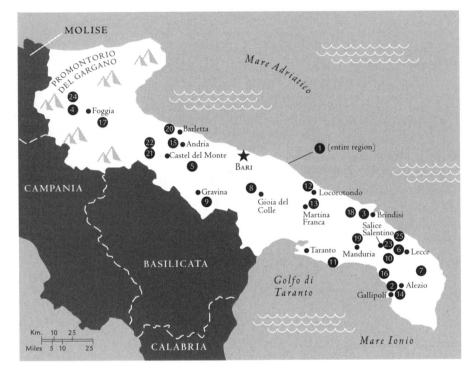

1	Aleatico di Puglia	13	Martina/Martina Franca
2	Alezio	14	Matino
3	Brindisi	15	Moscato di Trani
4	Cacc'e mmitte di Lucera	16	Nardò
5	Castel del Monte	17	Orta Nova
6	Copertino	18	Ostuni
7	Galatina	19	Primitivo di Manduria
8	Gioia del Colle	20	Rosso Barletta
9	Gravina	21	Rosso Canosa/Canisium
10	Leverano	22	Rosso di Cerignola
11	Lizzano	23	Salice Salentino
12	Locorotondo	24	San Severo
		25	Squinzano

leads us on a tour of some giant, bush-trained vines near the town of Salice Salentino. He describes the soils and methods of pruning and, every so often, he pulls down on the lower lid of his right eye with his index finger. He says that the thick-trunked *alberelli* in this particular vineyard are older than he is, and he does the thing with his eye again. He explains how many acres Taurino owns, and then the eye thing. How many varieties of grapes they have . . . eye thing.

This is the *Y'understand?* gesture. In some instances, it can also mean *Stai attento!* ("Beware!"), when the accompanying facial expression is suitably ominous. But Pino is using the *Y'understand?* version, which is ironic since his gravelly voice and dialect-flavored speech prevent us from understanding much of what he's saying. We nod yes anyway.

Continuing on to a small patch of big-berried table grapes, Pino does a sort of reverse karate-chop on himself, tapping his waist with the inside of his flattened hand (*I'm hungry*). He ducks under the trellis and returns with two large bunches of zibibbo grapes, widening his eyes and pushing an index finger into his cheek (*These are good*). As we munch on the grapes and walk along through the vineyard, we ask him about Cosimo Taurino, the widely admired proprietor of the estate, who passed away in 1999. Pino's eyes soften and he puts his hand to his heart for a moment, then he draws his thumb across his cheek and offers a knowing nod. This is the symbol for *furbo* ("sly, cunning"), which, based on his expression, Pino must mean in a good way. Apparently Taurino was a sharp businessman.

In the course of a half-hour tour, Pino covers what seems like the entire manual lexicon, as well as some subtle, semiverbal communica-tion: When he doesn't know the answer to something he blurts out a quick *boh*, an inflection used in place of *Non lo so* ("I don't know") all over Italy. When he knows something very well, or is in enthusiastic agreement with something someone has said, he replies with a rousing *woooop!* ("But of course!"). To review: *boh*, with an expulsion of air, for when you have no idea; *woooop*, with an intake of air, for when you know very well the person, place, or thing being discussed.

When it's time to leave, we tell Pino he's the most interesting vineyard man we've ever met. He laughs, looks skyward, and does the two-handed, pray-and-shake gesture, introducing a new variation: the *Ma dai!* ("Come on!"). We tell him we're not kidding and go on our way, feeling that little bit more Italian after the encounter. As we drive through some of the low-slung, sun-scorched villages of the Salentine peninsula, every group of old men playing cards in the shade, every gaggle of teenagers hanging out on their *motorini*, becomes a subject of study. The hands are really flying—or at least it seems that way.

Although both Calabria and Sicily reach closer to the equator, Puglia looks and feels most like the extreme south. This is probably because it is the flattest region in Italy, a fertile plain rivaled only by the Po Valley of Emilia-Romagna for productivity. Puglia is agriculture writ large: the biggest olive trees you'll ever see, the biggest wheat fields, the biggest vineyards, all of them rooted in iron-rich soils. The region is the principal source of the three Italian staples: bread, olive oil, and wine.

As in Venice, or the hills of Tuscany, Puglia seems to have its own type of light. Where Tuscany's is golden and diffuse, Puglia's is fiery and bright, whether it's bouncing off the rust-colored earth or gleaming in whitewashed hilltop villages. Summery towns such as Martina Franca and Gallipoli give Puglia the look of some outsize Greek isle, although the local culture is informed not just by the Greeks but by all of the historic occupants of the south: Lombards, Normans, Bourbons, and many others. Standing in sharp contrast to some of the boxy, bleached-out, Greek-looking villages are more ornate towns such as Martina Franca, Manduria, and Lecce, whose baroque palaces and churches evoke Rome and points even farther north.

Puglia has long run neck-and-neck with Sicily for the title of Italy's most prodigious wine producer. While in recent years Sicily has reclaimed the top spot, it is Puglia that seems more dominated by the co-op winery culture. Drive from Taranto to Lecce one late-August morning and you'll see huge industrial wineries with long lines of cars, trucks, and tractors out front. All of them are piled high with fresh-picked grapes and surrounded by men chatting and smoking cigarettes, waiting for their hauls to be weighed. As in Sicily, only a small percentage of Puglia's huge wine production is bottled and/or classified as DOC, leaving the rest to be shipped out as high-alcohol blending wine or concentrated grape must. But, as in Sicily, Puglia is in the midst of a gold rush, as more private investment—and hence wine in bottles, not tanker trucks—changes the face of the region.

As European Community and Italian-government subsidies for co-op wineries have largely dried up, the managers of these massive facilities, and their member grape-growers, face stark choices: change, sell, or go out of business. Co-ops have had to scale back production

and focus more on branded, bottled wines, while many grape growers have been content to either plant other crops or rip up their vines (and collect subsidies from the EC for doing so). Other growers are finding eager buyers for their properties, since the EC is not allowing any new planting of vineyards in Italy but, rather, allows only established vineyard estates to augment their plantings. So large Italian or foreign wine firms looking to make an investment in Puglia (of which there are many) can't just buy a wheat field and convert it to vines. The race is not so much for land but for *vineyard* land, which is typically replanted by the new owner.

"In both Sicily and Puglia, people are buying licenses to plant vineyards from firms that have them but for whatever reason have decided not to use them," says Renzo Cotarella, the general manager and chief winemaker for Tuscany's Antinori estate. Antinori recently took a big position in Puglia, purchasing two large vineyard properties and building a new winery in Minervino Murge, in the Castel del Monte DOC zone. Known as Vigneti del Sud, Antinori's Puglia operation markets wines under the Tormaresca brand name, sourcing grapes from a 250-acre vineyard in Minervino and another even larger holding in San Pietro Vernotico, not far from the coastal port of Brindisi. In addition to local grapes such as aglianico and negroamaro, the Vigneti del Sud farms (both of which grew grapes for local co-ops in the past) are being extensively planted with the likes of chardonnay and cabernet sauvignon.

"This area is ripe for development," says Cotarella, remarking on the relative ease and low cost of making wine in Puglia. "At this point in time [summer 2000], vineyards in the

Brindisi province are selling for fifteen million lire per hectare"—about three thousand dollars an acre. "In Grosseto, in southern Tuscany, it's twice as much. And in Bolgheri, in western Tuscany, it's ten times as much. We can make red wines of great quality down here in Puglia, and at a very competitive price." In the 1999 vintage, Antinori produced more than four hundred thousand bottles of Tormaresca. Their plan, of course, is to make millions.

"In Puglia, you have the advantage of working on a large scale. And unlike in Sicily, there's readily available water in Puglia," Cotarella continues. "Also, because Puglia is considered a depressed area, you get help from the EC to develop quality-oriented vineyards here, which helps you defray some of your costs." Ah, Italy . . . there's always an angle.

Some growers in Puglia have stepped outside of the co-op structure altogether and established relationships with market-savvy bottlers, such as Sicily's Calatrasi (which markets the Terrale line of wines) or partnerships, such as the one between American winemaker Mark Shannon and importer Neil Empson, whose A-Mano and Promessa wines have become bargain-priced sensations in the United States. Shannon and Empson essentially lease space in one of Puglia's large co-op wineries and buy grapes as they need them, creating high-quality, low-priced wines with very little in the way of overhead.

It could be argued that Puglia is evolving from a mass producer of bulk wine into a mass producer of cheap bottled wine: a subtle distinction, to be sure. Although there are a number of properties in the region producing good wines (most of them longer-established estates such as Taurino and Rivera), Puglia hasn't yet lived up to its billing as "the California of

Italy"—a moniker also attached, with more justification, to Sicily, which up to this point has capitalized more thoroughly on its incredible winemaking potential. Right now, Puglia is a great region to scour for everyday values, particularly deep, savory, well-priced reds from the local negroamaro or primitivo grapes. The truly great stuff remains a little more elusive, but the potential is undoubtedly there.

"The soils in particular are excellent here," says Cotarella, describing Puglia's rather consistent mixture of *terra rossa* (ferrous red clay and sand) and limestone. "It's the same kind of soil you see in places like Coonawarra in Australia. The minerals in the soils give the wine power, but the limestone underneath allows for good drainage to maintain acidity. You don't see that in a lot of flat regions; usually they are heavier soils. Here there's an excellent balance."

VINI BIANCHI
White Wines

Puglia has an awful lot of DOC zones for a region with such a paltry production of classified wine. This is especially true of white wine from Puglia, which is produced in abundance yet doesn't add up to much. A lot of it goes to vermouth blenders, while most of the wine that falls under DOC parameters remains firmly rooted in its home market.

The two largest white-wine DOCs in Puglia are Locorotondo and Martina Franca, which exemplify the myriad deficiencies of the DOC system in general and Puglia's in particular. Locorotondo and Martina Franca are neighboring communes near the Adriatic coast between Bari and Brindisi, part of a rolling plain famous for the conical-shaped stone dwellings known as *trulli*. The Locorotondo and Martina Franca DOC wines come from essentially identical soils, and are made from the same grapes—a blend based on the green, flinty verdeca, a local variety—yet they are treated as separate zones. On top of that, their wines are nearly impossible to find in bottles outside of the *trulli* district, save for those of the giant cooperative Cantina del Locorotondo. The two zones make nine hundred thousand gallons of wine a year. Where does it all go? We couldn't say, but somehow it all qualifies as DOC.

The other DOC whites of Puglia are similarly scarce, although for a more logical reason: They're produced in tiny quantities. Gravina, an inland DOC that hugs the Basilicata border, has been noted by wine writers as a solid white, but it is a rarity: Based on a random assortment of local and not-so-local grapes (malvasia, greco di tufo, bombino bianco, trebbiano toscano, and verdeca, among others), its production is largely confined to a large cooperative in Botromagno.

As DOC whites go, probably the most interesting wines are coming out of the Castel del Monte and Salice Salentino zones, whose disciplines allow for substantial amounts of chardonnay (there are also varietal whites from sauvignon, pinot bianco, and bombino bianco made in Castel del Monte). Chardonnay is on the rise on the southerly Salentine peninsula in particular, where it is found not only in Salice Salentino but in the Galatina Bianco DOC and a number of IGT- or VdT-designated bottlings. The chardonnays or chardonnay-based blends of Taurino, Pervini, Leone de Castris, and Francesco Candido are all good wines, but as of yet none of them will make you forget California. Like the other white wines of Puglia, they seem like afterthoughts in a region more naturally predisposed to big, jammy reds.

VINI ROSATI
Rosé Wines

Despite hundreds of miles of coastline and a cuisine rich in seafood—including a range of fragrant *brodetti* (fish soups) to rival anything from Greece or France—Puglia has a surprising dearth of good white wine to go with it. Luckily, there are a range of colorful, spicy rosés to sip alongside the local answer to *bouillabaisse*, and rarely does a food-and-wine combination work so well: The deep flavors of a rosé are well-suited to the assertive tastes of fish and shellfish. And when it comes to *rosati*, Puglia does not disappoint.

Some winemakers say that the *rosato* tradition of southern Italy—there are many excellent pink wines made in Abruzzo, Calabria, and Sicily as well—dates back to an era before fermentation temperatures could be controlled by refrigeration. Traditionally, making a full-fledged red wine, with an appropriate time to macerate on its skins, was difficult because the intense heat of the south induced "stuck" fermentations, in which yeasts stopped working as the temperature of the fermenting wine rose. In essence, the pink wine we know today may be the descendant of a half-made red from centuries ago.

These days, Puglian *rosati* are made either by macerating red grapes for a very short time before starting the fermentation, or by blending red and white musts together. The spicy negroamaro grape of the Salentine peninsula, most famous in Salice Salentino reds, makes an excellent *rosato* base, as does primitivo, whose dense color gives rosés an exceptional concentration.

One of the legendary *rosato* wines of Italy is the "Five Roses" brand from the Leone de Castris winery, a tangy negroamaro-based rosé that first debuted in 1923 and is still considered one of the best wines of its type in Italy. Other well-known *rosati* include the "Rosa del Golfo" of Damiano Calò in Alezio, and the "Mjère" *rosato* from his neighbor, Michele Calò (no relation), in Tuglie. Both wines, based on negroamaro, combine crisp cherry-fruit flavors with a dash of cinnamon and orange peel spice, striking a balance between refreshment and depth of flavor. These and a number of other worthy rosés are the unsung wines of the Italian south, obscured by their bigger red brethren and often passed over by American importers, who think the U.S. market is still hung over from white zinfandel. Too bad.

VINI ROSSI
Red Wines

The red-wine scene in Puglia is less complicated than it may look from the number of DOC zones strewn across the region. For all of the seeming diversity of Puglian wine, there are three main red grapes to remember: uva di troia, an unusually aromatic and deeply colorful red from the northern reaches; negroamaro, the most widely planted red in the region and the king of the Salento peninsula; and primitivo, which, after researchers at the University of California, Davis confirmed its genetic link to American red zinfandel, is one of the new Italian stars in American restaurants.

Uva di troia, so named for a small town west of Foggia where it is thought to have originated, is the least known of the trio. It factors into a handful of DOC reds, the best known of which are the Castel del Monte wines of Rivera in Andria. Rivera is one of the more historic properties in Puglia, and it was one of the first of the region's wineries to have a significant presence in the United States, especially with its "Il Falcone" Castel del Monte Riserva. Along with the nearby Torrevento and Santa Lucia estates, and now the new Antinori property, Rivera is the anchor of Castel del Monte, whose best wines hint at something more than sappy southern red. There are some who believe uva di troia is the most interesting red grape in Puglia, but even the Castel del Monte DOC doesn't always showcase it on its own: The wines can contain aglianico and montepulciano as well.

More firmly entrenched in Puglia is negroamaro, whose name means "black and bitter" and whose wines often follow suit—but in a good, licorice-like way. Probably the best-known negroamaro-based wines are the reds of the late Cosimo Taurino, whose 300-acre estate in Guagnano was for decades the only Puglian winery most Americans had ever heard of. Founded in 1972 and now run by Taurino's survivors—wife Rita, son Francesco, and daughter Rosanna—the winery is still the benchmark in Pugliese wine. Taurino garners wide praise not only for its earthy, perfumed Salice Salentinos but also for the negroamaro-based "Notarpanaro" blend, and "Patriglione," a red that incorporates some late-harvested negroamaro to give it a glycerine richness à la Amarone.

Negroamaro, as its name implies, is thick-skinned and deeply colored, giving it a somewhat tough, tannic personality that is softened and brightened by the addition of the more aromatic malvasia nera, the common partner to negroamaro in the DOC blends of the Salentine peninsula. In fact, as further evidence of Puglia's willy-nilly DOC structure, there are a whopping eleven classified reds that incorporate the negroamaro-malvasia nera combination: Alezio, Brindisi, Copertino, Galatina, Leverano, Lizzano, Matina, Nardò, Salice Salentino, and Squinzano. The majority of these zones are clustered next to one another near Lecce, and for the most part their wines—in those cases where commercial production actually exists—are difficult to tell apart. At a minimum, this overlap makes it easier for you as a consumer to know what you're getting: If you pick up a red wine from any of the above-named DOCs, you can be reasonably assured that it contains at least 50 percent negroamaro, along with a splash of malvasia nera.

A number of other well-known producers work along the same lines as Taurino, producing basic DOC wines such as Salice Salentino and augmenting those with VdT or IGT wines with *nomi di fantasia* (fantasy names). Francesco Candido's "Cappello di Prete" (negroamaro-malvasia nera) and "Duca d'Aragona" (negroamaro-montepulciano) bottlings complement his solid Salices, while Agricole Vallone, which makes both Salice Salentino and Brindisi Rosso reds, has attracted a lot of attention with its "Graticciaia," a deep red made from partially dried grapes. Michele Calò of the Alezio DOC complements his range with a single-vineyard, negroamaro-based blend called "Vigna Spano," another plump, savory Puglian red.

While negroamaro is considered the most structured, ageworthy red in Puglia, primitivo has emerged as the most consumer-friendly. Rich, soft, oak-aged primitivos have found an enthusiastic audience in the United States, at least in part because of their competitive prices. Aside from the intrigue of its relation to American zinfandel, primitivo has many of the characteristics American wine drinkers crave: sweet, soft tannins; plush, even syrupy fruit; and high alcohol. As expressed in DOCs such as Primitivo di Manduria (as well as in non-DOC bottlings), primitivo can be more than just a simple quaffing red, although for now that is its primary role.

The most significant primitivo producer of the moment is a company called Accademia dei Racemi, a consortium of five farm estates and two wineries in and around Manduria. Run by the brothers Gregorio and Fabrizio Perrucci, the company is centered around a large cooperative winery in Manduria called Pervini, owned by their father, and a winery the brothers built right next to Pervini, in which they vinify wines from their member estates. Under the Accademia dei Racemi umbrella are the wines of Felline, the Perruccis' vineyard in Manduria; Masseria Pepe, a small farm in Maruggio; Castel di Salve, a British-owned estate in Tricase, south of Lecce; and Sinfarossa, another small estate near Taranto. The Perrucci brothers oversee production at all four Accademia wineries and help market the Pervini wines, making them the big name in Pugliese primitivo.

"Thirty years ago, everyone in this region made their own wine," says Gregorio Perrucci. "My father started out as a broker for small family wineries, but once the co-ops got going in the sixties and seventies, that culture disappeared. What we're trying to do with Accademia is rediscover the individuality of Pugliese farms, but in a more financially viable context."

Primitivo, Perrucci notes, is an early-maturing variety, and has thinner skins and sweeter tannins than its counterpart in the Salentino, negroamaro. But it is richer in natural sugars and flavor compounds. "This is a grape that makes powerful wines," Perrucci says, "but they are very accessible when they are young."

The knock on primitivo is that it can be low in acid and excessively alcoholic, without the firm structure and dense concentration that characterizes the best negroamaro (and uva di troia, for that matter). Perrucci says that aging in small oak barrels definitely helps to rectify that, as does greater care in the vineyard. "We have this incredible resource here that very few regions have," he says, referring to the miles upon miles of old *alberelli* vines of primitivo throughout the Salentino, which recall the days of the ancient Greeks. Although the crosswinds of the Adriatic and Ionian seas help cool the vineyards of the Salento at night, it is still a scorchingly hot region; the tight, dense canopies of foliage offered by *alberelli*-trained vines help protect the grapes from overripening, so that they maintain a better balance of acidity and sugar.

As Perrucci explains, "With these old vines we can produce concentrated fruit, with good structure, but we have to guard against it becoming overripe. That's the biggest problem with Puglian reds: Most are cooked."

In the primitivos of Felline, A-Mano, and Sinfarossa, among others, the juicy core of black, spicy fruit is held in place by a frame of new oak. The modern sheen of these wines has given the region a much-needed face-lift. And they are the perfect reds to drink with rustic Puglian dishes such as *orecchiette* (ear-shaped pasta) with crumbled sausage and broccoli rabe, or the *pizza rustica* found in nearby Abruzzo that incorporates onions, capers, tomatoes, and anchovies. With the success these wines have had on the international market, it's likely that there will be more prospectors poking around in Puglia in the years to come.

VINI SPUMANTI E DOLCI
Sparkling and Sweet Wines

Unlike Sicily, to which it is so often compared, Puglia has no mass of sweet wines from which to choose. But there are a few notables. Thanks to continued dry weather through the fall and the aforementioned crosscurrents of the Adriatic and Ionian seas, the Salentine peninsula in particular is well suited to the *appassimento* (drying) of both red and white grapes. So along with some of the Amarone-style dry wines being marketed by Vallone and Pervini (Pervini's is named "Primo Amore"), there are provisions in the Primitivo di Manduria DOC for sweet and fortified versions of the wine. Some of these are made using the *appassimento* process, others by simply leaving grapes to hang and shrivel on the vines. Salice Salentino, too, can be made in sweet versions, and it's not a bad choice to pair with dry cheese such as aged *ricotta*, which is popular in Puglia.

Other sweet wines of Puglia include the rare Moscato di Trani DOC, made from moscato bianco, and the rarer red Aleatico di Puglia, a wine whose DOC covers the entire region but is all but lost to the world. Only about a dozen acres of vineyards are still registered under the DOC, and no wine was made in 1997. Think of it as one less thing to remember.

FAST FACTS: *P*UGLIA

PROVINCES	Bari (BA), Brindisi (BR), Foggia (FG), Lecce (LE), Taranto (TA)
CAPITAL	Bari
KEY WINE TOWNS	Lecce, Locorotondo, Manduria, Martina Franca, Salice Salentino
TOTAL VINEYARD AREA*	106,715 hectares, or 263,693 acres. Rank: 2nd
TOTAL WINE PRODUCTION*	7,236,000 hectoliters, or 191,175,693 gallons (2nd); 30% white;, 70% red
DOC WINE PRODUCED*	3.8% (17th)
SPECIALTY FOODS	*orecchiette* pasta; breads, often flavored; fennel; aged ricotta cheese; broccoli; cauliflower; eggplant; chickory; *cime di rapa* (broccoli rabe).
	*1997 figures. Rankings out of twenty regions total (Trentino–Alto Adige counted as one). Source: Istituto Statistica Mercati Agro-Alimentari (ISMEA), Rome.

KEY GRAPE VARIETIES

WHITES

BOMBINO BIANCO	Soft, light grape found in some measure in eight Puglian DOC wines, most notably Castel del Monte Bianco and Gravina.
VERDECA	Tart, vegetal, high-acid white, thought to be native to region. Widely planted in Puglia and used as a base in bulk wines and in the hyperproductive Martina Franca and Locorotondo DOCs.
CHARDONNAY	Widely planted international variety found in four Puglian DOCs, including the *bianco* of Salice Salentino.

OTHERS	TREBBIANO TOSCANO, used in a variety of blends, MALVASIA BIANCA (used in several blends).

REDS

NEGROAMARO	The most-planted red in Puglia, and the sixth-most planted red in Italy. Dark, thick-skinned, tannic, it is the base for eleven DOC reds, most in the southerly Salentine peninsula.
PRIMITIVO	Genetically linked to American zinfandel, an early-ripening, softly structured red used in varietal wines and blends.
MALVASIA NERA	Dark version of malvasia bianco. Combined with negroamaro in Salento DOC red blends such as Salice Salentino and Brindisi Rosso. There are two distinct clones, one from Brindisi and one from Lecce.
UVA DI TROIA	Native grape of northern Puglia, near Foggia. Thought to have been brought by the ancient Greeks from Troy (Troia). Aromatic and interesting, but on the wane. Used most notably in Castel del Monte reds.
OTHERS	MONTEPULCIANO, used in numerous DOC blends; SANGIOVESE, also used in numerous DOC blends; ALEATICO, rare red for sweet wines.

TOP VINTAGES IN PUGLIA, 1980—2000

Given its history as a producer of bulk wines, Puglia has not traditionally been a place in which vintages have been tracked very carefully. Besides, Puglia is blessed with one of the more consistent climates in Italy, lending it a California-like resistance to the whims of vintage. Yes, hail can be a threat in the Salento, but generally speaking, Puglia can rely, year in and year out, on hot, dry weather. And in general, Puglia does not produce any mass of wines that are capable of (or will benefit from) long aging. Puglian reds can be consumed young. Stick with recent vintages and don't worry too much about variance.

LA STRADA DEL VINO
WINE TOURING IN PUGLIA

Most people know Puglia as a jumping-off point for Greece from the Adriatic port of Brindisi, but little more. Generally speaking, Puglia is not as well equipped for tourism as, say, Tuscany, and there are very few wineries with facilities to receive visitors. Yet the towns of Martina Franca and especially Lecce, both on the Salentine peninsula, are true gems for anyone who enjoys architecture—the city is full of beautifully preserved baroque buildings—and good food and wine. Lecce is probably the most strategically oriented town in terms of seeing vineyards. Another town well worth a visit is the village of Gallipoli, on the Ionian coast.

DEGUSTAZIONI
TASTINGS

PRIMITIVO

A-Mano Primitivo, $

Sinfarossa Primitivo di Manduria "Zinfandel," $

Felline Primitivo di Manduria, $

Here are three expressions of primitivo, each a little deeper and richer than the last, all very juicy and accessible as young wines. Scents of licorice, black and red raspberries, and black pepper are on display in these wines, a push-pull of savory and sweet. On balance, they are easy-drinking wines with medium acidity and soft tannins, great for spicy pasta dishes that incorporate sausage or *peperoncini;* tannins and acidity tend to accentuate spice.

NEGROAMARO

Agricole Vallone Brindisi Rosso "Vigna Flaminia," $

Michele Calò Alezio Rosso "Mjère," $

Taurino "Notarpanaro," $

A little darker, a little firmer, a little tarrier, and a little more perfumed than its neighbor primitivo, negroamaro is also a little more crisply acidic and earthy. More of a rustic red than the slick primitivo, negroamaro is a wine that can stand up to a few years' aging. You'll note more dark tones of coffee and tobacco in these wines, particularly the Notarpanaro, a classic Puglian red and one of the best-known southern-Italian reds in the market.

La Cucina

FOOD FOR THE WINE

RECIPE BY MARIO BATALI

Only the Po valley can rival the long, flat, sun-baked plain of Puglia in agricultural output. Puglia's mineral-rich soil—a mixture of ferrous clay and sand over limestone—is ideal for big, flavorful vegetables, which the region has in abundance: broccoli rabe, cauliflower, all sorts of bitter greens, fennel, onions, and more. Puglia is Italy's largest producer of olive oil and a major bread baker as well, drawing on one of the country's biggest stands of wheat. You could plant a styrofoam packing peanut in the ground here and something might grow.

Given its long stretches of Adriatic and Ionian coastline, Puglia is also rich in seafood. But the pasta preparation below is more of the earth. The lasting impression of a drive through Puglia, especially in the south, is how the rust-colored soils reflect the waning afternoon light, creating the impression of a landscape on fire. The dish below draws on a staple local vegetable and points it up with some characteristic southern-Italian heat.

Orecchiette con Cavolfiore

ORECCHIETTE WITH CAULIFLOWER

2 tablespoons SALT
½ pound PANCETTA, cut into medium-to-large chunks (about 1 cup)
3 medium cloves GARLIC, crushed with the side of a knife
¼ cup extra-virgin OLIVE OIL
1 medium head CAULIFLOWER, cut into 1-inch florets, leaves and core included
1 teaspoon RED CHILI FLAKES
Freshly ground BLACK PEPPER to taste
1 pound ORECCHIETTE PASTA
½ pound RICOTTA SALATA, or other soft sheep's milk cheese, grated to yield 1 cup

SERVES 4

Place 6 quarts of water in a spaghetti pot, add 2 tablespoons of salt, and bring to a boil over high heat.

Meanwhile, place the pancetta, olive oil, garlic, and cauliflower pieces into a cold 12- to 14-inch sauté pan and set over medium heat. Cook the mixture, stirring regularly, until the cauliflower is soft, but not mushy, about 12 to 14 minutes. Remove from the heat and sprinkle with the chili flakes.

Cook the pasta according to package instructions and set aside ¼ cup of the cooking water. Drain the pasta and toss it into the pan with the cauliflower mixture. Add the reserved pasta water, place the pan back over high heat and cook until most of the liquid has evaporated, about 1 minute.

Remove the pan from the heat, add half of the grated cheese and toss to mix well. Divide among 4 plates and serve immediately with the remaining cheese on the side.

WINE RECOMMENDATION: A good primitivo would be a fine wine choice here, as would one of Puglia's excellent *rosati,* but the latter will be harder to find.

Basilicata

POWERHOUSE REDS FROM THE MIDDLE OF NOWHERE

— ❧ —

THE CAVE DWELLERS OF BARILE

It's Sunday morning in Barile, a light rain is falling, and as is usually the case on a Sunday in Italy, the streets are deserted. Barile is a melancholy sort of place to begin with, a lonely outcropping on Monte Vulture in northern Basilicata, and the weather isn't helping: From a distance the buildings seem to huddle together against the elements, mud creeping up their whitewashed flanks like tooth decay.

The only action at this hour is on the edge of town—literally an edge, as Barile is perched over a deep gorge—amid a network of caves (*gròtte*) dug into the volcanic hillside. Fronted with stonework and outfitted with metal doors, the caves are connected by access roads that zig-zag up the slope. Men on tractors haul cartloads of grapes along the muddy paths, while others buzz around their *gròtte*, dragging hoses, washing buckets, smoking cigarettes. The sweet-and-sour smell of fermenting wine hangs thick in the air.

Most of these people are small farmers who sell grapes to commercial wineries but keep a portion of their production for themselves,

using the *gròtte* as mini-wineries. Barile is the heart of the Aglianico del Vulture DOC zone, so there's plenty of homemade aglianico around. But there's also a big call for off-dry moscato *frizzante*, a classic farmer's wine from one of the most widely planted grapes in Italy.

It's early September, too early to harvest reds, so the focus is on moscato. In the darkness of their little caves, men and women shovel the big-berried grapes into rickety presses, shooing away bees and glancing warily at passersby. None of them has much to say until a gregarious, red-faced old-timer named Franco, whose wool cap has a hole so big it's more like a headband, invites us inside.

After a morning of not only making wine but sampling the already-made stuff, Franco and his friend, Vittorio, are a little worse for the wear. The arrival of guests gives them both a giddy burst of energy. Vittorio fetches a green bottle from the shadows, while Franco ceremoniously returns to his old basket press, his fingers as fat and pink as sausages while he pumps the handle. The crushed grapes ooze through the wooden slats, and a torrent of juice shoots out the bottom and collects in a big plastic tub. As rudimentary as the whole operation looks, however, Franco is no amateur: After a few pulls on the press, he dips a hydrometer (a device that measures sugar content) into the

THE DOC ZONES OF BASILICATA

1 Aglianico del Vulture

must, announcing with the confidence of a lab technician that the wine will be about 12 percent alcohol.

With a loud pop, Vittorio shoots a cork across the cave, washes out some crusty-looking glasses with a hose, and fills them to the brim. The wine has some brownish debris floating in it, but otherwise it's pretty good: lightly fizzy, appley, not too sweet. "You won't find this in any store," says Franco, clearly relishing his role as master of ceremonies. He invites a few more people into the *gròtta*, and soon there's a full-fledged wine tasting going on, everyone stamping their feet in the raw chill, downing glasses of moscato like water. It's ten in the morning.

Of course, home winemaking is hardly unusual in Italy, but nowhere is there a local culture quite like this. The *gròtte* of Barile were originally homes, excavated by Albanian refugees in the fifteenth century; in time they evolved into wine cellars (or, occasionally, garages), each of which is treated like a family heirloom. There are more than two hundred *gròtte* in Barile alone, and many others pockmarking the hillsides in neighboring villages, most of them home to some form of family wine production. In fact, Barile hosts a harvest festival every October, at which Franco and his neighbors sample one another's creations.

In some respects, these images are a dime a dozen—gnarled old farmhands, quaint hill towns, harvest festivals—but there's something extra-authentic about Barile. Whether because of the isolation of the area or its enduring poverty, Barile feels like a rural village from another time. Throughout nearly all of Italy it seems as though tourists have discovered everything, but the towns around Monte Vulture remain untrampled. Although there are some noteworthy archeological sites in the area, there aren't many touristy reasons to come to Basilicata. But then, that may be the best reason of all.

I VINI
The Wines

There is at least one good reason to come to Basilicata: Aglianico del Vulture. It's one of the great red wines of southern Italy, less famous than the aglianico-based Taurasi of neighboring Campania, but considered by many to be better.

Unfortunately, the small size of Basilicata and its wine industry has relegated Aglianico del Vulture to cult wine status—not cult wine in the sense of a boutique bottling of cabernet whose first vintage was three years ago, but cult wine in the sense of a historic local gem hunted down by real devotees.

Basilicata and aglianico have become synonymous, thanks not only to the quality of Aglianico del Vulture but to the lack of other wines to talk about; Aglianico del Vulture is the only DOC zone in the region. While moscato and malvasia are widely grown in Basilicata, the sparkling and sweet wines made from them are either *vini da contadini* (farmers' wines) or products for the local market. Paternoster, one of the two top commercial producers in Basilicata, bottles several white wines, but none are exported to the United States; D'Angelo, the other big name in the area, exports a white wine based on chardonnay and pinot bianco, but only in small quantities. On the whole, you're not likely to find much if any white wine from Basilicata in an American shop, and this is probably for the better.

Aglianico, however, is another story. The most significant concentration of vineyards is on the eastern face of Monte Vulture, a forty-three-hundred-foot spent volcano that looms over towns including Rionero, Barile, and Melfi. Covered in vines and chestnut groves at its midrange elevations, Monte Vulture seems to inject a brooding power into the grapes grown on it. A glass of young aglianico is dark and feral, like the wolves that still roam the hills in these parts, greeting you with a low, tannic growl.

"These are not wines to drink young," says Vito Paternoster, who runs the Paternoster family winery in Barile. The deeply colored aglianico grape is a tannic variety, thanks to its small berries and thick skin. But, as Paternoster explains, aglianico becomes supercharged in Monte Vulture's soil and climate. "We have a very unique combination here: On one hand, our vineyards are at relatively high altitudes"— eighteen hundred feet and up in Barile—"with steep grades, so we get good day-to-night temperature variations and good drainage. This helps preserve acidity. On the other hand, we have the intense sunlight of the south. This gives the power."

Donato D'Angelo, whose muscular, barrique-aged "Canneto" aglianico is probably the best-known wine from Basilicata, adds that while volcanic soils are rich in potassium (a critical vine nutrient), the key factor influencing wine in the Vulture is altitude. "Despite the fact that we're in the deep south, this is a cool climate," he says. "In fact, we probably have one of the latest harvests in Italy. We don't usually start with aglianico before October 20, and it's often much later." The longer growing season allows for more concentration and complexity of flavor to develop in the grapes, and

it shows in the wines. At its best, an Aglianico del Vulture is not only dense and powerful but exotically aromatic, much in the same way that Piedmont's Barolo melds power with perfume.

As with the nebbiolo of Barolo, questions remain as to where aglianico came from. The neighboring Campanians have effectively claimed it as their own—thanks to Naples, they've always been the center of power in the south. But there is strong evidence that humble old Basilicata was aglianico's original breeding ground. As with so much Italian viticultural history, the story is entertainingly imprecise.

There are now three theories of the origins of aglianico (see also the chapter on Campania). Two of the three hypotheses presume that the grape was brought by the Greeks in the form of seed, and that *aglianico* is a mutation of the word *hellenic*, or *ellenico* in Italian. The two Greek hypotheses diverge when it comes to aglianico's point of entry. One theory is that it came in through Metaponto (Metapontion), the one major Greek colony on Basilicata's tiny slice of Ionian coast, then migrated north through the Vulture, on to nearby Irpinia (the hills of Avellino, home of Taurasi), then farther north and east in Campania. The other suggests that the grape was brought first to Campania, possibly the Monte Massico area north of Naples, where it became the red *Falernum* (the modern-day Falerno del Massico), a wine highly prized by the Romans.

More recently, the conventional wisdom on aglianico has been challenged. Enology professor Attilio Scienza of the University of Milan is among those who believe that aglianico was a wild vine indigenous to the Italian peninsula, domesticated by native tribes as early as the Bronze Age and only later discovered and named by the Greeks. He says the name is derived not from *ellenico* but from the Greek word *eilanikos,* which translates roughly as a "vine that grows up trees." Regardless of which theory you believe, one thing about aglianico is certain: Aside from nebbiolo and sangiovese, there's no native Italian grape more capable of making powerful, interesting red wines.

Whereas the various Campanian aglianico DOCs (including Taurasi) allow for some blending of other grape varieties, Aglianico del Vulture is the grape on its own, with nothing to soften its tannic blow (or so the DOC and its producers say). The only problem is that there's not that much of it. Basilicata is one of Italy's smallest, least populous regions, and its reputation as a poor and inhospitable place still looms: It is essentially a clump of Apennines, and only 8 percent of the region's land is classified as plains. And while there have been economic improvements in recent years—a large Fiat factory in Lavello, near the Puglian border, is a recent industrial triumph—the wine industry has remained largely unchanged since the 1920s, when Paternoster and D'Angelo opened for business.

But there have been signs of new life. Winemaker and economics professor Francesco Sasso, who for years ran his family's large *cantina* in Rionero, sold out several years ago to a group of partners and focused his attentions on a smaller estate, Eubea, which produces some excellent aglianico under the Eubea–Covo dei Briganti label. Gerardo Giuratrabocchetti, a sheep and wheat farmer from Maschito, debuted his Cantine del Notaio brand in 1998 and quickly found a market for his limited-production, barrique-aged aglianico wines in the United States. Ditto for Michele Cutolo, a local doctor who makes his small-production Basilisco wines from family plots

near Rionero. The D'Angelo family has also branched out, marketing a value-priced line of aglianico-based wines from its Tenuta del Portale in Vulcano.

On a larger scale, a construction firm called Gruppo Pietrafessa has become a significant player in Vulture with its Tenuta della Quercia estate in Barile. And on the high plains of Venosa, near the Puglian border, perhaps the most significant new investment in Basilicata is taking shape. In October 2000, the massive Gruppo Italiano Vini (GIV), Italy's largest wine company, took control of a large vineyard property once owned by the Swiss conglomerate Winefood. At this writing, no new wines had yet been made at the estate, called Terra degli Svevi, but the arrival of a big name like GIV is important news for a backwater like Basilicata.

"In the past, most of the producers in Basilicata just sent wine anonymously to the north," says Vito Paternoster. "Now we've got a real reputation for aglianico, and maybe more people will be encouraged to do something on their own."

Looking at the current scene, it almost goes without saying that Aglianico del Vulture is one of the new generation of collectible wines from Italy. While your friends are battling it out for rare (and often incredibly expensive) Barolo and Brunello, you might consider checking out Paternoster's rare but relatively *inexpensive* "Rotondo" aglianico, D'Angelo's "Canneto" and "Vigna Caselle," or Notaio's "La Firma" Aglianico del Vulture. All of them are assertively aromatic, packed with black-berry fruit and wrapped in wooly blankets of tannin that will preserve them for years. If you care about the wine, not the show, Basilicata is a place to consider. Get there before everyone else.

FAST FACTS: *Basilicata*

PROVINCES	Matera (MT), Potenza (PZ)
CAPITAL	Potenza
KEY WINE TOWNS	Barile, Rionero in Vulture
TOTAL VINEYARD AREA*	10,848 hectares, or 26,805 acres. Rank: 17th
TOTAL WINE PRODUCTION*	481,000 hectoliters, or 12,708,058 gallons (17th); 27% white, 73% red
DOC WINE PRODUCED*	2.4% (19th)
SPECIALTY FOODS	*Luganica* sausage; *peperoncini* (both dried and vinegar-cured); Amaro Lucano (a bitter aperitif produced in Metaponto).

*1997 figures. Rankings out of twenty regions total (Trentino–Alto Adige counted as one). Source: Istituto Statistica Mercati Agro-Alimentari (ISMEA), Rome.

KEY GRAPE VARIETIES

WHITES

MALVASIA

Malvasia and Moscato are widely planted in Basilicata, but there is no DOC for them. Generally, wines made from these grapes are simple *vini da tavola* sold locally.

REDS

AGLIANICO

this dark, thick-skinned variety was thought to have been brought to Italy by the Greeks, its name derived from the term *hellenico* or *ellenico* ("Greek"). Others believe it was a native wild vine.

TOP VINTAGES IN BASILICATA, 1980–2000

As a general rule, Aglianico del Vulture producers age their wines much longer than the minimum one year required by DOC regulations, but even wines with three or four years on them are still likely to have a strong tannic bite. Top years: '82, '85, '88, '90, '92, '93, '95, '97, '98, '99.

LA STRADA DEL VINO
WINE TOURING IN BASILICATA

Like its neighbors Puglia and Calabria, Basilicata is somewhat off the beaten track for tourists. But as with any region of Italy, there are little country restaurants that amaze you with the freshness of their ingredients and the abundance of their menus. Within Basilicata's wine country, the one town of some touristic interest is Melfi, which was the first capital of the Normans when they ruled the Italian south. On the edge of town is one of the best restaurants you'll ever eat in: Novecento (0972-23-74-70), where you can load up on *lucanica* sausage and *burrata* (a mozzarella filled with raw curd that spills out like an egg yolk when you cut it open).

DEGUSTAZIONI
TASTINGS

AGLIANICO DEL VULTURE

Should you be tasting recent vintages of these wines, as you probably will, be ready for some ferrous, almost mouth-drying tannins. They're black and they bite, but they offer great aromatic complexity: lighter, higher-toned scents of violets and cherries mingle with telltale Aglianico notes of road tar, tobacco leaves, and coffee. These wines combine sweet and savory flavors much as nebbiolo does in Barolo and Barbaresco. When they're young, tame them with a hunk of sausage, a steak, or some pecorino cheese.

Paternoster
Aglianico del Vulture, $

D'Angelo
Aglianico del Vulture, $

La Cucina
FOOD FOR THE WINE
RECIPE BY MARIO BATALI

Essentially landlocked, save for small slices of Ionian and Mediterranean coasts, Basilicata has a land-based cuisine —and a poverty-driven one at that. In the rugged hills that consume the majority of the region, people have long eked out an existence on the most rudimentary of staples: dried pasta, cured meats, bread, and cheese.

Basilicata's two main contributions to the Italian table are spicy, dried *luganica* sausages, and dried or vinegar-cured *peperoncini*. Perhaps because they never had much to work with, the *Lucani* (as Basilicatans are called) like their food spicy. Peperoncini find their way into most dishes, including the long-cooked lamb stew called *cutturidde,* traditionally made from old, unsellable sheep, which accounts for the long cooking and strong flavoring.

The recipe below is a new take on a classic poor man's pasta—so *povera,* in fact, that it substitutes bread crumbs for cheese.

Spaghetti alla Luganica

1 pound SPAGHETTI

2 tablespoons SALT

1 pound SWEET LUGANICA SAUSAGE, removed from casings (Try to find luganica, because its rich flavor is hard to duplicate; if you can't find luganica, ask your butcher for another strongly flavored sweet sausage, preferably without fennel seeds.)

½ cup extra-virgin OLIVE OIL

4 GARLIC CLOVES, halved

4 DRIED CHILIES, whole, such as corno di bue

1 bunch ITALIAN PARSLEY, roughly chopped to yield ¼ cup loosely packed

½ cup toasted BREAD CRUMBS

SERVES 4

Place 6 quarts of water in a spaghetti pot, add 2 tablespoons salt, and bring to a boil over high heat.

Crumble the sausage roughly and place it in a 12- to 14-inch sauté pan with the olive oil, garlic, and chilis over medium heat. Cook until the sausage is fully cooked and has exuded most of the fat, about 8 to 10 minutes. Drain all but 4 tablespoons of the fat and set aside.

Cook the spaghetti according to package instructions and set aside ½ cup of the cooking water. Drain the pasta and toss into the pan with the sausage mixture and reserved cooking water. Place pan over high heat, add the parsley and cook, stirring, until most of the liquid has evaporated, about 1 minute. Season with salt and pepper to taste. Divide among 4 plates, each with its own chili pepper, sprinkle with toasted bread crumbs, and serve immediately.

WINE RECOMMENDATION: Aglianico del Vulture.

Calabria
The Great Unknown

———

Tying One On

Only when you see the process of making wine can you fully appreciate why it sometimes costs a lot of money. In fact, you have to wonder how wine can ever be cheap. Planting and maintaining a vineyard is a grueling, labor-intensive process of clearing boulders, driving stakes, grafting and training vines, and then, after the plants begin to flourish in soils too poor to support most other crops, trimming them obsessively so they don't produce too much. Never mind the costs of stainless steel fermenters and oak barrels: The vineyard alone is enough to break your back, physically and financially.

This thought comes to mind as Nicodemo Librandi starts the slow climb to a new vineyard site in the village of Rocca di Neto, shifting his dust-covered Rover into low gear as we bounce over clumps of freshly turned earth. Librandi's winery in Cirò Marina, just a few miles north of Rocca di Neto on Calabria's central Ionian coast, is the best-known property in the region; the family's vineyard holdings total more than five hundred acres, including this new piece in Rocca di Neto, a steep, winding ridge dotted with thousands of new rootstocks. Off in the distance a group of workers are hunched over the nascent stalks, sliding on their rumps from plant to plant. As we get closer we can see that they're in the process of grafting the one-year-old rootstocks.

Grafting is a process so tedious it's hard to imagine the workers ever finishing. Each has a bundle of straw tucked into his belt, and carries with him a large tin of foot-long twigs. These are vine "scions," or "fruiting canes," of gaglioppo, the chosen grape variety for the vineyard. Using small, razor-sharp paring knives, the workers carve notches out of the rootstocks, then slice buds off the scion canes and wedge the buds into the notches, fixing them in place with pieces of straw. Eventually, Librandi explains, the little piece of bud fuses with the rootstock and creates a new fruiting cane, from which the bunches of grapes are produced. This process, called chip budding, is obviously laborious and reputedly erratic (some grafts don't take). But, as with so much of viticulture, there's no better way to do it than by hand.

From the looks of things, these guys still have a long way to go: The vineyard spans more than ten hectares in total (about twenty-five acres), and is planted at a density of four thousand vines per hectare. Couple this with the blazing southern-Italian sun, which has bleached and cracked the soil and turned the

THE DOC ZONES OF CALABRIA

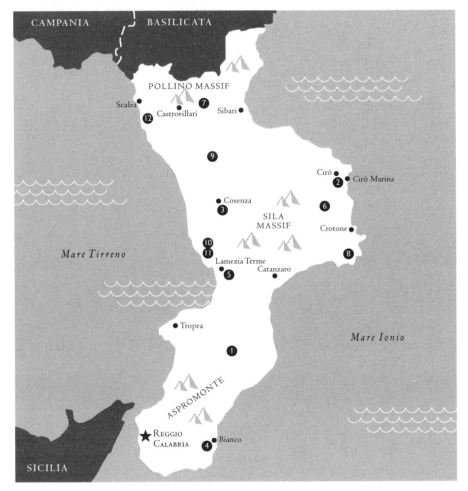

CAMPANIA   BASILICATA

POLLINO MASSIF

Scalea
⑦
⑫ Castrovillari   Sibari

⑨

Cirò
② Cirò Marina
⑥
Cosenza
③   SILA MASSIF
Crotone
⑩
⑪   ⑧
Lamezia Terme
⑤   Catanzaro

Mare Tirreno

Tropea

①

Mare Ionio

ASPROMONTE

★ REGGIO CALABRIA
④ Bianco

SICILIA

1	Bivongi	7	Pollino
2	Cirò	8	S. Anna di Isola Capo Rizzuto
3	Donnici	9	San Vito di Luzzi
4	Greco di Bianco	10	Savuto
5	Lamezia	11	Scavigna
6	Melissa	12	Verbicaro

nearby Neto River into a bed of stones, and suddenly wine doesn't seem so romantic. The workers, shaded only by their wide-brimmed straw hats, move swiftly from vine to vine, tying each one off with a neat, almost decorative bow. To the south the Ionian Sea is begging to be swum in, and these poor guys are sitting here in jeans and long-sleeved shirts, floating on a wave of parched earth. It'll be a good while before all of the new vines are grafted, and two years before they start producing wine-worthy grapes.

"You don't get immediate returns with wine," says Librandi, smiling ruefully as the grafters edge their way up the slope. "Everything you do is for four, five, ten years later. We can't change as fast as the market changes; we can only predict what might happen and then hope that it does."

And if it doesn't? "I don't know," he says with a chuckle. "Maybe we'll plant some wheat instead. But then there wouldn't be too much for these guys to do."

All of the inherent challenges of winemaking are amplified in Calabria, which is not only physically demanding but remains one of the more economically depressed parts of Italy. During the late forties, the region was the scene of some of the bloodiest peasant revolts against large feudal landowners, and was the first region in which an agrarian reform law was passed, in May 1950. But in many ways Calabria hasn't progressed much since then. Other than a trickle of tourist income in coastal towns such as Tropea and in ski resorts in the vast Sila mountain range, Calabria is still a predominantly agricultural economy. Whether it's grapes, figs, citrus fruits (including exotic stuff like citron and bergamot), or

olives, farmers in Calabria eke out a living in the rare pockets of flat (or semi-flat) land along the Ionian and Mediterranean coasts. Less than 10 percent of the region's surface area qualifies as plains, but somehow vegetables are a staple of the Calabrian table: peppers, eggplants, artichokes, and onions are all big crops, particularly toward the southern end of the region, which shares many physical and culinary similarities with Sicily.

When people talk about Calabrian wine, the discussion centers on its potential, not its actual output. Although it is far from the smallest wine-producing region in Italy, it may well be the most insignificant commercially speaking: There are twelve DOC zones here, but the majority produce only token amounts of wine. The only legitimate production center is Cirò, with around a dozen bottlers and about thirty thousand hectoliters a year in production. To the south of Cirò, the once-noteworthy DOC of Melissa has all but dried up, as have the zones of Donnici (south of Cosenza), Bivongi (in the toe of the boot, south of Catanzaro), and Pollino (a DOC in the Pollino mountains, historically known for light, tart reds, now barely known at all).

Calabria is one of the most rugged regions in Italy, and is rivaled only by Sardinia for long, lonely stretches of asphalt. Geographically, it is strikingly diverse: In the course of about forty-five minutes you can go from Cirò Marina, a dusty little beachside town on the Ionian, to San Giovanni in Fiore, which sits at three thousand feet in the thickly forested Sila range. One summer morning, on leaving the coastal town of Crotone, we saw a shirtless, sunburned old man picking *fichi d'india* (prickly pears) along the side of the road, using a tin can attached to the end of a broom handle; a half-hour later, we were dressed in sweaters and eating fresh porcini mushrooms and mountain cheeses in a café in the Sila, dwarfed by ancient firs and pines.

For all of their beauty, the Apennines divide and isolate Calabria in a more profound way than anywhere else on the peninsula: The Pollino Massif walls the region off from Basilicata to the north, while the Sila and Aspromonte ranges carve it in half. So many people have left Calabria over the years—including the ancestors of countless Italian-Americans—that it often feels abandoned. To someone passing through as a tourist, the region's jagged edges and precipitous drops are marvelous; to someone trying to make a living there, it's another story.

And yet Calabria seems as well suited as any region to high-quality wines, especially reds: Along the craggy coasts, the vineyards benefit from high altitudes, steep-sloping grades, temperate maritime climates, and low rainfall during the summer—not to mention mostly poor, well-drained soils. Nevertheless, viticulture has taken a back seat to citrus and olive groves, most likely because of the relative costs involved. So the number of readily available, noteworthy Calabrian wines can be counted on one hand. The viticultural gold rush that has swept through neighboring Puglia and Sicily hasn't yet reached Calabria, but there are some encouraging signs of new life.

Vini Bianchi
White Wines

Like its southern Mediterranean neighbors, Calabria is more naturally suited to red wines than to whites. But unlike its neighbors, Calabria doesn't turn out an ocean of white wine in spite of itself. Only 9 percent of the region's wine output is white, the majority of that based on greco, the ancient Greek vine so prominent throughout the Italian south.

No one has established precisely where greco and its related cultivars (called grechetto in Umbria and Lazio, grecanico in Sicily) first entered Italy, though it's possible that it was Crotone or Sibari in Calabria, two of the oldest Greek cities on the Italian mainland. Calabrians claim a particular strain of greco known as greco bianco (used most convincingly in sweet wines; see page 338), although it would be difficult to distinguish a Calabrian greco from a Campanian Greco di Tufo. It's certainly easier to find the latter, as only a token amount of Calabrian greco ever finds its way out of the region, most notably as the key blending ingredient in Cirò Bianco DOC whites.

Nine of the twelve DOC zones in Calabria include provisions for white wine, and all of these whites include greco in some significant (or dominant) percentage, along with an otherwise random cast of Italian characters, including the ever-present trebbiano toscano and malvasia bianca. Whites from greco vary widely in style, from crisp, piney, and resinous to more juicy, floral, and green appley. Because of a relative lack of winemaking technology in the south, Cirò Bianco and other greco-based wines can be perfectly pleasant summer whites but have a tendency to oxidize quickly, becoming nutty and more resinous. Of the handful of Calabrian whites actually available in noticeable commercial quantities, the *bianchi* of Librandi and Fattoria San Francesco, the Cirò zone's top two producers, are safe bets. To the west, in the Lamezia DOC zone, Cantine Lento and the up-and-coming Statti winery are turning out some good grecos as well. Should you encounter these rarities in a shop, chances are they'll be well priced and worth a shot, provided they are young; stick with the most recent vintage and you may find a new favorite picnic white.

VINI ROSSI
Red Wines

When it comes to Calabrian reds, even a seasoned Italian wine drinker knows the names Librandi and Cirò and little else. And frankly, there's not that much else to know. Calabrian red wine is still defined by Cirò, the quintessential hot weather red, which a lot of modern consumers have abandoned for inkier, sappier wines that coat the tongue like cough syrup. Cirò has its faults, as even its best producers will admit, but its crisp acidity and savory, spicy flavors win it points among those looking for a wine that conveys a sense of place.

That place is not as awe-inspiring as, say, the hills of Alba or the terraces of the Alto Adige. But it does have its own rustic charm. The classic Cirò DOC zone is centered on Cirò Marina, which has the faded, frayed-at-the-edges look of a once-popular resort, and its inland sibling Cirò, one of those classic Italian hill towns that looks from afar like a child's pile of building blocks, precariously perched and about to topple over. In between the two are arid, scrubby foothills dotted sporadically with vineyards, most of them bearing the top local red grape, gaglioppo.

The nearby Ionian helps to moderate the climate in Cirò, but this is without a doubt an unforgivingly hot and dry place during the vine-growing season. The vineyards of Cirò sit at fairly high altitudes—where slightly cooler nighttime temperatures help slow down the ripening process—and the soils are a favorable mix of calcareous clay, sand, and marl. Technically, this is the ideal environment for dense, dark, tongue-staining reds. But Cirò's wines don't fit that description: They tend instead to be lighter in color, often with tinges of orange from oxidation, with a soft, warm, diffuse feel on the palate. Lots of wine geeks use the word *jammy* to describe all manner of red wines, but Cirò is one of the better examples of the type of wine the term is intended to describe: Soft yet sharp, sweet yet sour, Cirò reds are most reminiscent of crushed wild berries, deeply flavorful but also a little mouth-puckering on occasion.

This is the image a lot of wine drinkers have of all southern-Italian reds: wines that have baked in the sun and taste as hot as their surroundings. Not all Cirò is this way, of course—just as not all primitivo from Puglia is cooked and jammy—but this is the image the wine is saddled with. As Cirò producers note, this is the result of a variety of factors: the natural environment, outmoded production techniques, and most notably, the raw ingredients involved.

"The gaglioppo grape has very light-colored pulp, and although its skins are very thick, it is not very high in tannin," says Nicodemo Librandi, whose Cirò wines not only put the DOC on the map in the United States but defy the notion that all Cirò reds are thin and cooked. "It is very hot here, so a lot of producers harvest before the grapes are fully ripe to maintain acidity. But it goes beyond that. With a grape like gaglioppo, which is very low in tannin, it is very difficult to get color and structure. You need a long maceration on the skins at controlled temperatures, and not all producers are willing to do that."

Librandi and others note that Cirò becomes thin and easily oxidized because producers traditionally exercised little control over fermentation temperatures. The higher the temperature, the more rapidly a grape must will oxidize, and the more rapidly the chemical reactions of fermentation will take place. In the absence of temperature regulation, a fermentation can literally bubble out of control, becoming so volatile that flavor and color compounds actually boil off. "If you don't control the temperature, the tannins just fall out," says Librandi. "And we're not working with a lot to begin with."

Among the producers of Cirò still active on the international market, Librandi and the relatively new Fattoria San Francesco (run by Francesco Siciliani, whose family owns the Caparra & Siciliani winery in Cirò Marina) are the benchmarks. They produce Cirò reds that highlight the good side of gaglioppo—its plush, red-berry fruit flavor and its slightly spicy aroma, above all else. Librandi has also resurrected a reputedly ancient grape variety called magliocco, bottling a wine from it called "Magno Megonico" that might best be described as a supercharged Cirò: It still lacks forceful tannin but is more weighty and fruity on the palate. These are not wines for long aging, but they are not wines to be overlooked, either. When treated right, gaglioppo has an almost pinot noir–like character, and can even hold up to a slight chill, which is a great way to drink light reds in the summer.

Outside of Cirò, the red wine options in Calabria are fairly scattered. Librandi has had considerable success beefing up gaglioppo with 40 percent cabernet sauvignon in its "Gravello" bottling. And a number of other producers are either striving to do more with gaglioppo or are planting other varieties to try to capitalize on the southern-Italian wine boom. On the west coast of Calabria, the adjacent DOCs of Lamezia, Scavigna, and Savuto are the other significant areas of red-wine production. Gaglioppo factors into those reds as well, but it isn't as dominant a percentage as in Cirò. The Sicilian nerello family makes an appearance in these reds, as do aglianico and sangiovese and, especially in Scavigna, a wide variety of other authorized grapes.

In Lamezia, producers such as Statti and Cantine Lento have followed Librandi's lead and combined gaglioppo with cabernet sauvignon, using the latter to compensate for what the former lacks—color and tannin. Statti's "Cauro" and Lento's "Federico II" are the kinds of rich, deeply colored reds that will make a mark in the U.S. market, both being immediately enjoyable and relatively affordable.

In Savuto, the best known (and perhaps only) producer is the Odoardi winery, headquartered in the heights of Nocera Terinese on Calabria's Mediterranean coast. There, brothers Giovanni and Gregorio Odoardi help gaglioppo along with doses of nerello cappuccio, greco nero, and sangiovese (along with a year's aging in French oak barriques). They also produce one of Calabria's heftiest reds from the neighboring Scavigna DOC, combining aglianico, cabernet sauvignon, cabernet franc, and merlot in a wine called "Vigna Garrone." (Created in 1994, probably just for the Odoardis, the Scavigna DOC's provisions are fairly loose as to which grapes can be used.) Along with Librandi's Gravello, "Vigna Garrone" is an example of the potential power of Calabrian reds, should more Calabrian winemakers choose to go for more extraction and structure in their wines.

"We've had very good results with some of the international varieties," notes Nicodemo Librandi. "But we're still pretty far behind just about every other region of Italy when it comes to viticulture. Here and there producers are striving for more quality, but it is not a broad movement. It's hard to catch up once you've fallen behind this far."

VINI DOLCI
Sweet Wines

Down in the most southerly reaches of the toe of the boot, in a town called Bianco on the Ionian coast, a rare sweet wine called Greco di Bianco still wins raves from wine critics, but those critics are likely to be Italians, and insiders at that. Honeyed and citrusy on the palate, the *appassimento*-style Greco di Bianco—whose only significant production comes from a winery called Vintripodi, in the village of Archi—is the kind of local oddity to look for on vacation, not in an American wine shop. Only about 300,000 bottles of this sweet nectar are produced per year. But should you find yourself in a restaurant in Reggio Calabria, waiting for the ferry to Messina, see if you can track down a glass. It's one of those rare birds in the world of wine, yet another in a long line of exotic species nearing extinction in the hills of Italy. Closer to home, you'll find token amounts of an *appassimento* wine from Librandi called "Le Passule," a rich, golden-amber dessert white made from a local variety called mantonico.

FAST FACTS: CALABRIA

PROVINCES	Catanzaro (CZ), Cosenza (CS), Crotone (CR), Reggio Calabria (RC), Vibo Valentina (VV)
CAPITAL	Reggio Calabria
KEY WINE TOWNS	Cirò; Lamezia
TOTAL VINEYARD AREA*	24,339 hectares, or 60,142 acres. Rank: 13th
TOTAL WINE PRODUCTION*	753,000 hectoliters, or 19,894,319 gallons (15th); 91% red/rosé, 9% white
DOC WINE PRODUCED*	4.8% (15th)
SPECIALTY FOODS	bergamot; eggplant; figs; lemons and citron; 'ndugghia (spreadable spicy sausage with peperoncini); peperoncini; zibbibo table grapes.

*1997 figures; rankings out of twenty regions total (Trentino–Alto Adige counted as one). Source: ISMEA (CK)

KEY GRAPE VARIETIES

WHITES

GRECO	A highly variable white with delicate aromas and a juicy texture. Calabrians claim a special strain of this Greek native called greco bianco, used in both dry whites (most notable Cirò Bianco) and a rare sweet wine from the extreme south of the region called Greco di Bianco.
MONTONICO	Found on Calabria's Calabrian coast, it's used locally in sweet wines, such as Librandi's "Le Passule."
OTHERS	TREBBIANO TOSCANO; MALVASIA BIANCA; CHARDONNAY.

	REDS
GAGLIOPPO	Soft and berryish, prone to oxidation if not treated with care, this is the principal red grape of Calabria and the base of its best-known DOC wine, Cirò. It is used in some percentage in all eleven of Calabria's red-wine DOCs.
MAGLIOCCO	A reputedly ancient vine, sometimes confused with gaglioppo. Also soft, with plush berry-scented fruit, but a little deeper and darker than gaglioppo. Producers such as Librandi have been experimenting with new wines from the grape.
OTHERS	AGLIANICO; CABERNET SAUVIGNON; MERLOT; NERELLO MASCALESE; NERELLO CAPPUCCIO.

TOP VINTAGES IN CALABRIA, 1980–2000

Calabrian whites, which are very rare in the United States, are best consumed as young as possible. On the red side, a good Cirò Classico Riserva, already aged three years before release, may hold up to a few more years in the bottle, but in general the soft tannins of the gaglioppo grape cause the wine to oxidize relatively quickly. When asked to recall the best years for his excellent Cirò wines, Nicodemo Librandi rated the following vintages as exceptional: 1980, '85, '88, '89, '90, '95, '97, '98, '99.

LA STRADA DEL VINO
WINE TOURING IN CALABRIA

Most of the action in Calabria is found along the region's Mediterranean coast, particularly in the towns of Cosenza, Tropea (probably Calabria's premier tourist town), and Reggio Calabria. But aside from Lamezia, where the Cantine Lento welcomes visitors (Via del Progresso 1; 0968-280-28), there's not a lot of wine-related stuff to do, other than eat *zibbibo* (moscato) grapes, which are sold all over as table grapes and are turned into all manner of homemade wines by the local restaurant owners. The Librandi winery in Cirò is also open to visitors (SS 106; 0962-315-18), though it sits in relative isolation on Calabria's central Ionian coast. Probably the most interesting aspect of Calabria is the Sila Massif, in the center of the region, highlighted by the mountain town of San Giovanni in Fiore. A detour up into the heights of the Sila might be an interesting thing to do before continuing on to Reggio and catching the ferry for Sicily.

DEGUSTAZIONI
TASTINGS

CIRÒ ROSSO

Librandi Cirò Rosso Classico, $

Fattoria San Francesco Cirò Rosso Classico "Ronco dei Quattroventi," $

Warm, soft, and savory are all adjectives to describe Cirò, which is not especially deep in color or structure but, as these wines illustrate, full of red-cherry and raspberry flavor. The principal difference between these wines is that San Francesco's "Ronco" spends a few months aging in French oak barriques, whereas Librandi's bottling is aged in stainless steel. There's a plushness to both wines, though the San Francesco's acidic edges have been rounded that little bit more by wood. In both wines the fruit is jammy and the texture soft, due to the naturally mild tannins of the gaglioppo grape. These are quaffing wines for grilled pizza, eggplant parmigiana, or other simple dishes, although both wines have a touch of earthy spice that seems tailor-made for some of Calabria's fiery preparations incorporating *peperoncini*.

La Cucina
FOOD FOR THE WINE

RECIPE BY MARIO BATALI

"Here in Calabria, everything we cook is *all'arrabbiata,*" says Salvatore Lento, whose winery in Lamezia Terme is one of Calabria's more progressive producers. Like their neighbors in Basilicata, Calabrians relied on heat from *peperoncini* to spice up an otherwise poor cuisine. One of the great local specialties of Calabria is a soft, spreadable sausage called *n'duja,* which is heavily dosed with *peperoncino* flakes.

Vegetables factor heavily into Calabrian cooking, particularly eggplant (this is the home of eggplant parmigiana), onions (especially the more pungent red onions), and tomatoes. Thanks no doubt to its proximity to Sicily, there are also an above-average number of desserts in the region, many of them incorporating almonds and honey, as in Sicily.

Peperoncini alla Calabrese

12 red or green ITALIAN FRYING PEPPERS
  or cubanelles
¼ cup plus 2 tablespoons extra-virgin
  OLIVE OIL
6 cloves GARLIC, sliced paper-thin
2 cups fresh BREAD CRUMBS
¼ cup chopped ITALIAN PARSLEY
SALT and PEPPER to taste
1 teaspoon RED CHILI FLAKES
½ pound young PROVOLONE CHEESE,
  grated

SERVES 4

Preheat the oven to 450°F.

Make an incision in each of the peppers from the stem 2 inches down toward the point. Carefully remove the ribs and seeds as best you can and set aside.

Place the olive oil and the garlic in a cool pan and place over medium heat. Cook until the garlic is light golden brown, about 2 minutes. Add the bread crumbs and the parsley and cook until the bread crumbs are toasted a light golden brown, stirring constantly, about 4 minutes. Place the toasted crumbs in a bowl to cool for 5 minutes.

Add the chili flakes and the grated cheese to the bread-crumb mixture and stir to mix well. Then, with a teaspoon, carefully stuff each of the peppers through the incision with as much of the cheese–bread crumb mixture as possible. Place the stuffed peppers on a cookie sheet and drizzle with the remaining oil. Season with salt and pepper to taste and place in oven to cook for 20 minutes, or until the skins start to blister and turn dark brown or black in spots. Remove and allow to cool 5 minutes before serving. These are excellent at room temperature.

WINE RECOMMENDATION: Calabria's best-known wine, Cirò, is a red that can stand up to a slight chill, and has a savory character that gives it an affinity for dishes with a little bit of heat. Cirò's soft tannins make it an especially good choice for spicy dishes, since tannins in wine tend to amplify hot spices.

Don't be afraid to throw a bottle of Cirò on ice a half-hour or so before serving the dish below: once you try it, the combination may become a regular part of your summer barbecue repertoire.

Sicilia

A New World of Wine

———⚜———

Birth of the Cool

Under a wicked August sun, Ignazio pilots his big BMW through a snarl of cars and motor scooters in downtown Palermo, one hand on the wheel and the other wrapped congenially around the passenger seat. As driving challenges go, Palermo may be second only to Naples in sheer chaos. But to Ignazio the near misses and tight squeezes of the ancient palm-lined streets are mere breaks in the conversation. When you're a Sicilian's guest you don't want for anything, least of all attention. Why would a little thing like life-threatening traffic keep him from looking us in the eyes when he speaks to us?

You sometimes see this kind of automotive artistry in New York cabbies, but they don't have Ignazio's flair: Puffing on a conical-shaped *toscano* cigar, his wild halo of silver curls flapping in the breeze, he has gotten onto the subject of Sicilian ice cream, for which his hands must occasionally abandon the wheel to make his point properly. We are on our way to Mondello, a relatively affluent suburb north of Palermo, to a bar he says has the best gelato in Italy.

"Sicilians are the only Italians with a real dessert culture," he explains, shouting over the nasal whine of the weaving *motorini* (scooters). "The Arabs introduced sherbet here, which they learned from the Chinese, and that gave way to gelato." Ignazio punctuates many of his pronouncements with *"Mi segui?"* (You follow me?) and a gentle jab to the ribs with his elbow. He points out a few buildings done in the Moorish style, their domed roofs giving the steaming streets the look of a North African casbah. "Most of the desserts we have are from the Arab culture, which is a big part of Sicilian culture."

For most Italians, and especially food and wine people, this kind of conversation is fairly standard fare. You hear a lot about how Italians are enraptured by food, in love with food, etc. But in general their approach to food (and wine) is surprisingly light on poetic flourishes. It's more scientific, historical, almost religious in its devotion to the "right" and "wrong" way to do things. Maybe it's the heavy Catholic influence in Italy, or just the weight of history, but Italians temper their passion for eating and drinking with an almost grave seriousness about it. If you settle for something that isn't *giusto* (just, correct) you are failing yourself and, to a degree, lowering your standing among your friends. Any Italian worth his salt has strong opinions on where to find the proper versions of whatever food he's looking for,

The DOC Zones of Sicilia

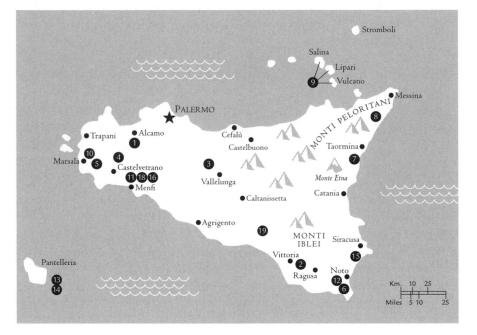

1 Alcamo
2 Cerasuolo di Vittoria
3 Contea di Sclafani
4 Contessa Entellina
5 Delia Nivolelli
6 Eloro
7 Etna
8 Faro
9 Malvasia delle Lipari
10 Marsala
11 Menfi

12 Moscato di Noto Naturale/
   Moscato di Noto
13 Moscato di Pantelleria
   Naturale/Moscato di Pantelleria
14 Moscato Passito di Pantelleria/
   Passito di Pantelleria
15 Moscato di Siracusa
16 Sambuca di Sicilia
17 Santa Margherita di Belice
18 Sciacca
19 Riesi*

*New in 2000–2001

even if it means traveling well out of his way to get some.

This is not to say there isn't a fast-food culture in Italy—it's growing all the time. But the percentage of people who think very carefully about everything they eat seems much higher in Italy than in America. So it is with Ignazio: There's properly made gelato—one with the appropriate *cremosità* (creaminess) and "recognizability of flavor"—and then there's the rest, which are to be avoided. "An industrial gelato is pumped full of air," he says with a wince. "A gelato *artigianale* is more concentrated, with natural flavor. It should taste like what it says it is."

Sicilian *gelato* is nevertheless somewhat leaner, he explains, than *gelati* from other parts of Italy, because it is either milk- or water-based, as opposed to cream-based. Milk is used for flavors such as almond or pistachio, while water is often preferred for fruit flavors including *cocomero* (watermelon), *mandarino* (tangerine), and *fichi d'india* (prickly pear). Then there's the granita, a simpler, soupier combination of churned ice, sugar, and either juice or some other natural flavoring (lemon and coffee are the two most popular).

"With *gelato* in particular, you look for natural colors," Ignazio says. "Is a pistachio nut bright green? No. So why is pistachio gelato bright green? *Mi segui?*"

He tucks the BMW into a highly illegal-looking parking spot and we're off to the practical part of the lesson: the ritual. As with "taking a coffee," the gelato break in Sicily is built into the day's schedule, like picking up the dry cleaning or dropping the kids off at school. On our arrival at his bar of choice, a bustling little place called Al Chiosco, he takes the liberty of ordering for us: a coffee granita,

an almond gelato, and a gelato *di fichi d'india,* along with three brioches. The counter man passes Ignazio the brioches, which he gently tears open, then plops in the scoops of granita and gelato. "This is the classic *palermitano* way," he says. "We do this for breakfast: You have a nice coffee granita in a brioche or maybe just some whipped cream inside. Then a gelato or a lemon granita in the afternoon." Either way, the brioche is a critical component.

The actual eating of these creations takes on a strangely serious tone as Ignazio (who takes the granita) awaits our reaction on the *gelati.* Standing outside the shop in the balmy Piazza Mondello, we find ourselves nodding thoughtfully, as if we were tasting an aged Barolo, and using wine-like descriptors: concentrated, balanced, and so on. It seems a little crazy to be thinking so critically about ice cream. Or is it?

"Even in Sicily you can't always find a proper gelato," Ignazio says, touching on the evils of artificial flavorings and reiterating his disdain for airy, "industrial" products. "But the tradition was born here. You don't find this taste anywhere else."

The best Sicilian *gelati* are those made from flavors indigenous to the island, which is as diverse geographically as it is culturally. Lemons, citrons, tangerines, oranges, almonds, pistachios—these are all huge crops in Sicily, as are less *gelato*-ready foods such as wheat, fava beans, artichokes, capers, olives, and, of course, wine and table grapes (most of the latter become raisins). Much of the island lies at a latitude more southerly than Tunisia's, and it is the hottest, driest region of Italy. And yet in its northern and eastern reaches, it is an extension of the Apennine mountain chain, with peaks that remain covered in snow for much of the winter. It isn't so much an island as a micro-continent, and it is bursting with produce all year round: a rainbow of citrus fruits in the winter; artichokes and young wheat in the spring; almonds and pistachios in August; grapes and olives in the fall.

Since the days of the Greeks, Sicily has been Italy's granary, and its reputation as an agricultural mass producer has carried over into wine. The island's most famous wine, Marsala, came into being mainly because the English merchant credited with creating it, John Woodhouse, needed to find a replacement for French claret during the eighteenth-century War of the Spanish Succession, which pitted Britain against France (this was when the market for Sherries, Madeiras, and Ports first developed as well).

Although Marsala became known not just as "filler" but as a world-class wine in its own right, Sicily has for centuries focused on the production of wine in bulk. The island is Italy's largest region and its most prolific wine producer (more than eight million hectoliters in 1997). But most Sicilian wine is shipped out in tankers as high-alcohol blending wine, to be used by producers in northern Italy and southern France. Sicily is also a major producer of concentrated grape musts, which are made by either cooking down or vacuum-evaporating the juice into a sappy sugar water. These are used for the same purpose as blending wines: to raise the alcohol levels of anemic wines made elsewhere. Of the huge production of Sicilian wine each year, only about 5 percent actually makes it into bottles, and only 2 percent of that is classified as DOC.

This somewhat anonymous wine culture stands in sharp contrast to one of the most richly diverse cuisines in Italy. Having seen more than its share of foreign rulers—including the Saracens, or Moors, who are credited with bringing not just ice cream but its precursor, sugar—and possessed of incredible agricultural resources, Sicily is a sensual feast. Pasta dishes are spiked with the likes of capers, mint, fennel, olives, and red peppers. Seafood is king—be it tuna, *pesce-spada* (swordfish), sardines, or anchovies—and the preparations are wild: chopped almonds, raisins, and citrus are all found in traditional Sicilian fish preparations, along with many of the other ingredients mentioned above. The prevailing cooking philosophy is *agrodolce* (sweet and sour), as exemplified by dishes such as caponata, the famous Sicilian casserole of eggplant, zucchini, olives, pine nuts, vinegar, and sugar.

To complement this complex cuisine, however, Sicilians mostly settled for flabby dry whites from Alcamo, on the western end of the island, and coarse, sun-baked reds from a variety of locations, including the volcanic slopes of Mount Etna in the east. Only its sweet wines—Marsala, along with the moscato- and malvasia-based nectars of Pantelleria, Lipari, and elsewhere—had any real market presence.

Along with neighboring Calabria, Sicily best exemplifies the enduring legacy of the *latifondo,* the system of land distribution and agricultural relationships that dominated the Italian south for centuries. Northern Italy was characterized by the *mezzadria* (sharecropping) model, where the peasantry at least had a stake in the land they were cultivating. But southern-Italian farms were much more oppressive. Sicily in particular was dominated by a relatively small number of large landowners, most of them noble families, for whom the Sicilian peasants were little more than indentured servants. After

Italy became a republic in 1946, the new government attempted to reverse the effects of the *latifondo* through the agrarian reforms of the early fifties. While a lot of land was appropriated from large landowners and redistributed to peasant families, it didn't lead to the rise of many private wine estates. Instead, those newly minted landowners who chose to grow grapes either sold their produce to the large Marsala houses or joined a cooperative winery, or *cantina sociale*. And more so than their counterparts elsewhere in Italy, these fledgling farmers also had the mafia to contend with.

The *cantina* movement exploded in the fifties and sixties, largely because of the failures of the agrarian reforms. The redistributed plots of land were too small to do individual farmers much good, so the Italian government's response was to subsidize the creation of cooperatives (not only for wine but other agricultural products). Propped up not only with government money but with contributions from the European Community, the ever-growing legion of co-ops became pumping stations for bulk wine to be shipped north, especially to France, which lost a key supply of blending wine when Algeria declared independence in 1962.

"Whatever vine produced the most tonnage, that's what the farmers planted," explains Diego Planeta. He is the president of one of Sicily's largest co-ops, Settesoli in Menfi, and also the patriarch of the Planeta winery in Sambuca, a private estate run by his daughter, Francesca, and nephew, Alessio. "In the beginning, cooperatives helped a lot, economically, because there were many small farmers in the fifties and sixties who otherwise wouldn't have found a market for their grapes. Very rarely were cooperatives managed by wine people.

They were built and run by politicians. And for a while, they could absorb as much as the farmers could grow."

This, of course, didn't last. Eventually, the bulk-wine market began to collapse, particularly when France found other sources for its own blending wines. (To compound grapegrowers' woes, Marsala began to fall out of favor in the market as well.) Only forward-looking co-ops such as Settesoli—which began marketing bottled dry wines in the early seventies—were positioned to survive.

"The result of the co-op system, by and large, was an immense amount of money spent by the community, no professional people coming out of the business, no enterprise, and quality was nonexistent," Planeta says. "Eventually, about ten years ago, the EC and government subsidies just disappeared altogether. Most of the co-ops went bankrupt, and of those that have survived, most have financial problems."

The co-op culture was pervasive enough that for much of the last three decades, the commercial wine scene in Sicily—excluding Marsala—was defined by two estates: the Corvo-Duca di Salaparuta property in Casteldaccia, which was controlled by the Sicilian regional government until the spring of 2001 (when it was sold to private investors), and the Conte Tasca d'Almerita estate in Vallelunga, better known as Regaleali. If you asked for a dry Sicilian white in the seventies and eighties, your choices were largely confined to either Corvo's "Columba Platino" or Regaleali's basic "Bianco," two clean, simple whites based on local grapes. For reds, the choices were more interesting, but no less limited: "Duca Enrico" from Corvo-Duca di Salaparuta or "Rosso del Conte" from Regaleali, both of which showcased Sicily's top native red, nero d'avola, to great effect.

But things have changed, and dramatically. The collapse of the co-op system has given way to a surge in private investment in vineyards and wineries. Many of these newcomers, in fact, are people whose families either grew grapes for or worked at a local co-op. Duca di Salaparuta's passing into private hands is highly symbolic, because Sicily has been gripped by land fever. "This is one of the few places in Italy where there has been land to be bought, and at a reasonable price," says Diego Planeta. Well-known wine firms are buying up big plots of land in Sicily, among them the Veneto's Zonin group (which purchased the 240-acre Principe di Butera estate in 1997), and the Hardy's wine conglomerate of Australia (which is involved in a highly successful joint venture with Sicily's Calatrasi). Among other brands, the Hardy's-Calatrasi partnership is known for the well-priced "Terrale" line of wines, which also includes some bottlings from Puglia.

Early pioneers from within Sicily included the Rallo family of Marsala, who sold their Rallo brand name in the mid-eighties. They then converted their Marsala *cantina* into a dry-wine facility, creating a range of excellent whites and reds from vineyards in Contessa Entellina, a half-hour inland from the town of Marsala. Another early arrival on the modern wine scene was the Lena family of Castelbuono, a village not far from Cefalù in the northeastern part of the island. The Lenas restored the twelfth-century Abbazia Sant'Anastasia in Castelbuono and introduced a line of mostly red wines in 1987.

In the nineties, it seemed like a new and noteworthy winery was opening every day. The Planeta estate, created from family vineyards

that once supplied the Settesoli co-op, debuted its first wines in 1995 and quickly became one of the most acclaimed properties in Italy. Another '95 debut was Ceuso "Vigna Custera," a powerful red blend created by Vincenzo, Giuseppe, and Antonino Melia of Alcamo, longtime grape growers for the local co-op who converted a family garage into a boutique winery. Then there's Salvatore Geraci, an architect by trade, who rescued the all-but-extinct Faro DOC in 1996 with the launch of his Palari-brand wines, sourced from a patchwork of old family vineyards in Messina.

And there's more. It is no exaggeration to say that, along with the Maremma region of southern Tuscany, Sicily is the hottest new frontier in Italian winemaking. "In my day, to sell a bottle of Sicilian wine was a drama," says Diego Planeta. "Now people are calling this place the Australia of Italy, the California of Italy. A good vintage, in certain areas of the world, is a miracle. Here, we don't get any rain after February. We have intense heat and sunlight. It's always windy and dry, so we don't have problems with rot. We can make great wine every year."

VINI BIANCHI
White Wines

Much of what you need to know about dry white wine in Sicily can be summed up with this statistic: Of the 330,000 acres of vineyards on the island (the largest total of any Italian region), nearly 60 percent are planted to catarratto, a fairly bland but extremely durable white grape. Catarratto is the base of a number of DOC whites, most notably Alcamo, in western Sicily. But its primary role is as a blending grape in Marsala and, more anonymously, as a staple of bulk-wine production, especially for vermouth houses in Piedmont. Technically, there are two varieties of catarratto—catarratto bianco comune and catarratto bianco lucido—but their differences are subtle. Although catarratto is found only on Sicily, it is the second-most planted grape in all of Italy.

When treated with care, catarratto can have a plush, spicy, almost beeswaxy character reminiscent of viognier, but very few producers are striving for important wines from the grape. It is low in acidity, making it difficult to showcase on its own; even in Alcamo DOC whites, it has lost ground in the blend to other local grapes such as inzolia (also known as ansonica) and grecanico, not to mention the increasingly popular chardonnay.

Aside from Alcamo, of which Rapitalà, Spadafora, and Pollara are making some solid examples, the only other DOC whites of note are those from the Etna zone, which combine catarratto with another variety unique to Sicily, carricante. In Etna, the pickings are similarly slim: Benanti, Murgo, and Barone Villagrande are the top producers, and, while their wines are more aromatic and crisp than the soft, melony wines of Alcamo, they too are lumped among the myriad light seafood whites being produced all over Italy. Because so many DOC wines have been stripped of any real character by producers striving to make as much as they can, the genuinely interesting versions are all but washed away in the deluge.

The benchmark whites of Sicily have long been made outside of DOC parameters, not only because of the difficulties associated with the catarratto grape but because their producers felt that DOC classifications would dilute the power of their brands. The Columba Platino from Corvo, for example, combines 80 percent inzolia with 20 percent grecanico, while Regaleali's Bianco is a mix of inzolia, catarratto, and a strain of grecanico that the Tasca family says is unique to their estate.

"Inzolia is probably the best of our native grapes on Sicily," says Giuseppe Tasca, the vineyard manager at Tasca d'Almerita-Regaleali. "In our *bianco*, we get the fruitiness and aroma from inzolia, the acidity from the Tasca variety, and the body from catarratto. But it is difficult to make a single-varietal wine from any of those three."

José Rallo, of the Donnafugata estate in Contessa Entellina, agrees. "Inzolia is fundamental to all of our white wines, because it has good fruitiness. But typically we need to pair it with something more aromatic or something with more body." Donnafugata makes a number of noteworthy blends that incorporate inzolia, including the inzolia-catarratto "Anthilia," and an exotic mix of inzolia, müller-thurgau, and sauvignon blanc called "Lighea."

There are, however, some single-variety wines from these indigenous grapes, the best of them from either inzolia or grecanico, a grape many believe to be related to the greco family of the Italian mainland. Of all the Sicilian natives, grecanico has the most penetrating acidity and freshness, even in a climate that can easily overripen just about anything you plant. "Grecanico is one of those classic Italian whites that matures very late, so it's good for Sicily," says Francesca Planeta, whose "Alastro" and "La Segreta" white blends combine grecanico with chardonnay.

Given the natural conditions in Sicily, the objective of most new-generation producers is white wines with more power. This has led to more planting of chardonnay, and in turn to the creation of the island's most celebrated white wine: the rich, barrel-fermented chardonnay of Planeta. "We have the perfect environment for great chardonnay," says Francesca Planeta, who in a relatively short time has become one of the young celebrities of Italian wine. "The difference in Sicily between now and ten years ago is that people are choosing the grapes that are best suited for this place, and being more careful about how they grow them. If there's been a change in the quality of Sicilian wine, and I think there has, it's all due to improvements in technology. The environment was always there."

Chardonnay is the white grape of the moment in Sicily. In the intense, dry heat of the southern Mediterranean, the grape ripens into a tropical fruit bomb, as exemplified not just by Planeta's bottlings but by the "La Fuga" Chardonnay of Donnafugata and the oak-fermented inzolia-chardonnay blend called "Bidis" made at Valle dell'Acate, in the southeastern zone of Vittoria. These are wines with the power and extraction of chardonnays of California and Australia, a comparison that is not lost on their makers. "As I travel around the world, I see that people don't really think of Sicily as being part of Italy," says Diego Planeta. "They think of it as its own place. And with the huge success of the New World, we're like a new New World country. Anything goes."

Practically speaking, the metamorphosis underway in Sicily makes for some highly variable choices in the wine shop. Although the island's future may well be peachy, pineappley, oak-kissed chardonnays, there are still plenty of Sicilian whites that cut a leaner figure. In many cases, these might be the better choices with some of the aggressively seasoned, citrus-tinged fish preparations of the island, especially *crudo* (raw seafood). A well-made Alcamo or Etna white, or maybe a varietal wine from inzolia or grecanico, won't wow you like a barrique-aged chardonnay, but neither will it clash with what you're eating. As more money and winemaking savvy find their way to the island, even the traditional whites are getting a new look. And as the commercial wine culture grows, the likes of Chile and Argentina are facing more serious competition from Sicily's new generation, who've got seemingly endless space and a generous winemaking climate at their disposal.

VINI ROSSI
Red Wines

Although Sicily still produces a greater percentage of white wines (a statistic skewed by Marsala), the real interest these days is in its deep, dark reds—particularly those made from the nero d'avola grape, whether bottled on its own or in blends with merlot, cabernet sauvignon, and especially syrah, to which it is often compared.

"With our climate, a lot of whites will ripen too fast," says Giuseppe Tasca of Regaleali. "But these are the perfect conditions for reds."

Although there are notable exceptions—such as the cool, moist, nearly continental climate of Mount Etna, a still-active volcano where chestnuts and pines grow at the higher elevations—Sicily has three things in abundance that red-wine grapes crave: heat, light, and dryness. At times, the island seems downright desertlike: The harsh North African *scirocco* kicks up dust and blurs the horizons, seemingly turning the scant summer rainfall to mud before it hits the ground. Prickly pear cacti line the highways, somehow drawing enough nutrients from the parched earth to produce their fiery yellow-orange fruit. "After February or March we hardly get any rain at all," says Giuseppe Tasca.

Sometimes, as in 1996, it can be *too* dry. But irrigation systems, fed by man-made lakes, help vintners keep their vines appropriately nourished. Access to water, in fact, is one of the key mitigating factors in the rapid development of Sicilian vineyards, and will ultimately limit just how much new planting there will be. But for those already established, there's a sense of being in the right place at the right time. "I would rather add the water I need at harvest time than to have too much rain," says Tasca.

Not that great red wine is a wholly recent phenomenon. Tasca d'Almerita's "Rosso del Conte" and Corvo's "Duca Enrico" are legendary Italian wines. Both are based on nero d'avola and both are lush, ageworthy reds that spend at least some time in French oak barriques. Now, not only are they getting some company, but the nero d'avola grape itself is attracting more serious attention.

"In the past, with Rosso del Conte and Duca Enrico, people talked about the wines as brands," says Count Lucio Tasca, Giuseppe's father, who was around when the gnarled *alberelli* (bush vines) of the Rosso del Conte vineyard were first planted, in 1959. "People didn't mention the grape when they talked about Rosso del Conte. Only now is nero d'avola being recognized."

By all accounts, nero d'avola is thin-skinned and susceptible to rot, as well as a late-ripener. "For us, nero d'avola is the last one to harvest," says Guiseppe Tasca. "It matures twenty days later than cabernet. Sometimes we harvest as late as the end of October or the beginning of November." Many vintners assert that only in Sicily can nero d'avola and other late-ripening varieties—such as cabernet sauvignon—reach proper maturity. "People have tried to plant nero d'avola in other parts of Italy but haven't had success," notes Lucio Tasca. "Anywhere you have the chance for rain at harvest, you won't do well with nero d'avola."

Other producers, such as Diego Planeta, say that not enough is known about the grape to make this assertion. "Some think that it came to us from the mainland," Planeta muses, referring to the grape's other name, calabrese, which suggests a link to Calabria. "How do we know there is not nero d'avola somewhere else under a different name, in the way that grecanico is probably greco or garganega?"

Although there is a smattering of nero d'avola in Calabria, it is essentially Sicily's alone. Named for a small town west of Siracusa, on the island's southeast coast, it is believed to have been brought by the Greeks (Siracusa was the second Greek colony on Sicily). It is the undisputed leader among the native red grapes of the island, although there are some excellent wines being made from the spicy, dark-hued nerello mascalese—most notably the Faro DOC blends of Palari and the popular *rosato* of Regaleali, both of which use the grape as their base. There's also the tart, bright, strawberry-scented frappato grape, which is combined with nero d'avola in the Cerasuolo di Vittoria DOC wines of southeastern Sicily.

Nero d'avola reds, meanwhile, fall into three main categories: those that are 100 percent nero d'avola, such as the varietal bottlings of the Morgante estate in Riesi, Donnafugata's "Mille e Una Notte," Regaleali's "Rosso del Conte," and Corvo's "Duca Enrico"; those that combine nero d'avola with cabernet, merlot, and/or syrah, such as Ceuso's "Vigna Custera," Planeta's "Santa Cecilia," and the wines of Abbazia Sant' Anastasia; and those of Cerasuolo di Vittoria, the one historic DOC zone in Sicily with an enduring reputation for quality reds.

Tasting through these diverse wines, it's difficult to pinpoint the precise character of nero d'avola. Generally speaking, it has a dark, tarry quality, with lots of black fruit aromas highlighted with scents of violets. It's also rich and well structured, with firm but silty tannins, which prompts many tasters to compare it with syrah.

"Many people think nero d'avola and syrah are related," says Giusto Occhipinti of COS, a leading estate in the Cerasuolo di Vittoria zone. "There are some who believe that syrah originated in Sicily. The theory is that it is related to nero d'avola and is named for the 'Sira' in Siracusa, not Shiraz in Persia." Whatever its true origins, vintners are finding different expressions of nero d'avola in different soils; some are spicy and firm, like Rhône syrah, others are plusher and juicier, like Aussie shiraz.

Occhipinti is closely studying nero d'avola, not just for his Cerasuolo di Vittoria wines but for his new estate, Vittoria, which will focus solely on single-vineyard nero d'avola. Having done a series of "micro-vinifications" from diverse vineyard plots in his area, he says the extreme southeastern tip of Sicily—where the soils are considerably sandier than those farther inland—is where nero d'avola is at its most potent.

Francesca Planeta is one of a number of producers who, like Occhipinti, believe that the sandy clays of the southeast (namely, the grape's original homeland west of Siracusa) is the place where nero d'avola reaches its peak. "There are two reasons why we have done more with merlot and cabernet up to this point," she offers. "First, our main estate in Sambuca has richer clays, and cabernet and merlot simply perform better there. But we purchased vineyard land in Noto [near Avola] because we feel that's where we can make something interesting from nero d'avola. The other reason we used the international varieties is because we needed to establish a reputation for Sicilian wines. We needed to attract people here with cabernet and merlot. Once we have established ourselves, then we can introduce them to nero d'avola."

But there is yet another reason why cabernet sauvignon, merlot, and syrah play such a prominent role in Sicily's new reds. "Strangely enough, with the local varieties such as nero d'avola, we don't have anything to go on when it comes to clonal material," says Alessio Planeta. "With the international grapes we had fifty different clones to choose from, so we could start with something of quality right away."

Until nero d'avola establishes itself in the minds of consumers (and likely even afterward), producers will continue to complement it with international varieties. At Planeta's vineyards in Sambuca, their focus is still as much on merlot, cabernet sauvignon, and syrah as it is on nero d'avola. At the Abbazia Sant'Anastasia, the Lenas make three blends— "Passomaggio" (nero d'avola with merlot); "Montenero" (nero d'avola with syrah and merlot); and "Litra" (nero d'avola and cabernet)— each of which is slicker than than the last.

Other producers, including Donnafugata, Calatrasi, Spadafora, and Colosi, are similarly enamored of this formula.

"To my knowledge, nero d'avola is the best of what we've found here in Sicily," concludes Diego Planeta. "But I have an opinion, which might be wrong, but I think that in a few years' time the whole world will be talking about Sicilian syrah. It's just like nero d'avola: It loves the heat."

Vini Dolci
Sweet Wines

Prior to the red-wine revolution of the nineties, Sicily was known principally for its sweet and fortified wines, especially Marsala, whose name (derived from the Arab phrase *marsah-el-Allah*, or "port of God") evokes the Arab past of the island and its culture. Sicilians have always had a wealth of wine choices to complement Saracen-inspired sweets such as cannoli (tubes of fried dough traditionally filled with cream cheese, sugar or honey, almond paste, and bits of candied fruit) and *cassata* (a liqueur-drenched sponge cake topped with sugar, ricotta, almond paste, and, again, candied fruit). Sicily is the first stop in Italy for the sweet-wine aficionado: There's Marsala, which can be nutty and dry or caramel sweet; Passito di Pantelleria, which captures the flavor of golden raisins in a bottle; and Malvasia delle Lipari, which tastes like fresh-picked apricots.

Although the best versions of each are increasingly scarce, Sicily's *vini dolci* not only hail from some of the most exotic locales in the world of wine but are (or were) made by some of Italy's most colorful personalities. The late Ignazio Miceli (he of the gelato run described previously) was instrumental in promoting the wines of Sicily and especially those of Pantelleria, the *scirocco*-swept island where moscato grows on close-cropped bush vines set in holes in the ground and protected by stone walls. The (also late) Carlo Hauner, a Milanese designer and artist, fell so in love with the Aeolian isle of Salina (where, incidentally, much of *Il Postino* was filmed) that he spent years purchasing tiny plots of land on which to grow malvasia. The legend is that it took two thousand separate contracts for Hauner to secure a mere forty acres of land on Salina, which is now controlled by his four children.

And then there's the excitable Marco DeBartoli, the one well-known artisan producer of Marsala in a town whose glory days are behind it. DeBartoli's Vecchio Samperi estate, which he founded in the late seventies after working in a number of much larger Marsala houses, is like an art-house movie theater set among the multiplexes. Creations of his such as the long-aged, unfortified "Vecchio Samperi" Marsala, and a luscious Passito di Pantelleria called "Bukkuram," are unlike any other wines in Italy or beyond.

What ultimately distinguishes the sweet wines of Sicily and its satellites are their places of origin: the dusty port of Marsala, which looks more Moroccan than Italian; the black sands of Pantelleria, the definition of a desert island; and the still-grumbling volcanoes of the Aeolian archipelago, a group of giant pumice stones jutting from the Mediterranean. The exotic flavors of the wines are a direct link to these distant places. And surprisingly, the wines are not that difficult to find.

Marsala

Forget for a minute the cheap Marsala used to sauce veal cutlets or flavor zabaglione cakes, and forget for a minute the premixed combinations of Marsala and egg cream or Marsala and coffee you might see in a Palermo ice-cream parlor. This is a wine that once stood alongside Sherry, Madeira, and Port as one of the great fortified wines of the world. While highly variable in style and quality, it can still be something special.

Marsala is a confusing category. The wines are categorized according to three variables: their color, their age, and their sweetness level. All Marsalas are either *oro* (gold), *ambra* (amber), or *rubino* (ruby), depending on the grapes they come from. *Oro* and *ambra* versions are made from white varieties, including the preferred grillo, the more prolific catarratto, and other local grapes such as inzolia and damaschino. The much rarer *rubino* versions are made from blends of red grapes, including perricone, nero d'avola (calabrese), and nerello mascalese (plus an allowed percentage of the above white grapes).

The age categories of Marsala are Fine, Superiore, and Vergine/Soleras. Fine Marsalas are the simplest, aged only one year (not necessarily in wood) and typically used for cooking. Superiore Marsalas are more luxurious, aged a minimum of two years (four years for Superiore Riserva) in large oak or chestnut casks. Many Superiore Marsalas carry Sherry-like descriptors such as SOM (Superior Old Marsala) and LP (London Particular), which harken back to Marsala's days as a British-controlled port.

Marsalas labeled as Vergine or Soleras are the most complex and longest-aged of the three main styles, with a basic Vergine/Soleras spending a minimum of five years in wood and a *stravecchio*, or *riserva*, spending a minimum of ten.

Both Fine and Superiore Marsalas can be *secco* (dry), *semisecco* (off-dry) or *dolce* (sweet), whereas Vergine/Soleras Marsalas are always dry, and are often made in the *solera* method, in which casks of wine of varying ages are blended together. These are the ultimate sipping Marsalas, with the oxidative notes of caramel, nuts, spice, orange peel, and other exotic flavors. A good Vergine or Soleras Marsala has the unctuous aroma of sweet wine, but in the mouth it is bone dry.

Aside from aging and sweetness level, the principal difference among Fine, Superiore, and Vergine/Soleras Marsalas is the method by which they are fortified. In the 1700s, Marsalas and their Spanish and Portugese counterparts were fortified—usually with grape brandy—so that they could withstand the long sea journey to Britain. The practice continues today, but in various forms. Some producers use either concentrated must, cooked-down must (*mosto cotto*), or a blend of brandy and fresh grape must called *sifone*, all of which raise the potential alcohol of the wine while diluting its essential character. In the top-end Vergine or Soleras versions of Marsala, only straight brandy is allowed to fortify the wine—as with great Port, the point is to produce a naturally sweet, powerful wine from exceptionally ripe grapes, wherein the addition of brandy merely arrests the fermentation and adds a few degrees of alcohol.

Because of the various ways in which the wine can be made, producers traditionally stretched the rules in order to stretch production, relying more on cooked or concentrated must (much of which was sourced outside of the DOC zone) and less on good-quality grapes from their own vineyards. Changes in the Marsala DOC discipline in 1984 restricted the use of these additives, and also prohibited the use of the word Marsala on the bottles of egg- and coffee-flavored concoctions. But, as with so much Italian wine, the production excesses of the seventies and eighties damaged the reputation of Marsala so much that production has never rebounded. Although the Marsala DOC is still the most prolific on the island, it is a shadow of its former self, with only a handful of brand-name producers still in operation. Among them are Florio, Pellegrino, and DeBartoli, whose Vecchio Samperi wines have the added distinction of being unfortified; they reach the minimum of 18 percent alcohol naturally, picking up their lusciously concentrated flavors from decades spent in wood. DeBartoli himself likes to drink his wines as apéritifs, maybe paired with roasted almonds, fresh sardines, or some cheese, preferring that the briny, oxidative flavors of the wine mingle with similarly savory flavors. Others might want to try these sippers with a hunk of bitter chocolate, to point up their caramel and nut character.

Malvasia delle Lipari

Although the DOC name cites the island of Lipari as the source, it's actually Lipari's neighbor, Salina, that provides the majority of the malvasia grapes used in the commercial production of this nectar of a wine. In the volcanic ash of these Aeolian islands, the malvasia grape plumps into a juicy evocation of the fruits of Sicily, its orangey color and flowery scents bringing to mind citrus blossoms. Most Malvasia delle Lipari, of which the best versions are made by Hauner, Caravaglio, and Colosi (all of which are exported to the United States), is a naturally sweet wine, with a minimum alcohol level of 11.5 percent. (There are richer, more alcoholic passiti incorporating dried grapes, and even a few fortified versions.) Best sipped with a slight chill, they are great with all the classic Sicilian desserts, especially those incorporating fruits: Of all the Sicilian vini dolci, the wines of Lipari, Salina, et al, are the most assertively fruity, and should be treated accordingly.

The Moscatos of Pantelleria and Beyond

Moscato (called zibibbo in Sicily, where it is also widely eaten as a table grape), is another widely planted and highly mutated grape, and is the base for the naturally sweet and passito wines of Pantelleria, which is only 52 miles from Cape Bon in Tunisia. Zibibbo is a popular table grape in southern Italy, producing big, bulbous berries despite the hot, dry conditions, which makes it an ideal grape for raisins as well. A good Moscato or Passito di Pantelleria is like biting into the plumpest golden raisin you can imagine.

Because of the harsh breezes off the North African desert, the preferred system of vine training on Pantelleria is the alberello (bush), in which the grape bunches are held close to the trunk of the plant and shaded by a tight canopy of leaves. Even with the protection of this canopy, the grapes are scorched and withered in the sun, then further dried on straw mats during the cool, dry autumn nights after the harvest, to concentrate their sugars. More honeyed and caramel-scented than their Aeolian-island cousin, the "raisin wines" of Pantelleria rival the Vin Santo of Tuscany as accompaniments for biscotti. In addition to Marco DeBartoli's "Bukkuram," there are great passiti being made by fireman/winemaker Salvatore

Murana, and by the Donnafugata estate, whose "Ben Ryé" bottling is one of the best examples of its type.

There are two other noteworthy moscato wines made on the main island of Sicily, but while DOC zones still exist for each they have all but disappeared from commercial distribution. Moscato di Noto, made in the southeastern Sicilian town of the same name, is considered perhaps the most prized wine of all the Sicilian stickies, but today only about seventy acres of vineyards are registered in the DOC zone. Moscato di Siracusa, an adjacent DOC zone, is also one for the history books, with only about five acres of registered vines still in existence. But should your travels take you to Siracusa, one of the most beautiful towns in southern Italy, you may have the pleasure of encountering one of these endangered species.

FAST FACTS: SICILIA

PROVINCES	Agrigento (AG), Caltanissetta (CL), Catania (CT), Enna (EN), Messina (ME), Palermo (PA), Ragusa (RG), Siracusa (SR), Trapani (TP)
CAPITAL	Palermo
KEY WINE TOWNS	Marsala; Messina; Noto; Ragusa
TOTAL VINEYARD AREA*	133,518 hectares, or 329,923 acres. Rank: 1st
TOTAL WINE PRODUCTION*	8,073,000 hectoliters, or 213,000,000 gallons (1st)
DOC WINE PRODUCED*	2.1% (20th)
SPECIALTY FOODS	almonds; pistachios; capers (especially on Pantelleria and the Aeolian islands); citrus fruits (lemons, oranges); tonno (tuna); pesce spada (swordfish).

*1997 figures. Rankings out of twenty regions total (Trentino–Alto Adige counted as one). Source: Istituto Statistica Mercati Agro-Alimentari (ISMEA), Rome.

KEY GRAPE VARIETIES

WHITES

CATARRATTO	One of the most heavily planted varieties in Italy, and yet it is found only in Sicily. Used in dry white blends from Alcamo and as a key blending ingredient in Marsala. It very occasionally makes interesting varietal wines.
GRECANICO	May be related to greco or garganega from the mainland. Principally a blending variety, it has good acidity and a fresh, appley flavor.
GRILLO	The historic base for Marsala; it is now on the wane.

INZOLIA (ANSONICA)	One of the better indigenous Sicilian whites, producing plump, dewy whites in the Alcamo DOC and used in most of the best *vini da tavola* (VdT) whites, such as Corvo's "Columba Platino."
MALVASIA	This well-traveled grape is thought to have been brought to Lipari by the Greeks. It gains uncommon depth of flavor in the volcanic ash of the Aeolian islands.
ZIBIBBO	The local name for muscat of Alexandria, or moscato bianco. This is a large-berried version of moscato used not only for wine but for table grapes and raisins.
OTHERS	CHARDONNAY; SAUVIGNON; MÜLLER-THURGAU; CARRICANTE, used in Etna Bianco DOC whites.

REDS

FRAPPATO	Light-colored, cherry-scented native grape with high acidity. It is occasionally made into light, bright reds and rosés on its own or blended with nero d'avola in the Cerasuolo di Vittoria DOC.
NERELLO MASCALESE	A spicy, deep-colored black grape used as the base of the Faro DOC blend and other reds of eastern Sicily.
NERO D'AVOLA (CALABRESE)	Sicily's most prominent native. The wines are deep and rich in black-fruit flavors, with a hint of exotic spice. Many wine-makers compare its character to that of syrah, with which it is often combined in blends.
OTHERS	NERELLO CAPPUCCIO, a local blending variety; PERRICONE, a deeply colorful blending variety; SYRAH; CABERNET SAUVIGNON; MERLOT.

TOP VINTAGES IN SICILY, 1980–2000

Benchmark Sicilian reds such as Corvo's "Duca Enrico" and Regaleali's "Rosso del Conte" have been known to be long agers, establishing the native nero d'avola grape as one of the "noble" vines of the Italian south. Great years in the eighties for those wines included 1985 and 1989. In the nineties, a new generation of deep, rich reds from producers such as Planeta and Donnafugata has some collectors making room in the cellars. The last three years of the decade (1997–'99) were all considered exceptional vintages, so pick up the latest releases with confidence.

LA STRADA DEL VINO
WINE TOURING IN SICILY

A wine tour of Sicily would most logically begin in the hectic confines of Palermo—an architecturally diverse city that has been cleaned up considerably in recent years. Then run east to Messina, and make sure to stop in Cefalù along the way; then south to Taormina (in the shadow of Mount Etna) and Siracusa (on the southeastern coast). There aren't many wineries to visit, but rather an incredible variety of seafoods and other delicacies to eat, plenty of interesting local wines to pair them with, and all of it in settings as dramatic as it gets in Italy. From Milazzo, west of Messina, you can catch the hydrofoil to the islands of Salina and Lipari, home of Sicily's famous sweet malvasias. Home cooks should also be aware of the excellent cooking school run by Anna Tasca Lanza at the sprawling Regaleali estate in Vallelunga, although that requires a journey inland.

DEGUSTAZIONI
TASTINGS

LIGHT WHITES

Corvo-Duca di Salaparuta "Columba Platino," $

Regaleali Bianco, $

Both of these wines include the inzolia and catarratto grapes, Sicily's two principal white varieties, in varying proportions (inzolia is the dominant variety in each). The Corvo wine in particular is exceptionally clean and fresh, with scents and flavors of green apple. The Regaleali builds on this, offering fleshier flavors of green melon and some citrus. The muted aromas and crisp yet rounded textures of these wines make them excellent apéritif choices, and they also make unobtrusive accompaniments to light seafood dishes.

FULL-BODIED WHITES

Donnafugata "La Fuga" Chardonnay, $–$$

Planeta Chardonnay, $$

Here are two increasingly popular restaurant wines, both of which show off the chardonnay grape at its biggest: rich, creamy, juicy, and full of the flavors of tropical fruits (bananas, pineapples, citrus). The principal difference is that the "La Fuga" is not aged in oak, whereas the Planeta wine spends some time in French barriques. These weighty whites need similarly rich food to stand up to them—maybe a thick grilled swordfish steak drizzled with olive oil.

NERO D'AVOLA

Abbazia Sant'Anastasia IGT Rosso, $

Regaleali "Rosso del Conte," $$

Duca di Salaparuta "Duca Enrico," $$$

This grouping starts simple, with the savory, spicy *rosso* from the well-regarded Santa Anastasia, then becomes more complex, with the two superstar reds of Sicily. If you are following the conventions of this book and seeking out the current vintages of these wines, note that the Regaleali and Duca di Salaparuta wines will be much older, as they are each aged for significant periods before release. This tasting will give you a feel for young nero d'avola versus old: See how its juicy raspberry flavors evolve into something more tarry and resiny over time. Other good nero d'avola producers include Morgante and Calatrasi, and the Cerasuolo di Vittoria wines of Valle dell'-Acate and COS are worth checking out, to compare how nero d'avola on its own stacks up against nero d'avola blended with the lighter frappato.

RED BLENDS

Ceuso "Vigna Custera," $$$

Planeta "Santa Cecilia," $$$

Palari Faro DOC Rosso, $$$

Though produced in smaller quantities, these reds represent Sicily's elite. They are highly variable, each of them evoking a great wine from another part of the world: The Ceuso wine, a blend of nero d'avola, merlot, and cabernet sauvignon, is reminiscent of a good Bordeaux; the Planeta wine, which combines syrah and nero d'avola, is a worthy substitute for Aussie Shiraz; and the Palari Faro, a blend of several indigenous Sicilian varieties, is a Mediterranean cousin to Châteauneuf-du-Pape. All three wines demonstrate how much flavor and power can be packed into a southern-Italian red, without becoming syrupy from overripening. Each is buttressed with some aging in French oak, and it shows. Pair them with something appropriately meaty.

PASSITO DI PANTELLERIA

Donnafugata "Ben Ryé" Passito di Pantelleria, $$

Salvatore Murana Passito di Pantelleria, $$

DeBartoli "Bukkarum" Passito di Pantelleria, $$$

Three wines are listed here, and any one of this group is a good orientation to the flavors of moscato *passito* as made on the remote island of Pantelleria. Plump and sweet, with hints of honey, cinnamon, caramel, and candied orange, these wines taste like some exotic Sicilian dessert in a bottle. They are fruity at their core and quite unctuous, but not so sweet that they'll clash with *siciliano* desserts such as cannoli (ricotta-stuffed pastry tubes) or *cassata* (a rich sponge cake containing a pantry-full of ingredients).

MALVASIA DELLE LIPARI

Hauner Malvasia delle Lipari, $$

Cantine Colosi Malvasia delle Lipari, $$

Cool and refreshing, not quite as thick and sappy as the *passiti* of Pantelleria, the amber nectars of Malvasia delle Lipari are wines with very clear aromas and flavors of ripe apricots. The aromas are also floral and citrusy (think orange blossoms), and there's a good backbone of acidity to check the sweetness.

MARSALA

Pellegrino Marsala Superiore "Sweet," $

Marco DeBartoli "Vecchio Samperi," $$$

Here are two ends of the very broad Marsala style spectrum. One wine is sweet, with a soft texture and plush flavors of almonds and caramel; the other is dry, with oxidative notes similar to those in a good fino or amontillado Sherry. The Pellegrino wine is more often woven into zabaglione cakes than it is sipped on its own, but the latter option should not be ruled out. The DeBartoli wine, like a good Sherry, might be put to use as an apéritif, where its briny acidity and dried fruit-and-nut flavors would complement what might be called a Sicilian answer to tapas: some sharp pecorino cheese, calamata olives, and maybe some classic Sicilian chick-pea fritters topped with anchovies.

La Cucina

FOOD FOR THE WINE

RECIPE BY MARIO BATALI

There are any number of ways to go when searching for a recipe or concept that is authentically *siciliano*. The incredible wealth of agricultural produce on the island leads to everything-but-the-kitchen-sink preparations such as Palermo's *paste con le sarde*—a mix of fresh sardines, onions, tomatoes, fennel, olive oil, sugar, currants, and pine nuts. Seafood dishes of *tonno* (tuna) and *pesce spada* (swordfish) are similarly complex affairs, with the island's prized capers often playing a significant role.

Unlike much of the rest of Italy, however, Sicily is especially rich in sweets to follow its unusually savory main courses. Myriad desserts are based on Sicilian specialties such as almonds, pistachios, and raisins, and as noted at the beginning of the chapter, gelato reaches the pinnacle of perfection on the island.

The preparation below is a conglomerate, of sorts, of a few *siciliano* specialties. First, there's the ingredients: raisins, fresh ricotta cheese (most famously used in Sicilian cannoli), and honey, all island staples. Then there's the technique: deep-frying. The Sicilian kitchen is full of *fritti*,

be they little deep-fried fritters of chickpea paste or large, meat-and-rice balls called *arancine*. Below is a *fritto dolce*, to be enjoyed alongside another Sicilian trademark: sweet wine.

NOTE: This recipe includes an overnight step.

Ricotta Fritta

1 cup golden RAISINS
1 cup MARSALA WINE
2 cups fresh RICOTTA CHEESE
1 piece CHEESECLOTH, 12-inch square
3 cups extra-virgin OLIVE OIL
1 cup FLOUR
2 large EGGS
1 teaspoon freshly ground BLACK PEPPER
½ teaspoon ground CINNAMON
½ cup POWDERED SUGAR, for dusting
½ cup WILDFLOWER HONEY, to drizzle

MAKES ABOUT 40 FRITTERS

Place the raisins and the marsala in a small bowl and allow the raisins to soak overnight. Place the ricotta in the center of the cheesecloth and tie it up like a hobo pack. Place a dowel, or any kitchen tool, over a deep kitchen bowl and suspend the pack of cheese with some string tied to the dowel. Put it in the refrigerator to drain overnight.

PREPARATION

Place the olive oil in a pot with tall sides or deep-fryer and heat to 370°F (you may need an oil thermometer).

Drain the raisins and set the extra marsala aside. Remove the ricotta from the cheesecloth and place it in a medium bowl. Add the raisins, flour, eggs, pepper, and cinnamon and stir to mix well. Using two tablespoons, form oval orbs about 2 inches long and drop them into the hot oil one at a time. Cook, 3 or 4 at a time, until a deep golden brown, about 3 minutes. Remove carefully with a slotted spoon to a plate lined with paper towels and dust with the powdered sugar. Continue until all of the dough is fried. Place the fritters on a plate, drizzle with honey, and serve immediately.

WINE RECOMMENDATION: A lightly chilled marsala or Malvasia delle Lipari.

Sardegna
The Big Mystery

—❧—

An Officer and a Gentleman

Before we caught the ferry to Olbia, more than one person said: Get a good map, go slow, and don't get lost. There are certain parts of Sardinia, most notably the Barbagia in the island's mountainous center, that are not only short on street signs but are apparently crawling with criminals. Some are illegal immigrants from Albania looking for a place to hide—and the hills of the Barbagia are as remote as it gets. Others are kidnappers who take people to the hills and hold them for ransom.

So we're feeling a little paranoid as we make our way toward Nuoro on SS 129. It's a hot and dusty drive, with no signs of a town anywhere on the immediate horizon. We pass a solitary shepherd sitting in the grass near the road, his flock off in the rocky pasture in the distance, and he follows the car with dark, suspicious eyes. Along the route there are a handful of the prehistoric stone-block dwellings known as *nuraghi*, most of them incredibly well preserved, as if the only civilizing attempt in the area since the Stone Age was the laying down of the asphalt for the superstrada. (If the shepherd hadn't been talking on a cell phone,

the feeling might have been more complete.)

Plus, the route is crawling with cops. Paranoia, it would seem, was not entirely unjustified. Nearly every crest of a hill has a *carabiniere* posted on the other side. In the course of about three miles, we're waved over three times.

Our car is a piece of junk—an old Fiat Chroma, the Ford Taurus of Fiats, noteworthy for being easy to steal. And our tags say Udine—the car is registered to our friend Valter in Friuli, on the far side of the mainland. So we are a natural target for the police. If we were Sardinian cops looking for contraband, we'd probably pull us over, too. Matters are complicated somewhat by our being Americans, although the process of explaining who we are and what we're doing here doesn't take too long. But it's still intimidating: Any one of these guys could bust us for the ten cases of wine samples we have in the trunk, but being American seems to help a lot. They just tell us to slow down and move on.

The third carabiniere is the most chatty. Emboldened by the relative congeniality of the first two encounters, we ask him what he's looking for. *"Extracommunitari,"* he says (illegals). Then, in perfect English: "And speeders. You know, you cannot travel more than one hundred kilometers per hour on Sardegna roads."

He ponders whether or not to write us up.

The DOC Zones of Sardegna

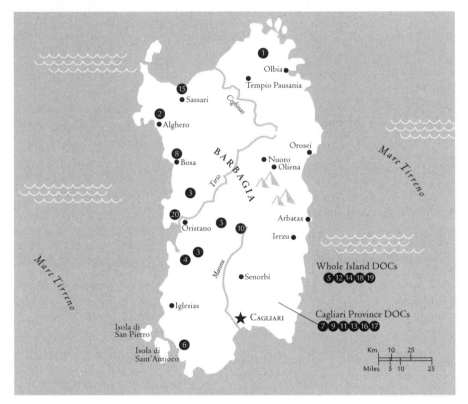

Whole Island DOCs
5 12 14 18 19

Cagliari Province DOCs
7 9 11 13 16 17

Km. 10 25
Miles 5 10 25

DOCG

1 Vermentino di Gallura

DOC

2 Alghero
3 Arborea
4 Campidano di Terralba/Terralba
5 Cannonau di Sardegna
6 Carignano del Sulcis
7 Girò di Cagliari
8 Malvasia di Bosa
9 Malvasia di Cagliari

10 Mandrolisai
11 Monica di Cagliari
12 Monica di Sardegna
13 Moscato di Cagliari
14 Moscato di Sardegna
15 Moscato di Sorso-Sennori
16 Nasco di Cagliari
17 Nuragus di Cagliari
18 Sardegna Semidano
19 Vermentino di Sardegna
20 Vernaccia di Oristano

But when he learns we're on a wine-and-food tour, his sense of duty is tested. He rattles off three nearby wineries and insists that we go to a particular restaurant outside Dorgali that serves *la cucina tipica* of the Barbagia. This is a key word, *tipica* (typical). Like so many Italians, our new carabiniere friend has a keen sense of the history of his hometown fare. (It's probably not much different than a North Carolina cop sounding off on the best barbecue, but this setting is so wild it seems somehow more meaningful.) He says that it is "very important" to try this restaurant. He even goes as far as to call ahead and tell them we're coming.

After a brisk handshake we take off, level off at an even hundred, and drive unmolested into Nuoro. After visiting a few *cantine* we decide to check out the restaurant, a fairly modern complex outside Dorgali that sits on a lonely, rocky bluff. The Mediterranean is a deep blue about ten kilometers to the east, while the surrounding hills are covered in the fragrant Mediterranean scrub known as *macchia*, some scattered vineyards, and olive groves. In a small stone-walled courtyard off to the side of the restaurant they are spit-roasting about six suckling pigs, freshly killed by the looks of things. The spits are arranged to form a teepee of pig flesh over a slow-burning pile of embers. The scents of the *macchia*—wild sage, mint, fennel, eucalyptus, myrtle—are hanging heavy in the air. There are a few bundles of myrtle twigs near the roasting pit, which are used to stoke the fire occasionally and to imbue the meat with their scent. The heady combination of roasting meat and fragrant herbs literally sticks to our clothes and follows us inside.

The restaurant is surprisingly ornate. It is more a party hall than a restaurant, with large chandeliers, a dance floor, and a picture window that looks to the Mediterranean. We talk a bit with the owner, mention the carabiniere episode, and within minutes a greatest hits of Barbagia cuisine starts arriving in waves from the kitchen. It begins with an old-time shepherd's dish called *pane frattau*, in which a piece of the island's famous unleavened flatbread, *pane carasau* (music paper), is briefly soaked in broth and topped with tomato, a poached egg, and grated pecorino. Then there are some pastas: *maccarones furriaos*, gnocchi with grated pecorino and saffron; and *anzellotti*, a pillow-like ravioli filled with fresh ricotta and *mentuccia*, a mintlike Mediterranean herb.

Next comes a heaping plate of lamb offal: *cordedda* (intestines), *cervelletta* (brain), and *tataliu* (heart). Simply cooked, with not much in the way of side dishes or garnishes to accompany them, the innards are pungent, their textures a little foreign. But in Sardinia this is the most *tipica* of the *cucina tipica*. As many have noted, Sardinia is nothing like its island neighbor to the south. Sardinia's food is first and foremost the food of the lonely, savage interior. Although tourists on the *Costa Smeralda* (Emerald Coast) to the north eat rock lobsters washed down with crisp vermentino wine, seafood preparations are a very recent phenomenon on the island; historically Sardinians avoided the coastal areas, fearing not only the malaria that once plagued them but the assorted foreign invaders—who, of course, eventually helped shape the cuisine and the culture.

Finally some suckling pig, or *porceddu*, arrives at the table. This is undoubtedly the signature dish of the island. The pig has been roasted so slowly and basted so frequently with its drippings that the skin is like a caramel-candy shell. The meat is fork-tender and exotically perfumed. We're drinking an earthy red Cannonau di Sardegna, a specialty of the Barbagia, and the combination is every bit as rustic, primal, and perfect as a red Burgundy with *côte du boeuf*. It's the kind of eating and drinking that gets the adrenaline flowing, making you feel like you're around some prehistoric campfire gnawing on a huge leg of mutton—even in a room painted sea foam green, with dainty fabric slipcovers on the chairs.

And there's still dessert after all that: *seadas*, a fried ravioli of sheep's-milk ricotta topped with a bitter, citrusy Sardinian honey. Just as we dig in, who walks into the adjacent bar but the carabiniere who sent us. He orders a *caffé* and comes right over to the table like a long-lost friend, beaming. "I told you, eh?" he says in English. "There aren't many Sardinian restaurants that serve the *real* Sardinian food."

It turns out that the owner of the restaurant is his brother-in-law, but we don't feel like we got taken. Just really full. And a little savage. The Barbagia will do that to you. Even if there are cut flowers on the table.

Of Italy's two Mediterranean isles, Sicily fits more seamlessly into the Italian whole. Sardinia has an aloofness that betrays its distance not only from the mainland (about eight hours on the express ferry, regardless of the jumping-off point) but also from its southern-Mediterranean neighbor. Although Sardinia and Sicily both have an other-worldly feel, Sardinia feels less like an Italian region with exotic ethnic touches, and more like an ethnicity unto itself. The wines that crop up in the island's boulder-strewn soils often have a similarly indefinable, incomparable quality.

Of course, Sardinia and Sicily have many similarities. Both sit in the path of the fierce north African *scirocco*, and both are subject to more intense heat and light than any wine region on the mainland. As such, they were historically known for thick, sweet dessert wines that recalled the fortified wines of Spain. Both have been defined in recent times by a cooperative winery culture, although Sardinia's co-ops were quicker to re-tool in the seventies and eighties and orient themselves toward bottled, "branded" wine. And both are incredibly diverse wine regions, by no means universally hot and dry but almost mini-continents unto themselves, capable of producing both rich, well-structured reds and aromatic, high-acid whites.

Sardinia, though, has not yet seen the boom in vineyard investment that Sicily has, for a variety of reasons. In the end, it may be too remote and sparsely populated to support any major wine revolution. But this is not to say that Sardinia hasn't captured the attention of the mainland: The Tuscan enologist Giacomo Tachis, of "Sassicaia" and Antinori fame, consults to the Argiolas and Santadi wineries in southern Sardinia, while *piemontese* winemaker Beppe Caviola has been lured to the northern shores of the island to work with Tenute Capichera. The Sella & Mosca estate in Alghero, with more than twelve hundred acres under vine, is one of the largest private wineries in Europe. And Sardinia's co-ops, among them Santadi and the Cantine del Vermentino, release wines that consistently win critical raves.

"Up until the 1950s, winemaking was really a farmhouse culture in Sardinia," explains Agostino Pisano, director of the Cantine della Trexenta, a leading cooperative based in the hills north of Cagliari. "Agriculture here was dominated by cereal grains since the time of the Romans. But after the Second World War there was a big push by the Italian government to plant vineyards here, as elsewhere. Most of the wineries now doing business in Sardinia were created during that time."

Like other regions heavily populated with co-ops (such as Sicily and Puglia), Sardinia has weathered tumultuous shifts in the marketplace. Says Pisano: "First we planted a tremendous amount of vineyards and made *vino da taglio*"—cutting wine, or bulk wine—"that was used by producers all over the mainland and in France. You can be sure that plenty of Roman Frascati was laced with nuragus from Sardegna. But of course the market for bulk wine dried up and suddenly we're ripping out everything we planted."

According to Pisano, the Trexenta co-op made about one hundred thousand hectoliters of wine in 1974, from more than two thousand acres of vines managed by the co-op's member-growers. Today, they produce about fifteen to twenty thousand hectoliters from roughly seven hundred acres of member vineyards. "It's like we've come full circle in only two decades," Pisoni says. "But the end result is that those who did remain in wine had to reengineer. Our first bottled wines came out in the mid-eighties. When you think about all the wine history on this island, that's incredible to consider.

"It took a while for Italian co-ops to figure this out, and some are still figuring it out, but we actually make more money now with much less production, because of the prices the wines can command in the market," he continues. "These days we have member-growers planting experimental vineyards and doing whatever else they can to modernize their farms. I think Sardinia was faster than most in making this change."

VINI BIANCHI
White Wines

Although the ancient Phoenicians, Sardinia's earliest foreign invaders, introduced winemaking to the island, the Spaniards left the most indelible mark on *il vino sardo*. Spain's Aragon Dynasty controlled Sardinia from the fourteenth to eighteenth centuries, and in that time they not only molded the regional dialect—Catalan Spanish is still spoken in Alghero, over dishes of paella, no less—but determined the future of the vineyards.

It is widely believed that Sardinia's best-regarded white grape, vermentino, is of Spanish origin. More certain is the parentage of the island's two top reds, cannonau and carignano, the former a synonym for Spain's garnacha (France's grenache), the latter the Italianized name for the carignan found in both Spain and France. The Spanish appear to have influenced not only the content of Sardinian wines but also the style, as evidenced by rarities such as Vernaccia di Oristano and Malvasia di Bosa, two DOC wines from the west coast of the island made in a Sherry style (see below).

Among the dry whites, the vermentino grape has emerged as Sardinia's star variety. In the northeastern region of Gallura in particular, where the vines must struggle to put down roots in granitic soils, vermentino can reach heights of concentration and aroma unequaled in the other parts of the Mediterranean. Although vermentino is by nature an assertively aromatic variety, in Sardinia it is especially evocative of the fragrant Mediterranean *macchia*, with its heady scents of wild herbs. As in Tuscany and Liguria, where it also thrives, vermentino is the wine to look for among the whites of Sardinia.

"It has a fairly big grape bunch, and it tends to fill up very quickly with water," says Mario Consorte, enologist at Sella & Mosca, whose "La Cala" Vermentino di Sardegna is a consistently clean, fragrant white. "Vermentino needs a very dry, well-ventilated climate, otherwise it's susceptible to breakage and rot."

Although the Vermentino di Sardegna DOC zone covers the entire island, the area best suited to the grape is widely agreed to be the Gallura region. Best known for its heavily developed *Costa Smeralda* (the Emerald Coast, a series of swank shoreline resorts developed by the Aga Khan in the sixties), the Gallura is nevertheless one of the loneliest, scrubbiest, rockiest wine regions in all of Italy. And yet Vermentino di Gallura has become the island's only DOCG classification, which was granted in 1996. Known also for its cork-oak trees, the Gallura—which consumes roughly the northeastern quarter of the island—brings out the best in the masochistic vermentino vine.

"Vermentino likes hot, and it likes dry," sums up Mario Ragnedda, co-owner of Tenute Capichera in Arzachena, probably the Gallura zone's top vermentino producer. "But the big issue is soil. It is a very vigorous, generous plant, and it needs the poorest soils possible in order to hold that vigor in check. Here we have a very thin layer of sandy topsoil over solid granite." Not far from the Capichera winery in Arzachena, in fact, is a giant prehistoric burial site known as the *tomba dei gigante* (tomb of the giants), in which giant slabs of granite are arranged in a dramatic arc at the crest of a steep hill.

At the same time, the Gallura is not quite as hot as some might think. Vineyard elevations in the region reach up to fifteen hundred feet. And while southern Sardinia is laid bare to the *scirocco*, the Gallura is more directly affected by cooler breezes from the north. Although still torrid and parched throughout the summer, the Gallura's vineyards benefit from the important fluctuation of day and night temperatures, enjoying a cooling each night that refreshes them and maintains acidity in the grapes.

While there are a number of tangy, flavorful wines made under the Vermentino di Sardegna appellation (Argiolas' "Costamolino" is an especially good one), the deepest expression of the grape is found among the Vermentino di Gallura DOCG wines. Leading the way are the plump, savory vermentinos of Capichera, in which the spicy fennel-and-sage aromatics of the wine are bolstered with a layer of juicy green-melon fruit. The same can be said for the two leading co-ops of Gallura, the Cantina Gallura in Tempio Pausania and the Cantina del Vermentino in Monti. The Gallura *cantina* is best known for a potent single-vineyard vermentino called "Canayli," among others; the Cantina del Vermentino has had great success in the United States with "Funtanaliras," also a powerfully perfumed, full-bodied white.

The proven superiority of the Gallura zone has also lured the giant Sella & Mosca firm, which purchased a vineyard and small winery in the zone a few years ago. Tasting the Sella & Mosca Vermentino di Gallura, called "Monteoro," alongside its benchmark "La Cala" Vermentino di Sardegna, clearly demonstrates the differences in depth and concentration: The La Cala is a light, clean, spicy white, with all of the requisite scrub-brushy vermentino aromas, while the "Monteoro" is decidedly juicier, fleshier, and more intense, its melony fruit flavors intertwined with herbal scents. "We get a level of depth and concentration in the vermentino of Gallura that we really can't get anywhere else," says Mario Consorte. "It's a function of low yields and a slightly longer growing season."

For the most part, vermentino is the dominant white variety in the northern half of Sardinia, while the lesser-regarded nuragus grape is more widespread in the southern reaches. Nuragus is mostly planted in the broad, hot Campidano plain that runs from Cagliari to Oristano, and is produced in such quantities that it rarely becomes more than a tartly acidic seafood white to serve as cold as possible. There are mouthwatering notes of sour apples and almonds in some of the better Nuragus di Cagliari DOC wines, which, along with their tooth-chattering acidity, lend them a kinship to wines such as Portugal's Vinho Verde and Spain's Albariño. Although much more difficult to find than the above-mentioned vermentino wines, the Nuragus di Cagliari wines of Argiolas (called "Sèlegas"), Meloni, and Trexenta are well worth a try on a hot summer day, when their refreshing acidity will liven up a calamari salad or some other light, lemony seafood preparation.

Rarer still are wines from the torbato grape, which is also of Spanish-French origin (it is known as tourbat in France). At the moment torbato is the nearly exclusive province of the Sella & Mosca estate, which has tried to revive interest in the variety. Although it is believed to have been a part of Sardinian viticulture since the sixteenth century, Consorte says torbato has all but disappeared, save for Sella & Mosca's "Terre Bianche" bottling. The wine is exotically aromatic, not unlike vermentino in that regard, and is more powerfully structured

than even the biggest Gallura white. Consorte views it not just as a good wine but as a link to Sardinia's somewhat mysterious vinous past. "It's possible that the Phoenicians brought it here first and only afterward did it get to France and Spain," Consorte says. "There's a rich viticultural heritage in Sardinia and only now are we beginning to understand it."

VINI ROSSI
Red Wines

There is slightly more red wine produced in Sardinia than white, and Sardinian reds divide neatly along geographic and stylistic lines, even more so than the whites. There's monica, a light, bright, berry-scented grape most common in the flatlands north of Cagliari; cannonau, a deeper, more flavorful variety grown everywhere, but considered at its best in the Barbagia hills south of Nuoro; and carignano, the inkiest and fruitiest of the group, which is more or less confined to the southwestern corner of the island, in a region known as the Sulcis. From these three grapes, Sardinia makes a surprisingly interesting spectrum of red wines.

The best known and most planted of the three is cannonau, which, according to legend, was imported to the island by Spanish conquerors in the thirteenth century. The grape is referred to as alicante (another synonym for grenache in Italy), and it appears to have taken on its new name during the Battle of Lepanto in 1571. During this sea clash—the Ottoman Turks against Spanish, Venetian, Genovese and other forces—the Spanish were said to have loaded ships with "courage, cannon, and Sardinian wine."

Sardinian cannonau is not especially colorful—it tends to begin browning at a fairly young age. But its rich and earthy flavors of tar, tobacco, and wild red berries make it an ideal accompaniment for the spit-roasted meats of the island. Cannonau's rustic flavors draw comparisons to Spanish Rioja (of which *garnacha* is a key component) and the spicy reds of the Languedoc in France. Sella & Mosca's Mario Consorte describes cannonau as a *vino selvatico* (wild wine)—a wine that, like the white vermentino, evokes its untamed surroundings.

Like vermentino, cannonau is well adapted to the often extreme heat and dryness of Sardinia. Although the Cannonau di Sardegna DOC zone covers the entire island, most producers agree that the ideal spots for cannonau are the foothills north and east of the Gennargentu mountains, running from Nuoro down to Capo Ferrato on the southeastern coast. There are three official subzones of the Cannonau di Sardegna DOC: Oliena, named for a town just south of Nuoro; Jerzu, farther south; and Capo Ferrato, farther south still. Situated in coastal hills with very mixed soils—granite, some clay, some volcanic material, and some sand—the vines are subject to withering Mediterranean heat but also cooling breezes from the inland mountains and points farther north. The result is a leathery, potent red with a good tannic grip, its only major flaw being its often faint hue.

"Cannonau is more concentrated here than grenache is in the Languedoc," says Mariano Murru, a young enologist who works at the Argiolas estate. "That is mainly a function of the heat. The only problem, really, is color. It's surprising to taste cannonau after you look at it, because it looks like it will be a light wine."

Probably the most critically acclaimed cannonau-based wine in Sardinia is a non-DOC red from Argiolas called "Turriga," a deeply concentrated, barrique-aged blend containing 85 percent cannonau and 15 percent of a combination of malvasia nera, carignano, and a Sardinian oddity called bovale sardo. This colorful supporting cast lends a deeper hue and a layer of juicy fat to the spicy, eucalyptus-scented cannonau, creating a wine that is dense, decadent, and complex.

Wines such as "Turriga" and Sella & Mosca's "Tanca Farrà (cannonau–cabernet sauvignon) put a modern sheen on a rustic variety, and while they have become the most sought-after cannonaus, they are not necessarily the best. Cannonau on its own is more medium-bodied, very similar to pinot noir in scale, with flavors of crushed wild berries and cherry kirsch overlain with leathery, herbal notes. Like vermentino, it is a wine that whets your appetite for food. Perhaps most interesting is the way even a young cannonau has the aromatic profile of a more mature red. Along with Sella & Mosca and Argiolas, there are a host of well-regarded cannonau producers throughout the island, including Giuseppe Gabbas and Alessandro Loi in the Barbagia and Tenute Soletta near Sassari.

And if cannonau is Sardinia's red-wine equivalent of vermentino, monica (another Spanish import) is the red-wine equivalent of the light white nuragus. Monica is grown throughout the southern half of the island, particularly on the Campidano plain north of Cagliari. There are two DOC zones for monica, one that covers the whole island and the other that is more specific to the Cagliari area. Monica has a buoyant cherry-berry flavor and is often good with a slight chill to tame its sometimes sharp acidity, and should be drunk young. Given the current fashion for big reds, it is not a wine exported in great quantities to the United States, although Argiolas' "Perdera" Monica di Sardegna (probably the most concentrated of the lot) is well distributed, as is the monica of Meloni Vini, a large winery situated just outside Cagliari.

Sardinia's red-wine trio is rounded out by carignano, typically the darkest and most powerful of the three. The Carignano del Sulcis DOC zone encompasses the southwestern corner of the island, where the fierce *scirocco* breezes sweep through the rugged hills, prompting most vintners to retain the classic *alberello* (bush vine) training system, wherein the plants are trained very low to the ground.

As noted in the *Oxford Companion to Wine*, the carignano grape is "high in everything—acidity, tannin, color, bitterness—except finesse and charm." This may be true. But in the carignano of Sulcis, the Sardinians have their "power red" to compete with everything from super-Tuscans to California cabernet. Planted in the sandy clays of the Sulcis region, the grape reaches brawny heights of concentration in wines such as "Terre Brune," a Carignano del Sulcis DOC made by the Cantina Sociale Santadi. A lot of people are surprised to learn that Santadi is a co-op when they taste "Terre Brune," a wine that is as black as the Sardinian night and every bit as mysterious. It's got some of the peppery spice of an Australian shiraz or a Rhône syrah, with a core of juicy fruit that gives it some accessibility as a young wine. Similarly buxom is the "Assajè" Carignano del Sulcis made by Tenute Capichera, from a small vineyard in the Sulcis region that the winery began leasing a few years ago to experiment with the variety.

Also growing in popularity in the Sulcis region is syrah, a vine well adapted to extreme heat and dryness. Santadi, in fact, has released a wine called "Shardana" that combines carignano with syrah to luscious effect—the wine goes down like hot cocoa. Unfortunately, Santadi is more or less the only game in town in Sulcis, a region with unlimited potential for powerhouse reds.

"We can get so much concentration in the grapes down there," says Mario Ragnedda of Capichera, who, at this writing, was planning the release of a new, barrique-aged carignano to take on "Terre Brune" (the first vintage will be '99). "The Sulcis could be the next Australia or Napa Valley."

VINI SPUMANTI E DOLCI
Sparkling and Sweet Wines

Looking at the DOC map of Sardinia is like a walk through a wine museum. It's filled with oddities, most of them sweet and fortified wines on the verge of extinction.

Given the intense heat and light of the island, Sardinia was traditionally predisposed toward thick, syrupy sweet wines, many of them based on the moscato and malvasia grapes. Today, there remain three DOC wines from moscato on the island: Moscato di Sardegna, a sparkling sweet white not unlike Moscato d'Asti in Piedmont; Moscato di Cagliari, made in sweet and fortified versions; and Moscato di Sorso-Sennori, which at this point exists in name only. From the malvasia grape comes Malvasia di Cagliari and the increasingly rare Malvasia di Bosa, which is made in a style reminiscent of Sherry—both dry and sweet. Other sweet sippers include Girò di Cagliari, a red that might substitute for tawny Port, and a variety of *amabile* (semisweet) and *dolce* (sweet) versions of grapes such as monica and vermentino. But these wines have become so marginalized they are all but impossible to find outside of Sardinia. In fact, they're not so easy to find in Sardinia.

The one fortified wine with some noteworthy production (and producers) is Vernaccia di Oristano, Italy's answer to Fino and Amontillado Sherry. The Attilio Contini winery in Cabras is widely regarded as the top producer of the wine, and his vernaccias really have no peer anywhere in Italy.

On the alluvial plains north of Oristano, current owner-winemaker Antonio Contini runs the winery with his brother, Paolo. They achieve a very high level of natural sugars in the vernaccia grapes (the grape is a different variety altogether from the vernaccia of San Gimignano in Tuscany), which are fermented into high-alcohol wines. The wines are placed in small chestnut casks that are filled to only 90 percent capacity, so that the beneficial film-forming yeast known as *flor* can form on the surface of the wines. Once all the fermentable sugars in the wine have been consumed, *flor* yeasts actually change their metabolism and begin to consume both oxygen and alcohol, forming a milky coating in the process. In small casks laid out in Contini's cool cellars, the wines maintain a fragile balance in which the evaporation of water from the casks balances out the consumption of alcohol by the *flor*, preventing the wine from turning into vinegar.

Contini's basic Vernaccia di Oristano is aged a minimum of six years in these small casks, its main difference from Sherry being that it is never topped off with younger wines (a process that, in Sherry-making, gives the yeast more nutrients to feed on). In the Contini wines, which include a bottling called "Antico Gregori" (a blend of wines of varying ages, including some that are thirty years old and more), the complex flavors of almonds, orange rind, tobacco, tea, and honey all intermingle in wines that hint at sweetness but finish dry. Antico Gregori, which reaches 19 percent alcohol naturally, tastes almost like Calvados, with a nutty, fruity intensity that brings to mind a good Amontillado Sherry.

One of Sardinia's few seafood specialties is *orata alla vernaccia,* a sauté of the small, white-fleshed Mediterranean sea bream finished with a healthy splash of Vernaccia di Oristano. The wine's raisiny, nutty intensity also makes it a great apéritif alongside the sharp sheep's-milk cheeses of the island and some salty olives. To drink it is to go to one of the most remote corners of Italian wine, although for American consumers it requires some extra effort to get there: Only about eighty thousand bottles of Vernaccia di Oristano are produced per year, so bottles come at a premium.

FAST FACTS: SARDEGNA

PROVINCES	Cagliari (CA), Nuoro (NU), Oristano (OR), Sassari (SS)
CAPITAL	Cagliari
KEY WINE TOWNS	Alghero, Cagliari, Oristano, Santadi, Tempio Pausania
TOTAL VINEYARD AREA*	43,331 hectares, or 107,070 acres. Rank: 8th
TOTAL WINE PRODUCTION*	1,062,000 hectoliters, or 28,058,124 gallons (12th); 43% white, 57% red.
DOC WINE PRODUCED*	15.6% (12th)
SPECIALTY FOODS	pecorino cheeses; *pane carasau* (unleavened flatbread); honey, including lavender and citrus-blossom; suckling pig; almonds; *sapa* (a sweet syrup made from reduced grape must); *bottarga* (dried mullet roe).

*1997 figures. Rankings out of twenty regions total (Trentino–Alto Adige counted as one). Source: Istituto Statistica Mercati Agro-Alimentari (ISMEA), Rome.

KEY GRAPE VARIETIES

WHITES

VERMENTINO	Its origins are debated, but it is widely believed to have come from Spain. Known for assertively fragrant whites from all over the island, but especially the Gallura zone in the northeast.
NURAGUS	Extremely vigorous variety, of ancient Phoenician origin, found mainly in the southern plains. High yields result in light, tartly acidic wines with aromatics reminiscent of vermentino, albeit not as dramatic.

VERNACCIA	Not to be confused with the vernaccia of San Gimignano (Tuscany), this plump, sugar-rich grape is used to make Sherry-style wines in Oristano.
MOSCATO AND MALVASIA	Both varieties are found in Sardinia, though most of the sweet, sparkling, and fortified wines made from them are nearing extinction.

REDS

MONICA	Lightly colored (and flavored) red of Spanish origin. Widely planted in the southern plains, it produces fresh, light, fruity reds.
CANNONAU (ALSO CANNONAO)	The Italian synonym for garnacha, or grenache. A hardy variety that produces wines with a decidedly leathery, earthy, even gamey personality. Fruit flavors are reminiscent of cherry kirsch and wild red berries. Medium-bodied.
CARIGNANO	Inky and rich, with firm tannins and more concentration than most cannonau. Found primarily in the southwestern corner of the island.
OTHERS	SYRAH, CABERNET SAUVIGNON, MERLOT.

TOP VINTAGES IN SARDINIA, 1980–2000

Some of Sardinia's big reds—such as Santadi's "Terre Brune," Sella & Mosca's "Marchese di Villamarina" cabernet sauvignon, and Argiolas's "Turriga"—will benefit greatly from several years (even five to ten years) of aging. Top recent red wine vintages on the island include 1996, '97, '99.

LA STRADA DEL VINO
WINE TOURING IN SARDINIA

There may be no more spectacular beachfront in all of Italy than the Costa Smeralda, which is centered on the town of Porto Cervo on the northeast coast. Essentially a string of resorts, it is a fairly exclusive hangout for wealthy Europeans who descend on the area in droves during *ferragosto,* a week in the middle of August when Italy all but closes down for vacation. Those is search of more wine-related activities will have to head elsewhere, and anyone wishing to truly explore the island should budget two weeks, whether wine is involved or not.

A logical first stop is the Sella & Mosca winery just outside of Alghero (Località I Piani, Alghero, 079-99-77-00, www.sellaemosca.com), which has a beautiful wine shop and a small museum of old wine tools and other artifacts. Base yourself in Alghero, where there are a number of excellent seafood restaurants (including La Lepanto). From Alghero, check out stunning coastal towns such as Stintino (at the extreme northwest corner of the island). Then head down to Cagliari and later, if you're game, return to Olbia via the rugged east coast (stopping perhaps at Orosei, home to some dramatic beaches and caves). In fact, for all of the wild, untamed stretches of Sardinia, its wineries are extremely well organized, with many keeping regular visitors hours. The DOC Wine Consortium of Sardinia publishes an excellent guide, in English, to the various wine zones of the island, complete with suggested itineraries, recommended restaurants, and useful phone numbers. Consorzio Vini DOC di Sardegna, Via dell'Artigianato 11, Cagliari; 070-24-11-40; www.sol.dada.it/consorzio-vinidoc.

DEGUSTAZIONI
TASTINGS

VERMENTINO

Sella & Mosca Vermentino di Sardegna "La Cala," $

Cantina del Vermentino Vermentino di Gallura "Funtanaliras," $

Tenute Capichera Vermentino di Gallura Classico, $

Start with the La Cala, the lightest and easiest of the lot: it has the requisite vermentino aromas of wild sage, fennel, and other aromatic herbs, balanced on a wave of refreshing acidity. "Funtanaliras" steps up the intensity somewhat, with a jolt of green-melon fruitiness to accent the herbal aromas, but finishes with a palate-cleansing chalkiness typical of the grape. The Capichera wine, a percentage of which is barrel-fermented, has a push-pull of creamy and spicy flavors. All are aromatic whites perfectly suited for the aggressively seasoned *zuppa di pesce* (fish soup) or other seafood preparations incorporating aromatic herbs. Vermentino is a great food wine.

Tenute Soletta Cannonau di Sardegna "Firmadu," $

Sella & Mosca Cannonau di Sardegna Riserva, $

Argiolas "Turriga," $$

CANNONAU

Again, this flight is arranged in ascending order, based on body. The Soletta wine shows off the wild-berry side of Cannonau, almost pinot noir–ish in its soft, plush fruitiness. The Sella & Mosca wine brings out some of the feral aspects of the grape, with more mature aromas of leather, tar, and pipe tobacco on top of a base of berry fruit. In "Turriga," a blend, both the color and flavor are much more intense, but the exotic eucalyptus aroma of the cannonau still shines through. These wines are great choices for grilled or roasted meats, especially suckling pig and lamb. Though tougher to find, other cannonaus worth seeking out include those of Giuseppe Gabbas, Argiolas, Alessandro Loi, and Attilio Contini.

Meloni Monica di Sardegna, $

Sella & Mosca "Raím," $$

Santadi Carignano del Sulcis "Terre Brune," $$$

OTHER REDS

This is a broad spectrum of wines, starting with the light, bright Monica and shifting abruptly to the richer carignano grape. The Monica, a good wine to serve with a chill, is all bright acid and light cherry flavor, perfect as a pasta wine or even a red for grilled fish. In "Raim," a blend of carignano and cabernet sauvignon, the volume is turned up a bit, with a more concentrated, plump flavor of crushed black raspberries. In "Terre Brune," the volume is turned up to ten in a deeply flavorful expression of carignano: blacker and bigger than "Raim," with tannins the consistency of ground cocoa, this powerhouse needs some spit-roasted meat to tame it. Sardinia is just the place for that.

La Cucina
FOOD FOR THE WINE
RECIPE BY MARIO BATALI

Countless food writers have remarked on the dearth of seafood dishes in Sardinia, despite its long, spectacular coastline. Although *aragosta* (lobster) and paella are popular dishes in coastal cities such as Alghero, Sardinian cuisine is without question dominated by the foods of shepherds and other hill dwellers.

Nothing says Sardinia quite like suckling pig—*porceddu* in the local parlance—which some inlanders still cook by burying it in the ground with wild herbs and hot rocks. Spit-roasting, meanwhile, is an art form on the island: a slow, deliberate process with lots of basting, so that the skin is crackling when done. The recipe below is sort of a city-boy's answer to *porceddu*, finished off with one of Sardinia's most celebrated exports—bitter honey—as a substitute for that crackling skin. Open a bottle of cannonau or carignano and imagine yourself under the stars in the Barbagia, checking on your flock by the light of a campfire. Make sure there's also plenty of pecorino cheese to nibble on and maybe some *pane carasau* (widely available in specialty food shops), which is especially good brushed with olive oil and sprinkled with salt.

Porchetta Sarda
ROAST PORK IN THE SARDINIAN STYLE

5-pound piece PORK LOIN, butterflied and lightly pounded to form a 10-by-7-inch square, about ½- to ¾-inch thick

4 tablespoons KOSHER SALT

12 large cloves GARLIC, cut into 4 pieces each

1 cup VERMENTINO WINE, or other dry white wine

12 fresh SAGE LEAVES, julienned

2 bunches ITALIAN PARSLEY, finely chopped

¼ cup plus two tablespoons extra-virgin OLIVE OIL

½ cup HONEY, preferably acacia or the bitter Sardinian variety, which can be found in specialty food shops

zest and juice of 1 LEMON

1 cup CHICKEN STOCK

SERVES 8 TO 10

Place the pork in a pan large enough to hold it comfortably and cover it with 3 tablespoons of the salt and 4 cups of water. Place in the refrigerator and allow it to brine overnight. Mash the cloves of garlic into a paste and put them into a cup or bowl with the wine. Allow to sit overnight at room temperature.

PREPARATION
Preheat oven to 450°F.

Rinse the pork under running water to remove the salt and dry it with paper towels. Place the garlic and wine mixture in a mixing bowl, and add the sage and parsley, then whisk in the ¼ cup of the olive oil. Season the meat inside with the remaining tablespoon of salt and rub the wine-garlic paste over the surface. Roll the pork like a jelly roll and tie with butchers' knots at 1-inch intervals.

Place the tied pork loin in a roasting pan just large enough to accommodate it. Mix the honey with the lemon juice and zest and brush the entire surface of the roast with a thin layer of the mixture and season with lots of freshly ground pepper. Place the pan in the oven and cook for 70 minutes, or until the internal temperature taken with a meat thermometer is 140°F. Baste every 15 minutes with the remaining honey mixture.

Remove from the oven and transfer to a cooling rack set over a plate. Let cool for 30 minutes. Place the roasting pan over medium heat and add the remnants of the basting mixture and the chicken stock to deglaze the pan, scraping up the dark bits stuck to the bottom. Bring to a boil and reduce to ⅔ cup. Pour through a strainer into a medium bowl and whisk in the remaining oil to form a light emulsion. Season to taste with salt and pepper and set aside. To serve, remove the twine and carve into 1-inch slices. Drizzle with sauce and serve at room temperature.

PART III

THE DATA

Appendix I

A Glossary of Italian Wine Terms: La Lingua del Vino

⎯⎯⎯ ❦ ⎯⎯⎯

The list below includes terms found regularly on Italian wine labels, many of which can say a lot about a wine, even if the producer or region is unfamiliar. Also listed are some non-Italian wine terms used in this book. What aren't included here are grape names, producer names, or region names, as they each have their own section. Phonetic spellings are included selectively.

ABBOCCATO Semisweet.

AGRONOMY The science of soil management and crop production.

ALBERELLO "Little tree" or "bush"; a term for a spur-trained bush vine. Bush vines, usually without any canes or other supports, are found in Puglia and Sicily in particular. Their compact size helps them resist strong winds, and their shape helps shade grapes from intense sunlight.

AMABILE (ah-MAH-bee-lay) Semisweet.

AMARO Bitter; used as a tasting term and as a name for an apéritif liqueur. The word is thought to be the root of the name *Amarone*, given to the dry red wines of Verona made from semi-dried grapes.

ANNATA Vintage.

ANTHOCYANINS Phenolic compounds that give color to red-wine grapes.

APPASSIMENTO (ah-pah-see-MEN-toh). The process of drying grapes, usually on straw mats (see

graticci) in airy lofts, to concentrate their sugars. Wines made from this process are usually rich and sweet, but in some instances can be dry, with only the perception of sweetness (as in the Amarone wines of Veneto). See also *passito*.

ARGILLA (ar-JEE-lah) Clay. Can be either heavy and hard to work or mixed with other components such as limestone and sand. Heavier clay soils are seen as undesirable because they retain too much water and can drown vines.

AZIENDA AGRICOLA (ah-zee-EN-dah ah-GREE-cola) A winery or estate that produces its wines from at least half estate-grown grapes.

BARRIQUE (bar-EEK) A 225-liter cask made of French oak. Also known as *botticella*.

BIANCO white wine.

BICCHIÈRE (pl. *bicchieri*; bick-YAIR-ay/ee) Glass.

BOTRYTIS A grape fungus that, in a specific form called *Botrytis cinerea*, can be beneficial. Under the right

conditions, botrytis doesn't simply rot grapes but instead initiates a chemical reaction in which tannins are consumed and glycerol is formed. When botrytis attacks in this way, it is called noble rot and the grapes it affects are made into glycerine-rich sweet wines.

BOTTE (pl. *botti*) Large cask for aging wine. Traditionally made from chestnut or Slavonian oak. Usually very large, a typical capacity being 50 hectoliters (about 5,000 bottles). Also called *fusto*.

BOTTIGLIA (boh-TEE-lia) Bottle.

BRICCO Piedmontese term for hilltop vineyard. Sometimes *bric*.

BRUT Dry sparkling wine. *Extra Brut* means very dry. See also *pas dosé*.

CALCAREOUS Any soil with a proportion of limestone mixed in. Typically a cool, well-drained soil that allows grapes to preserve their acidity.

CANTINA Winery/cellar.

CARAFFA Decanter.

CASCINA (ca-SHEE-na) Farmhouse. Often used as part of a winery name.

CAVATAPPI Corkscrew.

CHIARETTO (key-ah-REH-toe): A rosé wine, particularly one made in Bardolino in the Veneto.

CHINATO A bitter, aromatized wine made by infusing herbs into a base of Barolo wine.

CLASSICO (CLAH-see-coh) Classic. A term typically used to denote a historic area (for example, Chianti Classico) within a larger zone.

CLONE In grape terms, a population of vines propagated from the same "mother" plant.

COLLE/COLLINA (pl. *colli/colline*) Hill(s).

CONSORZIO An association, or consortium, of producers.

CONTADINO Farmer.

CORDONE SPERONATA A system of training vines along low wires, to take advantage of ground heat and to restrict production. Cordone differs from *guyot* in that there is a permanent branch from which buds (and eventually grapes) are formed.

CORPOSO Full-bodied.

CRÉMANT French term for a sparkling wine made outside of Champagne, but also used to denote a sparkling wine with slightly lower atmospheric pressure than that of a Champagne.

CRU Single vineyard.

CUVÉE French term for a blend of wines from different grapes.

DOC(G) *Denominazione di Origine Controllata (e Garantita)*, or denomination of controlled (and guaranteed) origin. The two highest Italian wine classifications (see section on "Decoding Italian Wine Laws," page 9, for a full discussion).

DEGUSTAZIONE (day-goo-staht-seeOH-nay) Wine tasting. Also *assaggio*.

DOLCE Sweet.

ENOLOGO (eh-NOH-lo-go) Winemaker.

ENOLOGY The study of wine and winemaking.

ENOTECA Wine shop or wine bar.

ENOTRIA Anglicized spelling of Oenotria, the ancient Greek name for Italy, which means "land of wine."

ETICHETTA (et-ee-KET-ah) Label.

ETTARO (AY-tah-ro) Hectare (see next column).

EXTRACT Technically, all of the solids in a wine, from sugars to minerals to glycerols. A wine said to be extracted has a full, syrupy feel on the palate, almost chewy. Reds have more extract than whites because they have more phenolic compounds.

FATTORIA A large wine estate. Traditionally, the *fattoria* was the central winery on a sharecropping farm, to which the various *poderi* (sharecroppers) would contribute a portion of their grapes.

FIASCO Flask, as in the straw-covered bottles of Chianti.

FORTIFICATO Fortified, also *liquoroso*. Refers to a wine, usually sweet, to which some spirits have been added.

FRESCO Fresh.

FRIZZANTE Lightly bubbly.

GALESTRO Name for the rocky, schist-like soils found in Tuscany. Also a name for a light white table wine made in Tuscany.

GIOVANE (JOH-vah-nay) young,

GRAPPA Brandy made from the skins, stems, seeds, and pulp of grapes after they are pressed. See also *vinaccia*.

GRAPPOLO Bunch of grapes.

GRATICCI Straw mats used to dry grapes in the *appassimento* process.

GUYOT System of training vines on low wires. Unlike *cordone speronata*, the main branch from which grapes hang is replaced every year. Both *guyot* and *cordone speronata* allow producers to plant vines more densely and to more carefully control the production of each vine.

HECTARE The standard unit of vineyard area in Europe. One hectare equals 2.471 acres.

IGT *Indicazione Geografica Tipica*, or geographic origin wine (see section on "Decoding Italian Wine Laws," page 9, for a full discussion).

IMBOTTIGLIATO ALL'ORIGINE Estate-bottled.

INVECCHIATO Aged.

LEES Solids that collect in a fermentation vessel, including spent yeast cells.

MACERATE/MACERAZIONE (mach-er-aht-see-OH-nay). Maceration, the process of leaving the skins in fermenting wine to extract color and tannin.

MARCHIO (MAR-key-oh) Proprietary name or brand.

MARL Cool, calcareous clay.

METODO CHARMAT The Charmat or tank method of sparkling winemaking, in which the secondary fermentation of the wine is carried out in a large pressurized tank.

METODO CLASSICO (MAY-toh-do CLAH-see-ko)/METODO CHAMPENOISE/METODO TRADIZIONALE The Champagne method, or *mèthode champenoise*, of sparkling winemaking, in which sugar and yeast are added to a base wine to induce a secondary fermentation in the bottle.

MOSTO Must.

MOSTO COTTO Literally, cooked must. Term used for grape must whose sugars are concentrated by heating; used to fortify certain types of Marsala wine.

MUFFA NOBILE (NOH-bee-lay) noble rot, or *botrytis cinerea*.

OCCHIO DI PERNICE Literally, "eye of the partrige." A term used for rose-colored Vin Santo made from a predominance of red grapes.

PAS DOSÉ Term used to describe very dry sparkling wines—those to which a final dose of liquor has not been added.

PASSITO Usually sweet wine from semi-dried grapes.

PERGOLA A system of vine training in which the vines are draped over high trellises, usually supported by pole arms. Differs from *tendone* (see below) in that the canopy of grapes is typically tilted upward, rather than lying flat. Widely used in Trentino–Alto Adige.

PHYLLOXERA A small aphid that attacks grapevines. Phylloxera destroyed most of the vineyards of Europe before the turn of the last century, and has wreaked considerable damage in California as well.

PODERE (POH-deh-reh) Small farm holding, traditionally of a sharecropper.

POLYPHENOLS/PHENOLS Chemical compounds found in abundance in wine, especially in the seeds, stems, and skins. They include pigments that give a wine color.

PROFUMO Scent.

RECIOTO A sweet wine made from semidried grapes. Term used primarily in the Veneto. See also *appassimento.*

RISERVA Reserve. Term used to describe a DOC(G) wine aged for a prescribed length of time.

RONCO (pl. *ronchi*) Another local term for hill(s) or hillside vineyard(s), used especially in Friuli–Venezia Giulia.

ROSATO Rosé wine.

ROSSO Red wine.

ROVERE (ROH-veh-ray) Oak.

SAPORE Flavor.

SCIROCCO Warm breeze from North Africa. Another phenomenon that affects the climate in much of southern Italy.

SECCO Dry.

SENTORE DI TAPPO To be corked, or spoiled from cork mold. *Sa di tappo* means "It is corked."

SFURSAT/SFORSATO A term used in Lombardy's Valtellina to describe a wine made using dried

grapes. A Sfursat/Sforsato wine is essentially the same as an Amarone, except that it is made from different grapes.

SIFONE Partially fermented grape must, containing as much as 25 percent pure alcohol, used to fortify some versions of Marsala wine.

SOLERA Typically associated with sherry, it is a system of topping off aging wines in barrels by adding fractions of younger wine. Also used in making Marsala.

SORÌ Piedmontese term for an especially well-exposed vineyard or slope.

SPUMANTE (pl. *spumanti*) Sparkling wine.

SUGHERO (SUE-ghe-ro) Cork (the material).

SUPERIORE A DOC wine that adheres to a certain higher standard (usually, but not always, higher natural alcohol).

TAPPO: Cork, as in a closure to a bottle (see *sentore di tappo*).

TENDONE System of training vines on high, flat trellises. Used in the plains to combat humidity by keeping grapes off the ground. Typically associated with mass production, although carefully cropped tendone vines can produce excellent grapes.

TENUTA Wine estate.

TERRENO Soil.

TERROIR French term that refers to the total natural environment of a vine, including the soil it's planted in, the climate of the area, and the aspect of the vineyard. The notion of terroir can be a vague one to grasp, but it essentially refers to a wine that exhibits characteristics unique to a particular place.

TRANQUILLO/VINO TRANQUILLO Still wine.

TUFA Corruption of the French *tuffeau*, which means calcareous rock.

UVA Grape.

UVAGGIO Blend of grapes.

VECCHIO Old or aged, sometimes an official term on labels that can be used only when a wine meets certain minimum aging requirements. Also *invecchiato* (*invecchiamento* is the aging process).

VENDEMMIA Harvest.

VENDEMMIA TARDIVA Late harvest, as in grapes that are allowed to hang on the vine to become super-ripe. Wines labeled *vendemmia tardiva* are most often sweet.

VIGNERON French word for "vine-grower."

VIGNETO Vineyard.

VIN(O) SANTO Literally "holy wine." Usually a semi-sweet to sweet dessert wine made from grapes that have been left to dry in lofts. Long-aged in small wood barrels, they pick up a distinctive nutty, resiny flavor.

VINACCIA Grape pomace, or the stems, seeds, skins, and pulp left after grapes are pressed.

VINO DA TAGLIO "Cutting wine" used for blending, mostly to bring alcohol levels up to required standards.

VINO DA TAVOLA Table wine, often anonymous bulk wine that isn't given DOC status. But sometimes a *vino da tavola*, or *VdT*, can be a high-end product (see section on "Decoding Italian Wine Laws").

VINO NOVELLO New, or *nouveau*, wine.

VITIGNO Vine variety.

VQPRD Acronym used on wine labels throughout the European Community to denote a "quality" wine made in a delimited region. VSQPRD for sparkling wines.

APPENDIX II
The Grapes: Le Uve

———— ❧ ————

The vineyards of Italy are the most diverse in the world, populated with so many grape varieties that no one knows for sure how many there are. Italy's Ministry of Agriculture and Forestry (MIRAF), based in Rome, has cataloged more than 350 grapes and deemed them "authorized" for planting and selling as wine. However, it is widely believed that there are more than 500 other varieties in circulation, some of them surely finding their way into the wines we drink. So while the following list of grapes is extensive, it by no means represents all the grapes one might encounter in Italy's vineyards.

According to the *Istituto Statistica Mercati Agro-Alimentari (ISMEA)*, a Rome-based organization, there are about 800,000 hectares (almost 2,000,000 acres) of vineyards currently in production throughout Italy. This is a slightly smaller total than either France or Spain, but it is about three times that of the United States. Moreover, from its 800,000 hectares, Italy produces the most wine per year of any country in the world.

Below is a list of authorized grape varieties in Italy, taken from the *Registro Nazionale delle Varietà Autorizzate e Raccomandate*, published by MIRAF. Not all of the authorized varieties are included here, because some are so rare as not to merit a mention. Those listed below contain the following information: grape type (*w* for white, *r* for red); the main region(s) in which the variety is cultivated; and a brief description of the variety, where appropriate. As a means of distinguishing them and to aid cross-referencing, all grape names are capitalized, unlike in the rest of the book.

ABBUOTO (R) Lazio.

AGLIANICO (R) Campania, Basilicata, other southern regions. Conventional wisdom is that this deeply colored, thick-skinned variety was brought to the Italian peninsula by the Greeks; Its name is derived from the term *hellenico* or *ellenico* (Greek). There is also a theory that it was a native wild vine that was later domesticated by the Greeks. Campania lays claim to it, but it's safe to call it native to Basilicata as well.

ALBANA (W) Emilia-Romagna. Native to the eastern half of Emilia-Romagna, historically linked to Rome, where the grape may have come from. Makes light dry whites and unctuous *passito* wines with scents of apricots and citrus.

ALBAROLA (W) Liguria. Light white used in the Cinque Terre.

ALEATICO (R) All regions. An unusual red that may be a mutation of *moscato*, or muscat. Makes sweet, perfumed reds in Lazio, Tuscany, and Puglia (among other regions), but is increasingly rare.

ALICANTE (R) Sardegna, Toscana. Synonym for Garnacha, or Grenache.

ALICANTE BOUSCHET (R) Various regions. French cross of Grenache and Petit Bouschet.

ANCELLOTTA (R) Emilia-Romagna. Deeply colored red used in blends with Lambrusco.

ANSONICA (W) Sicilia, Toscana. Synonym for Inzolia. Makes cool, clean whites with delicate aromas.

ARNEIS (W) Piemonte. Floral, citrusy white native to the Roero hills of Piedmont, where records of its cultivation date back to the 15th century.

ASPRINIO BIANCO (W) Campania. Light white used near Naples for crisp, dry wines and light sparklers.

BARBAROSSA (R) Emilia-Romagna. Rare native red made into a varietal wine by Fattoria Paradiso of Bertinoro.

BARBERA (R) Piedmont, Lombardia, Emilia-Romagna. Highly productive native of Piedmont known for its soft tannins. The second most planted red grape in Italy after Sangiovese.

BARBERA BIANCA (W) Piedmont, Lombardia, Emilia-Romagna. Rare white version of Barbera.

BARBERA SARDA (R) Sardegna.

BELLONE (W) Lazio. Used as a blending variety in a number of Lazio DOC whites.

BIANCAME (W) Marche, Umbria, Abruzzo. Possibly related to Trebbiano. Also known as Passerina or Bianchello.

BIANCHETTA GENOVESE (W) Liguria. Used in Golfo del Tigullio DOC blends.

BIANCHETTA TREVIGIANA (W) Trentino–Alto Adige.

BIANCO D'ALESSANO (W) Puglia. Used in DOC blends such as Gravina, Locorotondo, and Martina Franca.

BIANCOLELLA (W) Campania. A blending variety.

BLANC DE MORGEX (W) Valle d'Aosta. Superacidic white grown at high altitudes in the Valle d'Aosta.

BOMBINO BIANCO (W) Puglia, Emilia-Romagna. Light white, also called Pagadebit in Romagna and Campolese in Abruzzo.

BOMBINO NERO (R) Puglia.

BONARDA (R) Piedmont, Lombardia, Emilia-Romagna. Confusingly, this is a synonym for Croatina used in the Oltrepò Pavese and in the Colli Piacentini in Emilia-Romagna (DOC wines called Bonarda from Oltrepò Pavese are actually made from Croatina). Also confusing is the use of the name Bonarda Novarese in northern Piedmont; Bonarda Novarese is not Bonarda but Uva Rara, also found in Lombardia and Emilia. The real Bonarda, Bonarda Piemontese, is said to be nearly extinct.

BOSCO (W) Liguria. Light white from the Cinque Terre.

BOVALE GRANDE (R) Sardegna. Used as a synonym for Nieddera. Used mainly for blending.

BOVALE (R) Sardegna. Deeply colorful red, thought to be of Spanish origin. Some producers believe it is related to the French Mourvèdre. Used primarily as a blending variety.

BRACHETTO (R) Piemonte. Unusually aromatic red, found mainly in Roero, Asti, and Alessandria.

Makes mostly sweet wines, both still and sparkling.

CABERNET FRANC (R) All regions. Widely planted French cultivar, especially prominent in northeastern regions such as Veneto and Friuli, where it makes reds with a noticeably vegetal character.

CABERNET SAUVIGNON (R) All regions. Widely planted throughout Italy, it has become the base for some of the country's most famous (and most expensive) reds. This French grape has been in Italy since the early nineteenth century, if not before. However, Cabernet Sauvignon and its Bordeaux counterparts (Merlot, Cabernet Franc) became especially prominent in Italy after phylloxera destroyed most of Italy's vineyards at the end of the nineteenth century. Many vintners, especially those in the north and northeast, replanted heavily with these vines after phylloxera, in many cases abandoning native varieties.

CAGNINA NERA (R) Emilia-Romagna. Synonym for Refosco in Romagna.

CALABRESE (R) Sicilia. Synonym for Nero d'Avola. Makes dark, rich wines with a Syrah-like character.

CANAIOLO BIANCO (W) Toscana. Blending white, called Drupeggio in Umbria.

CANAIOLO NERO (R) Toscana. Productive red variety traditionally used in Chianti blends.

CANNONAO/CANNONAU (R) Sardegna. Italian name for Garnacha, or Grenache. Produces foresty, earthy reds with red-berry flavors.

CARIGNANO (R) Sardegna. Spanish-French import grown in

southwestern Sardinia. Makes plump, inky reds.

CARMENÈRE (R) Northern Italy. This French vine, once prominent in Bordeaux, is found in vineyards throughout the Veneto and Friuli, where it is often confused with Cabernet Franc. It lends a savory, herbaceous character to a variety of DOC red blends. It is especially prominent in the Vicenza area of the Veneto, where the new Vicenza DOC permits a varietal wine to be made from it.

CARRICANTE (W) Sicilia. Light, flinty white used in Etna DOC blends.

CATARRATTO BIANCO COMUNE (W) Sicilia. The most-planted white grape in Italy, despite being found in Sicily only. Traditionally used in Marsala blends, but can also make juicy, low-acid dry whites.

CATARRATTO BIANCO LUCIDO (W) Sicilia. As with Catarratto Bianco Comune, widely planted, but considered of higher quality than the Comune variety. Can occasionally recall Viognier with its spicy, beeswaxy aromas.

CESANESE COMUNE (R) Lazio. One of several sub-varieties used in spicy reds. The Comune is the larger-berried version.

CESANESE D'AFFILE (R) Lazio. Native grape of Lazio used to make spicy, aromatic reds.

CHARDONNAY (W) All regions. Burgundy's favorite son is so durable and versatile (and commercially viable) that few Italian vintners can avoid planting at least a little. It was likely introduced to Italy at the turn of the last century after phylloxera

struck, and its ease of use has made it one of the more popular white grapes from the top to the toe of the boot.

CHIAVENNASCA (R) Lombardia. Name for Nebbiolo in Lombardia's Valtellina.

CILIEGIOLO (R) Toscana. Bright, cherry-scented red often used in unique varietal wines. Grown also in Liguria and elsewhere.

CLAIRETTE (W) Sardegna, Toscana. Thought to be native to southeastern France, it is used in blends.

COCOCCIOLA (W) Abruzzo. Used widely in Abruzzo IGT wines.

CODA DI VOLPE BIANCA (W) Campania. Named "tail of the fox" by Pliny because of the shape of its grape clusters. It is used in Vesuvio DOC blends (among others) and in varietal bottlings. Chalky and aromatic.

COLORINO (R) Toscana. As the name implies, a deeply colorful red traditionally used as a blending ingredient to add stuffing to Chianti.

CORNALLIN (R) Valle d'Aosta.

CORTESE (W) Piedmont. A native of Piedmont, it is the base of Gavi DOCG whites.

CORVINA (R) Veneto. Dark and spicy, it is the principal red grape in the Valpolicella DOC blend (also used for Amarone della Valpolicella and Recioto della Valpolicella).

CORVINONE (R) Veneto. Thought to be a subvariety or clone of the Corvina of Valpolicella, while others consider it a distinct variety. It has larger berries than Corvina and produces more juice, prompting

many producers to substitute it for Corvina in their wines.

CROATINA (R) Emilia-Romagna, Lombardia. Dark, plummy variety found in the Oltrepò Pavese and Colli Piacentini DOCs, where it is confusingly referred to as Bonarda. Also grown in Piedmont, where it is blended with the real Bonarda.

DAMASCHINO (ALSO DAMASKINO) (W) Sicilia.

DOLCETTO (R) Piemonte, Liguria. The name means "little sweet one," in reference to its sweet taste when ripe. Deeply colored but with soft tannins, the variety ripens early and produces soft, fruity, accessible reds with plush black-fruit flavors. Considered native to Piedmont. Called Ormeasco in Liguria.

DURELLA (R) Veneto, Toscana.

ERBALUCE (W) Piemonte. High-acid variety grown in the northerly reaches of Piedmont near Valle d'Aosta, particularly the town of Caluso north of Turin. Makes crisp, dry whites and sharp, fragrant sparklers.

FALANGHINA (W) Campania. Thought to have been brought by the ancient Greeks, it may get its name from the Latin word *phalanga*, meaning stake or pole, in reference to the early Greek method of training vines to poles.

FAVORITA (W) Piemonte. Used as a blending variety in Piedmont. May be related to Vermentino.

FIANO (W) Campania. Grown in Campania since antiquity. Spicy, smoky, and crisp, it is probably the most assertively aromatic and fullest bodied of the region's whites.

FORASTERA (W) Campania. A specialty of the island of Ischia.

FORTANA (R) Emilia-Romagna. Deeply colorful and tart, used as a blending variety.

FRANCONIA (R) Friuli-Venezia Giulia. Of German origin. Also known as Blaufränkish or Limberger, it is used sparingly in Friuli.

FRAPPATO (R) Sicilia. Light, brightly aromatic red found in southeastern Sicily. A key component in the Cerasuolo di Vittoria DOC blend.

FREISA (R) Piemonte. Lightly colored, high-acid variety, made mostly into fizzy, often sweet, reds.

FUMIN (R) Valle d'Aosta. Dark and plush, with soft tannins, it is one of Valle d'Aosta's premier varieties, vinified as both a varietal wine and in blends.

GAGLIOPPO (R) Calabria. Softly tannic, lightly colored red, used as the base of Cirò DOC reds.

GAMAY (R) Veneto, Tuscany, Umbria. French grape grown throughout Italy. Vinified as a varietal wine in Umbria's Colli del Trasimeno DOC.

GARGANEGA (W) Veneto. One of Italy's most planted white grapes, it is the base of Soave DOC wines.

GIRÒ (R) Sardegna. Of Spanish origin, like many of Sardinia's grapes. Used in rare, Port-style reds made near the city of Cagliari.

GRECANICO DORATO (W) Sicilia. Crisp, appley white possibly related to the Greco of the mainland.

GRECHETTO (W) Umbria, Tuscany, Lazio. Possible related to Greco, it is considered native to Umbria, where it makes many of the region's top whites. It is being used in greater proportions in Orvieto DOC blends.

GRECHETTO ROSSO (R) Umbria, Toscana, Lazio.

GRECO (W) Campania. Brought by the Greeks, this ancient vine may well be the progenitor not only of like-named varieties such as Grechetto, Grecanico, and Garganega, but also of the vast Trebbiano family. It is best known as the base of Campania's Greco di Tufo.

GRECO BIANCO (W) Calabria. A distinct subvariety used in rare sweet wines from southern Calabria, as well as in a handful of dry whites.

GRECO NERO (R) Calabria. Dark version of Greco, mainly used for blending.

GRIGNOLINO (R) Piedmont. Native of the Monferrato hills, it makes light, tangy reds sometimes compared to Beaujolais. Increasingly rare.

GRILLO (W) Sicilia. Plump white widely planted in western Sicily, where it is used in Alcamo and Marsala DOC blends, among others.

GROPPELLO DI MOCASINA (R) Lombardia. Found in Lake Garda area. A type of Groppello is also found in northern Tuscany.

GROPPELLO DI SANTO STEFANO (R) Lombardia.

GROPPELLO GENTILE (R) Lombardia.

GUARNACCIA (R) Campania. Subvariety of Grenache found on the island of Ischia.

IMPIGNO (W) Puglia. Base of the Ostuni DOC whites of Puglia.

INCROCIO BRUNI 54 (W) Marche. *Incrocio* means cross, in this case a cross of Verdicchio and Sauvignon. Very rare.

INCROCIO MANZONI 2.15 (R) Veneto, Friuli–Venezia Giulia. Cross of Prosecco and Cabernet Sauvignon.

INCROCIO MANZONI 6.0.13 (W) Veneto, Friuli–Venezia Giulia. Cross of Riesling and Pinot Bianco. The number at the end was assigned by the person who created the crossing.

INCROCIO TERZI (R) Lombardia. Cross of Barbera and Cabernet Franc.

KERNER (W) Alto Adige. Cross of Schiava and Riesling.

LACRIMA (R) Marche, Calabria. In the Marche, Lacrima di Morro d'Alba is a plump, Gamay-like grape so named because its skins are prone to bursting and sending "tears" (*lacrime*) of juice running down the bunches. In Calabria, Lacrima is a sometime synonym for Gaglioppo.

LAGREIN (R) Trentino–Alto Adige. Distinctive, herbaceous red native to Bolzano. Made as both a plump *dunkel* (red) and a spicy, aromatic *kretzer* (rosé).

LAMBRUSCO (R) Emilia-Romagna, Lombardia, Trentino. Believed to be a native wild vine (*vitis silvestris*) that may have been first domesticated and turned into wine by the Etruscans. It has a number of subvarieties (see below), and is typically vinified in a *frizzante* style to create a compatibility with the hearty cuisine of Emilia-Romagna, its principal growing area.

Subvarieties include: Lambrusco a Foglia Frastagliata, found in Trentino; Lambrusco di Sorbara; Lambrusco Grasparossa; Lambrusco Maestri; Lambrusco Marani; Lambrusco Montericco; Lambrusco Salamino; and Lambrusco Viadanese.

LUMASSINA (W) Liguria. Light white found around Savona in Liguria.

MACERATINO (W) Marche. Possibly related to Greco, a light white used in the fading Colli Maceratesi DOC.

MAGLIOCCO CANINO (R) Calabria. Ancient red native to Calabria, making a comeback in the cellars of producers such as Librandi.

MALBECH/MALBEC (R) All regions. Dark, tannic Bordeaux variety used in much the same way it was used in France: as a means of beefing up blends.

MALVASIA (W) All regions. Along with Trebbiano and Moscato, the Malvasia family of grapes is one of the most diffuse in Italy, with many permutations (see following entries). It is thought to have originated in Greece.

MALVASIA BIANCA (W) Lazio, Umbria, Tuscany. Subvariety of Malvasia used in a range of DOC blends. Especially popular for Vin Santo.

MALVASIA BIANCA DI BASILICATA (W) Basilicata. Subvariety of Malvasia unique to the Basilicata region.

MALVASIA BIANCA DI CANDIA (W) Lazio. Subvariety of Malvasia, makes aromatic yet dry whites in a variety of DOC zones. Often blended with Trebbiano.

MALVASIA DEL LAZIO (W) Lazio. Subvariety of Malvasia, considered of lesser quality than the more assertive Malvasia Bianca di Candia.

MALVASIA DI CASORZO (R) Piemonte. Very light, pinkish red used in *frizzante*-style sweet rosés and reds.

MALVASIA DI LIPARI (W) Sicilia. Among the subvarieties of Malvasia best known for its sweet wines. Produces an apricot-scented nectar in the volcanic soils of Lipari, an island off the northeast coast of Sicily.

MALVASIA DI SARDEGNA (W) Sardegna. Subvariety of Malvasia used in sweet, apricot-scented whites.

MALVASIA DI SCHIERANO (W) Piemonte.

MALVASIA ISTRIANA (W) Friuli–Venezia Giulia. One of the most distinctive subvarieties of Malvasia, producing crisp, well-structured dry whites with hints of white flowers, citrus, and peach.

MALVASIA NERA DI BASILICATA (R) Basilicata. Dark, tannic red used in blending.

MALVASIA NERA DI BRINDISI (R) Puglia. A major variety on the Salentine peninsula of southern Puglia. Its somewhat sweet black fruit offsets the bitter chocolate flavors of Negroamaro in regional blends such as Salice Salentino and Brindisi Rosso.

MALVASIA NERA DI LECCE (R) Puglia. A subvariety of Malvasia unique to the Lecce area of the Salentine peninsula. Also used primarily in blends with Negroamaro.

MALVASIA ROSA (R) Trentino–Alto Adige.

MAMMOLO (R) Toscana. Violet-scented red once used as a blending grape in Chianti and Montepulciano. Increasingly rare.

MARSIGLIANA NERA (R) Calabria. Used as a blending grape in the Lamezia area.

MARZEMINO (R) Trentino–Alto Adige. Very dark, abundantly fruity variety that is vinified in both dry and sweet styles. Some theories say it is of Austrian origin, others assert that the grape was an ancient Greek vine that arrived in the region via the Adige River.

MERLOT (R) All regions. Used on its own and in blends, this highly productive and adaptable Bordeaux vine (introduced to Italy at the turn of the last century, if not before) is now the third most planted red grape in Italy behind Sangiovese and Barbera.

MOLINARA (R) Veneto. Traditionally the third grape in the Valpolicella DOC blend (in addition to Corrina and Rondinella). Tart and tannic. Increasingly being phased out in favor of Corvina or other varieties.

MONICA (R) Sardegna. Lightly colored (and lightly flavored) red of Spanish origin. Widely planted in the southern Sardinian plain of Campidano.

MONTEPULCIANO (R) Abruzzo, Marche. One of the most-planted red grapes in Italy, it is characterized by a very deep, purplish color. Its tannins are sweet, its flavors jammy and soft. The variety reaches its greatest heights in the Montepulciano d'Abruzzo and Rosso Cònero DOCs.

MONTONICO BIANCO (W) Calabria. Also called Mantonico. Used in sweet nectars such as Librandi's "Le Passule."

MONTÙ (R) Emilia-Romagna. Also called Montuni. Found on the Pò plain.

MOSCADELLO (W) Toscana. Subvariety of Moscato found in Montalcino, used in thick, sweet whites.

MOSCATELLO (W) All regions. Large-berried version of Moscato, also known as Muscatel.

MOSCATO BIANCO (W) All regions, especially Piedmont. Italian name for Muscat Blanc à Petits Grains, the oldest and some say best variety of Muscat. It has smaller berries than the Muscat of Alexandria (called Zibbibo in Italy). Moscato Bianco is the most planted and highest regarded of the diverse and diffuse Moscato family, which includes dozens of distinct varieties. Also known as Moscato Canelli.

MOSCATO DI SCANZO (W) Lombardia.

MOSCATO GIALLO (W) Trentino–Alto Adige. Called Gold-muskateller in German, it makes uniquely flavorful dry wines with crisp acidity.

MOSCATO NERO DI ACQUI (R) Piemonte.

MOSCATO ROSA (R) Trentino–Alto Adige. Unique red subvariety of Moscato with very thin skins that produces rose-colored, semi-sweet wines of distinctive character.

MOSTOSA (W) Lazio. Light white used in blends. Also found in Adriatic regions, including the Colli Rimini in Emilia-Romagna.

MÜLLER-THURGAU (W) All regions, especially Trentino. Famed German cross of Riesling and Sylvaner is at its best in the heights of Trentino, but these days it reaches all the way down to Sicilia.

NASCO (W) Sardegna. Light white found near Cagliari.

NEBBIOLO (R) Piedmont, Lombardia, Valle d'Aosta. Along with Sangiovese, this is Italy's most noble red grape, used in the often ethereal wines of Barolo and Barbaresco. Considered native to Piedmont, records of its cultivation date back to the 1300s. Late-ripening and sensitive to adverse vintage conditions, it nevertheless produces Italy's most uniquely perfumed and powerful reds. Called Chiavennasca in Lombardia's Valtellina, Spanna in northern Piedmont, and Picotendro in Valle d'Aosta.

NEGRARA (R) Veneto. Negrara Trentina is the most common subvariety.

NEGRETTO (R) Italian synonym for the Négrette of Southwest France.

NEGROAMARO (R) Puglia. One of the most planted reds in Italy, it is the base for Salice Salentino and numerous other reds of the Salentine peninsula. The name means "black and bitter," and the wines are typically deeply colored and brawny, with hints of exotic spice. There's also a subvariety called Negroamaro Precoce.

NERELLO CAPPUCCIO (R) Sicilia. A blending variety found mainly in eastern Sicily, near Etna.

NERELLO MASCALESE (R) Sicilia. Dark, spicy, perfumed red grape best known as the base of the Faro DOC blend.

NERETTA CUNEESE (R) Piemonte.

NERETTO DI BARIO (R) Piemonte.

NERO BUONO (R) Lazio. Used as a blending variety in DOCs such as Castelli Romani and Cori.

NERO D'AVOLA (R) Sicilia. The most important red grape of Sicily, also called Calabrese. Produces dark, thick, exotic reds that often bring to mind Australian Shiraz or Rhône Syrah.

NEYRET (R) Valle d'Aosta.

NIEDDERA (R) Sardegna. Synonym for Bovale, a dark red of Spanish origin. Made occasionally into a varietal wine.

NIEDDU MANNU (R) Sardegna.

NOCERA (R) Calabria, Sicilia. Blending variety found in southeast Calabria and northeast Sicily. Used in Faro and Bivongi DOC blends.

NOSIOLA (W) Trentino. Native of Trentino used to make distinctive, high-acid dry whites.

NURAGUS (W) Sardegna. Extremely vigorous variety, of ancient Phoenician origin, found mainly in the southern plains of Sardinia. High yields result in light, tartly acidic wines.

OLIVELLA NERA (R) Campania, Lazio. Synonym for Sciascinoso.

ORTRUGO (W) Emilia-Romagna. Simple white found in the Colli Piacentini.

OSELETA (R) Veneto. A local vine being revived by the Masi estate in the Valpolicella, it produces dense, dark, perfumed reds.

OTTAVIANELLO (R) Puglia.

PAGADEBIT (W) Emilia-Romagna. Synonym for Bombino Bianco.

PAMPANUTO (W) Puglia. Light white used in the *bianco* of the Castel del Monte DOC.

PASCALE (R) Sardegna. Very rare red of Cagliari.

PASSERINA (W) Marche. Synonym for Biancame.

PECORELLO (W) Calabria.

PECORINO (W) Marche, Abruzzo. Firm, fine white, but plantings are on the wane.

PELAVERGA (R) Piemonte. Increasingly rare light red used to make fizzy, berry-scented wines.

PERRICONE (R) Sicilia. Popular blending grape in Sicily.

PETITE ARVINE (W) Valle d'Aosta. A specialty of the Swiss Valais, also found in the Valle d'Aosta. Makes lightly colored, tart, flinty dry whites, and occasionally sweet wines.

PETIT ROUGE (R) Valle d'Aosta. Light, fruity, Gamay-like red used in light wines that often lean toward rosé in style.

PETIT VERDOT (R) All regions. Prized for its inky color and tannic structure, this Bordeaux blending workhorse performs a similar role throughout Italy.

PICOLIT (W) Friuli–Venezia Giulia. Though difficult to grow, this native grape of Friuli–Venezia

Giulia is famed for rich, honeyed sweet wines. It is also used to round out dry white blends, lending a creamy, beeswaxy character.

PIEDIROSSO (R) Campania. Found in a variety of Campania's DOC wines, this light red (so named for its "red feet," or red stalks) is used mostly as a blending ingredient.

PIGATO (W) Liguria. Thought to be of Greek origin, it is largely confined to the western Ligurian Riviera, most densely planted around Albenga. Sharp, herbal, and distinctive.

PIGNOLA (W) Lombardia. White grape of the northerly Valtellina DOC.

PIGNOLETTO (W) Emilia-Romagna. Crisp, aromatic white grown around Bologna.

PIGNOLO (R) Friuli–Venezia Giulia. A grape considered native to Friuli–Venezia Giulia, it was all but extinct before a group of producers —Walter Filiputti, Girolamo Dorigo, and the Zamò family— took cuttings from the vineyards of the Abbey of Rosazzo and reintroduced the vine to the world. Its wines are dense, dark, and often impenetrably tannic when young, but have intriguingly exotic aromas of black fruits and wintry spices. More producers in the zone are now experimenting with the variety, which some believe will become Friuli's most powerful, ageworthy red.

PINELLA (W) Veneto. Rare white used occasionally in Colli Euganei DOC blends.

PINOT BIANCO (W) All regions, and especially in the north. The Italian version of Pinot Blanc has been

planted throughout the country since the early 1800s. The best versions of this semiaromatic variety are produced in Friuli–Venezia Giulia and Alto Adige (where it is alternately called Weissburgunder).

PINOT GRIGIO (W) All regions. Given the commercial success of wine made from this grape, it's surprising to learn that the variety does not rank among the twenty most-planted in Italy. So named for its grayish tint when ripe (*grigio* means gray), this variety (known as Pinot Gris in France) is extremely productive and highly variable in character. These days, it is usually characterized by delicate aromas and a cool, clean texture. In the past, the darkish skins of the grapes led to wines that were coppery in color (*ramato*), but the arrival of more advanced winemaking technology has all but eliminated that. Many producers, especially those in Friuli–Venezia Giulia, feel that the grape is typically harvested too early (a by-product of mass production) and that, when grown and vinified with care, it can produce a more full-bodied, complex wine.

PINOT NERO (R) All regions. France's Pinot Noir is not typically very interesting in Italy, although it has shown class in isolated instances in Piedmont, Lombardia (Oltrepò Pavese), and Alto Adige.

POLLERA NERA (R) Liguria.

PORTOGHESE (R) Italian name for German Portugeiser, or Blauer Portugeiser.

PRIE BLANC/ROUGE (W, R) Valle d'Aosta.

PRIMITIVO (R) Puglia. Proven by a genetic study to be the parent of America's Zinfandel, this Puglian specialty has become an extremely popular variety in soft, spicy, sun-baked reds from the Salentine Peninsula.

PROCANICO (W) Umbria. Name given to a particular clone of Trebbiano in Umbria.

PROSECCO (W) Veneto, Friuli–Venezia Giulia. Possibly of Friulian origin, this light, peach-scented, late-ripening white is well known as a base for the *spumanti* of Valdobbiadene.

PRUGNOLO GENTILE (R) Toscana. Considered a distinct subvariety of Sangiovese unique to Montepulciano (see also Sangiovese).

QUAGLIANO (R) Piemonte. Rare red used in sweet sparklers.

RABOSO PIAVE (R) Veneto. Dark red native to the Piave plain in Veneto.

RABOSO VERONESE (R) Veneto. Subvariety of Raboso native to Verona.

REBO (R) Trentino. Cross of Marzemino and Merlot. Found in Trentino, named for Rebo Rigotti, the agronomist who created it.

REFOSCO DAL PEDUNCOLO ROSSO (R) Friuli–Venezia Giulia. The name means "Refosco with the red stalks," and the variety is considered the best of the Refosco subvarieties. Produces dark, tannic, spicy reds with a decided black-fruit character.

REFOSCO NOSTRANO (R) Friuli–Venezia Giulia, Veneto, Emilia-Romagna (where it is called Cagnina).

RIBOLLA GIALLA (W) Friuli–Venezia Giulia. One of Friuli's pre-mier native varieties, probably brought to the area via Slovenia from Greece. The grape makes firm, floral whites, especially in zones such as Rosazzo in the Colli Orientali DOC. Known as Rebula in Slovenia. Ribolla Nera is a synonym for Schioppettino.

RIESLING ITALICO (W) Friuli–Venezia Giulia, Veneto, Trentino–Alto Adige, Lombardia. Not considered a relative of true German riesling, this is the lesser-regarded of the two Rieslings found in Italy. Makes some interesting light, aromatic whites.

RIESLING or RIESLING RENANO (W) Friuli–Venezia Giulia, Veneto, Trentino–Alto Adige, Lombardia. The Italian name for Rhine (Renano) or Johannisberg Riesling. As with most of the Germanic varieties, it is made in a drier, crisper style in Italy than it is in Germany or Alsace.

ROLLO (W) Liguria. May be related to the Rolle of France's Languedoc.

RONDINELLA (R) Veneto. The second of the three grapes used in the Valpolicella DOC blend, used to add color and body.

ROSSESE (R) Liguria. Savory, spicy red native to the western Ligurian Riviera, most notably the town of Dolceacqua.

ROSSIGNOLA (R) Veneto. A minor blending variety in Bardolino and Valpolicella DOC blends.

ROSSOLA NERA (R) Lombardia. Also called Rossara.

ROUSSANNE (W) Toscana, Liguria. A Rhône Valley native that occasionally finds its way into Italian blends and varietal bottlings.

RUCHÈ (R) Piemonte. Unique to Piedmont's Asti area, it makes fruity, floral, sweet-scented reds with soft tannins.

SAGRANTINO (R) Umbria. Unique to a group of five communes centered around Montefalco, in central Umbria, this dark, spicy, exotic variety is on the comeback trail after having all but faded away. Only about 250 acres of the vine exist, but it makes one of Italy's most distinctive and powerful reds.

SANGIOVESE (R) All regions. Italy's most noble and most diffuse red grape, the base of Chianti Classico, Vino Nobile di Montepulciano (where it is called Prugnolo), Brunello di Montalcino (where it is called Brunello) and Morellino di Scansano (Morellino). It is considered a native wild vine (*vitis silvestris*) that was first discovered by the Etruscans in the Apennines between Tuscany and Romagna. Its telltale character is an aroma of black cherries buttressed by scents of wood smoke, tar, and herbs.

SAUVIGNON (W) All regions. Highly versatile French variety (the Italians drop the "blanc" from the name) being made in a range of styles throughout Italy. The best versions are typically found in Friuli–Venezia Giulia, Trentino–Alto Adige, and Tuscany.

SCHIAVA (R) Trentino–Alto Adige. Also called Vernatsch. The dominant red of Trentino–Alto Adige, used to make light, simple reds often served with a slight chill. Subvarieties include Schiava Gentile and Schiava Grigia.

SCHIOPPETTINO (R) Friuli–Venezia Giulia. A rare native red of Friuli–Venezia Giulia, it is sometimes compared to Syrah due to its pepperiness on the palate. Though often forbiddingly tannic, the dark, violet-scented variety evolves into a warm, rich red with time. Like Pignolo, it is returning to favor in Friuli after having been thrown over for international varieties such as Cabernet Sauvignon and Merlot.

SCIASCINOSO (R) Campania, Lazio. Used as a blending variety in Campania Vesuvio DOC and in Lazio.

SEMIDANO (W) Sardegna. Light white of the Cagliari area.

SÉMILLON (W) All regions. Not widely used, but it occasionally turns up in fleshy blends with Sauvignon, à la Bordeaux.

SPANNA (R) Piemonte. Synonym for Nebbiolo.

SUSUMANIELLO (R) Puglia. Blending grape in Brindisi DOC.

SYLVANER VERDE (W) Trentino–Alto Adige. More readily associated with Alsace, this rich and aromatic variety makes steely, minerally, petrol-scented whites, particularly in the Valle d'Isarco in the Alto Adige.

SYRAH (R) All regions. Also called Shiraz. Probably of Persian origin, this Rhône Valley and Aussie stalwart is gaining popularity throughout Italy, mainly due to its resistance to intense heat. From Sicily to Lazio, the Tuscan Maremma, and beyond, Syrah is factoring more and more prominently into both blends and varietal bottlings.

TANNAT (R) All regions. Dark and very tannic red variety better known as an ingredient in southwest-French wines such as Madiran.

TAZZELENGHE (R) Friuli—

Venezia Giulia. Sharply acidic red (the name means "tongue cutter") native to eastern Friuli.

TEMPRANILLO (R) Toscana. This Spanish import is catching on in the Tuscan Maremma, among other places.

TEROLDEGO (R) Trentino. Possibly a relative of Marzemino, and therefore possibly of Greek origin. Now better regarded than Marzemino, it is mostly confined to the Campo Rotaliano plain of northern Trentino, where it is made into a deep-purple, tarry red with a distinctive personality.

TERRANO (R) Friuli–Venezia Giulia. Synonym for Refosco in the Carso DOC region of Friuli.

TIMORASSO (W) Piemonte. Sharply acidic, aromatic white used for light whites and for grappa production.

TOCAI FRIULANO (W) Friuli–Venezia Giulia. The top native white of Friuli, it is not to be confused with Tokay of Alsace or Tokaji from Hungary. It is its own unique cultivar, distantly related to Sauvignon Blanc. Its wines combine a decided mineral quality with scents of pear and peach. The EC has declared that the grape name must be changed in order to avoid confusion with other Tocai/Tokay wines of the world. At this writing, the name Friuliano was the leading candidate.

TOCAI ROSSO (R) Veneto.

TORBATO (W) Sardegna. Rare white of French origin.

TRAMINER (W) Friuli–Venezia Giulia, Veneto, Trentino–Alto Adige. The name is said to be derived from the town of Termeno (Tramin) in the Alto Adige, where

the variety is believed to have originated. Traminer is considered the parent of the more widespread Gewürztraminer, which has spread most famously to Alsace but also to other parts of the world. The basic Italian Traminer is less aromatic than Gewürztraminer (the prefix *gewürz* means spicy, as a means of distinguishing the two). Traminer Aromatico is the Italian name for Gewürztraminer.

TRAMINER AROMATICO (W) Friuli–Venezia Giulia, Veneto, Trentino–Alto Adige. Italian name for Gewürztraminer. Typically, Italian versions of the wine are very aromatic but not as oily and rich as their Alsatian counterparts.

TREBBIANO (W) All regions. The largest family of white grapes in Italy, with countless subvarieties (see following entries). Its origins are widely debated. Known as Ugni Blanc in France, it is extremely prolific and usually produces pale, light whites.

TREBBIANO DI SOAVE (W) Veneto, Lombardia. Also called Trebbiano di Lugana, it is considered among the best of the Trebbiano subvarieties, producing distinctive whites in Lugana and adding class to Soave DOC blends (when producers choose to use it). The more productive Trebbiano Toscano has edged it out in a lot of places, most notably Soave.

TREBBIANO GIALLO (W) Lazio subvariety of Trebbiano.

TREBBIANO MODENESE (W) Emilia-Romagna subvariety of Trebbiano.

TREBBIANO ROMAGNOLO (W) Emilia-Romagna subvariety of Trebbiano.

TREBBIANO SPOLETINO (W) Umbrian subvariety of Trebbiano.

TREBBIANO TOSCANO (W) Tuscan subvariety, far and away the most planted of the family. It factors into countless DOC blends throughout Italy, and especially Tuscany.

UVA DI TROIA (R) Puglia. Native grape of northern Puglia, near Foggia. Thought to have been brought by the ancient Greeks, thus the name *Troia* (Troy). Aromatic and interesting, but on the wane. Used most notably in Castel del Monte reds.

UVA RARA (R) Lombardia. Synonym for Piedmontese Bonarda. Not to be confused with the Bonarda of Lombardia, which is actually Croatina.

VELTLINER (W) Trentino–Alto Adige. One of Austria's greats makes an occasional appearance in Italy, particularly in the Alto Adige.

VERDEA (W) Emilia-Romagna. White grape found in the Colli Piacentini.

VERDECA (W) Puglia. Tart white found in DOC wines such as Locorotondo and Gravina, though much of the wine made from the variety is said to go toward vermouth production.

VERDELLO (W) Sicily, Umbria. High-acid blending white in both Sicily and Umbria. Despite sharing the same name, the grapes in the two regions are not considered related.

VERDICCHIO (W) Marche. One of Italy's better-regarded native grapes, it produces crisp, full-flavored whites with distinctive aro-

mas of pine and herbs. It may be related to either Greco or Trebbiano (genetic studies, in fact, have linked it closely to the Trebbiano di Soave subvariety). Its two principal areas of production are the low hills west of Jesi, in central Marche, and a higher pre-Apennine basin farther inland, centered on the commune of Matelica.

VERDISO (W) Veneto. Brightly aromatic white found in several DOC zones around Treviso, including the Colli di Conegliano.

VERDUZZO FRIULANO (W) Friuli–Venezia Giulia. A unique white native to the hills of Friuli, it produces both chalky, somewhat tannic dry whites and honeyed sweet wines. Its prime territory is considered the area of Ramandolo in the Colli Orientali del Friuli DOC.

VERDUZZO TREVIGIANO (W) Veneto. A subvariety of Verduzzo found on the Piave plain of the Veneto.

VERMENTINO (W) Liguria, Toscana, Sardegna. Surely one of Italy's most distinctive native whites, it is a savory, crisply acidic grape that captures some of the herbal aromas of the Mediterranean scrub that grows alongside it. Extremely durable and resistant to both heat and drought, it thrives in coastal zones such as the Tuscan Maremma and Sardegna's rock-strewn Gallura region.

VERMENTINO NERO (R) Sardegna. Red version of Vermentino. Very rare.

VERNACCIA DI ORISTANO (W) Sardegna. A high-acid white used to make Sherry-style wines in the town of Oristano in Sardegna.

VERNACCIA DI S. GIMIGNANO (W) Toscana. Delicately aromatic white grown around the medieval town of San Gimignano. The Vernaccia di San Gimignano DOC was one of Italy's first.

VERNACCIA NERA (R) Dark version of Vernaccia.

VERNATSCH (R) See Schiava.

VESPAIOLA (W) Veneto. High in natural sugars, this plump and fragrant white is best known for the Torcolato sweet wines in the Breganze DOC zone.

VESPOLINA (R) Piemonte, Lombardia. Blending variety found in northern Piedmont, where it is often combined with Nebbiolo and Bonarda. Known as Ughetta in Lombardia, where it is grown sparingly in the Oltrepò Pavese.

VIEN DE NUS (R) Valle d'Aosta. Extremely rare red used in blends around the town of Nus.

VIOGNIER (W) All regions. Plump, waxy, aromatic French native gaining in popularity all over Italy.

VITOVSKA (W) Friuli–Venezia Giulia. A chalky, aromatic white native to the Carso region.

ZIBIBBO (W) Sicilia, Calabria. Italian name for Muscat/Moscato of Alexandria, an ancient member of the highly variable muscat/moscato family. Juicier, more alcoholic and less aromatic than Moscato Bianco. Best known in the *passito* wines of the island of Pantelleria, off the west coast of Sicily.

Appendix III
A Directory of DOC(G) and IGT Zones

———— ❦ ————

As described in "La Légge" (pages 9–12), Italy's wines are classified in a number of ways. A *Denominazione di Origine Controllata*, or DOC, denotes a wine made within an officially delimited geographic zone, from an officially prescribed grape or blend of grapes. Even more rigidly controlled are those wines labeled with a *Denominazione di Origine Controllata e Garantita*, or DOCG. Wines labeled with an *Indicazione Geografica Tipica*, or IGT, are subject to fewer controls over their grape blends and production methods, but nevertheless must come from a specific geographic area.

Below is a list of the DOCG, DOC, and IGT designations as of October 2001. Because these designations are constantly being revised, and because new designations are constantly being created, this list may not include every single denomination currently on the books in Italy (indeed, there were several new DOC designations being considered by Italy's National DOC Committee at this writing, as well as several DOCs that were under consideration for elevation to DOCG status). The following list is a quick reference to wines that in many cases carry only their DOC (or DOCG) name—a place name more often than not—and nothing else to identify them. Provided below are the prescribed grape blend(s) for each DOC(G), along with information about the production zone and any mandated aging requirements. Many DOC designations—Friuli's Collio, for example—include prescriptions for a wide variety of wine types. So in addition to the grapes used in the various DOC wines (note: grape names are capitalized here), the various styles are documented in the key below. The listings for each region are alphabetical, although it should be noted that any DOCGs in a region are listed first. The year each DOC(G) was created is in parentheses.

Since IGT wines are most often varietals with no aging requirements, we simply list the IGT zones with brief descriptions of where they're located and the styles of wines permitted.

DOC AND DOCG WINE ZONES BY REGION

Abruzzo

CONTROGUERRA DOC (1996)
ZONE: Northernmost Abruzzo, on the border with Marche, centered on the commune of Controguerra. **GRAPES:** *Bianco:* Trebbiano Toscano min. 60%; Passerina min. 15%; other white grapes max. 25%. *Rosso:* Montepulciano min. 60%; Merlot and/or Cabernet Sauvignon min. 15%; other red grapes max. 25%. *Spumante:* Trebbiano min. 60%; Verdicchio and/or Pecorino min. 30%; other white grapes max. 10%. *Passito Bianco:* Malvasia and/or Passerina min. 60%; other white grapes max. 40%. *Passito Rosso:* Montepulciano min. 60%; other red grapes max. 40%. *Moscato Amabile:* Moscato min. 85%. *Varietal Whites:* min. 85% of stated variety; wines from Passerina, Malvasia, Riesling, Chardonnay. *Varietal Reds:* min. 85% of stated variety; wines from Cabernet, Ciliegiolo, Merlot, Pinot Nero. **AGING:** Rosso Riserva: min. 2 yrs (min. 6 mos. in bottle). **WINE TYPES:** dw (also frizzante); spdw; sw; dr (also novello); sr

MONTEPULCIANO D'ABRUZZO DOC (1968)
ZONE: Spreading across all four of Abruzzo's provinces, from the southern border with Molise to the northern border with Marche and inland toward the Apennines. **GRAPES:** Montepulciano min. 85%. **AGING:** Rosso Riserva: min. 2 yrs. (min. 6 mos. in wood). **WINE TYPES:** dr; ros

MONTEPULCIANO DI ABRUZZO COLLINE TERAMANE DOC (1995)
ZONE: A subzone of the all-encompassing Montepulciano DOC, the Colline Teramane ranges from the city of Teramo eastward to the Adriatic, reaching toward the Marche border to the north and toward Pescara to the south. **GRAPES:** Montepulciano min. 90%; Sangiovese max. 10%. **AGING:** Riserva: min. 3 yrs. **WINE TYPES:** dr

TREBBIANO D'ABRUZZO DOC (1972)
ZONE: Similar parameters to Montepulciano d'Abruzzo zone, spreading across all four Abruzzo provinces. **GRAPES:** Trebbiano d'Abruzzo and/or Trebbiano Toscano min. 85%. **WINE TYPES:** dw

Alto Adige

ALTO ADIGE COLLI DI BOLZANO/SÜDTIROL BOZNER LEITEN (SUBZONE) DOC (1975)
ZONE: Subzone of Alto Adige (Südtirol), east of the Adige River and extending upward to points just south of the Isarco River. **GRAPES:** Schiava min. 90%; remainder Lagrein and/or Pinot Nero. **WINE TYPES:** dr

ALTO ADIGE LAGO DI CALDARO/SÜDTIROL KALTERERSEE (SUBZONE) DOC (1970)
ZONE: While the Lago di Caldaro/Kalterersee DOC extends into neighboring Trento, producers can add "Alto Adige/Südtirol" to the denomination when the wine hails from a specific area within the Alto Adige close to Lake Caldaro. In order to be considered an "Alto Adige Lago di Caldaro," a wine must hail from the communes of Appiano, Caldaro, Termeno, Cortaccia, Vadena, Egna, Montagna, Ora, or Bronzolo. **GRAPES:** Schiava min. 85%; Pinot Nero and/or Lagrein max. 15%. **WINE TYPES:** dr

ALTO ADIGE MERANESE/SÜDTIROL MERANER (SUBZONE) DOC (1975)
ZONE: Subzone of Alto Adige (Südtirol), covering both sides of the Adige River near Merano, northwest of Bolzano. Altitudes range from 300 to 650 m on slopes

oriented mainly south and southwest. **GRAPES:** Schiava 100%. **WINE TYPES:** dr

ALTO ADIGE SANTA MADDALENA/SÜDTIROL ST. MAGDALENER (SUBZONE) DOC (1975)

ZONE: Subzone of Alto Adige (Südtirol), comprising a swath of vineyards north of Bolzano at the confluence of the Isarco and Adige Rivers. **GRAPES:** Schiava min. 90%; remainder Lagrein and/or Pinot Nero. **WINE TYPES:** dr

ALTO ADIGE/SÜDTIROL (WITH GRAPE VARIETY ONLY) DOC (1975)

ZONE: Takes in most of the province of Bolzano, following the contours of the Adige River from the border with Trentino up to Merano. Stretches east and north of Bolzano but does not include the Isarco River valley up toward Bressanone (see Valle Isarco/Eisacktaler subzone, below). Soils: sand and limestone at lower elevations; more gravel and clay higher up. Elevations: from 300 to 1,000 m. Seven subzones total (see below). **GRAPES:** Wines labeled Alto Adige/Südtirol with indication of grape variety must contain min. 95% of that variety (Schiava min. 85%; wines labeled with two grapes, i.e. Cabernet-Lagrein, min. 80% of those varieties, with predominant variety listed first). *Varietal Whites:* Malvasia; Moscato Giallo (Goldmuskateller); Pinot Bianco (Weissburgunder); Pinot Grigio (Rülander); Chardonnay; Riesling Italico (Welschriesling); Riesling; Müller-Thurgau; Sylvaner; Sauvignon; Traminer/Gewürztraminer. *Varietal Reds:* Moscato Rosa (Rosenmuskateller, also *passito*); Lagrein (red called scuro, or dunkel; rosé called rosato, or kretzer); Merlot; Cabernet Franc; Cabernet Sauvignon; Cabernet-Lagrein; Cabernet-Merlot; Lagrein-Merlot; Pinot Nero (Blauburgunder or Spätburgunder); Schiava (Vernatsch). *Alto Adige Spumante:* blend of Pinot Bianco and/or Pinot Nero and/or Chardonnay required, min. 20% Pinot Nero for Spumante Rosato. *Alto Adige Bianco or Weiss:* Chardonnay and/or Pinot Bianco and/or Pinot Grigio min. 75%, with no one more than 70% of total. **AGING:** Spumante: min. 20 mos. in bottle (riserva spumante min. 42 mos.). Riserva reds: min. 2 yrs. **WINE TYPES:** dw; sw; spw; ros; dr; sr; spr

ALTO ADIGE TERLANO/SÜDTIROL TERLANER (SUBZONE) DOC (1975)

ZONE: Subzone of Alto Adige (Südtirol), primarily west of the Adige in a broad area around Terlano, as well as a small swath east of the Adige northwest of Bolzano. **GRAPES:** *Bianco* (grape variety not specified): Pinot

Bianco and/or Chardonnay min. 50%; remainder can include Riesling Italico, Riesling, Sauvignon, Sylvaner, Müller-Thurgau max. 50%; "other" authorized white grapes max. 10%. *Varietal Whites:* min. 90% of stated variety; wines from Pinot Bianco, Chardonnay, Riesling Italico, Riesling, Sauvignon, Sylvaner, Müller-Thurgau; **WINE TYPES:** dw

ALTO ADIGE VALLE ISARCO/SÜDTIROL EISACKTALER (SUBZONE) DOC (1975)

ZONE: Subzone of Alto Adige (Südtirol), along the banks of the Isarco River between Bolzano and Bressanone (Brixen). High-altitude sites mostly on the west bank of the river, facing south-southeast. The northernmost DOC zone in Italy. **GRAPES:** *Varietal Whites:* min. 90% of stated variety and max. 10% other authorized white grapes. wines from Traminer Aromatico (Gewürztraminer); Pinot Grigio (Rülander); Veltliner; Sylvaner; müller-thurgau; Kerner. *Klausner Laitacher:* blend of Schiava and/or Portoghese and/or Lagrein and/or Pinot Nero from communes of Barbiano, Chiuso, Velturno and Villandro. **WINE TYPES:** dw; dr

ALTO ADIGE VALLE VENOSTA/SÜDTIROL VINSCHGAU (SUBZONE) DOC (1993)

ZONE: Subzone of Alto Adige (Südtirol), along the northern banks of the Adige River as it turns west after Merano. Centered around the commune of Naturno. **GRAPES:** Varietal whites from Chardonnay; Kerner; müller-thurgau; Pinot Bianco (Weissburgunder); Pinot Grigio (Rülander); Riesling; Traminer Aromatico (Gewürztraminer). Varietal reds from Pinot Nero; Schiava. Wines must contain min. 90% of stated variety. **WINE TYPES:** dw; dr

LAGO DI CALDARO/KALTERERSEE DOC (1970)

ZONE: Begins around Lake Caldaro, west of Adige River, and extends down into northern Trentino. DOC zone shared with Trentino. Generally lower-lying slopes with vineyards not exceeding 600 m elevation. Also treated as a subzone of Alto Adige when wine hails from specific area (see Alto Adige Lago di Caldaro subzone). **GRAPES:** Schiava min. 85%; Pinot Nero and/or Lagrein max. 15%. **WINE TYPES:** dr

VALDADIGE/ETSCHTALER DOC (1975)

ZONE: A vast zone following the Adige River from Bolzano (Alto Adige) to Trento (Trentino) to Verona (Veneto). While taking in much of the provinces of Bolzano and Trento, it only extends to the communes of Brentino, Belluno, Dolcè and Rivoli Veronese in the province of Verona, yet production is concentrated in Trentino and Veneto. A broader appellation than either the Trentino or Alto Adige zones. **GRAPES:** *Bianco:* Pinot Bianco, Pinot Grigio, Riesling Italico, müller-thurgau and/or Chardonnay min. 20%; remainder mix of Bianchetta Trevigiana, Trebbiano Toscano, Nosiola, Vernaccia and Garganega. *Rosato and Rosso:* Schiava and/or Lambrusco min. 30% (min. 20% Schiava); remainder mix of Merlot, Pinot Nero, Lagrein, Teroldego, Negrara. *Pinot Grigio:* min. 85% of named variety; max. 15% "other" authorized white grapes. *Pinot Bianco:* min. 85% of named variety; max. 15% other. *Chardonnay:* min. 85% of named variety; max. 15% other. *Schiava:* min. 85% of named variety; max. 15% other authorized red grapes. **WINE TYPES:** dw; ros; dr

Basilicata

AGLIANICO DEL VULTURE DOC (1971)
ZONE: A broad territory north of Potenza, encompassing area around Monte Vulture to northwest and stretching toward Puglian border. Mostly volcanic soils near Rionero and Barile, more clay in the high plains near Venosa. **GRAPES:** Aglianico 100%. **AGING:** Normal: 1 yr. Vecchio: 3 yrs., min. 2 in wood. Riserva: 5 yrs., min. 2 in wood. **WINE TYPES:** dr; sr; spr

Calabria

BIVONGI DOC (1996)
ZONE: A small cluster of hills south of Catanzaro, set in from the Ionian coast, at elevations up to 800 m. **GRAPES:** *Bianco:* Greco Bianco, Guardavalle (Uva Greca) and/or Montonico 30% to 50%; Malvasia Bianca and/or Ansonica 30% to 50%; other recommended white grapes max. 30%. *Rosato and Rosso:* Gaglioppo and/or Greco Nero 30% to 50%; Nocera and/or Calabrese (Nero d'Avola) 30% to 50%; other authorized red grapes max. 10%; other authorized white grapes max. 15%. **AGING:** Rosso Riserva: min. 2 yrs. **WINE TYPES:** dw; ros; dr (also novello)

CIRÒ DOC (1969)
ZONE: The Ionian coast of Calabria, centered on the communes of Cirò and Cirò Marina. Soils: mix of marl, clay and sand. Classico zone comprised of Cirò and Cirò Marina only. **GRAPES:** *Bianco:* Greco Bianco min. 90%; Trebbiano Toscano max. 10%. *Rosato and Rosso:*

Gaglioppo min. 95%; Trebbiano Toscano and/or Greco Bianco max. 5%. **AGING:** Rosso: min. 9 mos. Classico Riserva/Classico Superiore Riserva: min. 2 yrs. **WINE TYPES:** dw; ros; dr

DONNICI DOC (1975)
ZONE: Band of hills just south of Cosenza, in eastern Calabria. **GRAPES:** *Bianco:* Montonico Bianco min. 50%; Greco Bianco, Malvasia Bianca, and/or Pecorello Bianco max. 30%; other authorized white grapes max. 20%. *Rosato and Rosso:* Gaglioppo min. 50%; Greco Nero min. 10%; Malvasia Bianca, Greco Bianco, Montonico Bianco, and/or Pecorello Bianco max. 10%; other authorized white and red grapes max. 20%. **AGING:** Rosso Riserva: min. 2 yrs. (min. 6 mos. in wood). **WINE TYPES:** dw; ros; dr (also novello)

GRECO DI BIANCO DOC (1980)
ZONE: Southernmost Puglia, on the Ionian coast. **GRAPES:** Greco di Bianco min. 95%; other whites max. 5%. **AGING:** min. 1 yr. **WINE TYPES:** sw

LAMEZIA DOC (1978)
ZONE: Stretch of Mediterranean coast and inland valleys south of Cosenza, flanking the Armato River. Soils: mostly alluvial. **GRAPES:** *Bianco:* Greco Bianco max. 50%; Trebbiano Toscano max. 40%; Malvasia min. 20%; other authorized white grapes max. 30%. *Rosato and Rosso:* Nerello Mascalese and/or Nerello Cappuccio 30% to 50%; Gaglioppo and/or Magliocco 20% to 25%; Greco Nero and/or Marsigliana Nera 25% to 35%; other red grapes max. 20%. *Greco:* min. 85% Greco; other authorized white grapes max. 15%. **AGING:** Rosso Riserva: min. 3 yrs. (min. 6 mos. wood, 6 mos. bottle). **WINE TYPES:** dw; ros; dr

MELISSA DOC (1979)
ZONE: Central Ionian coast of Calabria, between the communes of Cirò and Crotone. Soils: clays, sands and marl. **GRAPES:** *Bianco:* Greco Bianco 80% to 95%; Trebbiano Toscano and/or Malvasia Bianca 5% to 20%. *Rosso:* Gaglioppo 75% to 95%; Greco Nero, Greco Bianco, Trebbiano Toscano, Malvasia Bianca 5% to 25%. **AGING:** Rosso Superiore: min. 2 yrs. **WINE TYPES:** dw; dr

POLLINO DOC (1975)
ZONE: Plateau in northernmost Calabria beneath the Pollino massif, which separates Calabria from Basilicata. Soils: clay, marl and sandstone. **GRAPES:** Gaglioppo min. 60%; Greco Nero, Malvasia Bianca and/or

Guarnaccia Bianca min. 20% (white grapes max. 20%).
AGING: Superiore: min. 2 yrs. WINE TYPES: dr

SANT'ANNA DI ISOLA CAPO RIZZUTO DOC (1979)
ZONE: The central Ionian coast of Calabria, surrounding the coastal commune of Isola di Capo Rizzuto. Soils: predominantly alluvial, with patches of sand. GRAPES: *Rosso and Rosato:* Gaglioppo 40% to 60%; Nocera, Nerello Mascalese, Nerello Cappuccio, Malvasia Nera, Malvasia Bianca, and/or Greco Bianco 40% to 60% (white grapes no more than 35% of total). AGING: WINE TYPES: ros; dr

SAN VITO DI LUZZI DOC (1994)
ZONE: North-central Calabria, centered on commune of Luzzi, north of Cosenza. GRAPES: *Bianco:* Malvasia Bianca 40% to 60%; Greco Bianco 20% to 30%; other white grapes max. 40%. *Rosato and Rosso:* Gaglioppo min. 70%; Malvasia max. 10%; Greco Nero, Sangiovese, and/or other red grapes max. 30%. WINE TYPES: dw; ros; dr

SAVUTO DOC (1975)
ZONE: The Savuto River valley, south of Cosenza, running from high hills inland to Mediterranean coast. Soils: clay, marl and sandstone. GRAPES: *Rosso and Rosato:* Gaglioppo 35% to 45%; Greco Nero, Nerello Cappuccio, Magliocco Canino, and/or Sangiovese 30% to 40% (max. 10% Sangiovese); Malvasia Bianca and/or Pecorino max. 25%. AGING: Superiore: min. 2 yrs. WINE TYPES: ros; dr

SCAVIGNA DOC (1994)
ZONE: Sandwiched between Savuto and Lamezia DOCs on central Mediterranean coast of Calabria. Soils: clay and marl. GRAPES: *Bianco:* Trebbiano Toscano max. 50%; Chardonnay max. 30%; Greco Bianco max. 20%; Malvasia Bianca max. 10%; other authorized white grapes max. 35%. *Rosso and Rosato:* Gaglioppo max. 60%; Nerello Cappuccio max. 40%; other authorized red grapes max. 40%. WINE TYPES: dw; ros; dr

VERBICARO DOC (1995)
ZONE: Northern Mediterranean coast of Calabria. GRAPES: *Bianco:* Greco Bianco min. 30%; Malvasia Bianca max. 40%; Guarnaccia Bianca max. 30%; other authorized white grapes max. 30%. *Rosso and Rosato:* Gaglioppo and/or Greco Nero 60% to 80%; Malvasia Bianca, Guarnaccia Bianca and/or Greco Bianco

min. 20%; other authorized red grapes max. 20%. AGING: Rosso Riserva: min. 3 yrs. WINE TYPES: dw; ros; dr

Campania

TAURASI DOCG (DOC 1970; DOCG 1991)
ZONE: High hills east of Avellino, flanking the Calore River. Soils: calcareous marl mixed with volcanic deposits. GRAPES: Aglianico min. 85%; other red grapes max. 15%. AGING: Min. 3 yrs. (min. 1 yr. in wood). Riserva: Min. 4 yrs. (min. 18 mos. in wood). WINE TYPES: dr

AGLIANICO DEL TABURNO/TABURNO DOC (1986)
ZONE: Hills west and north of Benevento, in north-central Campania. GRAPES: *Aglianico del Taburno Rosso, Rosato, and Novello:* Aglianico min. 85%. Taburno *Bianco:* Trebbiano Toscano 40% to 50%; Falanghina 30% to 40%; other white grapes max. 30%. *Taburno Rosso:* Sangiovese 40% to 50%; Aglianico 30% to 40%; other red grapes max. 30%. *Varietal Whites:* Min. 85% of stated variety. Whites from Falanghina, Greco, Coda di Volpe. *Varietal Reds:* Red from Piedirosso min. 85%. *Spumante:* Coda di Volpe and/or Falanghina 60% to 70%; other white grapes max. 40%. AGING: Rosso: min. 2 yrs. (min. 3 yrs including min. 6 mos. in wood for riserva). WINE TYPES: dw; spdw; ros dr (also novello).

AVERSA DOC (1993)
ZONE: An area near the Campanian coast north of Naples, centered on the commune of Aversa. GRAPES: *Aversa Asprinio:* Min. 85% Asprinio; max. 15% other varieties. *Aversa Asprinio Spumante:* 100% Asprinio. WINE TYPES: dw; spdw

CAMPI FLEGREI DOC (1994)
ZONE: Area just north of Naples, including the outer limits of the city itself. GRAPES: *Bianco:* Falanghina 50% to 70%; Biancolella and/or Coda di Volpe 10% to 30%; other authorized grapes max. 30%. *Falanghina:* Falanghina min. 90%. *Rosso:* Piedirosso (Pér e Palummo) 50% to 70%; Aglianico and/or Sciascinoso 10% to 30%; other authorized grapes max. 30%. *Piedirosso (or Pér e Palummo):* Piedirosso (Pér e Palummo) min. 90%. AGING: Min. 2 yrs. for Piedirosso/Pér e Palummo Riserva. WINE TYPES: dw; spdw; dr (also novello); sr

CAPRI DOC (1977)
ZONE: The island of Capri. GRAPES: *Bianco:* Falanghina and Greco, with Greco comprising max. 50% of total. *Rosso:* Piedirosso min. 80%. WINE TYPES: dw; dr

CASTEL SAN LORENZO DOC (1991)
ZONE: A cluster of hills flanking the Calore River, southeast of the city of Salerno, centered on the commune of Castel San Lorenzo. GRAPES: *Bianco:* Trebbiano Toscano 50% to 60%; Malvasia Bianca 30% to 40%; other authorized grapes max. 20%. *Rosso and Rosato:* Barbera 60% to 80%; Sangiovese 20% to 30%; other authorized grapes max. 20%. *Barbera:* Barbera min. 85%. *Moscato and Moscato Spumante:* Moscato Bianco min. 85%. AGING: Min. 2 years for Barbera Riserva. WINE TYPES: dw; dr; ros; spsw; sw (also the designation Moscato Lambiccato for wines with exceptional concentration)

CILENTO DOC (1989)
ZONE: A vast stretch of the hilly southern Campanian coast, reaching to the border with Basilicata. GRAPES: *Bianco:* Fiano 60% to 65%; Trebbiano Toscano 20% to 30%; Greco Bianco and/or Malvasia Bianca 10% to 15%; other authorized grapes max. 10%. *Rosso:* Aglianico 60% to 75%; Piedirosso and/or Primitivo 15% to 20%; Barbera 10% to 20%; other authorized grapes max. 10%. *Rosato:* Sangiovese 70% to 80%; Aglianico 10% to 15%; Primitivo and/or Piedirosso 10% to 15%; other authorized grapes max. 10%. *Aglianico:* Aglianico min. 85%. AGING: Aglianico min. 1 yr. WINE TYPES: dw; dr; ros

COSTA D'AMALFI DOC (1995)
ZONE: The often steep slopes of the Amalfi coast, taking in 13 communes. There are three designated subzone designations: Furore (for wine from the communes of Furore, Praiano, Conca dei Marini, and/or Amalfi); Ravello (for wine from the communes of Ravello, Scala, Minori, and/or Atrani); and Tramonti (for wine from the communes of Tramonti and/or Maiori). GRAPES: *Bianco:* Falanghina and Biancolella min. 60%, with Falanghina min. 40%; other authorized grapes max. 40%. *Rosso and Rosato:* Piedirosso min. 40%; Sciascinoso and/or Aglianico max. 60%; other authorized red grapes max. 40%. AGING: Red wines with subzone designation min. 2 yrs. to be called Riserva. WINE TYPES: dw; dr; ros

FALERNO DEL MASSICO DOC (1989)
ZONE: The volcanic slopes of Monte Massico on the north coast of Campania, reaching to the border with Lazio. GRAPES: *Bianco:* Falanghina 100%. *Rosso:* Aglianico 60% to 80%; Piedirosso 20% to 40%; Primitivo and/or Barbera max. 20%. *Primitivo:* Primitivo min. 85%; Aglianico, Piedirosso, and/or Barbera max. 15%. AGING: Riserva Reds: min. 2 yrs. (min. 1 yr. in wood). WINE TYPES: dw; dr

FIANO DI AVELLINO DOC (1978)
ZONE: Central Campania, in the thickly wooded hills around the commune of Avellino. GRAPES: Fiano min. 85%; Greco, Coda di Volpe and/or Trebbiano Toscano max. 15%. WINE TYPES: dw

GALLUCCIO DOC (1997)
ZONE: Northwestern Campania, hugging the border with Lazio, taking in seven communes, including that of Galluccio. Abuts Falerno del Massico DOC to the northeast. GRAPES: *Bianco:* Falanghina min. 70%; other authorized white grapes max. 30%. *Rosso and Rosato:* Aglianico min. 70%; other authorized red grapes max. 30%. AGING: Rosso may not be released before June 1 of year succeeding vintage. Riserva: min. 2 yrs. (min. 1 yr. in wood). WINE TYPES: dw; dr; ros

GRECO DI TUFO DOC (1970)
ZONE: Tufaceous volcanic hills north of the commune of Avellino, taking in a small area centered on the commune of Tufo. GRAPES: Greco 85% to 100%; Coda di Volpe max. 15%. WINE TYPES: dw; spdw

GUARDIA SANFRAMONDI/GUARDIOLO DOC (1993)
ZONE: A small cluster of towns north of Benevento, one of which is Guardia Sanfromondi. The zone is within the confines of the larger Solopaca DOC. GRAPES: *Bianco:* Malvasia Bianca di Candia 50% to 70%; Falanghina 20% to 30%; other white grapes max. 10%. *Falanghina:* Falanghina min. 90%; other white grapes max. 10%. *Rosso and Rosato:* Sangiovese min. 80%; other red grapes max. 20%. *Spumante:* Falanghina min. 70%; other white grapes max. 30%. *Aglianico:* Aglianico min. 90%; other red grapes max. 10%. WINE TYPES: dw; spdw

ISCHIA DOC (1966)
ZONE: The island of Ischia, off the coast of Naples. GRAPES: *Bianco:* Forastera 45% to 70%; Biancolella 30% to 55%; other white grapes max. 15%. *Rosso:*

Guarnaccia 40% to 50%; Piedirosso 40% to 50%; other red grapes max. 15%. *Forastera:* Forastera min. 85%; other white grapes 15%. *Biancolella:* Biancolella min. 85%; other white grapes max. 15%. *Piedirosso/Per e Palummo:* Piedirosso (Per e Palummo) min. 85%; other red grapes max. 15%. **AGING:** Min. 30 days in bottle for whites; min. 90 days in bottle for reds. **WINE TYPES:** dw; spdw; dr; dr

PENISOLA SORRENTINA DOC (1994)
ZONE: The Sorrento Peninsula, south of Naples. The communes of Gragnano and Lettere are treated as official subzones. **GRAPES:** *Bianco:* Falanghina, Biancolella, and/or Greco Bianco min. 60%, with Falaghina component no less than 40%; other white grapes max. 40%. *Rosso:* Piedirosso (Pér e Palummo), Sciascinoso, and/or Aglianico min. 60%, with Piedirosso component no less than 40%; other red grapes max. 40%. **WINE TYPES:** dw; dr (also frizzante); sr (frizzante).

SANNIO DOC (1997)
ZONE: A vast area of northern Campania in and around Benevento, reaching north and east toward the border with Molise. **GRAPES:** *Bianco:* Trebbiano Toscano min. 50%; other white grapes max. 50%. *Rosso:* Sangiovese min. 50%; other red grapes max. 50%. *Metodo Classico Spumante:* Aglianico, Greco, and/or Falanghina. *Varietal Whites:* Min. 85% of stated variety. Wines from Coda di Volpe, Falanghina, Fiano, Greco, Moscato. *Varietal Reds:* Min. 85% of stated variety. Wines from Aglianico, Barbera, Piedirosso, Sciascinoso. **AGING:** Metodo Classico Spumante: Min. 1 yr. **WINE TYPES:** dw; spdw; sw (frizzante); ros (also frizzante); spros; sros (frizzante); dr (also frizzante and novello); sr (frizzante); spdr

SANT'AGATA DEI GOTI DOC (1993)
ZONE: A small area due west of Benevento, in north-central Campania. **GRAPES:** *Bianco:* Falanghina 40% to 60%; Greco 40% to 60%; other white grapes max. 20%. *Rosso and Rosato:* Aglianico 40% to 60%; Piedirosso 40% to 60%; other red grapes max. 20%. *Varietal Whites:* Min. 90% of stated variety. Wines from Falanghina, Greco. *Varietal Reds:* Min. 90% of stated variety. Wines from Aglianico, Piedirosso. **AGING:** Aglianico min. 2 yrs. (min. 2 yrs. plus 1 yr. in bottle for Riserva). Piedirosso Riserva min. 2 yrs. **WINE TYPES:** dw; sw; ros; dr (also novello for all types)

SOLOPACA DOC (1973)
ZONE: The Calore River Valley northwest of Benevento, in north-central Campania. **GRAPES:** *Bianco:*

Trebbiano Toscano 40% to 60%; Falanghina, Coda di Volpe, Malvasia Toscana, and/or Malvasia di Candia for the remainder. *Falanghina:* Falanghina min. 85%; other white grapes max. 15%. *Rosso and Rosato:* Sangiovese 50% to 60%; Aglianico 20% to 40%; other red grapes, including Piedirosso and Sciasinoso, max. 30%. *Aglianico:* Aglianico min. 85%; other red grapes max. 15%. *Spumante:* Falanghina min. 60%; other white grapes max. 40%. **AGING:** Aglianico min. 10 mos.; Rosso Superiore min. 1 yr. in wood. **WINE TYPES:** dw; spdw; ros; dr

VESUVIO DOC (1983)
ZONE: Volcanic slopes of Mount Vesuvius, south of Naples. The "Lacryma Christi" designation is given to whites, red, and rosés, sparkling, still, and sweet, of superior alcohol content. **GRAPES:** *Bianco* (also *Lacryma Christi Bianco*): Coda di Volpe and/or Verdeca min. 80%, with a minimum 35% of Coda di Volpe; Falanghina and/or Greco max. 20%. *Rosso and Rosato* (also *Lacryma Christi Rosso and Rosato*): Piedirosso and/or Sciascinoso min. 80%, with Piedirosso no less than 50% of total; Aglianico max. 20%. **WINE TYPES:** dw; spdw; sw; ros; spros; dr; spdr; sr

Emilia-Romagna

ALBANA DI ROMAGNA DOCG (DOC 1967; DOCG 1987)
ZONE: Stretch of hills between Bologna and Rimini, in the Romagnan half of Emilia-Romagna. Soils: marl and/or sandy clays. **GRAPES:** Albana 100%. **AGING:** Passito cannot be released before April 1 of yr. succeeding vintage. **WINE TYPES:** dw; sw

BOSCO ELICEO DOC (1989)
ZONE: Reclaimed marsh east of Ravenna. Soils: mix of sandy clay and alluvial material. **GRAPES:** *Bianco:* Trebbiano min. 70%; Sauvignon and/or Malvasia Bianco di Candia max. 30%; other white grapes max. 5%. *Sauvignon:* Sauvignon min. 85%. *Merlot:* Merlot min. 85%. *Fortana:* Fortana min. 85%. **WINE TYPES:** dw (also frizzante); sw; dr (also frizzante); sr

CAGNINA DI ROMAGNA DOC (1988)
ZONE: A band of Romagnan hills stretching from Faenza to Rimini. **GRAPES:** Cagnina (Refosco or Terrano) min. 85%. **WINE TYPES:** sr

COLLI BOLOGNESE CLASSICO PIGNOLETTO DOC (1997)

ZONE: Hills more directly south of Bologna, abutting Colli Bolognesi zone. GRAPES: Pignoletto min. 85% AGING: wine cannot be released before April 1 of year succeeding vintage. WINE TYPES: dw

COLLI BOLOGNESI DOC (1975)

ZONE: Pre-Apennine hills south and west of Bologna, centered on the commune of Monte San Pietro. Soils: mix of clay and marl. There are seven subzone designations within the DOC, used to distinguish geographic origins of certain varietal wines: Colline di Riosto; Colline Marconiane; Zola Predosa; Monte San Pietro; Colline di Oliveto; Terre di Montebudello; Serravalle. GRAPES: *Bianco:* Albana 60% to 80%; Trebbiano Romagnolo 20% to 40%. *Varietal Whites:* Min. 85% of stated variety. Wines from Chardonnay; Pignoletto; Pinot Bianco; Riesling Italico; Sauvignon. *Varietal Reds:* Min. 85% of stated variety. Wines from Cabernet Sauvignon; Barbera; Merlot. Varietal wines may be labeled with one of 7 subzone designations, with slight variations in grape percentages for each. AGING: Barbera, Cabernet Sauvignon Riserva: min. 1 yr. Barbera, Cabernet Riserva w/subzone designation: min. 3 yrs. (often with min. time in wood). WINE TYPES: spdw; dw (also frizzante); sw; dr (also frizzante)

COLLI D'IMOLA DOC (1997)

ZONE: Hills around the town of Imola, east of Bologna. GRAPES: *Bianco and Rosso:* Any combination of authorized grapes. *Varietal Whites:* Min. 85% of stated variety. Wines from Chardonnay, Pignoletto, Trebbiano. *Varietal Reds:* Min. 85% of stated variety. Wines from Barbera, Cabernet Sauvignon, Sangiovese AGING: Riserva Reds: min. 18 mos. WINE TYPES: dw (also frizzante); sw; dr (also frizzante and novello); sr

COLLI DI FAENZA DOC (1997)

ZONE: Pre-Apennine hills south of Faenza, east of Bologna on the Via Emilia. GRAPES: *Bianco:* Chardonnay 40% to 60%; Pignoletto, Pinot Bianco, Sauvignon and/or Trebbiano 40% to 60%. *Rosso:* Cabernet Sauvignon 40% to 60%; Ancellotta, Ciliegiolo, Merlot and/or Sangiovese 40% to 60%. *Pinot Bianco:* Pinot Bianco 100%. *Trebbiano:* Trebbiano 100%. *Sangiovese:* Sangiovese 100%. AGING: Rosso/Sangiovese: min. 6 mos. (min. 2 yrs. for riserva). WINE TYPES: dw; dr

COLLI DI PARMA DOC (1982)

ZONE: Apennine foothills south of Parma. GRAPES: *Rosso:* Barbera 60% to 75%; Bonarda (Croatina) 25% to 40%; other red grapes max. 15%. *Malvasia:* Malvasia Bianca di Candia 85% to 100%. *Sauvignon:* Sauvignon 100%. WINE TYPES: dw (also frizzante); sw; spdw; spsw; dr (also frizzante)

COLLI DI RIMINI DOC (1996)

ZONE: Coastal hills in the southeastern-most part of Emilia-Romagna. GRAPES: *Bianco:* Trebbiano Romagnolo 50% to 70%; Biancame and/or Mostosa 30% to 50%; other white grapes max. 20%. *Rebola:* Pignoletto min. 85%. *Rosso:* Sangiovese 60% to 75%; Cabernet Sauvignon 15% to 25%; other red grapes max. 25%. *Cabernet Sauvignon:* Cabernet Sauvignon min. 85%. *Biancame:* Biancame min. 85%. AGING: Cabernet Sauvignon Riserva min. 2 yrs. WINE TYPES: dw; sw; dr

COLLI DI SCANDIANO E DI CANOSSA DOC (1996)

ZONE: Band of hills between Parma and Modena, taking in the city of Reggio. GRAPES: *Bianco:* Sauvignon 40% to 80%; remainder Malvasia di Candia, Trebbiano Romagnolo, Pinot Bianco and/or Pinot Grigio (min. 85% Sauvignon for classico). *Varietal Whites:* Min. 85% stated variety. Wines from Sauvignon; Malvasia; Pinot Bianco; Chardonnay. *Varietal Reds:* Min. 85% of stated variety. Wines from Lambrusco Grasparossa; Lambrusco Montericco; Cabernet Sauvignon; Marzemino; Malbo; Pinot Nero. *Passito:* Sauvignon min. 90%. AGING: Cabernet Sauvignon Riserva: Min. 2 yrs. (min. 8 mos. in wood). WINE TYPES: dw; spdw; sw; ros; dr (also frizzante)

COLLI PIACENTINI DOC (1967)

ZONE: Apennine foothills south of Piacenza, including valleys of the Tidone, Trebbia, Nure, and Arda rivers. Each of these four river valleys has its own subzone designation, which is attached to some wines: Gutturnio (includes Tidone River valley); Trebbiano Val Trebbia (Trebbia); Val Nure (Nure), and Monterosso Val d'Arda (Arda). Soils are predominantly sandy clays. GRAPES: *Gutturnio:* Barbera 55% to 70%; Croatina (Bonarda) 30% to 45%. *Monterosso Val d'Arda:* Malvasia di Candia and Moscato Bianco 20% to 50%; Trebbiano Romagnolo 20% to 50%; other white grapes max. 30%. *Trebbiano Val Trebbia:* Ortrugo 35% to 65%; Malvasia di Candia and Moscato Bianco 10% to 20%; Trebbiano Romagnolo 15% to 30%; other white grapes max. 15%.

Val Nure: Malvasia di Candia 20% to 50%; Trebbiano Romagnolo and Ortrugo 20% to 65%; other white grapes max. 15%. *Novello:* Pinot Nero and/or Barbera and/or Croatina (Bonarda) min. 60%; other red grapes max. 40%. *Vin Santo:* Malvasia di Candia and/or Ortrugo and/or Sauvignon and/or Marsanne and/or Trebbiano min. 80%. *Vin Santo di Vigoleno:* Marsanne and/or Bervedino and/or Sauvignon and/or Ortrugo and/or Trebbiano Romagnolo min. 60%. *Pinot Spumante:* Pinot Nero min. 85%; Chardonnay max. 15%. *Varietal Wines:* Min. 85% of stated variety. Wines from Ortrugo; Barbera; Bonarda; Malvasia; Pinot Nero; Pinot Grigio; Sauvignon; Cabernet Sauvignon; Chardonnay. **AGING:** Gutturnio: Min. 9 mos. Gutturnio Riserva: Min. 2 yrs. (min. 3 mos. in wood). Vin Santo: Min. 4 yrs. (min. 3 yrs. in wood). Vin Santo di Vigoleno: Min. 5 yrs. (min. 4 yrs. in wood). **WINE TYPES:** dw (also frizzante); sw; spdw; ros; spros; dr (frizzante and abboccato); sr; spdr

LAMBRUSCO DI SORBARA DOC (1970)
ZONE: Plains just north of Modena, centered on commune of Sorbara. Soils: clays with alluvial sands and gravel. **GRAPES:** Lambrusco di Sorbara min. 60%; Lambrusco Salamino 40%. **WINE TYPES:** ros (frizzante); dr (frizzante); sr (frizzante)

LAMBRUSCO GRASPAROSSA DI CASTELVETRO DOC (1970)
ZONE: Plains south of Modena, including communes of Sassuolo and Castelvetro. Soils: sandy calcareous clays. **GRAPES:** Lambrusco Grasparossa min. 85% **WINE TYPES:** ros (frizzante); dr (frizzante); sr (frizzante)

LAMBRUSCO SALAMINO DI SANTA CROCE DOC (1970)
ZONE: Plains north of Modena, reaching to the banks of the Po River. **GRAPES:** Lambrusco Salamino min. 90%. **WINE TYPES:** ros (frizzante); dr (frizzante); sr (frizzante)

PAGADEBIT DI ROMAGNA DOC (1988)
ZONE: Much of the Romagnan part of Emilia-Romagna, from Bologna to Rimini. Overlaps several other DOCs, including Sangiovese di Romagna and Trebbiano di Romagna. Subzone designation for wines made in commune of Bertinoro. **GRAPES:** Bombino Bianco (Pagadebit) min. 85%. **WINE TYPES:** dw; sw

REGGIANO DOC (1971)
ZONE: Plains surrounding city of Reggio Emilia and reaching north toward the Po. Soils: clay mixed with sand and alluvial gravel. **GRAPES:** *Lambrusco Rosso/Rosato/Novello:* Lambrusco Marani, Lambrusco Salamino, Lambrusco Montericco, Lambrusco Maestri and/or Lambrusco di Sorbara min. 85%; Ancellotta max. 15%. *Lambrusco Salamino Rosso:* Lambrusco Salamino min. 85%. Rosso/Rosso Novello: Ancellotta 50% to 60%; Lambrusco (various types) remainder. *Bianco Spumante:* Lambrusco 100%. **WINE TYPES:** spdw; dr (frizzante); ros (frizzante); sr (frizzante); dr (novello)

RENO DOC (1987)
ZONE: A broad swath of plain between Modena and Imola, including area around Bologna. **GRAPES:** *Bianco:* Albana and/or Trebbiano Romagnolo min. 40%; other white grapes max. 60%. *Pignoletto:* Pignoletto min. 85%. *Montuni:* Montù min. 85%. **WINE TYPES:** dw (frizzante); sw (frizzante)

ROMAGNA ALBANA SPUMANTE DOC (1995)
ZONE: Same as Albana di Romagna DOCG. This DOC reserved only for spumante wines. **GRAPES:** Albana 100%. **WINE TYPES:** spsw

SANGIOVESE DI ROMAGNA DOC (1967)
ZONE: Pre-Apennine hills stretching from southeast of Bologna down to the Adriatic near Rimini. Vineyards also extend to plains north of Via Emilia. Soils are sandy, marly clays, changing to more alluvial material. **GRAPES:** Sangiovese 85% to 100% **AGING:** Riserva: Min. 2 yrs. **WINE TYPES:** dr (also novello)

TREBBIANO DI ROMAGNA DOC (1973)
ZONE: Similar to Sangiovese di Romagna. **GRAPES:** Trebbiano Romagnolo 85% to 100%. **WINE TYPES:** dw (also frizzante); spdw; spsw

Friuli–Venezia Giulia

RAMANDOLO DOCG (2000–2001)
ZONE: Small area near Tarcento, within Colli Orientali DOC. **GRAPES:** Verduzzo min. 90%. **WINE TYPES:** sw

CARSO DOC (1985)
ZONE: The sliver of Italian territory that runs from the Isonzo River to the city of Trieste, on the border with Slovenia. Soils: chalky limestone and red sands. **GRAPES:** *Wines designated Carso without mention of variety:* Terrano min. 70%; other authorized red grapes max. 30%. *Varietal Wines:* Min. 85% of stated variety. *Whites:*

Chardonnay; Malvasia Istriana; Pinot Grigio; Sauvignon; Traminer; Vitovska. *Reds:* Cabernet Franc; Cabernet Sauvignon; Merlot; Refosco dal Peduncolo Rosso; Terrano. **WINE TYPES:** dw; dr

COLLI ORIENTALI DEL FRIULI DOC (1970)

ZONE: Literally "eastern hills of Friuli," a band of hills following the contours of the Julian Alps, running from Manzano (southeast of Udine) to Tarcento (north of Udine). Soils: calcareous marl and sandstone. There are three delimited subzones: (1) Ramandolo, in the extreme north, near Tarcento; (2) Cialla, east of Cividale near the Slovenian border; (3) Rosazzo, in the hills of the commune of the same name, southeast of Udine. **GRAPES:** *Bianco, Rosato and Rosso:* any mixture of following grapes, excluding aromatic varieties. *Varietal Wines:* Min. 85% of stated variety. *Whites:* Chardonnay; Malvasia Istriana; Picolit; Pinot Bianco; Pinot Grigio; Ribolla Gialla; Riesling Renano; Sauvignon; Tocai Friulano; Traminer Aromatico; Verduzzo Friulano. *Reds:* Cabernet; Cabernet Franc; Cabernet Sauvignon; Merlot; Pignolo; Pinot Nero; Refosco; Schioppettino; Tazzelenghe. *Ramandolo:* Verduzzo 100%. *Cialla:* varietal wines from Picolit; Ribolla Gialla; Verduzzo; Refosco; Schioppettino. *Rosazzo:* varietal wines from Picolit; Ribolla Gialla; Pignolo. **AGING:** Riserva wines: min. 2 yrs. **WINE TYPES:** dw; sw; ros; dr

COLLIO GORIZIANO/COLLIO DOC (1968)

ZONE: A strip of hills marking Italy's border with Slovenia (the historic zone includes a substantial amount of vineyards now in Slovenia). Zone stretches from Gorizia west to Cormòns and north along the east bank of the Judrio River. Also a small cluster of vineyards near Farra d'Isonzo. Soils: marl and sandstone. **GRAPES:** *Bianco and Rosso:* one or more of following grapes, of like color; müller-thurgau or Traminer max. 20%. *Varietal Wines:* Must be 100% of stated variety. *Whites:* Chardonnay; Malvasia Istriana; müller-thurgau; Picolit; Pinot Bianco; Pinot Grigio; Ribolla Gialla; Riesling Renano; Riesling Italico; Sauvignon; Tocai Friulano; Traminer Aromatico. *Reds:* Cabernet Franc; Cabernet Sauvignon; Merlot; Pinot Nero. **AGING:** Riserva whites: min. 2 yrs. Riserva reds: min. 3 yrs. (min. 6 mos. in wood). **WINE TYPES:** dw; sw; dr

FRIULI ANNIA DOC (1995)

ZONE: Sandwiched between the Aquilea and Latisana DOCs on Friuli's Adriatic coast. Soils: mix of gravel/ alluvial material and sandy clays. **GRAPES:** *Bianco, Rosato, Rosso:* one or more of following grapes, of like color.

Varietal Wines: min. 90% of stated variety. *Whites:* Chardonnay; Malvasia Istriana; Pinot Bianco; Pinot Grigio; Sauvignon; Tocai Friulano; Traminer Aromatico; Verduzzo. *Reds:* Cabernet Franc; Cabernet Sauvignon; Merlot; Refosco del Peduncolo Rosso. **AGING:** Riserva Reds: min. 2 yrs. (1 yr. in wood). **WINE TYPES:** dw (also frizzante); spdw; sw; ros; dr

FRIULI AQUILEIA DOC (1975)

ZONE: Friuli's Adriatic basin, centered on ancient roman town of Aquileia. Plains running from the Grado lagoon up toward Udine. Soils: sandy clays mixed with gravel and limestone. **GRAPES:** *Bianco:* one or more of following varieties. *Rosso:* one or more of following varieties. *Rosato:* Merlot 100%. *Varietal Wines:* min. 90% of stated variety. *Whites:* Chardonnay; Malvasia Istriana; müller-thurgau; Pinot Bianco; Pinot Grigio; Riesling Renano; Sauvignon; Tocai Friulano; Traminer Aromatico; Verduzzo. *Reds:* Cabernet; Cabernet Franc; Cabernet Sauvignon; Merlot; Refosco. **AGING:** Riserva Reds: min. 2 yrs. **WINE TYPES:** dw (also frizzante); spdw; ros; dr (also novello)

FRIULI GRAVE DOC (1970)

ZONE: The vast central plain of Friuli, straddling the Tagliamento River and encompassing both Udine and Pordenone. Soils: alluvial terrain, ranging from gravel near river and sandy loam further west. **GRAPES:** *Bianco, Rosato, Rosso:* one or more of following varieties of like color, excluding aromatic varieties. *Varietal Wines:* min. 90% of stated variety. *Whites:* Chardonnay; Pinot Bianco; Pinot Grigio; Riesling Renano; Sauvignon; Tocai Friulano; Traminer Aromatico; Verduzzo. *Reds:* Cabernet; Cabernet Franc; Cabernet Sauvignon; Merlot; Pinot Nero; Refosco. *Spumante:* Chardonnay, Pinot Bianco min. 75%; Pinot Nero max. 15%; other white grapes max. 10%. **AGING:** Riserva min. 2 yrs. **WINE TYPES:** dw (also frizzante); spdw; ros; dr (also novello)

FRIULI ISONZO DOC (1974)

ZONE: Sandwiched between the Collio and Carso DOCs. A high alluvial plain, with more gravel and limestone at its northern reaches and richer sandy loams as it follows the Isonzo river south. **GRAPES:** *Bianco, Rosato, Rosso:* one or more of following varieties of like color, excluding aromatic varieties. *Varietal Wines:* 100% of stated variety. *Whites:* Chardonnay; Malvasia Istriana; Moscato Giallo; Moscato Rosa; Pinot Bianco; Pinot Grigio; Riesling Italico; Riesling Renano; Sauvignon; Tocai Friulano; Traminer Aromatico; Verduzzo. *Reds:* Cabernet; Cabernet

Franc; Cabernet Sauvignon; Franconia; Merlot; Pinot Nero; Refosco; Schioppettino. *Vendemmia Tardiva:* late-harvest wines can be made from Tocai Friulano; Sauvignon; Verduzzo Friulano; Pinot Bianco and Chardonnay. **WINE TYPES:** dw (also frizzante); sw; ros (also frizzante); dr

FRIULI LATISANA DOC (1975)

ZONE: The east bank of the Tagliamento River, in southwestern Friuli, abutting the border with Veneto. Includes both alluvial soils and sandy loam, reaching out to the resort town of Lignano Sabbiadoro on the Adriatic. **GRAPES:** *Bianco, Rosso:* one or more of following varieties of like color, excluding aromatic varieties. *Rosato:* Merlot 70% to 80%; Cabernet Franc; Cabernet Sauvignon and/or Refosco 20% to 30%. *Varietal Wines:* min. 90% of stated variety. *Whites:* Chardonnay; Malvasia Istriana; Pinot Bianco; Pinot Grigio; Riesling Renano; Sauvignon; Tocai Friulano; Traminer Aromatico; Verduzzo. *Reds:* Cabernet; Cabernet Franc; Cabernet Sauvignon; Franconia; Merlot; Pinot Nero; Refosco. *Spumante:* Chardonnay, Pinot Bianco and/or Pinot Nero min. 90%; other white grapes max. 10%. **AGING:** Riserva reds: min. 2 yrs. **WINE TYPES:** dw (also frizzante); spdw; sw; ros (also frizzante); dr (also frizzante)

LISON-PRAMAGGIORE DOC
SEE LISTING UNDER VENETO

Lazio

ALEATICO DI GRADOLI DOC (1972)

ZONE: A series of communes on the north shore of Lake Bolsena, in northern Lazio, near the border with Tuscany and Umbria. **GRAPES:** Aleatico 100%. **AGING:** Liquoroso: min. 6 mos. Liquoroso Riserva: min. 3 yrs. (min. 2 yrs. in wood). **WINE TYPES:** sr; fr

APRILIA DOC (1966)

ZONE: Coastal plain south of Rome, including the communes of Nettuno, Aprilia and Latina. Soils: sandy clay and alluvial material. **GRAPES:** Varietal White from Trebbiano (min. 95%). Varietal Reds from Sangiovese and Merlot (min. 95%). **WINE TYPES:** dw; dr

ATINA DOC (1999)

ZONE: Southern Lazio, in hills around the commune of Atina, east of Frosinone. **GRAPES:** *Atina Rosso:* Cabernet Sauvignon min. 50%; Syrah min. 10%; Merlot min. 10%; Cabernet Franc min. 10%; other authorized red

grapes max. 20%. *Atina Cabernet:* Cabernets Sauvignon and Franc min. 85%. **AGING:** Rosso and Cabernet Riserva: min. 2 yrs. (min. 6 mos. in wood). **WINE TYPES:** dr

BIANCO CAPENA DOC (1975)

ZONE: North of Rome on the west bank of the Tiber River, centered on the commune of Capena. **GRAPES:** Malvasia (di Candia, del Lazio, Toscana) max. 55%; Trebbiano (Toscano, Romagnolo, Giallo) min. 25%; Bellone and/or Bombino max. 20%. **WINE TYPES:** dw; sw

CASTELLI ROMANI DOC (1996)

ZONE: All-encompassing DOC just south of Rome, taking in the volcanic hills known as the Colli Albani. Includes towns such as Frascati, Marino and other hill towns founded in the Middle Ages as refuges for Roman nobles. **GRAPES:** *Bianco:* Malvasia and Trebbiano min. 70%; other authorized grapes max. 30%. *Rosso:* Cesanese, Merlot, Montepulciano, Nero Buono and/or Sangiovese min. 85%; other authorized grapes max. 15%. *Rosato:* must be blend of preceding red and white grapes; proportions may vary. **WINE TYPES:** dw (also frizzante); ros (also frizzante); dr (also novello); sw; sr

CERVETERI DOC (1974)

ZONE: Arid coastal hills northwest of Rome, reaching from the commune of Cerveteri up past Civitavecchia to Tarquinia. Soils: calcareous clay with some volcanic material. **GRAPES:** *Bianco:* Trebbiano Toscano (Procanico) and/or Trebbiano Giallo min. 50%; Malvasia di Candia and/or Malvasia del Lazio max. 35%; other white grapes max. 30%. *Rosso and Rosato:* Sangiovese and Montepulciano min. 60% (min. 25% each); Cesanese Comune max. 25%; other red grapes max. 30%. **WINE TYPES:** dw (also frizzante); sw; ros (also frizzante); dr (also novello); sr

CESANESE DEL PIGLIO/PIGLIO DOC (1973)

ZONE: Pre-Apennine hills between Rome and Frosinone, centered on the commune of Piglio. **GRAPES:** Cesanese min. 90%. **WINE TYPES:** dr (also frizzante and spumante); spdr; sr

CESANESE DI AFFILE/AFFILE DOC (1973)

ZONE: Pre-Apennine hills between Rome and Frosinone, known as the Ciociara. High-altitude vineyards of calcareous clay and rock. **GRAPES:** Cesanese min. 90%. **WINE TYPES:** dr; sr

CESANESE DI OLEVANO ROMANO DOC (1973)

ZONE: Part of the trio of high-altitude DOCs in the Ciociara range between Rome and Frosinone. **GRAPES:** Cesanese min. 90%. **WINE TYPES:** dr (also frizzante); sr

CIRCEO DOC (1996)

ZONE: Southern coast of Lazio, reaching from Latina to Terracina. **GRAPES:** *Bianco (all types):* Malvasia di Candia max. 30%; Trebbiano Toscano min. 60%; other white grapes max. 30%. *Rosso and Rosato (all types):* Merlot min. 85%. *Circeo Trebbiano:* Trebbiano min. 85%. *Circeo Sangiovese and Sangiovese Rosato:* Sangiovese min. 85%. **WINE TYPES:** dw (also frizzante); ros (also frizzante); dr (also novello and frizzante); sw; sr

COLLI ALBANI DOC (1970)

ZONE: Part of the Castelli Romani south of Rome, a zone of hills on the western edge of Lake Albano. Soils: volcanic. **GRAPES:** Malvasia di Candia max. 60%; Trebbiano (Toscano, Giallo, Romagnolo, di Soave) 25% to 50%; Malvasia del Lazio 5% to 45%; other white grapes (except Moscato) max. 10%. **WINE TYPES:** dw; spdw; sw

COLLI DELLA SABINA DOC (1996)

ZONE: Hills on the right bank of the Tiber from north of Rome all the way to the border with Umbria. **GRAPES:** *Bianco and Spumante:* Trebbiano Toscano and/or Giallo min. 40%; Malvasia di Candia and/or Malvasia del Lazio min. 40%; other white grapes max. 20%. *Rosso/Rosato/Novello:* Sangiovese 40% to 70%; Montepulciano 15% to 40%; other red grapes max. 30%. **WINE TYPES:** dw (also frizzante); spdw; spsw; ros (also frizzante); dr (also frizzante and novello)

COLLI ETRUSCHI VITERBESI DOC (1996)

ZONE: A large swath of northern Lazio reaching from Viterbo to the border of Tuscany and surrounding Lake Bolsena. **GRAPES:** *Bianco:* Malvasia Lazio or Toscana max. 30%; Trebbiano Toscano (Procanico) 40% to 80%; other white grapes max. 30%. *Rosso and Rosato:* Montepulciano 20% to 45%; Sangiovese 50% to 65%; other red grapes max. 30%. *Varietal Wines:* Whites from Procanico; Grechetto; Rossetto; Moscatello. Reds from Grechetto; Sangiovese; Violone; Canaiolo; Merlot. All varietal wines min. 85% of stated variety. **WINE TYPES:** dw (also frizzante); sw(also frizzante); ros (also frizzante); swros (also frizzante); dr (also novello and frizzante); sr (also frizzante)

COLLI LANUVINI DOC (1971)

ZONE: The southwestern sector of the Alban Hills south of Rome, reaching from Lake Nemi to Aprilia. Soils: volcanic. **GRAPES:** Malvasia Bianca di Candia max. 70%; Trebbiano (Toscano, Verde, Giallo) min. 30%; other white grapes max. 10%. **WINE TYPES:** dw; sw

CORI DOC (1971)

ZONE: Southeastern-most edge of the Castelli Romani, just north of the city of Latina. **GRAPES:** *Bianco:* Malvasia di Candia max. 70%; Trebbiano Toscano max. 40%; Bellone and/or Trebbiano Giallo max. 30%. *Rosso:* Montepulciano 40% to 60%; Nero Buono 20% to 40%; Cesanese 10% to 30%. **WINE TYPES:** dw; sw; dr

EST! EST!! EST!!!
DI MONTEFIASCONE DOC (1966)

ZONE: Volcanic slopes ringing Lake Bolsena, in northern Lazio. **GRAPES:** Trebbiano Toscano (Procanico) 65%; Malvasia Bianca Toscana 20%; Rossetto (Trebbiano Giallo) 15%. **WINE TYPES:** dw; sw

FRASCATI DOC (1966)

ZONE: The heart of the Alban Hills south of Rome, north of Lake Albano. Volcanic soils. **GRAPES:** Malvasia Bianca di Candia and/or Trebbiano Toscano min. 70%; Greco and/or Malvasia del Lazio max. 30%; other white grapes max. 10%. **WINE TYPES:** dw; sw

GENAZZANO DOC (1992)

ZONE: Ciociaria hills between Rome and Frosinone. Genazzano is the westernmost DOC in a cluster that includes Cesanese di Piglio and Cesanese d'Affile. **GRAPES:** *Bianco:* Malvasia di Candia 50% to 70%; Bellone and Bombino 10% to 30%; Trebbiano Toscano, Pinot Bianco and other white grapes max. 40%. *Rosso:* Sangiovese 70% to 90%; Cesanese 10% to 30%; other red grapes max. 20%. **WINE TYPES:** dw; dr; sw; sr

MARINO DOC (1970)

ZONE: Western edge of the Alban Hills south of Rome, centered on the commune of Marino. **GRAPES:** Malvasia Bianca di Candia max. 60%; Trebbiano (Toscano, Romagnolo, Giallo and/or di Soave) 25% to 55%; Malvasia del Lazio 5% to 45%; other authorized white grapes max. 10%. **WINE TYPES:** dw; sw

MONTECOMPATRI-COLONNA/
MONTECOMPATRI/COLONNA DOC (1973)

ZONE: Part of the Alban hills south of Rome, wedged

between Frascati and Zagarolo DOCs. **GRAPES:**
Malvasia (Bianca di Candia and/or Puntinata) max. 70%;
Trebbiano (Toscano, Verde and/or Giallo) min. 30%;
Bellone and/or Bonvino max. 10%. **WINE TYPES:**
dw; sw

ORVIETO DOC
SEE LISTING UNDER UMBRIA

TARQUINIA DOC (1996)
ZONE: Vast section of coastal Lazio from Rome to bor-
der with Tuscany. Envelops Cerveteri DOC. Soils: sandy
clays w/ limestone and volcanic material. **GRAPES:**
Bianco: Trebbiano Toscano (Procanico) and/or Trebbiano
Giallo min. 50%; Malvasia di Candia and/or Malvasia
del Lazio max. 35%; other white grapes (except Pinot
Grigio) max. 30%. *Rosso and Rosato:* Sangiovese and
Montepulciano min. 60% (no less than 25% of either);
Cesanese Comune max. 25%; other authorized red
grapes max. 30%. **WINE TYPES:** dw; sw; ros; dr (also
novello); sr

VELLETRI DOC (1972)
ZONE: A southern chunk of the Castelli Romani, centered on the commune of Velletri. Soils: volcanic.
GRAPES: *Bianco and Spumante:* Malvasia max. 70%; Trebbiano Toscano min. 30%; Bellone, Bonvino and other
white grapes max. 20%. *Rosso:* Sangiovese 10% to 45%;
Montepulciano 30% to 50%; Cesanese Comune and/or
d'Affile min. 10%; other red grapes max. 30%. **AGING:**
Rosso Riserva min. 2 yrs. **WINE TYPES:** dw; spdw; sw;
dr; sr

VIGNANELLO DOC (1992)
ZONE: East of Viterbo, abutting the Tiber River as it
runs into Lazio from Umbria. Soils, calcareous clay and
volcanic material. **GRAPES:** *Bianco:* Trebbiano (Giallo
and/or Toscano) 60% to 70%; Malvasia Bianca (di
Candia and/or di Chianti) 20% to 40%; other white
grapes max. 10%. Greco: Greco min. 85%. *Rosso and
Rosato:* Sangiovese 40% to 60%; Ciliegiolo 40% to 50%;
other red grapes max. 20%. **AGING:** Rosso Riserva min.
2 yrs. (min. 1 yr. in bottle). **WINE TYPES:** dw; spdw;
ros; dr

ZAGAROLO DOC (1973)
ZONE: The northeastern edge of the Castelli Romani,
southeast of Rome. **GRAPES:** Malvasia max. 70%;
Trebbiano min. 30%; Bellone and/or Bonvino max.
10%. **WINE TYPES:** dw; sw

Liguria

CINQUE TERRE/CINQUE TERRE SCIACCHETRÀ DOC (1973)
ZONE: The steep slopes above the coastal towns of
Riomaggiore, Vernazza and Monterosso, in the area
known as the "five lands," or Cinque Terre. There are
three subzones: Costa de Sera; Costa de Campu; and
Costa da Posa. Soils: calcareous sands on hand-built
terraces. **GRAPES:** Bosco min. 40%; Albarola and/or
Vermentino max. 40%; other authorized white grapes
max. 20%. **AGING:** Sciacchetrà: min. 1 yr. (min. 3 yrs.
for Sciacchetrà Riserva). **WINE TYPES:** dw; sw

COLLI DI LUNI DOC (1989)
ZONE: Straddles Liguria and Tuscany along Mediterranean where the two regions meet, but centered around
La Spezia in Liguria. Soils: calcareous clays in hills flanking Magra River. **GRAPES:** *Bianco:* Vermentino min.
35%; Trebbiano Toscano 25% to 40%; other white
grapes max. 30%. *Vermentino:* Vermentino (max. 10%
other whites). *Rosso:* Sangiovese 60% to 70%; Canaiolo
Nero and/or Ciliegiolo min. 15%; other red grapes max.
25% (max. 10% Cabernet Sauvignon). **AGING:** Rosso
Riserva: min. 2 yrs. **WINE TYPES:** dw; dr

COLLINE DI LEVANTO DOC (1995)
ZONE: Coastal vineyards adjacent to Cinque Terre to
the northwest, situated in the communes of Levanto,
Bonassola, Framura and Deiva Marina. Soils: calcareous
sand and clay, similar to Cinque Terre. **GRAPES:** *Bianco:*
Vermentino min. 40%; Albarola min. 20%; Bosco min.
5%; other authorized white grapes max. 35%. *Rosso* (also
novello): Sangiovese min. 40%; Ciliegiolo min. 20%; other
authorized red grapes 20% to 40%. **WINE TYPES:** dw;
dr (also novello)

GOLFO DEL TIGULLIO DOC (1997)
ZONE: Coastal and interior hills surrounding the Gulf
of Tigullio, centered on the communes of Portofino,
Santa Margherita and Rapallo and spreading east, north,
and west. **GRAPES:** *Bianco:* Vermentino 20% to 70%;
Bianchetta Genovese 20% to 70%; other approved
nonaromatic white grapes max. 40%. *Rosso/Rosato:*
Ciliegiolo 20% to 70%; Dolcetto 20% to 70%; other
approved nonaromatic red grapes max. 40%. *Bianchetta
Genovese:* min. 85% Bianchetta. *Vermentino:* Min. 85% Vermentino. *Ciliegiolo:* min. 85% Ciliegiolo. *Moscato/Moscato
Passito:* Moscato 100%. *Passito:* any mix of approved
white grapes. *Spumante:* any mix of approved white grapes.

AGING: Passito: min. I yr. **WINE TYPES:** dw (also frizzante); spdw; sw; ros (also frizzante); dr (also frizzante and novello)

RIVIERA LIGURE DI PONENTE DOC (1988)

ZONE: A vast stretch of western Liguria, reaching from Genoa to the border with France and taking in both coastal and inland vineyard sites. Production centered in province of Imperia, though there are 3 subzones: Riviera dei Fiore, covering the westernmost communes of Liguria including Dolceacqua, Diano Castello and Imperia; Albenga/Albenganese, centered around the commune of Albenga, between Imperia and Genoa; and Finale/Finalese, centered on the commune of Finale Ligure and reaching toward Genoa. **GRAPES:** *Varietal Whites (Vermentino, Pigato):* min. 95% of stated variety. *Varietal Reds (Rossese, Ormeasco):* min. 95% of stated variety. *Ormeasco Sciac-trà:* 95% Ormeasco vinified as rosé. **AGING:** Ormeasco Superiore min. I yr. **WINE TYPES:** dw; ros; dr

ROSSESE DI DOLCEACQUA/DOLCEACQUA DOC (1972)

ZONE: Westernmost Liguria, centered on the commune of Dolceacqua and reaching into foothills of Ligurian Alps. Soils: calcareous clays. **GRAPES:** Rossese min. 95%. **AGING:** Superiore: min. I yr. **WINE TYPES:** dr

VAL POLCÈVERA DOC (1999)

ZONE: A small river valley north of Genoa. Subzone denomination Coronata attached to white wines from a specific part of the zone near Genoa. **GRAPES:** *Bianco* (also *spumante, passito* and *Coronata subzone*): Vermentino, Bianchetta Genovese and/or Albarola min. 60%; Pigato, Rollo and/or Bosco max. 40%. *Bianchetta Genovese:* min. 85% Bianchetta Genovese. *Vermentino:* min. 85% Vermentino. *Rosso/Rosato:* Dolcetto, Sangiovese and/or Ciliegiolo min. 60%; Barbera max. 40%. **WINE TYPES:** dw (also frizzante); spdw; sw; ros (also frizzante); dr (also novello and frizzante)

Lombardia

FRANCIACORTA DOCG (DOC 1967; DOCG 1995)

ZONE: Low hills south of Lake Iseo, between Bergamo and Brescia. Soils: glacial moraine. **GRAPES:** Chardonnay and/or Pinot Nero and/or Pinot Bianco (min. 15% Pinot Nero for rosato; Satèn is a term used to describe a

crèmant-style wine from 100% Chardonnay). **AGING:** 18 mos. in bottle. Wine cannot be released until 25 mos. after the vintage of the youngest wine in cuvée. Vintage Wines: Min. 30 mos. in bottle, wine cannot be sold until 37 mos. from vintage. **WINE TYPES:** spdw; spros

VALTELLINA SUPERIORE DOCG (DOC 1968; DOCG 1998)

ZONE: Steep slopes on the banks of the Adda River near Sondrio, in northern Lombardy. Superiore designation given to wines from a twenty-kilometer stretch of vineyards between Sondrio and Teglio. Official subzones, from west to east, are Sassella (near Sondrio), Grumello, Inferno, Valgella. Soils: pebbly, rocky, silty clays. **GRAPES:** Chiavennasca (Nebbiolo) min. 90%. **AGING:** Min. 2 yrs. (min. I yr. in wood). Min. 3 yrs. for Riserva. **WINE TYPES:** dr

BOTTICINO DOC (1968)

ZONE: Gentle slopes east of Brescia. **GRAPES:** Barbera min. 30%; Schiava min. 10%; Marzemino min. 20%; Sangiovese min. 10%; other red grapes max. 10%. **AGING:** Riserva min. 2 yrs. **WINE TYPES:** dr

CAPRIANO DEL COLLE DOC (1980)

ZONE: Small swath of hills south of Brescia, centered on commune of Capriano del Colle. **GRAPES:** *Bianco and Trebbiano:* Trebbiano di Soave (or other Trebbianos) min. 85%. *Rosso:* Sangiovese min. 40%; Marzemino min. 35%; Barbera min. 3%; Merlot and/or Incrocio Terzi max. 15%. **AGING:** Rosso Riserva min. 2 yrs. **WINE TYPES:** dw (also frizzante); dr (also novello)

CELLATICA DOC (1968)

ZONE: Low hills just west of Brescia, flanked by Franciacorta DOC. **GRAPES:** Marzemino min. 30%; Barbera min. 30%; Schiava min. 10%; Incrocio Terzi min. 10%; other red grapes max. 10%. **AGING:** Superiore min. I yr. **WINE TYPES:** dr

GARDA DOC
SEE LISTING UNDER VENETO

GARDA COLLI MANTOVANI DOC (1976)

ZONE: Hills south of Lake Garda reaching toward city of Mantova. **GRAPES:** *Bianco:* Garganega max. 35%; Trebbiano (all types) max. 35%; Chardonnay max. 35%; Sauvignon and/or Riesling max. 15%. *Rosato and Rosso:* Merlot max. 45%; Rondinella max. 40%; Cabernet max. 20%. *Varietal Whites:* Min. 85% of stated variety. Wines from Chardonnay; Pinot Bianco; Pinot Grigio;

Sauvignon. *Varietal Reds:* Min. 85% of stated variety. Wines from Cabernet (Sauvignon and/or Franc); Merlot. AGING: Cabernet and Merlot Riserva min. 2 yrs. (min. 1 yr. in wood). WINE TYPES: dw; ros; dr

LAMBRUSCO MANTOVANO DOC (1987)

ZONE: Broad section of Po plain south of Mantova. Two subzones: Viadanese-Sabbionetano and Oltrepò Mantovano. GRAPES: Lambrusco Viadanese, Lambrusco Maestri, Lambrusco Marani, and/or Lambrusco Salamino min. 85%; Lambrusco di Sorbara, Lambrusco Grasparossa, Ancellotta and/or Fortana max. 15%. WINE TYPES: dr (frizzante); sr (frizzante); ros (frizzante) sros (frizzante)

LUGANA DOC (1967)

ZONE: On the south shore of Lake Garda, predominantly in Lombardy (including Sirmione) but with a sliver of territory extending into Veneto. Low hills and plains. Soils: Calcareous clay. GRAPES: Trebbiano di Lugana min. 90%; other authorized white grapes max. 10%. WINE TYPES: dw; spdw

OLTREPÒ PAVESE DOC (1970)

ZONE: Apennine foothills in southwestern corner of Lombardy. Soils: Calcareous clays. Subzones of Buttafuoco and Sangue di Giuda cover communes of Broni; Stradella; Canneto Pavese; Montescano; Castana; Cigognola, and Pietra de' Giorgi in northeastern part of zone. GRAPES: *Spumante:* Pinot Nero min. 70%; Chardonnay, Pinot Grigio and/or Pinot Bianco max. 30%. *Rosso/ Rosato/Buttafuoco/Sangue di Giuda:* Barbera 25% to 65%; Croatina 25% to 65%; Uva Rara, Vespolina (Ughetta) and/or Pinot Nero max. 45%. *Bonarda:* Croatina 85% to 100%. *Barbera:* Barbera 85% to 100%. *Riesling Italico:* Riesling Italico min. 85%. *Riesling Renano:* Riesling Renano min. 85%. *Cortese:* Cortese min. 85%. *Moscato:* Moscato Bianco min. 85%. *Pinot Nero:* Pinot Nero min. 85%. *Pinot Grigio:* Pinot Grigio min. 85%. *Chardonnay:* Chardonnay min. 85%. *Sauvignon:* Sauvignon min. 85%. *Cabernet Sauvignon:* Cabernet Sauivignon min. 85%. *Liquoroso/Passito:* Moscato Bianco min. 85%. *Malvasia:* Malvasia min. 85%. AGING: Spumante min. 18 mos. in bottle, cannot be released before 24 mos. from vintage. Moscato Passito min. 8 mos. Rosso Riserva min. 2 yrs. WINE TYPES: dw (also frizzante); dr (also frizzante); ros; sw (also frizzante); spdw

RIVIERA DEL GARDA BRESCIANO/GARDA BRESCIANO DOC (1977)

ZONE: Western shores of Lake Garda. GRAPES: *Bianco:* Riesling Italico and/or Riesling Renano up to 100%; other white grapes up to 20%. *Rosso and Chiaretto:* Groppello 30% to 60%; Sangiovese 10% to 25%; Marzemino 5% to 30%; Barbera 10% to 20%; other red grapes max. 10%. Groppello: Groppello min. 85%. WINE TYPES: dw; spdw; ros; spros; dr (also novello)

SAN COLOMBANO AL LAMBRO/SAN COLOMBANO DOC (1984)

ZONE: Low hills north of the Po east of Pavia, not far from Oltrepò Pavese zone. GRAPES: Croatina 30% to 45%; Barbera 25% to 40%; Uva Rara 5% to 15%; other red grapes max. 15%. WINE TYPES: dr

SAN MARTINO DELLA BATTAGLIA DOC (1970)

ZONE: Southern shores of Lake Garda, intertwined with Lugana DOC. GRAPES: Tocai Friulano min. 80%; other white grapes max. 20%. WINE TYPES: dw; sw

TERRE DI FRANCIACORTA DOC (1995)

ZONE: Equivalent to Franciacorta DOCG. Terre di Franciacorta designation reserved for nonsparkling whites and reds. GRAPES: *Bianco:* Chardonnay and/or Pinot Bianco and/or Pinot Nero up to 100%. *Rosso:* Cabernet Sauvignon and Cabernet Franc min. 25%; Barbera min. 10%; Nebbiolo min. 10%; Merlot min. 10%; other red grapes max. 10%. WINE TYPES: dw; dr

VALCALEPIO DOC (1976)

ZONE: Hills running from west of Bergamo down to banks of Iseo River in east, abutting Franciacorta DOCG. GRAPES: *Bianco:* Pinot Bianco and Chardonnay 55% to 80%; Pinot Grigio 20% to 45%. *Rosso:* Cabernet Sauvignon 25% to 60%; Merlot 40% to 75%. *Moscato Passito:* Moscato di Scanzo/Moscato 100%. AGING: Rosso min. 1 yr. (min. 3 mos. in wood). Rosso Riserva min. 3 yrs. (min. 1 yr. in wood). Moscato Passito min. 2 yrs. WINE TYPES: dw; dr; sw

VALTELLINA DOC (1968)

ZONE: Steep, high-altitude slopes along Adda River in northern Lombardy, reaching from Ardenno and Tirano. Soils: silty clays mixed with pebbles and sand. Valtellina Superiore DOCG reserved for 4 specific subzones. GRAPES: Chiavennasca (Nebbiolo) min. 80%; other red grapes max. 20%. AGING: Min. 6 mos. Sfursat/ sforsato min. 2 yrs. WINE TYPES: dr

Marche

BIANCHELLO DEL METAURO DOC (1969)
ZONE: Hills running west to east along the Metauro River, in northern Marche. Soils: sandy clays. **GRAPES:** Bianchello (Biancame) min. 95%. **WINE TYPES:** dw

COLLI MACERATESI DOC (1975)
ZONE: Hills in the province of Macerata, south of Ancona. **GRAPES:** Maceratino min. 80%; Trebbiano Toscano, Verdicchio, Malvasia Toscana, and/or Chardonnay max. 20%. **WINE TYPES:** dw

COLLI PESARESI DOC (1972)
ZONE: Band of hills in northeastern Marche, fanning out from the seaside town of Pesaro. **GRAPES:** *Rosso and Rosato:* Sangiovese min. 70%. *Bianco:* Trebbiano Toscano, Verdicchio, Biancame, Pinot Grigio, Pinot Nero, Riesling Italico, Chardonnay, Sauvignon, and/or Pinot Bianco min. 75%. *Varietal Whites:* min. 85% of stated variety. Wines from Trebbiano; Biancame; Roncaglia. *Sangiovese:* Sangiovese min. 85%. *Focara Rosso:* Pinot Nero, Cabernet Franc, Cabernet Sauvignon and/or Merlot min. 50%; other red grapes max. 25%; Sangiovese max. 50%. *Focara Pinot Nero:* Pinot Nero min. 90%. **AGING:** Riserva Reds min. 2 yrs. **WINE TYPES:** dw; ros; dr (also novello)

ESINO DOC (1995)
ZONE: The Esino River basin, taking in much of the communes of Ancona and Macerata. **GRAPES:** *Bianco:* Verdicchio min. 50%; other white grapes max. 50%. *Rosso:* Sangiovese and/or Montepulciano min. 60%; other red grapes max. 40%. **WINE TYPES:** dw (also frizzante); dr (also novello)

FALERIO DEI COLLI ASCOLANI DOC (1975)
ZONE: A sizeable chunk of southern Marche, surrounding the city of Ascoli Piceno. **GRAPES:** Trebbiano Toscano 20% to 50%; Passerina 10% to 30%; Pecorino 10% to 30%; other white grapes max. 20%. **WINE TYPES:** dw

LACRIMA DI MORRO/LACRIMA DI MORRO D'ALBA DOC (1985)
ZONE: Hills north and slightly west of Ancona. **GRAPES:** Lacrima min. 85%. **WINE TYPES:** dr (also frizzante); sr

OFFIDA DOC (2000–2001)
ZONE: Southern Marche, around town of Offida. **GRAPES:** Whites from Passerina and Pecorino, Rosso from Montepulciano and Cabernet. **WINE TYPES:** dw; dr; sw

ROSSO CÒNERO DOC (1967)
ZONE: The hills around Monte Cònero in central Marche, including the communes of Ancona, Offagna, Camerano, Sirolo, Numana, and parts of Catelfidardo and Osimo. Soils: chalky clays. **GRAPES:** Montepulciano min. 85%; Sangiovese max. 15%. **AGING:** Riserva min. 2 yrs. **WINE TYPES:** dr

ROSSO PICENO DOC (1968)
ZONE: A vast stretch of Marche, running all the way from Senigallia, north of Ancona, down to Ascoli Piceno. **GRAPES:** Montepulciano 35% to 70%; Sangiovese 30% to 50%; other red grapes max. 15%. **AGING:** Superiore min. 1 yr. **WINE TYPES:** dr (also novello)

VERDICCHIO DEI CASTELLI DI JESI DOC (1968)
ZONE: Gentle hills west of Ancona, fanning westward from the commune of Jesi. Soils: calcareous clays. **GRAPES:** Verdicchio min. 85% for all types. **AGING:** Riserva min. 2 yrs. (min. 6 mos. in bottle). **WINE TYPES:** dw; spdw; sw

VERDICCHIO DI MATELICA DOC (1967)
ZONE: High pre-Apennine valley west of Ancona, centered on the commune of Matelica. **GRAPES:** Verdicchio min. 85%. **AGING:** Riserva min. 2 yrs. (min. 4 mos. in bottle). **WINE TYPES:** dw; spdw; sw

VERNACCIA DI SERRAPETRONA DOC (1971)
ZONE: Small band of hills west of Macerata. **GRAPES:** Vernaccia Nera min. 85%. **WINE TYPES:** spdr; spsr

Molise

BIFERNO DOC (1983)
ZONE: Much of the eastern half of Molise, reaching from Campobasso to the Adriatic, bisected by the Biferno River. **GRAPES:** *Bianco:* Trebbiano Toscano 65% to 70%; Bombino Bianco 25% to 30%; Malvasia Bianca 5% to 10%. *Rosso and Rosato:* Montepulciano 60% to 70%; Trebbiano Toscano 15% to 20%; Aglianico 15% to 20%; other white or red grapes max. 5%. **AGING:** Rosso Riserva min. 3 yrs. **WINE TYPES:** dw; ros; dr

MOLISE/DEL MOLISE DOC (1998)
ZONE: The region of Molise. **GRAPES:** Varietal

whites, reds, and rosés. Whites from Chardonnay, Falanghina, Greco Bianco, Moscato Bianco, Pinot Bianco, Sauvignon, Trebbiano. Reds from Aglianico, Cabernet Sauvignon, Montepulciano, Sangiovese, Tintilia. *Spumante:* Chardonnay, Pinot Bianco, and/or Moscato. *Spumante with Varietal Mention:* Min. 85% of stated variety. **AGING:** Min. 2 yrs. (min. 6 mos. in wood). **WINE TYPES:** dw; spdw; sw; dr (also novello); sr

PENTRO DI ISERNIA DOC (1983)

ZONE: Two separate zones flanking the inland Molise town of Isernia. One zone is to the north, in the Verrino River Valley, the other to the south and southwest of Isernia. **GRAPES:** *Bianco:* Trebbiano Toscano 60% to 70%; Bombino Bianco 30% to 40%; other white grapes max. 10%. *Rosso and Rosato:* Montepulciano 45% to 55%; Sangiovese 45% to 55%; other red grapes max. 10%. **WINE TYPES:** dw; ros; dr

Piemonte

ASTI DOCG (1967)

ZONE: A broad swath of the Langhe and Monferrato hills south and southeast of the commune of Asti, including parts of the provinces of Asti, Cuneo, and Alessandria. Includes sparkling (Asti Spumante) and semisparkling (Moscato d'Asti) wines which are sweet or semisweet. **GRAPES:** Moscato Bianco 100%. **WINE TYPES:** sw (frizzante); spsw

BARBARESCO DOCG (DOC 1966; DOCG 1980)

ZONE: Undulating hills in three communes east and northeast of Alba: Barbaresco, Neive, and Treiso. Soils are predominantly calcareous marls as in Barolo. **GRAPES:** Nebbiolo 100%. **AGING:** Min. 2 yrs. (min. 1 yr. in wood); Riserva min. 4 yrs. **WINE TYPES:** dr

BAROLO DOCG (DOC 1966; DOCG 1980)

ZONE: A swath of the Langhe hills southwest of the town of Alba, taking in 11 communes in total. Soils are predominantly marls rich in limestone, and the top wines in the DOCG are said to hail from the communes of Monforte d'Alba, Serralunga d'Alba, Castiglione Falletto, Barolo, and La Morra. Barolo Chinato is an aromatized wine made from a base of Barolo wine, traditionally consumed as a digestif. **GRAPES:** Nebbiolo 100%. **AGING:** Min. 3 yrs. (min. 2 yrs. in wood); Riserva min. 5 yrs. **WINE TYPES:** dr

BRACHETTO D'ACQUI/ACQUI DOCG (DOC 1969; DOCG 1996)

ZONE: The Monferrato hills southeast of the town of Asti, including communes in the Belbo and Bormida river valleys, in the provinces of Asti and Alessandria, respectively. Key towns include Acqui Terme and Strevi. Overlaps the Asti DOCG, among others. **GRAPES:** Brachetto 100%. **WINE TYPES:** sr (also frizzante); spsr

GATTINARA DOCG (DOC 1967; DOCG 1990)

ZONE: A band of mostly south-facing slopes north of the city of Vercelli, centered on the commune of Gattinara. **GRAPES:** Nebbiolo (locally called Spanna) min. 90%; Vespolina max. 4%; Bonarda max. 10%. **AGING:** Min. 3 yrs. (min. 1 yr. in wood); Riserva min. 4 yrs. (min. 2 yrs. in wood). **WINE TYPES:** dr

GAVI/CORTESE DI GAVI DOCG (1974; DOCG 1988)

ZONE: Hills stretching from Novi Ligure, in southeastern Piedmont, down toward the border with Liguria. The center of the zone is the small commune of Gavi. **GRAPES:** Cortese 100%. **AGING:** Superiore 1 yr. **WINE TYPES:** dw (also frizzante); spdw

GHEMME DOCG (DOC 1969; DOCG 1995)

ZONE: Hills east of the Sesia River, north of the city of Vercelli, centered on the commune of Ghemme. **GRAPES:** Nebbiolo (Spanna) min. 75%; Vespolina and/or Uva Rara max. 25%. **AGING:** Min. 3 yrs. (min. 20 mos. in wood, min. 9 mos. in bottle); Riserva min. 4 yrs. (min. 25 mos. in wood, min. 9 mos. in bottle). **WINE TYPES:** dr

ALBUGNANO DOC (1997)

ZONE: Four communes in the hills east of Turin, all of which are nevertheless in the province of Asti: Albugnano, Pino d'Asti, Castelnuovo Don Bosco, and Passerano Marmorito. **GRAPES:** Nebbiolo min. 85%; Freisa, Barbera, and/or Bonarda max. 15%. **AGING:** Superiore min. 1 yr. (min. 6 mos. in oak barrels). **WINE TYPES:** dr (also frizzante and abboccato); ros

BARBERA D'ALBA DOC (1970)

ZONE: A vast area centered on the town of Alba, reaching north and west into the Roero hills, east toward the Belbo River and south toward Monforte d'Alba. The zone essentially straddles the Tanaro River, spreading to the east and west. **GRAPES:** Barbera 100%. **AGING:** Superiore min. 1 yr. in oak or chestnut barrels. **WINE TYPES:** dr

BARBERA D'ASTI DOC (1970)

ZONE: Abuts the Barbera d'Alba DOC to the northeast and spreads further north, east, and west, with the commune of Asti as its center. The zone extends as far as Castelnuovo Don Bosco in the west (on the border with the Torino province) and north to the banks of the Po River near Casale Monferrato. **GRAPES:** Barbera 85% to 100%; Freisa, Grignolino, and/or Dolcetto max. 15%. **AGING:** Wines cannot be released until March of year succeeding vintage year. Superiore min. 1 yr. (min. 6 mos. in wood). **WINE TYPES:** dr

BARBERA DEL MONFERRATO DOC (1970)

ZONE: Essentially all of the Monferrato Hills, including much of the area covered by the Barbera d'Asti DOC and extending farther east into Alessandria and down toward Gavi. **GRAPES:** Barbera 85% to 100%; Freisa, Grignolino, and/or Dolcetto max. 15%. **AGING:** Superiore min. 1 yr. (min. 6 mos. in wood). **WINE TYPES:** dr (also frizzante and abboccato)

BOCA DOC (1969)

ZONE: North of the city of Novara on the right bank of the Sesia River, including the communes of Boca, Maggiora, Cavallirio, Prato Sesia, and Grignasco. One of the most northerly DOCs in Piedmont. **GRAPES:** Nebbiolo (Spanna) 45% to 70%; Vespolina 20% to 40%; Bonarda (Uva Rara) max. 20%. **AGING:** Min. 3 yrs. (min. 2 yrs. in wood). **WINE TYPES:** dr

BRAMATERRA DOC (1979)

ZONE: Abuts Gattinara DOC to the north and west, on the west side of the Sesia River in northern Piedmont. **GRAPES:** Nebbiolo (Spanna) 50% to 70%; Croatina 20% to 30%; Bonarda and/or Vespolina 10% to 20%. **AGING:** Min. 2 yrs. (min. 18 mos. in wood); Riserva min. 3 yrs. (min. 2 yrs. in wood). **WINE TYPES:** dr

CANAVESE DOC (1996)

ZONE: A band of hills flanking the Dora Baltea River northeast of Turin. Overlaps the Erbaluce di Caluso DOC. **GRAPES:** *Bianco:* Erbaluce 100%. *Rosso and Rosato:* Nebbiolo, Barbera, Freisa, and/or Neretto min. 60%; other authorized red grapes max. 40%. *Varietal Reds:* Min. 85% of stated variety. Wines from Nebbiolo and Barbera. **WINE TYPES:** dw; ros; dr (also novello)

CAREMA DOC (1967)

ZONE: Small cluster of hills flanking the Dora Baltea River, northeast of Turin. Zone is confined to the commune of Carema, on Piedmont's border with Valle d'Aosta. **GRAPES:** Nebbiolo (Spanna) min. 85%; other authorized red grapes min. 15%. **AGING:** Min. 3 yrs. (min. 2 yrs.. in wood); Riserva min. 4 yrs. (min. 30 mos. in wood, min. 1 yr.. in bottle). **WINE TYPES:** dr

COLLI TORTONESI DOC (1973)

ZONE: Hills in and around the town of Tortona, in easternmost Piedmont, reaching toward the border with Lombardy. Adjacent to Lombardy's Oltrepò Pavese DOC. **GRAPES:** *Bianco:* any mixture of white grapes authorized in Alessandria province. *Rosso:* any mixture of red grapes authorized in Alessandria province. *Chiaretto (rosé):* any mixture of red grapes authorized in Alessandria province. *Cortese and Cortese Spumante:* Cortese min. 85%. *Barbera:* Barbera min. 85%. *Dolcetto:* Dolcetto min. 85%. **AGING:** Barbera Superiore min. 1 yr. (min. 6 mos. in wood). **WINE TYPES:** dw (also frizzante); spdw; ros; dr (also frizzante and novello)

COLLINA TORINESE DOC (1999)

ZONE: Hills flanking the Po River right around the city of Turin. **GRAPES:** *Rosso:* Barbera min. 60%; Freisa min. 25%; other red grapes max. 15%. *Varietal Reds:* Min. 85% of stated variety. Wines from Barbera; Bonarda; Malvasia di Schierano; Pelaverga (Cari). **AGING:** Min. 3 yrs. (min. 20 mos. in wood, min. 9 mos. in bottle); Riserva min. 4 yrs. (min. 25 mos. in wood, min. 9 mos. in bottle). **WINE TYPES:** dr (also novello and frizzante); ros (also novello and frizzante); sros; sr

COLLINE NOVARESI DOC (1994)

ZONE: A broad band of hills north of Novara, east of the Sesia River. Zone overlaps several other DOCs, including Fara, Ghemme, and Boca, and extends further east. **GRAPES:** *Bianco:* Erbaluce 100%. *Rosso:* Nebbiolo min. 30%; Uva Rara max. 40%; Vespolina and/or Croatina max. 30%. *Varietal Reds:* Min. 85% of stated variety. Wines from Nebbiolo (Spanna); Uva Rara (Bonarda); Vespolina; Croatina; Barbera. **WINE TYPES:** dw (also frizzante); dr (also frizzante)

COLLINE SALUZZESI DOC (1996)

ZONE: A small band of hills flanking the Po River between Cuneo and Turin, including the communes of Pagno, Piasco, Saluzzo, and six others. **GRAPES:** *Rosso:* Nebbiolo, Pelaverga, and/or Barbera min. 60%; other red grapes max. 40%. *Varietal Reds:* 100% of stated variety. Wines from Pelaverga; Quagliano. **WINE TYPES:** dr; sr (also frizzante); spsr

CORTESE DELL'ALTO MONFERRATO DOC (1992)
ZONE: A broad portion of the Alto Monferrato hills, namely those south of Alessandria and Asti reaching toward the Apennines that separate Piedmont from Liguria. **GRAPES:** Cortese min. 85%. **WINE TYPES:** dw (also frizzante); spdw

COSTE DELLA SESIA DOC (1996)
ZONE: Abuts Gattinara DOC to the west, including a number of communes between Biella and Gattinara. **GRAPES:** *Bianco:* Erbaluce 100%. *Rosso and Rosato:* Nebbiolo, Bonarda, Vespolina, Croatina, and/or Barbera min. 50%. *Varietal Reds:* Min. 85% of stated variety. Wines from Nebbiolo (Spanna); Vespolina; Bonarda (Uva Rara); Croatina. **WINE TYPES:** dw; ros; dr

DOLCETTO D'ACQUI DOC (1972)
ZONE: Hills flanking the Bormida River southeast of Asti, running from the border with Liguria up past Acqui Terme. Soils: calcareous clays. **GRAPES:** Dolcetto 100%. **AGING:** Superiore min. 1 yr. **WINE TYPES:** dr

DOLCETTO D'ALBA DOC (1974)
ZONE: Parts of the Langhe hills east of the Tanaro River, extending to the southwest, northeast, and east of the city of Alba. **GRAPES:** Dolcetto 100%. **AGING:** Superiore min. 1 yr. **WINE TYPES:** dr

DOLCETTO D'ASTI DOC (1974)
ZONE: Hills southeast of the town of Asti, overlapping somewhat with the Moscato d'Asti DOC. Key communes include Bubbio, Canelli, and other communes east of the Belbo River. **GRAPES:** Dolcetto 100%. **AGING:** Superiore min. 1 yr. **WINE TYPES:** dr

DOLCETTO DELLE LANGHE MONREGALESI DOC (1974)
ZONE: Flanks the Dolcetto di Dogliani zone to the west and south, following the Tanaro River toward Mondovì and Ceva. This is one of the southernmost appellations in Piedmont, reaching close to the mountainous border with Liguria. **GRAPES:** Dolcetto 100%. **AGING:** Superiore min. 1 yr. **WINE TYPES:** dr

DOLCETTO DI DIANO D'ALBA/DIANO D'ALBA DOC (1974)
ZONE: A small zone centered on the commune of Diano d'Alba, sandwiched between the city of Alba and the Barolo DOCG zone to the southwest. **GRAPES:** Dolcetto 100%. **AGING:** Superiore min. 1 yr. **WINE TYPES:** dr

DOLCETTO DI DOGLIANI DOC (1974)
ZONE: Hills beginning at the southern end of the Barolo DOCG and extending south along the east bank of the Tanaro River, centered on the commune of Dogliani. **GRAPES:** Dolcetto 100%. **AGING:** Superiore min. 1 yr. **WINE TYPES:** dr

DOLCETTO DI OVADA DOC (1972)
ZONE: Sandwiched between the Dolcetto d'Acqui and Gavi DOC(G)s southeast of Asti. **GRAPES:** Dolcetto 100%. **AGING:** Superiore min. 1 yr. **WINE TYPES:** dr

ERBALUCE DI CALUSO/CALUSO DOC (1967)
ZONE: Hills of glacial moraine flanking the Dora Baltea River, northeast of Turin. Key communes are Caluso and Canavese. **GRAPES:** Erbaluce 100%. **AGING:** Passito min. 4 yrs. (5 yrs. for Passito Riserva). **WINE TYPES:** dw; spdw; sw

FARA DOC (1969)
ZONE: Hills east of the Sesia River, just north of the city of Novara. Lies south of the Ghemme and Sizzano DOC(G)s. **GRAPES:** Nebbiolo (Spanna) 30% to 50%; Vespolina 10% to 30%; Bonarda (Uva Rara) max. 40%. **AGING:** Min. 3 yrs. (min. 2 yrs. in wood). **WINE TYPES:** dr

FREISA D'ASTI DOC (1972)
ZONE: Hills extending throughout much of Asti province, including those north, south, east, and west of the city of Asti. **GRAPES:** Freisa 100%. **AGING:** Superiore min. 1 yr. **WINE TYPES:** dr (also frizzante); sr (also frizzante); spsr

FREISA DI CHIERI DOC (1973)
ZONE: Hills just east of Turin, centered on the commune of Chieri. **GRAPES:** Freisa 100%. **AGING:** Superiore min. 1 yr. **WINE TYPES:** dr (also frizzante); sr (also frizzante); spsr

GABIANO DOC (1983)
ZONE: A small zone north of Asti, near the Po River, centered on the commune of Gabiano. **GRAPES:** Barbera 90% to 95%; Freisa and/or Grignolino 5% to 10%. **AGING:** Riserva min. 2 yrs. **WINE TYPES:** dr

GRIGNOLINO D'ASTI DOC (1973)
ZONE: Hills north and south of the city of Asti.

GRAPES: Grignolino min. 90%; Freisa max. 10%.
WINE TYPES: dr

GRIGNOLINO DEL MONFERRATO CASALESE DOC (1974)
ZONE: Abuts Grignolino d'Asti to the north, reaching toward the south bank of the Po River. Extends east to the commune of Casale Monferrato, which sits on the Po. GRAPES: Grignolino min. 90%; Freisa max. 10%. WINE TYPES: dr

LANGHE DOC (1994)
ZONE: The Langhe Hills, taking in a broad area around the city of Alba, mostly east of the Tanaro River. Overlaps many DOC(G)s, including Barolo, Barbaresco, and Roero Arneis. GRAPES: *Bianco and Rosso:* any authorized grapes for province of Cuneo. *Varietal Whites:* 100% of stated variety. Wines from Arneis; Chardonnay; Favorita. *Varietal Reds:* 100% of stated variety. Wines from Nebbiolo; Dolcetto. WINE TYPES: dw; dr (also frizzante); sr (also frizzante)

LESSONA DOC (1976)
ZONE: Just west of the Bramaterra DOC, north of Vercelli. Centered on the commune of Lessona. GRAPES: Nebbiolo (Spanna) min. 75%; Vespolina and Bonarda max. 25%. AGING: Min. 2 yrs. (min. 1 yr. in wood). WINE TYPES: dr

LOAZZOLO DOC (1992)
ZONE: The commune of Loazzolo, south of Asti in the Monferrato hills. Falls within the boundaries of the Moscato d'Asti DOCG, among others. GRAPES: Moscato Bianco 100%. AGING: Min. 2 yrs. WINE TYPES: sw (passito-style)

MALVASIA DI CASORZO D'ASTI DOC (1968)
ZONE: A small zone situated midway between Asti and Canale Monferrato. GRAPES: Malvasia di Casorzo min. 90%; Barbera, Freisa, and/or Grignolino max. 10%. AGING: Superiore min. 1 yr. WINE TYPES: ros (also frizante); sros; spsros; sr (also frizzante); spsr

MALVASIA DI CASTELNUOVO DON BOSCO DOC (1973)
ZONE: Northwest of Asti in hills centered on the commune of Castelnuovo Don Bosco. GRAPES: Malvasia di Schierano min. 85%; Freisa max. 15%. AGING: Superiore min. 1 yr. WINE TYPES: ros (also frizzante); sros; spsros; sr (also frizzante); spsr

MONFERRATO DOC (1994)
ZONE: The broad band of hills running from the border of Liguria down past Alessandria and Asti and toward the banks of the Po to the north. GRAPES: *Bianco and Rosso:* any mix of authorized grapes in the provinces of Asti and Alessandria. *Chiaretto/Ciaret:* Barbera, Bonarda, Cabernet Franc, Cabernet Sauvignon, Freisa, Grignolino, Pinot Nero and/or Nebbiolo min. 85%. *Dolcetto:* Dolcetto min. 85%. *Freisa:* Freisa min. 85%. *Monferrato Casalese:* Cortese min. 85%. WINE TYPES: dw (also frizzante); ros (also frizzante); dr (also frizzante)

NEBBIOLO D'ALBA DOC (1970)
ZONE: Hills on both sides of the Tanaro River near Alba, but excluding those within the Barbaresco and Barolo DOCGs. Takes in most of the Roero DOC GRAPES: Nebbiolo 100%. AGING: Secco min. 1 yr. WINE TYPES: dr; sr; spdr

PIEMONTE DOC (1994)
ZONE: All of winemaking Piedmont. GRAPES: *Piemonte:* Chardonnay, Pinot Bianco, Pinot Grigio, and/or Pinot Nero in any combination, vinified as a spumante. *Piemonte Moscato/Moscato Passito:* Moscato Bianco 100%. *Varietal Whites:* Min. 85% of stated variety. Wines from Chardonnay; Cortese; Pinot Bianco; Pinot Grigio. *Varietal Reds:* Min. 85% of stated variety. Wines from Barbera; Bonarda; Grignolino; Brachetto; Pinot Nero. AGING: Moscato Passito min. 1 yr. WINE TYPES: dw; spdw; sw; spsw; dr (also novello); sr; spsr

PINEROLESE DOC (1996)
ZONE: A small zone southwest of Turin, north of the Po. GRAPES: *Rosso and Rosato:* Barbera, Bonarda, Nebbiolo, and/or Neretto min. 50%; other red grapes max. 50%. *Pinerolese Ramie:* Avanà 30%; Avarengo min. 15%; Neretto min. 20%; other red grapes max. 35%. *Varietal Reds and Rosés:* Min. 85% of stated variety. Wines from Barbera, Bonarda, Freisa, Dolcetto, Doux d'Henry. WINE TYPES: dr (also frizzante); ros (also frizzante); sros

ROERO DOC (1985)
ZONE: Steep, often thickly forested hills west of Alba. GRAPES: *Roero Arneis:* Arneis 100%. *Roero:* Nebbiolo 95% to 98%; Arneis 2% to 5%. AGING: Roero cannot be released until June of the year succeeding vintage year WINE TYPES: dw; spdw; dr

RUBINO DI CANTAVENNA DOC (1970)
ZONE: A small zone north of Asti on the banks of the

Po, including the commune of Gabiano. Geographically roughly equivalent to the Gabiano DOC.. **GRAPES:** Barbera 75% to 90%; Grignolino and/or Freisa max. 25%. **AGING:** Wine cannot be released until Dec. 31 of the year following the vintage year. **WINE TYPES:** dr

RUCHÉ DI CASTAGNOLE MONFERRATO DOC (1987)
ZONE: Just northeast of the city of Asti, centered on the commune of Castagnole Monferrato. **GRAPES:** Ruché min. 90%; Barbera and/or Brachetto max. 10%. **WINE TYPES:** dr; sr

SIZZANO DOC (1969)
ZONE: The commune of Sizzano, northwest of Novara on the right bank of the Sesia River. Immediately south of Ghemme DOCG. **GRAPES:** Nebbiolo (Spanna) 40% to 60%; Vespolina 15% to 40%; Bonarda (Uva Rara) max. 25%. **AGING:** Min. 3 yrs. (min. 2 yrs. in wood). **WINE TYPES:** dr

VALSUSA DOC (1997)
ZONE: A cluster of hills north of the Dora Baltea River west of Turin, not far from the border with France. **GRAPES:** Avanà, Barbera, Dolcetto, and/or Neretto min. 60%; other red grapes max. 40%. **WINE TYPES:** dr

VERDUNO PELAVERGA/VERDUNO DOC (1995)
ZONE: Overlapping the northern limit of the Barolo DOCG, centered on the commune of Verduno. Includes parts of La Morra and Roddi d'Alba. **GRAPES:** Pelaverga min. 85%; other red grapes max. 15%. **AGING:** Min. 6 mos. **WINE TYPES:** dr (also frizzante)

Puglia

ALEATICO DI PUGLIA DOC (1973)
ZONE: Encompasses all the DOC zones of Puglia. **GRAPES:** Aleatico min. 85%; Negroamaro, Malvasia Nera and/or Primitivo max. 15%. **AGING:** min. 6 mos. (min. 3 yrs. for riserva). **WINE TYPES:** sr; fr

ALEZIO DOC (1983)
ZONE: A small cluster of communes in southwestern Puglia, including Gallipoli, Alezio and Tuglie. Soils: red clays and sands over limestone. **GRAPES:** Negroamaro min. 80%; Malvasia Nera, Sangiovese and/or Montepulciano max. 20%. **AGING:** Rosso Riserva: min. 2 yrs. **WINE TYPES:** ros; dr

BRINDISI DOC (1979)
ZONE: Centered on the coastal port of Brindisi in southeastern Puglia and extending inland toward Mesagne. Soils: red soils on a limestone base. **GRAPES:** Negroamaro min. 70%; Malvasia Nera, Susumaniello, Montepulciano and/or Sangiovese max. 30% (Sangiovese no more than 10% of total). **AGING:** Rosso Riserva: min. 2 yrs. **WINE TYPES:** ros; dr

CACC'E MMITTE DI LUCERA DOC (1975)
ZONE: Centered on the commune of Lucera, north of Foggia. Soils: calcareous clay and sand. **GRAPES:** Uva di Troia 35% to 60%; Montepulciano, Sangiovese and/or Malvasia Nera 25% to 35%; Trebbiano Toscano, Bombino Bianco, and/or Malvasia del Chianti 15% to 30%. **WINE TYPES:** dr

CASTEL DEL MONTE DOC (1971)
ZONE: Occasionally high slopes surrounding the commune of Castel del Monte west of Bari, reaching toward the border with Basilicata. Soils: ferrous red soils over limestone. **GRAPES:** *Bianco:* Pampanuto up to 100%; Chardonnay up to 100%; Bombino Bianco up to 100%; other nonaromatic white varieties max. 35%. *Rosso:* Uva di Troia up to 100%; Aglianico up to 100%; Montepulciano up to 100%; other authorized red grapes max. 35%. *Rosato:* Bombino Bianco up to 100%; Aglianico up to 100%; Uva di Troia up to 100%; other authorized red grapes up to 35%. *Varietal Whites:* min. 90% of stated variety; wines from Bombino Bianco; Chardonnay; Pinot Bianco; Sauvignon. *Varietal Reds:* min. 90% of stated variety; wines from Bombino Nero; Uva di Troia; Cabernet; Pinot Nero; Aglianico. *Varietal Rosato:* from min. 90% Aglianico. **AGING:** Riserva Red: min. 2 yrs. (min. 1 yr. in wood). **WINE TYPES:** dw (also frizzante); ros (also frizzante); dr (also novello)

COPERTINO DOC (1976)
ZONE: Just south of the Salice Salentino DOC, near Lecce in southern Puglia. Soils: red clays over limestone. **GRAPES:** Negroamaro min. 70%; Malvasia Nera, Montepulciano, and/or Sangiovese max. 30% (Sangiovese no more than 15% of total). **AGING:** Rosso Riserva min. 2 yrs. **WINE TYPES:** ros; dr

GALATINA DOC (1997)
ZONE: South of Lecce on the Salentine peninsula, centered on the commune of Galatina. Soils: red clay and sand over limestone. **GRAPES:** *Bianco:* Chardonnay min. 55%; other authorized white grapes max. 45%. *Chardonnay:* Chardonnay min. 85%. *Rosato and Rosso:* Negroamaro

min. 65%; other authorized red grapes max. 35%.
Negroamaro: Negroamaro min. 85%. **AGING:** Negroamaro Riserva min. 2 yrs. (min. 6 mos. in wood). **WINE
TYPES:** dw (also frizzante); ros (also frizzante); dr
(also novello)

GIOIA DEL COLLE DOC (1987)
ZONE: A broad swath of central Puglia south of Bari,
reaching from the border with Basilicata toward Bari and
the Adriatic. Abuts Castel del Monte and Gravina zones.
GRAPES: *Bianco:* Trebbiano Toscano 50% to 70%; other
authorized white grapes 30% to 50%. *Rosato and Rosso:*
Primitivo 50% to 60%; Montepulciano, Sangiovese,
Negroamaro and/or Malvasia Nera 40% to 50% (Mal-
vasia max. 10%). *Primitivo:* Primitivo 100%. *Aleatico:*
Aleatico min. 85%. **AGING:** Aleatico min. 6 mos.
Aleatico Riserva: min. 2 yrs. (min. 1 yr. in wood).
Primitivo Riserva min. 2 yrs. **WINE TYPES:** dw; ros; dr;
sr; fr

GRAVINA DOC (1983)
ZONE: Central Puglia, west of Bari near border with
Basilicata. Centered on commune of Gravina in Puglia.
GRAPES: Malvasia del Chianti 40% to 65%; Greco di
Tufo and/or Bianco d'Alessano 35% to 60%; Bombino
Bianco, Trebbiano Toscano, and/or Verdeca max. 10%.
WINE TYPES: dw; spdw; sw

LEVERANO DOC (1979)
ZONE: The commune of Leverano, west of Lecce in
southern Puglia. Abuts Copertino DOC to the west and
Salice Salentino DOC to the south. **GRAPES:** *Bianco and
Bianco Passito and Vendemmia Tardiva:* Malvasia Bianca min.
50%; Bombino Bianco max. 40%; other authorized
white grapes max. 30%. *Malvasia Bianca:* Malvasia Bianca
min. 85%. *Rosso and Rosato:* Negroamaro min. 50%; Malvasia Nera, Montepulciano, and/or Sangiovese max.
40%; other authorized red grapes max. 30%. *Negroamaro
and Negroamaro Rosato:* Negroamaro min. 85% **AGING:**
Rosso Riserva: min. 2 yrs. **WINE TYPES:** dw; sw; ros;
dr (also novello)

LIZZANO DOC (1988)
ZONE: South of Taranto, centered on the commune
of Lizzano. **GRAPES:** *Bianco:* Trebbiano Toscano 40%
to 60%; Chardonnay and/or Pinot Bianco min. 30%;
Malvasia Bianca max. 10%; Sauvignon and/or Bianco di
Alessano max. 25%. *Rosso and Rosato:* Negroamaro 60%
to 80%; Montepulciano, Sangiovese, Bombino Nero
and/or Pinot Nero max. 40%; other red grapes max.
10%. *Negroamaro Rosso and Rosato:* Negroamaro min. 85%.

Malvasia Nera: Malvasia Nera min. 85%. **WINE TYPES:**
dw (also frizzante); spdw; ros; spros; dr (also novello)

LOCOROTONDO DOC (1969)
ZONE: South of Bari near the Adriatic coast, centered
on the commune of Locorotondo. Soils: red clay and
sand on a limestone base. **GRAPES:** Verdeca 50% to
65%; Bianco d'Alessano 35% to 50%; Fiano, Bombino
Bianco and/or Malvasia Toscana max. 5%. **WINE
TYPES:** dw; spdw

MARTINA/MARTINA FRANCA DOC (1969)
ZONE: Adjacent to Locorotondo zone south of Bari,
centered on commune of Martina Franca. **GRAPES:**
Verdeca 50% to 65%; Bianco d'Alessano 35% to 50%;
Fiano, Bombino Bianco and/or Malvasia Toscana max.
5%. **WINE TYPES:** dw; spdw

MATINO DOC (1971)
ZONE: Abuts Alezio DOC in southern Puglia, extend-
ing inland from Alezio toward the commune of Matino.
Soils: red clays and sands on a limestone base. **GRAPES:**
Negroamaro min. 70%; Malvasia Nera and/or San-
giovese max. 30%. **WINE TYPES:** ros; dr

MOSCATO DI TRANI DOC (1974)
ZONE: Broad rolling plain called Le Murge between
Foggia and Bari, in north-central Puglia. **GRAPES:**
Moscato Bianco min. 85% **AGING:** Naturale: min. 6
mos. Liquoroso: min. 1 yr. **WINE TYPES:** sw; fw

NARDÒ DOC (1987)
ZONE: The communes of Nardò and Porto Cesareo,
along the Gulf of Taranto west of Lecce. **GRAPES:**
Negroamaro min. 80%; Malvasia Nera and/or Montepulciano max. 20% **AGING:** Rosso Riserva: min. 2
yrs. **WINE TYPES:** ros; dr

ORTA NOVA DOC (1984)
ZONE: Northern plains of Puglia, just south of Foggia.
Soils: calcareous clay and sand. **GRAPES:** Sangiovese
min. 60%; Uva di Troia, Montepulciano, Lambrusco
and/or Trebbiano max. 40% (Lambrusco and Trebbiano
max. 10%) **WINE TYPES:** ros; dr

OSTUNI DOC (1972)
ZONE: Adriatic coast and inland communes north of
Brindisi, abutting Martina Franca DOC to east. Soils:
red clays on a limestone base. **GRAPES:** *Bianco:* Impigno
50% to 85%; Francavilla 15% to 50%; Bianco Alessano
and/or Verdeca max. 10%. *Ottavianello:* Ottavianello
min. 85%; Negroamaro, Malvasia Nera, Notar

Domenico and/or Susumariello max. 15%. **WINE TYPES:** dw; dr

PRIMITIVO DI MANDURIA DOC (1974)
ZONE: A broad plain between Taranto and Brindisi in southern Puglia, centered on commune of Manduria. Soils: red clay and sand on limestone base. **GRAPES:** Primitivo 100%. **AGING:** Rosso and Dolce Naturale: min. 9 mos. Liquoroso: min. 2 yrs. **WINE TYPES:** dr; sr; fr

ROSSO BARLETTA DOC (1977)
ZONE: Swath of Adriatic coastal plains and inland communes between Foggia and Bari. **GRAPES:** Uva di Troia min. 70%; Montepulciano, Sangiovese and/or Malbech max. 30% (Malbech max. 10% of total). **AGING:** Invecchiato: min. 2 yrs. (min. 1 yr. in wood). **WINE TYPES:** dr

ROSSO CANOSA/CANISIUM DOC (1979)
ZONE: Near Castel del Monte DOC in central Puglia, centered on the commune of Canosa. **GRAPES:** Uva di Troia min. 65%; Montepulciano and/or Sangiovese max. 35% (Sangiovese max. 15% of total); other authorized red grapes max. 5%. **AGING:** Riserva min. 2 yrs. (min. 1 yr. in wood). **WINE TYPES:** dr

ROSSO DI CERIGNOLA DOC (1974)
ZONE: Northern plains of Puglia, south of Foggia. Soils: calcareous clays and sand. **GRAPES:** Uva di Troia min. 55%; Negroamaro 15% to 30%; Sangiovese, Barbera, Montepulciano, Malvasia and/or Trebbiano Toscano max. 15%. **AGING:** Riserva min. 2 yrs. in wood. **WINE TYPES:** dr

SALICE SALENTINO DOC (1976)
ZONE: Named for commune of Salice Salentino, a commune northwest of Lecce on the Salentine peninsula. Soils: red clay and sand on a limestone base. **GRAPES:** *Bianco:* Chardonnay min. 70%; other authorized white grapes max. 30%. *Pinot Bianco:* Pinot Bianco min. 85%; Chardonnay and/or Sauvignon max. 15%. *Rosso and Rosato:* Negroamaro min. 80%; Malvasia Nera max. 20%. *Aleatico:* Aleatico min. 85%; Negroamaro, Malvasia Nera and/or Primitivo max. 15%. **AGING:** Aleatico min. 6 mos. Aleatico Riserva min. 2 yrs. Rosso Riserva min. 2 yrs. (6 mos. in wood). **WINE TYPES:** dw (also frizzante); spdw; spros; ros (also frizzante); dr (also novello); sr; fr

SAN SEVERO DOC (1968)
ZONE: Rolling plains north of Foggia, in northern Puglia, reaching toward border with Molise. **GRAPES:** *Bianco:* Bombino Bianco 40% to 60%; Trebbiano Toscano 40% to 60%; Malvasia Bianca and/or Verdeca max. 20%. *Rosato and Rosso:* Montepulciano d'Abruzzo 70%-100%; Sangiovese max. 30%. **WINE TYPES:** dw; ros; dr

SQUINZANO DOC (1976)
ZONE: Coastal plains on Salentine peninsula, between Lecce and Brindisi. Soils: red clays and sand over limestone. **GRAPES:** Negroamaro min. 70%; Malvasia Nera and/or Sangiovese max. 30% (Sangiovese no more than 15% of total). **AGING:** Rosso Riserva min. 2 yrs. (6 mos. in wood). **WINE TYPES:** ros; dr

Sardegna

VERMENTINO DI GALLURA DOCG (DOC 1975; DOCG 1996)
ZONE: Vineyards reaching up to 500m elevation in the rocky northeast corner of Sardinia. The Coghinas River, west of Tempio Pausania, forms western border. Soils: sandy clays over granite base. **GRAPES:** Vermentino min. 95%; other white grapes max. 5%. **WINE TYPES:** dw

ALGHERO DOC (1995)
ZONE: Plains between Alghero and Sassari, in northwestern Sardinia. **GRAPES:** *Bianco, Rosato and Rosso:* any authorized grapes. *Varietal Whites:* min. 85% of stated variety. Wines from Chardonnay; Sauvignon; Torbato; Vermentino. *Varietal Reds:* Min. 85% of stated variety. Wines from Cabernet Sauvignon and/or Franc and/or Carmenère; Sangiovese; Cagnulari. **AGING:** Liquoroso: min. 3 yrs (5 yrs. for riserva). **WINE TYPES:** dw (also frizzante); spdw; sw; ros (also frizzante); dr (also novello); spdr; sr

ARBOREA DOC (1987)
ZONE: A vast chunk of west-central Sardinia, flanking the Tirso River as it runs down to Oristano. Soils: predominantly alluvial. **GRAPES:** *Trebbiano:* Min. 85% trebbiano. *Sangiovese Rosso and Rosato:* min. 85% sangiovese. **WINE TYPES:** dw (also frizzante); sw; ros; dr

CAMPIDANO DI TERRALBA/TERRALBA DOC (1975)
ZONE: Plains south of Oristano, on the southwest coast of Sardinia. **GRAPES:** Bovale min. 80%; Pascale di Cagliari, Greco Nero, and/or Monica max. 20%.

AGING: Min. 6 mos. (release Mar. 31 of year succeeding vintage). WINE TYPES: dr

CANNONAU DI SARDEGNA DOC (1972)

ZONE: The entire island of Sardinia. The subzone Oliena or Nepente di Oliena is reserved for wines made in the commune of Oliena, just south of Nuoro near the Gennargentu mountains. The subzone Capo Ferrato is reserved for wines made in several communes in the extreme southeastern corner of the island. The subzone Jerzu is reserved for wines made in the communes of Jerzu and Cardedu, in the Barbagia region. GRAPES: Cannonau min. 90%; other red grapes max. 10%. AGING: Wine cannot be released until April 1 of yr. succeeding vintage. Riserva: min. 2 yrs. (min. 6 mos. in wood). Liquoroso: min. 10 mos. (min. 6 mos. in wood). WINE TYPES: dr; ros; sr; fr

CARIGNANO DEL SULCIS DOC (1989)

ZONE: The Sulcis region of southwestern Sardinia, including the islands of Sant'Antioco and San Pietro. Soils: sandy clays. GRAPES: Carignano min. 85%; other red grapes max. 15%. AGING: *Rosso:* min. 3 mos. in bottle. Rosso Riserva and Superiore: min. 2 yrs. (min. 6 mos. in bottle). Passito: min. 6 mos. (min. 3 mos. in bottle). Wines may not be released before Nov. 1 of the year succeeding the vintage year. WINE TYPES: dr (also novello); sr; ros

GIRÒ DI CAGLIARI DOC (1972)

ZONE: The majority of southwestern Sardinia, comprising an entire swath of the island and low hills west and south of the Gennargentu mountains. GRAPES: Girò min. 95%. AGING: Wines cannot be released before July 1 of yr. succeeding vintage. Liquoroso Riserva: min. 2 yrs. (min. 1 yr. in wood). WINE TYPES: sr; fr

MALVASIA DI BOSA DOC (1972)

ZONE: Small coastal zone north of Oristano known as the Planargia hills. GRAPES: Malvasia di Sardegna min. 95%. AGING: All versions min. 2 yrs. WINE TYPES: dw; sw; fw

MALVASIA DI CAGLIARI DOC (1972)

ZONE: The majority of southwestern Sardinia, comprising the entire Campidano plain and low hills west and south of the Gennargentu mountains. GRAPES: Malvasia di Sardegna min. 95%. AGING: Wines cannot be released before July 1 of yr. succeeding vintage. Liquoroso Riserva: min. 2 yrs. (min. 1 in wood). WINE TYPES: dw; sw; fw

MANDROLISAI DOC (1981)

ZONE: Near the geographic center of Sardinia in the Barbagia hills. Soils: rocky. GRAPES: Bovale Sardo min. 35%; Cannonau 20% to 35%; Monica 20% to 35%. AGING: Rosso Superiore: min. 2 yrs. (min. 1 in wood). WINE TYPES: dr; ros

MONICA DI CAGLIARI DOC (1972)

ZONE: The majority of southwestern Sardinia, comprising the entire Campidano plain and low hills west and south of the Gennargentu mountains. GRAPES: Monica min. 95%. AGING: Wines cannot be released before July 1 of yr. succeeding vintage. Liquoroso Riserva: min. 2 yrs. (min. 1 in wood). WINE TYPES: dr; sr; fr

MONICA DI SARDEGNA DOC (1972)

ZONE: The entire island of Sardinia. GRAPES: Monica min. 85%; other red grapes max. 15%. AGING: Wines cannot be released before Mar. 31 of yr. succeeding vintage. Superiore: 1 yr. WINE TYPES: dr (also frizzante); sr

MOSCATO DI CAGLIARI DOC (1972)

ZONE: The majority of southwestern Sardinia, comprising the entire Campidano plain and low hills west and south of the Gennargentu mountains. GRAPES: Moscato Bianco min. 95%. AGING: Wines cannot be released until Mar. 1 of yr. succeeding vintage. Liquoroso Riserva: 1 yr. WINE TYPES: sw; fw

MOSCATO DI SARDEGNA DOC (1979)

ZONE: The entire island of Sardinia. Subzone designations include Tempio or Tempio Pausania for wines from that commune, and Gallura for wines of the Gallura region in the northeastern part of the island. GRAPES: Moscato Bianco min. 90%. WINE TYPES: spsw

MOSCATO DI SORSO-SENNORI DOC (1972)

ZONE: The neighboring communes of Sorso and Sennori, near the coast of Sardinia north of Sassari. GRAPES: Moscato Bianco min. 95%. AGING: Wines may not be released until Mar. 1 of yr. succeeding vintage. WINE TYPES: sw; fw

NASCO DI CAGLIARI DOC (1972)

ZONE: The majority of southwestern Sardinia, comprising the entire Campidano plain and low hills west and south of the Gennargentu mountains. GRAPES: Nasco min. 95%. AGING: Wines cannot be released until July 1 of yr. succeeding vintage. Liquoroso Riserva: min. 2 yrs. (1 yr. in wood). WINE TYPES: dw; sw; fw

NURAGUS DI CAGLIARI DOC (1974)
ZONE: The majority of southwestern Sardinia, comprising the entire Campidano plain and low hills west and south of the Gennargentu mountains. GRAPES: Nuragus 85% to 100%; other white grapes max. 15%. WINE TYPES: dw (also frizzante); sw

SARDEGNA SEMIDANO DOC (1995)
ZONE: The entire island of Sardinia. Subzone denominations include Mogoro for a cluster of communes between Cagliari and Oristano. GRAPES: Semidano min. 85%; other white grapes max. 15%. WINE TYPES: dw; spdw; spsw; sw

VERMENTINO DI SARDEGNA DOC (1988)
ZONE: The entire island of Sardinia. GRAPES: Vermentino min. 85%; other white grapes max. 15%. WINE TYPES: dw; spdw; sw

VERNACCIA DI ORISTANO DOC (1971)
ZONE: Mostly alluvial plains and river valleys around the town of Oristano, on the west coast of Sardinia. GRAPES: Vernaccia di Oristano 100%. AGING: Min. 2 yrs. in wood. Superiore: min. 3 yrs. in wood. Riserva: min. 4 yrs. in wood. GRAPES: 1971

Sicilia

ALCAMO DOC (1972)
ZONE: Southwest of Palermo, reaching from the Gulf of Castellamare to the commune of Alcamo and points farther inland. Soils: fairly heavy clay and limestone in rolling hills. GRAPES: *Bianco (also Spumante and Vendemmia Tardiva)*: Catarratto min. 60%; Ansonica/Inzolia, Grillo, Grecanico, Chardonnay, Müller-Thurgau, and/or Sauvignon max. 40%; other authorized grapes max. 20%. *Classico*: Catarratto min. 80%; other authorized grapes max. 20%. *Rosato/Rosato Spumante*: Mix of Nerello Mascalese, Calabrese/Nero d'Avola, Sangiovese, Frappato, Perricone, Cabernet Sauvignon, Merlot, and/or Syrah. *Rosso/Rosso Novello/Rosso Riserva*: Calabrese/Nero d'Avola min. 60%; Frappato, Sangiovese, Perricone, Cabernet Sauvignon, Merlot, and/or Syrah max. 40%; other authorized grapes max. 10%. *Varietal Whites*: Catarratto, Ansonica/Inzolia, Grillo, Grecanico, Chardonnay, müller-thurgau, Sauvignon: Min. 85% of stated variety. *Varietal Reds*: Calabrese/Nero d'Avola, Cabernet Sauvignon, Merlot, Syrah: Min. 85% of stated variety. For Vendemmia Tardiva grapes must not be harvested before Sept. 15. AGING: Rosso Riserva min. 2 yrs. (min. 6 mos. in wood barrels). WINE TYPES: dw; spdw; sw; ros; spros; dr (also novello)

CERASUOLO DI VITTORIA DOC (1973)
ZONE: Southeast coast of Sicily running from the communes of Gela to Comiso and inland past Acate. Soils: Iron-rich clay over limestone with more sand to the east and south of zone. GRAPES: Nero d'Avola (Calabrese) max. 60%; Frappato min. 40%; Grosseto Nero and/or Nerello Mascalese max. 10%. WINE TYPES: dr

CONTEA DI SCLAFANI DOC (1996)
ZONE: Southeast of Palermo in occasionally high (500 m and up) hills centered on commune of Vallelunga. Soils: clay with some limestone. GRAPES: *Bianco*: Catarratto, Inzolia (Ansonica) and/or Grecanico min. 50%; other authorized white grapes max. 50%. *Rosso*: Nero d'Avola (Calabrese) and/or Perricone min. 50%; other authorized red grapes max. 50%. *Rosato*: Nerello Mascalese min. 50%; other authorized grapes up to 50%. *Varietal Whites*: Min. 85% of stated variety; wines from Inzolia (Ansonica); Catarratto; Grecanico; Grillo; Chardonnay; Pinot Bianco; Sauvignon. *Varietal Reds*: Min. 85% of stated variety; wines from Nero d'Avola (Calabrese); Perricone; Cabernet Sauvignon; Pinot Nero; Syrah; Merlot; Sangiovese. *Spumante*: Allowed for all white grapes and Rosato. *Dolce/Vendemmia Tardiva*: All white grapes eligible, with or without mention of grape name. AGING: Riserva Reds: min. 2 yrs. Vendemmia Tardiva: min. 18 mos. (min. 6 mos. in wood). WINE TYPES: dw; spdw; sw; ros; spros; dr (also novello)

CONTESSA ENTELLINA DOC (1993)
ZONE: Centered on the commune of Contessa Entellina, about 35 miles south of Palermo. Soils: calcareous clays. GRAPES: *Bianco*: Inzolia (Ansonica) min. 50%; Catarratto, Grecanico, Chardonnay, müller-thurgau, Sauvignon, Pinot Bianco and/or Grillo max. 50%. *Rosso and Rosato*: Nero d'Avola (Calabrese) and/or Syrah min. 50%; other authorized red grapes max. 50%. *Varietal Whites*: min. 85% of stated variety; wines from Chardonnay; Grecanico; Inzolia (Ansonica); Sauvignon. *Varietal Reds*: min. 85% of stated variety; wines from Cabernet Sauvignon; Merlot; Pinot Nero. *Ansonica Vendemmia Tardiva*: Min. 85% Ansonica (Inzolia). AGING: Riserva Reds: min. 2 yrs. (min. 6 mos. in wood). Vendemmia Tardiva: min. 18 mos. (min. 6 mos. in wood). WINE TYPES: dw; sw; ros; dr

DELIA NIVOLELLI DOC (1998)
ZONE: A large chunk of westernmost Sicily, within the

boundaries of the Marsala DOC and running from commune of Marsala inland to Salemi. Soils: predominantly clay. **GRAPES**: *Bianco:* Grecanico, Inzolia (Ansonica) and/or Grillo min. 65%; other authorized white grapes max. 35%. *Rosso:* Nero d'Avola (Calabrese), Perricone (Pignatello), Merlot, Cabernet Sauvignon, Syrah and/or Sangiovese min. 65%; other authorized red grapes max. 35%. *Spumante:* mix of Grecanico, Chardonnay, Inzolia (Ansonica), Damaschino and/or Grillo; or, varietal spumante permitted if min. 85% of stated variety. *Varietal Whites:* Min. 85% of stated variety; wines from Chardonnay; Damaschino; Grecanico; Grillo; Inzolia (Ansonica); müller-thurgau; Sauvignon. *Varietal Reds:* min. 85% of stated variety; wine from Nero d'Avola (Calabrese); Merlot; Perricone (Pignatello); Cabernet Sauvignon; Syrah; Sangiovese. **AGING**: Riserva Reds min. 2 yrs. **WINE TYPES**: dw; spdw; dr (also novello)

ELORO DOC (1994)

ZONE: The southeasternmost tip of Sicily, overlapping Moscato di Noto DOC. The subzone Pachino refers to commune of Pachino, at the extreme southeastern tip of the island. Soils: sandy, chalky clays. **GRAPES**: *Rosso and Rosato:* Nero d'Avola (Calabrese), Perricone (Pignatello) and/or Frappato min. 90%. *Varietal Reds:* Min. 90% of stated variety; wines from Nero d'Avola (Calabrese); Perricone (Pignatello); Frappato. *Eloro Pachino:* Nero d'Avola min. 80%; Perricone (Pignatello) and/or Frappato max. 20%. **AGING**: Pachino min. 6 mos. Riserva Reds min. 2 yrs. (min. 6 mos. in wood). **WINE TYPES**: ros; dr

ETNA DOC (1968)

ZONE: Arc of eastern, northern, and southern slopes of Mount Etna. Bianco Superiore specifically from commune of Milo. Soils: volcanic. **GRAPES**: *Bianco:* Carricante min. 60%; Catarratto max. 40%; Trebbiano, Minella and/or other authorized white grapes max. 15%. *Bianco Superiore:* Min. 80% Carricante. *Rosato and Rosso:* Nerello Mascalese min. 80%; Nerello Cappuccio max. 20%; other grapes, red or white, max. 10%. **WINE TYPES**: dw; ros; dr

FARO DOC (1976)

ZONE: Commune of Messina, in northeasternmost Sicily. Named for lighthouse (*faro*) at Capo Peloro, on the Straits of Messina. Soils: sandy clays and volcanic ash. **GRAPES**: Nerello Mascalese 45% to 60%; Nocera 5% to 10%; Nerello Cappuccio 15% to 30%; Calabrese (Nero d'Avola), Gaglioppo and/or Sangiovese max. 15%. **AGING**: Min. 1 yr. **WINE TYPES**: dr

MALVASIA DELLE LIPARI DOC (1973)

ZONE: The Aeolian archipelago off the northeast coast of Sicily, including the islands of Lipari, Salina, Vulcano and Stromboli, among others. Soils: volcanic. **GRAPES**: Malvasia di Lipari min. 95%; Corinto Nero 5% to 8%. **AGING**: Passito min. 9 mos. Liquoroso min. 6 mos. **WINE TYPES**: sw

MARSALA DOC (1969; MODIFIED 1984)

ZONE: A large chunk of western Sicily taking in coastal ports of Marsala and Trapani and reaching well inland. Soils: silty clays. **GRAPES**: *Oro and Ambra Versions:* Mix of Grillo, Catarratto, Ansonica (Inzolia), and/or Damaschino. *Rubino Versions:* Mix of Perricone (Pignatello), Nero d'Avola (Calabrese), and/or Nerello Mascalese, plus max. 30% white grapes. **AGING**: Fine min. 1 yr. Superiore min. 2 yrs. Superiore Riserva min. 4 yrs. Vergine (Soleras) min. 5 yrs. Vergine (Soleras) Riserva (Stravecchio) min. 10 yrs. **WINE TYPES**: fw; fr

MENFI DOC (1995)

ZONE: Southwestern coast near commune of Menfi. Subzone denomination Feudo dei Fiori used for some whites; subzone denomination Bonera used for some reds. **GRAPES**: *Bianco:* Inzolia (Ansonica), Chardonnay, Catarratto and/or Grecanico min. 75%; other authorized white grapes max. 25%. *Feudo dei Fiori:* Chardonnay and/or Inzolia (Ansonica) min. 80%; other white grapes max. 20%. *Varietal Whites:* Min. 85% of stated variety; wines from Chardonnay; Grecanico; Inzolia (Ansonica). *Rosso:* Nero d'Avola, Sangiovese, Merlot, Cabernet Sauvignon and/or Syrah min. 70%; other red grapes max. 30%. *Bonera:* Cabernet Sauvignon, Merlot, Nero d'Avola, Sangiovese and/or Syrah min. 85%. *Varietal Reds:* Min. 85% of stated variety. Wines from Nero d'Avola; Sangiovese; Cabernet Sauvignon; Merlot; Syrah. *Vendemmia Tardiva:* Chardonnay, Catarratto, Inzolia (Ansonica) and/or Sauvignon 100%. **AGING**: Bonera min. 1 yr. Bonera, Rosso and Varietal Red Riserva min. 2 yrs. **WINE TYPES**: dw; ros; dr

MOSCATO DI NOTO DOC (1974)

ZONE: Dry, gentle slopes and plains in southeastern Sicily, including the communes of Noto, Pachino, and Avola. Soils: sandy, silty clays. **GRAPES**: Moscato Bianco 100%. **AGING**: Liquoroso: min. 5 mos. **WINE TYPES**: sw; spsw

MOSCATO DI PANTELLERIA DOC (1971)

ZONE: The island of Pantelleria, between Sicily and

Tunisia. Soils: volcanic. **GRAPES**: Zibibbo (Moscato) 100%. **WINE TYPES**: sw; fw

MOSCATO DI SIRACUSA DOC (1973)
ZONE: Southeastern Sicily, taking in the entire commune of Siracusa. Soils: sandy, siliceous clays. **GRAPES**: Moscato Bianco 100%. **WINE TYPES**: sw

PASSITO DI PANTELLERIA DOC (1971)
ZONE: The island of Pantelleria, between Sicily and Tunisia. Soils: volcanic. **GRAPES**: Zibibbo (Moscato) 100%. **AGING**: Extra min. 1 yr. **WINE TYPES**: sw; fw

RIESI DOC (2000–2001)
ZONE: South-central Sicily. **GRAPES**: Whites from Inzolia and Chardonnay, reds from Nero d'Avola and Cabernet. **TYPES**: dw; ros; dr

SAMBUCA DI SICILIA DOC (1995)
ZONE: Southwestern Sicily, centered in the hills of the commune of Sambuca. Soils: calcareous clays. **GRAPES**: *Bianco:* Ansonica (Inzolia) 50% to 75%; Catarratto and/or Chardonnay 25% to 50%; other white grapes, except for Trebbiano Toscano, max. 15%. *Rosato and Rosso:* Nero d'Avola (Calabrese) 50% to 75%; Nerello Mascalese, Sangiovese, and/or Cabernet Sauvignon 25% to 50%; other red grapes max. 15%. *Chardonnay:* min. 85% Chardonnay. *Cabernet Sauvignon:* min. 85% Cabernet. **AGING**: Rosso min. 6 mos. Riserva min. 2 yrs. (min. 6 mos. in wood). **WINE TYPES**: dw; ros; dr

SANTA MARGHERITA DI BELICE DOC (1996)
ZONE: Southwestern Sicily, on slopes east of the Belice River. **GRAPES**: *Bianco:* Ansonica (Inzolia) 30% to 50%; Grecanico and/or Catarratto 50% to 70%; other authorized white grapes max. 15%. *Rosso:* Nero d'Avola (Calabrese) 20% to 50%; Sangiovese and/or Cabernet Sauvignon 50% to 80%; other red grapes max. 15%. *Varietal Whites:* min. 85% of stated variety; wines from Catarratto; Grecanico; Ansonica (Inzolia). *Varietal Reds:* min. 85% of stated variety; wines from Nero d'Avola (Calabrese); Sangiovese. **WINE TYPES**: dw; dr

SCIACCA DOC (1998)
ZONE: The southwest coast of Sicily, centered on the commune of Sciacca. Subzone Rayana used on some whites. **GRAPES**: *Bianco:* Inzolia (Ansonica), Grecanico, Chardonnay and/or Catarratto min. 70%; other authorized white grapes max. 30%. *Riserva Rayana:* Inzolia and/or Catarratto min. 80%; other authorized white grapes max. 20%. *Varietal Whites:* min. 85% of stated variety; wines from Inzolia; Grecanico; Chardonnay. *Rosato and*

Rosso: Merlot, Cabernet Sauvignon, Nero d'Avola, and/or Sangiovese min. 70%; other red grapes max. 30%. *Varietal Reds:* min. 85% of stated variety. Wines from Merlot; Cabernet Sauvignon; Nero d'Avola; Sangiovese. **AGING**: Riserva Rayana and Rosso Riserva min. 2 yrs. (min. 6 mos. in wood). **WINE TYPES**: dw; ros; dr

Toscana

BRUNELLO DI MONTALCINO DOCG (DOC 1966; DOCG 1980)
ZONE: Like an island on land, Montalcino rises up about 20 miles south of Siena, bounded by the Ombrone and Orcia rivers. Mix of continental and Mediterranean climates. Soils: calcareous clay in northern part of zone, sandier clay further south. Altitudes reach over 500 m. **GRAPES**: Sangiovese "Brunello" 100%. **AGING**: minimum 2 yrs. in oak barrels (no specified size); total of 4 yrs., 5 for riserva, including a required 6 mos. in bottle. Wine can't be released for sale until Jan. 1 of the year 5 years from the vintage year (i.e. a 1996 Brunello can't be released until after Jan 1, 2001). 6 yrs. for riserva. **WINE TYPES**: dr

CARMIGNANO DOCG (DOC 1975; DOCG 1990)
ZONE: On the eastern face of Monte Albano, about 10 miles west of Florence, centered around commune of same name. **GRAPES**: Sangiovese min. 50%; Canaiolo Nero up to 20%; Cabernets Franc and Sauvignon, individually or together, from 10% to 20%; Trebbiano Toscano, Canaiolo Bianco, and Malvasia del Chianti, individually or together, up to 10%; other authorized red grapes up to 10%. **AGING**: min. 8 mos. in barrels of chestnut or oak, 12 mos. for riserva. Total aging: wine cannot be released until June of the year 2 yrs. from vintage (i.e. 1996 vintage released June 1998); riserva wines cannot be released until Sept. 29 of the third year after harvest year (i.e. a 2000 riserva is released Sept. 29, 2003). **WINE TYPES**: dr

CHIANTI DOCG (DOC 1967; DOCG 1984)
ZONE: A vast zone in central Tuscany, stretching from Pisa to Arezzo to Siena. Subzones: Chianti Colli Aretini; Chianti Colli Fiorentini; Chianti Colli Senesi; Chianti Colline Pisane; Chianti Montalbano; Chianti Rufina; Chianti Montispertoli (in province of Firenze). **GRAPES**: Sangiovese, 75% to 100%; Canaiolo Nero up to 10%; Trebbiano Toscano and/or Malvasia del Chianti up to 10%; other authorized red grapes up to 10% of total.

AGING: Wines marked Chianti or Chianti Colli Aretini, Colli Senesi, Colline Pisane and Montalbano cannot be released until March 1 of the year immediately following the vintage; wines called Colli Fiorentini, Rúfina, Montespertoli or Superiore cannot be released until June 1 of the year succeeding vintage. Min 2 yrs. aging for riserva. WINE TYPES: dr

CHIANTI CLASSICO DOCG (DOC 1967; DOCG 1984; MODIFIED 1996)

ZONE: Densely forested hills between Florence and Siena. Bounded approx. by Florence-Siena superstrada (SS2) to west and communes of Gaiole and Castelnuovo Berardenga to east. Soils: predominantly sandstone at higher altitudes, calcareous clay at lower altitudes; altitudes range from 250 to 600 meters. GRAPES: Sangiovese 75% to 100%; Canaiolo Nero up to 10%; Trebbiano Toscano and/or Malvasia Bianca 0% to 6%; other authorized red grapes up to 15%. AGING: Min 1 yr. (wines cannot be sold until Oct. the year after harvest); Min. 2 yrs. plus 3 mos. in bottle for riserva. Riserve typically released in the spring of third year after vintage year. WINE TYPES: dr

VERNACCIA DI SAN GIMIGNANO DOCG (DOC 1966; DOCG 1993)

ZONE: Centered on commune of San Gimignano, northwest of Siena just outside Chianti Classico DOCG. High altitudes and chalky soils. GRAPES: Vernaccia di San Gimignano, with other nonaromatic approved white varieties up to 10%. AGING: Min 12 mos. for riserva, including 4 mos. in bottle. WINE TYPES: dw

VINO NOBILE DI MONTEPULCIANO DOCG (DOC 1966; DOCG 1980)

ZONE: Gentle, more open slopes (in comparison to Chianti Classico) ranging from 250 to 600 m around commune of Montepulciano, bounded by Orcia and Chiana rivers. GRAPES: Sangiovese (Prugnolo Gentile), min. 70%; Canaiolo Nero up to 20%; up to 20% of other recommended grapes for province of Siena, not to include more than 10% white varieties and not to include Malvasia del Chianti or "aromatic" white varieties. AGING: Min. 2 yrs., starting the Jan. 1 after vintage. Options: (1) 24 mos. in wood; (2) 18 mos. min. in wood, remainder in other container; (3) 12 mos. min. in wood plus 6 mos. min. in bottle, remainder in another container. Riserva: min. 3 yrs.; 6 mos. bottle aging required (same wood aging options apply). WINE TYPES: dr

ANSONICA COSTA DELL'ARGENTARIO DOC (1995)

ZONE: Extreme south of Tuscany on Mediterranean coast, abutting border with Lazio and including Isola del Giglio. GRAPES: Ansonica (Inzolia) min. 85%; other authorized white grapes up to 15%. WINE TYPES: dw

BARCO REALE DI CARMIGNANO/CARMIGNANO DOC (1994)

ZONE: Centered on town of Carmignano, due west of Florence. GRAPES: *Barco Reale/Carmignano/Rosato di Carmignano:* Sangiovese, min. 50%; Canaiolo Nero up to 20%; Cabernet Franc and/or Sauvignon from 10% to 20%; Trebbiano Toscano, Canaiolo Bianco, and/or Malvasia up to 10%; other authorized red grapes up to 10%. *Vin Santo di Carmignano:* Trebbiano Toscano and/or Malvasia Bianca min. 75%; other authorized white grapes up to 25%. *Vin Santo di Carmignano Occhio di Pernice:* Sangiovese min. 50%; other authorized white and red grapes up to 50%. AGING: Vin Santo (regular and "Occhio di Pernice"): Min. 3 yrs (riserva 4 yrs.) in wood barrels no larger than 3 hl. WINE TYPES: dr; ros; Vin Santo

BIANCO DELL'EMPOLESE DOC (1989)

ZONE: Straddles Arno River west of Florence, centered in commune of Empoli. GRAPES: Trebbiano Toscano min. 80%; other approved white grapes up to 20% (max. 8% Malvasia del Chianti). AGING: Vin Santo min. 3 yrs in wood barrels no larger than 5 hl. WINE TYPES: dw; Vin Santo

BIANCO DELLA VALDINIEVOLE DOC (1976)

ZONE: Between Pistoia and Lucca, northwest of Firenze. GRAPES: Trebbiano Toscano min. 70%; Malvasia del Chianti, Canaiolo Bianco, and/or Vermentino up to 25%; other authorized white grapes up to 5%. AGING: Vin Santo della Valdinievole: min. 3 yrs in wood barrels no larger than 2 hl. WINE TYPES: dw; Vin Santo

BIANCO DI PITIGLIANO DOC (1966)

ZONE: Volcanic soils in extreme south of Tuscany, stretching roughly from Scansano to Tuscany's border with Lazio. GRAPES: Trebbiano Toscano 50% to 80%; Greco, Malvasia Bianca, and/or Verdello up to 20%; Grechetto, Chardonnay, Sauvignon Blanc, Pinot Bianco, and Riesling Italico individually up to 15%, together no more than 30%; other authorized white grapes up to 10%. WINE TYPES: dw; spdw

BIANCO PISANO DI SAN TORPÈ DOC (1980)
ZONE: Between Empoli and Pisa, south of Arno River, stretching toward Montescudaio. **GRAPES:** Trebbiano Toscano min. 75%; other authorized white grapes up to 25%. **AGING:** Bianco: 3 to 4 mos. (cannot be released until Jan. 31 of year succeeding harvest). Vin Santo: min. 3 yrs. (4 for riserva) in wood barrels no larger than 2 hl. **WINE TYPES:** dw; Vin Santo

BOLGHERI/BOLGHERI SASSICAIA DOC (1983)
ZONE: Commune of Castagneto Carducci, including village of Bolgheri, on Tuscan coast between Livorno and Grosseto. Mix of hills and flatlands. **GRAPES:** *Bolgheri Bianco:* Trebbiano Toscano 10% to 70%; Vermentino 10% to 70%; Sauvignon 10% to 70%; other authorized white grapes up to 30%. *Bolgheri Sauvignon:* min. 85% Sauvignon, max. 15% other authorized white grapes. *Bolgheri Vermentino:* min. 85% Vermentino, max. 15% "other." *Bolgheri Rosato and Rosso:* Cabernet Sauvignon 10% to 80%; Merlot up to 70%; Sangiovese up to 70%; other red varieties up to 30%. *Bolgheri Vin Santo Occhio di Pernice:* Sangiovese 50% to 70%; Malvasia Nera 30% to 50%; other red varieties up to 30%. *Bolgheri Sassicaia:* Cabernet Sauvignon min. 80%; other red varieties max. 20%. **AGING:** Rosso Superiore: min. 2 yrs. (1 mo. in wood; min. 6 mos. in bottle). Vin Santo Occhio di Pernice: min. 3 yrs. (4 yrs. for riserva) in wood barrels no larger than 5 hl. Sassicaia: min. 18 mos. in 225 l barrique; 6 mos. in bottle before release. **WINE TYPES:** dw; dr; Vin Santo

CANDIA DEI COLLI APUANI DOC (1981)
ZONE: Northern coast of Tuscany near border of Liguria, in hillside vyds. overlooking Mediterranean. **GRAPES:** *All Versions:* Vermentino 70% to 80%; Albarola 10% to 20%; Trebbiano Toscano and/or Malvasia Bianca up to 20% (Malvasia max. 5%). **AGING:** Vin Santo: min. 3 yrs. in wood barrels no larger than 5 hl. **WINE TYPES:** dw; sw; Vin Santo

CAPALBIO DOC (1999)
ZONE: Hilly areas in the southern part of Grosseto province, including commune of Capalbio, often following contours of Grosseto-Roma train line. Clay-dominated soils. **GRAPES:** *Bianco and Vin Santo:* Trebbiano Toscano min. 50%; other authorized white grapes max. 50%. *Vermentino:* Vermentino min. 85%; other whites max. 15%. *Rosato, Rosso and Rosso Riserva:* Sangiovese min. 50%; other authorized red grapes max. 50%. *Cabernet Sauvignon:* Cabernet Sauvignon min. 85%; other reds max. 15%. *Sangiovese:* Sangiovese min. 85%;

other reds max. 15%. **AGING:** Bianco, Vermentino, and Rosato: wine not released until Dec. 31 of vintage year. Rosso Riserva min. 2 yrs. (6 mos. in wood). Cabernet Sauvignon and Sangiovese: min. 6 mos. Vin Santo: min. 3 yrs. (2 yrs. in wood containers no larger than 3 hl.). **WINE TYPES:** dw; dr; Vin Santo

COLLI DELL'ETRURIA CENTRALE DOC (1990)
ZONE: Concurrent w/ much of Chianti DOCG; hillside vineyards in provinces of Arezzo, Firenze, Pistoia, and Siena, across a vast stretch of central Tuscany. **GRAPES:** *Bianco:* Trebbiano Toscano, min. 50%; Chardonnay, Pinot Bianco/Grigio, Vernaccia, Malvasia, and/or Sauvignon up to 50%; other authorized white grapes up to 25%. *Rosso and Rosato:* Sangiovese min. 50%; Cabernets Sauvignon and Franc, Merlot, Pinot Nero, and/or Canaiolo Nero up to 50%; other red grapes up to 25%. *Rosso Novello:* Sangiovese min. 50%; Canaiolo Nero, Merlot, Gamay, and/or Ciliegiolo up to 50%; other red grapes up to 25%. *Vin Santo:* Trebbiano Toscano and/or Malvasia min. 70%; other white grapes max. 30%. *Vin Santo Occhio di Pernice:* Sangiovese min. 50%; other white/red grapes up to 50%. **AGING:** Bianco, Rosato, and Novello: no min. Rosso: released Feb. 1 in year succeeding vintage. Vin Santo: min. 3 yrs. (4 yrs. for riserva) in wood barrels no larger than 5 hl. **WINE TYPES:** dw; ros; dr (also novello); Vin Santo

COLLI DI LUNI DOC
SEE LISTING UNDER LIGURIA

COLLINE LUCCHESI DOC (1968)
ZONE: Hills around Sercio River in communes of Lucca, Capannori, and Porcari in northern Tuscany. **GRAPES:** *Bianco:* Trebbiano Toscano 45% to 70%; Greco, Grechetto, Vermentino, and/or Malvasia up to 45%; Chardonnay and/or Sauvignon up to 30%; other white varieties up to 15%. *Vermentino:* Vermentino min. 85%; other whites max. 15%. *Sauvignon:* Sauvignon min. 85%; other whites max. 15%. *Rosso:* Sangiovese 45% to 70%; Canaiolo and/or Ciliegiolo up to 30%; Merlot max. 15%; other red grapes max. 15% (Aleatico and Moscato max. 5%). *Merlot:* Merlot min. 85%; other reds max 15% (no Aleatico or Moscato). *Sangiovese:* Merlot min. 85%; other reds max 15% (no Aleatico or Moscato). *Vin Santo:* authorized white grapes. *Vin Santo Occhio di Pernice:* authorized red grapes. **AGING:** Rosso, Merlot, and Sangiovese: min. 2 yrs. for Riserva. Vin Santo: min. 3 yrs. in wood barrels no larger than 5 hl. **WINE TYPES:** dw; dr

CORTONA DOC (1999)

ZONE: Comprises much of the commune of Cortona, southeast of Arezzo. Mostly heavier clay and alluvial soils. **GRAPES:** *Rosato:* Sangiovese 40% to 60%; Canaiolo Nero 10% to 30%; other authorized red grapes max. 30%. *Vin Santo:* Trebbiano Toscano, Grechetto and/or Malvasia min. 80%; other whites max. 20%. *Vin Santo Occhio di Pernice:* Sangiovese and/or Malvasia Nera min. 80%; other grapes max. 20%. *Varietal Wines:* All contain min. 85% of variety named; max. 15% of other varieties (of same color) permitted. **AGING:** reds min. 6 mos. Vin Santo min. 3 yrs. (5 yrs., incl. 6 mos. in bottle, for riserva; 8 yrs., incl. 6 mos. in bottle, for "Occhio di Pernice"). **WINE TYPES:** dw; ros; dr; Vin Santo

ELBA DOC (1967)

ZONE: The red soils of the island of Elba, off the south Tuscan coast. **GRAPES:** *Aleatico:* Aleatico 100%. *Ansonica and Ansonica Passito:* Ansonica (Inzolia) min. 85%; other whites max. 15%. *Bianco, Spumante, and Vin Santo:* Trebbiano Toscano (Procanico) min. 50%; Ansonica and/or Vermentino max. 50%; other whites max. 20%. *Moscato:* Moscato 100%. *Rosso, Rosato, and Vin Santo Occhio di Pernice:* Sangiovese min. 60%; other red/white grapes max. 40% (max. 10% white). **AGING:** Rosso riserva: min. 24 mos. (12 mos. in wood). Vin Santo: min. 3 yrs. (4 yrs. for riserva) in wood barrels no larger than 5 hl. **WINE TYPES:** dw; spdw; sw; ros; dr; Vin Santo

MONTECARLO DOC (1969)

ZONE: Sandy, calcareous, low-lying slopes between Lucca and Pistoia. **GRAPES:** *Bianco and Vin Santo:* Trebbiano Toscano 40% to 60%; Sémillon, Pinot Gris, Pinot Bianco, Vermentino, Sauvignon, and Roussane 40% to 60% (no more than 10% of any single one). *Rosso and Vin Santo Occhio di Pernice:* Sangiovese 50% to 75%; Canaiolo Nero 5% to 15%; Ciliegiolo, Colorino, Malvasia Nera, Sjriak, Cabernets Franc and Sauvignon, and/or Merlot 10% to 15%; other red and white grapes max. 20%. **AGING:** Rosso riserva: min. 2 yrs. (min. 6 mos. in bottle). Vin Santo: min. 3 yrs. (4 yrs. for riserva) in wood barrels no larger than 5 hl. **WINE TYPES:** dw; dr; Vin Santo

MONTECUCCO DOC (1998)

ZONE: About 10 to 15 miles north of the city of Grosseto, in hills west of Ombrone River. **GRAPES:** *Bianco:* Trebbiano Toscano min. 60%; other authorized white grapes max. 40%. *Vermentino:* Vermentino min. 85%; other whites max. 15%. *Rosso:* Sangiovese min. 60%; other reds max 40%. *Sangiovese:* Sangiovese min. 85%; other reds max. 15%. **AGING:** Bianco and Vermentino: can be released Feb. 1 succeeding vintage. Rosso and Sangiovese: can be released Apr. 1 succeeding vintage; min. 2 yrs. (18 mos. in wood) for Rosso or Sangiovese riserva. **WINE TYPES:** dw; dr

MONTEREGIO DI MASSA MARITTIMA DOC (1994)

ZONE: northwest of Grosseto, taking in a stretch of Mediterranean coast from Castiglione della Pescia to Follonica and stretching inland toward Roccastrada and Massa Marittima. Said to be a zone attracting big-name investment. **GRAPES:** *Bianco:* Trebbiano Toscano min. 50%; Vermentino, Malvasia, and/or Ansonica (Inzolia) max. 30%; other authorized white grapes, singly (15%) or collectively (30%). *Vermentino:* Vermentino, min. 90%; other whites max. 10%. *Rosato, Rosso:* Sangiovese, min. 80%; other reds singly (max. 10%) or collectively (max. 20%). *Vin Santo:* Trebbiano Toscano and/or Malvasia min. 70%; other whites max. 30%. *Vin Santo Occhio di Pernice:* Sangiovese 50% to 70%; Malvasia Nera 10% to 50%; other red grapes max. 30%. **AGING:** Rosso riserva: min. 2 yrs. (min. 6 mos. in wood; 3 mos. in bottle). Vin Santo: min. 3 yrs. (4 yrs. for riserva) in wood barrels no larger than 5 hl. **WINE TYPES:** dw; ros; dr (also novello); Vin Santo

MONTESCUDAIO DOC (1976)

ZONE: A few miles north of Bolgheri DOC along the Tuscan coast, east of the Via Aurelia. **GRAPES:** *Bianco and Vin Santo:* Trebbiano Toscano min. 50%; other authorized white grapes max. 50%. *Varietal Whites:* Min. 85% of stated variety; max. 15% of other whites. *Rosso:* Sangiovese min. 50%; other approved reds max. 50%. *Varietal Reds:* Min. 85% of stated variety; max. 15% of other reds. **AGING:** Rosso riserva: min. 2 yrs. (min. 3 mos. in bottle). Vin Santo: min. 4 yrs. (min. 18 mos. in wood barrels no larger than 5 hl.). **WINE TYPES:** dw; dr; Vin Santo.

MORELLINO DI SCANSANO DOC (1978)

ZONE: Band of hills between Ombrone and Albenga rivers in southern Tuscany, centered around commune of Scansano, southeast of Grosseto. **GRAPES:** Sangiovese (Morellino), 85% to 100%; other authorized red grapes max. 15%. **AGING:** Rosso Riserva min. 2 yrs. (min. 1 in wood). **WINE TYPES:** dr

MOSCADELLO DI MONTALCINO DOC (1984)

ZONE: Hillside vineyards in the commune of Montalcino, south-central Tuscany, home also to Brunello di Montalcino and Rosso di Montalcino. **GRAPES:** Moscato Bianco 85% to 100%; other authorized whites max. 15%. **AGING:** Vendemmia Tardiva: min. 1 yr. **WINE TYPES:** sw; spsw

ORCIA DOC (2000)
ZONE: Between Montalcino and Montepulciano DOCs, north of Orcia River in central Tuscany, stretching from Chianciano toward Siena. **GRAPES:** *Bianco:* Trebbiano Toscano min. 50%; other authorized white grapes max. 50%. *Rosso and Rosso Novello:* Sangiovese min. 60%; other grapes max. 40% (max. 10% white grapes). Vin Santo: Trebbiano Toscano and/or Malvasia Bianca min. 50%; other white grapes max. 50%. **AGING:** Bianco and Rosso: can be released March 1 in yr. succeeding vintage. Vin Santo: min. 3 yrs. **WINE TYPES:** dw; dr (also novello); Vin Santo

PARRINA DOC (1971)
ZONE: A small zone on the Mediterranean coast in the extreme south of Tuscany, centered around the coastal town of Orbetello. **GRAPES:** *Bianco:* Trebbiano Toscano (Procanico) 30% to 50%; Ansonica (Inzolia) and/or Chardonnay 30% to 50%; other authorized white grapes max. 20%. *Rosato and Rosso:* Sangiovese min. 70%; other reds max. 30%. **AGING:** Rosso: can be released June 1 of year succeeding vintage. Rosso Riserva: min. 2 yrs. (1 yr. in wood). **WINE TYPES:** dw; ros; dr

POMINO DOC (1983)
ZONE: A tiny zone in a part of the commune of Rúfina, east of Florence. Essentially a one-producer (Frescobaldi) denomination. **GRAPES:** *Bianco:* Pinot Bianco and/or Chardonnay 60% to 80%; Trebbiano Toscano max. 30%; other authorized white grapes max. 15%. *Rosso:* Sangiovese 60% to 75%; Canaiolo, Cabernets Sauvignon and Franc 15% to 25%; Merlot 10% to 20%; other reds max 15%. *Vin Santo:* can be either bianco or rosso, based on above grape blends. **AGING:** Rosso: min. 1 yr. (6 mos. in chestnut or oak casks). Vin Santo: min. 3 yrs. in wood casks no larger than 4 hl. **WINE TYPES:** dw; dr; Vin Santo

ROSSO DI MONTALCINO DOC (1983)
ZONE: Corresponds to DOCG zone for Brunello di Montalcino. **GRAPES:** Sangiovese (Brunello) 100% **AGING:** 1 yr. **WINE TYPES:** dr

ROSSO DI MONTEPULCIANO DOC (1988)
ZONE: Corresponds to Vino Nobile di Montepulciano

DOCG zone. **GRAPES:** Sangiovese (Prugnolo Gentile) min. 70%; Canaiolo Nero max. 20%; other authorized grapes max. 20% (max. 10% of white grapes). **AGING:** 6 mos. **WINE TYPES:** dr

SAN GIMIGNANO DOC (1996)
ZONE: Corresponds to Vernaccia di San Gimignano DOC: the hills of the commune of San Gimignano, northwest of Siena in central Tuscany. **GRAPES:** *Rosso:* Sangiovese min. 50%; other authorized red grapes max. 50%. *Rosato:* Sangiovese min. 60%; Canaiolo Nero max. 20%; Trebbiano Toscano, Malvasia del Chianti, and/or Vernaccia max. 15%; other reds. max 15%. *Sangiovese and Sangiovese Rosato:* Sangiovese min. 85%; other reds max. 15%. *Vin Santo:* Malvasia max. 50%; Trebbiano Toscano min. 30%; Vernaccia max. 20%; other whites max. 10%. **AGING:** Rosso: min. 6 mos.; riserva min. 2 yrs. Vin Santo: min. 3 yrs. (min. 4 mos. in bottle). **WINE TYPES:** dr (also novello); ros; Vin Santo

SANT'ANTIMO DOC (1996)
ZONE: Named for the Sant'Antimo abbey in the commune of Montalcino, this DOC encompasses the entire commune of Montalcino and represents an effort by the area's producers to "classify" all of the wines made in the commune. **GRAPES:** *Bianco:* locally authorized grapes. *Rosso (also novello):* locally authorized grapes. *Vin Santo:* Trebbiano Toscano and/or Malvasia min. 70%; other authorized white grapes max. 30%. *Vin Santo Occhio di Pernice:* Sangiovese 50% to 70%; Malvasia Nera 30% to 50%; other grapes max. 30%. *Varietal Whites and Reds:* wines carrying grape name (i.e. Chardonnay) contain min. 85% of that variety, max. 15% of other authorized varieties. **AGING:** Vin Santo: min. 3 yrs. (riserva 4 yrs.) in wood casks no larger than 4 hl. **WINE TYPES:** dw; dr; Vin Santo

SOVANA DOC (1999)
ZONE: A sliver of southernmost Tuscany, abutting border with Lazio, northeast of commune of Pitigliano. **GRAPES:** *Rosso and Rosato:* Sangiovese min. 50%; other varieties max. 50%. *Varietal Reds:* wines with varietal name (i.e. Aleatico) contain min. 85% of stated variety, max. 15% of other approved varieties. **AGING:** Riserva Reds with varietal name: min. 24 mos. (6 mos. in bottle). **WINE TYPES:** ros; dr

VAL D'ARBIA DOC (1985)
ZONE: A band of hills fanning out from Siena both north and south, taking in southern parts of Chianti

Classico and stretching down toward Montalcino. Follows contours of Arbia River. **GRAPES:** Trebbiano Toscano and Malvasia del Chianti 70% to 90%; Chardonnay 10% to 30%; other authorized white grapes max. 15%. **AGING:** Vin Santo: min. 3 yrs. in wood casks no larger than 2 hl. **WINE TYPES:** dw; Vin Santo

VAL DI CORNIA (ALSO VAL DI CORNIA SUVERETO) DOC (1989)
ZONE: A coastal DOC straddling the Cornia River, which empties into the Mediterranean near Piombino, about 50 miles south of Livorno. Suvereto is a subzone of the DOC, centered on the commune of the same name, from which producers can make four varietal red wines. **GRAPES:** *Bianco:* Trebbiano Toscano min. 50%; Vermentino max. 50%; other authorized whites up to 20%. *Rosso and Rosato:* Sangiovese min. 50%; Cabernet Sauvignon and/or Merlot up to 50%; other authorized reds up to 20%. *Varietal Whites and Reds:* min. 85% of grape variety named (i.e. Ciliegiolo, Vermentino); max 15% of other authorized white or red varieties. *Aleatico Passito:* 100% Aleatico. *Ansonica Passito:* 100% Ansonica (Inzolia). **AGING:** Sangiovese, Merlot, Cabernet Sauvignon, and Rosso superiore: min. 18 mos. (min. 6 mos. in wood); min. 24 mos. for riserva. Suvereto Reds: min. 26 mos. (min. 15 mos. in wood casks no larger than 30 hl; min. 6 mos. in bottle). **WINE TYPES:** dw; sw; dr; sr

VALDICHIANA DOC (1972)
ZONE: Gentle hills near Tuscany's border with Umbria, between Arezzo and Montepulciano. **GRAPES:** *Bianco and Bianco Vergine:* Trebbiano Toscano min. 20%; Chardonnay, Pinot Bianco, Grechetto and/or Pinot Grigio up to 80%; other authorized white varieties up to 15%. *Chardonnay:* min. 85% Chardonnay, max. 15% other whites. *Grechetto:* min. 85% Grechetto, max. 15% other whites. *Rosso and Rosato:* Sangiovese min. 50%; Merlot and/or Syrah max. 50%; other authorized red grapes max. 15%. *Sangiovese:* Min. 85% Sangiovese, max. 15% other reds. *Vin Santo:* Trebbiano Toscano and/or Malvasia Bianca min. 50%; other authorized white grapes max. 50%. **AGING:** Vin Santo: min. 3 yrs (4 yrs. for riserva) with min. 2 yrs. in wood casks no larger than 5 hl. **WINE TYPES:** dw; spdw; dr; Vin Santo

VIN SANTO DEL CHIANTI DOC (1997)
ZONE: Corresponds to vast Chianti DOCG (see listing), including subzones Colli Aretini, Colli Fiorentini, Colli Senesi, Colline Pisane, Montalbano, Rúfina and Montespertoli. **GRAPES:** *Vin Santo:* Trebbiano Toscano and/or Malvasia min. 70%; other authorized white grapes max. 30%. *Vin Santo Occhio di Pernice:* Sangiovese min. 50%; other authorized red or white grape max. 50%. **AGING:** Vinification and aging carried out in wood casks (caratelli) of no more than 5 hl. Min. aging 3 yrs. (4 yrs. for riserva). **WINE TYPES:** Vin Santo

VIN SANTO DEL CHIANTI CLASSICO DOC (1995)
ZONE: Corresponds to Chianti Classico DOCG. **GRAPES:** *Vin Santo:* Trebbiano Toscano and/or Malvasia min. 70%; other authorized white grapes max. 30%. *Vin Santo Occhio di Pernice:* Sangiovese min. 50%; other authorized red or white grape max. 50%. **AGING:** Vinification and aging carried out in wood casks (caratelli) of no more than 5 hl. Min. aging 3 yrs. (4 yrs. for riserva). **WINE TYPES:** Vin Santo

VIN SANTO DI MONTEPULCIANO DOC (1996)
ZONE: Corresponds to Vino Nobile di Montepulciano DOCG. **GRAPES:** *Vin Santo:* Malvasia Bianca, Grechetto (Pulcinculo) and/or Trebbiano Toscano min. 70%; other authorized white varieties max. 30%. *Vin Santo Occhio di Pernice:* Sangiovese min. 50%; other authorized grapes max. 50%. **AGING:** Vinification and aging carried out in wood casks (caratelli) of no more than 3 hl. (smaller for riserva and "occhio di pernice"). Min. aging 3 yrs. (5 yrs. for riserva, 8 yrs. for "occhio di pernice"). **WINE TYPES:** Vin Santo

Trentino

CASTELLER DOC (1974)
ZONE: Stretching from the border of Veneto to the border of Alto Adige; a vast zone taking in both the valley floor and surrounding slopes up to 600 m. **GRAPES:** Schiava min. 30%; Lambrusco max. 60%; Merlot, Lagrein, and/or Teroldego max. 20%. **WINE TYPES:** dr

LAGO DI CALDARO/CALDARO DOC (1970)
ZONE: DOC overlaps with Alto Adige, with most of the classic vineyards in Alto Adige near Lake Caldaro. Trentino's share is in northern part of region in communes of Rovere della Luna; Faedo; San Michele all' Adige; Lavis; Giovo; Lisignano; Cembra. **GRAPES:** Schiava min. 85%; Pinot Nero and/or Lagrein max. 15%. **WINE TYPES:** dr

TEROLDEGO ROTALIANO DOC (1971)

ZONE: The sandy, gravelly plain (Campo Rotaliano) between Mezzacorona and Mezzolombardo in northern Trentino. At the confluence of the Adige and Noce rivers. **GRAPES:** Teroldego 100%. **AGING:** min. 2 yrs. for riserva. **WINE TYPES:** dr; ros

TRENTINO DOC (1971)

ZONE: An all-encompassing DOC that takes in the whole province of Trento, covering more than 20 types of wines. **GRAPES:** *Bianco:* Chardonnay and/or Pinot Bianco, min. 80%; Sauvignon, müller-thurgau and/or Incrocio Manzoni max. 20%. *Rosato (Kretzer):* Schiava, Teroldego and/or Lagrein, with no one exceeding 70% of total. *Rosso:* Cabernet Franc and/or Cabernet Sauvignon, Merlot. *Varietal Wines:* Min. 85% of stated variety, max. 15% of other authorized grapes of same color. *Whites:* Chardonnay; Moscato Giallo; müller-thurgau; Nosiola; Pinot Bianco; Pinot Grigio; Riesling Italico; Riesling Renano; Sauvignon; Traminer Aromatico (Gewürztraminer). *Reds:* Moscato Rosa; Cabernet; Cabernets Sauvignon and Franc; Lagrein (either scuro/dunkel or rosato/kretzer); Marzemino; Merlot; Pinot Nero; Rebo. *Vin Santo:* Nosiola 100%. **AGING:** Reds: min. 6 mos. Bianco, Rosso, Chardonnay, Pinot Bianco, Riesling, Sauvignon, Cabernet Franc, Cabernet Sauvignon, Merlot, Pinot Nero, Lagrein, and Marzemino min. 2 yrs. for riserva. Vin Santo: min. 3. yrs. **WINE TYPES:** dw; dr; ros; vin santo

TRENTINO SORNI (SUBZONE) DOC (1971)

ZONE: Billed as the smallest DOC zone in Italy, though it is now treated more as a subzone than a stand-alone DOC. Vineyards are located on steep, high slopes within the communes of Lavis (where the village of Sorni is located), Giovo and San Michele all'Adige. **GRAPES:** *Bianco:* Nosiola, müller-thurgau, Sylvaner, Pinot Bianco, Pinot Grigio, and/or Chardonnay. *Rosso:* Teroldego, Schiava and/or Lagrein. **WINE TYPES:** dw; dr

TRENTO DOC (1993)

ZONE: Consistent with the Trentino DOC geographically. Trento DOC discipline created specifically for sparkling wines made using the *metodo classico* (Champagne method). **GRAPES:** Varying percentages of Chardonnay, Pinot Bianco, Pinot Nero, and/or Pinot Meunier. **AGING:** Min. 15 mos. on the lees in bottle; 24 mos. for vintage-dated wines; 36 mos. for riserva. **WINE TYPES:** spdw; spros

VALDADIGE/ETSCHTALER DOC
SEE LISTING UNDER ALTO ADIGE

Umbria

MONTEFALCO SAGRANTINO DOCG (DOC 1980; DOCG 1992)

ZONE: South of Perugia in central Umbria, centered on the communes of Montefalco and Bevagna. Soils: calcareous clays. **GRAPES:** Sagrantino 100% **AGING:** Secco: 30 mos. (min. 12 mos. in wood). Passito: 30 mos. **WINE TYPES:** dr; sr

TORGIANO ROSSO RISERVA DOCG (1990)

ZONE: The right bank of the Tiber River southeast of Perugia, centered on the commune of Torgiano. Soils: calcareous clays. **GRAPES:** Sangiovese 50% to 70%; Canaiolo 15% to 30%; Trebbiano Toscano max. 10%; other red grapes max. 10%. **AGING:** Min. 3 yrs. **WINE TYPES:** dr

ASSISI DOC (1997)

ZONE: Hills east of Perugia, centered on the commune of Assisi. **GRAPES:** *Bianco:* Trebbiano 50% to 70%; Grechetto 10% to 30%; other white grapes max. 40%. *Grechetto:* Grechetto min. 85%. *Rosso and Rosato:* Sangiovese 50% to 70%; Merlot 10% to 30%; other red grapes max. 40%. **WINE TYPES:** dw; ros; dr (also novello)

COLLI ALTOTIBERINI DOC (1980)

ZONE: Slopes on either side of the Tiber River north of Perugia. **GRAPES:** *Bianco:* Trebbiano Toscano 75% to 90%; Malvasia del Chianti max. 10%; other white grapes max. 15%. *Rosso and Rosato:* Sangiovese 55% to 70%; Merlot 10% to 20%; other red grapes max. 15%. **WINE TYPES:** dw; ros; dr

COLLI AMERINI DOC (1989)

ZONE: Hills in southern Umbria near Terni, reaching to the banks of the Tiber on the border with Lazio. **GRAPES:** *Bianco:* Trebbiano Toscano 70% to 85%; Grechetto, Verdello, Garganega, and/or Malvasia Toscana max. 30% (max. 10% Malvasia); other white grapes max. 15%. *Rosso and Rosato:* Sangiovese 60% to 80%; Montepulciano, Ciliegiolo, Canaiolo, Merlot and/or Barbera max. 35% (Merlot max. 10%); other red grapes max. 15%. *Malvasia:* Malvasia Toscana min. 85%. **WINE TYPES:** dw; ros; dr (also novello)

COLLI DEL TRASIMENO/TRASIMENO DOC (1972)

ZONE: Hills surrounding Lake Trasimeno, west of Perugia near the border with Tuscany. **GRAPES:** *Grechetto:*

Grechetto min. 85%. *Merlot:* Merlot min. 85%. *Cabernet Sauvignon:* Cabernet Sauvignon min. 85%. *Gamay:* Gamay min. 85%. *Bianco/Vin Santo:* Trebbiano min. 40%; Grechetto, Chardonnay, Pinot Bianco, and/or Pinot Grigio min. 30%; other white grapes max. 30%. *Rosso and Rosato:* Sangiovese min. 40%; Ciliegiolo, Gamay, Merlot, and/or Cabernet min. 30%; other red grapes max. 30%. *Spumante Classico:* Chardonnay, Pinot Grigio, Pinot Bianco, Pinot Nero, and/or Grechetto min. 70%; other white grapes max. 30%. *Bianco Scelto:* Vermentino, Grechetto, Chardonnay, Pinot Grigio, Pinot Bianco, Sauvignon, and/or Riesling min. 85%; other white grapes max. 15%. *Rosso Scelto:* Gamay, Cabernet Sauvignon, Merlot, and/or Pinot Nero min. 85%; other red grapes max. 15%. **AGING:** Rosso, Rosato, Bianco and Bianco Scelto: min. 6 mos. Rosso Scelto: min. 1 yr. Rosso Riserva: min. 2 yrs. (min. 4 mos. in wood). Vin Santo: min. 18 mos. in wood. **WINE TYPES:** dw (also frizzante); spdw; ros; dr (also frizzante and novello); Vin Santo

COLLI MARTANI DOC (1988)

ZONE: Broad basin south of Perugia, bounded by the Tiber to the west. Todi subzone centered on the small commune of Todi in the southwestern corner of the zone. **GRAPES:** *Trebbiano:* Trebbiano min. 85%; Trebbiano Spoletino, Grechetto, Malvasia Bianca di Candia, Malvasia Bianca del Chianti, Garganega, and/or Verdicchio max. 15%. *Grechetto and Grechetto di Todi:* Grechetto min. 85%; Trebbiano Toscano; Trebbiano Spoletino, Malvasia Bianca di Candia, Malvasia Bianca del Chianti, Garganega, and/or Verdicchio max. 15%. *Sangiovese:* Sangiovese min. 85%; Canaiolo, Ciliegiolo, Barbera, Merlot, Montepulciano, other red and white grapes max. 15%. **AGING:** Sangiovese: min. 1 yr. (2 yrs., with 1 yr. in wood, for riserva). **WINE TYPES:** dw; dr

COLLI PERUGINI DOC (1981)

ZONE: Hills on the west bank of the Tiber west of Perugia, abutting the Colli del Trasimeno DOC. **GRAPES:** *Bianco and Vin Santo:* Trebbiano Toscano min. 50%; other white grapes max. 50%. *Spumante:* Grechetto, Chardonnay, Pinot Bianco, Pinot Nero, and/or Pinot Grigio min. 80%; other white grapes max. 20%. *Rosso and Rosato:* Sangiovese min. 50%; other red grapes max. 50%. *Varietal Whites:* Min. 85% of stated variety. Wines from Chardonnay; Grechetto; Pinot Grigio; Trebbiano. *Varietal Reds:* Min. 85% of stated variety. Wines from Cabernet Sauvignon; Merlot; Sangiovese. **WINE TYPES:** dw; spdw; ros; dr (also novello); Vin Santo

LAGO DI CORBARA DOC (1998)

ZONE: Hills surrounding Lake Corbara, in southwestern Umbria (overlapping Orvieto DOC). **GRAPES:** *Rosso:* Cabernet Sauvignon, Merlot, and/or Pinot Nero min. 70%; Aleatico, Barbera, Cabernet Franc, Canaiolo, Cesanese, Ciliegiolo, Colorino, Dolcetto, and/or Montepulciano max. 30%. *Varietal Reds:* Min. 85% of stated variety. Wines from Cabernet Sauvignon; Merlot; Pinot Nero. **WINE TYPES:** dr

MONTEFALCO DOC (1979)

ZONE: South of Perugia in central Umbria, centered on the communes of Montefalco and Bevagna. Soils: calcareous clays. **GRAPES:** *Bianco:* Grechetto min. 50%; Trebbiano Toscano 20% to 35%; other white grapes for remainder. *Rosso:* Sangiovese 60% to 70%; Sagrantino 10% to 15%; other red grapes for remainder. **AGING:** *Rosso:* Min. 18 mos. (30 mos. for riserva, min. 12 mos. in wood). **WINE TYPES:** dw; dr

ORVIETO DOC (1971)

ZONE: Hills up to 500 meters surrounding the town of Orvieto, southwest of Perugia, and extending into neighboring Lazio. The classico zone is in the center, closer to Orvieto, and includes areas around Lake Corbara. Soils: mix of sand, clay, limestone over volcanic tufa. **GRAPES:** Trebbiano Toscano (Procanico) 40% to 60%; Verdello 15% to 25%; Grechetto, Canaiolo Bianco (Drupeggio) and/or Malvasia Toscana for remainder (Malvasia max. 20% of total). **WINE TYPES:** dw; sw

ROSSO ORVIETANO/ORVIETANO ROSSO DOC (1998)

ZONE: Roughly equivalent to the Orvieto DOC but extending to include a larger area, reaching to the border with Tuscany. **GRAPES:** *Rosso:* Min. 70% of Aleatico, Cabernet Franc, Cabernet Sauvignon, Canaiolo, Ciliegiolo, Merlot, Montepulciano, Pinot Nero and/or Sangiovese. *Varietal Reds:* Min. 85% of stated variety. Wines from Aleatico; Cabernet Franc; Cabernet Sauvignon; Canaiolo; Ciliegiolo; Merlot; Montepulciano; Pinot Nero; Sangiovese. **WINE TYPES:** dr; sr

TORGIANO DOC (1968)

ZONE: Small cluster of hills around the commune of Torgiano, immediately southeast of Perugia. **GRAPES:** *Bianco:* Trebbiano Toscano 50% to 70%; Grechetto 15% to 40%; other white grapes max. 15%. *Rosso:* Sangiovese 50% to 70%; Canaiolo 15% to 30%; Trebbiano Toscano max. 10%; other red grapes max. 15%. *Rosato:* Sangiovese 50% to 70%; Canaiolo 15% to 30%; Trebbiano Toscano max. 10%; other red grapes max. 15%. *Varietal Whites:* Min. 85% of stated variety. Wines from Chardonnay; Pinot Grigio; Riesling Italico. *Varietal Reds:* Min. 85% of stated variety. Wines from Cabernet Sauvignon; Pinot Nero. *Spumante:* Chardonnay 40% to 50%; Pinot Nero 40% to 50%; other white grapes max. 15%. **WINE TYPES:** dw; spdw; ros; dr

Valle d'Aosta

VALLE D'AOSTA DOC

ZONE: Slopes on either side of the Dora Baltea River throughout the Valle d'Aosta region, ranging from 800 to 1,200-plus meters elevation and extending roughly from Morgex in the west to the border with Piedmont in the east. There are seven geographic subzones, which may or may not appear on the label: Morgex et La Salle (high-elevation vineyards in the communes of Morgex and La Salle, at the western end of the region near Mont Blanc); Enfer d'Arvier (slopes flanking the Dora Baltea in the towns of Arvier, Mombet, and Bouse); Torrette (often high-altitude slopes flanking the Dora Baltea at Quart, Aymavilles, Villeneuve, and several other communes just west of the city of Aosta); Nus (just east of Aosta, centered on the commune of Nus); Chambave (east of Aosta, centered on the commune of Chambave); Arnad-Monjovet (slopes along the Dora Baltea as it makes a southward turn toward Piedmont, including those in the communes of Arnad, Monjovet, and five others); Donnaz/Donnas (named for the commune of the same name near where the Dora Baltea enters Piedmont). **GRAPES:** *Bianco/Blanc:* Any approved varieties. *Rosso/Rouge:* Any approved varieties. *Rosato/Rosé:* Any approved varieties. *Varietal Wines:* Min. 90% of stated variety. Whites from müller-thurgau; Pinot Grigio; Chardonnay; Petite Arvine; Pinot Noir. Reds from Gamay; Pinot Nero; Premetta; Fumin; Petite Rouge. *Blanc de Morgex et de La Salle:* Blanc de Morgex 100%. *Chambave:* Moscato Bianco (Muscat Blanc) 100%. *Chambave Rouge:* Petit Rouge 60%; Dolcetto, Gamay, and/or Pinot Nero min. 25%; other red grapes max. 15%. *Nus/Nus Malvoisie:* Pinot Grigio (Pinot Gris/Malvoisie) 100%. *Nus Rosso/Rouge:* Vien de Nus min. 50%; Petit Rouge and/or Pinot Nero min. 30%; other red grapes max. 20%. *Arnad-Monjovet:* Nebbiolo (Picotendro) min. 70%; Dolcetto, Vien de Nus, Pinot Nero, Neyret, and/or Freisa max. 30%. *Torrette:* Petit Rouge min. 70%; other red grapes max. 30%. *Donnas/Donnaz:* Nebbiolo (Picotendro) min. 85%; Freisa and/or Neyret max. 15%. *Enfer d'Arvier:* Petit Rouge min. 85%;

other red grapes max. 15%. **AGING:** Bianco/Rosso/Rosato: 3 mos. Varietal Whites: 3 mos. Varietal Reds: 6 mos. (3 mos. for Premetta). Blanc de Morgex: 3 mos. Chambave Muscat: 3 mos. Chambave Rouge: 6 mos. Nus Malvoisie: 3 mos. Nus Rosso: 6 mos. Arnad-Monjovet: 8 mos. (12 mos. for Superiore). Torrette: 6 mos. (8 mos. for Superiore). Donnas: 24 mos. Enfer d'Arvier: 6 mos. **WINE TYPES:** dw (also frizzante); sw; ros (also frizzante); dr (also frizzante)

Veneto

BARDOLINO SUPERIORE DOCG (DOC 1968; DOCG 2001)

ZONE: The southeastern shores of Lake Garda, taking in 16 communes in the province of Verona, including Bardolino, Garda, Peschiera, and Sommacampagna. Sandier soils further north, heavier clays further south. **GRAPES:** Corvina 35% to 65%; Molinara 10% to 40%; Negrara max. 10%; Rossignola, Barbera, Sangiovese, and/or Garganega max. 15%. **AGING:** Min. 1 yr. **WINE TYPES:** dr

RECIOTO DI SOAVE DOCG (DOC 1968; DOCG 1992)

ZONE: East of Verona in the hills around the commune of Soave, including the Alpone, Illasi, Mezzane, and Tramigna valleys. The smaller classico zone is the band of hills between the towns of Soave and Monteforte d'Alpone. **GRAPES:** Garganega, min. 70%; Pinot Bianco, Chardonnay, and/or Trebbiano di Soave max. 30% (of this 30%, a max. of 15% can be other types of Trebbiano, i.e. Trebbiano Toscano). **AGING:** Wines cannot be sold until Sept. 1 of yr. following vintage. **WINE TYPES:** sw; spsw

BAGNOLI DI SOPRA/BAGNOLI DOC (1995)

ZONE: South and southeast of the city of Padova, in flatlands stretching toward the Adige River. Classico designation for wines from the commune of Bagnoli only. Soils: sandy-alluvial with some limestone. **GRAPES:** Spumante Bianco and Rosato: Chardonnay min. 20%; Raboso min. 40%. *Bianco:* Chardonnay min. 30%; Tocai Italiano and/or Sauvignon min. 20%; Raboso (vinified as white) min. 10%; other authorized white grapes max. 10%. *Rosato:* Raboso Piave and/or Raboso Veronese min. 50%; Merlot max. 40%; other authorized red grapes max. 10%. *Rosso:* Merlot 15% to 60%; Cabernet Franc and/or Carmenere and/or Cabernet Sauvignon min.

15%; Raboso Piave/Veronese min. 15%; other authorized red grapes max. 10%. Friularo Rosso: Raboso Piave min. 90%; other authorized reds max. 10%. Merlot and Cabernet: varietal wines with min. 85% of said variety. Rosso Passito: Raboso Piave and/or Raboso Veronese min. 70%. AGING: Rosso, Friularo and Varietal Red Riserva: min. 2 yrs. (1 yr. in oak barrels). Passito: min. 2 yrs. in oak barrels. WINE TYPES: dw; spdw; ros; spros; dr; sr

ARCOLE DOC (2000–2001)
ZONE: Area south and east of Verona. GRAPES: Wide array of varietal whites and reds.

BARDOLINO DOC (1968)
ZONE: See Bardolino DOCG. GRAPES: Corvina 35% to 65%; Rondinella 10% to 40%; Molinara 10% to 20%; Negrara max. 10%; Rossignola, Barbera, Sangiovese and/or Garganega max. 15%. WINE TYPES: dr (also novello and frizzante); ros; spros

BIANCO DI CUSTOZA DOC (1971)
ZONE: Gentle hills and plains southeast of Lake Garda. Soils: Predominantly a clay and limestone mix. Some sand. GRAPES: Trebbiano Toscano 20% to 45%; Garganega 20% to 40%; Tocai Friulano 5% to 30%; Cortese, Malvasia Toscana, Riesling Italico, Pinot Bianco, and/or Chardonnay 20% to 30%. WINE TYPES: dw; spdw

BREGANZE DOC (1969)
ZONE: Low hills and alluvial plains north of city of Vicenza, centered around commune of Breganze and stretching north and east up to Brenta River. Soils: calcareous clay at higher elevations, gravel on alluvial plains. GRAPES: Bianco: Tocai Friulano 85% to 100%; other authorized white grapes max. 15%. Rosso: Merlot 85% to 100%; other authorized red grapes max. 15%. Varietal Wines: min. 85% of stated variety. Whites: from Chardonnay; Sauvignon; Vespaiolo; Pinot Grigio; Pinot Bianco. Reds: from Cabernet; Cabernet Sauvignon; Marzemino; Pinot Nero. Torcolato: Vespaiolo 100%, produced as passito. AGING: Riserva Reds: Min. 2 yrs. Torcolato: Min. 1 yr. WINE TYPES: dw; dr; sw

COLLI BERICI DOC (1973)
ZONE: A band of hills south-southwest of Vicenza, reaching toward Soave and Gambellara DOCs to west. Part of a string of ancient volcanoes that includes Colli Euganei. GRAPES: All wines except spumante carry varietal designation. Chardonnay: Min. 85%; Pinot Bianco

max. 15%. Garganega: Min. 90%; Trebbiano di Soave max. 10%. Tocai Italico: Min. 90%; Garganega max. 10%. Sauvignon: Min. 90%; Garganega max. 10%. Pinot Bianco: Min. 85%; Pinot Grigio max. 15%. Spumante: Garganega min. 50%; Pinot Grigio, Pinot Bianco, Chardonnay and/or Sauvignon max. 50%. Reds: Merlot: 100%. Tocai Rosso: Min. 85%; Garganega max. 15%. Cabernet: Cabernet Franc and/or Sauvignon 100%. AGING: Cabernet Riserva: min. 3 yrs. WINE TYPES: dw; spdw; dr

COLLI DI CONEGLIANO DOC (1993)
ZONE: North of Treviso, running from Valdobbiadene to Conegliano then north to Vittorio Veneto. Refrontolo designation only for wines from communes of Refrontolo, Pieve di Soligo, and San Pietro di Feletto, about midway between Valdobbiadene and Conegliano. Torchiato di Fregona designation only for wines from communes of Fregona, Sarmede, and Cappella Maggiore. GRAPES: Bianco: Incrocio Manzoni 6.0.13 min. 30%; Pinot Bianco and/or Chardonnay min. 30%; Sauvignon and/or Riesling Renano max. 10%. Rosso: min. 10% each of Cabernet Franc, Cabernet Sauvignon, Marzemino, and Merlot, with Merlot no more than 40% of total; Incrocio Manzoni 2.15 max. 10%. Refrontolo Passito: Marzemino min. 95%; max. 5% other authorized red grapes. Torchiato di Fregona Passito: Prosecco min. 30%; Verdiso min. 30%; Boschera min. 25%; other authorized white grapes up to 15%. AGING: Bianco: min. 6 mos. Rosso: min. 2 yrs. (6 mos. in wood). Refrontolo: min. 6 mos. (min. 3 mos. in bottle). Torchiato: min. 1 yr. (min. 3 mos. in bottle). WINE TYPES: dw; dr; sw; sr

COLLI EUGANEI DOC (1969)
ZONE: Cluster of hills southwest of Padova. Soils: volcanic/calcareous clay mix. GRAPES: Bianco: Garganega 30% to 50%; Prosecco 10% to 30%; Tocai Friulano and/or Sauvignon 20% to 40%; Pinella, Pinot Bianco, Riesling Italico, and/or Chardonnay max. 20%. Rosso: Merlot 60% to 80%; Cabernet Franc, Cabernet Sauvignon, Barbera, and/or Raboso 20% to 40%. Fior d'Arancio: Moscato Giallo min. 95%. Serprino: Prosecco min. 90%. Varietal Wines: Min. 90% of stated variety; 95% for Moscato. Whites: Chardonnay; Moscato; Pinello(a); Pinot Bianco; Tocai Italico. Reds: Cabernet; Cabernet Franc; Cabernet Sauvignon; Merlot. AGING: Riserva Reds: Min. 2 yrs. (min. 6 mos. in oak). Flor d'Arancio Passito: min. 1 yr. WINE TYPES: dw; spdw; dr (also novello); sw

GAMBELLARA DOC (1970)
ZONE: Southwest of Vicenza, adjacent to Soave DOC

zone. A smaller Classico zone is contained within DOC boundaries. **GRAPES:** Garganega 80% to 100%; other authorized white grapes max. 20%. **AGING:** Vin Santo: min. 2 yrs. **WINE TYPES:** dw; sw; vin santo

GARDA/GARDA CLASSICO DOC (1996)

ZONE: The southern shores of Lake Garda and spreading through the Valpolicella hills to the east. A large zone that includes parts of the provinces of Verona in Veneto, and Mantova and Brescia in Lombardy. Classico zone is limited to the area near Brescia. **GRAPES:** *Garda:* Varietal whites and reds, all calling for a min. 85% of stated variety. *Whites:* Garganega; Pinot Bianco; Pinot Grigio; Chardonnay; Tocai Friulano; Riesling Italico; Riesling; Cortese; Sauvignon. *Reds:* Barbera; Cabernet; Cabernet Franc; Cabernet Sauvignon; Corvina; Marzemino; Merlot. *Garda Classico:* 4 wine types: *Bianco:* Riesling min. 70%; other authorized white grapes max. 30%. *Rosso (also Chiaretto):* Gropello min. 30%; Marzemino min. 5%; Sangiovese min. 5%; Barbera min. 5%; other authorized red grapes max. 10%. *Groppello:* Groppello min. 85%; other authorized grape varieties max 15%. **AGING:** Groppello Riserva: min. 2 yrs. (min. 3 mos. in bottle). **WINE TYPES:** dw; dr; spdw; ros; spros

LESSINI DURELLO DOC (1987)

ZONE: A broad zone north of the Valpolicella and Soave DOCs, in the hills of the Monti Lessini. **GRAPES:** Durello min. 85%; Garganega, Trebbiano di Soave, Pinot Bianco, Pinot Nero, and/or Chardonnay max. 15%. **WINE TYPES:** dw; spdw

LISON-PRAMAGGIORE DOC (1971)

ZONE: Northeasternmost corner of Veneto and a slice of western Friuli south of Pordenone. Soils: calcareous clays. **GRAPES:** *Bianco:* Tocai Friulano 50% to 70%; other authorized white grapes max. 50%. *Rosso (also Rosato):* Merlot 50% to 70%; other authorized red grapes max. 50%. *Lison/Lison Classico:* Tocai Friulano min. 85%; other authorizes white grapes max. 15%. *Varietal Wines:* Min. 85% of stated variety. Whites: Pinot Bianco; Chardonnay; Pinot Grigio; Riesling Italico; Riesling Renano; Sauvignon; Verduzzo. Reds: Merlot; Malbech; Cabernet; Cabernet Franc; Cabernet Sauvignon; Refosco. **WINE TYPES:** dw (also frizzante); spdw; sw; dr (also novello); ros

LUGANA DOC
SEE LISTING UNDER LOMBARDIA

MERLARA DOC (2000–2001)

ZONE: Between Verona and Lake Garda. **GRAPES:** Whites from Tocai and Malvasia, reds frm Cabernet, Marzemino, and Merlot.

MONTELLO E COLLI ASOLANI DOC (1977)

ZONE: Slopes west of the Piave River, centered on the commune of Monfumo northwest of Treviso. **GRAPES:** *Rosso:* Merlot 40% to 60%; Cabernet Franc 20% to 30%; Cabernet Sauvignon 10% to 20%; other authorized red grapes max. 15%. *Varietal Wines:* Must contain min. 85% of stated variety. *Whites:* Prosecco; Chardonnay; Pinot Bianco; Pinot Grigio. *Reds:* Cabernet; Cabernet Franc; Cabernet Sauvignon; Merlot. **AGING:** Superiore Reds: min. 2 yrs. (with min. 6 mos. in wood). **WINE TYPES:** dw; spdw; dr

PROSECCO DI CONEGLIANO-VALDOBBIADENE DOC (1969)

ZONE: A band of hills between the communes of Conegliano and Valdobbiadene, in northeastern Veneto. Slopes are steeper and higher to the west near Valdobbiadene, gentler towards Conegliano, where they open onto an alluvial plain. Wines from vineyards in the village of San Pietro di Barbozza, near Valdobbiadene, can take the Superiore di Cartizze designation. There are about 250 acres of vines registered under the Cartizze designation. **GRAPES:** Prosecco min. 85%; Pinot Bianco, Pinot Grigio, Chardonnay, and/or Verdiso max. 15%; Verdiso alone max. 10%. **WINE TYPES:** dw (also frizzante); spdw

SAN MARTINO DELLA BATTAGLIA DOC (1970)

ZONE: A small zone on the southern shores of Lake Garda, within Lugana DOC, reserved for wines from Tocai Friulano. Soils: calcareous clays. Shared with Lombardy. **GRAPES:** Tocai Friulano min. 80%; other authorized white grapes max. 20%. **WINE TYPES:** dw; fw

SOAVE DOC (1968)

ZONE: East of Verona in the hills around the commune of Soave, including the Alpone, Illasi, Mezzane, and Tramigna valleys. The smaller classico zone, first delimited in 1931, is a band of hills between the towns of Soave and Monteforte d'Alpone. Soils: volcanic mixed with calcareous clays in classico zone, more alluvial in southern and western reaches near Adige River. **GRAPES:** Garganega min. 70%. Pinot Bianco, Chardonnay, and/or Trebbiano di Soave max. 30%. Of this 30%, max. 15% can be other types of Trebbiano, i.e. Trebbiano Toscano. **AGING:** Superiore: cannot be released before March 1 of year succeeding vintage. **WINE TYPES:** dw; spdw

VALDADIGE/ETSCHTALER DOC
SEE LISTING UNDER ALTO ADIGE

VALPOLICELLA/RECIOTO DELLA VALPOLICELLA DOC (1968)
ZONE: A series of valleys just north of the city of Verona, which fan out from the Lessini Mountains. The Classico zone is the western part closer to Lake Garda, taking in the communes of Sant'Ambrogio, San Pietro, Marano, Fumane, and Negrar. Valpantena designation attached to wines from Pantena valley, running through the commune of Grezzana in eastern part of zone. Soils: volcanic tufa throughout much of the classico, mixing with calcareous clays and, further east near Illasi, alluvial material. **GRAPES:** Corvina 40% to 70%; Rondinella 20% to 40%; Molinara 5% to 25%; Rossignola, Negrara Trentina, Barbera, and/or Sangiovese max. 15%; max. 5% other authorized red grapes. **AGING:** Superiore: min. I yr. Amarone: min. 2 yrs. **WINE TYPES:** dr; sr; spsr

VICENZA DOC (2000–2001)
ZONE: Province of Vicenza. **GRAPES:** A wide range of varietal whites and reds.

VINI DEL PIAVE/PIAVE DOC (1971)
ZONE: A vast alluvial plain north and northeast of Venice, bisected by the Piave River. **GRAPES:** Varietal wines containing min. 95% of stated variety. **AGING:** Cabernet/Cabernet Sauvignon Riserva: min. 2 yrs. (min. I yr. in wood). Merlot/Pinot Nero Riserva: min. 2 yrs. (min. 6 mos. in wood). Raboso Riserva: min. 3 yrs. (min. I yr. in wood). **WINE TYPES:** dw; dr

IGT ZONES
BY REGION

Abruzzo

ALTO TIRINO
ZONE: Interior uplands south of the Gran Sasso, centered on the commune of Ofena. **WINE TYPES:** dw (also frizzante); sw; ros (also frizzante and novello); dr (also frizzante and novello); sr

COLLI APRUTINI
ZONE: A vast stretch of the northern coast of Abruzzo.

WINE TYPES: dw (also frizzante); sw; ros (also frizzante and novello); dr (also frizzante and novello); sr

COLLI DEL SANGRO
ZONE: Hills flanking the Sangro River in southern Abruzzo. **WINE TYPES:** dw (also frizzante); sw; ros (also frizzante and novello); dr (also frizzante and novello); sr

COLLINE FRENTANE
ZONE: The southern reaches of Abruzzo. **WINE TYPES:** dw (also frizzante); sw; ros (also frizzante and novello); dr (also frizzante and novello); sr

COLLINE PESCARESI
ZONE: The province of Pescara, in central Abruzzo. **WINE TYPES:** dw (also frizzante); sw; ros (also frizzante and novello); dr (also frizzante and novello); sr

COLLINE TEATINE
ZONE: The coastal sector of southern Abruzzo, in the province of Chieti. **WINE TYPES:** dw (also frizzante); sw; ros (also frizzante and novello); dr (also frizzante and novello); sr

DEL VASTESE/HISTONIUM
ZONE: Southern Abruzzo, near the border of Molise. **WINE TYPES:** dw (also frizzante); sw; ros (also frizzante and novello); dr (also frizzante and novello); sr

TERRE DI CHIETI
ZONE: The province of Chieti, in southern Abruzzo. **WINE TYPES:** dw (also frizzante); sw; ros (also frizzante and novello); dr (also frizzante and novello); sr

VALLE PELIGNA
ZONE: Interior uplands around L'Aquila. **WINE TYPES:** dw (also frizzante); sw; ros (also frizzante and novello); dr (also frizzante and novello); sr

Alto Adige

MITTERBERG TRA CAURIA E TEL/MITTERBERG ZWISCHEN GFRILL UND TOLL O MITTERBERG
ZONE: Province of Bolzano **WINE TYPES:** dw (also frizzante); ros (also frizzante); dr (also frizzante and novello)

VIGNETI DELLE DOLOMITI/WEINBERG DOLOMITEN
ZONE: A vast zone stretching from Bolzano (Alto Adige) to Belluno (Veneto), generally following the con-

tours of the Dolomites. **WINE TYPES**: dw (also frizzante); ros(also frizzante); dr (also frizzante and novello)

Basilicata

BASILICATA
ZONE: Region of Basilicata. **WINE TYPES**: dw (also frizzante); dr(also frizzante); ros(also frizzante)

GROTTINO DI ROCCANOVA
ZONE: Wine must come from vineyards in province of Potenza, specifically the 3 communes of Roccanova, Castronuovo di Sant'Andrea, and Sant'Arcangelo, **WINE TYPES**: dw; dr; ros; sw; sr

Calabria

ARGHILLÀ
ZONE: Southern Calabria, including communes of Calanna, Campo Calabro, Fiumara and Villa San Giovanni. **WINE TYPES**: ros (also novello); dr (also novello)

CALABRIA
ZONE: The entire region of Calabria. **WINE TYPES**: dw (also frizzante); sw; ros; dr (also frizzante); sr

CONDOLEO
ZONE: Central Ionian coast of Calabria, centered on commune of Mandatoriccio, north of Cirò. **WINE TYPES**: ros (also novello); dr (also novello)

COSTA VIOLA
ZONE: Mediterranean coast of Calabria just north of Reggio Calabria. **WINE TYPES**: dw; ros (also novello); dr (also novello)

ESARO
ZONE: A cluster of communes north of Cosenza, in central Calabria. **WINE TYPES**: dw; ros (also novello); dr (also novello)

LIPUDA
ZONE: Central Ionian coast of Calabria, including communes of Cirò and Melissa. **WINE TYPES**: dw (also frizzante); ros (also frizzante and novello); dr (also frizzante)

LOCRIDE
ZONE: Southern Ionian coast of Calabria, including

coastal town of Bianco. **WINE TYPES**: dw; ros; dr (also novello)

PALIZZI
ZONE: The southernmost tip of Calabria. **WINE TYPES**: ros; dr (also novello)

PELLARO
ZONE: Southernmost Calabria, near Reggio Calabria. **WINE TYPES**: ros; dr (also novello)

SCILLA
ZONE: Communes of Scilla, on the southern Calabrian coast north of Reggio Calabria. **WINE TYPES**: ros; dr (also novello)

VAL DI NETO
ZONE: The Neto River valley on the central Ionian coast of Calabria. Used by many Cirò producers, including Librandi. **WINE TYPES**: dw (also frizzante); sw; ros (also frizzante); dr (also frizzante and novello); sr

VALDAMATO
ZONE: The Lamato River valley south of Cosenza, roughly equivalent geographically to the Lamezia DOC. **WINE TYPES**: dw (also frizzante); sw; ros (also frizzante); dr (also frizzante and novello); sr

VALLE DEL CRATI
ZONE: The Crati River Valley in north-central Calabria. **WINE TYPES**: dw; sw; ros; dr (also novello); sr

Campania

COLLI DI SALERNO
ZONE: The province of Salerno in southern Campania. **WINE TYPES**: dw (also frizzante); sw; ros (also frizzante); sros; dr (also frizzante and novello); sr

DUGENTA
ZONE: The commune of Dugenta in northern Campania, in the province of Benevento. **WINE TYPES**: dw; ros; dr (also novello)

EPOMEO
ZONE: The Island of Ischia. **WINE TYPES**: dw (also frizzante); sw; ros (also frizzante); sros; dr (also frizzante and novello); sr

IRPINIA
ZONE: The province of Avellino in central Campania, in which the Taurasi and Greco di Tufo DOCs are located,

among others. **WINE TYPES:** dw (also frizzante); sw; ros (also frizzante); sros; dr (also frizzante and novello); sr

PAESTUM
ZONE: Named for the ancient Greek city on the Campanian coast south of Salerno. **WINE TYPES:** dw (also frizzante); sw; ros (also frizzante); sros; dr (also frizzante and novello); sr

POMPEIANO
ZONE: The province of Naples, excluding the island of Ischia. **WINE TYPES:** dw (also frizzante); sw; ros (also frizzante); sros; dr (also frizzante and novello); sr

ROCCAMONFINA
ZONE: Hills in a series of communes, including that of Roccamonfina, in the province of Caserta, northeast of Naples. **WINE TYPES:** dw (also frizzante); sw; ros (also frizzante); sros; dr (also frizzante and novello); sr

TERRE DEL VOLTURNO
ZONE: Hills of northwesternmost Campania, bounded by the Volturno River. **WINE TYPES:** dw (also frizzante); sw; ros (also frizzante); sros; dr (also frizzante and novello); sr

Emilia-Romagna

BIANCO DI CASTELFRANCO EMILIA
ZONE: Plains between Bologna and Modena. **WINE TYPES:** dw (also frizzante)

EMILIA/DELL'EMILIA
ZONE: The western half of Emilia-Romagna, encompassing both hills and plains in six provinces. **WINE TYPES:** dw; dr (also novello); ros

FORLÌ
ZONE: The province of Forlì, east of Bologna. **WINE TYPES:** dw (also frizzante); dr (also frizzante and novello); ros (also frizzante)

FORTANA DEL TARO
ZONE: Encompasses the entire Parma province, including the city of Parma. **WINE TYPES:** dr (also frizzante and novello)

MODENA/PROVINCIA DI MODENA
ZONE: The province of Modena, west of Bologna. **WINE TYPES:** dw (also frizzante); dr (also frizzante and novello); ros (also frizzante)

RAVENNA
ZONE: The province of Ravenna, along the Adriatic coast east of Bologna. **WINE TYPES:** dw (also frizzante); dr (also frizzante and novello); ros (also frizzante)

RUBICONE
ZONE: Hills and plains straddling the Via Emilia between Bologna and Forlì. **WINE TYPES:** dw (also frizzante); dr (also frizzante and novello); ros (also frizzante)

SILLARO/BIANCO DEL SILLARO
ZONE: Hills and plains between Bologna and Rimini; roughly equivalent to Sangiovese/Trebbiano di Romagna DOC. **WINE TYPES:** dw (also frizzante and novello)

TERRE DI VELEJA
ZONE: A series of communes south of Piacenza; roughly equivalent to Colli Piacentini DOC zone. **WINE TYPES:** dw (also frizzante); dr (also frizzante); ros (also frizzante)

VAL TIDONE
ZONE: The Tidone River valley, southwest of Piacenza. **WINE TYPES:** dw (also frizzante); dr (also frizzante)

Friuli–Venezia Giulia

ALTO LIVENZA
ZONE: Western Friuli plains, in province of Pordenone, and continuing into the province of Treviso in northeastern Veneto. **WINE TYPES:** dw (also frizzante); ros (also frizzante); dr (also frizzante and novello)

DELLE VENEZIE
ZONE: Taking in much of the Tre Venezie, including the province of Trento and all provinces in the regions of Veneto and Friuli–Venezia Giulia. **WINE TYPES:** dw (also frizzante); dr (also frizzante and novello); rosato (also frizzante)

VENEZIA GIULIA
ZONE: all of Friuli–Venezia Giulia winemaking area. **WINE TYPES:** dw (also frizzante); ros (also frizzante); dr (also frizzante and novello)

Lazio

CIVITELLA D'AGLIANO
ZONE: The commune of Civitella d'Agliano, northeast of Viterbo near the border with Umbria. **WINE TYPES:**

dw (also frizzante); ros (also frizzante); dr (also novello and frizzante)

COLLI CIMINI
ZONE: A cluster of communes south of Viterbo near Lake Vico, reaching eastward toward the Tiber River. **WINE TYPES:** dw (also frizzante and novello); ros (also frizzante); dr (also novello and frizzante)

FRUSINATE/DEL FRUSINATE
ZONE: The entire province of Frosinone, southeast of Rome. **WINE TYPES:** dw (also frizzante); ros (also frizzante); dr (also novello and frizzante)

LAZIO
ZONE: The entire Lazio region. **WINE TYPES:** dw (also frizzante); ros (also frizzante); dr (also novello and frizzante)

NETTUNO
ZONE: The communes of Anzio and Nettuno, on the Mediterranean coast south of Rome. **WINE TYPES:** dw (also frizzante); ros (also frizzante); dr (also frizzante)

Liguria

COLLINE SAVONESI
ZONE: The entire province of Savona, between Genoa and Imperia. **WINE TYPES:** dw (also frizzante); sw; ros; dr (also novello)

Lombardia

ALTO MINCIO
ZONE: Flanking Mincio River, which runs through Mantova south of Lake Garda. **WINE TYPES:** dw (also frizzante); sw; dr (also frizzante and novello); sr; ros (also frizzante)

BENACO BRESCIANO
ZONE: Western shores of Lake Garda. **WINE TYPES:** dw (also frizzante); dr (also novello)

BERGAMASCA
ZONE: Stretch of hills surrounding Bergamo and reaching east toward Brescia and north to the Orobie Alps. **WINE TYPES:** dw; dr (also novello); ros

COLLINA DEL MILANESE
ZONE: Low hills on north bank of Po River southeast of Milano. **WINE TYPES:** dw (also frizzante); sw; ros (also frizzante); dr (also frizzante and novello)

MONTENETTO DI BRESCIA
ZONE: Small stretch of hills east of Brescia. **WINE TYPES:** dw (also frizzante); dr (also novello)

PROVINCIA DI MANTOVA
ZONE: The entire province of Mantova, encompassing stretch of plains south of Lake Garda. **WINE TYPES:** dw (also frizzante); sw; dr (also frizzante and novello); sr; ros (also frizzante)

PROVINCIA DI PAVIA
ZONE: The province of Pavia, in southwestern Lombardy. **WINE TYPES:** dw (also frizzante); dr (also frizzante and novello); ros (also frizzante)

QUISTELLO
ZONE: A handful of communes in the province of Mantova, south of Lake Garda. **WINE TYPES:** dw (also frizzante); dr (also frizzante and novello); ros (also frizzante)

RONCHI DI BRESCIA
ZONE: Hills of Brescia and seven communes to its east. **WINE TYPES:** dw (also frizzante); sw; dr (also novello)

SABBIONETA
ZONE: Small chunk of Po plain southwest of Mantova. **WINE TYPES:** dw (also frizzante); dr (also frizzante and novello); ros (also frizzante)

SEBINO
ZONE: Hills west and north of Brescia, including parts of Franciacorta and Cellatica DOCs. **WINE TYPES:** dr (also novello); sr; dw

TERRAZZE RETICHE DI SONDRIO
ZONE: Banks of Adda River, in northern Lombardy. Roughly equivalent to Valtellina DOC(G). **WINE TYPES:** dw; ros (also frizzante); dr (also novello)

Marche

MARCHE
ZONE: The entire Marche region. **WINE TYPES:** dw (also frizzante); ros (also frizzante); dr (also frizzante and novello)

Molise

OSCO/TERRE DEGLI OSCI
ZONE: The province of Campobasso, comprising the eastern and less mountainous half of Molise. WINE TYPES: dw (also frizzante); sw; ros (also frizzante); dr (also frizzante and novello)

ROTAE
ZONE: The province of Isernia, comprising the interior uplands of Molise. WINE TYPES: dw (also frizzante); sw; ros (also frizzante); dr (also frizzante and novello)

Puglia

DAUNIA
ZONE: Northern plains of Puglia; province of Foggia. WINE TYPES: dw (also frizzante); sw; ros (also frizzante); dr (also frizzante); sr

MURGIA
ZONE: The province of Bari, in central Puglia. WINE TYPES: dw (also frizzante); sw; ros (also frizzante); dr (also frizzante); sr

PUGLIA
ZONE: All provinces of Puglia. WINE TYPES: dw (also frizzante); sw; ros (also frizzante); dr (also frizzante); sr

SALENTO
ZONE: Southern peninsula of Puglia, including provinces of Brindisi, Lecce, and Taranto. WINE TYPES: dw (also frizzante); sw; ros (also frizzante); dr (also frizzante); sr

TARANTINO
ZONE: Province of Taranto, in southern Puglia. WINE TYPES: dw (also frizzante); sw; ros (also frizzante); dr (also frizzante); sr

VALLE D'ITRIA
ZONE: Swath of Salentine peninsula in southern Puglia running from Taranto in west to Ostuni in east. WINE TYPES: dw (also frizzante); sw; ros (also frizzante); dr (also frizzante); sr

Sardegna

BARBAGIA
ZONE: The Barbagia hills in central Sardinia, on the western edge of the Gennargentu massif. WINE TYPES: dw (also frizzante); dr (also frizzante and novello); ros (also frizzante)

COLLI DI LIMBARA
ZONE: Much of the Gallura region of northeastern Sardinia, including the communes of Tempio Pausania, Arzachena, and Olbia. WINE TYPES: dw (also frizzante); dr (also frizzante and novello); ros (also frizzante)

ISOLA DEI NURAGHI
ZONE: The entire island of Sardinia. WINE TYPES: dw (also frizzante); dr (also frizzante and novello); ros (also frizzante)

MARMILLA
ZONE: A cluster of communes on the Campidano plain between Cagliari and Oristano. WINE TYPES: dw (also frizzante); dr (also frizzante and novello); ros (also frizzante)

NURRA
ZONE: Plains and coastal areas in the extreme northwest corner of the island, taking in the communes of Alghero, Sassari, Porto Torres, and others. WINE TYPES: dw (also frizzante); dr (also frizzante and novello); ros (also frizzante)

OGLIASTRA
ZONE: The eastern edge of the Gennargentu Massif, including ecommunes such as Tortoli and Jerzu, on the east coast south of Nuoro. WINE TYPES: dw (also frizzante); dr (also frizzante and novello); ros (also frizzante)

PARTEOLLA
ZONE: A swath of the Campidano plain north and northwest of Cagliari, including communes such as Dolianova, Monastir, and Sarramanna. WINE TYPES: dw (also frizzante); dr (also frizzante and novello); ros (also frizzante)

PLANARGIA
ZONE: A small coastal sector between Oristano and Sassari, in west-central Sardinia. WINE TYPES: dw (also frizzante); dr (also frizzante and novello); ros (also frizzante)

PROVINCIA DI NUORO
ZONE: The entire province of Nuoro, in central Sardinia. WINE TYPES: dw (also frizzante); dr (also frizzante and novello); ros (also frizzante)

ROMANGIA
ZONE: Coastal sector northeast of Sassari. WINE TYPES: dw (also frizzante); dr (also frizzante and novello); ros (also frizzante)

SIBIOLA
ZONE: Low hills due north of Cagliari, near the commune of Dolianova. WINE TYPES: dw (also frizzante); dr (also frizzante and novello); ros (also frizzante)

THARROS
ZONE: The entire province of Oristano, in west-central Sardinia. WINE TYPES: dw (also frizzante); dr (also frizzante and novello); ros (also frizzante)

TREXENTA
ZONE: The Trexenta hills north of Cagliari, including communes of Senorbi and Selegas. WINE TYPES: dw (also frizzante); dr (also frizzante and novello); ros (also frizzante)

VALLE DEL TIRSO
ZONE: The Tirso River valley in west-central Sardinia, just north of Oristano. WINE TYPES: dw (also frizzante); dr (also frizzante and novello); ros (also frizzante)

VALLI DI PORTO PINO
ZONE: The southwestern corner of Sardinia, including the communes of Santadi and Teulada. WINE TYPES: dw (also frizzante); dr (also frizzante and novello); ros (also frizzante)

Sicilia

CAMARRO
ZONE: Western Sicily, in province of Trapani. WINE TYPES: dw (also frizzante); dr (also frizzante and novello); ros (also frizzante)

COLLI ERICINI
ZONE: Northwestern Sicily, between Trapani and Alcamo. WINE TYPES: dw (also frizzante); dr (also frizzante); ros (also frizzante)

FONTANAROSSA DI CERDA
ZONE: The commune of Cerda, about 30 miles southeast of Palermo. WINE TYPES: dw (also frizzante); dr (also frizzante and novello); ros (also frizzante)

SALEMI
ZONE: The commune of Salemi, in western Sicily

between Marsala and Alcamo. WINE TYPES: dw (also frizzante); dr (also frizzante and novello); ros (also frizzante)

SALINA
ZONE: The Aeolian island of Salina, off the northeast coast of Sicily. WINE TYPES: dw (also frizzante); dr (also frizzante and novello); ros (also frizzante)

SICILIA
ZONE: The entire island of Sicily. WINE TYPES: dw (also frizzante); dr (also frizzante and novello); ros (also frizzante); fw; fr

VALLE BELICE
ZONE: Slopes east of the Belice River in southwestern Sicily, taking in the communes of Menfi, Contessa Entellina, and Santa Margherita Belice, among others. WINE TYPES: dw (also frizzante); dr (also frizzante and novello); ros (also frizzante)

Toscana

ALTA VALLE DELLA GREVE
ZONE: Overlaps with northwestern chunk of Chianti Classico zone, following contours of Greve River from San Casciano to Panzano. WINE TYPES: dw; ros; dr (also novello)

COLLI DELLA TOSCANA CENTRALE
ZONE: A vast swath of Central Tuscany, taking in the provinces of Arezzo, Firenze, Pistoia, Prato, and Siena. WINE TYPES: dw (also frizzante); ros; dr (also novello)

MAREMMA TOSCANA
ZONE: Taking in the whole province of Grosseto along the south coast of Tuscany. WINE TYPES: dw (also frizzante); ros; dr (also novello)

TOSCANA/TOSCANO
ZONE: The whole of Tuscany, encompassing Provinces of Arezzo, Firenze, Grosseto, Livorno, Lucca, Massa Carrara, Pisa, Pistoia, Prato, Siena. WINE TYPES: dw (also frizzante and abboccato); ros (also abboccato); dr (also novello and abboccato)

VAL DI MAGRA
ZONE: The northwesternmost sliver of Tuscany, from the Apuan Alps near Carrara to the border with Liguria. WINE TYPES: dw; ros; dr

Trentino

ATESINO
ZONE: Province of Trento.

DELLE VENEZIE
ZONE: Taking in much of the ancient Tre Venezie, including the province of Trento and all provinces in the regions of Veneto and Friuli–Venezia Giulia. WINE TYPES: dw (also frizzante); dr (also frizzante and novello); ros (also frizzante)

VALLAGARINA
ZONE: The southern part of Trentino and the province of Verona in the Veneto. WINE TYPES: dw (also frizzante); dr (also frizzante and novello); ros (also frizzante)

VIGNETI DELLE DOLOMITI/WEINBERG DOLOMITEN
SEE LISTING UNDER ALTO ADIGE

Umbria

ALLERONA
ZONE: Southern Umbria, encompassing the communes of Allerona, Casteviscardo, and Castelgiorgio. WINE TYPES: dw (also frizzante and novello); sw; ros (also frizzante and novello); dr (also frizzante and novello)

BETTONA
ZONE: The commune of Bettona, near Torgiano southeast of Perugia. WINE TYPES: dw (also frizzante); ros (also novello); dr (also novello)

CANNARA
ZONE: The communes of Bettona, Bevagna, and Cannara, along the Topino River southeast of Perugia. WINE TYPES: dr; sr

NARNI
ZONE: Southernmost Umbria, including communes of Narni, Terni, and several others reaching toward border with Lazio. WINE TYPES: dw (also frizzante); sw; ros (also frizzante and novello); dr (also novello); sr

SPELLO
ZONE: The commune of Spello, between Assisi and Foligno east of Perugia. WINE TYPES: dw; ros; dr

UMBRIA
ZONE: The entire region of Umbria. WINE TYPES: dw (also frizzante and novello); sw; ros (also frizzante and novello); dr (also frizzante and novello); sr

Veneto

ALTO LIVENZA
ZONE: Northeastern Veneto and western Friuli, taking in eight communes in province of Treviso and six in province of Pordenone. WINE TYPES: dw (also frizzante); dr (also frizzante); ros (also frizzante)

COLLI TREVIGIANI
ZONE: Hills north of Treviso, following contours of Piave River in communes of Nervesa, Pederoba and others. WINE TYPES: dw (also frizzante); dr (also frizzante and novello); ros (also frizzante)

CONSELVANO
ZONE: Roughly consistent with Bagnoli DOC. WINE TYPES: dw (also frizzante); dr (also frizzante and novello); ros (also frizzante)

DELLE VENEZIE
ZONE: Taking in much of the ancient Tre Venezie, including the province of Trento and all provinces in the regions of Veneto and Friuli–Venezia Giulia. WINE TYPES: dw (also frizzante); dr (also frizzante and novello); ros (also frizzante)

MARCA TREVIGIANA
ZONE: The entire province of Treviso. WINE TYPES: dw (also frizzante); dr (also frizzante and novello); ros (also frizzante)

PROVINCIA DI VERONA/VERONESE
ZONE: The entire province of Verona. WINE TYPES: dw (also frizzante); dr (also frizzante and novello); ros (also frizzante)

VALLAGARINA
ZONE: SEE LISTING UNDER TRENTINO

VENETO
ZONE: The region of Veneto. WINE TYPES: dw (also frizzante); sw; dr (also frizzante and novello); sr; ros (also frizzante)

VENETO ORIENTALE
ZONE: The eastern and northeastern reaches of the Veneto region, taking in the provinces of Treviso and Venezia. WINE TYPES: dw (also frizzante); dr (also frizzante and novello); ros (also frizzante)

VIGNETI DELLE DOLOMITI/WEINBERG DOLOMITEN
SEE LISTING UNDER ALTO ADIGE

APPENDIX IV
The Producers: Le Aziende

—— ❧ ——

There are more wineries in Italy than we care to count. More than a million grape-growers have some form of commercial production, and, according to one source, some fifty thousand wineries produce wine countrywide. The number of these wineries that actually bottle wine for sale is much less, but even so, it would be impossible to catalog them all.

At this point in time, an amazing number of Italian wine brands, large and small, are finding their way into the United States. Some estates are so tiny that their American importers sell their entire allocations before the wines even hit the docks. Yet as the market expands—and it's expanding every year—new and notable Italian wines pour (or trickle) onto our shores.

What follows is a highly subjective listing of some seven hundred Italian wine estates, all of which (unless otherwise noted) are available in some quantity in the United States. The wineries are listed alphabetically. Also included is the region each winery hails from, and the commune and province (province's abbreviation is in parentheses) in which the winery is based. Further, any DOC(G)s used by the estate are listed, as a point of reference.

In instances where the winery name is the name of a person, for example, "Elio Altare"—then it is listed alphabetically under the last name, as "Altare, Elio." Of course, many Italian winery names begin with words such as *Tenuta, Fattoria, Villa,* and so on. In instances where it was felt that *Fattoria* or *Tenuta* were vital components to the winery name (for some wineries, it is a key element of the brand name, for others, not), then they are listed under *Fattoria . . .* or *Tenuta . . .* There are also instances where a winery has two widely used names, i.e. the name of their brand and the name of the proprietor. In such instances, we've chosen the more widely used name and put the second name in parentheses. As a general guideline, consider both the proprietor's name as well as any prefixes when searching for it in this guide.

A MACCIA
LIGURIA; RANZO (IM)
DOC(G)s: Riviera Ligure di
  Ponente
Loredana Faraldi's tiny estate in the
hills of Ranzo is known primarily
for a tangy, aromatic pigato. She
also makes great olive oil.

A-MANO
PUGLIA; SAN MARZANO (LE)
American winemaker Mark Shannon, in partnership with an Italian
marketing firm, created this highly
successful, value-priced brand. The
lush, jammy A-Mano primitivo is a
crowd-pleaser priced to buy by the
case.

ABBAZIA DI NOVACELLA
ALTO ADIGE; VARNA (BZ)
DOC(G)s: Alto Adige Valle
  d'Isarco/Südtirol Eisacktaler
This Augustinian monastery,
founded in 1142, is 40 kilometers
from the Brenner Pass to Austria.
One of the northernmost wine estates in Italy, its specialty is perfumed, high-acid whites from
varieties such as sylvaner and
gewürztraminer. In total, the abbey
owns a number of vineyards, including some around Bolzano, so the
native red lagrein is also a specialty.

ABBAZIA SANTA ANASTASIA
SICILIA; CASTELBUONO (PA)
Set in the hills of Castelbuono, a
few minutes inland from the spectacular north coast near Cefalù, the
vineyards here are a mix of sandy
clay and limestone in which the
Lena family have not only nero
d'avola but syrah, cabernet sauvignon, and merlot. The wines are a
slick series of IGT blends, combining nero d'avola with merlot ("Passomaggio"), syrah ("Montenero"),
and cabernet ("Litra").

ABBONA, MARZIANO ED ENRICO
PIEMONTE; DOGLIANI (CN)
DOC(G)s: Dolcetto di Dogliani;
  Barbaresco; Barbera d'Alba;
  Barolo
One of the key wineries in the
Dogliani zone, with several different
dolcettos including the top-end
"Bricco S. Bernardo" and the Beau-
jolais-like "Vigneto Munta." The
estate also makes well-priced, acces-
sible Barolo and Barbaresco from
small holdings in those zones.

ABRATE, LUCA
PIEMONTE; BRÀ (CN)
DOC(G)s: Barbera d'Alba;
  Nebbiolo d'Alba; Roero
Based west of Alba in Brà, this artisan producer makes wines in both
the Roero and Alba areas, most notably a lush and affordable Barbera
d'Alba called "Ouitin." Arneis and
nebbiolo are also specialties and, like
the barberas, are good values.

ABRIGO, ORLANDO
PIEMONTE; TREISO (CN)
DOC(G)s: Barbaresco; Barbera
  d'Alba; Langhe Rosso
Brawny Barbaresco from several different cru vineyards. Also worth
checking out are the Barbera d'Alba
"Montersino" and the woody, full-
bodied Langhe Rosso "Livraie"
(100% merlot).

ACCORDINI, STEFANO
VENETO; S. PIETRO IN CARIANO
  (VR)
DOC(G)s: Amarone della
  Valpolicella; Recioto della
  Valpolicella; Valpolicella Classico
A boutique Amarone producer run
by brothers Tiziano and Daniele
Accordini. Their "Acinatico" and "Il
Fornetto" Amarones are examples of
the more elegant, more readily
drinkable, less extracted style of

Amarone. Small production.

ACCORNERO E FIGLI
PIEMONTE; VIGNALE MONFERRATO
  (AL)
DOC(G)s: Barbera del Monferrato
A Barbera specialist in the Monferrato DOC. A highlight is the dense
"Bricco Battista" Barbera del Monferrato, concentrated and smoky
from a touch of wood aging. The
super-fruity "Giulin" is also noteworthy.

ACQUABONA
TOSCANA; PORTOFERRAIO (LI)
DOC(G)s: Elba
The best-known winery on the island of Elba, off the Tuscan coast.
Oddities such as the sweet red
aleatico and simple dry whites from
vermentino and ansonica (inzolia)
are among the highlights—although
you'll probably have to vacation on
the island to find them.

ADANTI
UMBRIA; BEVAGNA (PG)
DOC(G)s: Montefalco
A solid lineup of Umbrian reds,
highlighted by a spicy Sagrantino di
Montefalco and several proprietary
blends, including "Arquata Rosso"
(cabernets sauvignon and franc,
merlot, barbera) and "Nispero"
(sangiovese, cabernet sauvignon,
barbera).

ALESSANDRIA, F.ILLI
PIEMONTE; VERDUNO (CN)
DOC(G)s: Barolo; Barbera d'Alba;
  Langhe
Small producer known for its
"Monvigliero" cru Barolo. Like
other Verduno wines (such as those
of Burlotto), these Barolos are ap-
proachable when young.

ALESSANDRIA, GIANFRANCO
PIEMONTE; MONFORTE D'ALBA
(CN)
DOC(G)s: Barolo; Barbera d'Alba
A tiny estate, with around 10 acres of vineyard, that bottled its first commercial vintage in 1991. Powerful, limited-production Barolos (the cru wine is "San Giovanni") and Barbera d'Alba are the principal offerings.

ALLEGRINI
VENETO; FUMANE (VR)
DOC(G)s: Valpolicella Classico;
 Amarone della Valpolicella;
 Recioto della Valpolicella
One of the biggest names in Valpolicella, known primarily for rich and powerfully built Amarone as well as the IGT red "La Poja," a wine that showcases the local corvina grape in all of its dark, coffee-scented splendor. "La Poja" is unique, in fact, in achieving exceptional concentration without incorporating any dried-grape wine or ripasso methodology in its production. The value-priced "Palazzo della Torre" (which includes 30% dried grapes) is a fruity and fun Valpolicella with more meat than most, and the "La Grola" (corvina-rondinella-sangiovese-syrah) is another solid red.

ALTARE, ELIO
PIEMONTE; LA MORRA (CN)
DOC(G)s: Barolo; Langhe Rosso;
 Barbera d'Alba; Dolcetto d'Alba
Since the mid-seventies, Elio Altare has been one of the deans of wine-making in the Barolo zone. He and contemporaries such as Luciano Sandrone, Domenico Clerico, and Roberto Voerzio were among the first winemakers in the area to travel to other winemaking regions (namely Burgundy and Bordeaux) in an effort to modernize their own operations, and since then they have

been at the forefront of Barolo-making. Altare's estate in the heights of La Morra is known primarily for the aromatic, sinewy "Vigneto Arborina" Barolo, a wine as complex and tightly wound as its maker. Altare also makes Barolo from the Brunate cru south of La Morra, and a Langhe DOC nebbiolo called "Arborina," among other wines.

ALTESINO
TOSCANA; MONTALCINO (SI)
DOC(G)s: Brunello di Montalcino
Known for characteristically firm and fine Brunellos that need a good amount of aging before they start to express themselves. They also make a well-regarded Vin Santo and some super-Tuscan red blends.

AMBROSINI, LORELLA
TOSCANA; SUVERETO (LI)
DOC(G)s: Val di Cornia
Maker of a range of unusual red blends in the Suvereto area, an increasingly popular spot on the south Tuscan coast. Top wines are "Riflesso Antico" (100% montepulciano) and Subertum (sangiovese-merlot).

ANSELMI
VENETO; MONTEFORTE D'ALPONE
(VR)
DOC(G)s: Soave
Although he is one of the of the most acclaimed producers of Soave, Roberto Anselmi decided several years ago to shun the DOC designation for his top wines because of what he perceived to be flaws in the production discipline for the zone. His whites—namely the progressively richer trio of "San Vincenzo," "Capitel Foscarino" and "Capitel Croce"—demonstrate how rich and flavorful the garganega grape can be when treated with care. The "I Capitelli" Recioto di Soave is one of

the best examples of its type. Consistent, well-priced wines.

ANTANO, MILZIADE
UMBRIA; BEVAGNA (PG)
DOC(G)s: Montefalco; Sagrantino
 di Montefalco
Producer of some of the most evocative Montefalco wines. The Rossos are generously dosed with the sagrantino grape, making them more complex than most, while the Sagrantino di Montefalco DOC wines, of which there are three, are spicy and singular. A boutique winery in the top rank.

ANTINORI
TOSCANA; FIRENZE (FI)
DOC(G)s: Bolgheri; Brunello di
 Montalcino; Chianti Classico;
 Orvieto Classico; Vino Nobile di
 Montepulciano
An estate that's too far-reaching to be neatly summarized here. The Antinoris are Florentine nobles who've produced wine since the 1300s, and today the empire extends throughout Tuscany and Umbria as well as Piedmont and Puglia. Current chief Piero Antinori has been one of the most dynamic figures in Italian wine, having helped create the super-Tuscan category with the introduction of "Tignanello" (80% sangiovese, 20% cabernet) in 1971, and having helped propel the Chianti Classico zone out of its doldrums by challenging the DOC's established norms. Today, the Antinori holdings include three estates in Chianti Classico (Santa Cristina, Badia a Passignano, Pèppoli), one in Bolgheri (Tenuta Belvedere), one in Piedmont (Prunotto), one in Umbria (Castello della Sala), one in Montepulciano (Braccesca), one in Montalcino (Pian delle Vigne), and a newly established estate in Puglia (Vigneti del Sud). The company's

wines run the gamut, from reliable, low-priced wines such as the white "Galestro" and "Pèppoli" Chianti Classico, to higher-end wines such as "Solaia" (80% cabernet, 20% sangiovese), Pian delle Vigne Brunello, and the benchmark Tenute Marchese Antinori Chianti Classico Riserva.

ANTONELLI-SAN MARCO
UMBRIA; MONTEFALCO (PG)
DOC(G)s: Sagrantino di
   Montefalco (also Passito); Rosso
   di Montefalco; Colli Martani
Another of Montefalco's best (if lesser-known) producers. Antonelli's rich, brambly Sagrantinos and Port-like Sagrantino Passito are tough to find but worth the effort.

ANTONIOLO
PIEMONTE; GATTINARA (VC)
DOC(G)s: Gattinara
A top property in Gattinara, with two cru wines: the "Osso San Grato," considered the most powerful and ageworthy, and the "San Francesco," typically a little more accessible in its youth. There's also the white Erbaluce di Caluso.

APOLLONIO
PUGLIA; LECCE AREA
DOC(G)s: Copertino; Salice
   Salentino
Value-priced reds from negroamaro and primitivo are a specialty. Check out the Salice Salentino and the Primitivo "Terragnolo" for everyday drinking.

ARGIANO
TOSCANA; MONTALCINO (SI)
DOC(G)s: Brunello di Montalcino
Powerful Brunello and a super-Tuscan called "Solengo" (a sinewy blend of sangiovese, cabernet, syrah, and merlot), are the top wines.

Ranks among the biggest names in Montalcino.

ARGIOLAS
SARDEGNA; SERDIANA (CA)
DOC(G)s: Cannonau di Sardegna;
   Monica di Sardegna; Nuragus di
   Cagliari; Vermentino di Sardegna
From vineyards situated in the Trexenta hills north of Cagliari, the Argiolas family turns out some of Sardegna's best wines, especially reds. With the help of famed enologist Giacomo Tachis and an exotic array of local grapes—cannonau (grenache), carignano (carignane), bovale (similar to mourvèdre), and monica—Argiolas is best known for "Turriga," a blend of cannonau, malvasia, carignano, and bovale that captures the wild, untamed nature of the area. The "Costamolino" vermentino is a reliable light white.

ARMANI
VENETO; DOLCE (VR)
A maker of unusual wines from north of Verona. The top wine is the IGT Corvara Rosso (50% cabernet sauvignon, 50% corvina).

ARTIMINO
TOSCANA; ARTIMINO (FI)
DOC(G)s: Carmignano; Chianti
   Montalbano
A noted producer of Carmignano. The estate, located in the town of Artimino, has a country hotel and restaurant on-site.

AVIGNONESI
TOSCANA; MONTEPULCIANO (SI)
DOC(G)s: Vino Nobile di
   Montepulciano; Vin Santo
The Falvo family holdings include four estates, with the home base in Montepulciano, the zone they helped make famous. Vino Nobile is still the wine Avignonesi is best

known for, but the rich, long-aged, and very rare Vin Santo is probably the most sought-after. Still, lush and modern reds remain the specialty. Try the super-Tuscan "Desiderio" (merlot with a touch of cabernet) and "50&50" (sangiovese-merlot), the latter made in collaboration with a Chianti estate called Capanelle (which supplies the sangiovese).

AZELIA
PIEMONTE; CASTIGLIONE
   FALLETTO (CN)
DOC(G)s: Barolo; Barbera d'Alba;
   Dolcetto d'Alba
Luigi Scavino's small property is known for its modern, fleshy, new-oak-aged Barolos. Luigi is the cousin of Enrico Scavino, current proprietor of the Paolo Scavino estate (got all that?).

BADIA A COLTIBUONO
TOSCANA; GAIOLE IN CHIANTI
   (SI)
DOC(G)s: Chianti Classico
Run by brother-sister team Roberto and Emanuela Stucchi, this historic estate is known for Chianti as well as a varietal sangiovese called Sangioveto. Descendants of the de' Medicis, the Stucchis run a restaurant and gift shop on the grounds of their eleventh-century abbey, a popular tourist destination. A new, space-age winery was completed in 1999, and winemaking consultant Luca D'Attoma came on board in 2000, ensuring more muscular, modern reds in the future.

BADIA DI MORRONA
TOSCANA; TERRICCIOLA (PI)
DOC(G)s: Chianti
A western Tuscan estate known for "N'Antia" (a blend of sangiovese, cabernet, and merlot) and "Vignalta" (all sangiovese).

BALTER
Trentino; Rovereto (TN)
DOC(G)s: Trento Brut; Trentino
Nicola Balter's small property in Rovereto, south of Trento, is best known for its Trento Brut sparkler from chardonnay. There's also a red, "Barbanico," made from cabernet, merlot, and lagrein, that has won critical praise.

BALTIERI
Veneto; Mizzole (VR)
DOC(G)s: Valpolicella; Amarone della Valpolicella
Small, family-run estate in Valpolicella. The limited-production "Sortilegio" Amarone is good and well priced.

BANFI VINI (VIGNE REGALI)
Piemonte; Strevi (AL)
DOC(G)s: Asti; Brachetto d'Acqui; Dolcetto d'Acqui; Gavi
The Piedmont arm of the mammoth American-owned Banfi company, which is better known for the Castello Banfi estate in Montalcino. This property is focused on fun and fizzy wines such as the unusual red sparkler Brachetto d'Acqui and classic Asti Spumante. Probably the best-known wine here is the superclean, steely Gavi "Principessa Gavi," a bargain-priced sipping white.

BARBERANI (VALLESANTA)
Umbria; Baschi (TR)
DOC(G)s: Orvieto Classico; Lago di Corbara
A top Orvieto producer, as evidenced by its consistently excellent "Calcaia" bottling. Other wines include a good varietal grechetto and a red blend, "Foresco," that blends sangiovese and cabernet sauvignon in barrique.

BARBERO, PIETRO
Piemonte; Moasca (AT)
DOC(G)s: Barbera d'Asti; Gavi; Monferrato
A small estate with holdings near Asti and in Gavi. The specialty is rich and well-structured barbera, as evidenced by the Barbera d'Asti "La Vignassa."

BARONCINI
Toscana; San Gimignano (SI)
DOC(G)s: Vernaccia di San Gimignano; Chianti Colli Senesi; Morellino di Scansano
Typical of many estates in San Gimignano, Baroncini has expanded its horizons: Not only does it produce well-regarded Vernaccia di San Gimignano but a number of Chiantis and, more notably, a fruity Morellino di Scansano from an estate it owns in the red-hot southern Maremma.

BARONE CORNACCHIA
Abruzzo; Torano Nuovo (TE)
DOC(G)s: Montepulciano d'Abruzzo; Trebbiano d'Abruzzo
Good, inexpensive Montepulciano d'Abruzzo. Try the "Poggio Varano" in particular.

BASILISCO
Basilicata; Rionero in Vulture (PZ)
DOC(G)s: Aglianico (PZ)
A small, recently established winery run by Michele Cutolo, who is making Aglianico del Vulture in a fruity, barrique-aged style. A little pricey for what it is, but good.

BASTIANICH
Friuli; Premariacco (UD)
DOC(G)s: Colli Orientali del Friuli
The winery owned by the co-author of this book, Joseph Bastianich. Located near Buttrio, the small property boasts a stand of vines that are more than 50 years old, which produce exceptionally concentrated fruit for the range of cool and fruity whites crafted by consultant Maurizio Castelli and an on-site team that includes Emilio del Medico and Wayne Young. Castelli uses a small percentage of late-harvested fruit in some of the varietal whites, leading to the creation of "Tocai Plus," a luscious, peach-scented tocai friulano, and "Pinot Plus," a pinot grigio—based white with a similarly full-bodied approach. The showpiece is the white blend "Vespa Bianco," a mix of chardonnay, picolit, and sauvignon, some fermented in stainless steel and some in new oak; it's a creamy, honeyed, and complex white with power to spare. "Vespa Rosso" is a spicy and savory merlot-based red, and there are more new creations in the offing. A new red, a blend of refosco, pignolo, and cabernet franc made in the *appassimento* style, is also on the way. It will be called "Calabrone."

BATASIOLO
Piemonte; La Morra (CN)
DOC(G)s: Barolo; Barbera d'Alba; Dolcetto d'Alba; Langhe
Attractively priced Barolo and Barbera d'Alba (among other things). The top wine is the Barolo "La Corda della Briccolina."

BATTISTOTTI
Trentino; Nomi (TN)
DOC(G)s: Trentino
A small property whose highlights include two Trentino rarities well worth trying out: the dry red marzemino and the sweet moscato rosa. The marzemino, a red with an exotic mix of red and black berry flavors, is a soft and jammy wine. The moscato rosa has great acidity to complement its rosy, grenadine-like flavors.

BAVA

PIEMONTE; COCCONATO D'ASTI
(AT)

DOC(G)s: Barolo; Barbera d'Asti;
Gavi; Monferrato; Moscato
d'Asti

A relatively large Piedmontese producer with a diverse production that
includes Moscato d'Asti, Gavi di
Gavi, and Barolo. Barbera d'Asti is
also a specialty, with several different bottlings to choose from—
"Piano Alto," "Stradivario," and
"Arbest." Pricing can get expensive
at the high end.

BEGALI, LORENZO

VENETO; SAN PIETRO IN CARIANO
(VR)

DOC(G)s: Valpolicella; Amarone
della Valpolicella; Recioto della
Valpolicella

A small farmstead winery that produces medium-bodied, well-balanced Amarone. Begali's sweet
Recioto is also a great example of
how a wine can have both depth and
finesse at the same time.

BEL COLLE

PIEMONTE; VERDUNO (CN)

DOC(G)s: Barolo; Barbera d'Alba;
Dolcetto d'Alba

Verduno is on the outskirts of
prime Barolo territory (it's just
north of La Morra), and the Monvigliero vineyard produces consistently round, fruit-driven
Barolos—as exemplified by Bel
Colle's version. Other offerings
include Barbaresco and Barbera
d'Alba.

BELLAVISTA

LOMBARDIA; ERBUSCO (BS)

DOC(G)s: Franciacorta; Terre di
Franciacorta

A spectacular modern winery (it
would look more at home in Cali-

fornia, in fact) owned by construction titan Vittorio Moretti. Along
with nearby Ca' del Bosco, this is
the estate that established Franciacorta as a serious player in the world
of sparkling wine. Wines such as the
"Gran Cuvée Brut" and the finely
structured "Gran Cuvée Rosé" can
stand alongside the wines of Champagne—that is, if wine drinkers
could overcome long-standing preju-
dices. Try also the "Convento del-
l'Annunciata" Chardonnay, one of
the estate's Terre di Franciacorta
DOC wines.

BELLENDA

VENETO; VITTORIO VENETO (TV)

DOC(G)s: Prosecco di Conegliano-
Valdobbiadene; Colli Trevigiani

A noteworthy maker of prosecco,
along with a handful of less convincing Veneto wines. The sparklers
are nice, and some are available in
half-bottles.

BENANTI

SICILIA; VIAGRANDE (CT)

DOC(G)s: Etna

Benanti is one of the few commercial producers making a go of it on
the black-lava slopes of Mount
Etna. The "Pietramarina" is a fresh,
flinty white from carricante. On the
red side, the wines are based primarily on the local nerello mascalese,
intriguingly fragrant and spicy if a
bit tannic.

BERA, F.LLI

PIEMONTE; NEVIGLIE (CN)

DOC(G)s: Asti; Barbera d'Alba;
Langhe; Moscato d'Asti

Among the best small-scale producers of Asti and Moscato d'Asti.
Also known for deeply extracted
barberas. A good find, but it will
take some looking.

BERLUCCHI, GUIDO & CO.

LOMBARDIA; CORTEFRANCA (BS)

DOC(G)s: Franciacorta; Terre di
Franciacorta

Considered the birthplace of Franciacorta sparkling wine and still a
leading estate in the zone, despite
the recent passing of proprietor
Guido Berlucchi. It was the mid-
sixties when a consultant enologist
named Franco Ziliani, while working for the Berlucchi estate (one of
maybe five commercial wineries in
the zone at the time), decided to try
his hand at Champagne-style
sparklers from some of Berlucchi's
pinot noir grapes. The results paved
the way for a new wine zone to rise
out of essentially nothing. Today,
the Berlucchi wines remain models
of firmness and finesse, particularly
the "Cuvée Imperiale Brut."

BERSANO

PIEMONTE; NIZZA MONFERRATO
(AT)

DOC(G)s: Barbera d'Asti; Barolo;
Barbaresco; Brachetto d'Acqui;
Gavi; Monferrato

A large wine house whose product
line runs the Piedmontese gamut.
Barbera d'Asti is a specialty.

BERTANI

VENETO; NEGRAR (VR)

DOC(G)s: Valpolicella; Valpolicella
Valpantena; Amarone della
Valpolicella; Soave

Founded in 1857, this is one of
Italy's oldest commercial wineries
and was one of the pioneering producers of Amarone in the Veneto.
Bertani Amarone exemplifies the
more classic take on the wine—it is
aged in large vats, for longer periods
(up to 10 years) before it is released,
resulting in a more leathery, coffee-
scented wine with notes of dried
(rather than fresh) fruits. From the

winery's Villa Novare estate come a host of more modern wines, including the new "Ognisanti" Valpolicella, an oaky but richly fruity red that debuted with the '97 vintage, and the "Villa Novare" Cabernet Sauvignon. The Valpolicella Valpantena DOC red called "Secco Bertani" is a benchmark example of the ripasso style.

BIGI

UMBRIA; ORVIETO (TR)
DOC(G)s: Orvieto; Est! Est!! Est!!! di Montefiasconi; Vino Nobile di Montepulciano
One of the estates in the wide-ranging Gruppo Italiani Vini (GIV) portfolio, this historic property is one of Orvieto's top wineries. Orvieto Classico (especially the "Torricella") is the key wine, but there are also varietal whites from grechetto and some sangiovese as well. Supercheap.

BINDELLA

TOSCANA; MONTEPULCIANO (SI)
DOC(G)s: Vino Nobile di Montepulciano
Swiss-born Rudolph Bindella established this estate in 1984, and has kept the product line simple, producing two wines: a consistently good, concentrated Vino Nobile, along with the table wine "Vallocaia," combining sangiovese (prugnolo) with a touch of cabernet sauvignon.

BIONDI-SANTI (IL GREPPO)

TOSCANA; MONTALCINO (SI)
DOC(G)s: Brunello di Montalcino
One of the most legendary wine estates in all of Italy, and considered the birthplace of the "brunello" clone of sangiovese. The cellars at this striking property, which is run by Jacopo Biondi-Santi (with the help of winemaking consultant Vittorio Fiore), contain vintages dating back to the 1800s. The Brunellos here are made in a classical style, featuring more rustic complexity than modern sheen. On the other hand, some of the estate's newer super-Tuscan wines, notably the all-sangiovese "Sassoalloro" and the sought-after cabernet-sangiovese blend "Schidione," are softer, juicier, and aged in barriques.

BISCI

MARCHE; MATELICA (MC)
DOC(G)s: Verdicchio di Matelica
Situated in the high hills of the Matelica zone, not far from the Apennines that separate Le Marche and Umbria, this winery produces fragrant, high-toned whites from the verdicchio grape. The Verdicchio di Matelica "Vigneto Fogliano" is a highlight, a great choice for seafood.

BISOL & FIGLI, DESIDERIO

VENETO; VALDOBBIADENE (TV)
DOC(G)s: Prosecco di Valdobbiadene; Talento Brut
Firm and well-structured Prosecco di Valdobbiadene wines, great for apéritifs. Check out the "Brut Crede" and the Cartizze.

BISSON, ENOTECA

LIGURIA; CHIAVARI (GE)
DOC(G)s: Golfo del Tigullio
Situated on the Gulf of Tigullio, not far from the resort town of Portofino, this wine shop/winery turns out some fine and fragrant vermentino and pigato. The "Vigna Erta" line is the one to look for. On the red side, there's a spicy red called "Il Musaico," based on the local ormeasco (dolcetto).

BOCCADIGABBIA

MARCHE; CIVITANOVA MARCHE (MC)
DOC(G)s: Rosso Piceno
A rising-star estate in the Marche region, which got its start making the traditional Rosso Piceno DOC but has branched out into international wines based on cabernet sauvignon, chardonnay, and pinot noir (pinot nero). The flagship wine is a rich and toasty cabernet sauvignon called "Akronte," which epitomizes the new-generation reds coming out of the Marche these day: Deep and inky, full-bodied but with soft tannins, and with a healthy dollop of new oak aging, it's a wine to compete with the soft and juicy reds of Chile, Argentina, or California.

BOFFA, ALFIERO

PIEMONTE; SAN MARZANO (AT)
DOC(G)s: Barbera d'Asti
A medium-size estate specializing in Barbera d'Asti, of which it has a number of different versions, either from single vineyards or incorporating particular production techniques.

BOGLIETTI, ENZO

PIEMONTE; LA MORRA (CN)
DOC(G)s: Barolo; Barbera d'Alba; Dolcetto d'Alba; Langhe
The wines of this estate are great finds in the ever-pricier world of Barolo—velvety, accessible, and affordable. Enzo and Gianni Boglietti produce three cru Barolos: "Brunate," "Case Nere," and "Fossati." They're examples of the more delicate, aromatic style of Barolos made around the commune of La Morra.

BOGONI

VENETO; MONTEFORTE D'ALPONE (VR)
DOC(G)s: Soave; Recioto di Soave
The wines of this small estate illustrate how enjoyable Soave can be when handled with care and made in

small, manageable quantities. Carlo Bogoni makes fresh and fruity Soaves with character, and they are very cheap.

BOLLA
VENETO; VERONA (VR)
DOC(G)s: Bardolino; Soave;
    Valpolicella; Amarone della
    Valpolicella
Founded in 1883, this well-known Veronese house is one of the largest-selling Italian wine brands in the United States. Everyone knows Bolla for its bargain-basement Soave (and the TV ads that publicized it), but many forget that Bolla was the first producer to label and market an Amarone wine (the 1950 vintage). These days, Bolla may not be fashionable, but the top-end "Tufaie" Soave and the Amarone are serious wines.

BOLOGNA, GIACOMO
See Braida.

BONCI
MARCHE; CUPRAMONTANA (AN)
DOC(G)s: Verdicchio dei Castelli di
    Jesi
Solid Verdicchio dei Castelli di Jesi, especially the "San Michele Vineyards" bottling.

BORGO CONVENTI
FRIULI; FARRA D'ISONZO (GO)
DOC(G)s: Collio; Friuli Isonzo
A typically wide-ranging Friulian lineup of fresh varietal whites, including tocai friulano, sauvignon, chardonnay, and spicy riesling and traminer. There's also a Bordeaux-style red blend called "Braida Nuova."

BORGO DEL TIGLIO
FRIULI; CORMONS (GO)
DOC(G)s: Collio
Nicola Manferrari is a soft-spoken guy, content to let his flinty, fine,

perfumed whites do the talking. Among his specialties are flinty tocai and exotically aromatic malvasia. His Malvasia "Selezione" is one of the best examples of the variety.

BORGO MARAGLIANO
PIEMONTE; LOAZZOLO (AT)
DOC(G)s: Loazzolo; Moscato
    d'Asti
Moscato is the focus here, but this small winery also produces a well-regarded dry sparkler from chardonnay and pinot noir called "Brut Giuseppe Galliano" (so named for the proprietor).

BORGO SALCETINO
TOSCANA; RADDA IN CHIANTI (SI)
DOC(G)s: Chianti Classico
Owned by the Livon family of Friuli–Venezia Giulia. Modern, supple Chianti Classico.

BORGO SAN DANIELE
FRIULI; CORMONS (GO)
DOC(G)s: Friuli Isonzo
This estate is not yet firmly established in the States, but it is one to keep an eye out for. The house style favors rich, ripe wines with plenty of extract, as evidenced by chewy whites such as the potent pinot grigio, the juicy tocai friulano, and the buttery blend "Arbis Bianco," a mix of tocai, pinot bianco, chardonnay, and sauvignon. On the red side, the soft and fruity "Gortmarin" (cabernet-merlot) is among the fruitier and fuller reds to be found up here.

BORGOGNO, GIACOMO & FIGLI
PIEMONTE; BAROLO (CN)
DOC(G)s: Barolo; Barbera d'Alba;
    Dolcetto d'Alba
One of the more historic Barolo estates and one of the larger landowners in the town of Barolo itself. Their traditionally styled Barolos

are blended from a variety of cru sites. One of the house specialties is the occasional rerelease of older vintages culled from stocks set aside at the winery.

BOSCAINI
VENETO; MARANO (VR)
DOC(G)s: Soave; Valpolicella;
    Amarone della Valpolicella
Dario Boscaini (brother of Masi's Sandro) runs this family estate, known for inexpensive Valpolicella and Amarone. Valpolicella is a particular specialty—check out the excellent "San Ciriaco" and the ripasso-style "Santo Stefano." The Amarone "Ca' de Loi" is also a great value.

BOSCARELLI
TOSCANA; MONTEPULCIANO (SI)
DOC(G)s: Vino Nobile di
    Montepulciano
While many new-generation Montepulciano estates go for superripe, chocolatey wines, the De Ferrari family toes a more traditional line, with Vino Nobiles that showcase the more earthy, foresty, tightly wound side of sangiovese (here called prugnolo). In good vintages they are exceptionally complex, and they typically need some time to come around. Maurizio Castelli consults.

BOTROMAGNO
PUGLIA; GRAVINA DI PUGLIA (BA)
DOC(G)s: Gravina
A co-op known for light, delicately aromatic whites from the Gravina DOC. Clean, simple, and inexpensive.

BOVIO, GIANFRANCO
PIEMONTE; LA MORRA (CN)
DOC(G)s: Barolo; Barbera d'Alba;
    Dolcetto d'Alba; Langhe
Gianfranco Bovio is not only a winemaker but the proprietor of

one of Piedmont's best restaurants, Belvedere. His earthy, perfumed, finely structured Barolos—from the Gattera and Arborina vineyards—are textbook examples of the more elegant style of La Morra–area wines. And the prices are reasonable.

BRAIDA DI GIACOMO BOLOGNA
PIEMONTE; ROCCHETTA TANARO (AT)
DOC(G)s: Barbera d'Asti; Brachetto d'Acqui; Dolcetto d'Alba; Langhe; Moscato d'Asti; Monferrato

These days, the barbera grape has a fairly prestigious image, thanks to a wide array of powerful, luxurious reds being made from it. But it wasn't always that way: It was once a rustic, high-acid filler until the late Giacomo Bologna demonstrated how good it could be if treated with care in the vineyard then aged in small oak barrels to compensate for its lack of tannic structure. Bologna's "Bricco dell'Uccellone" is a landmark wine (whose price has shot up accordingly) that continues to rank among the deepest and most flavorful barberas around. Other offerings include the Langhe DOC red "Il Baciale," a blend of barbera and pinot nero. A landmark estate.

BRICCO MONDALINO
PIEMONTE; VIGNALE MONFERRATO (AL)
DOC(G)s: Barbera d'Asti; Barbera del Monferrato

A small winery in the Monferrato hills specializing in ripe and rich barberas. The biggest is the barrique-aged "Il Bergantino," but the basic Barbera del Monferrato is no slouch and a good buy.

BRICCO ROCCHE; BRICCO ASILI
PIEMONTE; CASTIGLIONE FALLETTO (CN)
DOC(G)s: Barolo; Barbaresco

The Ceretto family chose to "brand" their Barolos and Barbarescos with the names of their most prized vineyard sites, and to build a winery at each site as well. As such, their Bricco Rocche line includes a Barolo from the Bricco Rocche vineyard, and their Bricco Asili line includes a Barbaresco called "Bricco Asili–Bricco Asili." In all, the Bricco Rocche winery turns out three cru Barolos: the powerful "Bricco Rocche," the plush "Brunate," and the more austere "Prapò." At Bricco Asili, there are also three offerings: the formidable "Bricco Asili," followed by the more delicate "Fasét" and "Bernardot" bottlings. In their youth, the Ceretto wines tend to be tough and tannic, brimming with potential energy. Give them time. (See also Ceretto.)

BRIGALDARA
VENETO; SAN PIETRO IN CARIANO (VR)
DOC(G)s: Valpolicella; Amarone della Valpolicella; Recioto della Valpolicella

Good Valpolicella wines across the board. A small estate focused on quality, its specialties include the Valpolicella "Il Vegro" (dosed with cabernet and aged an extra year before release).

BRIGL, JOSEF
ALTO ADIGE; APPIANO/EPPAN (BZ)
DOC(G)s: Alto Adige

The full range of varietal whites and reds is available from this relatively large Alto Adige winery. Solid chardonnays, sauvignons, merlots, and lagreins at low prices.

BROGLIA
PIEMONTE; GAVI (AL)
DOC(G)s: Gavi

Some of the better, more fruit-driven Gavi to be found. The "Bruno Broglia" builds on the traditionally lean frame of Gavi by adding a percentage of barrel-fermented cortese, giving the wine a buttery kick.

BROVIA
PIEMONTE; CASTIGLIONE FALLETTO (CN)
DOC(G)s: Barolo; Barbera d'Alba; Dolcetto d'Alba; Roero Arneis

Muscular Barolos from the Rocche, Villero, and Monprivato crus, all located within the commune of Castiglione, on the eastern side of the Barolo DOC. Brovia is also known for a super-rich Dolcetto d'Alba called "Solatio" and an aromatic arneis.

BRUNA
LIGURIA; RANZO (IM)

Though difficult to find in the States (its distribution, like that of all Ligurian wines, is spotty), the wines of this estate are considered some of the region's most structured and aromatic. Hearty whites from the spicy pigato grape—of which there are several—are a specialty. Worth a try if you happen upon them. Rossese di Dolceacqua is also made.

BRUNELLI
VENETO; S. PIETRO IN CARANO (VR)
DOC(G)s: Amarone della Valpolicella; Recioto della Valpolicella

Potent and sappy Amarones are the specialty of this property, as evidenced by the dynamite "Campo dei Titari." The style is super-fruity, almost Port-like in its extract, with a creamy sheen that suggests aging in smaller, newer oak barrels. The Valpolicella Classico "Pa Riondo" is also interesting, as is the white bianco passito called "Re Sol."

BRUNELLI, GIOVANNI
Toscana; Montalcino (SI)
DOC(G)s: Brunello di Montalcino
An unsung small Brunello producer making warm, smooth wines at affordable prices. Worth a look.

BUCCI
Marche; Ostra Vetere (AN)
DOC(G)s: Verdicchio dei Castelli di Jesi
The standard-bearer of the Jesi DOC, with a range of perfumed, well-structured verdicchios that emphasize elegance and bright acidity. The "Villa Bucci" Riserva is a rare example of a verdicchio that can age, holding on to its freshness for many years in bottle.

BUIATTI, LIVIO E CLAUDIO
Friuli; Buttrio (UD)
DOC(G)s: Colli Orientali del Friuli
Solid, inexpensive varietal, including pinot grigio, pinot bianco, tocai, and refosco.

BURLOTTO, G. B.
Piemonte; Verduno (CN)
DOC(G)s: Barolo; Barbera d'Alba
Looking for a great buy in Barolo? Check out the round and accessible Barolo "Vigneto Cannubi" from this Verduno estate, at the northern tip of the Barolo DOCG zone. The "Monvigliero" is cheaper still, if less convincing.

BUSSIA SOPRANA
Piemonte; Monforte d'Alba (CN)
DOC(G)s: Barolo; Barbera d'Alba
A small estate named for one of the top vineyards in Monforte d'Alba. Cru Barolos include bottlings from the Vigna Colonnello and Mosconi crus.

BUSSO, PIERO
Piemonte; Neive (CN)
DOC(G)s: Barbaresco; Barbera d'Alba; Dolcetto d'Alba; Langhe
A typically small Langhe estate of about 14 acres, where the Busso family makes two intense Barbarescos, both of which strike a balance between the traditional and modern style. The reasonably priced "Vigna Borgese" is a characteristically fine and firm Barbaresco, the "Bricco Mondino" a little chunkier. The Dolcetto "Vigna Majano" is also noteworthy.

BUSSOLA, TOMMASO
Veneto; Negrar (VR)
DOC(G)s: Valpolicella; Amarone della Valpolicella; Recioto della Valpolicella
A boutique producer of Valpolicella wines, in a supercharged modern style. The "BG" line is more affordably priced, the "TB" a little higher end, but both offer luscious takes on Valpolicella, Amarone, and Recioto. Highly recommended.

CA' BIANCA
Piemonte; Alice Bel Colle (AL)
DOC(G)s: Barolo; Barbera d'Asti; Dolcetto d'Acqui; Gavi; Moscato d'Asti
Owned by the Gruppo Italiano Vini (GIV) conglomerate, this large estate has a diversified production: solid and inexpensive Barolo; plump and flavorful Gavi; and a Barbera d'Asti priced for everyday drinking.

CA' DEI FRATI
Lombardia; Sirmione (BS)
DOC(G)s: Lugana
Located at the southern tip of Lake Garda, this Lugana specialist offers great value. The fragrant and fine Lugana "I Frati" is a terrific white to buy by the case for summer sipping. There are also some barrel-fermented white blends, highlighted by "Tre Filer" (trebbiano, chardonnay, sauvignon).

CA' DEL BAIO
Piemonte; Treiso (CN)
DOC(G)s: Barbaresco; Barbera d'Alba; Langhe; Moscato d'Asti
This artisan producer offers great value in Barbaresco, producing two excellent wines from the Asili cru. One is an earthy, traditional style called "Slavonia" (so named because it is aged in larger Slavonian oak casks) the other a fatter, modern style evocatively named "Barrique." There's also Langhe Nebbiolo and Barbera d'Alba, among other things, and not a bad wine in the bunch.

CA' DEL BOSCO
Lombardia; Erbusco (BS)
DOC(G)s: Franciacorta; Terre di Franciacorta
Along with Bellavista, this is the showpiece of Franciacorta and one of the most high-tech (and prolific) wineries in Italy. The sparklers made here offer great value across the board, from the basic Franciacorta Brut to more high-end sparklers such as the "Cuvée Annamaria Clementi." All the wines are made in the classic Champagne method and are based largely on chardonnay, although most of the cuvées include pinot noir and sometimes pinot bianco. Still wines from chardonnay and pinot noir (pinot nero) are also offered, and they are as acclaimed as the sparklers. Try a Ca' del Bosco wine alongside a good Champagne and see for yourself what a great bargain Franciacorta can be (relatively speaking, anyway).

CA' DI FRARA
LOMBARDIA; MORNICO LOSANA
(PV)
DOC(G)s: Oltrepò Pavese
A leading winery in the Oltrepò Pavese DOC, with a typically wide array of whites and reds. Look for the pinot grigio "V.T." for an ultra-luscious take on that normally reticent variety, and for the riesling renano, a local specialty. The deep local red, bonarda, is also well done.

CA' VIOLA
PIEMONTE; MONTELUPO ALBESE
(CN)
DOC(G)s: Dolcetto d'Alba; Langhe
Proprietor Beppe Caviola is a popular young winemaking consultant, and his eponymous estate is known for intense, inky reds. His dolcettos, particularly the fruit bomb "Barturot," challenge traditional perceptions of what dolcetto is supposed to be: Is it light, plush, Beaujolais-like wine, or is it black and luscious like Caviola's? Obviously, it can be both. And don't miss the "Bric du Luv" Langhe Rosso, a blend of barbera and pinot noir that tastes like liquid chocolate, or the plush "Rangone" pinot noir. All are pricey and somewhat rare.

CA' ROME
PIEMONTE; BARBARESCO (CN)
DOC(G)s: Barbaresco; Barbera
d'Alba; Barolo
A small, family-run estate perched atop the Rabajà vineyard of Barbaresco. The "Maria di Brun" Barbaresco is the winery's top offering, although the estate is also known for two cru Barolos—"Rapet" and "Vigna Cerretta"—from vineyards in the Serralunga area.

CA' RONESCA
FRIULI; DOLEGNA DEL COLLIO
(GO)
DOC(G)s: Collio; Colli Orientali
del Friuli
Solid wines, especially the sauvignons and tocais.

CA' RUGATE
VENETO; MONTEFORTE D'ALPONE
(VR)
DOC(G)s: Soave; Valpolicella
Another place to look for more serious, carefully crafted Soave. Offerings include the crisp and aromatic "Monte Fiorentine" and the richer, barrel-fermented "Monte Alto."

CADIVIN
SICILIA; PARTINICO (PA)
DOC(G)s: Alcamo
Cadivin was created by two young brothers, Diego and Alberto Cusumano, who set aside a corner of a mammoth cooperative near Alcamo to make value-priced bottled wines. The co-op remains a major supplier of bulk wine, but the Cusumanos have combined family vineyard holdings with those of contract growers to create the Cadivin brand. Fresh, friendly whites from inzolia and savory reds from nero d'avola are the focus.

CAGGIANO, ANTONIO
CAMPANIA; TAURASI (AV)
DOC(G)s: Taurasi
Architect Antonio Caggiano had previously grown grapes to sell to other wineries, but in 1990 he began bottling his production. His labyrinthine, grottolike winery was constructed entirely from materials salvaged from the 1980 earthquake that devastated Avellino. The specialty here is earthy, spicy Taurasi, as well as two potent IGT wines based on the aglianico grape. Dry and

sweet whites from fiano and greco round out the small portfolio.

CALATRASI (TERRALE, ALLORA; D'ISTINTO, TERRE DI GINESTRA)
DOC(G)s: Sicilia; San Cipirello
(PA)
Maurizio Miccichè and his brother Giuseppe founded this estate in 1980 and have created four different product lines: "Terrale," which includes IGT wines from both Sicily and Puglia; "Terra di Ginestra," another value-priced line of Sicilian whites and reds; "Allora," varietal Puglian wines; and "D'Istinto," the highest-end, with a rich syrah as the highlight. The D'Istinto wines are produced in partnership with BRL Hardy of Australia. Calatrasi has its own marketing arm based in Vashon, Washington, and Terrale in particular has attracted a following in the United States for its everyday values.

CALÒ, MICHELE
PUGLIA; TUGLIE (LE)
DOC(G)s: Alezio
Located in Tuglie, in the southern reaches of Puglia, this little-known winery is like many others in Puglia—blessed with an ample supply of old, bush-trained vines, but still catching up in terms of technique. The Calò reds, all based on negroamaro with a touch of malvasia nera, are headlined by the savory, concentrated "Vigna Spano."

CANDIDO
PUGLIA; SANDONACI (BR)
DOC(G)s: Salice Salentino
In a region dominated by large co-ops, Francesco Candido's relatively small winery is one place to look for more serious Puglian reds. The Salice Salentinos are among the best available, and rarer reds such as

"Duca d'Aragona" (negroamaro-montepulciano) and "Cappello di Prete" (negroamaro–malvasia nera) make the case that negroamaro is more interesting than the more popular primitivo.

CANEVEL SPUMANTI
Veneto; Valdobbiadene (TV)
DOC(G)s: Prosecco di
    Valdobbiadene; Cartizze;
    Colli di Conegliano
Bargain-priced prosecco for weddings or other large-scale entertaining.

CANTALUPO
Piemonte; Ghemme (NO)
DOC(G)s: Ghemme
Proof that great nebbiolo wines don't all come from Barolo and Barbaresco. This northern Piedmont winery is the anchor of the Ghemme DOC, its offerings highlighted by the cocoa-scented Ghemme "Collis Breclamae," one of three cru wines.

CANTELE
Puglia; Lecce (LE)
DOC(G)s: Salice Salentino
A very large estate near Lecce that buys in grapes for its wide variety of Salice Salentinos and other Salento IGT wines. The Salice Salentino Riserva is serviceable, as is the plump primitivo. Bargain prices make it easy to experiment.

CANTINA DEI PRODUTTORI NEBBIOLO DI CAREMA
Piemonte; Carema (TO)
DOC(G)s: Carema
A co-op with a bunch of tiny member-growers, who contribute nebbiolo grapes from their rocky vineyards near Piedmont's border with the Valle d'Aosta. This winery and the private estate of Luigi Ferrando are the key players in the Carema DOC zone. Check out

these wines for a more perfumed, delicate take on nebbiolo as compared to Barolo.

CANTINA DI TERLANO
Alto Adige; Terlano/Terlan (BZ)
DOC(G)s: Alto Adige
Yet another of Alto Adige's excellent cooperative wineries, with an extensive product line. Spicy red wines from lagrein and pinot nero are noteworthy, and there are, of course, a host of cool and fragrant varietal whites from gewürztraminer, pinot bianco, and sauvignon.

CANTINA PRODUTTORI SAN MICHELE APPIANO/ST. MICHAEL EPPAN
Alto Adige; Appiano/Eppan (BZ)
DOC(G)s: Alto Adige/Südtirol
This picturesque cantina, founded in 1907, looks more like a ski resort than a winery. It is among the best of the Alto Adige co-ops, producing a vast array of wines. Pinot bianco is a particular strength (especially the "Schulthauser"), and the basic chardonnay is a great example of what the variety tastes like unadorned by wood. In general, the "Classic" wines emphasize acidity and fruit, while the single-vineyard and "Sanct Valentin" wines bring on a bit more oak—but not too much. As for reds, "Sanct Valentin" Pinot Nero is the star, one of the best Italian pinots available.

CANTINA PRODUTTORI SANTA MADDALENA / ST. MAGDALENER
Alto Adige; Bolzano
DOC(G)s: Alto Adige
Another of Alto Adige's co-op wineries, with a particularly broad and interesting range of products. Superclean varietal whites from

chardonnay, sauvignon (try the "Mockhof"), and pinot bianco are complemented by reds from lagrein (especially the "Perlhof"), cabernet ("Mumelterhof"), and the schiava-based Santa Maddalena DOC. Reliable, varietally true, and inexpensive.

CANTINA PRODUTTORI VALLE ISARCO
Alto Adige; Chiusa/Klausen (BZ)
DOC(G)s: Alto Adige
Located north of Bolzano along the Isarco River, this co-op makes lean and racy whites from cool, high-altitude vineyards. It is one of a very few wineries to work with the veltliner grape (related to Austria's grüner veltliner) and also makes aromatic wines from pinot bianco, pinot grigio, gewürztraminer (try the "Aristos"), and sylvaner.

CANTINA SOCIALE DEL VERMENTINO
Sardegna; Monti (SS)
DOC(G)s: Vermentino di Gallura DOCG
One of Sardegna's excellent co-ops, sourcing grapes from more than 250 member-growers. The specialty here is potent, herb-scented vermentino, as exemplified by the "Funtanaliras" Vermentino di Gallura DOCG. A lot of wine for very little money.

CANTINA SOCIALE DELLA TREXENTA
Sardegna; Senorbì (CA)
DOC(G)s: Cannonau di Sardegna; Monica di Sardegna; Moscato di Cagliari; Nuragus di Cagliari; Vermentino di Sardegna
Founded in 1956 by 26 local farmers, this co-op didn't start bottling until the mid-'80s. The production is large and mostly middle-of-the-road, but there are a few finds: Can-

nonau di Sardegna is a specialty, and the red blend "Tanca Su Conti," aged 18 months in barrique and two years in bottle before release, is noteworthy. Among whites, the "Tanca Su Contissa" Vermentino is solid.

CANTINA SOCIALE DI SANTADI
Sardegna; Santadi (CA)
DOC(G)s: Carignano del Sulcis; Monica di Sardegna; Nuragus di Cagliari
The best example of the high quality of Sardegna's co-op wineries. In fact, this may be Sardegna's top estate, thanks to its array of dense, juicy reds based on the carignano grape. The best known of these is "Terre Brune," a Carignano del Sulcis DOC wine that is consistently beefy and ageworthy. There are a host of other slick wines that summon thoughts of Aussie shiraz—the new "Shardana" is one (it incorporates some syrah in its blend). Among the whites, the vermentino-chardonnay blend "Villa Chiesa" is interesting.

CANTINA SOCIALE DORGALI
Sardegna; Dorgali (NU)
DOC(G)s: Cannonau di Sardegna
In the heart of Sardegna's Barbagia, said to be ground zero for the best cannonau, this *cantina sociale* turns out a range of friendly, fresh reds based on the variety.

CANTINA SOCIALE GALLURA
Sardegna; Tempio Pausania (SS)
DOC(G)s: Vermentino di Gallura
Another northern Sardegna co-op, specializing in vermentino. Three different Vermentino di Gallura DOC wines are produced—"Canayli," "Piras," and "Mavriana"—along with a handful of other specialties, including a unique

Sardinian take on nebbiolo. "Balajana" is a barrique-aged, non-DOC vermentino.

CANTINA TOLLO
Abruzzo; Tollo (CH)
DOC(G)s: Montepulciano d'Abruzzo; Trebbiano d'Abruzzo
A large cooperative winery, with more than 1,200 members, producing bargain-priced Montepulciano d'Abruzzo and Trebbiano d'Abruzzo. The top of the line is the Montepulciano d'Abruzzo "Cagiolo." Simple, fruity wines.

CANTINA VITICOLTORI DI CALDARO/KALTERN
Alto Adige; Caldaro/Kaltern (BZ)
DOC(G)s: Alto Adige
The co-op of the village of Caldaro/Kaltern, known especially for its rich and spicy gewürztraminers. Pinot nero and cabernet are also well regarded.

CANTINE DEL NOTAIO
Basilicata; Rionero in Vulture (PZ)
DOC(G)s: Aglianico del Vulture
Gerardo Giuratrabocchetti had always grown grapes on his farm in Maschito, in northern Basilicata, but it wasn't until the mid-'90s that he decided to do something "commercial" with them. Giuratrabocchetti now makes small quantities of hand-crafted aglianico, having debuted his first vintage in 1998. His two wines—one an Aglianico del Vulture DOC, the other an IGT Aglianico—are differentiated by length of their maceration and length of time spent in wood (the IGT is shorter on both counts).

CAPEZZANA
Toscana; Carmignano (PO)
DOC(G)s: Carmignano
A beautiful hilltop estate owned by the Contini-Bonacossi family. Capezzana is best known for its rich and rustic Carmignano, but there's also a jammy super-Tuscan called "Ghiaie della Furba" and even a chardonnay. The real gems are the consistently good Vin Santo and a delicious, full-bodied olive oil.

CAPICHERA
Sardegna; Arzachena (SS)
DOC(G)s: Vermentino di Gallura; Carignano del Sulcis
The Gallura zone in northeastern Sardinia is the home of this white-wine specialist. Three levels of Vermentino di Gallura DOC are made, starting with the crisp, spicy "Vigna 'Ngena" and finishing with the plumper, rounder "Vendemmia Tardiva," which, despite the name, is not a sweet wine.

CAPPELLANO
Piemonte; Serralunga d'Alba (CN)
DOC(G)s: Barolo; Barbera d'Alba; Dolcetto d'Alba; Langhe
Barolo and Barbera d'Alba "Gabutti" are wines to look for. Cappellano is also known for the unusual Barolo chinato.

CAPRAI, ARNALDO
Umbria; Montefalco (PG)
DOC(G)s: Montefalco; Sagrantino di Montefalco
The Caprai family poured a lot of money into their high-tech Montefalco estate, and have attracted lots of international attention to both themselves and to the once-dormant Montefalco zone. Caprai Sagrantino di Montefalco is now a well-known wine in the States, a slick and chocolatey red in which the oak in-

fluence is heavy but not overwhelming. Whether it's a simple Montefalco Rosso or the reserve selection Sagrantino di Montefalco "25 Anni," Caprai wines can be consumed either immediately or years down the line.

CARAVAGLIO
Sicilia; Lipari (ME)
DOC(G)s: Malvasia delle Lipari
Right up there with Hauner when it comes to rich, honeyed Malvasia delle Lipari.

CARMIGNANI, FUSO
Toscana; Montecarlo (LU)
DOC(G)s: Montecarlo
Another of Lucca's freewheeling producers (probably the most freewheeling, in fact), with oddly named wines such as "For Duke," a sangiovese-syrah blend (named for Duke Ellington). The Montecarlo Rosso DOC "Sassonero" includes syrah as well, while the Montecarlo Bianco "Stati d'Animo" ("Feelings") is a creamy, barrique-aged white.

CAROBBIO
Toscana; Panzano in Chianti (FI)
DOC(G)s: Chianti Classico
Consistently good Chianti Classico.

CARPENÈ MALVOTTI
Veneto; Conegliano (TV)
DOC(G)s: Prosecco di Conegliano
The birthplace of prosecco as we know it today (see the Veneto chapter for more on this). The basic Prosecco di Conegliano "Extra Dry" is a great house pour.

CARPINETA FONTALPINO
Toscana; Castelnuovo
  Berardegna (SI)
DOC(G)s: Chianti Colli Senesi
A boutique estate owned by Gioia

Cresti, producing a Chianti Colli Senesi DOC and a barrique-aged super-Tuscan called "Do Ut Des" (cabernet-merlot-sangiovese).

CARPINETO
Toscana; Greve in Chianti (FI)
DOC(G)s: Chianti Classico;
  Brunello di Montalcino;
  Vernaccia di San Gimignano;
  Vino Nobile di Montepulciano;
  Orvieto
A large estate with a diverse production, including whites from San Gimignano and Orvieto. There's a good Vino Nobile di Montepulciano, an inexpensive table wine called "Dogajolo" (sangiovese-cabernet), and a line of wines called "Farnito," highlighted by a peppery cabernet sauvignon.

CASA ALLE VACCHE
Toscana; San Gimignano (SI)
DOC(G)s: Chianti Colli Senesi;
  Vernaccia di San Gimignano
Inexpensive everyday wines, highlighted by the Chianti Colli Senesi DOC "Cinabro."

CASA EMMA
Toscana; Barberino Val d'Elsa (FI)
DOC(G)s: Chianti Classico
Not far from Isole e Olena, this small estate of the Bucalossi family makes some deep, sleekly styled Chianti Classico of its own. Check out the riserva bottling in particular. "Soloio" is a chocolatey, chunky varietal merlot that leaves no doubt it was aged in barriques.

CASAL THAULERO
Abruzzo; Roseto degli Abruzzi (TE)
DOC(G)s: Montepulciano d'Abruzzo; Trebbiano d'Abruzzo
Bargain-priced picnic wines from montepulciano and trebbiano.

CASALE DEL GIGLIO
Lazio; Le Ferriere (LT)
Located in the fertile flatlands south of Rome, this high-tech estate is producing rich, Aussie-style whites and reds on a large scale. The barrel-fermented Chardonnay "Antinoo" is a ripe and tropical white in the California/Australia mode, as are most of the reds from merlot, cabernet sauvignon, petit verdot (!), and syrah (which they call shiraz). These are good, readily accessible wines and they keep getting better.

CASALE-FALCHINI
Toscana; San Gimignano (SI)
DOC(G)s: Vernaccia di San
  Gimignano; Chianti Colli Senesi
One of the first producers to pump up the anemic Vernaccia di San Gimignano by fermenting it in wood. More interesting are the estate's reds, including the super-Tuscans "Campora" (100% cabernet) and "Paretaio" (sangiovese).

CASALFARNETO
Marche; Serra de'Conti (AN)
DOC(G)s: Verdicchio dei Castelli di Jesi
A good, small, lesser-known producer of fruity and clean Verdicchio dei Castelli di Jesi. Try the "Gran Casale."

CASALOSTE
Toscana; Panzano in Chianti (FI)
DOC(G)s: Chianti Classico
High-end Chianti Classico, particularly the "Don Vincenzo" Riserva.

CASANOVA DI NERI
Toscana; Montalcino (SI)
DOC(G)s: Brunello di Montalcino
An admired small-scale producer known for inky, sleek Brunello di Montalcino in the modern, barrique-aged style.

CASCINA BONGIOVANNI

PIEMONTE; CASTIGLIONE FALLETTO (CN)

DOC(G)s: Barolo; Dolcetto d'Alba; Langhe

A tiny winery run by winemaker Davide Mazzone, whose Barolo "Pernanno" is a new-generation Barolo aged in barriques. Solid wines across the board.

CASCINA CA' ROSSA

PIEMONTE; CANALE (CN)

DOC(G)s: Barbera d'Alba; Roero

An estate based in the Roero DOC that does a lot of things well: There's some delicious, citrusy arneis (the best is the "Merica"); a warm, soft Roero DOC red from nebbiolo called "Audinaggio"; and a light, frizzante brachetto called "Birbét." All are great finds.

CASCINA CASTLÈT

PIEMONTE; COSTIGLIOLE D'ASTI (AT)

DOC(G)s: Barbera d'Asti; Barbera del Monferrato; Monferrato; Moscato d'Asti

A barbera specialist near the town of Asti, with a number of different bottlings featuring the grape. The Monferrato Rosso DOC "Policalpo" is a fruity blend of barbera and cabernet sauvignon.

CASCINA CHICCO

PIEMONTE; CANALE (CN)

DOC(G)s: Barbera d'Alba; Langhe; Nebbiolo d'Alba; Roero

A progressive small winery in the Roero hills with a diverse range of well-made wines. The powerful Barbera d'Alba "Bric Loira" has gotten a fair amount of press, as has the Nebbiolo d'Alba "Mompissano." The brachetto grape is also a specialty.

CASCINA FONDA

PIEMONTE; MANGO (CN)

DOC(G)s: Asti; Moscato d'Asti; Barbera d'Alba; Dolcetto d'Alba; Piemonte

One of a large number of small producers making handcrafted Asti and Moscato d'Asti, but you'll probably have to go to Piedmont to sample them.

CASCINA LA BARBATELLA

PIEMONTE; NIZZA MONFERRATO (AT)

DOC(G)s: Barbera d'Asti; Monferrato Rosso

A leading estate in the Monferrato zone, known for its smooth and silky red blend called "Sonvico" (barbera–cabernet sauvignon–pinot nero). Also the rich Barbera d'Asti "La Vigna dell'Angelo." Serious wines from a boutique producer.

CASCINA LA MADDALENA

PIEMONTE; ROCCAGRIMALDA (AL)

DOC(G)s: Dolcetto di Ovada; Barbera del Monferrato; Monferrato Rosso

A specialist in the rare Dolcetto di Ovada, grown at the southeastern edge of the Monferrato hills, not far from Gavi. Big and berried reds.

CASCINA LUISIN

PIEMONTE; BARBARESCO (CN)

DOC(G)s: Barbaresco; Barbera d'Alba; Dolcetto d'Alba

An excellent small producer of Barbarescos in an accessible, fruit-forward style. The "Rabajà" bottling is the top dog, and there are also some excellent barberas.

CASCINA MORASSINO

PIEMONTE; BARBARESCO (CN)

DOC(G)s: Barbaresco; Barbera d'Alba; Dolcetto d'Alba; Langhe

A small and respected Barbaresco producer. Their wine from the

Ovada cru, right below the town of Barbaresco, is their best-regarded wine. They also make good, inexpensive dolcetto and barbera.

CASCINA ORSOLINA

PIEMONTE; MONCALVO (AT)

DOC(G)s: Barbera d'Asti; Grignolino d'Asti; Monferrato; Piemonte

A small estate known for the inky Barbera d'Asti "Bricco dei Cappuccini" and a Monferrato Rosso blend called "Sole" (barbera–merlot–pinot nero).

CASCINA VANO

PIEMONTE; NEIVE (CN)

DOC(G)s: Barbaresco; Barbera d'Alba; Langhe

A tiny winery in the heights of Neive with concentrated and complex Barbaresco and Barbera d'Alba. Proof that there are good wines around every corner in Piedmont, though you'll probably have to go there to drink them.

CASE BASSE

TOSCANA; MONTALCINO (SI)

DOC(G)s: Brunello di Montalcino

Gianfranco Soldera's tiny estate is a cult favorite for its intense, rustic, long-aging Brunellos. They're pricey but powerful, elusive but evocative.

CASÒN HIRSCHPRUNN

ALTO ADIGE; MAGRÉ/MARGREID (BZ)

DOC(G)s: Bianco/Rosso Mitterberg IGT

Purchased by Alois Lageder in 1991 (it previously belonged to the diocese of Trento), this 17th-century property is a rare chateau-style winery in the heavily fragmented Alto Adige, surrounded by 32 hectares of its own vineyards. From it Lageder produces four wines, two "first-growths" and two "second-growths," in the spirit of Bordeaux. The "firsts" are the rich, tropical "Contest Bianco" (pinot grigio–chardonnay) and the lush "Casòn Rosso" (a merlot-based blend), while the "seconds" are "Etelle Bianco" and "Corolle Rosso" (the blends are similar, though these wines are generally aged for a shorter time in oak).

CASTEL DE PAOLIS
LAZIO; GROTTAFERRATA (RM)
DOC(G)s: Frascati
With the help of Attilio Scienza of the University of Milan and consultant Franco Bernabei, the Santarelli family has transformed its estate from anonymous grape grower to leading winery. They've received praise for the red blends "I Quattro Mori" and "Campo Vecchio," both of which combine syrah, merlot, petit verdot, and cabernet sauvignon. They've also taken Frascati DOC in new directions, pumping up their Frascati's with untraditional grapes such as viognier and sémillon.

CASTELGIOCONDO
TOSCANA; MONTALCINO (SI)
DOC(G)s: Brunello di Montalcino
The huge Montalcino estate (more than 250 acres) owned by the Frescobaldi family, of Marchese de' Frescobaldi fame. The Brunello here is consistently potent and made in a chocolatey, oak-influenced style. There's also a varietal merlot from the estate called "Lamaione."

CASTELL 'IN VILLA
TOSCANA; CASTELNUOVO
  BERARDEGNA (SI)
DOC(G)s: Chianti Classico
Good Chianti Classico and an elegant super-Tuscan called "Santacroce" that blends sangiovese with cabernet sauvignon. There's also a Sherry-ish Vin Santo worth trying.

CASTELLARE DI CASTELLINA
TOSCANA; CASTELLINA IN CHIANTI
  (SI)
DOC(G)s: Chianti Classico
A small estate located just west of Castellina, owned by publishing magnate Paolo Panerai. The wines, most notably the Chianti Classicos, are elegant and perfumed takes on the sangiovese grape. The limited-production "I Sodi di San Niccolò" is a *vino da tavola* blending sangiovese and malvasia nera.

CASTELLARI BERGAGLIO
PIEMONTE; ROVERETO DI GAVI
  (AL)
DOC(G)s: Gavi; Gavi di Rovereto
Bergaglio's barrel-fermented "Pilin" once again carries the Gavi DOCG designation after years of being bottled as an IGT. In general, this is one of Gavi's better producers, extracting more than average from the reticent cortese grape. Check out "Fornaci" and "Vignavecchia" as well.

CASTELLO BANFI
TOSCANA; MONTALCINO (SI)
DOC(G)s: Brunello di Montalcino;
  Sant'Antimo
This well-known property is owned by the Mariani family of Long Island, New York, who began acquiring land in Montalcino in 1978. The Marianis were (and are) the importers of Riunite Lambrusco, among other brands, and the success they enjoyed prompted them to become winemakers in their own right. Today, the Castello Banfi estate is centered on the beautifully renovated Poggio alle Mura castle south of Montalcino, where the Marianis turn out rich, powerful Brunello di Montalcino on a grand scale. Other key wines include luxurious, oak-tinged red blends such as "Summus" (sangiovese-syrah-cabernet) and

"Excelsus" (cabernet-merlot). At the lower end of the price spectrum, there's the reliable IGT red called "Centine" (mostly sangiovese) and a newish varietal syrah called "Colvecchio." See also "Banfi Vini ('Vigne Regali') listing.

CASTELLO D'ALBOLA
TOSCANA; RADDA IN CHIANTI (SI)
DOC(G)s: Chianti Classico
Solid, consistent, low-priced Chianti and a decent super-Tuscan named "Acciaiolo" (sangiovese 60%, cabernet 40%). The winery is owned by the giant Zonin group, which is based in the Veneto.

CASTELLO DEI RAMPOLLA
TOSCANA; PANZANO IN CHIANTI
  (FI)
DOC(G)s: Chianti Classico
One of the wineries perched on the famed "Conca d'Oro" (golden shell) south of Panzano, in the Chianti Classico zone. Proprietors Luca and Maurizia DiNapoli carry on an artisan tradition of winemaking handed down by their father, Alceo, who died some years ago. It's still primarily a farmhouse-style operation, and the wines have the taste of being made by hand: they are fruity and slick, but also earthy, smoky, complex. In addition to dark and brooding Chianti Classico, the estate is known for two highly sought-after red blends: "Sammarco" (90% cabernet sauvignon, 10% sangiovese) and "Vigna d'Alceo" (85% cabernet sauvignon, 15% petit verdot), the latter introduced in the 1996 vintage. The super-Tuscans are collector's reds and are priced accordingly.

CASTELLO DEL ROMITORIO
TOSCANA; MONTALCINO (SI)
DOC(G)s: Brunello di Montalcino
Flashy Brunello di Montalcino is

the focus, but there's also a sangiovese-cabernet blend called
"Romito del Romitorio" that's attracting some attention to this small
estate.

CASTELLO DELLA PANERETTA
Toscana; Barberino Val D'Elsa
(FI)
DOC(G)s: Chianti Classico
Solid Chianti Classico along with a
varietal sangiovese called "Quattro-
centenario" and a somewhat rare
canaiolo-based wine, "Le Terrine."

CASTELLO DELLA SALA
Umbria; Ficulle (TR)
DOC(G)s: Orvieto Classico
A scenic property and the one that
gave Orvieto a dose of fashion
sense. Owned by Tuscany's Marchese
Antinori, the winery is known not
so much for Orvieto but for a balanced, barrique-aged chardonnay-
grechetto blend called "Cervaro
della Sala." The wine has great acidity and clear fruit flavors, as well as
a distinctive minerality picked up
from the tufaceous soils of the
zone. There's also an excellent late-
harvest dessert wine, "Muffato della
Sala," made from botrytis-affected
sauvignon blanc, grechetto, traminer,
and riesling. Pinot nero, sauvignon,
and, yes, Orvieto Classico round out
the line.

CASTELLO DI AMA
Toscana; Gaiole in Chianti
(SI)
DOC(G)s: Chianti Classico
Excellent but pricey Chianti and a
celebrated varietal merlot called
"Vigneto L'Apparita." Purchased in
the 1970s by a consortium of four
families, it is run by Lorenza Sebasti
and her winemaker husband, Marco
Pallanti. Surely one of Chianti's
most beautiful wineries, its top
Chianti is the barrique-aged cru

"Vigneto Bellavista." Look also for
their excellent sangiovese rosé.

CASTELLO DI BROLIO
(BARONE RICASOLI)
Toscana; Gaiole in Chianti
(SI)
DOC(G)s: Chianti Classico
The amiable barone Francesco Ricasoli, a descendant of Bettino Ricasoli (who at this same castle in
Gaiole created the original formula
for Chianti in the 1870s), has revitalized this estate. The Brolio winery
had fallen out of family hands for a
time, but upon reclaiming it in
1993 Francesco Ricasoli set out to
make serious reds. The Castello di
Brolio Chianti Classico is a rich and
luxurious sangiovese, a far cry from
the thin, acidic Chiantis of decades
ago. The super-Tuscan "Casalferro"
(all sangiovese) is a collector's item.
Carlo Ferrini is the consulting enologist.

CASTELLO DI CACCHIANO
Toscana; Gaiole in Chianti
(SI)
DOC(G)s: Chianti Classico
A well-regarded Chianti Classico es-
tate run by Giovanni Ricasoli,
known for its deeply flavorful ris-
erve, "Millennio."

CASTELLO DI FARNETELLA
Toscana; Sinalunga (SI)
DOC(G)s: Chianti Colli Senesi
Located west of Siena in Sinalunga,
this estate run by Giuseppe Mazzo-
colin (of Fattoria di Felsina fame)
and well-known consultant Franco
Bernabei has an offbeat product
line. A good Chianti Colli Senesi is
the anchor, but then there's the
pinot nero–based "Nero di Nubi," a
varietal sauvignon, and even a
dessert wine from the rare moscato
rosa.

CASTELLO DI FONTERUTOLI
Toscana; Castellina in Chianti
(SI)
DOC(G)s: Chianti Classico
An acclaimed Tuscan property—and
a town unto itself—owned by the
Mazzei family, another of the region's prominent noble names.
Fonterutoli is a luxury brand, readily associated with deep, well-
structured, velvety reds made by the
consultant Carlo Ferrini, one of
Tuscany's most acclaimed enologists.
The Chianti Classico Riserva is a
perfect example of a "modern" Chianti, aged in new oak (giving it a
chocolatey richness) and incorporating a touch of cabernet sauvignon
in the blend. The "Siepi" super-
Tuscan, a sangiovese-merlot blend
from a vineyard of the same name,
is also a slick and powerful wine.
More widely available is the excellent *annata* Chianti and the "Poggio
alla Badiola" sangiovese. The Mazzei
have also invested in the south-
Tuscan Maremma, making a plush
Morellino di Scansano at their new
Belguardo estate.

CASTELLO DI MELETO
Toscana; Gaiole in Chianti
(SI)
DOC(G)s: Chianti Classico
Reasonably priced and well-made
Chianti Classico. There's also a rich,
oak-tinged super-Tuscan red called
"Fiore."

CASTELLO DI NEIVE
Piemonte; Neive (CN)
DOC(G)s: Barbaresco
Austere Barbarescos from a winery
located in an ancient castle in the
commune of Neive. Also good
arneis.

CASTELLO DI QUERCETO

Toscana; Greve in Chianti (FI)
DOC(G)s: Chianti Classico
Lean and aromatic Chianti and a host of super-Tuscan reds, including the all-sangiovese "La Corte" and the blend "Querciolaia."

CASTELLO DI SELVOLE

Toscana; Castelnuovo
  Berardegna (SI)
DOC(G)s: Chianti Classico
A well-regarded small producer of Chianti Classico. There's also the 100% sangiovese "Barullo."

CASTELLO DI SPESSA

Friuli; Capriva del Friuli
  (GO)
DOC(G)s: Collio
Located in a beautiful castle in Capriva, not far from the legendary Schiopetto estate, Castello di Spessa offers elegant whites (and a few reds) at reasonable prices. Pinot bianco is a specialty, vinified in a clean, firm, and minerally style, and there's also good tocai, ribolla, sauvignon . . . all the usual Friulian suspects. A reliable house.

CASTELLO DI TASSAROLO

Piemonte; Tassarolo (AL)
DOC(G)s: Gavi; Monferrato
One of the better known (and biggest) Gavi producers. Marchese Paolo Spinola's castle in the village of Tassarolo was once a state unto itself; now it is one of the more prolific and high-tech producers of Gavi, crafting all of its wines from 100% cortese. There's the juicy Gavi Tassarolo "S" (15% of which is barrel-fermented), the single-vineyard "Vignavecchia," and the chunky, all-barrique, single-vineyard "Alborina." A white blend called "Ambrogio Spinola" (cortese-chardonnay-sauvignon-sémillon) is an interesting addition.

CASTELLO DI VERRAZZANO

Toscana; Greve in Chianti (FI)
DOC(G)s: Chianti Classico
First established in the seventh century and acquired by the Cappellini family in 1953, this is a benchmark Chianti estate. Rich and smoky Chianti Classico and the long-aging "Sassello" super-Tuscan (100% sangiovese). The family's wines and other produce are all on the menu at their Cantinetta dei Verrazzano, a fun café in the heart of Florence.

CASTELLO DI VICCHIOMAGGIO

Toscana; Greve in Chianti (FI)
DOC(G)s: Chianti Classico
Smooth and velvety Chianti from a beautiful castle in Greve, which also has a restaurant on-site. The Chianti Classico Riserva "La Prima" is a consistently excellent wine. "Ripa delle More" is 100% sangiovese, "Ripa delle Mandorle" a silky blend of sangiovese with 20% cabernet sauvignon.

CASTELLO DI VOLPAIA

Toscana; Radda in Chianti (SI)
DOC(G)s: Chianti Classico
One of the landmark estates in Chianti Classico, a tiny medieval village that was essentially bought outright by the Mascheroni family in the late-sixties. Easily one of the zone's most beautiful properties, its vineyards lie at some of Chianti Classico's highest altitudes, lending the wines of the estate a lean, racy, perfumed character. This is classically proportioned Chianti, made by one of Tuscany's sangiovese purists, Maurizio Castelli.

CASTELLUCCIO

Emilia-Romagna; Modigliana
  (FC)
DOC(G)s: Sangiovese di Romagna
An estate partly owned by the Tus-
can winemaking consultant Vittorio Fiore, and managed by his son. Located high in the pre-Apennine hills east of Bologna, the estate is known for heady, perfumed sangiovese from vineyards in the shadow of the Tosco-Emiliano Apennines. These are dense, well-structured reds, highlighted by two vineyard selections: the "Ronco dei Ciliegi" sangiovese, typically firm and fine with more perfume, and "Ronco delle Ginestre," typically a little fuller and richer (according to the younger Fiore, this has mostly to do with the relative positioning of the vineyards). These are Romagnan sangioveses of the top rank, complemented by two racy sauvignon blancs, "Lunaria" and "Ronco del Re." Quantities are limited, so snap these wines up if you can find them.

CATALDI MADONNA

Abruzzo; Ofena (AQ)
DOC(G)s: Montepulciano
  d'Abruzzo; Trebbiano d'Abruzzo
One of the few estates located in Abruzzo's high plains near L'Aquila, this remote winery makes great Montepulciano d'Abruzzo. Try the limited-production "Toni" in particular: If you think Montepulciano d'Abruzzo is just supermarket wine, this black beauty will change your mind. The pink Cerasuolo is also especially good.

CAVALLERI

Lombardia; Erbusco (BS)
DOC(G)s: Franciacorta; Terre di
  Franciacorta
An excellent producer of Franciacorta sparklers, including a remarkable "Collezione Rosé" (about 85% chardonnay, 15% pinot nero), and the blanc de blancs "Pas Dosé." Stands alongside Bellavista and Ca' del Bosco as one of the best and brightest in the region.

CAVALLOTTO (TENUTA BRICCO BOSCHIS)
PIEMONTE; CASTIGLIONE FALLETTO (CN)
DOC(G)s: Barolo; Barbera d'Alba; Dolcetto d'Alba; Langhe

As the estate name suggests, the Cavollotto family sources its grapes from the Bricco Boschis vineyard in Castiglione Falletto. There are three cru Barolos, "Bricco Boschis," "San Giuseppe," and "Colle Sud-Ovest," all made in a more traditional style, with long aging in large oak barrels before release—funky, fine, zesty Barolos. Also a handful of other Alba wines.

CAVIT
TRENTINO; TRENTO (TN)
DOC(G)s: Trento Brut; Trentino; Teroldego Rotaliano

Best known in the States for clean and well-priced pinot grigio and Trento Brut DOC sparklers, this winery—not just a cooperative but a consortium of several cooperatives—hits all the Trentino bases. It is pretty well regarded not only for its sparklers (which are great values) but for classic Trentino reds such as marzemino, teroldego, and lagrein.

CECCHI (VILLA CERNA)
TOSCANA; CASTELLINA IN CHIANTI (SI)
DOC(G)s: Chianti Classico; Morellino di Scansano

One of Chianti Classico's biggest properties, known for plump and juicy wines year in and year out. Cecchi's *annata* Chianti is a reliable choice for a barbecue, while the riserva "Villa Cerna" is a serious wine in good vintages. The Cecchi family has recently branched out into the Scansano area, producing the soft and fruity "Valle delle Rose" Morellino di Scansano—another great bargain.

CENNATOIO
TOSCANA; PANZANO IN CHIANTI (FI)
DOC(G)s: Chianti Classico

Fine, floral Chianti Classico is the focus of this small, well-regarded estate, which makes a wide variety of Chianti bottlings. There are also a number of super-Tuscans, including "Mammolo" (70% merlot, 30% sangiovese) and "Arcibaldo" (50% sangiovese, 50% cabernet sauvignon). Also Vin Santo.

CERETTO
PIEMONTE; ALBA (CN)
DOC(G)s: Barolo; Barbaresco; Langhe; Nebbiolo d'Alba; Barbera d'Alba; Dolcetto d'Alba

The Ceretto family owns seven different vineyards and controls those around its home base in Alba. The result is a wide array of wines, from the bright and fruity Arneis "Blangé" (one of the best-known arneis whites around) to the brawny Barolos of their Bricco Rocche estate. At Bricco Rocche the Cerettos make three cru Barolos: "Bricco Rocche," "Brunate," and "Prapò." At their Bricco Asili estate in Barbaresco, they have three single-vineyard Barbarescos: "Bricco Asili," "Bernardot," and "Faset." These are characteristically dense and compact wines that require some time to open up. One of the biggest names in Piedmont, with good reason.

CESANI, VINCENZO
TOSCANA; SAN GIMIGNANO (SI)
DOC(G)s: Vernaccia di San Gimignano; Chianti Colli Senesi

This estate produces some of San Gimignano's best wine, from its fat and floral vernaccias to the sangiovese-based red called "Luenzo," a rich and chocolatey treat.

CESARI
VENETO; VERONA (VR)
DOC(G)s: Amarone della Valpolicella; Soave

A large producer of inexpensive Verona wines, including Soave and Valpolicella. The estate's Amarone "Il Bosco" is a surprising wine—a lot of Amarone for relatively little money.

CESARI, UMBERTO
EMILIA-ROMAGNA; CASTEL S. PIETRO TERME (BO)
DOC(G)s: Albana di Romagna; Sangiovese di Romagna; Trebbiano di Romagna

Headquartered just east of Bologna, this is one of Emilia-Romagna's best-known producers. The sweet Albana di Romagna Passito "Colle del Re" is the most acclaimed wine, followed by the dry red Sangiovese di Romagna. Solid and inexpensive.

CESCONI
TRENTINO; LAVIS (TN)
DOC(G)s: Trentino

A tiny estate that has gained particular notice for its reds from cabernet and merlot. There's also an array of excellent whites, including pinot grigio, sauvignon, traminer, and chardonnay. Not firmly established in the States at this writing.

CEUSO
SICILIA; ALCAMO (TP)

Although the Alcamo area in western Sicily was traditionally white-wine country, the Melia brothers of Ceuso—whose winery is a converted garage—focus on reds. Their "Vigna Custera" (nero d'avola–cabernet-merlot) is sourced from vineyards near Alcamo, and is one of the most luxurious, complex reds coming out of Sicily.

CHIARLO, MICHELE

PIEMONTE; CALAMANDRANA (AT)
DOC(G)s: Barbera d'Asti; Barolo; Barbaresco; Gavi; Langhe; Monferrato; Moscato d'Asti

One of the largest estates in Piedmont, with vineyard holdings throughout the Langhe and Monferrato hills. The huge Chiarlo product line is highlighted by its lean, elegant Barolo "Cerequio" and the deeper "Cannubi," along with the austere Barbaresco "Asili." Also noteworthy are the Moscato d'Asti "Nivole" (one of the best wines of its type) and the rich, barrel-aged Barbera d'Asti "La Court." The red blend "Countacc!" (nebbiolo-barbera-cabernet) also has some devoted fans in the States.

CIACCI PICCOLOMINI D'ARAGONA

TOSCANA; MONTALCINO (SI)
DOC(G)s: Brunello di Montalcino; Sant'Antimo

Ciacci's "Vigna di Pianrosso" Brunello is a great wine to seek out, as it has the two things you want in a good Brunello di Montalcino: power and perfume. The Sant'Antimo DOC-labeled "Fabius" (a syrah) is a more chocolatey, immediately drinkable wine to enjoy while the power-packed Brunellos age.

CIGLIUTI

PIEMONTE; NEIVE (CN)
DOC(G)s: Barbaresco; Barbera d'Alba; Dolcetto d'Alba; Langhe

Typical of Barbarescos from the commune of Neive, the Cigliutti wines are firm and tannic, not yielding a lot in their youth but undoubtedly loaded with energy. Renato Cigliuti is a widely respected, farmhouse-scale producer whose "Serraboella" Barbaresco consistently wines critical raves.

There's also a good Barbera d'Alba from the Serraboella vineyard, among other wines.

CIMA

TOSCANA; MASSA (MA)
DOC(G)s: Candia dei Colli Apuani

Based in the Candia hills near Massa, not far from where Tuscany meets Liguria, this ascendant estate is run by energetic young winemaker Aurelio Cima. Crisp, vermentino-based whites (both Candia dei Colli Apuani DOC as well as IGT) are a specialty. There's also an interesting red from merlot ("Montervo") and a blend of sangiovese and the rare massaretta called "Romalbo."

CITRA

ABRUZZO; ORTONA (CH)
DOC(G)s: Montepulciano d'Abruzzo; Trebbiano d'Abruzzo

A large co-op known for cheap quaffing wines, although some (like the Montepulciano d'Abruzzo) are surprisingly good.

CLERICO

PIEMONTE; MONFORTE D'ALBA (CN)
DOC(G)s: Barolo; Langhe; Barbera d'Alba

Sexy and highly sought-after Barolos are the trademark of this small estate, but there's also great barbera ("Tre Vigne") and plump dolcetto ("Visadi") to drink while you're waiting for Domenico Clerico's big-boned Barolos to age. Of his three cru Barolos, the rarest and most powerful is the "Percristina," while the "Ciabot Mentin Ginestra" is more readily accessible. Like a lot of high-end Barolo, it's pricey and relatively rare.

CO.VI.O.

UMBRIA; ORVIETO (TR)
DOC(G)s: Orvieto Classico

The name is short for Cooperative Vitivinicola Orvieto, a cooperative winery with a good range of whites and reds. There are several good Orvieto wines to choose from, along with a raft of other wines.

COCCI GRIFONI

MARCHE; RIPATRANSONE (AP)
DOC(G)s: Rosso Piceno; Falerio dei Colli Ascolani

An established producer of southern-Marche whites and reds. Decent Rosso Picenos highlighted by the new "Il Grifone."

COGNO, ELVIO

PIEMONTE; NOVELLO (CN)
DOC(G)s: Barolo; Barbera d'Alba; Dolcetto d'Alba; Langhe

Classic Barolo, with all the evocative scents of dried fruits, tobacco, leather, spice, etc. The signature wine is the Barolo "Ravera" from a cru located due south of the town of Barolo. Good barberas and dolcettos as well.

COL D'ORCIA

TOSCANA; MONTALCINO (SI)
DOC(G)s: Brunello di Montalcino; Sant'Antimo

One of the best-known wineries in Montalcino, and one of the best values in Brunello. Owned by the Piedmontese vermouth-maker Cinzano, this state-of-the-art facility turns out deep, dark, coffee-scented Brunello di Montalcino that is nevertheless accessible in its youth. The fruity Rosso di Montalcino is a wine to snap up by the case. Excellent, consistent wines that are relatively easy to find. Maurizio Castelli consults.

COLLAVINI, EUGENIO

FRIULI; CORNO DI ROSAZZO
(UD)

DOC(G)s: Collio; Colli Orientali del Friuli

A wide range of inexpensive varietal whites and reds are made at this estate. The "Collezione Privata" line is definitely the way to go here, whether it's chardonnay, tocai, sauvignon, or pinot grigio.

COLLE DEI BARDELLINI

LIGURIA; IMPERIA (IM)

DOC(G)s: Riviera Ligure di Ponente

One of the best-known Ligurian wineries, owned by Genovese restaurateurs Pino and Luigi Sola. Both vermentino and pigato are excellent here, redolent of the herbal Mediterranean scrub and ready for a plate of fragrant pesto-drenched pasta. Check out the "Vigna U Munte" Vermentino in particular.

COLLE PICCHIONI (PAOLA DIMAURO)

LAZIO; MARINO (RM)

DOC(G)s: Marino

Paola DiMauro, a well-known cook and restaurateur, got into winemaking as a hobbyist years ago and soon became one of Lazio's most important vintners. Her small estate south of Rome, which she runs with her son, Armando, is known for light yet expressive whites from the Marino DOC (similar to Frascati) as well as some deep, savory red blends of cabernet sauvignon and merlot. The Bordeaux-style "Vigna del Vassallo" is complex and concentrated, an eye-opening red wine in a region known for watery whites.

COLMELLO DI GROTTA

FRIULI; FARRA D'ISONZO (GO)

DOC(G)s: Collio; Friuli Isonzo

Not well known in the States, but a good source of varietal whites from chardonnay, tocai, sauvignon, and pinot grigio. Also notable is "Rondon," a blend of chardonnay, sauvignon, and pinot grigio.

COLOSI

SICILIA; MESSINA (ME)

DOC(G)s: Malvasia delle Lipari; Passito di Pantelleria

Known primarily for sweet wines (Malvasia delle Lipari in particular), but lately the estate has also created some fruity, bargain-priced dry wines, particularly reds.

COLPETRONE

UMBRIA; GUALDO CATTANEO (PG)

DOC(G)s: Montefalco

Part of a consortium of wineries and other agricultural concerns owned by the SAI Insurance company, which also includes Fattoria del Cerro in Montepulciano. Colpetrone, like Fattoria del Cerro, is known for dense, dark, deeply extracted reds. The Montefalco Rosso is an excellent value.

COLTERENZIO/ SCHRECKBICHL

ALTO ADIGE;
CORNAIANO/GIRLAN (BZ)

DOC(G)s: Alto Adige–Südtirol

Characteristic of Alto Adige's co-ops, Colterenzio aims for quality, not just quantity. Established in 1960 by a group of 28 growers, it takes its name from the small hamlet southwest of Bolzano where it is based, and now sources grapes from more than 300 member-growers. The whites are consistently good, particularly the gewürztraminer and pinot bianco; in all, the cantina produces a wide range of wines across three price tiers (check out the "Weisshaus" line), with lots of great finds, both red and white.

CONSORZIO VITICOLTORI ASSOCIATI DEL VULTURE

BASILICATA; BARILE (PZ)

DOC(G)s: Aglianico del Vulture

CSAV is a state-owned co-op. Run by Sergio Paternoster (brother of Vito of the nearby Paternoster winery), the winery sells in bulk and in bottles, and many of the latter are pretty respectable. The Aglianico del Vulture "Pietre Neve" and "Carpe Diem" are spicy, savory, and fruit-driven—solid, well-priced reds with a rustic appeal.

CONTADI CASTALDI

LOMBARDIA; ADRO (BS)

DOC(G)s: Franciacorta; Terre di Franciacorta

A sparkling new sparkling-wine house owned by Vittorio Moretti (Bellavista) and his son-in-law, Martino DeRosa. The basic Franciacorta Brut is a consistent winner at a fair price, measuring up pretty well to much more expensive wines from Champagne. And the elegant Satén is smooth and elegant.

CONTE ZANDOTTI

LAZIO; ROME (RM)

DOC(G)s: Frascati

One of the better Frascati producers. Top wines include the Frascati "Cannellino" and a red blend called "La Petrosa."

CONTERNO, ALDO

PIEMONTE; MONFORTE D'ALBA (CN)

DOC(G)s: Barolo; Barbera d'Alba; Dolcetto d'Alba; Langhe

Aldo Conterno is the son of the late, great Giacomo Conterno and the brother of Giovanni Conterno, the proprietor of the Giacomo Conterno estate across town in Monforte. The two brothers split up the family holdings a long time ago, as they didn't see eye to eye on how to make Barolo. Aldo's striking cantina is perched on the prized Bussia Soprana vineyard in Monforte, from which he makes some of the most critically acclaimed, powerfully structured Barolos available. His single-vineyard "Vigna Colonnello" and "Vigna Cicala" Barolos are complemented, in exceptional vintages, by the Riserva "Gran Bussia," which spends three years in Slavonian oak casks, two years in stainless steel and a year in bottle before it is released. These are not fully modern Barolos in that they don't incoporate aging in small oak barriques, but they do have a sheen and depth that comes from fully ripe fruit sourced from great vineyards. Conterno is also known for the immediately pleasurable "Il Favot" Langhe DOC Nebbiolo, and for some potent, well-structured Langhe Chardonnay as well. In all, there are about a dozen wines, all of them highly sought-after.

CONTERNO, GIACOMO
Piemonte; Monforte d'Alba (CN)
DOC(G)s: Barolo; Barbera d'Alba; Dolcetto d'Alba
Located just outside the Monforte town center, this legendary winery is run by Giovanni Conterno (older brother of Aldo, with whom he parted ways back in 1969). He and his son, Roberto, continue to make Barolo the old-fashioned way—that is, by leaving the wines to macerate on their skins for extended periods during fermentation, and carrying out said fermentations in very large casks. This results in wine with less forward fruitiness but more of the earthy, tarry, rosy aromas of the nebbiolo grape. Conterno's "Monfortino," made only in exceptional vintages, is one of those landmark

wines that has no peer when at its peak. The standard "Cascina Francia" bottling is benchmark Barolo in its own right, and the simpler, fruitier dolcetto and barbera are there to drink while you wait for the Barolos to age.

CONTERNO FANTINO
Piemonte; Monforte d'Alba (CN)
DOC(G)s: Barolo; Barbera d'Alba; Dolcetto d'Alba; Langhe
Founded in 1982 by Diego Conterno and Guido Fantino, this medium-size estate in Monforte produces sleek, modern Barolos that are aged in new wood. The chocolate-rich "Vigna del Gris" and "Sorì Ginestra" Barolos are quickly snapped up by collectors and restaurants, but the luscious Langhe Rosso called "Monprà" (a blend of nebbiolo, barbera, and cabernet sauvignon) is more widely available and well worth a try. Barbera, dolcetto, and a very good chardonnay round out the product line.

CONTERNO, PAOLO
Piemonte; Monforte d'Alba (CN)
DOC(G)s: Barolo; Barbera d'Alba; Dolcetto d'Alba; Langhe
A respected Barolo producer with wines hailing from the south-facing Ginestra vineyard, producing ripe and supple wines.

CONTI FORMENTINI
Friuli; San Floriano del Collio (GO)
DOC(G)s: Collio
A spectacular winery-restaurant–golf course in the heights of San Floriano, near the border with Slovenia. Its large production includes good Collio varietal wines at good prices.

CONTI ZECCA
Puglia; Leverano (LE)
DOC(G)s: Salice Salentino
One of Puglia's largest estates, known for Salice Salentino and the cabernet-negroamaro blend called "Nero."

CONTINI, ATTILIO
Sardegna; Cabras (OR)
DOC(G)s: Vernaccia di Oristano; Cannonau di Sardegna; Vermentino di Sardegna
Contini is Sardinia's most celebrated producer of Vernaccia di Oristano, a wine that bears a strong resemblance to Spanish Sherry. The vernaccia grape is considered indigenous to the area (not to be confused with the vernaccia of San Gimignano), though the method of production may well have been brought by the Spaniards, who controlled Sardinia for centuries. Also worth checking out are Contini's dry reds from cannonau and the dark, savory niedddera, a rare local variety.

CONTRATTO, GIUSEPPE
Piemonte; Canelli (AT)
DOC(G)s: Asti; Barbera d'Asti; Barolo
One of the best-regarded producers of Asti spumante, this historic cellar in Canelli is owned by Antonella and Carlo Bocchino, better known for their popular grappas. In addition to classic semi-sweet Asti, the Contratto estate has focused more attention on crisp, structured dry sparklers made in the Champagne method. There's also an unusually fine Asti made in the Champagne method and a rich red Barbera d'Asti called "Solus Ad," among other offerings.

COOS, DARIO
Friuli; Nimis (UD)
DOC(G)s: Colli Orientali del Friuli
Noteworthy for its production of the rare white verduzzo, a lush and exotic sweet wine, from the tiny Ramandolo subzone. Friuli's other famous sweet white, picolit, is also a specialty at this out-of-the-way property.

COPPO, FELICE
Piemonte; Mombello Monferrato (AL)
DOC(G)s: Barbera del Monferrato
Good barbera from a small estate near Asti.

COPPO, LUIGI E FIGLI
Piemonte; Canelli (AT)
DOC(G)s: Barbera d'Asti; Piemonte
The mark of consultant Riccardo Cotarella can be felt on the sleek modern wines from this estate, which specializes in Barbera d'Asti. The "Pomorosso" bottling is plump and fruity, with a sheen of new oak, as is the less expensive "Camp du Rouss." In a nod to the international market, the winery also produces several chardonnays, among them the buttery "Monteriolo."

CORDERO DI MONTEZEMOLO
Piemonte; La Morra (CN)
DOC(G)s: Barolo
Elegant and aromatic Barolos from La Morra. The top cru is the "Vigna Enrico VI," a rich and accessible Barolo at a reasonable price.

CORINO, GIOVANNI
Piemonte; La Morra (CN)
DOC(G)s: Barolo; Barbera d'Alba; Dolcetto d'Alba
Renato Corino, son of Giovanni, directs the winemaking at this small La Morra estate, which bottles

wines from top crus, including Giachini and the Vigneto Arborina (the latter made most famous by Elio Altare). The style is modern, fruit-forward, barrique-aged.

CORONCINO
Marche; Staffolo (AN)
DOC(G)s: Verdicchio dei Castelli di Jesi
Lucio Canestrari is a verdicchio specialist, crafting four distinct wines from the grape: his base-level "Staffilo," which is green, piney, and grassy; "Il Bacco," the principal wine of the estate, round and pear-scented; the fleshier, softer "Il Coroncino," a closer selection of grapes from the Coroncino and Cerrete vineyards.

CORREGGIA, MATTEO
Piemonte; Canale (CN)
DOC(G)s: Barbera d'Alba; Nebbiolo d'Alba; Roero
One of the best producers in the Roero area, Matteo Correggia is well liked by the critics, who have heaped praise on his dense, barrel-aged "Marun" Barbera d'Alba, one of those new-generation barberas with power to spare. He also makes excellent arneis and a rosy, dry brachetto called "Anthos." Solid wines across the board from a boutique winery.

CORTE RUGOLIN
Veneto; Marano di Valpolicella (VR)
DOC(G)s: Valpolicella; Amarone della Valpolicella; Recioto della Valpolicella
A small-scale estate in the Valpolicella Classico zone, producing the area's classic trio of reds. All the wines are solid, with the Valpolicella ripasso meriting special mention. Pricing is reasonable.

CORTE SANT'ALDA
Veneto; Mezzane di Sotto (VR)
DOC(G)s: Valpolicella; Amarone della Valpolicella; Recioto della Valpolicella
Located in the Val di Mezzane, at the eastern edge of the Valpolicella DOC, Corte Rugolin is one of those wineries other winemakers mention when you ask them what they drink when they don't drink their own. Proprietor Marinella Camerani has high-altitude vineyards producing deeply concentrated fruit for her wines, which are headlined by a massive Amarone. The fruit-driven Valpolicella Superiore is no slouch, either, and the Recioto della Valpolicella is deeply concentrated.

CORTESE, GIUSEPPE
Piemonte; Barbaresco (CN)
DOC(G)s: Barbaresco; Barbera d'Alba; Dolcetto d'Alba; Langhe
Inexpensive Barbaresco from the Rabajà cru is a highlight, but there's also Barbera and Dolcetto d'Alba for everyday drinking.

COTTANERA
Sicilia
A new project in the Mount Etna area producing some big reds from syrah, merlot, and other varieties. One to watch.

COS
Sicilia; Comiso Caltagirone (RG)
DOC(G)s: Cerasuolo di Vittoria
COS is one of the leaders of the Cerasuolo di Vittoria DOC zone, its name an amalgam of the surnames of its founders. The estate produces spicy, berried Cerasuolo (a blend of the local grapes nero d'avola and frappato) and more modern reds based on cabernet and merlot.

COSTA, TEO
PIEMONTE; CASTELLINALDO (CN)
DOC(G)s: Barbera d'Alba;
  Nebbiolo d'Alba; Roero
A good producer based in the Roero hills with a diverse and interesting production. Barbera d'Alba is a specialty, as is Roero Arneis.

COSTANTI, ANDREA
TOSCANA; MONTALCINO (SI)
DOC(G)s: Brunello di Montalcino
A classic small-scale Montalcino winery, run by the hands-on Andrea Costanti. Big and bold Brunello di Montalcino is complemented by a consistently excellent Rosso di Montalcino, which is no wimp itself. Small-production wines with big flavors and big price tags.

CUOMO, MARISA
CAMPANIA; FURORE (SA)
DOC(G)s: Costa d'Amalfi
Here's where you turn when you want a taste of the Amalfi coast—and, more specifically, of the ancient falanghina grape. Marisa Cuomo's fresh and fragrant Costa d'Amalfi DOC wines, the Furore "Fiorduva" and the Ravello, are proof that light wines can be deeply flavorful.

D'ANCONA
SICILIA; PANTELLERIA (TP)
DOC(G)s: Moscato di Pantelleria;
  Passito di Pantelleria
Another excellent sweet-wine producer on the exotic isle of Pantelleria.

D'ANGELO
BASILICATA; RIONERO IN VULTURE
  (PO)
DOC(G)s: Aglianico del Vulture
Donato D'Angelo's wines are the standards by which all other Basilicata wines are judged. There's not only a classic Aglianico del Vulture

DOC but also the single-vineyard "Vigna Caselle" (only made in top vintages) and "Canneto," also 100% Aglianico from the estate's best old vines. The new "Serra delle Querce" (debuted with the '98 vintage) aims to soften the hard edges of Aglianico with 30% merlot, but on the whole D'Angelo is about big, black wines that need some time to evolve.

DAL FARI
FRIULI; CIVIDALE DEL FRIULI
  (UD)
DOC(G)s: Colli Orientali del Friuli
A solid lineup of varietal whites and reds, clean and correct. A highlight is the super-white "Bianco delle Grazie" (chardonnay-sauvignon-tocai-riesling), which has a good creamy taste with some exotic aromas to go with it.

DARIO D'ANGELO
ABRUZZO; GIULIANOVA (TE)
DOC(G)s: Montepulciano
  d'Abruzzo; Trebbiano d'Abruzzo
Montepulciano and Trebbiano d'Abruzzo.
The price is right.

DE BARTOLI (VECCHIO SAMPERI)
SICILIA; MARSALA (TP)
DOC(G)s: Marsala; Moscato di
  Pantelleria; Passito di Pantelleria
A rare artisan producer of the fortified Marsala, a wine that has long since fallen out of fashion (thanks in large part to the heavy industrialization of its production). Marco DeBartoli is one of those quirky, uncompromising characters who's content to make wines for a small cult following: his "Vecchio Samperi" Marsala is a lavish wine made in the style of a fine sherry, while his sweet Passito di Pantelleria, called "Bukkarum," is one of the

most famous and sought-after dessert wines in Italy. Distribution is very spotty.

DECONCILIIS
CAMPANIA; PRIGNANO CILENTO
  (SA)
An up-and-coming southern-Italian cantina located in the relatively uncharted Cilento zone on the Campania coast. From high-altitude vineyards looking out toward the Mediterranean, Bruno DeConciliis specializes in full-bodied, fruit-forward wines from aglianico, which, in the relatively hot climate of the Cilento, makes wines that are a little more accessible than young wines from Taurasi. The signature red is the 100% aglianico "Naima" (named for a John Coltrane song). Another specialty is a ripe, barrel-fermented fiano called "Perella."

DECUGNANO DEI BARBI
UMBRIA; ORVIETO (TR)
DOC(G)s: Orvieto Classico; Lago
  di Corbara
One of the more highly regarded Orvieto wineries, thanks especially to the success of the barrel-fermented "IL" Orvieto Classico Superiore. The basic Orvieto is no slouch, and there's a red blend called "IL" that combines montepulciano, sangiovese, and canaiolo.

DEI
TOSCANA; MONTEPULCIANO (SI)
DOC(G)s: Vino Nobile di
  Montepulciano
A small estate with good Vino Nobile di Montepulciano and the lush super-Tuscan "Sancta Caterina," a blend of sangiovese (prugnolo), syrah, and cabernet sauvignon.

DELTETTO
Piemonte; Canale (CN)
DOC(G)s: Barbera d'Alba; Langhe; Roero
A respected producer of mostly Roero DOC wines. The Roero Arneis wines are good examples of their type, while the barrique-aged "Braja" (nebbiolo) is a highlight among the reds.

DESSILANI
Piemonte; Fara Novarese (NO)
DOC(G)s: Fara; Gattinara; Ghemme
A large and important producer in the Novara-Verceli hills of northern Piedmont, producing wines from the little-used Fara DOC (nebbiolo-based), along with solid Gattinara and Ghemme. Check out the two Faras—"Caramino" and "Lochera"—for a different, more delicate take on the nebbiolo grape.

DESTEFANIS
Piemonte; Montelupo Albese (CN)
DOC(G)s: Dolcetto d'Alba; Barbera d'Alba; Langhe; Nebbiolo d'Alba
Plump, inky dolcettos and other modern wines that bear the mark of consultant Beppe Caviola.

DI LENARDO
Friuli; Gonars (UD)
DOC(G)s: Friuli Grave
People love wines that cost $10 but taste much more expensive, and this producer makes a lot of them. Quirky Massimo Di Lenardo gives his rich and extracted whites weird names, such as the Grave Chardonnay "Woody" (why should be obvious enough) and the Tocai Friulano "Toh!" But across the board, the whites in particular have depth that defies their paltry price tags.

DIEVOLE
Toscana; Castelnuovo Berardegna (SI)
DOC(G)s: Chianti Classico
A quirky Chianti producer known for a sappy, fruit-driven style. In addition to rich Chianti Classico (notably the "Novecento" bottling), there are a range of big, oaky super-Tuscans, headlined by the all-sangiovese "Broccato."

DIMAJO NORANTE
Molise; Campomarino (CB)
DOC(G)s: Biferno Rosso
Sandwiched between Campania and Abruzzo, Alessio DiMajo's Molise wine estate leans more toward the former. DiMajo makes crisp and fragrant varietal whites from the Campanian trio of greco, falanghina, and fiano, while also favoring the aglianico grape on the red side. His top red, "Don Luigi" (aglianico blended with montepulciano), bears the sleek, chocolatey stamp of consultant winemaker Riccardo Cotarella. So does the well-priced "Ramitello" (also montepulciano-aglianico), a velvety yet rustic southern-Italian red. This is really the only Molise wine estate with significant distribution overseas.

DIPOLI, PETER
Alto Adige; Egna/Ora (B2)
DOC(G)s: Alto Adige
A small producer who has attracted a lot of attention for his red wines, particularly a merlot called "Ygum" and a cabernet-merlot blend called "Fihl." They are powerful wines, infused with some of menthol-like flavors typical of Alto Adige reds, but more powerful and concentrated than most of their Alto Adige counterparts. Quantities are very limited—look for it in restaurants.

DITTAJUTI, CONTE LEOPARDI
Marche; Numana (AN)
DOC(G)s: Rosso Cònero
One of the better estates in the Rosso Cònero DOC, producing plump and fruity reds that showcase montepulciano in all its inky, sweet glory. Great values.

DONNAFUGATA
Sicilia; Marsala (TP)/Contessa Entellina (PA)
DOC(G)s: Contessa Entellina; Marsala Superiore; Moscato di Pantelleria; Passito di Pantelleria
The Rallo name was built around Marsala, which the family has produced since the 1850s, but these days the focus is on dry wines. Spurred by Gabriella Rallo's inheritance of vineyard land in the hills between Marsala and Palermo, the family sold the Rallo brand name in 1983 and transformed its huge Marsala cantina into a facility specializing in luxurious white blends and nero d'avola–based reds under the Donnafugata brand name. Highlights are the tropical "La Fuga" Chardonnay and the rich "Tancredi" Rosso, a barrique-aged blend of nero d'avola and cabernet sauvignon. Donnafugata also produces succulent Moscato and Passito di Pantelleria from estate-owned vines on that island.

DORIGATI
Trentino; Mezzacorona (TN)
DOC(G)s: Teroldego Rotaliano; Trento Brut; Trentino
One of Trentino's better interpreters of the rare teroldego grape, as evidenced by the tarry and complex red called "Diedri." Solid pinot grigio and chardonnay are also on offer.

DORIGO
FRIULI; BUTTRIO (UD)
DOC(G)s: Colli Orientali del Friuli
Among the best (and most prolific) red wine producers in Friuli, and no slouch with whites, either. The broad Dorigo portfolio includes the ultimate expression of the rare native pignolo grape, as well as a dark and stormy refosco and a luxurious cabernet-merlot blend called "Montsclapade," so named for one of Dorigo's top vineyards. Other native reds such as tazzelenghe and schioppettino receive royal treatment here as well, each given a healthy dose of barrique aging to lend them added heft. The whites are typically heady and juicy, with ample notes of oak—the best are the tropical "Ronc di Juri" Chardonnay and potent "Ronc di Juri" Ribolla Gialla. You'll most likely find them in restaurants, as they are rare.

DREI DONÀ TENUTA LA PALAZZA
EMILIA-ROMAGNA; FORLÌ (FO)
DOC(G)s: Sangiovese di Romagna
An ultramodern winery with a lineup of boldly international wines. Topping the list is the super-concentrated "Magnificat" Cabernet Sauvignon, a wine that brings the Napa Valley to mind with its combination of fruit richness and silty tannins. "Il Tornese" is also built in a California style, with lots of creamy oak framing the rich tropical fruit. "Graf Noir" is Drei Donà's answer to the super-Tuscans, a sleek sangiovese-cabernet blend built on the same scale as the Magnificat. But don't overlook the Sangiovese di Romagna wines: they are among the best of their type.

DUCA DI SALAPARUTA (CORVO)
SICILIA; CASTELDACCIA (PA)
"Corvo" means crow in Italian, a name the nobleman Giuseppe Alliata gave to his vineyard land east of Palermo, which was full of ravens. Alliata was the seventh Duke of Salaparuta and the one who established a winery in 1824, which the family operated until the mid-1950s, when the Sicilian regional government took over. The Ente Siciliano per la Promozione Industriale has directed the production of Corvo–Duca di Salaparuta wines for the past four decades (a sale to private owners was imminent at this writing), building the brand into one of the biggest in Italy. While Corvo is thought of as a bargain house, there are some gems among the mass of wine produced—namely, the justly famous "Duca Enrico," a 100% nero d'avola that shows off the spicy, luxuriously berried fruit of the variety.

EINAUDI, LUIGI
PIEMONTE; DOGLIANI (CN)
DOC(G)s: Barolo; Dolcetto di Dogliani; Langhe
Luigi Einaudi was the first president of the Italian Republic, and his namesake wine estate in Dogliani is now run by his niece, Paola, and her husband. More than a dozen wines are produced at this expansive estate, including the trendy Langhe Rosso "Luigi Einaudi" (a blend of nebbiolo, barbera, cabernet, and merlot). Dolcetto di Dogliani is also a specialty, and there's a good and moderately priced Barolo from the estate's piece of the famed Cannubi vineyard. A reliable name.

ERCOLE VELENOSI
MARCHE; ASCOLI PICENO (AP)
DOC(G)s: Rosso Piceno; Falerio di Colli Ascolani
An increasingly popular and interesting winery with one foot in the Marche and one in California. Tropically fruity chardonnay is one highlight of this estate's diverse production, which also includes plump Rosso Piceno, the best being the "Roggio del Filare." There's a lot of experimenting going on here—with different grapes and techniques—so keep an eye on them.

EUBEA (FRANCESCO SASSO)
BASILICATA; RIONERO IN VULTURE (PZ)
DOC(G)s: Aglianico del Vulture
Francesco Sasso is no newcomer to Basilicata wine: his family began making wine here in 1925 and Francesco was intimately involved with the winery until the early '90s. In '95 he sold the Sasso brand, by then a well-known one. Then in '97 he reentered the wine world, albeit on a smaller scale: He bought a plot of vines near Rionero and focused on making small quantities of aglianico under the Eubea/Francesca Sasso trademark, named for his daughter. Look for the "Covo dei Briganti" bottling.

FALESCO
LAZIO; MONTEFIASCONE (VT)
DOC(G)s: Est! Est!! Est!!! di Montefiascone
A boutique winery in northern Lazio owned by well-traveled consultant Riccardo Cotarella, who is based in neighboring Umbria. Falesco's potent, barrel-aged "Montiano" (100% merlot) has become a sought-after cult wine, but the real find here may be the fruity, fun "Vitiano," a blend of cabernet, merlot, and sangiovese. Whites include the

DOC Est! Est!! Est!!! and a varietal grechetto.

FANTI (LA PALAZZETTA)
TOSCANA; MONTALCINO (SI)
DOC(G)s: Brunello di Montalcino
Flavio Fanti is a hands-on grower-producer whose deep, dark Brunellos (and Rossos) are consistently good.

FANTI (SAN FILIPPO)
TOSCANA; CASTELNUOVO
DELL'ABATE (SI)
DOC(G)s: Brunello di Montalcino
One of a number of small producers in the tiny village of Castelnuovo dell'Abate, south of Montalcino, where the more southerly vineyards produce plumper, rounder Brunellos. With the help of young consultant Stefano Chioccioli, this estate is producing limited quantities of deeply concentrated wines.

FANTINEL
FRIULI; PRADAMANO (UD)
DOC(G)s: Colli Orientali del
   Friuli; Collio; Friuli Grave
A *négociant*-style producer with a wide range of bargain-priced whites and reds. The top wines come from the "Sant'Helena" range, and include pinot bianco, pinot grigio, sauvignon, and chardonnay.

FANTINO, ALESSANDRO E GIAN NATALE
PIEMONTE; MONFORTE D'ALBA
   (CN)
DOC(G)s: Barolo; Barbera d'Alba
This estate's "Vigna dei Dardi" Barolo, named for its cru near Bussia in Monforte d'Alba, is one of the great values in Barolo. It's well structured and complex, with all the classic aromas and flavors of nebbiolo, and fairly accessible when young. The Fantinos also make good bar-

bera and an unusual nebbiolo passito.

FARNESE
ABRUZZO; ORTONA (CH)
DOC(G)s: Montepulciano
   d'Abruzzo; Trebbiano d'Abruzzo
A characteristically huge (though privately held) Abruzzo estate with vineyard holdings all over the region. The calling card is everyday wines from trebbiano and montepulciano. The Montepulciano d'Abruzzo "Opis" has the most stuffing.

FASSATI
TOSCANA; MONTEPULCIANO (SI)
DOC(G)s: Vino Nobile di
   Montepulciano
A large and pretty reliable estate in Montepulciano, owned by the Fazi-Battaglia company of the Marche. Good, fruity Vino Nobile at an affordable price.

FATTORIA AMBRA
TOSCANA; CARMIGNANO (PO)
DOC(G)s: Carmignano
Ranks alongside Capezzana as one of the best in the Carmignano DOC. Young winemaker Giuseppe Rigolli makes full and smooth reds based on sangiovese and cabernet sauvignon. Check out the riserva wines in particular: "Le Vigne Alte" (made from the estate's highest-elevation vineyards) and "Elzana."

FATTORIA DEI BARBI
TOSCANA; MONTALCINO (SI)
DOC(G)s: Brunello di Montalcino
One of the historic estates of Montalcino, known for burly, complex, somewhat austere Brunello di Montalcinos (although in recent years the style has gotten fatter and oakier). Still reasonably priced, these wines are a great introduction to Brunello—from the "base" bottling

up to the Riserva "Vigna del Fiore." At the lower end of the scale, Barbi has some great values in its fruity "Brusco dei Barbi" (mostly sangiovese) and "Rosso dei Barbi" (all sangiovese) wines. The estate, run by the Colombini-Cinelli family, is also developing wines from a new estate in the Scansano area.

FATTORIA DEL BUONAMICO
TOSCANA; MONTECARLO (LU)
DOC(G)s: Montecarlo
One of the better estates in the Lucca area, producing a diverse and international array of wines, including a deep and spicy syrah and a cabernet-merlot blend, both of them carrying the "Il Fortino" moniker. There's also a cool pinot bianco called Vasario, and a red blend called "Cercatola," a mix of cabernets sauvignon and franc, sangiovese, and syrah. Interesting wines.

FATTORIA DEL CERRO
TOSCANA; MONTEPULCIANO (SI)
DOC(G)s: Vino Nobile di
   Montepulciano; Chianti Colli
   Senesi
An admired Montepulciano property owned by the agribusiness arm of Italy's SAI insurance company. The dense, sappy Vino Nobile "Antica Chiusina" is characteristic of the house style, which emphasizes weighty extract and a healthy dose of oak. Other notable reds include the "Poggio Golo" merlot.

FATTORIA DI FELSINA
TOSCANA; CASTELNUOVO
   BERARDEGNA (SI)
DOC(G)s: Chianti Classico
Elegant and aromatic Chianti Classico is the specialty of this famed estate, which also produces the critic's favorite "Fontoalloro," a sangiovese capable of very long aging. Rather than go for the big, oaky,

fruit bomb, Felsina opts for refinement and balance. The "Vigneto Rancia" Chianti Classico Riserva is a great example of this.

FATTORIA DI MONTECHIARI
Toscana; Montecarlo (LU)
DOC(G)s: Montecarlo
Another interesting winery from the Lucca area, joining the likes of Wandanna, Fubbiano, and Buonamico in producing international-style reds. Montechiari is all about varietal wines, producing cabernet sauvignon, chardonnay, and pinot nero—all of them round and immediately accessible.

FATTORIA DI PETROIO
Toscana; Castelnuovo
  Berardegna (SI)
DOC(G)s: Chianti Classico
Fleshy, fruity, well-priced Chianti Classico.

FATTORIA LE TERRAZZE
Marche; Numana (AN)
DOC(G)s: Rosso Cònero
Perhaps the best examples of Rosso Cònero come from this estate, which is run by the eccentric Antonio Terni. The plump and purple "Sassi Neri" Rosso Cònero is a rich, barrel-aged red from 100% montepulciano, as is the very rare "Visions of J," an even denser Rosso Cònero named for a Bob Dylan song (Terni is a self-described "Bobcat"). The non-DOC "Chaos" is another luscious, immediately drinkable red from montepulciano, syrah, and merlot. Attilio Pagli is the consulting enologist.

FATTORIA MANTELLASSI
Toscana; Magliano in Toscana
  (GR)
DOC(G)s: Morellino di Scansano
One of the early arrivals in the Grosseto area of southern Tuscany,

this estate produces some of the best Morellino di Scansano available. There's also a super-fruity red called "Querciolaia," made from the softly contoured alicante (grenache) grape. Great values.

FATTORIA NITTARDI
Toscana; Castellina in Chianti
  (SI)
DOC(G)s: Chianti Classico
Good, reliable Chianti Classico wines, vintage after vintage.

FATTORIA PARADISO
Emilia-Romagna; Bertinoro
  (FC)
DOC(G)s: Sangiovese di Romagna;
  Albana di Romagna
The landmark wine estate of Romagna, with an agriturismo and an excellent restaurant on-site. The Pezzi family has become well known for a variety of wines, most notably the Albana di Romagna Passito called "Gradisca," a rich and apricot-scented sweet wine that is among the best of its type. As with a number of other estates in the hills east of Bologna, the focus for red wines is on the sangiovese grape. Paradiso's "Vigna delle Lepri" is a smoky and fruity red, a benchmark Romagnan wine that remains relatively affordable. Another interesting red is "Barbarossa," from a rare native grape of the same name that the Pezzis have nursed back to life.

FATTORIA POGGIOPIANO
Toscana; San Casciano Val di
  Pesa (FI)
DOC(G)s: Chianti Classico
A small Chianti Classico estate that has won a lot of praise for its super-Tuscan "Rosso di Sera," a blend of sangiovese and the all-but-forgotten colorino.

FATTORIA SAN FRANCESCO
Calabria; Cirò (KR)
DOC(G)s: Cirò
A relatively new Calabrian winery owned by Francesco Siciliani, whose family owns the Caparra & Siciliani estate, one of the classic Cirò houses (those wines are not available in the States). The San Francesco property is like an airplane hangar, outfitted with the latest technology, and the Ciròs produced there have a freshness rarely found in this appellation. The "Ronco dei Quattroventi" and "Donna Madda" Ciròs have a plush, berried quality that bring pinot noir to mind. And the whites are clean and refreshing. A great addition to a somewhat limited wine scene in Calabria.

FATTORIA ZERBINA
Emilia-Romagna; Faenza (RA)
DOC(G)s: Albana di Romagna;
  Sangiovese di Romagna;
  Trebbiano di Romagna
Probably the top producer in Romagna, with a diverse production that includes one of the best Albana di Romagna sweet wines—the silky "Scacco Matto"—as well as some of the most chocolate-rich sangiovese-based reds in the zone. The "Marzieno" Ravenna Rosso is an inky, blackberry-scented blend of sangiovese with a touch of cabernet sauvignon, a wine to rival some of the sangiovese-cabernet blends of neighboring Tuscany. The Sangiovese di Romagna DOC "Pietramora" is spicy and satisfying as well.

FAZI-BATTAGLIA
Marche; Castelplano (AN)
DOC(G)s: Rosso Cònero;
  Verdicchio dei Castelli di Jesi
The wines that got America acquainted with Verdicchio dei Castelli di Jesi. In the seventies and

eighties this industrial-scale winery marketed whites packaged in fish- and amphora-shaped bottles. That's not exactly fashionable anymore, but it had its desired effect. When people think of Italian whites for seafood, verdicchio often gets the call. And Fazi-Battaglia has some decent whites to choose from, most notably "Le Moie," a bright and aromatic selection, and "Riserva San Sisto," which is plumped up with oak. Among the reds, the Rosso Cònero "Passo San Lupo" is a solid choice. They're not fashionable wines, but they're not bad.

FELLINE
PUGLIA; MANDURIA (TA)
DOC(G)s: Primitivo di Manduria
Another of the wineries under the umbrella of the Accademia dei Racemi, a Manduria-based consortium that promotes the wines of a variety of small Puglian estates. Felline's Primitivo di Manduria is one of the better examples to be found, soft and immediately drinkable, while the IGT red "Alberello" lends the structure of negroamaro (50% of the blend) to the sweet, sappy fruit of primitivo. Like most of the better Puglian wines, it remains a great value given the quality.

FELLUGA, LIVIO
FRIULI; CORMONS (GO)
DOC(G)s: Colli Orientali del Friuli (also Rosazzo subzone)
Livio Felluga was one of the early pioneers of modern Friulian wine-making, along with contemporaries such as Mario Schiopetto. The trademark Felluga style—crisp, clean, varietally expressive white made using controlled-temperature fermentation—has been widely imitated over the last several decades, but the Felluga family continues to set standards: The estate's "Terre

Alte" (tocai–pinot bianco–sauvignon) is one of the best-known Friulian whites, an aromatic and well-structured wine made entirely in stainless steel. In recent years the estate has focused considerable attention on reds from their vineyards in Rosazzo (predominantly the "Sossò" merlot), but the whites remain more appealing. Their sweet picolit is among Friuli's best, and their basic dry tocai friulano is textbook.

FELLUGA, MARCO
FRIULI; GRADISCO D'ISONZO (GO)
DOC(G)s: Collio
One of the larger houses in Friuli, producing clean, consistent wines at reasonable prices. The basic tocai friulano, which can be had for under $20, is a serious white, and the chardonnay and pinot grigio are also very good. The white blend "Molamatta" is a fleshy, creamy blend of tocai, ribolla gialla, and pinot grigio. Less convincing are the reds, although the "Carantan" (a Bordeaux blend) is better than most in the area.

FERRANDO, LUIGI
PIEMONTE; IVREA (TO)
DOC(G)s: Canavese; Carema; Erbaluce di Caluso
The anchor of the Carema DOC. Ferrando's rustic reds from nebbiolo are sought out by fans of this fickle grape, while the high-toned whites from the erbaluce grape offer a tooth-chattering alternative to buttery chardonnays. Check out the "black label" Erbaluce di Caluso (which is fattened with a little barrel fermentation) and don't miss the sweet Erbaluce Passito called "Solativo."

FERRARI
TRENTINO; TRENTO (TN)
DOC(G)s: Trento Brut
The Lunelli family's huge, modern winery looks a little bit like a suburban office complex, but inside are some of Italy's best sparkling wines—all made in the classic Champagne method. The firmly structured, vintage-dated "Giulio Ferrari Riserva del Fondatore" (all chardonnay) is the top-of-the-line choice, and it remains a bargain in comparison to Champagne.

FEUDI DI SAN GREGORIO
CAMPANIA; SORBO SERPICO (AV)
DOC(G)s: Fiano di Avellino; Greco di Tufo; Taurasi; Sannio
Probably Campania's most dynamic winery, at least in terms of the variety of wines on offer. Classic Campania reds such as Taurasi (several good ones) and Lacryma Christi are complemented by a host of more custom-crafted wines, such as the rich and honeyed "Cutizzi" Greco di Tufo (which incorporates some late-harvested fruit for depth) and the Fiano di Avellino "Pietracalda" (same premise). Another highlight is "Serpico," a burly aglianico that ranks among the best (and most ageable) wines made from the grape. Riccardo Cotarella consults.

FILIPUTTI, WALTER
FRIULI; MANZANO IN ROSAZZO (UD)
DOC(G)s: Colli Orientali del Friuli
A former journalist, Walter Filiputti took up residence in the historic Abbazia di Rosazzo some years ago and launched his eponymous array of wines. It's a fairly even mix of whites and reds, highlighted by the white blend "Poesis" (chardonnay-tocai-picolit) and the reds "Ronco dei Domenicani" (a cabernet-based blend) and "Ronco dei Benedettini"

(merlot). Pricing and availability are both decent.

FILOMUSI GUELFI
Abruzzo; Popoli (PE)
DOC(G)s: Montepulciano d'Abruzzo

A relatively young and small estate near Pescara producing limited quantities of good Montepulciano d'Abruzzo. A lot of wine for the money.

FIRRIATO
Sicilia; Paceco (TP)
DOC(G)s: Alcamo; Etna

A relatively new winery whose red blend "Camelot" (cabernet sauvignon and merlot) has attracted a lot of attention. The estate's production is diverse, including a simple Alcamo Bianco and a smooth Etna Rosso. The "Santagostino Rosso" is an in-vogue blend of nero d'avola and syrah. A winery to watch.

FLORIO
Sicilia; Marsala (TP)
DOC(G)s: Marsala

A large Marsala house whose better, Sherry-style bottlings are not exported (at least not in significant quantities).

FOLONARI, AMBROGIO E ALBERTO
Toscana; Firenze (FI)
DOC(G)s: Chianti Classico

A new firm created from the split up of the Folonari family of Ruffino. Ambrogio and Alberto Folonari now control the former Ruffino entities Cabreo (known for its popular, internationally styled super-Tuscan wines) and Nozzole (a Chianti house), among others. See also Ruffino.

FONTANA CANDIDA
Lazio; Monteporzio Catone (RM)
DOC(G)s: Frascati

One of the best-known Italian wine brands in America. While production is large-scale, it can nevertheless be interesting. The top-end Frascatis, such as the "Terre dei Grifi" and "Santa Teresa," are not exactly white Burgundies, but they're pretty appealing, fragrant whites. They may not be especially fashionable, but the Fontana Candida wines are consistent and inexpensive.

FONTANA, GRAZIANO
Trentino; Faedo (TN)
DOC(G)s: Trentino

Nervous, fragrant, high-toned white with lots of acidic backbone are the calling card of this hidden gem. Located in the heights of Faedo (also the home of the more famous Pojer & Sandri), Graziano Fontana builds aroma and structure into varietal whites from sauvignon, traminer, chardonnay, and müller-thurgau (a particular specialty). On balance, the sauvignon and müller are probably the most interesting, and pricing is very reasonable.

FONTANABIANCA
Piemonte; Neive (CN)
DOC(G)s: Barbaresco; Barbera d'Alba; Dolcetto d'Alba; Langhe

Not well known in the States, but yet another small Piemontese winery making good wine. The limited-production Barbaresco "Sorì Burdin" is the top bottling.

FONTANAFREDDA
Piemonte; Serralunga d'Alba (CN)
DOC(G)s: Barolo; Barbaresco; Barbera d'Alba; Nebbiolo d'Alba

With more than 240 acres of vineyards and production of nearly a million bottles a year of Barolo alone, this Piedmontese landmark is fairly well known in the U.S. Founded in the late-1800s by Emmanuele Guerreri, son of King Victor Emmanuel II, this estate dominates the Serralunga d'Alba area, bottling Barolos from an array of different vineyards. The Barolo "Vigna La Rosa" is a benchmark for Italian-wine lovers, and in general the Fontanafredda wines are well made, if not earth-shattering. Everything from fruity dolcetto to fizzy Asti is produced here, with mixed results.

FONTODI
Toscana; Panzano in Chianti (FI)
DOC(G)s: Chianti Classico

The Manetti family, tile-makers who supplied the materials for most of the cathedral roofs in the Florence area, acquired this estate in the 1960s. It is one of Chianti's flagship wineries, overlooking the sunsplashed bowl of vineyards beneath the village of Panzano in Chianti, and it is best known for the tarry "Flaccianello della Pieve," one of the first all-sangiovese super-Tuscans. The Chianti Classico "Vigna del Sorbo" is also a powerful, coffee-scented evocation of sangiovese.

FORADORI
Trentino; Mezzolombardo (TN)
DOC(G)s: Teroldego Rotaliano

Considered the top producer of teroldego, this winery is run by young Elisabetta Foradori, who continues to experiment with this unusual, hard-to-ripen variety. Foradori's "Granato" (100% teroldego) is one of the most unique Italian reds around, a black and brooding wine set apart by the unique aromas of the variety. The "basic" Teroldego Rotaliano is a more affordable introduction to the grape.

FORCHIR
Friuli; San Giorgio della Richinvelda (PN)
DOC(G)s: Friuli Grave
Huge wine house in Grave producing bargain-priced varietal.

FORTETO DELLA LUJA
Piemonte; Loazzolo (AT)
DOC(G)s: Loazzolo; Monferrato Rosso; Piemonte Brachetto
Giancarlo Scaglione is widely admired for the diverse lineup of mostly sweet wines he crafts at his small farmstead winery near Canelli. He takes the often pedestrian moscato grape to great heights, as evidenced by the Sauternes-like richness and smokiness of his Loazzolo DOC "Piasa Rischei," a late-harvest moscato aged in wood. His delicate, strawberry-scented brachetto, "Pian di Sogni," is another gem, and the Moscato d'Asti "Piasa San Maurizio" is one of the best frizzanti around. Awesome artisan wines.

FRESCOBALDI
Toscana; Firenze (FI)
DOC(G)s: Brunello di Montalcino; Chianti; Chianti Rufina; Pomino
Frescobaldi is a noble Tuscan family with roots going back more than 1,000 years. The family's winemaking history goes back almost as far, but it wasn't until the 1960s that brothers Vittorio, Ferdinando, and Leonardo really modernized the business. Today, the Frescobaldi empire spans nine estates covering more than 1,800 acres of vineyard land. The gems are the Castelgiocondo property in Montalcino (acquired in 1989) and the Nipozzano estate in the Rufina zone, the latter turning out one of the consistently great bargains in Italian wine: the Castello di Nipozzano Chianti Rufina Riserva. Other Frescobaldi highlights include the spicy Pomino Rosso DOC and the cabernet sauvignon "Mormoreto," also from the Nipozzano property. Frescobaldi is also a partner with American Robert Mondavi in Luce della Vite, a brand based out of Castelgiocondo in Montalcino. The Luce wine is a sappy, slick sangiovesemerlot blend.

FUNTANIN
Piemonte; Canale (CN)
DOC(G)s: Barbera d'Alba; Langhe; Roero
A Roero-area producer specializing in full-bodied reds from barbera and nebbiolo. The Roero Arneis "Pierin di Soc" is a citrusy white.

GABBAS, GIUSEPPE
Sardegna; Nuoro (NU)
DOC(G)s: Cannonau di Sardinia
Sole proprietorships are rare in the co-op-dominated wilds of Sardegna, especially tiny estates like that of Giuseppe Gabbas. His three wines, all based on cannonau (grenache), might summon to mind pinot noir. The fresh, fine "Lillovè" Cannonau DOC is the purest expression of the variety (it sees no oak), while the blends "Dule" and "Arbeskia" plump it up with cabernet and other grapes.

GAGLIARDO, GIANNI
Piemonte; La Morra (CN)
DOC(G)s: Barolo; Dolcetto d'Alba; Langhe
A respected producer of Barolo based in La Morra. The top bottling, "Le Preve," is not a cru wine but rather a blend of fruit from La Morra and Castiglione Falletto. Other offerings include savory whites from the rare favorita grape.

GAGLIOLE
Toscana; Castellina in Chianti (SI)
A Swiss lawyer, appropriately named Thomas Bar, owns this small estate. The estate's potent and savory "Rosso" is an IGT wine made from sangiovese with a touch of cabernet sauvignon.

GAJA, ANGELO
Piemonte; Barbaresco (CN)
DOC(G)s: Barbaresco; Langhe
The biggest name in Italian wine, period. Since the 1960s, Angelo Gaja has been considered the premier winemaking innovator in Italy. He is the first one in Piedmont credited with the modernization of Barbaresco and Barolo wines, having pioneered the use of controlled-temperature fermentation (to help reduce oxidation in the wines) and small-cask aging (to stabilize color and preserve fruitiness). His Barbarescos and ever-expanding raft of other wines are tightly allocated and eye-poppingly expensive, but in good years (such as '85, '89, '90, and '97, to name a few) they are among the best red wines made anywhere in the world. Gaja's signature wines are his compact, highly perfumed Barbarescos, although recently he opted to take the "Barbaresco" name off of his three well-known cru wines—"Sorì San Lorenzo," "Sorì Tildin," and "Costa Russi." He says he did it because people were ignoring his "base" Barbaresco, which he considers an excellent product. Others contend he switched to the Langhe DOC so he could have more freedom to blend in international grapes such as cabernet sauvignon. Based on tastings of the most recent vintages, it doesn't seem as if cabernet enters the mix: The distinctive, heady per-

fume of nebbiolo is still a Gaja calling card. His wide range of wines also includes the Langhe Nebbiolo "Sperss" (once a Barolo DOCG); two rich and structured chardonnays; and of course barberas, dolcettos, and blends, all of them labeled with colorful brand names. Gaja has also developed estates in Tuscany, both in Montalcino (Pieve Santa Restituta) and more recently in Bolgheri (Ca' Marcanda, where he is just now coming on the scene with his take on super-Tuscan wine). Everything he makes is top of the line, and priced accordingly.

GALARDI (TERRA DI LAVORO)
Campania; Sessa Aurunca (CE)
One of Campania's cult wineries, with a small-production, supercharged red everyone is scrambling to buy. The Galardi winery is set among magnificent chestnut groves in the high hills of Sessa Aurunca, in northwestern Campania, and on a clear day the Mediterranean can be seen in the distance. From the estate's vineyards come deeply concentrated aglianico, piedirosso, and other grapes (such as cabernet sauvignon) used to make the lone wine "Terra di Lavoro." This is a black, brooding, long-aging red—one of the south's very best wines. Try it if you can find it.

GARCHE DEL BARONE
Sicilia; Pantelleria (TP)
DOC(G)s: Moscato di Pantelleria; Passito di Pantelleria
A new operation on Pantelleria connected to the Falvo family of Avignonesi in Tuscany, whose wine-marketing firm, Classica, has holdings all over Italy. Garche del Barone makes luscious Moscato di Pantelleria ("Khafur"), Passito di Pantelleria ("Le Leave del Kuttinar"), and an unusual dry zibbibo ("Luciri").

GAROFOLI
Marche; Loreto (AN)
DOC(G)s: Verdicchio dei Castelli di Jesi; Rosso Cònero
One of the more historic wineries in the Marche, specializing in verdicchio but marketing a wide range of local wines. The Verdicchio dei Castelli di Jesi "Podium" is easily one of the best wines of its type, with all of the herbal, citrusy aromatic of the grape but a weightiness of extract that separates it from an often thin pack. The "Macrina" Verdicchio is also quite good. Garofoli also makes sparkling versions of verdicchio (along with several other dry selections), and solid Rosso Cònero, among other wines. If you want, you can still get the verdicchio in a fish bottle.

GASTALDI
Piemonte; Neive (CN)
DOC(G)s: Barbaresco; Dolcetto d'Alba; Langhe
Ripe and accessible Barbaresco is the specialty of this boutique estate, which is also known for good chardonnay-based whites, plush dolcettos and, in exceptional vintages, the nebbiolo-based "Rosso Gastaldi."

GATTI, PIERO
Piemonte; San Stefano Belbo (CN)
DOC(G)s: Langhe; Piemonte
The late Piero Gatti worked with Piedmont's fun grapes: the sweet, peachy moscato; the spicy, strawberry-scented brachetto; and the violet-hued freisa. Lightly sparkling moscato is a specialty, but the freisa—one of the few wines of its type to be found in the States—is also worth trying. The "Verbeia" blends barbera and freisa.

GEOGRAFICO
Toscana; Gaiole in Chianti (SI)
DOC(G)s: Chianti Classico; Chianti Colli Senesi; Vino Nobile di Montepulciano; Brunello di Montalcino
A co-operative winery producing a wide range of cheap, serviceable reds and whites. The most serious bottling is the Chianti Classico "Montegiachi," definitely a good wine for the money.

GERMANO, ETTORE
Piemonte; Serralunga d'Alba (CN)
DOC(G)s: Barolo; Barbera d'Alba; Dolcetto d'Alba; Langhe
A good, modern Piedmontese lineup, running the gamut from the rich Barolo "Prapò" to decent dolcettos and barberas to Langhe DOC chardonnay.

GHISOLFI, ATTILIO
Piemonte; Monforte d'Alba (CN)
DOC(G)s: Barolo; Barbera d'Alba; Dolcetto d'Alba; Langhe
Notable barbera and dolcetto, along with a new Langhe Rosso DOC called "Alta Bussia," a barbera-nebbiolo blend. The Barolo "Bricco Visette" is solid. A small estate.

GIACOSA, BRUNO
Piemonte; Neive (CN)
DOC(G)s: Barbaresco; Barolo; Dolcetto d'Alba; Roero Arneis
One of the Langhe's enduring classics, based in the commune of Neive in the Barbaresco DOCG but cultivating vineyards in both Barolo and Barbaresco. Bruno Giacosa is a traditionalist, producing big-boned and somewhat austere wines aged for long periods in large casks before release. Giacosa's "Falletto" and "Vigna Rionda" Barolos—from

crus in the commune of Ser-ralunga—are probably the most powerful of the lot. There's also the Barolos "Rocche" and "Villero" (both from Castiglione Falletto) and the Barbaresco "Santo Stefano." Another specialty of the house is a fragrant, silky Roero Arneis, one of the best wines of its type.

GIACOSA, CARLO
PIEMONTE; BARBARESCO (CN)
DOC(G)s: Barbaresco; Barbera d'Alba; Dolcetto d'Alba
The Barbaresco-based Giacosas have vineyards in most of the commune's top crus, and their Barbaresco wines include the meaty "Montefico" and "Narin." Barbera is also a specialty here.

GIACOSA F.LLI
PIEMONTE; NEIVE (CN)
DOC(G)s: Barbaresco; Barolo; Barbera d'Alba; Langhe
A *négociant*-style producer (i.e., they buy grapes) known for a good Barbaresco from the Rio Sordo cru in the commune of Barbaresco. Other wines include the Barbera d'Alba "Maria Gioana."

GINI
VENETO; MONTEFORTE D'ALPONE (VR)
DOC(G)s: Soave
In the top rank of Soave producers, with a house style that favors super-ripe garganega and a touch (and sometimes more than a touch) of oak. The best place to start is with the Soave "La Froscà" (a portion of which is barrel-fermented) and move up to the rich and honeyed Soave "Contrada Selvarenza" (all of which is barrel-fermented). Along with the wines of Inama, these are some of the fullest-bodied Soaves available.

GRAF ENZENBERG (TENUTA MANINCOR)
ALTO ADIGE; CALDARO/KALTERN (BZ)
DOC(G)s: Alto Adige-Südtiroler; Terlaner
Originally, Count Michael Goëss-Enzenberg sold grapes to local co-ops, but he began selling wines under the Manincor-Graf Enzenberg label in 1996. Check out the moscato giallo (goldmuskateller) and the "Mason" Pinot Noir, one of the better Italian pinots around. "Cuvée Sophie," named for Enzenberg's wife, is a luscious, oak-tinged white blend.

GRASSO, ELIO
PIEMONTE; MONFORTE D'ALBA (CN)
DOC(G)s: Barolo; Barbera d'Alba; Dolcetto d'Alba; Langhe
Good and affordable Barolo, highlighted by the powerful "Runcot" and the more delicate "Ginestra Case Maté." Also solid Barbera d'Alba and Langhe Chardonnay.

GRASSO, SILVIO
PIEMONTE; LA MORRA (CN)
DOC(G)s: Barolo; Barbera d'Alba; Dolcetto d'Alba
Sleek and modern Barolos from the southwest-facing La Morra crus of Luciani and Manzoni. Federico Grasso's style incorporates some new oak, particularly in the Barbera d'Alba "Fontanile." Limited quantities.

GRATTAMACCO
TOSCANA; CASTAGNETO CARDUCCI (LI)
DOC(G)s: Bolgheri
One of the pioneering estates in the Bolgheri area of coastal Tuscany, having arrived on the scene just after Marchese Mario Incisa della Rocchetta of Tenuta San Guido (Sassi-

caia), and just before the Marchese's nephew, Lodovico Antinori (Ornellaia). The Grattamacco property is a farmstead operation, with two principal wines: the opulent Rosso, a blend of sangiovese and cabernet sauvignon, and the crisp and clean Bianco, which is vermentino-based. These are evocative wines, not as well known as some of their Bolgheri brethren and therefore not as pricey. Maurizio Castelli consults.

GRAVNER
FRIULI; OSLAVIA (GO)
DOC(G)s: Collio
The leader of a Slovenian brat pack, of sorts, that included neighbors Stanko Radikon and the Bensa brothers of La Castellada. They decided in the eighties to move away from making traditional cold-fermentation whites in stainless steel and instead go for more Burgundian-style wines incorporating fermentation and aging in French oak. Gravner's whites are difficult to find (like their reclusive maker), but they represent some of the most powerful and complex whites to be found anywhere in Italy. Wines such as Gravner's barrel-fermented ribolla gialla demonstrate how a "woody" wine can also be fruity, firm, and brightly acidic. These wines have a tightly coiled power to them that brings to mind white Burgundy, and they are priced accordingly. Lately, though, he has dramatically changed his style, preferring minimal intervention in the vineyards and cellar.

GREPPONE MAZZI
TOSCANA; MONTALCINO (SI)
DOC(G)s: Brunello di Montalcino
The Montalcino estate controlled by Tenimenti Ruffino. Good, modern Brunello.

GROTTA DEL SOLE
CAMPANIA; QUARTO (NA)
DOC(G)s: Asprinio d'Aversa;
   Campi Flegrei; Fiano di Avellino;
   Greco di Tufo

Naples-area winery with some decent, inexpensive wines, including Lacryma Christi both white and red. The Greco di Tufo is probably their best wine, but the falanghina is also good.

GRUPPO ITALIANO VINI
VENETO; CALMASINO (VR)
DOC(G)s: Various

GIV sells more than 60 million bottles a year from the following producers: Nino Negri (Valtellina, Lombardia); Santi (Valpolicella, Veneto); Lamberti (Verona area, Veneto); Folonari (Verona area, Veneto); Conti Formentini (Collio, Friuli–Venezia Giulia); Melini (Chianti Classico, Toscana); Machiavelli (Chianti Classico, Toscana); Bigi (Orvieto, Umbria); Fontana Candida (Frascati, Lazio). It is the largest wine company in Italy, controlling more than 700 hectares of owned or rented vineyards and selling more than 60 million bottles a year. Its member estates have varying degrees of autonomy, but all coordinate their efforts with technical director Emilio Pedron.

GUALDO DEL RE
TOSCANA; SUVERETO (LI)
DOC(G)s: Val di Cornia

The area around Suvereto, near Tuscany's southern coast, is one to keep an eye on. Gualdo del Re is one of a number of up-and-coming wineries in the area (others include Tua Rita and San Giusto). Interesting, savory reds such as the "Re Nero" (merlot–pinot nero) and "Federico Primo" (cabernet-merlot-sangiovese) join well-priced Val di Cornia DOC bottlings, both white and red.

HAAS, FRANZ
ALTO ADIGE;
   MONTAGNA/MONTAN (BZ)
DOC(G)s: Alto Adige

Franz Haas is a well-known consultant and scholar, and his namesake estate is one of the biggest and most respected brand names in the Alto Adige. His is a characteristically wide range of wines, both white and red. Highlights include the reds from the "Schweizer" line: Merlot, Pinot Nero, and the sweet Moscato Rosa, which is a specialty. Whites are headlined by gewürztraminer and pinot bianco. Good wines across the board. Haas also markets a line of wines under the "Kris" brand name.

HAUNER
SICILIA; SANTA MARINA, ISOLA
   SALINA (ME)
DOC(G)s: Malvasia delle Lipari;
   Cerasuolo di Vittoria

When Brescian artist Carlo Hauner visited the Aeolian island of Salina in 1963, he didn't want to leave—he ended up settling there in the early '70s, and began acquiring vineyards with which to produce the local sweet wine. Salina's vineyards were divided among countless families, and legend has it that Hauner signed some 2,000 contracts in acquiring his 20 hectares of vines. The volcanic soils of Salina are home to the sweet, fragrant malvasia with which the Hauner name has become synonymous. To complement the two Malvasia delle Lipari wines (one a natural late-harvest sweet wine, the other a passito incorporating grapes dried on reed mats), the Hauner estate, now run by the late founder's children, produces a number of good dry whites and reds.

HOFSTÄTTER
ALTO ADIGE; TERMENO/TRAMIN
   (BZ)
DOC(G)s: Alto Adige

As you might expect from a winery located in the suspected birthplace of gewürztraminer, Hofstätter is a great source of flinty, apricot-scented whites from this grape. Not to mention chardonnay, pinot bianco, pinot grigio, and, most notably, one of the better Italian takes on pinor noir (the "S. Urbano" bottling). One of Alto Adige's best.

I CAMPETTI
TOSCANA; MASSA MARITTIMA
   (GR)
DOC(G)s: Monteregio di Massa
   Marittima

A small southern-Tuscan winery with a couple of interesting wines on offer: the "Castruccio" Rosso (a blend of sangiovese, colorino, canaiolo, and ciliegiolo), a savory southern red with good concentration; and the oily and fragrant viognier, a decadent white.

I PAGLIERI (ROAGNA)
PIEMONTE; BARBARESCO (CN)
DOC(G)s: Barbaresco; Barolo;
   Langhe

A small but modern-thinking producer whose ripe and leathery Barbarescos and Barolos remain reasonably priced. The Barbaresco cru "Paje" is the richest, spiciest wine in the bunch, while the "La Rocca e Pira" Barolo is broader and more brooding. "Opera Prima" is a blend of different vintages of barrique-aged nebbiolo.

ICARDI
PIEMONTE; CASTIGLIONE TINELLA
   (CN)
DOC(G)s: Barolo; Barbera d'Alba;
   Langhe; Monferrato; Piemonte

A creative producer with a wide

range of Alba and Asti wines, including several selections of ripe and rich Barbera d'Alba, interesting Langhe Rosso DOC wines such as "Nej" (all pinot nero) and "Bricco del Sole" (barbera-nebbiolo-barbera), even some Moscato d'Asti. There's also Barolo, but the red blends tend to be more interesting.

IL POGGIOLINO
TOSCANA; SAMBUCA DI
    TAVARNELLE (FI)
DOC(G)s: Chianti Classico
Tasty, affordable Chianti Classico.

IL POGGIONE
TOSCANA; MONTALCINO (SI)
DOC(G)s: Brunello di Montalcino
A landmark winery in Montalcino with a long history of tightly wound, long-aging Brunellos. The late Pierluigi Talenti (whose eponymous estate is also profiled) was long the guiding force here, but that job is now in the hands of Fabrizio Bindocci. These wines are a great introduction to classic Brunello, while the new "San Leopoldo" (sangiovese–cabernet sauvignon) is a nod to modern trends.

IL VESCOVINO
TOSCANA; PANZANO IN CHIANTI
    (FI)
DOC(G)s: Chianti Classico
Funky, meaty Chianti Classico and a super-Tuscan called "Merlotto," which blends sangiovese with cabernet sauvignon.

IL VIGNALE
PIEMONTE; NOVI LIGURE (AL)
DOC(G)s: Gavi; Monferrato Rosso
Pleasant, floral Gavi (particularly the "Vigne Alte") priced for casual occasions.

ILLUMINATI
ABRUZZO; CONTROGUERRA (TE)
DOC(G)s: Controguerra;
    Montepulciano d'Abruzzo;
    Trebbiano d'Abruzzo
One of the top producers of Montepulciano d'Abruzzo, this small, family-run estate in the northern Abruzzo village of Controguerra is best known for "Lumen," an inky, luscious blend of montepulciano and cabernet sauvignon that carries the new Controguerra DOC designation. The Montepulciano d'Abruzzo wines, particularly the single-vineyard "Zanna," are great examples of how complex and age-worthy montepulciano can be.

INAMA
VENETO; SAN BONIFACIO (VR)
DOC(G)s: Soave; Colli Berici
Young Stefano Inama has caught some flack for his super extracted, barrel-fermented take on Soave, but he continues to win new fans with each vintage. His single-vineyard Soave "Foscarino" is as ripe and rich a take on the garganega grape as you'll find, and the Soave "Vigneto du Lot" (100% barrel-fermented) is even richer. From the nearby Colli Berici DOC, Inama also produces an excellent cabernet sauvignon called "Bradisismo."

INNOCENTI, VITTORIO
TOSCANA; MONTEFOLLONICO (PI)
DOC(G)s: Vino Nobile di
    Montepulciano; Vin Santo
Top-rated Vin Santo and similarly admired Vino Nobile di Montepulciano from an artisan producer.

ISOLE E OLENA
TOSCANA; BARBERINO VAL D'ELSA
    (FI)
DOC(G)s: Chianti Classico
Located at the western edge of the Chianti Classico DOC in the heights of Barberino Val d'Elsa, Isole e Olena is a special place. Proprietor/winemaker Paolo DeMarchi is widely admired for his research on the sangiovese grape, from which he crafts excellent Chianti Classico as well as the super-Tuscan "Cepparello," the latter a tightly allocated item in the States. Powerful cabernet sauvignon and syrah are also specialties here.

JERMANN
FRIULI; VILLANOVA DI FARRA
    (GO)
Silvio Jermann is the still the biggest star in a region increasingly filled with noteworthy names, thanks mostly to the success of the luscious white blend "Vintage Tunina" (a field blend of chardonnay, sauvignon, picolit, and a few other unnamed varieties). Working outside the realm of DOC, Jermann has helped to define Friulian wine as bigger, fruitier, and more ageworthy than the traditional Italian norm. His product line is extensive: the tropical, all-steel "Tunina" is complemented by the creamy, barrel-aged "Capo Martino" (pinot bianco-malvasia-tocai-picolit) and a host of dewy, fresh varietal wines (check out the "Dreams" chardonnay in particular). These are some of Italy's best and most famous whites.

KANTE, EDI
FRIULI; DUINO AURISINA (TS)
DOC(G)s: Carso
Edi Kante's rabbit hole of a winery bores down into the limestone-rich earth of the Carso zone, a sliver of land that connects Trieste with the rest of Friuli–Venezia Giulia. Kante's varietal whites (especially the exotic malvasia istriana and powerful sauvignon) are as good as it gets: Although he uses a lot of barrel fermentation, Kante has a knack for

creating wines with a balance of acidity, fruit, and wood flavors. The oak influence in his wines is beautifully moderated, allowing varietal characteristics to shine through.

KEBER, EDI
Friuli; Cormons (GO)
DOC(G)s: Collio
A tiny but noteworthy producer in the Collio DOC, known for excellent tocai friulano, bianco, and a plump merlot.

KEBER, RENATO
Friuli; Cormons (GO)
DOC(G)s: Collio
A small, well-regarded Collio producer with a particular affinity for pinot grigio, pinot bianco, and tocai friulano. Keber's whites are rich and well structured, with the Collio Bianco "Beli Grici" (pinot bianco, ribolla gialla, sauvignon, tocai) at the top of the list. The varietal wines carrying the "Grici" designation (chardonnay, tocai, merlot) are partially fermented in barrique, and it shows.

KUEN HOF (PETER PLIEGER)
Alto Adige;
  Bressanone/Brixen (BZ)
DOC(G)s: Alto Adige Valle
  Isarco/Südtirol-Eisacktaler
Peter Plieger is a specialist in aromatic varieties, producing balanced, exotically perfumed wines from his tiny winery near Bressanone. His farmstead cantina is cut into an impossibly steep-sloping vineyard of about 550 meters elevation. Everything he makes, from his spicy grüner veltliner to the honeyed, floral gewürztraminer, is worth a try, if you can find any—production is extremely limited.

LA BIANCARA
Veneto; Gambellara (VI)
DOC(G)s: Gambellara
Gambellara is just east of the Soave DOC, and the local grape is the same—garganega. The La Biancara wines are juicy and well-made expressions of garganega—ripe and dewy. The rich, barrel-fermented "Pico dei Lorenti" tacks on a dose of tropical fruitiness to garganega's typically sinewy frame, while the sweet Recioto di Gambellara is a honeyed nectar well worth the extra effort it will take to find.

LA BOATINA
Friuli; Cormons (GO)
DOC(G)s: Collio
Good varietal wines, including ribolla gialla, chardonnay, and pinot bianco. The jammy red blend "Picol Maggiore" (merlot–cabernet sauvignon–cabernet franc) has the spicy, somewhat vegetal flavors often found in Friulian reds.

LA BRACCESCA
Toscana; Montepulciano (SI)
DOC(G)s: Vino Nobile di
  Montepulciano
The Montepulciano arm of the giant Antinori firm, producing ripe and stylish Vino Nobile as well as a juicy merlot. A fast-expanding brand that offers consistent value.

LA BRANCAIA
Toscana; Castellina in Chianti
  (SI)
DOC(G)s: Chianti Classico
Swiss adman Bruno Widmehr purchased his first property in Chianti in 1981, and the grapes grown on his vineyards in Castellina were vinified by his good friends, the Mazzeis, at the nearby Castello di Fonterutoli. These days, Bruno's winemaker daughter Barbara (with help from famed consultant Carlo Ferrini) makes the slick, dark-toned La Brancaia wines in a sparkling new subterranean cellar. The estate continues with two wines: a ripe, rich, thoroughly modern Chianti Classico and the super-Tuscan "La Brancaia," a blend of 60% sangiovese, 30% merlot, and 5% cabernet. New wines from a newly acquired plot in the Maremma are forthcoming.

LA CADALORA
Trentino; Ala (TN)
DOC(G)s: Trentino
Good, clean varietal wines with the characteristic perfumy quality of the north. Solid pinot grigio, chardonnay, etc., priced at by-the-case levels.

LA CALONICA
Toscana; Montepulciano (SI)
DOC(G)s: Vino Nobile di
  Montepulciano
A lesser-known Vino Nobile producer making the wines in fruit-forward modern style. Super-Tuscan offerings include the barrique-aged "Signorelli" (merlot) and "Girifalco" (sangiovese).

LA CAPPUCCINA
Veneto; Monteforte d'Alpone
  (VR)
DOC(G)s: Soave; Recioto di Soave
One of the more historic wineries in the Verona area, and one of the better producers of Soave. The proprietors are definitely after the international market with their Soave Superiore "San Brizio," which is aged in oak, and the "Fontego," which includes some chardonnay in the mix. But the wines are solid, and the prices are good. Other offerings include reds from cabernets franc and sauvignon.

LA CARRAIA
UMBRIA; ORVIETO (TR)
DOC(G)s: Orvieto Classico
Part-owned by well-traveled consultant Riccardo Cotarella, this Orvieto-based winery not only makes good Orvieto Classico wines (try the "Poggio Calvelli") but also the "super-Umbro" red called "Fobiano," a single-vineyard blend of cabernet sauvignon and merlot.

LA CASTELLADA
FRIULI; GORIZIA (GO)
DOC(G)s: Collio
Part of a like-minded clique of producers (with Slovenian leanings) that includes Josko Gravner, Stanko Radikon, and Edi Kante, proprietors Nicolò and Giorgio Bensa aim for a Burgundian style in their wines. Their "Bianco della Castellada," a blend of tocai, pinot grigio, chardonnay, and sauvignon, is deeply concentrated and smoky from its fermentation in French barriques. These are big wines from a beautiful, bucolic borderland.

LA CHIARA
PIEMONTE; GAVI (AL)
DOC(G)s: Gavi
The barrel-fermented Gavi "Vigneto Groppella" is an unusually plump and tropical Gavi.

LA FIORITA (LAMBORGHINI)
UMBRIA; PANICALE (PG)
DOC(G)s: Colli del Trasimeno
Yes, that Lamborghini. Run by Patrizia Lamborghini (daughter of car titan Ferruccio), this Lake Trasimeno winery specializes in chunky, rich red blends. There's "Trescone," which combines sangiovese, ciliegiolo, and merlot, and the denser, darker "Campoleone," a 50-50 sangiovese-merlot mix. "Campoleone" has its cult followers thanks to high marks in the press, making it difficult to find.

LA GIUSTINIANA
PIEMONTE; GAVI (AL)
DOC(G)s: Gavi; Asti; Brachetto d'Acqui
Good, perfumed Gavis from the area's biggest estate, along with a barrel-fermented cortese and some wines from brachetto and moscato. Some big, dry barberas are coming as well.

LA LASTRA
TOSCANA; SAN GIMIGNANO (SI)
DOC(G)s: Vernaccia di San Gimignano; Chianti Colli Senesi
An emerging name in San Gimignano, with a powerful, fruit-driven Vernaccia di San Gimignano Riserva and an interesting red, "Rovaio" (cabernet-merlot-sangiovese).

LA MADONNINA (CASA VINICOLA TRIACCA)
TOSCANA; GREVE IN CHIANTI (FI)
DOC(G)s: Chianti Classico
Acquired in the early seventies by the Triacca family of Sondrio, Lombardia, this historic Chianti estate produces the 100% sangiovese "Riserva La Madonnina." For something slicker, try the Chianti "Vigna La Palaia," dosed with 15% cabernet and aged in new barriques.

LA MASSA
TOSCANA; PANZANO (FI)
DOC(G)s: Chianti Classico
A critically acclaimed estate in Panzano whose "Giorgio Primo" Chianti Classico is one of the better examples of new generation Chianti: Dense and deeply extracted, with an intensity to rival most super-Tuscans, it's a Chianti you'd rather age for a while rather than sip thoughtlessly with pizza.

LA MONACESCA
MARCHE; MATELICA (MC)
DOC(G)s: Verdicchio di Matelica
The premier estate in the Matelica zone. The base Verdicchio di Matelica is characteristically firm and fine, high-toned in the style of the zone. The white blend "Mirum," a blend of verdicchio, chardonnay, and sauvignon, is creamier, more appley and rich, but still the emphasis is on freshness (no oak). On the red side, there's a sangiovese-merlot called "Camerte" that is definitely worth a try.

LA PALAZZOLA
UMBRIA; STRONCONE (TR)
A well-regarded Umbrian estate producing a range of lush reds, including a merlot, a pinot nero, and several blends. There's also an excellent sweet wine called "V.T."

LA PODERINA
TOSCANA; MONTALCINO (SI)
DOC(G)s: Brunello di Montalcino; Moscadello di Montalcino
Part of the group of wineries owned by SAI Agricola, the agriculture branch of the large SAI insurance firm. Ripe and accessible Brunellos and Rossos are complemented by a late-harvest Moscadello di Montalcino.

LA RAMPA DI FUGNANO
TOSCANA; SAN GIMIGNANO (SI)
DOC(G)s: Vernaccia di San Gimignano; Chianti Colli Senesi
A notable, relatively new estate in San Gimignano, producing a range of stylish wines. The Vernaccia di San Gimignanos (the aromatic "Alata" and the more full-bodied "Privato") are above average, for sure, but it's the reds that have gotten the most attention. The "Gisèle" merlot has won high marks, as has the "Bombereto" sangiovese.

LA SALA

TOSCANA; SAN CASCIANO VAL DI
 PESA (FI)
DOC(G)s: Chianti Classico
A small and well-regarded winery
run by hands-on proprietor Laura
Baronti. Her Chianti Classicos are
elegant and reasonably priced.

LA SCOLCA

PIEMONTE; GAVI (AL)
DOC(G)s: Gavi
The benchmark wine of Gavi is this
estate's Gavi di Gavi "Etichetta
Nera" (black label), which proprietor Giorgio Soldati crafts in a floral, flinty style. The estate also
makes some surprisingly good
sparklers from the cortese grape.

LA SPINETTA

PIEMONTE; CASTAGNOLE LANZE
 (AT)
DOC(G)s: Barbaresco; Barbera
 d'Asti; Moscato d'Asti;
 Monferrato Rosso
La Spinetta's proprietor, Giorgio
Rivetti, is one of the darlings of the
Italian (and American) wine press.
He makes the quintessential "modern" Piedmont wines: they're loaded
with rich, ripe fruit (thanks to rigor-
ous selections in the vineyard), are
nearly black with extract (thanks to
high-tech vinification methods), and
they have a chocolatey sheen from
aging in new oak barriques. Rivetti
produces three single-vineyard
Barbarescos—"Vigneto Gallina,"
Vigneto Starderi," and "Vigneto
Valeirano"—all of them styled to
be drunk either immediately or 20
years down the line. The Barbera
d'Asti "Ca' di Pian" is an unfiltered
monster in its own right, and the red
blend "Pin" (nebbiolo-barbera-
cabernet) is another decadent
mouthful. Moscato d'Asti is another
specialty, and now Rivetti is experimenting with sauvignon and

chardonnay. It's all pricey stuff, and
made in limited quantities.

LA STOPPA

EMILIA-ROMAGNA
RIVERGARO (PC)
DOC(G)s: Colli Piacentini
The Colli Piacentini, or the hills of
Piacenza, is not a well-known wine
zone. La Stoppa is considered one
of the key estates, based on the
strengths of its red wines from
cabernet sauvignon and barbera.
The cabernet "Stoppa" is most definitely worth a try, as is the barbera,
but the real gems of this estate are
two sweet wines: the rare "Buca
delle Canne," from late-harvest
sémillon, and "Vigna del Volta," a
passito malvasia. In "Vigna del
Volta," which is a relative bargain
and readily available, there's a penetrating apricot sweetness cleansed by
a crisply acidic finish, the mark of
any good dessert wine. Try it with
biscotti or maybe tossed into some
fresh berries.

LA TENAGLIA

PIEMONTE; SERRALUNGA DI CREA
 (CN)
DOC(G)s: Barbera d'Asti;
 Grignolino del Monferrato
 Casalese; Piemonte
Tuscan consultant Attilio Pagli
works with this Asti-area estate,
making it a winery to watch. The
specialty is ink-black barberas and
the rare, berry-scented grignolino
grape. International varieties such as
chardonnay and syrah are also finding their way into bottles.

LA TOGATA

TOSCANA; MONTALCINO (SI)
DOC(G)s: Brunello di Montalcino
The limited-production Brunello di
Montalcino made here is still aged
in large oak, lending it an elegance
and harmony not always found in

some of the more modern, barrique-aged monsters of the day. In a
nod to fashion, though, this small
estate brought in some small barrels
for its full-bodied varietal sangiovese
called "Azzurreta."

LA TOSA

EMILIA-ROMAGNA; VIGOLZONE
 (PC)
DOC(G)s: Colli Piacentini
Often referred to in the same breath
as La Stoppa, since the top wine
here, too, is a cabernet sauvignon.
"Luna Selvatica" is rich and ripe and
immediately accessible, the emphasis
being on forward fruit. The Gutturnio (a DOC blend of barbera
and bonarda) is brightly fruity and
crisply acidic, and the white sauvignon is good as well.

LA VALENTINA

ABRUZZO; SPOLTORE (PE)
DOC(G)s: Montepulciano
 d'Abruzzo; Trebbiano d'Abruzzo
Simple, solid Abruzzo wine, priced
right for barbecues or other casual
occasions.

LA VIARTE

FRIULI; PREPOTTO (UD)
DOC(G)s: Colli Orientali del Friuli
A wide range of good varietal
whites (chardonnay, sauvignon,
tocai, ribolla, pinots grigio and
bianco) along with a tropically
fruity blend called "Sìum" (ver-
duzzo-picolit). Red blends include
natives such as tazzelenghe and
schioppettino.

LA VIS

TRENTINO; LAVIS (TN)
DOC(G)s: Trentino
A co-op known for a wide range of
well-priced wines, both white and
red. Check out the pinot grigio,
chardonnay, cabernet sauvignon, and
pinot nero from the "Ritratti" line.

LAGEDER
ALTO ADIGE; MAGRÈ/MARGREID (BZ)
DOC(G)s: Alto Adige-Südtirol; subzones Terlaner and St. Maddalena/Magdalener
From a spectacular spot in Magrè, the most southerly German-speaking village in Europe, Alois Lageder makes more than 30 different wines—the best being crisp, clean, perfumed whites from chardonnay, pinot bianco, and pinot grigio. Lageder is probably the biggest private producer in the Alto Adige, and a visit to the sleekly designed, eco-friendly winery (it is partially solar-powered) is recommended. The reds, especially the tarry "Lindenburg" lagrein and the cabernets from the Löwengang and Römigberg estates, are also well regarded.

LAMBRUSCHI, OTTAVIANO
LIGURIA; CASTELNUOVO MAGRA (SP)
DOC(G)s: Colli di Luni
This is considered the top spot in the Colli di Luni DOC, for whatever that's worth. Solid, savory whites from vermentino to drink cold with fritto misto.

LAMOLE & VILLA VISTARENNI
TOSCANA; GAIOLE IN CHIANTI (SI)
DOC(G)s: Chianti Classico
Owned by the Veneto-based Santa Margherita group, this winery is a good source of inexpensive, everyday Chiantis, most notably the Chianti Classico "Lamole di Lamole," so named for a sub-zone of Chianto Classico near Greve.

LANARI
MARCHE; ANCONA (AN)
DOC(G)s: Rosso Cònero
Rosso Cònero is typically thought of as soft, supple and fruity wine (which it is), but as the barrique-aged wines of Lanari demonstrate, it can also have depth and structure. His Rosso Cònero "Fibbio" in particular is an ultrarich red, loaded with black fruit flavor and framed by grainy tannins.

LE BOCCE
TOSCANA; PANZANO IN CHIANTI (FI)
DOC(G)s: Chianti Classico; Vin Santo
Good and affordable Chianti Classico—a lot of wine for the money.

LE CALCINAIE
TOSCANA; SAN GIMIGNANO (SI)
DOC(G)s: Vernaccia di San Gimignano; Chianti Colli Senesi
Noted wines include the Vernaccia di San Gimignano "Vigna ai Sassi" and the super-Tuscan red "Teodoro" (sangiovese-merlot).

LE CINCIOLE
TOSCANA; PANZANO IN CHIANTI (FI)
DOC(G)s: Chianti Classico
It's often said that Chianti Classicos from Panzano are among the more perfumed and elegant, thanks at least in part to the high elevations of the vineyards. Le Cinciole's wines are distinguished by their perfumy aromas of cherry and rose petals, and by their crisp acidity. Great food wines with pure sangiovese flavors.

LE CORTI-CORSINI
TOSCANA; SAN CASCIANO VAL DI PESA (FI)
DOC(G)s: Chianti Classico
Rich and full-bodied Chianti Classico, most with a touch of new oak aging.

LE DUE TERRE
FRIULI; PREPOTTO (UD)
DOC(G)s: Colli Orientali del Friuli
An artisan estate specializing in blends. The "Sacrissassi Bianco" is a tropical, fragrant blend of sauvignon, ribolla gialla, and tocai, while the "Sacrissassi Rosso"—definitely one of Friuli's more serious reds—combines refosco and schioppettino, aged in barrique. They are hard-to-find specialties that are well worth seeking out, including perhaps Italy's best pinot noir.

LE FILIGARE
TOSCANA; BARBERINO VAL D'ELSA (FI)
DOC(G)s: Chianti Classico
A winery with a long history of top-level Chianti Classico. Great consistency from vintage to vintage, both with the Chianti and with the super-Tuscan "Le Rocce" (sangiovese–cabernet sauvignon).

LE FONTI
TOSCANA; PANZANO IN CHIANTI (FI)
DOC(G)s: Chianti Classico
Limited-production Chianti (all of which is made as riserva) and a sangiovese-cabernet blend called "Fontissimo."

LE FRACCE
LOMBARDIA; CASTEGGIO (PV)
DOC(G)s: Oltrepò Pavese
A leading estate in the Oltrepò Pavese, a DOC near the border with Emilia-Romagna that is attracting more and more attention in the United States. Bonarda is a key grape here, and the Le Fracce "La Rubiosa" is a good example, along with the regular DOC bottling. Other highlights include spicy riesling renano (another Oltrepò Pavese specialty) and pinot grigio.

LE FRAGHE
VENETO; COLOMBARA (VR)
DOC(G)s: Bardolino; Valdadige
A small estate near Lake Garda that is considered one of the better producers of Bardolino. There are also some good varietal whites from garganega and chardonnay.

LE MACCHIOLE
TOSCANA; BOLGHERI (LI)
DOC(G)s: Bolgheri
One of the Bolgheri boutiques, producing a sought-after cabernet sauvignon called "Paleo," among other wines. The powerful "Scrio" syrah is another hot item, as is the "Messorio" merlot. High-end super-Tuscan reds (and whites) with price tags to match, they tend to sell out fast.

LE MACCHIONE
TOSCANA; MONTEPULCIANO (SI)
DOC(G)s: Vino Nobile di
    Montepulciano
An artisan producer of super-charged Vino Nobile di Montepulciano. Definitely worth looking around for.

LE MURELLE
TOSCANA; LUCCA (LU)
DOC(G)s: Colline Lucchese
Like most of its Lucca neighbors, this estate doesn't feel constrained by tradition and focuses on wines from international grapes—sauvignon, chardonnay and, most recently cabernet sauvignon (the "Niffo" bottling).

LE PUPILLE
TOSCANA; MAGLIANO IN TOSCANA
    (GR)
DOC(G)s: Morellino di Scansano
Husband-and-wife team Elisabetta Geppetti and Stefano Rizzi have brought some flash to Morellino di Scansano, producing some of the zone's slickest and most structured wines. The "Poggio Valente" Morellino di Scansano Riserva is a serious wine, as is the super-Tuscan "Saffredi," a blend of cabernet, merlot, and alicante (grenache). The base-level Morellino is a fantastic value to compete with the cheap, supple reds of Chile and California.

LE RAGOSE
VENETO; NEGRAR (VR)
DOC(G)s: Valpolicella; Amarone
    della Valpolicella; Recioto della
    Valpolicella; Garda
With grapes sourced from high-elevation vineyards, Le Ragose's Amarones tend to be lean and fine, more spicy and earthy than many of their more fruit-driven counterparts. Ditto for the estate's Valpolicellas, which are typically made in a more classical style. The "Le Sassine" Valpolicella is made in the ripasso method.

LE SALETTE
VENETO; FUMANE (VR)
DOC(G)s: Valpolicella; Amarone
    della Valpolicella; Recioto della
    Valpolicella
Good Valpolicella and some excellent, well-balanced Amarone, especially the "La Marega" bottling. Small production.

LE TRAME
TOSCANA; CASTELNUOVO
    BERARDEGNA (SI)
DOC(G)s: Chianti Classico
Winemaker Giovanna Morganti's father, Enzo, was the longtime director at the giant San Felice winery, right across from where Giovanna's small stand of vineyards now sits. A sangiovese purist, she makes a small amount of Chianti Classico that strikes a balance between modern ripeness and heft and traditional earthiness and aromatic complexity.

It is not typically exported to the States (although that may soon change), but it is worth seeking out on a tour of Chianti Classico. Among the best Chianti Classicos we tasted.

LE VELETTE
UMBRIA; ORVIETO (TR)
DOC(G)s: Orvieto Classico
Solid Orvieto whites, along with a handful of red blends. The highlight among the latter is the sangiovese-cabernet blend "Calanco." There's also a new varietal merlot called "Gaudio."

LE VIGNE DI ZAMÒ
FRIULI; MANZANO (UD)
DOC(G)s: Colli Orientali del Friuli
The Zamò family, with the help of consultant Franco Bernabei, make a wide variety of whites and reds from assorted vineyard holdings concentrated in Rosazzo. A specialty is tocai friulano (especially the single-vineyard "Vigne Cinquant' Anni"), but Zamò is also known for reds—the well-known "Ronco dei Roseti" (a Bordeaux blend) as well as the often great pignolo. A stylish, reliable winery.

LENTO
CALABRIA; LAMEZIA TERME (CZ)
DOC(G)s: Lamezia
Although hard to find in the States, this estate's wines are worth mentioning simply because they rank among the best in a region with slim pickings. Based on the west-central Calabrian coast, the winery's Lamezia DOC Rosso (from gaglioppo, nerello cappuccio, and other local grapes) is a soft and pleasant red. The "Federico II," from cabernet sauvignon, is solid, as is the cool and clean Lamezia Greco, one of the better Calabrian whites.

LEONE CONTI
EMILIA-ROMAGNA; FAENZA (RA)
DOC(G)s: Albana di Romagna;
  Sangiovese di Romagna; Colli di
  Faenza

Another top-level producer of San-giovese di Romagna, with two different bottlings: the "Poderepozzo Le Betulle" and the "Contiriserva." These are fruity, jammy sangiovese wines, complemented by the estate's range of sweet and dry whites from albana.

LEONE DE CASTRIS
PUGLIA; SALICE SALENTINO (LE)
DOC(G)s: Salice Salentino

The anchor of the Salice Salentino DOC and one of Puglia's pioneering private producers. The winery is best known for the spicy, deep "Five Roses" rosé, a great example of southern-Italian rosato and one of Italy's best-known brand names. The winery's Salice Salentinos (especially "Majana") are also worth a try.

LES CRÊTES
VALLE D'AOSTA; AYMAVILLES
  (AO)
DOC(G)s: Valle d'Aosta

Really the only commercial producer in the Valle d'Aosta whose wines can be found in any quantity in the States. Charismatic proprietor Constantino Charrère is best known for his flavorful chardonnays, especially the rich, barrel-fermented "Cuvée Bois." Perhaps more appealing, however, is the chardonnay "Cuvée Frissonière," which is only partially barrel-fermented. Also worth a try are the light red "Fumin," and the peppery, Rhône-like "Coteau Latour," a red made from 100% syrah.

LIBRANDI
CALABRIA; CIRO MARINA (KR)
DOC(G)s: Ciro

The leading winery in Calabria and the standard-bearer of Cirò, Calabria's best-known DOC. A large estate with multiple vineyard sites, it has been run by the Librandi family since the 1950s. Librandi's classic Cirò wines define the style: plush and berried, with crisp acidity and a touch of earthy spice. The newish "Gravello" plumps up the native gaglioppo grape with cabernet sauvignon, while the rich, shiraz-like "Magno Megonio" is a revival of an ancient variety called magliocco. Rosés and whites are all solid, too, as is the sweet "Le Passule."

LIS NERIS-PECORARI
FRIULI; SAN LORENZO (GO)
DOC(G)s: Friuli Isonzo

Alvaro Pecorari's Isonzo DOC wines (mostly whites) are arranged in three tiers: those made all in stainless steel and labeled simply with the grape name; those that include both a vineyard designation and a portion of barrel-fermented wine ("Gris" Pinot Grigio, "Picól" Sauvignon); and those that are 100% barrel-fermented, single-vineyard wines ("Dom Picól," Sauvignon Chardonnay "Sant'Jurosa"). The latter can be a little over-the-top; the midrange stuff strikes a better balance, and the all-steel wines are clean and correct. Excellent varietal whites.

LISINI
TOSCANA; MONTALCINO (SI)
DOC(G)s: Brunello di Montalcino

A simple, small, farmstead-style winery producing angular, aromatic Brunello di Montalcino (also Rosso, of course). Look especially for the single-vineyard "Ugolaia," which is

tightly wound in its youth but smooth and elegant with time.

LIVERNANO
TOSCANA; RADDA IN CHIANTI (SI)

Owned by Swiss dentist Carlo Montanari, this is one of the many small, modern estates that have popped up throughout Tuscany in recent years, well equipped and committed to making limited amounts of great wine (a parallel might be drawn to some of the boutique estates capturing all the press in California). Livernano's "Puro Sangue" (all sangiovese) and "Livernano Rosso" (cabernet-merlot-sangiovese) are undoubtedly stylish, smooth reds, ripe and clean and rounded out with new oak.

LIVÓN
FRIULI; SAN GIOVANNI AL
  NATISONE (UD)
DOC(G)s: Collio; Colli Orientali
  del Friuli

A relatively large Friulian estate with vineyard holdings in both Collio and Colli Orientali del Friuli. The best-known (and most acclaimed) white is "Braide Alte," a creamy, oak-tinged blend of chardonnay, sauvignon, picolit, and moscato giallo. In general, the Livón whites are superripe and often barrel-fermented to boot, as evidenced by the creamy "Braide Mate" Chardonnay and the "Valbuins" Sauvignon. There are some deep, funky reds, too, including Tiareblù (merlot-cabernet) and "Riul" Refosco.

LOACKER (SCHWARHOF SANTA GIUSTINA)
ALTO ADIGE; BOLZANO
DOC(G)s: Alto Adige

Characteristic of the Alto Adige, this family-owned estate produces a wide range of varietal wines, including pinot grigio, gewürztraminer, and lagrein. Rainer Loacker also owns the Corte Pavone estate in Montalcino, Tuscany.

LOI, ALBERTO
SARDEGNA; CARDEDU (NU)
DOC(G)s: Cannonau di Sardegna
Soft, earthy Cannonau di Sardegna DOC reds from the Barbagia region. A small producer with a tiny distribution in the States.

LONGARIVA
TRENTINO; ROVERETO (TN)
DOC(G)s: Trentino
One of Trentino's great artisan estates, though one that has yet to establish a presence in the States. Great varietal whites from pinot bianco, pinot grigio (especially the copper-colored "Graminé"), and chardonnay are complemented by classic Trentino reds such marzemino and cabernet sauvignon. There's also a pinot noir. Someone is going to import these wines at some point (if they aren't already), so keep an eye out.

LUCE DELLE VITE
TOSCANA; MONTALCINO (SI)
The Montalcino-based joint venture between Tuscany's Marchesi di Frescobaldi and California's Robert Mondavi winery. There's a soft, California-ish richness to the wines, both the top-of-the-line "Luce" and the more affordable "Lucente" (both are sangiovese-merlot blends)

LUNGAROTTI
UMBRIA; TORGIANO (PG)
DOC(G)s: Torgiano
When you think of Umbria, this estate is the first one to come to mind. The late Giorgio Lungarotti was the one who put Umbrian wines on the map, producing warm, long-aged sangioveses and sangiovese-cabernet blends long before the current wave of "super-Umbro" wines started showing up. The flagship Lungarotti wines are the Rubesco Riserva "Vigna Monticchio," a sangiovese-canaiolo blend aged a year in barrel and five years in bottle before release, and "San Giorgio," a sangiovese-cabernet blend that undergoes a similar aging regimen. This long bottle aging is somewhat unique and tends to set Lungarotti apart from today's superripe crowd: The Lungarotti wines tend to be more leathery, fine, and mature-tasting, with secondary aromas of earth and dried fruits lending the wines great complexity. The product line is way too extensive to list here: there are 20 wines and a handful of food products, including great olive oil.

LUPI
LIGURIA; PIEVE DI TECO (IM)
DOC(G)s: Riviera Ligure di Ponente
Western-Ligurian estate known for pigato, vermentino, and Rossese di Dolceacqua. Not available in the States at this writing.

MACHIAVELLI
TOSCANA; SAN CASCIANO VAL DI PESA (FI)
DOC(G)s: Chianti Classico
One of the estates owned by the Gruppo Italiano Vini (GIV), and one of the better ones at that. The Chianti Classico "Vigna di Fontalle Riserva" has long been a critics' favorite.

MACULAN
VENETO; BREGANZE (VI)
DOC(G)s: Breganze
Fausto Maculan literally put the Breganze DOC zone on the map, creating luscious whites and reds from the gentle hills north of Vicenza. Starting with the whites, his basic Breganze di Breganze (pinot bianco–tocai) is a fleshy and fragrant white, as is the newer "Pinot & Toi," made from the same varieties (he also makes several beefy chardonnays). Maculan's rich (and expensive) reds are headlined by the powerful cabernet sauvignon called "Ferrata." But the real stars are a trio of luscious late-harvest dessert wines: "Dindarello" (100% moscato); "Torcolato" (100% vespaiola); and "Acininobili" (vespaiola-garganega).

MADONIA, GIOVANNA
EMILIA-ROMAGNA; BERTINORO (FC)
DOC(G)s: Sangiovese di Romagna; Albana di Romagna Passito
At its best, Sangiovese di Romagna is a deeply fruity alternative to Chianti Classico, as exemplified by the range of sangioveses made at this estate. The best example is the smoky and rich Sangiovese di Romagna "Ombroso," a wine with all the power of a Riserva Chianti, but without the price tag. There's also a passito from albana and a chunky dry merlot called "Sterpigno," but "Ombroso" is the real find here.

MAFFINI, LUIGI
CAMPANIA; SAN MARCO DI CASTELLABATE (SA)
Along with Bruno DeConciliis, Luigi Maffini is drawing attention to the Cilento area of southern Campania. He's best known for a superripe take on the fiano grape called "Kràtos" and two red blends of aglianico and piedirosso— "Klèos" and "Cenito." Hard to find but worth the search.

MANZONE, GIOVANNI
PIEMONTE; MONFORTE D'ALBA (CN)
DOC(G)s: Barolo; Barbera d'Alba; Dolcetto d'Alba; Langhe

Sleek and concentrated Barolos from a little-known cru called Gramolere in the commune of Monforte. Manzone's small production includes the base "Gramolere" as well as the "Bricat Le Gramolere" (from a hilltop site) and a Barolo Riserva, made only in exceptional years. Barbera and dolcetto are also made, bearing the "La Serra" vineyard designation.

MARCARINI
PIEMONTE; LA MORRA (CN)
DOC(G)s: Barolo; Barbera d'Alba;
    Dolcetto d'Alba; Langhe
Smooth and refined Barolo from two of La Morra's classic cru sites, Brunate and La Serra, the latter typically very approachable as a young wine. There's also an especially good dolcetto, "Boschi di Berri," among the range of Langhe wines on offer.

MARCHESI ALFIERI
PIEMONTE; SAN MARTINO ALFIERI
    (AT)
DOC(G)s: Barbera d'Asti;
    Monferrato; Piemonte
A beautiful Baroque castle in which the San Germano family now makes a range of respectable Asti reds, notably barbera, the funky grignolino, and some pinot noir (used in the "San Germano" bottling).

MARCHESI DI BAROLO
PIEMONTE; BAROLO (CN)
DOC(G)s: Barolo; Barbera d'Alba;
    Dolcetto d'Alba; Moscato d'Asti
This is one of the Barolo zone's largest and most historic estates. Some believe it is the birthplace of the wine, which is said to have been first made here by the noble Falletti family in the nineteenth century. With upwards of 300,000 bottles a year in production—including six different cru Barolos from the commune of Barolo—this is a readily

available brand that offers consistent quality. A good introduction to classic Barolo.

MARCHESI DI GRESY
PIEMONTE; BARBARESCO (CN)
DOC(G)s: Barbaresco; Dolcetto
    d'Alba; Langhe; Moscato d'Asti
Made up of three estates in the Langhe and Monferrato hills, the Marchesi di Gresy home base is its Martinenga estate, which sits in a wide basin, surrounded by Barbaresco's famous Asili and Rabajà vineyards. Alberto di Gresy's powerful, tightly wound Barbarescos are sourced from the Martinenga, Gaiun-Martinenga, and Camp Gros–Martinenga vineyards. The latter is considered the top of a line that also includes Dolcetto d'Alba, a nice Langhe Chardonnay, and Moscato d'Asti from the estate's La Serra property. A consistent performer.

MARCHESI PANCRAZI (TENUTA DI BAGNOLO)
TOSCANA; MONTEMURLO (PO)
Marchese Vittorio Pancrazi's 15th-century estate west of Florence specializes in pinot noir, which is said to have been planted here by accident in the mid-'70s. Pancrazi's "Villa Bagnolo" was called the "best pinot noir in Italy" by one critic, but it won't make you forget Burgundy—or California, for that matter. Pancrazi also makes a rare varietal colorino (called "Casaglia").

MARCHETTI
MARCHE; ANCONA (AN)
DOC(G)s: Rosso Cònero;
    Verdicchio dei Castelli di Jesi
Small producer in the Ancona area specializing in Rosso Cònero.

MARENCO
PIEMONTE; STREVI (AL)
DOC(G)s: Brachetto d'Acqui;
    Barbera d'Asti; Dolcetto d'Acqui;
    Moscato d'Asti
Best known for dessert wines from the white moscato and red brachetto, this estate also makes some solid barberas and dolcettos. Good prices.

MARENGO, MARIO
PIEMONTE; LA MORRA (CN)
DOC(G)s: Barolo; Dolcetto d'Alba
Serious but very limited-production Barolo (about 5,000 bottles a year) from the Brunate cru in La Morra.

MARION
VENETO; SAN MARTINO BUON
    ALBERGO (VR)
DOC(G)s: Valpolicella
A newish estate run by Stefano Campedelli, with help from winemaking consultant Celestino Gaspari. The top wine at the moment is an unusually powerful Valpolicella, which might be more accurately described as a small-scale Amarone. Try it if you can find it.

MARTELLI & BUSDRAGHI
TOSCANA; SUVERETO (LI)
DOC(G)s: Val di Cornia
An up-and-coming southern-Tuscan producer headquartered in Suvereto, within the Val di Cornia DOC. They make a good, savory IGT vermentino called "Incontri" and two solid red blends, "Il Granato" (60% sangiovese, 40% merlot) and "Incontri" Val di Cornia DOC Rosso (cabernet-merlot-sangiovese).

MARTILDE
LOMBARDIA; ROVESCALA (PV)
DOC(G)s: Oltrepò Pavese
A creative winery with a wide array of products, the best of them rich and fruit-driven reds from bonarda

and barbera. They tend to hold their barberas in bottle for some time before release, lending a mature, leathery character to the otherwise sappy red fruit flavors. The same goes for the bonarda reds, of which the tarry, tobacco-scented "Zaffo" is probably the best example.

MARTINETTI, FRANCO M.
PIEMONTE; TORINO (TO)
DOC(G)s: Colli Tortonesi; Barbera d'Asti; Gavi; Monferrato
Franco Martinetti is sort of a contract winemaker, making a range of wines without actually having a winery of his own. His big-boned Barbera d'Asti "Montruc" is a perennial critical favorite, as is the Monferrato Rosso "Sul Bric" (barbera-cabernet). These are rich, barrique-aged reds of serious structure (and serious prices).

MASCARELLO, BARTOLO
PIEMONTE; BAROLO (CN)
DOC(G)s: Barolo; Barbera d'Alba; Dolcetto d'Alba
Bartolo Mascarello is a Barolo legend, a Yoda-like figure who dispenses wisdom and kindness to all who enter his humble cantina. His namesake wine is a paragon of old-school Barolo, unadorned by new oak and redolent not only of the nebbiolo grape but of the ground it grows in. This is Barolo at its most natural, a pure expression of ripe fruit from low-yielding vineyards, with no other bells or whistles attached. There's also evocative barbera and dolcetto to drink while you wait for Mascarello's perfumy yet powerful Barolos to mature.

MASCARELLO, GIUSEPPE E FIGLIO
PIEMONTE; MONCHIERO (CN)
DOC(G)s: Barolo; Barbera d'Alba; Dolcetto d'Alba; Langhe

Earthy, aromatic, more traditionally styled Barolo from a trusted producer. The product line here is varied, with the top-end Barolo "Monprivato" joined by several barberas, a dolcetto, and some freisa to boot.

MASCIARELLI
ABRUZZO; SAN MARTINO SULLA MARRUCINA (CH)
DOC(G)s: Montepulciano d'Abruzzo; Trebbiano d'Abruzzo
Unquestionably one of Abruzzo's top producers, Gianni Masciarelli makes rich, deeply extracted whites and reds. If you're looking for a great value, pick up the "Marina Cvetic" Montepulciano d'Abruzzo (named for Masciarelli's wife): deep, dark, and rich, with a touch of earthy complexity to complement the black berry fruit. More impressive (though more expensive) is the rare "Villa Gemma," another Montepulciano d'Abruzzo that completely defies the grape's image as a simple supermarket quaffer. Masciarelli also makes better-than-average Trebbiano d'Abruzzo and a plump, oaky chardonnay.

MASI AGRICOLA
VENETO; GARGANAGO DI VALPOLICELLA (VR)
DOC(G)s: Valpolicella Classico; Amarone della Valpolicella; Recioto della Valpolicella
Headed by the gregarious Sandro Boscaini, this is one of the Veneto's largest and most prestigious estates, known for a wide variety of whites and reds—and headlined by a range of deeply concentrated Amarones. Boscaini is a real ambassador for the Valpolicella zone (having taught more than a few American journalists everything they know about Amarone), and his single-vineyard "Mazzano" Amarone is among the

more powerful, complex, and age-worthy wines of its type. The Masi line also includes Valpolicella and Amarone made from grapes grown at the Serego Alighieri estate, a lavish Veronese villa still owned by descendants of the poet Dante. Check out the Valpolicella "Serego Alighieri" and the superrich "Vaio Armaron Serego Alighieri" Amarone. Another Masi gem is "Campofiorin," a ripasso-style Valpolicella that offers great value year in and year out.

MASO CANTANGHEL
TRENTINO; CIVEZZANO (TN)
DOC(G)s: Trentino
Known as much for its fantastic country restaurant as for its wines, this small winery has a range of well-made whites and reds. The "Vigna Piccola" Chardonnay and the "Rosso di Pila" Cabernet are highlights, although you may have to venture to Trento to find them.

MASO POLI
TRENTINO; SAN MICHELE ALL'ADIGE (TN)
DOC(G)s: Trentino; Sorni
A tiny estate headquartered within the Sorni subzone, on the steep slopes of San Michele all'Adige. Steely, fragrant whites are a specialty, including pinot grigio and a blend called "Costa Erta."

MASSA VECCHIA
TOSCANA; MASSA MARITTIMA (GR)
DOC(G)s: Monteregio di Massa Marittima
A south-Tuscan estate with a black and beautiful cabernet sauvignon called "La Fonte di Pietrarsa." Other wines include the odd "Le Veglie di Neri," a dessert red based on the rare aleatico grape.

MASSERIA PEPE
PUGLIA; MARUGGIO (TA)
DOC(G)s: Primitivo di Manduria
A small estate specializing in soft, juicy primitivo. Part of the Accademia dei Racemi group, its top wine is the Primitivo di Manduria "Dunico," a good example of the brambly cherry fruit and soft tannins of primitivo.

MASTROBERARDINO
CAMPANIA; ATRIPALDA (AV)
DOC(G)s: Fiano di Avellino; Lacryma Christi; Taurasi
Campania's best-known winery, a trailblazing estate that established the Taurasi DOCG as the "Barolo of the south." Mastroberardino's Taurasi "Radici" is still one of the most concentrated and complex Taurasis around, showcasing the black berry fruit and exotic spiciness of the aglianico grape. Flinty white Fiano di Avellino is another specialty, as are the classic Lacryma Christi (the name means "tears of Christ") wines that helped make Mastroberardino famous. In all, the estate makes a wide array of varietal reds and whites alongside its DOC offerings.

MASTROJANNI
TOSCANA; MONTALCINO (SI)
DOC(G)s: Brunello di Montalcino
Deeply flavorful, velvety Brunello di Montalcino at a fair price, Mastrojanni Brunello is typically accessible when young yet capable of long aging. Modern in style but not overblown, it's got everything you'd want in a Brunello while remaining affordable. Another great red from sangiovese master Maurizio Castelli.

MASUT DA RIVE
FRIULI; MARIANO DEL FRIULI (GO)
DOC(G)s: Friuli Isonzo

Wines from the Isonzo DOC are increasingly characterized by a weight of extract on the palate that isn't found as readily in the slightly cooler heights of Collio and Colli Orientali. Masut da Rive's Fabrizio Gallo illustrates this with plump, blowsy whites from chardonnay (especially the "Maurus") and pinot bianco, as well as some chunky reds.

MECELLA, ENZO
MARCHE; FABRIANO (AN)
DOC(G)s: Rosso Cònero; Verdicchio di Matelica
One of the deans of Marche winemaking, whose small estate features interesting handcrafted wines. Mecella employs barrique aging in many of his selections, including the Verdicchio di Matelica "Antico di Casa Fosca" and the Rosso Cònero "Rubelliano." Also notable is the red blend "Braccano," a brightly fruity mix of ciliegiolo and merlot. Not all of the wines are distributed in the States.

MEDICI, ERMETE & FIGLI
EMILIA-ROMAGNA; REGGIO EMILIA (RE)
DOC(G)s: Lambrusco Reggiano
Don't rule out Lambrusco until you've tasted the dry and detailed versions made here. Deeply fruity yet tangy and spicy, Medici's "Concerto" is a classic accompaniment to a plate of prosciutto di Parma or parmigiano. Don't be afraid: just try it. Medici also makes a delicate and delicious dry white from malvasia called "Daphne."

MELINI
TOSCANA; POGGIBONSI (SI)
DOC(G)s: Chianti Classico; Vernaccia di San Gimignano
A large estate that belongs to the Gruppo Italiani Vini (GIV). Some of the lower-priced bottlings are su-

permarket wines, but there are a few gems, namely the Chianti Classico Riserva "La Selvanella" (from a single vineyard) and the fragrant Vernaccia di San Gimignano "Le Grillaie." Consistent wines, good values.

MELONI VINI
SARDEGNA; SELARGIUS (CA)
DOC(G)s: Cannonau di Sardegna; Girò; Monica di Sardegna; Moscato di Cagliari; Vermentino di Sardegna
A large, privately owned estate outside of Cagliari, with a varied assortment of well-priced wines. Highlights include the Vermentino di Sardegna "Astice" and a range of light, smoky reds based on the monica grape.

MEZZOCORONA
TRENTINO; MEZZOCORONA (TN)
DOC(G)s: Trento Brut; Trentino; Teroldego Rotaliano
A huge Trentino cooperative known first and foremost for its sparkling wines, particularly those bearing the "Rotari" brand name. They are cheap and decent, perfect for weddings and what not, and are complemented by a range of white and red still wines: crisp and clean pinot grigio and chardonnay for the whites, teroldego and merlot for the reds.

MIANI
FRIULI; BUTTRIO (UD)
DOC(G)s: Colli Orientali del Friuli
A tiny farmhouse winery whose rich, decadent wines (especially whites) are cult favorites. Proprietor Enzo Pontoni is what you'd call a *garagiste*, making his full-bodied wines by hand (and then pricing them accordingly). His syrupy, peach-scented tocai friulano is held up as one of the best examples of a

wine from that grape. The "Miani Rosso," a blend of merlot, cabernet sauvignon, and tazzelenghe, is like liquid chocolate. Ditto for the varietal merlot. These are hard-to-find wines, but worth the search (keep your eyes peeled for more wines from the red refosco in the future).

MICELI
SICILIA; PALERMO (PA)
DOC(G)s: Alcamo; Passito di
  Pantelleria
The late Ignazio Miceli was a major force in promoting Sicilian wines abroad, and his eponymous wine-making company lives on, specializing in sweet wines from Pantelleria. Check out the slightly sparkling Garighe Zibbibo and the Passito di Pantelleria "Tanit."

MIONETTO
VENETO; VALDOBBIADENE (TV)
DOC(G)s: Prosecco di
  Valdobbiadene
A huge firm with a vast array of different sparkling and semi-sparkling wines available in the U.S. One of the best is a non-DOC sparkler from prosecco called Sergio MO, an exceptionally dry, fine, and well-structured take on the grape. Naturally, there are several different Prosecco di Valdobbiadene bottlings, as well as a top-end Cartizze, and a number of traditional wines made in the semi-sparkling frizzante style. One is an interesting, Lambrusco-like frizzante red made from marzemino. There are also some bargain-priced still wines.

MOCCAGATTA
PIEMONTE; BARBARESCO (CN)
DOC(G)s: Barbaresco; Barbera
  d'Alba; Dolcetto d'Alba; Langhe
Brothers Franco and Sergio Minuto are known for their rich, sleek Bar-

barescos from three different vine-yard holdings: the top-end "Vigneto Cole" (the rarest and most critically praised); the powerful "Basarin"; and the more accessible "Bric Balin." Their barbera from the Basarin vineyard is also a knockout. Modern Barbaresco at still-affordable prices.

MOLETTIERI, SALVATORE
CAMPANIA; MONTEMARANO (AV)
DOC(G)s: Taurasi
A small Taurasi producer, making small amounts of densely concentrated red. Ageworthy wines from high-altitude vineyards, highlighted by the Taurasi "Vigna Cinque Querce."

MOLINO, MAURO
PIEMONTE; LA MORRA (CN)
DOC(G)s: Barolo; Barbera d'Alba;
  Dolcetto d'Alba; Langhe
A new-generation Barolo producer whose luxurious "Vigna Conca" Barolo (from a south-facing cru in La Morra) is well worth the extra effort it will take to find it. Molino is part of a clique of relatively young Barolo makers whose wines are sleek, pricey, and produced in limited quantities—but the quality is undeniable. Ditto for the excellent Barbera d'Alba and Langhe Rosso DOC blend called "Acanzio" (nebbiolo-barbera).

MONCHIERO CARBONE
PIEMONTE; CANALE (CN)
DOC(G)s: Barbera d'Alba; Langhe;
  Roero
Another of Roero's better producers, making lush and modern wines. The Barbera d'Alba "MonBirone" is a rich and oaky red, as is the Roero Rosso "Srü." Check out the white from arneis as well.

MONSANTO
TOSCANA; BARBERINO VAL D'ELSA
  (FI)
DOC(G)s: Chianti Classico
Earthy, aromatic, classic Chianti from one of the historic estates in the region. The Riserva Chianti Classico "Il Poggio" is noteworthy, while the super-Tuscans "Tinscvil" (sangiovese-cabernet) and "Nemo" (all cabernet) are decent.

MONTE, PAOLO
PIEMONTE; DIANO D'ALBA (CN)
DOC(G)s: Diano d'Alba
Good reds from the little-used Diano d'Alba DOC.

MONTEVERTINE
TOSCANA; RADDA IN CHIANTI (SI)
Sergio Manetti's "Le Pergole Torte," a sangiovese, is a cult favorite—not only for its evocative aromas and long aging potential, but for its arty labels that change with each vintage. This is one of the classic super-Tuscan wines (it is said to be the first barrique-aged pure sangiovese ever made), and is tightly allocated. A collector's wine.

MONTEVETRANO
CAMPANIA; SAN CIPRIANO PIA-
  CENTINO (SA)
Photographer Silvia Imparato's hobby estate near Salerno has been a darling of the wine media since its inception in the mid-'90s. This is thanks in part to the fame of consulting enologist Riccardo Cotarella, but owes primarily to the intense flavors of the estate's sole wine, "Montevetrano." This blend of aglianico, merlot, and cabernet sauvignon is one of those small-production cult wines that wine collectors scramble to acquire, but not without good reason: It is definitely luscious stuff.

MONTI

PIEMONTE; MONFORTE D'ALBA
(CN)

DOC(G)s: Barbera d'Alba; Langhe

A small estate specializing in barbera, although Barolos are said to be
in the works.

MONTORI, CAMILLO

ABRUZZO; CONTROGUERRA (TE)

DOC(G)s: Controguerra;
Montepulciano d'Abruzzo;
Trebbiano d'Abruzzo

Among the elite montepulciano
producers in Abruzzo, headquartered within the new Controguerra
DOC. Montori's "Fonte Cupa"
Montepulciano d'Abruzzo is a
benchmark, and the montepulciano-
cabernet blend "Leneo d'Oro" (a
Controguerra DOC wine) is chunky
and slick. Good and cheap.

MONTRESOR

VENETO; VERONA (VR)

DOC(G)s: Bianco di Custoza;
Lugana; Soave; Valpolicella;
Amarone della Valpolicella

A large Veronese wine house producing the full range of Verona
whites and reds. Inexpensive store
brands.

MORGANTE

SICILIA; GROTTE (AG)

With the help of consultant Riccardo Cotarella, the Morgante family turns out two slick, barrel-aged
nero d'avola wines, one aged four
months in new barriques, the other
for a year. Both show off the luscious black fruit of the variety,
though for some the sweetness from
the new wood may be a bit much.

MORGASSI SUPERIORE

PIEMONTE; GAVI (AL)

DOC(G)s: Gavi

Founded in 1990, this creative-
minded estate isn't content to pro-

duce just simple Gavi. There are also
some stylish reds from syrah
("Tamino") and cabernet/barbera
("Sarastro").

MORI, GIACOMO

TOSCANA; SAN CASCIANO DEI
BAGNI (SI)

DOC(G)s: Chianti

A hidden gem; good Chianti at fair
prices. The "Castelrotto" is aged in
barrique, lending it extra weight.
Warm, fruity reds with cool labels
to boot.

MORIS FARMS

TOSCANA; MASSA MARITTIMA
(GR)

DOC(G)s: Morellino di Scansano

Moris Farms was making Morellino
di Scansano well before it got
trendy, but even with all the big Tuscan names rushing to the Maremma,
the Moris wines still hold up. The
soft and juicy Morellino is a great
value for everyday, and the "Av-
voltore" (sangiovese-cabernet-syrah)
is a knockout.

MORMORAIA

TOSCANA; SAN GIMIGNANO (SI)

DOC(G)s: Vernaccia di San
Gimignano

As with some of his neighbors in
San Gimignano, Mormoraia proprietor Giuseppe Passoni is focusing as
much attention on slick super-
Tuscan reds as on traditional Vernaccia di San Gimignano. While he's
got an excellent version of the latter,
along with the white blend "Ostria
Grigia" (vernaccia-chardonnay),
there's also "Neitea," a red blend of
sangiovese and cabernet.

MORODER, ALESSANDRO

MARCHE; ANCONA (AN)

DOC(G)s: Rosso Cònero

One of the biggest names in Marche
wine, and with good reason: The

Moroder Rosso Còneros are sappy
and rich, and toasty from their time
in new oak. The top wine is
"Dorico," a "selection" as opposed
to a single-vineyard wine. Dark and
brooding, it also has the benefit of
being readily available and reasonably priced.

MOVIA

SLOVENIA

Dobrove, Slovenia

Founded in 1820, Movia anchors
the Slovenian side of the historic
Collio wine zone, which was divided
when new national borders where
drawn after the Second World War.
Thanks to friends in high places—
namely Marshall Tito, who was a
fan—the property remained in family hands even when Communist Yu-
goslavia otherwise nationalized the
industry. Winemaker Ales Kristancic
is both French- and Italian-trained,
his calling card being complex, oak-
aged white wines. Kristancic's style
is to leave his wines long enough in
barriques so that the oak flavors in
the wine actually recede. Whether
it's a chardonnay, the native rebula
(ribolla), or a blend, Movia's whites
show how oak can be used as a tool,
rather than a weapon. Ditto for the
reds.

MURANA

SICILIA; PANTELLERIA (TP)

DOC(G)s: Moscato di Pantelleria;
Passito di Pantelleria

Farmer and local fireman Salvatore
Murana cultivates not just zibibbo
for his passito wines but also capers,
tomatoes, and olives in the volcanic
soils of Pantelleria. Murana makes
both a Moscato di Pantelleria,
which incorporates zibibbo dried
for short periods, and two bottlings
of Passito di Pantelleria, which not
only utilize more deeply concen-

trated fruit but also see a year's aging in oak barrels.

MURI-GRIES, CANTINE CONVENTO
Alto Adige; Bolzano (BZ)
DOC(G)s: Alto Adige
A Benedictine monastery that is one of the better-regarded producers of lagrein, a dark, plush, and spicy red when vinified with care. The Muri-Gries lagreins are full of black berry fruit and aromatic notes of cigar box and tar, undeniably unique. A handful of varietal whites round out the abbey's product line, along with a rosato lagrein.

MUSSO, WALTER
Piemonte; Barbaresco (CN)
DOC(G)s: Barbaresco; Barbera d'Alba; Dolcetto d'Alba; Langhe
Great-value Albese wines, especially the Barbaresco "Rio Sordo," which is a lot of wine for the money. Other wines include barbera, dolcetto, and chardonnay, all very reasonably priced.

NERVI
Piemonte; Gattinara (VC)
DOC(G)s: Gattinara
A historic property, founded at the beginning of the century, and the home of some rich and complex reds from nebbiolo. Try Nervi's "Vigneto Molsino" Gattinara DOC alongside a good Barolo wine for a look at how nebbiolo expresses itself in different environments. Nervi wines are relative bargains and they're known to age well.

NIEDRIST, IGNAZ
Alto Adige;
    Cornaiano/Girlan (BZ)
DOC(G)s: Alto Adige
A small, widely admired artisan producer known for his spicy, assertively aromatic riesling. He also

experiments considerably with reds, the best results coming with pinot noir. Very little, if any, distribution in the States.

NINO FRANCO
Veneto; Valdobbiadene (TV)
DOC(G)s: Prosecco di Valdobbiadene
The prosecco wines made by Primo Franco are among the best available. Unlike the general mass of light, sweetish sparklers in Valdobbiadene, wines such as Franco's "Rustico" and "Primo Franco" are more firmly structured and full-bodied, with an appealing minerality and acidity. Great for aperitifs.

NINO NEGRI
Lombardia; Chiuro (SO)
DOC(G)s: Valtellina Superiore, Valtellina Sforsato, Valtellina Superiore Grumello, Sassella & Inferno
Founded in 1897 by innkeeper Nino Negri, this mountain winery is one of the oldest commercial estates in Italy. Run for the last 30 years by inscrutable enologist Casimiro Maule, Negri anchors the wine scene in the Valtellina. The winery's range is based almost entirely on nebbiolo (or chiavennasca, as it is called here), highlighted by the rich, complex "Sfursat 5 Stelle," aged 16 months in barrique and another 6 months in bottle. For other examples of nebbiolo from this extreme northern latitude, check out Negri's cru wines: Sassella "La Tense," Grumello "Vigna Sassorosso," and the Inferno "Mazér." This is nebbiolo at its most perfumed, every bit as complex as Barolo, if a little less powerful.

NOZZOLE
Toscana; Firenze (FI)
DOC(G)s: Chianti Classico
Serviceable Chianti from a property once controlled by Ruffino and now run by Ambrogio and Alberto Folonari, who recently acquired Nozzole, Cabreo, and other properties in a separation of family holdings. See also Ruffino.

OASI DEGLI ANGELI
Marche; Cupra Marittima (AP)
A trendy boutique estate on the south coast of the Marche, with a couple of super-Marchigiano wines that have attracted a good amount of hype. To their credit, they focus on the local montepulciano grape in their star wine, "Kurni," a purple-black monster with fruit and power to spare. It is luscious, to be sure, one of those supple yet potent reds that would make a great short-term ager (maybe two to three years).

OBERTO, ANDREA
Piemonte; La Morra (CN)
DOC(G)s: Barolo; Barbera d'Alba; Dolcetto d'Alba; Langhe
A lesser-known gem whose Barolo "Vigneto Rocche," among other wines, can stand alongside wines that cost three times as much. From Barolo to barbera to dolcetto, everything is well made and well priced.

OCONE
Campania; Ponte (BN)
DOC(G)s: Sannio; Solopaca; Taburno
In the shadow of Monte Taburno (1400 m), Domenico Ocone continues a 90-year family tradition of winemaking in the Sannio hills east of Benevento. His spicy, high-acid whites from falanghina, greco, and coda di volpe (check out the white "VinGiocondo" blend) are best for

aperitifs or light seafood dishes. The aglianico-based reds are solid, both savory and fruity, distinguished by hints of tobacco on the nose and palate.

ODDERO, F.ILLI
Piemonte; La Morra (CN)
DOC(G)s: Barolo; Barbaresco; Dolcetto d'Alba; Langhe
A winery with a long history in the region, and one of the largest producers at that, turning out upwards of 150,000 bottles per year. Top wines include the Barolo "Vigna Rionda" and a rustic cabernet sauvignon called "Furestè."

ODDERO, MASSIMO
Piemonte; Diano d'Alba (CN)
DOC(G)s: Barolo; Barbaresco; Diano d'Alba; Gavi
Located due south of Alba in Diano d'Alba—essentially wedged between the Barolo and Barbaresco DOCs, this small property makes both Barolo and Barbaresco along with dolcetto, barbera, some Gavi, and a warm and fruity red blend called "Rosso del Notaia" (nebbiolo-barbera-cabernet).

ODOARDI
Calabria; Nocera Terinese (CZ)
DOC(G)s: Scavigna; Savuto Superiore
Odoardi's high-altitude coastal vineyards southwest of Cosenza turn out two monster barrique-aged reds, "Vigna Garrone" (Scavigna DOC; blend of aglianico, cabernet, and merlot) and "Vigna Mortilla" (Savuto DOC; blend of gaglioppo, nerello, sangiovese, and others). The sweet zibbibo "Valeo" is as honeyed and rich as passito wines come. A top Calabrian property, newly available in the States.

ORLANDI CONTUCCI PONNO
Abruzzo; Roseto degli Abruzzi (TE)
DOC(G)s: Montepulciano d'Abruzzo; Trebbiano d'Abruzzo
A winery right on the cusp of entering the American market at this writing. Young Marina Orlandi Contucci, with the help of consultant Donato Lanati, flanks her more traditional Abruzzese wines (Trebbiano/Montepulciano d'Abruzzo) with some international bottlings, particularly a dark and luscious cabernet-based blend called "Liburnio." The all-cabernet "Colle Funaro" is also noteworthy. Moderate pricing.

ORNELLAIA
Toscana; Bolgheri (LI)
DOC(G)s: Bolgheri
Founded by Marchese Lodovico Antinori (raffish brother of Antinori's Piero) in the early 1980s, this is one of the great super-Tuscan estates. On a plot not far from the famed Sassicaia estate (run by his uncle, the late Marchese Mario Incisa della Rocchetta), Lodovico planted cabernet sauvignon, merlot, and later sauvignon, believing the maritime hills of Bolgheri were similar to those of Bordeaux. "Ornellaia," a cabernet-merlot blend, debuted with the great 1985 vintage, and has become an auction-house staple. Since most of the wine is snapped up by collectors before it hits the docks, expect to pay up for it. More affordable are the second red, "Le Volte" (sangiovese–cabernet sauvignon) and the excellent "Poggio alle Gazze" sauvignon blanc. In 2000, California's Mondavi winery bought an interest in this landmark estate, though no new wines were in the offing at this writing.

ORSOLANI
Piemonte; San Giorgio Canavese (TO)
DOC(G)s: Erbaluce di Caluso; Caluso Passito
Looking for something different? The steely, acidic erbaluce grape is the focus of this northern-Piedmont estate, which turns it into a fragrant and fine dry white, a nervous and surprising sparkler, and a luscious-yet-refreshing sweet wine. The Caluso Passito "Sulé," made sweet by drying the grapes on straw mats, is a highlight—its spicy, nutty, resiny sweetness is cleaned up nicely by the refreshing natural acidity of the erbaluce variety. But don't miss the Champagne-method "Cuvée Storica" and dry white "Vignot S. Antonio."

PACENTI, SIRO
Toscana; Montalcino (SI)
DOC(G)s: Brunello di Montalcino
A very small property run by young winemaker Giancarlo Pacenti, whose dense and succulent Brunellos are made in an oak-kissed modern style. Rare and pricey, but undeniably delicious.

PAITIN
Piemonte; Neive (CN)
DOC(G)s: Barbaresco; Barbera d'Alba; Dolcetto d'Alba; Langhe
Named for one of the great cru vineyards of the Barbaresco zone, this well-established family winery is definitely one to seek out. The "Sorì Paitin" Barbaresco is a muscular red that will reward long aging; the Dolcetto d'Alba "Sorì Paitin" and Barbera d'Alba "Serra Boella" are there to drink while you wait. Prices are not too bad.

PALARI

SICILIA; SAN STEFANO BRIGA (ME)

DOC(G)s: Faro

Sicily's Faro DOC is named for a lighthouse that overlooks the Straits of Messina. There's lots of wine history in this area, but by the mid-1980s Faro was nearly extinct as a source of commercial wine—until local architect Salvatore Geraci revived production in his grandfather's vineyards in Santo Stefano Briga. These gnarled old vines produce obscure local varieties such as nerello mascalese and cappuccio, which Geraci and consultant Donato Lanati make into earthy, spicy, complex wines that have invited comparisons to Châteauneuf-du-Pape and even Burgundy. Palari's concept is simple: a first (Faro DOC) and second wine ("Rosso del Soprano"), produced from different selections of the same grapes.

PALAZZONE

UMBRIA; ORVIETO (TR)

DOC(G)s: Orvieto Classico

Another Orvieto estate that has focused as much (if not more) attention on red wines from international varieties. The estate's "Armaleo" is a barrique-aged blend of cabernets sauvignon and franc, a rich and savory red that has consistently wowed the wine press (for whatever that's worth). Another noteworthy wine is the sweet "Muffa Nobile," a late-harvested sauvignon made in the grand tradition of Orvieto sweet wines. Among the Orvietos, check out the "Campo del Guardiano."

PALOMBO, GIOVANNI

LAZIO; ATINA (FR)

DOC(G)s: Atina

Going it somewhat alone in the village of Atina near Frosinone, Giovanni Palombo has attracted considerable attention for his well-made whites and reds that look to Bordeaux for inspiration. The white blend "Somiglio" (sauvignon-sémillon) is aromatic and creamy, a luscious white, while the cabernet sauvignon-based "Duca Cantelmi" is one of Lazio's deepest and best reds. A winery to watch.

PANIZZI, GIOVANNI

TOSCANA; SAN GIMIGNANO (SI)

DOC(G)s: Vernaccia di San Gimignano

If the wine critics are to be believed, this is the heavy hitter in San Gimignano, boasting a reserve-level vernaccia with both fruit intensity and oaky accents to spare. Even at the high end, the prices are very fair.

PARUSSO, ARMANDO

PIEMONTE; MONFORTE D'ALBA (CN)

DOC(G)s: Barolo; Barbera d'Alba; Dolcetto d'Alba; Langhe

Current chief Marco Parusso took over this family property in the mid-eighties, and is typically mentioned along with modern-thinking producers such as Enrico Scavino, Domenico Clerico, and Luciano Sandrone. The Parusso wines have all the hallmarks of new-generation Piedmont wines: forward fruit (and lots of it), a certain slickness, and softness imparted by new oak. In a word, density. The standard Langhe lineup is offered, from Dolcetto and Barbera to cru Barolo ("Vigna Munie" is considered the top).

PASQUA

VENETO; VERONA (VR)

DOC(G)s: Soave; Valpolicella; Amarone della Valpolicella

Another huge wine house in Verona. Soave is a specialty, and other notable wines include the Valpolicella "Vigneti di Casterna" and the Amarone "Cecilia Baretta."

PATERNOSTER

BASILICATA; BARILE (PZ)

DOC(G)s: Aglianico del Vulture

A landmark southern-Italian cantina. Headquartered in Barile, at the foot of Monte Vulture, the winery's base-level Aglianico del Vulture is rosy and spicy, while the rarer "Rotondo" (a single-vineyard Aglianico that debuted with the '97 vintage) and "Don Anselmo" (the best Aglianicos from the estate) are powerful wines that merit some aging—if you can find them.

PECCHENINO, F.ILLI

PIEMONTE; DOGLIANI (CN)

DOC(G)s: Dolcetto di Dogliani; Langhe

Intense and inky wines from dolcetto are a Dogliani specialty, as evidenced by the product line at this family farm. The Dolcetto di Dogliani "Sirì d'Jermu" is one of a number of wines the Pecchenino brothers craft from the variety, all of them mouth-coating reds that can (and should) be cracked open right away.

PECORARI, PIERPAOLO

FRIULI; SAN LORENZO ISONTINO (GO)

Pierpaolo Pecorari shuns DOC in favor of the Venezia-Giulia IGT, enabling him to source grapes from all over for his large production. The wide range of varietal whites are consistent from vintage to vintage and varietally correct. Good wines to buy by the case for parties.

PELISSERO

PIEMONTE; TREISO (CN)

DOC(G)s: Barbaresco; Barbera d'Alba; Dolcetto d'Alba; Langhe

Yet another example of how much

good wine there is to be found in the Langhe. This medium-size property is best known for the critically acclaimed Barbaresco "Vanotu," but just about everything they make has plenty of muscle: try the Barbera d'Alba "I Piani" and the Dolcetto "Augenta" if your budget doesn't permit springing for the Barbarescos.

PELLEGRINO
Sicilia; Marsala (TP)
DOC(G)s: Alcamo; Marsala; Moscato di Pantelleria; Passito di Pantelleria

Among the best-known (and best-regarded) Marsala houses, and a producer of a wide range of other wines, most notably Passito di Pantelleria, of which Pellegrino turns out a luscious and well-priced version.

PEPE, EMIDIO
Abruzzo; Torano Nuovo (TE)
DOC(G)s: Montepulciano d'Abruzzo

A cult classic. This tiny cantina is known to its small but devoted group of followers as a source of rustic, handcrafted reds from montepulciano. Emidio Pepe and family make Montepulciano d'Abruzzo in an earthy, complex style (they still crush grapes by foot), and the wines are known to age well. These are old-fashioned, exotic reds that are worth a try if you come across them on a restaurant list. They're not cheap, by the way.

PERTIMALI (LIVIO SASSETTI)
Toscana; Montalcino (SI)
DOC(G)s: Brunello di Montalcino

Smoky and rich Brunello and and especially full-bodied Rosso di Montalcino.

PERTINACE, VIGNAIOLI ELVIO
Piemonte; Treiso (CN)
DOC(G)s: Barbaresco; Barbera d'Asti; Dolcetto d'Alba; Langhe

A cooperative winery drawing grapes from more than a dozen member-growers. The principal wines are Barbarescos, made from an assortment of vineyard sites. The "Nervo," from a south-facing slope, is probably the biggest and broadest of the bunch, but on the whole these wines are marked by finesse. The Langhe Rosso "Pertinace" (nebbiolo-barbera-cabernet) is a spicy, silky red—a good buy.

PERVINI
Puglia; Manduria (TA)
DOC(G)s: Primitivo di Manduria

A characteristically huge Puglian winery run by Gregorio and Fabrizio Perrucchi, who use it as their home base for their Accademia dei Racemi, a consortium that consults to and helps market wines from a variety of smaller Puglian estates. Pervini is best known for soft and savory Primitivo di Manduria, particularly "Archidamo," an archetypal primitivo. The tarry "Bizantino Rosso" is a blend of primitivo and negroamaro. Both are great everyday reds, ready to go on release.

PETROLO
Toscana; Mercatale Valdarno (AR)

Young proprietor Luca Sanjust makes varietal sangiovese, merlot, and blends from a property located outside of the Chianti Classico zone to the east. He prefers the rich, sappy international style, best exemplified by his top wine, the black-as-night "Galatrona" merlot. There's also the full-bodied "Torrione" sangiovese, itself no wimp. But the most interesting wine may be the more savory, soft, yet affordable "Terre di Galatrona" (sangiovese-merlot). A good boutique producer.

PETRUCCO
Friuli; Buttrio (UD)
DOC(G)s: Colli Orientali del Friuli

A small family winery with the full complement of Friulian varietal wines, among them an exceptional ribolla gialla, fine sauvignon, and good tocai and pinot grigio. Reds include a single-vineyard merlot called "Vigna del Balbo."

PIAN DELLE VIGNE
Toscana; Montalcino (SI)
DOC(G)s: Brunello di Montalcino

The Montalcino estate acquired in 1993 by the Antinori wine house. The few vintages that have been released show plenty of promise.

PIANCORNELLO
Toscana; Montalcino (SI)
DOC(G)s: Brunello di Montalcino

Tiny property south of Montalcino with some good Brunello and Rosso, along with an inexpensive red blend called "Poggio dei Lecci."

PIEROPAN, LEONILDO
Veneto; Soave (VR)
DOC(G)s: Soave; Recioto di Soave

A lot of people think of Soave is little more than yellow water, but then they try the floral, elegant Soaves of Leonildo Pieropan and are converted. It's almost a rite of passage: taste Pieropan's single-vineyard wines (the "Vigneto Calvarino" and the top-of-the-line, 100% garganega "La Rocca") and suddenly "Soave" is no longer a dirty word. A true artisan producer with some luscious recioto wines as well.

PIETRAFITTA
Toscana; San Gimignano (SI)
DOC(G)s: Vernaccia di San Gimignano; Vin Santo

Long-established San Gimignano estate with a variety of different vernaccias, some of them barrel-fermented (like the "Vigna La Costa" Riserva) to lend them more heft.

PIEVE DEL VESCOVO
Umbria; Corciano (PG)
DOC(G)s: Colli del Trasimeno
An American-owned estate near Lake Trasimeno, with consultant Riccardo Cotarella on hand to help with the winemaking. In typical Colli di Trasimeno fashion, the wines are funky blends: "Luccaio" is a warm and inviting blend of merlot, cabernet sauvignon, gamay, ciliegiolo, and canaiolo, aged in barrique. The "Etesiasco" Bianco is a similar soup, incorporating trebbiano, chardonnay, grechetto, and other varieties.

PIEVE SANTA RESTITUTA
Toscana; Montalcino (SI)
DOC(G)s: Brunello di Montalcino
Piedmont's Angelo Gaja is the man behind this recently established estate.

PIGHIN, F.ILLI
Friuli; Pavia di Udine (UD)
DOC(G)s: Friuli Grave; Collio
A large estate with holdings in both the Grave and Collio DOCs. There are some decent wines in the bunch, and the Grave wines are bargains.

PIO CESARE
Piemonte; Alba (CN)
DOC(G)s: Barolo; Barbaresco; Langhe; Nebbiolo d'Alba; Barbera d'Alba; Dolcetto d'Alba
One of the larger and more historic Barolo houses, having diversified into Barbaresco and various other DOC and non-DOC whites and reds. Current proprietor Pio Boffa owns a variety of choice vineyard

sites, including "Ornato" near Serralunga d'Alba, the source of his plush and powerful Barolo "Ornato." His Barbaresco "Il Bricco" is another single-vineyard gem. The base-level wines—from Barolo and Barbaresco to Barbera d'Alba and Dolcetto d'Alba—are all textbook examples of their respective appellations.

PIOVENE PORTO GODI, CONTE ALESSANDRO
Veneto; Villaga (VI)
DOC(G)s: Colli Berici
Located between Verona and Vicenza in the little-known Colli Berici DOC, whose volcanic soils have proved hospitable to Bordeaux varieties such as cabernet sauvignon and sauvignon blanc. Porto Godi makes good examples of both, along with some tangy merlot and a range of other local whites. A winery on the rise.

PIRA
Piemonte; Dogliani (CN)
DOC(G)s: Barbera d'Alba; Dolcetto di Dogliani; Langhe
Another of Dogliani's dolcetto specialists. Good barbera, too.

PIRA & FIGLI (CHIARA BOSCHIS)
Piemonte; Barolo (CN)
DOC(G)s: Barolo
A small and historic estate that faded with the death of proprietor Luigi Pira in 1980, but was brought back to prominence by the Boschis family, owners of Borgogno, who acquired it outright in 1990. In contrast to the more traditional wines of Borgogno, the current Pira wines are fruit-forward and pumped up with new oak. Check out the acclaimed Barolo "Cannubi," if you can find it.

PIRA, LUIGI
Piemonte; Serralunga d'Alba (CN)
DOC(G)s: Barolo; Dolcetto d'Alba
Yet another Pira, this one situated in Serralunga, where the Marenca and Margheria vineyards produce round, big-boned Barolos given extra muscle from new oak. Limited production.

PLANETA
Sicilia; Menfi/Sambuca di Sicilia (AG)
DOC(G)s: Cerasuolo di Vittoria
Planeta wines debuted in 1995 and quickly joined Italy's elite. Diego Planeta, the longtime head of the large Settesoli co-op in Menfi, is the not-so-invisible hand behind his family's private estate, which is run by his daughter, Francesca, and nephew, Alessio (with enologist Carlo Corino). Full-bodied, tropically fruited whites (especially the popular chardonnay) and rich, international reds the specialties. Check out the Merlot and the "Santa Cecilia," the latter combining nero d'avola with syrah.

PLIGER, PETER
See Kuen Hof.

PLOZNER
Friuli; Spilimbergo (PN)
DOC(G)s: Friuli Grave
A large producer of Grave DOC wines. Solid and consistent varietal whites (and a few reds) priced right for weddings or parties. The wines are always clean and correct, and often surprisingly flavorful for the price.

PODERE CAPACCIA
Toscana; Radda in Chianti (SI)
DOC(G)s: Chianti Classico
A longtime favorite of the critics, the "Querciagrande" Sangiovese is

this estate's top wine, followed closely by some savory and complex Chianti Classico.

PODERE IL PALAZZINO
Toscana; Gaiole in Chianti (SI)
DOC(G)s: Chianti Classico
Consistently good Chianti Classico that shows off the smoky, spicy side of sangiovese, as opposed to the increasingly popular fruit-bomb side. Try the "Grosso Sanese" Riserva.

PODERE LANCIOLA II
Toscana; Impruneta (FI)
DOC(G)s: Chianti Classico; Chianti Colli Fiorentini
An estate just outside of Florence with some decent wines, notably the sangiovese–cabernet sauvignon blend "Terricci." The Chianti Classico "Le Masse di Greve" is also notable.

PODERE POGGIO SCALETTE
Toscana; Greve in Chianti (FI)
Owned by veteran Tuscan winemaking consultant Vittorio Fiore, this small property makes a limited-production varietal sangiovese called "Il Carbonaione." A little overhyped, but good.

PODERI COLLA
Piemonte; Alba (CN)
DOC(G)s: Barolo; Barbaresco; Langhe; Nebbiolo d'Alba; Dolcetto d'Alba; Barbera d'Alba
A large estate with a variety of vineyards throughout the Langhe, including the "Dardi Le Rose" cru in Monforte d'Alba (source of a solid Barolo of the same name) and the "Tenuta Roncaglia" in Barbaresco. Another highlight among the Colla reds is "Bricco del Drago," a soft and accessible mix of dolcetto and nebbiolo that was one of the first super-Langhe blends on the market.

POGGERINO
Toscana; Radda in Chianti (SI)
DOC(G)s: Chianti Classico
A gem. Located just down the street from the famed Montevertine property, Piero Lanza's tiny farmhouse winery quietly turns out powerful Chianti Classico. Whether it's a basic *annata* or the potent Riserva "Bugialla," Lanza goes for dense concentration in his sangiovese. His wines are typically aged not in barriques but in larger *tonneaux*, and not all of them are new; rather than craft a sweet, oaky confection, he makes wine that is both rustic and slick at the same time. Pricey but worth it.

POGGIO AL SOLE
Toscana; Tavarnelle Val di Pesa (FI)
DOC(G)s: Chianti Classico
Well-regarded Chianti Classico, especially the dense "Casasilia" Riserva, along with a varietal syrah and a cabernet-merlot blend called "Seraselva."

POGGIO ANTICO
Toscana; Montalcino (SI)
DOC(G)s: Brunello di Montalcino
One of the leading estates of Montalcino, producing earthy, complex wines. There's also a great restaurant on-site.

POGGIO SALVI
Toscana; Sovicille (SI)
DOC(G)s: Chianti Colli Senesi; Vin Santo
Among other things, the wines of this estate are great values. The Chianti Colli Senesi is a warm, round red for everyday, but the real find is the Vin Santo, which might bring to mind a fine Sherry with its crisp acidity and almondy flavor.

POJER & SANDRI
Trentino; Faedo (TN)
DOC(G)s: Trentino
Probably the best known (and best regarded) of Trentino's wineries. Located in the heights of Faedo, this winery/distillery produces a wide range of fragrant whites, crisp sparklers, delicate reds, and smooth grappas. Check out the whites first, particularly those based on the exotic local varieties: müller-thurgau, nosiola, and traminer. They are typically nervous and perfumed, great whites for dishes laced with mountain herbs. Also worth a try is the fruit-bomb late-harvest white called "Essenzia."

POLENCIC, ISIDORO
Friuli; Cormons (GO)
DOC(G)s: Collio
Yet another Collio producer known for consistent quality, be it a tocai, pinot bianco, or pinot grigio, among others.

POLIZIANO
Toscana; Montepulciano (SI)
DOC(G)s: Vino Nobile di Montepulciano; Morellino di Scansano
Originally founded in 1961 and focused on inexpensive Chianti Colli Senesi wines, this estate took a new tack when Federico Carletti took over from his father in 1980, fresh out of enology school. Through vineyard acquisitions and extensive investments in a high-tech cellar, Carletti has built Poliziano into a luxury brand, known for dark and luscious barrique-aged Vino Nobile di Montepulciano. Carletti works with the consultant Carlo Ferrini, who has a knack for giving wines a certain sheen—not just of new oak but of ripe, clean fruit flavors that coat the tongue. Poliziano's powerful "Asinone" Vino Nobile now car-

ries a hefty price tag, but there are few if any Vino Nobiles elsewhere in the zone that can match its intensity. A new Poliziano-owned estate, Lohsa, is turning out plush Morellino di Scansano DOC red, with more to come in the future.

PRÀ, GRAZIANO
VENETO; MONTEFORTE D'ALPONE (VR)
DOC(G)s: Soave; Recioto di Soave
One of Soave's boutique producers, with a range of wines that defy Soave's still-entrenched image as an insipid white. The basic Soave Classico Superiore is fruity and fresh, with lots of personality, and the product line builds from there: The "Monte Grande" is fermented and aged in wood, albeit large barrels, so that it gets just a kiss of creamy, toasty flavor to complement the fruit. More over-the-top is the "Colle S. Antonio," which incorporates some late-harvested fruit and is fermented and aged in small barriques. This is a rich and buttery Soave, an atypical but undeniably bold bottle.

PRAVIS
TRENTINO; LASINO (TN)
DOC(G)s: Trentino
A large estate hitting all the Trentino hot-buttons, bottling clean and correct wines from nosiola, müllerthurgau, and a variety of reds, including syrah, cabernet sauvignon, and the rare rebo.

PRIMOSIC
FRIULI–VENEZIA GIULIA; OSLAVIA (GO)
DOC(G)s: Collio
An artisan producer of cool, classy Collio whites, including a barrel-fermented super-white called "Klin" (chardonnay-sauvignon-ribolla). The varietal whites with the "Gmajne"

designation (ribolla gialla and chardonnay in particular) are worth the extra effort it will take to find them.

PRINCIC, ALESSANDRO
FRIULI; CORMONS (GO)
DOC(G)s: Collio
The Princic family is one of Friuli's best known, and widely respected. Proprietor Sandro Princic is following in the footsteps of his father, the legendary Doro, in making varietal whites in a cool, clean, varietally correct style. Doro Princic was one of the early pioneers in Friulian wine, and today the Princic label can still be relied upon for stylish, delicate whites and reds. Try the excellent tocai friulano for starters, then move on to the malvasia, then the full-bodied pinot bianco. The reds are generally a little less interesting.

PRINCIPIANO, FERDINANDO
PIEMONTE; MONFORTE D'ALBA (CN)
DOC(G)s: Barolo; Barbera d'Alba
Ferdinando Principiano is a young up-and-comer in the Barolo zone, producing big yet accessible Barolos from two crus near Monforte: "Boscareto" and "Le Coste." A good Barbera d'Alba rounds out the short product line.

PRODUTTORI DEL BARBARESCO
PIEMONTE; BARBARESCO (CN)
DOC(G)s: Barbaresco
Many American wine lovers have been introduced to Barbaresco by way of this well-run cooperative winery (run by Aldo Vacca), which sources grapes from its member-growers to make a wide range of cru Barbarescos. Consistency and fair prices are the hallmarks of the winery, and should you want to taste your way through some of Bar-

baresco's greatest crus (for comparison and contrast), you can do it all here: there's Barbaresco from Rabajà, Montestefano, Moccagatta, and Rio Sordo, to name a few. Textbook Barbaresco made in a traditional style.

PROMESSA
PUGLIA; SAN MARZANO (LE)
American expat Mark Shannon's second label in Puglia, with lush, bargain-priced sangiovese, negroamaro, and primitivo.

PROVENZA
LOMBARDIA; DESENZANO DEL GARDA (BS)
DOC(G)s: Garda; Lugana
A winery on the Lombardy side of Lake Garda, specializing in fragrant, flinty Lugana DOC whites. Also notable is a Garda Chiaretto (rosé) that has a nice rosy, spicy flavor. There are also sparkling versions of Lugana.

PRUNOTTO
PIEMONTE; ALBA (CN)
DOC(G)s: Barolo; Barbaresco; Barbera d'Alba; Dolcetto d'Alba; Nebbiolo d'Alba
A wide range of good wines are made at this large and long-established wine house, which was acquired some time ago by Tuscany's Antinori firm. Rich and heady Barolos from crus such as "Bussia" and "Cannubi" top the list, but there's also Barbaresco, Dolcetto d'Alba, and most notably two single-vineyard barberas that are well worth seeking out, the "Pian Romualdo" and the "Costamiòle."

PUIATTI, VITTORIO
FRIULI; FARRA D'ISONZO (GO)
DOC(G)s: Collio
Generally delicate whites that don't incorporate wood. The late Vittorio Puiatti was a well-known figure in

Friulian wine, and his son Giovanni now carries on the family tradition. Whether it's ribolla gialla, pinot bianco, pinot grigio, or sauvignon, the wines are clean and affordable. The Puiattis also own an estate in Tuscany.

QUERCIA AL POGGIO
Toscana; Barberino Val d'Elsa (FI)
DOC(G)s: Chianti Classico
Fine, fragrant Chiantis from high-elevation vineyards at the western edge of the Chianti Classico zone.

QUERCIABELLA
Toscana; Greve in Chianti (FI)
DOC(G)s: Chianti Classico
Perched high above Greve in Chianti, this beautiful estate, under the direction of Sebastiano Castiglioni, is one of Chianti Classico's best. The wines, made by soft-spoken enologist Guido de Santi, are full and ripe but elegant, the products of high-altitude vineyards and a wine-making philosophy that emphasizes balance. Querciabella Chianti Classico is a deliciously smoky, savory take on sangiovese, while the firmly structured "Camartina" combines sangiovese with cabernet sauvignon. The "Batár" Chardonnay is a rich and buttery nod to current white-wine fashion, and the excellent Vin Santo "Orlando" has a richness and complexity matched by few others. An ultramodern winery where everything is done well.

QUINTARELLI, GIUSEPPE
Veneto; Negrar (VR)
DOC(G)s: Valpolicella; Amarone della Valpolicella; Recioto della Valpolicella
Giuseppe Quintarelli is the dean of Veronese winemakers. His Amarone is the standard by which all others are judged, and is priced accordingly—but if there was ever a reason to spend a lot of money on wine, Quintarelli provides one with Amarones that are consistently luxurious and complex, yet balanced. A Quintarelli Amarone is first and foremost about the exotic aromas only a dried-grape wine can deliver, also exemplified by his Amarone-style "Alzero," made from cabernet franc. For an introduction to the Quintarelli style, go for the more accessibly priced Valpolicella (typically incorporating a touch of Amarone) or the "Rosso Ca' del Merlo."

RADIKON
Friuli; Oslavia (GO)
DOC(G)s: Collio
From his tiny farmhouse winery in the hills of Oslavia, looking east to Slovenia, Stanko Radikon produces some of the most evocative Friulian wines available. His style is Burgundian, incorporating some barrel-fermentation for the whites and barrel aging for the reds. His white lineup includes a powerfully built ribolla gialla, its rich appley fruit carried on a raft of bright acidity, while his white blend "Oslavje" (chardonnay, ribolla gialla, tocai friulano, sauvignon) also boasts incredible richness and structure. On the red side, Radikon's barrique-aged merlot is a sought-after cult wine to rival the merlot-based reds of Pomerol.

RAINOLDI, ALDO
Lombardia; Chiuro (SO)
DOC(G)s: Valtellina; Valtellina Superiore; Valtellina Sforsato
This small family operation turns out some of the most evocative wines in the Valtellina, whether traditional reds aged in large Slovenian oak *botti* or modern, fruit-forward wines aged in barrique. Giuseppe Rainoldi has his young nephew,

Aldo, on board as enologist, and together they take nebbiolo to heights many in Barolo would envy. Check out some of the more traditional *riserve*, such as the Sassella Riserva and Inferno Riserva, for superfine nebbiolo with scents of everything from dried cherries and mushrooms to Earl Grey tea. For more size, trade up to the barrique-aged Sfursat "Fruttaio Ca' Rizzieri."

REDI
Toscana; Montepulciano (SI)
DOC(G)s: Vino Nobile di Montepulciano; Vin Santo
Located right in the town of Montepulciano, Redi is a brand name given to the top wines of the Vecchia Cantina, a local cooperative with more than 300 member-growers. The top Vino Nobile is the brawny "Briarero," and there's also a good Vin Santo.

REGALEALI
See Tasca d'Alimerita.

RENATO RATTI (ANTICHE CANTINE DELL'ABBAZIA DELL'ANNUNZIATA)
Piemonte; La Morra (CN)
DOC(G)s: Barolo; Barbera d'Alba; Dolcetto d'Alba; Monferrato; Nebbiolo d'Alba
The late Renato Ratti, who died in 1988, is referred to in one text as "The Father of Modern Barolo." It was Ratti who in the 1960s concluded that most Barolo was too tannic and too oxidized, thanks to what he felt were overly long maceration periods and overly long aging in dirty, creaky wood barrels. Ratti helped revolutionize Barolo by introducing controlled temperature fermentations in stainless steel, shortening the maceration period, and aging the wines less. The rounder, more accessible, more

fruit-forward style of Barolo lives on in the Ratti wines today, which might be described as modern but not ultramodern. Ratti's trademark wines include the elegant "Marcenasco" Barolo, the "Occhetti" Nebbiolo d'Alba (a great buy), and the dark, coffeeish "Villa Pattono," an unusual red blend from a property the family owns in the Monferrato DOC. These are classic Piedmont wines, and they're affordable. Pietro Ratti has been at the helm of this estate for many years now, and the wines keep getting better.

REVELLO
PIEMONTE; LA MORRA (CN)
DOC(G)s: Barolo; Barbera d'Alba; Dolcetto d'Alba
A small and stylish estate assisted by the consultant Beppe Caviola, who is known for wines of great depth. The Revello Barolo "Giachini," and the base-level Barolo for that matter, are big wines—accessible now but surely better in 10 years. The Dolcetto d'Alba and Barbera d'Alba wines are well made.

RIECINE
TOSCANA; GAIOLE IN CHIANTI (SI)
DOC(G)s: Chianti Classico
Clean and fruity Chiantis complemented by the more full-bodied "La Gioia," a varietal sangiovese.

RINALDI, GIUSEPPE
PIEMONTE; BAROLO (CN)
DOC(G)s: Barolo; Barbera d'Alba
One of Barolo's enduring classics, producing Barolo from the well-known crus of Brunate and Cannubi. If you like a more classically styled Barolo, a wine with some of the earthy, leathery, spicy aromatics of the nebbiolo grape, then these reasonably priced wines are for you. Rinaldi also produces a rich yet rustic Barbera d'Alba, among other wines.

RISECCOLI
TOSCANA; GREVE IN CHIANTI (FI)
DOC(G)s: Chianti Classico
Well-structured Chianti Classicos that are moderately expensive.

RIVERA
PUGLIA; ANDRIA (BA)
DOC(G)s: Castel del Monte
One of Puglia's top estates, characteristically large (about 1.5 million bottles a year). Known for a dark and well-structured red called "Il Falcone," a Castel del Monte DOC combining uva di troia and montepulciano. The estate does just about everything well, including primitivo ("Triusco") and aglianico ("Cappellaccio"). Still very affordable, and very good.

ROAGNA
See I. Paglieri.

ROCCA, ALBINO
PIEMONTE; BARBARESCO (CN)
DOC(G)s: Barbaresco; Barbera d'Alba; Dolcetto d'Alba; Langhe
Angelo Rocca makes monster Barbarescos in the modern style—superextracted through the use of a roto-fermenter, aged in barrique, but most of all properly ripe. The "Vigneto Brich Ronchi," his top Barbaresco cru, is as densely concentrated and tannic as ground espresso. Give his wines time, and you'll be rewarded.

ROCCA BERNARDA
FRIULI; PREMARIACCO (UD)
DOC(G)s: Colli Orientali del Friuli
A good and diverse production that includes one of the best picolits available, if you can find it. Firm and fruity dry whites are solid across the board, from tocai to chardonnay to pinot grigio.

ROCCA, BRUNO
PIEMONTE; BARBARESCO (CN)
DOC(G)s: Barbaresco; Barbera d'Alba; Dolcetto d'Alba; Langhe
Just down the street from Albino Rocca (no relation), this estate is known for powerful Barbaresco from the "Rabajà" and "Coparossa" vineyard sites. Although difficult to find, these are sleek and very potent Barbarescos for long-term cellaring.

ROCCA DELLE MACIE
TOSCANA; CASTELLINA IN CHIANTI (SI)
DOC(G)s: Chianti Classico
A large Chianti Classico estate known for consistency and fair prices. Chianti Classico and Chianti Classico Riserva are always fruity, soft, and serviceable. The more serious "Ser Gioveto" is a pure sangiovese with a little more heft.

ROCCA DI CASTAGNOLI
TOSCANA; GAIOLE IN CHIANTI (SI)
DOC(G)s: Chianti Classico
Serious, structured Chianti Classico. The estate, which has more than 375 acres of vineyards, sells most of . . . produce to *négociants*, but reserves its best fruit for its well-priced Chiantis.

ROCCA DI FABBRI
UMBRIA; MONTEFALCO (PG)
DOC(G)s: Montefalco Rosso; Sagrantino di Montefalco; Colli Martani
Good reds from the Montefalco DOC, and a new super-Umbro wine called "Faroaldo," a blend of sagrantino and cabernet sauvignon.

ROCCA DI MONTEGROSSI
TOSCANA; GAIOLE IN CHIANTI (SI)
DOC(G)s: Chianti Classico; Vin Santo

Small-production winery set in what was once a lookout post for the Barone Ricasoli family castle in Gaiole. Now run by Marco Ricasoli, the estate's small, carefully crafted production includes fine Chianti Classico, and a luscious sangiovese-based super-Tuscan called "Geremia." Rounding out the list is a rich Vin Santo, which is aged for five years in thirteen-gallon casks before release, lending it great intensity.

ROCCHE COSTAMAGNA
PIEMONTE; LA MORRA (CN)
DOC(G)s: Barolo; Barbera d'Alba; Dolcetto d'Alba
Value-priced reds—by Piedmont standards, anyway—include a solid Barolo.

ROCCHE DEI MANZONI
PIEMONTE; MONFORTE D'ALBA (CN)
DOC(G)s: Barolo; Langhe
Proprietor Valentino Migliorini is considered one of Barolo's modernists, in that he has never skimped on the new oak in his Barolos and other wines. His wines are deeply extracted, even showy, and as such are very hard to resist. The top cru wine is the Barolo "Cappella di Santo Stefano," but the more widely available "Vigna Big" and "Vigna d'la Roul" (the most delicate of the three) are no slouches. Migliorini also makes several delicious red blends, among them "Bricco Manzoni" (80% nebbiolo, 20% barbera), "Varo" (80% barbera, 20% nebbiolo), and "Quatr Nas" (nebbiolo-cabernet-merlot–pinot noir). His "Pinonero" pinot noir is also slick, and his *méthode champenoise* sparkler "Brut Zero" (all chardonnay) is one of Italy's better bubblies.

RODANO
TOSCANA; CASTELLINA IN CHIANTI (SI)
DOC(G)s: Chianti Classico
An excellent, reliable, and affordable house. What more could you want? There's a chocolatey, dark-robed intensity to just about everything this winery turns out, be it a simple Chianti Classico or one of its two super-Tuscans, "Monna Claudia" (sangiovese-cabernet) or "Lazzicante" (merlot).

RODDOLO, FLAVIO
PIEMONTE; MONFORTE D'ALBA (CN)
DOC(G)s: Barolo; Barbera d'Alba; Dolcetto d'Alba; Nebbiolo d'Alba
A boutique producer with about 12 acres of vineyards, from which he makes stylish and concentrated Barolos and other Langhe standards. Quantities of everything are extremely limited, particularly the cabernet sauvignon "Bricco Appiani," one of the few varietal cabernets to be found in these parts.

ROMANO DAL FORNO
VENETO; ILLASI (VR)
DOC(G)s: Valpolicella; Amarone della Valpolicella; Recioto della Valpolicella
Romano Dal Forno's wines are, in a word, humongous. He takes the idea of dense vineyard planting to the extreme, claiming to plant 11,000 vines per hectare, each of which produces a minuscule amount of superconcentrated grapes. In the cellar, Dal Forno ages his Valpolicellas, Amarones, and Reciotos in barriques, lending them even greater concentration. The Dal Forno Amarone is one step shy of Port, the Recioto an absolute bomb (it's not fortified, but tastes like it), and

the Valpolicella (which includes some Amarone blended in) is as rich as most producers' Amarones. These have become cult wines, and their prices reflect this.

RONCHI DI MANZANO
FRIULI; MANZANO (UD)
DOC(G)s: Colli Orientali del Friuli
A relatively young estate whose proprietor, Roberta Borghese, has a penchant for big, funky, barrique-aged reds and lush, tropically fruity whites. Her "Ronc di Subule" Merlot in good vintages is like liquid chocolate, as is the cabernet-merlot blend "Le Zuccule." Like the reds, the whites see time in barrique, lending even the basic tocai friulano a smoky, creamy note. The sweet picolit is a knockout as well.

RONCO DEI TASSI
FRIULI; CORMONS (GO)
DOC(G)s: Collio
A leading estate in the Collio DOC, headed up by talented winemaker Fabio Coser. His whites are extracted and creamy on the palate, yet firmly structured, as evidenced by his dewy tocai friulano, potent sauvignon, and white blend "Fosarin," a mix of malvasia, tocai, and barrel-fermented pinot bianco. On the red side, "Cjarandon," based on merlot, is ripe and rich.

RONCO DEL GELSO
FRIULI; CORMONS (GO)
DOC(G)s: Friuli Isonzo
Friuli's Isonzo DOC is definitely a region to watch, and Ronco del Gelso is one of its leading lights. The wines of this estate are full bodied and expressive, examples of the greater heights of concentration that are possible in the Isonzo's slightly warmer climes. The rich pinot grigio "Sot Lis Rivis" is a far

cry from the flabby, watery pinot grigios that are held up as the industry standard. The rest of Giorgio Badin's varietal whites follow suit: There's a plump and peachy tocai; a steely sauvignon, and a spicy riesling, among others.

RONCO DEL GNEMIZ
FRIULI; SAN GIOVANNI AL NATISONE (UD)
DOC(G)s: Colli Orientali del Friuli
There's a tightly coiled intensity to the wines of this estate that lends them a long life: Even several years from the vintage, the varietal whites have brisk acidity and good, minerally freshness. Try the chalky tocai first, then the plumper yet firmly acidic chardonnay (a good, clean, varietally true take on the variety). The "Rosso del Gnemiz" (a Bordeaux blend) is less exciting. Stick with the whites. Prices are fair.

RONCO DELLE BETULLE
FRIULI; MANZANO (UD)
DOC(G)s: Colli Orientali del Friuli
A boutique estate with prime vineyards in the hills of Rosazzo, not far from the historic Abbazia di Rosazzo. There's a delicious, minerally tocai, a full-bodied pinot bianco, and a white blend, "Narciso Bianco," that combines pinot bianco, tocai, and sauvignon to luxurious effect. Rosazzo is considered to be Friuli's key subzone for reds, though the "Narciso Rosso" (cabernet-merlot) doesn't make an especially strong case for that.

ROSA DEL GOLFO
PUGLIA; ALEZIO (LE)
A small estate in southern Puglia specializing in spicy, deep, unusually expressive rosés from blends of negroamaro and malvasia nera. Good whites from verdeca are also notable.

ROSSO, GIGI
PIEMONTE; CASTIGLIONE FALLETTO (CN)
DOC(G)s: Barolo; Barbaresco; Barbera d'Alba; Dolcetto d'Alba; Gavi; Roero Arneis
One of the larger houses in the Barolo zone, producing everything from classically styled Barolo to whites from Roero and Gavi. The top Barolo is "Arione," from a vineyard in Serralunga, which has decent depth. All of the wines are very reasonably priced.

RUFFINO
TOSCANA; PONTASSIEVE (FI)
DOC(G)s: Chianti Classico; Brunello di Montalcino
One of Italy's largest wine firms, and one of the best-known Italian wine brands in America, thanks to the immense popularity of the plush Chianti Classico "Riserva Ducale Oro." Founded by the Folonari family, of Brescia, in 1913, Ruffino has long used a combination of estate-owned vineyards and brought-in grapes to produce a vast array of wines. The Chianti wines are the best known, whether they carry the Ruffino, Santedame, or Nozzole labels, but there is also Brunello di Montalcino (from the firm's Il Greppone Mazzi estate), Vino Nobile (Lodola Nuova and Gracciano), and super-Tuscans made under the "Cabreo" brand. Recently, two branches of the family split up the Ruffino holdings in what was said to be an amicable parting, leaving Luigi Folonari with the Ruffino, Lodola Nuova, Santedame, and Greppone Mazzi; and Ambrogio and Alberto Folonari with Cabreo, Nozzole, Gracciano, and several other properties. The latter Folonaris have to be pleased that the popular "Cabreo Il Borgo" (sangiovese-

cabernet) and "Cabrea La Pietra" (chardonnay) wines are under their control, while from Nozzole they have another popular super-Tuscan in "Il Pareto," a cabernet sauvignon.

RUGGERI & C.
VENETO; VALDOBBIADENE (TV)
DOC(G)s: Prosecco di Valdobbiadene
Round and tasty proseccos, perfect for aperitifs, with all the peachy softness of the prosecco grape on display. The Extra Dry "Giall'Oro" is the basic bottling, a fine and balanced sparkler for any festive occasion.

RUGGERI CORSINI
PIEMONTE; MONFORTE D'ALBA (CN)
DOC(G)s: Barbera d'Alba
A barbera specialist known for rich, silky-smooth wines from the grape. Check out the "Armujan" in particular.

RUSSIZ SUPERIORE
FRIULI; CAPRIVA DEL FRIULI (GO)
DOC(G)s: Collio
A beautiful hilltop winery owned by Friulian powerhouse Marco Felluga (younger brother of Livio). The best-regarded wine here is the luscious tocai friulano, and there are a number of other varietal whites to choose from. The red blend "Riserva degli Orzoni" (a blend of cabernets sauvignon and franc) and the straight cabernet franc are both unique reds, comparable to some of the cabernet franc–based reds of France's Loire.

SALADINI PILASTRI
MARCHE; SPINETOLI (AP)
DOC(G)s: Rosso Piceno; Falerio dei Colli Ascolani
Good Rosso Piceno (most notably

the "Conte Saladino") and a red blend, "Pregio del Conte," that combines aglianico and montepulciano.

SALCHETO
TOSCANA; MONTEPULCIANO (SI)
DOC(G)s: Vino Nobile di Montepulciano
A small property producing solid, classically styled Vino Nobile di Montepulciano.

SALVIONI (LA CERBAIOLA)
TOSCANA; MONTALCINO (SI)
DOC(G)s: Brunello di Montalcino
Super-exclusive, super-powerful, super-expensive Brunello di Montalcino from a tiny boutique winery. This is one of those wines you read a lot about but don't necessarily see, because collectors and restaurants gobble up most of what little there is. If you see it on a list and feel like splurging, chances are you won't be disappointed.

SAN BIAGIO
MARCHE; MATELICA (MC)
DOC(G)s: Verdicchio di Matelica
A relative newcomer to the Marche wine scene, with a citrusy Verdicchio di Matelica and two red blends: "Bragnolo" (ciliegiolo-sangiovese) and "Grottagrifone" (cabernet-merlot). Nothing to write home about yet, but consultant Riccardo Cotarella is said to be on board.

SAN FABIANO CALCINAIA
TOSCANA; CASTELLINA IN CHIANTI(SI)
DOC(G)s: Chianti Classico
One of a number of new-generation estates aided by the hawkeyed consultant Carlo Ferrini (others include Fonterutoli and Poliziano). In addition to Chianti Classico with more than its share of toasty new oak, there's the buzzed-about "Cerviolo

Rosso" (sangiovese-merlot-cabernet), one of a growing crop of superextracted super-Tuscan wines looking to California for inspiration.

SAN FELICE
TOSCANA; CASTELNUOVO BERARDEGNA (SI)
DOC(G)s: Chianti Classico
Located down in the southeastern corner of the Chianti Classico zone, this historic estate is part of a swanky resort village, replete with high-end restaurant, tennis courts, etc. The San Felice wines are well known among American consumers, particularly the Chiantis. San Felice's "Poggio Rosso" Riserva is a consistently full-bodied and elegant take on Chianti Classico. There's also the acclaimed "Vigorello," a sangiovese with a touch of cabernet, and Brunello di Montalcino from other Chianti Classico vineyards of theirs.

SAN GERVASIO
TOSCANA; PALAIA (PI)
DOC(G)s: Chianti
An estate not far from Pisa producing a number of stylish reds, including "A Sirio," a varietal sangiovese, and "I Renai," a new bottling based on merlot.

SAN GIUSTO A RENTENNANO
TOSCANA; GAIOLE IN CHIANTI (SI)
DOC(G)s: Chianti Classico
Housed in a ninth-century fortress, this small-scale operation makes robust Chianti Classico and a potent barrique-aged sangiovese called "Percarlo." There's also some exceptional Vin Santo.

SAN ROMANO
PIEMONTE; DOGLIANI (CN)
DOC(G)s: Dolcetto di Dogliani

Dogliani, just south of the Barolo DOCG, is thought to be the birthplace of dolcetto. San Romano is one of the area's dolcetto specialists, making a number of extremely full-bodied dolcettos. The top gun is the dense, alcohol-rich "Vigna del Pilone," an example of the super-extracted, barrique-aged style of dolcetto that's now fashionable in Piedmont.

SANDRONE, LUCIANO
PIEMONTE; BAROLO (CN)
DOC(G)s: Barolo; Barbera d'Alba; Dolcetto d'Alba; Nebbiolo d'Alba
Both Luciano Sandrone and his wife had worked at Marchesi di Barolo before acquiring a tiny plot of land outside the village of Barolo in 1977. Since then, the Sandrone winery has become the archetypal Barolo boutique, with a small production of rich, handcrafted, super-sleek Barolos and other wines. Sandrone could be called a modernist in that he opts for shorter macerations, shorter aging, and at least some new wood for his wines (although he, like Enrico Scavino, has come to prefer larger 500-liter *tonneaux* over 225-liter barriques). This is Barolo at its most luxurious, especially the top cru "Cannubi Boschis," from a choice plot on the southeast-facing Cannubi cru outside Barolo. The only problem is how little there is of it around. More readily available is his excellent Dolcetto d'Alba and a soft, accessible Nebbiolo d'Alba called Valmaggiore. A class act that's worth paying a little more for.

SANT'ELENA
FRIULI; GRADISCO D'ISONZO (GO)
DOC(G)s: Friuli Isonzo
A small estate acquired in 1997 by

the New York–based wine importer Dominic Nocerino of Vinifera Imports. With the help of consultant Franco Bernabei, he is concentrating on reds from cabernet and merlot aged in barrique (their names are "Ròs di Rôi" and "Tato"). There's a also a pinot grigio and a chardonnay-sauvignon blend called "JN."

SANTA LUCIA
Puglia; Corato (BA)
DOC(G)s: Castel del Monte
A lesser-known gem. Castel del Monte is probably the most interesting DOC wine in Puglia, and Santa Lucia makes some of the best. The Castel del Monte Riserva is dark and spicy, thanks to a dash of malbec along with the traditional uva di troia and montepulciano. Santa Lucia is also one of the few producers to make the rare sweet red Aleatico.

SANTA MARGHERITA
Veneto; Fossato di
    Portogruaro (VE)
DOC(G)s: Alto Adige; Valdadige;
    Lison-Pramaggiore
One of Italy's largest wine firms, and the one that turned pinot grigio into a brand. Although the production at this estate includes a variety of whites and reds (carrying various Veneto, Trentino, and Alto Adige DOC designations), the wine that defines it is its pinot grigio, of which more than 5 million bottles a year are now produced.

SANTAVENERE (CASA VINICOLA TRIACCA)
Toscana; Montepulciano (SI)
DOC(G)s: Vino Nobile di
    Montepulciano
A one-wine estate in Montepulciano acquired in 1990 by the Triacca family of Valtellina. Vineyards span 33 hectares, with plans for more

plantings and an expanded cellar at this writing.

SANTI
Veneto; Illasi (VR)
DOC(G)s: Valpolicella; Amarone
    della Valpolicella; Soave
Part of the Gruppo Italiano Vini (GIV) conglomerate, this is a well-regarded Valpolicella estate making solid Valpolicellas and Amarones. The Amarone "Proemio" is a luxurious wine that can stand up to some of the bigger names, while the Valpolicellas are simpler and less expensive wines for more casual occasions.

SARACCO, PAOLO
Piemonte; Castiglione Tinella
    (CN)
DOC(G)s: Moscato d'Asti; Langhe
Surely one of the best producers of Moscato d'Asti, Paolo Saracco also has a deft touch with dry whites. Before moving onto dessert, check out his Langhe Chardonnay "Bianch del Luv": a well-structured, minerally chardonnay that might bring a good Chablis to mind.

SARTARELLI
Marche; Poggio San Marcello
    (AN)
DOC(G)s: Verdicchio dei Castelli di
    Jesi
Considered one of the top (if not the top) producers of Verdicchio dei Castelli di Jesi, this estate's three wines are arranged in ascending order of richness: the basic DOC bottling is limey and bright; the "Tralivio" is a little fuller and fruitier (the result of a closer selection in the vineyard); and the "Balciana" has an almost tropical fruit quality, thanks to a small percentage of late-harvested fruit. While the "Balciana" has attracted the most critical raves, it's the "Tralivio,"

thanks to its elegance and balance, that is the more interesting wine.

SARTORI
Veneto; Negrar (VR)
DOC(G)s: Soave; Valpolicella;
    Amarone della Valpolicella
With roots in the Valpolicella zone going back more than 100 years, this large firm continues to turn out value-priced Veneto wines at a clip of about 10 million bottles per year. Among the offerings are a host of inexpensive varietal wines, along with more serious stuff like the Amarone "Corte Bra." In general, these are party, or picnic wines, and priced to move.

SASSETTI, LIVIO
See Pertimali.

SASSOTONDO
Toscana; Sovana (GR)
DOC(G)s: Bianco di Pitigliano
A relatively new estate in southern Tuscany with some exceptional and interesting wines. The pet grape here is the rare ciliegiolo, found sporadically in the Tuscan Maremma and a handful of other regions, which Sassotondo showcases in its "San Lorenzo" bottling. There's a bright, berried, slightly spicy quality to the wine, and good depth. The Sassotondo Rosso is essentially a lighter version of the "San Lorenzo." There's also a sangiovese, "Franze," and a trebbiano-based Bianco di Pitigliano DOC. A great find.

SATTA, MICHELE
Toscana; Castagneto Carducci
    (LI)
DOC(G)s: Bolgheri
An artisan producer and contemporary of such Bolgheri greats as Lodovico Antinori and Piermario Cavallari. His Bolgheri Rosso "Piastraia" (cabernet-merlot-sangiovese-

syrah) and the all-sangiovese "Vigna al Cavaliere" remain relative values in comparison to some of their Bolgheri brethren. The brisk white "Costa di Giulia," a vermentino-sauvignon blend, is a terrific seafood white.

SCAGLIOLA
PIEMONTE; CALOSSO (AT)
DOC(G)s: Barbera d'Asti; Moscato d'Asti; Langhe; Piemonte
Dense and chunky barrique-aged Barbera d'Asti is a specialty here (the "SanSi" in particular is a big wine). The diverse production also includes a good Langhe Chardonnay and highly regarded Moscato d'Asti.

SCARBOLO
FRIULI–VENEZIA GIULIA; PAVIA DI UDINE (UD)
DOC(G)s: Friuli Grave
Home not only to grapes but to a small-scale pork butchery and a bustling neighborhood restaurant, Valter Scarbolo's winery turns out some of the best wines in the Grave DOC. Top picks include his round, luxurious tocai, clean and varietally true chardonnay, and a tarry refosco called "Campo del Viotto." An up-and-coming property offering great value.

SCARPA (ANTICA CASA VINICOLA)
PIEMONTE; NIZZA MONFERRATO (AT)
DOC(G)s: Barbera d'Asti; Brachetto d'Acqui; Dolcetto d'Acqui; Barolo
Noteworthy for its championing of Piedmontese oddities such as the strawberry-scented red brachetto, which it makes in both dry and sweet versions, and the funky, fruity grignolino. Production is very diverse, however, and even includes some Barolo.

SCAVINO, PAOLO
PIEMONTE; CASTIGLIONE FALLETTO (CN)
DOC(G)s: Barolo; Barbera d'Alba; Dolcetto d'Alba; Langhe
Scavino's Barolos are some of the most distinctive and powerful available. His cru wines include the sinewy "Bric del Fiasc," the tiny-production "Cannubi," and the rarer even "Rocche dell'Annunziata." Winemaker/proprietor Enrico Scavino also markets "Carobric," an assemblage of grapes from the above crus (the name is an assemblage as well). Also worth checking out are his barbera and the Langhe Rosso "Corale" (nebbiolo-barbera—cabernet sauvignon).

SCHIOPETTO
FRIULI; CAPRIVA DEL FRIULI (GO)
DOC(G)s: Collio
Founder Mario Schiopetto is credited with introducing controlled-temperature fermentation to Friuli, and with it the style of clean, high-acid, varietally true white wine for which Friuli has become famous. Now run by Mario's twin sons and daughter, Schiopetto is still best known for its flinty, minerally tocai friulano. But the wide array of Schiopetto wines also includes excellent pinot bianco, malvasia, pinot grigio, and the acclaimed "Podere dei Blumeri" Sauvignon. The white blend "Blanc des Rosis" (tocai–pinot bianco–malvasia-sauvignon) is vinified exclusively in stainless steel.

SCRIMAGLIO, FRANCO E MARIO
PIEMONTE; NIZZA MONFERRATO (AT)
DOC(G)s: Barbera d'Asti; Monferrato Rosso
Lots of different barbera wines are made here, highlighted by the Bar-bera d'Asti "Bricco S. Ippolito." In all, there are about a half dozen different barbera bottlings, all of them good and affordable.

SCUBLA, ROBERTO
FRIULI; PREMARIACCO (UD)
DOC(G)s: Colli Orientali del Friuli
A small-scale producer of rich, well-structured whites (one of many in the Collio). Specialties include a full-bodied pinot bianco and tocai friulano. The unusual "Bianco Pomédes" combines late-harvest tocai, pinot bianco, and partially dried riesling, all aged in barrique.

SEBASTE, MAURO
PIEMONTE; ALBA (CN)
DOC(G)s: Barolo; Barbaresco; Dolcetto d'Alba; Roero Arneis
A solid, wide-ranging lineup that includes Barolo from the Prapo cru in Serralunga (probably their top wine), along with Barbaresco, Roero Arneis, and two well-priced Dolcetto d'Albas.

SEGHESIO
PIEMONTE; MONFORTE D'ALBA (CN)
DOC(G)s: Barolo; Barbera d'Alba; Dolcetto d'Alba; Langhe
Perched on a hilltop overlooking Serralunga d'Alba, this winery, run by brothers Aldo and Riccardo Seghesio, is a source of elegant, reliable Barolo, of which "Vigneto La Villa" is their most acclaimed wine. As with the Barolos, the excellent Barbera d'Alba is aged in new oak barriques.

SELLA & MOSCA
SARDEGNA; ALGHERO (SS)
DOC(G)s: Alghero; Vermentino di Sardegna; Vermentino di Gallura; Cannonau di Sardegna
This behemoth property, with more than 1,500 acres under vine, a

chapel, museum, wine shop, and numerous guest houses, is one of the largest wine estates in Europe. Founded in 1899 by two Piedmontese men who ventured to Alghero on a hunting trip, the estate was a vine nursery in its early years. Commercial wine production commenced in earnest in the 1950s. The Bonomi family acquired the estate in 1978 and revitalized the vineyards and winery, building production to 6 million bottles a year. And yet the wines—including the fresh and fragrant Vermentino "La Cala," the spicy Cannonau Riserva, and the luscious, elegant "Marchese di Villamarina" Cabernet Sauvignon—do not taste mass-produced.

SELVAPIANA
TOSCANA; PONTASSIEVE (FI)
DOC(G)s: Chianti Rufina; Vin
  Santo
This estate has a long history in the tiny Rufina zone, which lies due east of Florence in the high hills around Pontassieve. The wines here are great bargains, packed with ripe and savory fruit flavor. The "Riserva Bucerchiale" and "Fornace" bottlings are billed as the top wines, but its hard to beat the straight Chianti Rufina for pure enjoyment. There's also some excellent Vin Santo.

SERAFINI & VIDOTTO
VENETO; NERVESA DELLA
  BATTAGLIA (TV)
Situated somewhat out of the DOC mainstream in a village near Treviso, this boutique estate is trying to emulate the great chateaus of Bordeaux with its tarry, spicy reds based on cabernet sauvignon and merlot. "Il Rosso dell'Abbazia," so named for the historic abbey in which the winery is housed, is deeply colorful and well structured, a consistent favorite of the Italian wine cognoscenti.

"Phigaia" is a fruity and simple second wine. They're nice, but not ready to take on Bordeaux just yet.

SERTOLI SALIS
LOMBARDIA; TIRANO (SO)
DOC(G)s: Valtellina; Valtellina
  Superiore; Valtellina Sforsato
Housed in the Palazzo Salis, built by Swiss nobles in the 1700s, this winery was one of the first commercial bottlers in Italy, with labels going back to the mid-1800s. However, winemaking ceased here in 1908 and wasn't revived until 1989, when descendants of the founding family and private investors restarted the operation. Winemaker Claudio Introini, a Valtellina veteran, emphasizes fresh berry fruit in his nebbiolos, preferring shorter aging periods in oak and a longer rest in bottle before release.

SETTESOLI
SICILIA; MENFI (AG)
Settesoli includes 6,500 hectares of vines tended by 2,300 growers. It is the largest *cantina sociale* in Italy, and one of the first in Italy to set aside a portion of its production to be bottled and sold under a trademark. Diego Planeta is the president (since 1972) and Carlo Corino the consulting enologist. There are now two Settesoli brands: "Mandrarossa" (seven wines) and "Inycon" (seven wines), featuring simple, fruity varietals with everything from chardonnay to nero d'avola.

SETTIMO, AURELIO
PIEMONTE; LA MORRA (CN)
DOC(G)s: Barolo
A small estate producing Barolo from the Rocche cru, among other wines.

SINFAROSSA
PUGLIA; AVETRANA (TA)
DOC(G)s: Primitivo di Manduria
Part of the Accademia dei Racemi consortium, this primitivo specialist plays up the relationship of primitivo and American zinfandel by labeling one of its wines "Zinfandel." It's a rich and chocolatey red in an American mode, as is its Primitivo di Manduria sibling. Old-vine concentration at a reasonable price.

SOLDERA
SEE CASE BASSE

SOLETTA
SARDEGNA; FLORINAS (SS)
DOC(G)s: Cannonau di Sardegna;
  Vermentino di Sardegna
A small and relatively new estate run by the Soletta family, whose vineyards are in northern Sardinia near Sassari. The specialty here is cannonau, best exemplified by the smooth, smoky Cannonau di Sardegna "Firmadu." Great value.

SOTTIMANO
PIEMONTE; NEIVE (CN)
DOC(G)s: Barbaresco; Barbera
  d'Alba; Dolcetto d'Alba
Not a big name in the States, but one worth hunting around for. Several austere and powerfully built Barbarescos are made, including the "Cottà Vigna Brichet," "Pajoré Vigna Lunetta," and "Fausoni Vigna del Salto."

SPADAFORA
SICILIA; MONREALE (PA)
DOC(G)s: Alcamo
At his growing estate in the hills south of Palermo, Francesco Spadafora focuses on freshness in his wines, whether they're chalky, flinty whites from catarratto or inzolia or savory reds based on nero d'avola.

SPERI
Veneto; San Pietro in Cariano (VR)
DOC(G)s: Valpolicella; Amarone della Valpolicella; Recioto della Valpolicella

This well-known winery in Valpolicella blends traditional and modern winemaking techniques to create Valpolicellas and Amarones that have both power and harmony. The Amarone "Monte Sant'Urbano" is a single-vineyard wine aged for four years in small oak casks, which helps preserve its color intensity and add toasty flavors. The Valpolicella "La Roverina" is also a single-vineyard wine, aged a year in oak, and the "Sant'Urbano" Valpolicella is like a mini-Amarone, employing the *ripasso* method to add depth and complexity.

SPINELLI
Abruzzo; Atessa (CH)
DOC(G)s: Montepulciano d'Abruzzo

Super-cheap Montepulciano di Abruzzo, Trebbiano d'Abruzzo, and Montepulciano Cerasuolo. The "Terra d'Aligi" line isn't bad.

SPORTOLETTI
Umbria; Spello (PG)
DOC(G)s: Assisi

A respected estate near Assisi, and yet another client of Terni-based consultant Riccardo Cotarella. The "Villa Fidelia" wines are the headliners, and the Grechetto di Assisi is also decent.

STATTI
Calabria; Lamezia (CZ)
DOC(G)s: Lamezia

An up-and-coming property managed by two young brothers, whose expansive family farm is outside Lamezia Terme. The estate's top red, "Cauro," is a plush, modern blend of the local gaglioppo with cabernet sauvignon, and it's only a matter of time before it turns up more readily in the States. Same goes for the juicy Lamezia Greco, an expressive white from Calabria's version of the greco grape.

STROZZI, GUICCIARDINI
Toscana; San Gimignano (SI)
DOC(G)s: Vernaccia di San Gimignano

The light white Vernaccia di San Gimignano has taken a back seat here to big, rich, super-Tuscan reds, including "Millani" (sangiovese-cabernet-merlot), "Selvascura" (mostly merlot), and "Sodole" (all sangiovese). Tarry and potent (especially the Sodole), these wines all show a pretty heavy oak influence. If you like black, chocolatey reds, these are the wines for you.

STRUZZIERO
Campania; Venticano (AV)
DOC(G)s: Fiano di Avellino; Taurasi

Classic Campania reds and whites. The Fiano di Avellino is the best-regarded wine.

STURM, OSCAR
Friuli; Cormons (GO)
DOC(G)s: Collio

A small farmstead winery with a consistent track record with chardonnay and sauvignon, among other varieties.

TAMELLINI
Veneto; Soave (VR)
DOC(G)s: Soave; Recioto di Soave

An excellent Soave producer, known for wines with crisp acidity and bright aromas. Great values.

TASCA D'ALMERITA (REGALEALI)
Sicilia; Vallelunga Pratameno (CL)

Along with Corvo, this is the best-known wine house in Sicily, a sprawling farm owned by the Tasca d'Almerita family. Count Lucio Tasca and son Giuseppe continue to produce one of southern Italy's greatest reds in the nero d'avola–based "Rosso del Conte," as well as a good cabernet and a spicy rosato that has become a cult favorite (among many others). The estate is also home to Anna Tasca Lanza's acclaimed cooking school.

TAURINO
Puglia; Guagnano (LE)
DOC(G)s: Salice Salentino

The late Cosimo Taurino was a legend in Puglia—truly the producer who put Puglian wines on the map. Taurino's tangy Salice Salentino and the rich and tarry "Notarpanaro" (mostly negroamaro) are well known to American consumers, and continue to be consistent values. The pricier "Patriglione," a negroamaro–malvasia nera blend that incorporates some dried fruit à la Amarone, is one of Puglia's densest and most expressive reds.

TAVIGNANO
Marche; Cingoli (MC)
DOC(G)s: Verdicchio dei Castelli di Jesi; Rosso Piceno

Good verdicchio wines, particularly the "Misco" bottling.

TEDESCHI
Veneto; San Pietro in Cariano (VR)
DOC(G)s: Valpolicella Classico; Amarone della Valpolicella; Recioto della Valpolicella

One of the most consistent (and technologically advanced) wineries in the Valpolicella zone, turning out excellent reds year after year. Tedeschi's Amarone "Monte Olmi" is one of the best values in the category, a complex and flavorful wine in a medium-bodied style. The "La Fabriseria" Amarone is richer and more extracted, a better choice for cheese. The "Capitel S. Rocco" Valpolicella Ripasso is a spicy everyday quaffer.

TENIMENTI ANGELINI (TREROSE)
Toscana; Montepulciano (SI)
DOC(G)s: Vino Nobile di
    Montepulciano
This firm, which also owns the Val di Suga estate in Montalcino (see below), is making some excellent Vino Nobile di Montepulciano, as evidenced by its rich, coffee-scented "Simposio," one of two Vino Nobile selections.

TENIMENTI D'ALESSANDRO
Toscana; Cortona (AR)
DOC(G)s: Cortona
The Cortona area, which was recently given a DOC designation, lies just north of Montepulciano. It's a hot area for vineyard investment, thanks at least in part to the success of Massimo D'Alessandro's wines. His "Podere Il Bosco," a warm and rich syrah, has any number of wine firms in the area thinking that Cortona is the next Australia. That's probably an exaggeration, but the rich reds and whites of Tenimenti D'Alessandro suggest good things to come.

TENUTA BELTRAME
Friuli; Bagnaria Arsa (UD)
DOC(G)s: Friuli Aquilea
Sauvignon is a specialty here—both the white sauvignon blanc and the red cabernet sauvignon, the latter showing better-than-average depth in an area infamous for thin, weedy reds. Beltrame is the best-regarded winery in the Aquilea DOC, and the wines are relative bargains for the quality they offer.

TENUTA BELVEDERE
Toscana; Bolgheri (LI)
DOC(G)s: Bolgheri
The Bolgheri estate of Piero Antinori, recently equipped with a space-age underground cantina. The ripe and supple "Guado al Tasso" Bolgheri Rosso (a blend of cabernet sauvignon, merlot, and syrah) is a consistently excellent wine, while the reasonably priced vermentino is a savory and fragrant white for seafood.

TENUTA BONZARA
Emilia-Romagna; Monte San
    Pietro (BO)
DOC(G)s: Colli Bolognesi
The Colli Bolognesi (located just southwest of Bologna) are said to be a hotbed for cabernet sauvignon, but as of yet there hasn't been too much evidence to support the claim. The best examples so far have come from Tenuta Bonzara, whose consulting enologist Stefano Chioccioli crafts ripe, fruit-driven wines at Francesco Lambertini's small hillside property. Generally speaking, the Bonzara reds (which also include the "Rocca di Bonacciara" Merlot) have ample fruit but don't have the burly, dense structure of some of the great Tuscan cabernets. But they would seem to be on their way, and the wines are still affordable.

TENUTA CAPARZO
Toscana; Montalcino (SI)
DOC(G)s: Brunello di Montalcino
Always reliable, Tenuta Caparzo wines have an aristocratic quality about them. They're rich but not overblown, and aromatic in a way many Brunellos are not—that is, in a fruity and fresh way. The Brunello "La Casa," if you can find (and afford) it, is the wine to collect.

TENUTA DEL PORTALE
Basilicata; Rionero in Vulture
    (PZ)
DOC(G)s: Aglianico del Vulture
An estate owned by the D'Angelo family of Rionero. Good Aglianico del Vulture, as well as a plump 100% aglianico called "Vulcano" and a longer-aged varietal aglianico called "Le Vigne a Capanno." Great values.

TENUTA DEL TERRICCIO
Toscana; Castellina Marittima
    (PI)
A boutique winery not far from Pisa. Geared toward the international market, it is known for the potent super-Tuscans called "Lupicaia" (barrique-aged cabernet sauvignon and merlot) and "Tassinaia" (a shorter-aged blend of cabernet, merlot, and sangiovese). Serious wines, for sure, so be prepared to pay up.

TENUTA GIUNCHEO
Liguria; Camporosso (IM)
DOC(G)s: Riviera Ligure di
    Ponente
A leading Ligurian estate, specializing in savory, aromatic whites from vermentino and pigato. The basic DOC bottlings have lots of structure and character, while the Vermentino "Eclis" is an attempt to pump up the variety with barrel fermentation. There's also the spicy red Rossese di Dolceacqua.

TENUTA IL BOSCO
Lombardia; Zenevredo (PV)
DOC(G)s: Oltrepò Pavese
An Oltrepò Pavese estate owned by the Zonin group of the Veneto. Good pinot nero, bonarda, and a variety of regional sparklers.

TENUTA LE QUERCE
BASILICATA; RIONERO IN VULTURE (PZ)
DOC(G)s: Aglianico del Vulture
Financed by the local firm Gruppo Pietrafesa, this new winery is worth noting because of its scale—it has the potential to become one of the larger wineries in the area. The well-known consultant Severino Garofano (of Taurino fame) oversees the newly planted vineyards. Pietrafesa markets wines under the Sasso brand (having acquired that Rionero-based winery in 1997); its best-known products are "Il Viola" and "Federico II." It remains to be seen how the Sasso/Le Querce branding situation works itself out.

TENUTA LODOLA NUOVA
TOSCANA; MONTEPULCIANO (SI)
DOC(G)s: Vino Nobile di Montepulciano
Owned by the Ruffino wine firm, this estate makes solid Vino Nobile and Rosso di Montalcino.

TENUTA ROCCACCIA
TOSCANA; PITIGLIANO (GR)
DOC(G)s: Bianco di Pitigliano
Located in Pitigliano, in extreme southern Tuscany near its border with Lazio, this is a winery to watch. The story is a familiar one in Italy these days. Up until a few years ago, its proprietors, the Goracci family, sold their grapes to a local co-op. Now they have decided to produce wine in bottles, and the results are exciting. Topping the list is a bright, berried blend of sangiovese and ciliegiolo called "Fontenova," which is aged in barrique. This is ripe, plump, uniquely aromatic wine at a fair price. Snap it up if you see it.

TENUTA ROVEGLIA
LOMBARDIA; POZZOLENGO (BS)
DOC(G)s: Lugana
A leading producer of the aromatic white Lugana, probably the ultimate expression of the trebbiano grape.

TENUTA SAN GUIDO
TOSCANA; BOLGHERI (LI)
DOC(G)s: Bolgheri Sassicaia
As noted in the Tuscany chapter of this book, this was the estate that started the whole super-Tuscan trend. Mario Incisa della Rochetta first planted cabernet sauvignon at the Tenuta San Guido in the late-'40s, intending to make some Bordeaux-style wine for his own consumption, but by the early '70s "Sassicaia" had become a commercial phenomenon. This is probably the most sought-after collector's wine in Italy, as it is known to age exceptionally well. What distinguishes it most from the ever-growing pack of super-Tuscans is its elegance and reserve—there's plenty of flavor there, it's just in a tightly bound package.

TENUTA SAN LEONARDO
TRENTINO; AVIO (TN)
DOC(G)s: Trentino
Located in southern Trentino, this beautiful estate is owned by Marchese Carlo Guerreri Gonzaga, who has modeled his winery after a Bordeaux chateau. His top wine, "San Leonardo" (cabernet sauvignon–merlot) is considered one of Italy's best Bordeaux-style blends.

TENUTA SANT' ANTONIO
VENETO; COLOGNA AI COLLI (VR)
DOC(G)s: Valpolicella; Amarone della Valpolicella
Although headquartered outside the Valpolicella Classico zone, this relatively new winery near Illasi has fast become a big name in Valpolicella thanks to its big, slick wines. The Valpolicella "Monti Garbi" incorporates a touch of Amarone for body, while the newer Valpolicella "La Bandina" achieves its depth without the use of any dried fruit. The Amarone "Campo dei Gigli" is a good example of the modern take on Amarone—rich and chocolatey, with a sheen of vanilla from its aging in small oak barrels.

TERRA DEGLI SVEVI
BASILICATA; VENOSA (PZ)
Recently acquired by the Veneto-based Gruppo Italiano Vini (GIV), it was once controlled by the Swiss conglomerate Winefood. Not much is known yet about the wines that will be produced, but GIV's involvement makes it an estate to watch.

TERRABIANCA
TOSCANA; RADDA IN CHIANTI (SI)
DOC(G)s: Chianti Classico
Owners Robert and Maja Guldener traded in their lives as successful Swiss professionals for that of winemakers in Tuscany, and their estate is consistently praised for its luxurious wines, most of them barrique-aged reds based on sangiovese. The Chianti Classico Riserva "Vigna della Croce" is a good place to start, after which you might build up to the sexy but pricey "Campaccio," a sangiovese-cabernet blend. An increasingly popular estate with a long track record for quality.

TERRE BIANCHE
LIGURIA; DOLCEACQUA (IM)
DOC(G)s: Riviera Ligure di Ponente; Rossese di Dolceacqua
A leading western-Ligurian producer. Solid pigato and vermentino, as well as the light red Rossese di Dolceacqua.

TERRE DEL CEDRO
EMILIA-ROMAGNA; OSPEDALETTO
DI CORIANO (RN)
DOC(G)s: Sangiovese di Romagna;
Trebbiano di Romagna
Good sangiovese made under the
direction of famed consultant Riccardo Cotarella. There are three different bottlings, all well priced, with
the barrique-aged "Zarricante" occupying the top spot.

TERRE ROSSE
LIGURIA; FINALE LIGURE (SV)
DOC(G)s: Riviera Ligure di
Ponente
Like just about all Ligurian wines,
these will be difficult to find in the
States, but the producer is worth
mentioning. The intense, herbal
pigato is the specialty here, along
with its cousin, vermentino. Great
seafood whites if you can locate
them (maybe on your next trip to
San Remo).

TERREDORA
CAMPANIA; MONTEFUSCO (AV)
DOC(G)s: Fiano di Avellino; Greco
di Tufo; Taurasi
The product of a split of the Mastroberardino family holdings (one
side of the family got the brand
name, the other got the vineyards).
Terredora, run by Walter, Paolo,
Lucio, and Daniela Mastroberardino, is a new brand sourcing
grapes from prized old vines. The
Taurasi is a standout, as is the IGT
aglianico "Il Principio." Greco di
Tufo is also a particular strength of
this estate—check out the "Terre
degli Angeli" bottling.

TERUZZI & PUTHOD
TOSCANA; SAN GIMIGNANO (SI)
DOC(G)s: Vernaccia di San
Gimignano
This estate is a reference point, a
standard: If you've had only one

Vernaccia di San Gimignano in your
life, it was probably this one. Then
there's the crisp and fragrant "Terre
di Tufi" IGT, a vernaccia-based
blend that spends a little time
plumping up in French oak barriques. These are simple but flavorful whites, great for a *zuppa di pesce*
or countless other seafood dishes.

TIEFENBRUNNER
ALTO ADIGE;
CORTACCIA/KURTATSCH (BZ)
DOC(G)s: Alto Adige
Among the largest and best-known
wineries in the Alto Adige, with a
typically broad-ranging product line.
The cabernet sauvignon "Linticlarus" is one of several critically
acclaimed cabernets grown in the
Alto Adige, but, like its peers
(Lageder's "Cor," Elena Walch's
"Castel Ringberg"), it has a green,
bell-peppery character that may be
off-putting to California cabernet
fans. More exciting are the Tiefenbrunner whites, including the pinot
grigio, pinot bianco, sauvignon blanc,
and "Linticlarus" Chardonnay.

TOMMASI
VENETO; S. PIETRO IN CARIANO
DOC(G)s: Valpolicella; Amarone
della Valpolicella; Recioto della
Valpolicella
One of the classic Amarone-makers,
known for a more traditional house
style that favors the leathery, spicy,
earthy flavors that come from long
aging in large oak.

TORMARESCA (VIGNETI DEL
SUD)
PUGLIA; SAN PIETRO VERNOTICO
(BA)
DOC(G)s: Castel del Monte
The huge new estate owned by Tus-
cany's Antinori. Tormaresca is the
brand name attached to the tropi-
cally fruity "Bianco," made from

chardonnay, and the "Rosso" from
aglianico, cabernet, and merlot. The
estate spans more than 1,200 acres
in Castel del Monte and Brindisi,
meaning that the bargain-priced
Tormaresca wines will be available
in ample quantities.

TORRE ROSAZZA
FRIULI; MANZANO (UD)
DOC(G)s: Colli Orientali del Friuli
A well-known name in Friuli, producing a wide range of wines (more
than a dozen) at affordable prices.
The reds are especially well regarded,
particularly the "L'Altromerlot"
Merlot. All the standard Friulian
whites are represented, all of them
good values for casual sipping.

TORREVENTO
PUGLIA; CORATO (BA)
DOC(G)s: Castel del Monte
Another solid producer of the rich
red Castel del Monte (their "Vigna
Pedale" is 100% uva di troia) and
other reds and whites.

TRAVAGLINI
PIEMONTE; GATTINARA (VC)
DOC(G)s: Gattinara
Probably the Gattinara producer
best known to Americans, this rustic
nebbiolo in the odd-shaped bottle is
still a reliable standard. Check out
the new "Tre Vigne" Gattinara,
crafted from fruit selected from
three choice vineyards; the Gattinara
Riserva is also worth a try. In either
case, don't expect a fruit bomb, but
rather a wine that seems to draw
flavor right out of the ground it
grows in.

TRE MONTI
EMILIA-ROMAGNA; IMOLA (BO)
DOC(G)s: Albana di Romagna;
Colli d'Imola; Sangiovese di
Romagna; Trebbiano di Romagna
An up-and-coming property mak-

ing the full range of Romagna wines in high style. Their "super-Romagnolo" is the Colli d'Imola "Boldo," a blend of sangiovese and cabernet sauvignon. It is a rich if slightly mentholated complement to their Sangiovese di Romagna "Thea," which seems like a more complete wine. Both sweet and dry whites from albana are also offered, along with the light Trebbiano di Romagna.

TRIACCA
LOMBARDIA; VILLA DI TIRANO (SO)
DOC(G)s: Valtellina; Valtellina Superiore; Valtellina Sforsato
The striking La Gatta estate, a former Dominican convent cut into a steep hillside near Tirano, is the spiritual home of Triacca. Domenico Triacca is an energetic viticulturist and technician: He creates his unique "Prestigio" wine by cutting the cordons of select nebbiolo vines and leaving the grapes to dry on these cut branches for a good month after the normal harvest. This and his more traditional Sforsato are wines that combine fruity richness with the aromatic complexity typical of the region. Triacca also operates estates in Chianti Classico (La Madonnina, acquired in 1969) and Montepulciano (Santavenere, acquired in 1990).

TUA RITA
TOSCANA; SUVERETO (LI)
A relatively recent arrival on the Tuscan wine scene, but one that made a big splash. Located in the red-hot Suvereto area, south of Livorno on the coast, the small estate named for proprietor Rita Tua has definitely gotten a good read on the international market. The most sought-after wine is the "Redigaffi," a sappy yet structured 100% merlot that the

wine critics have gone crazy for (and of which they make very little). Other offerings include the "Giusto di Notri" and "Perlato del Bosco" red blends. All are fairly pricey.

UCCELLIERA
TOSCANA; MONTALCINO (SI)
DOC(G)s: Brunello di Montalcino
A tiny and very well run farm in Montalcino owned by young upstart Andrea Cortonesi. Forwardly fruity Brunello and Rosso di Montalcino comprise the estate's lineup.

UMANI RONCHI
MARCHE; OSIMO (AN)
DOC(G)s: Verdicchio dei Castelli di Jesi; Rosso Cònero
When it comes to brand recognition and sheer output, this is the most important estate in the Marche, with an ever-expanding array of good, well-priced wines. The Verdicchio dei Castelli di Jesi "Casal di Serra" is a ripe and unusually powerful expression of the grape, while "Le Busche" combines verdicchio with chardonnay to interesting effect. Among the many reds, the top wines are the luscious Rosso Cònero "Cùmaro," and the even more luscious red blend "Pelago." The basic Rosso Cònero "San Lorenzo" is one of the great values in Italian wine.

VAGNONI
TOSCANA; SAN GIMIGNANO (SI)
DOC(G)s: Chianti Colli Senesi; Vernaccia di San Gimignano
Inexpensive whites and reds from San Gimignano.

VAJRA, G. D.
PIEMONTE; BAROLO (CN)
DOC(G)s: Barolo; Barbera d'Alba; Dolcetto d'Alba; Langhe
Vajra wines blend modern and traditional winemaking techniques, and

are typically readily accessible as young wines, broad and somewhat Burgundian in their flavor profile. The winery has holdings in three Barolo commune vineyards: Le Coste, Fossati, and Bricco delle Viole. The last makes the most consistently good Barolo. Prices are fair.

VAL DI SUGA
TOSCANA; MONTALCINO (SI)
DOC(G)s: Brunello di Montalcino
Super-powerful Brunello di Montalcino, particularly the monster bottling "Vigna del Lago."

VAL CERASA
SICILIA
A newish estate on Mount Etna with some great values on reds.

VALDIPATTA
TOSCANA; MONTEPULCIANO (SI)
DOC(G)s: Vino Nobile di Montepulciano
This small estate, run by the Caporali family, offers great value in Vino Nobile. The wines are rich and accessible, fruity and modern, and are now joined by several super-Tuscans: "Tre Fonti" is an interesting blend of cabernet, sangiovese (prugnolo), and canaiolo, while the "Trincerone" combines canaiolo with merlot.

VALENTINI, EDOARDO
ABRUZZO; LORETO APRUTINO (PE)
DOC(G)s: Trebbiano d'Abruzzo; Montepulciano d'Abruzzo
The reclusive Edoardo Valentini has developed a reputation as one of the most uncompromising artisans in the world of Italian wine. He has elevated wines generally known as simple quaffers (Montepulciano/Trebbiano d'Abruzzo) into cult classics that sell out quickly when he gets around to releasing them. His wines generally receive considerable

bottle age before they go on sale, and it's not uncommon for Valentini to hold back the release of certain vintages if he doesn't think they're ready. Valentini Trebbiano d'Abruzzo is typically round and creamy yet powerfully structured; it has no peer in the category. The Montepulciano d'Abruzzo is as plump and fruity as any from the region while also boasting an earthy, smoky complexity. The pink Cerasuolo is also a standout.

VALLAROM
Trentino; Avio (TN)
DOC(G)s: Trentino
Owned by the family of professor Attilio Scienza of the University of Milan, this winery has a deft touch with both whites and reds. The blend "Campi Sarni" is a typically savory, spicy Trentino red, the pinot noir crisp and aromatic, the marzemino more exotically fruity. On the white side, chardonnay is a specialty.

VALLE DELL'ACATE
Sicilia; Acate (RG)
DOC(G)s: Cerasuolo di Vittoria
The up-and-coming Valle dell'Acate estate focuses considerable attention on the frappato grape, not only blending it with the richer nero d'avola for Cerasuolo but bottling it on its own to showcase its bright, fresh, cherry-scented character.

VALLE DELL'ASSO
Puglia; Galatina (LE)
DOC(G)s: Galatina; Salice Salentino
Soft, spicy, and bargain-priced blends of negroamaro and primitivo from the Salentine peninsula.

VALLONA
Emilia-Romagna; Castello Serravalle (BO)

Good cabernet and chardonnay from the colli Bolognesi.

VALLONE
Puglia; Lecce (LE)
DOC(G)s: Brindisi; Salice Salentino
A characteristically large Puglian estate focused on the classic Salentine peninsula blend of negroamaro and malvasia nera. In addition to a good basic Salice Salentino, the Vallone estate is known for the VdT "Gratticciaia," a negroamaro-malvasia blend that incorporates semidried fruit to give it an Amarone-like richness. The Brindisi Rosso DOC "Vigna Flaminio" is dark and juicy.

VARALDO
Piemonte; Barbaresco (CN)
DOC(G)s: Barbaresco; Barbera d'Alba; Dolcetto d'Alba; Langhe
A producer of outstanding wines across the board, highlighted by powerful yet accessible Barbarescos such as the "Bricco Libero," its top wine. Good barbera, dolcetto, and freisa complement the powerhouse Barbarescos.

VECCHIE TERRE DI MONTEFILI
Toscana; Panzano (FI)
DOC(G)s: Chianti Classico
An always-reliable estate producing fine Chianti Classico, along with the sangiovese-cabernet blend "Bruno di Rocca," and an unsual white blend called "Vigna Regis" (a fruit cocktail of chardonnay, sauvignon, and gewürztraminer).

VEGA (D'ANTICHE TERRE)
Campania; Manocalzati (AV)
DOC(G)s: Greco di Tufo; Fiano di Avellino; Taurasi
Good examples of the inland Campania DOC wines of Greco di Tufo, Fiano di Avellino, and especially

Taurasi, here vinified in an earthy, traditional style.

VEGLIO, MAURO
Piemonte; La Morra (CN)
DOC(G)s: Barolo; Barbera d'Alba; Dolcetto d'Alba; Langhe
A range of top-flight Barolo is made at this artisanal estate, with three cru wines from the commune of La Morra ("Arborina," "Gattera," and "Rocche") and one from the commune of Barolo ("La Villa"). It would be difficult to assign roles for each of them—much more fun to taste for yourself. The wines are fruit-driven and powerfully structured. The same goes for the excellent barberas and dolcettos.

VENICA & VENICA
Friuli; Dolegna del Collio (GO)
DOC(G)s: Collio
Brothers Gianni and Giorgio Venica run this winery and *agriturismo* not far from Italy's border with Slovenia. The wide range of wines includes excellent chardonnay, pinot grigio, tocai, and especially sauvignon, most notably the single-vineyard "Ronco delle Mele"—a powerful sauvignon redolent of mandarin oranges and wild herbs. "Tre Vignis" is a creamy blend of tocai, chardonnay, and sauvignon, and the "Rosso delle Cime" (cabernet-merlot-refosco) is among of the better Friulian reds.

VENTURINI
Veneto; San Pietro in Cariano (VR)
DOC(G)s: Valpolicella; Amarone della Valpolicella; Recioto della Valpolicella
Great values in Valpolicella, Amarone, and Recioto. The Venturini Amarone holds to a moderate scale, deeply flavorful without being

sappy and sweetish. It's an Amarone you might consider alongside a main course of steak or osso buco, as opposed to reserving it for the cheese. In general, everything the winery makes is solid.

VERCESI DEL CASTELLAZZO
Lombardia; Montù Beccaria (PV)
DOC(G)s: Oltrepò Pavese
Good whites and reds from the Oltrepò Pavese, an interesting DOC in southwestern Lombardia. The tarry, black fruit-flavored bonarda grape is a specialty (try the "Fatila" bottling), and there's also a very good pinot nero (pinot noir), called "Luogo dei Monti."

VERDI, BRUNO
Lombardia; Canneto Pavese (PV)
DOC(G)s: Oltrepò Pavese
If you're in the market for some interesting, off-the-beaten-track wines, this is a good place to start. Bruno Verdi's wide range of Oltrepò Pavese DOC wines are interesting and usually quite good. Among the whites, the steely riesling renano "Vigneto Costa" is a highlight, while the reds are headlined by a dense and tarry bonarda (try the "Cavariola" Riserva). Barbera is another specialty.

VIBERTI, ERALDO
Piemonte; La Morra (CN)
DOC(G)s: Barolo; Barbera d'Alba; Dolcetto d'Alba
A good, small Barolo estate also known for ripe, oak-kissed barberas. The Barbera d'Alba "Vigna Clara" is well regarded.

VIBERTI, OSVALDO
Piemonte; La Morra (CN)
DOC(G)s: Barolo; Barbera d'Alba; Dolcetto d'Alba; Langhe

Solid range of Langhe wines, including a Barolo from the Bricco delle Viole cru and well-priced barbera and dolcetto.

VICARA
Piemonte; Rosignano Monferrato (AL)
DOC(G)s: Barbera del Monferrato; Monferrato
The name Vicara is an amalgam of the last names of the three partners, Visconti, Cassinis, and Ravizza. Each own vineyards that contribute fruit to their Monferrato DOC wines, which include a sleek blend of barbera, cabernet, and nebbiolo called "Rubello." Also noteworthy is the Barbera dell'Monferrato "Cantico della Crosia," a clean and fruit-rich red with superb varietal character. Great buys.

VIE DI ROMANS
Friuli; Marion del Friuli (GO)
DOC(G)s: Friuli Isonzo
Another star winery from the Isonzo DOC zone, and one of Friuli's most acclaimed estates. Powerfully aromatic sauvignon is a specialty (try the fruity "Vieris" or the woodier "Piere"), and the white blend "Flors di Uis" is one of the top super-whites: a blend of malvasia, chardonnay, and riesling vinified in stainless steel, "Flors di Uis" is from the more aromatic school of Friulian white blends. The "Ciampagnis Vieris" Chardonnay is also excellent, as is the full-bodied, barrel-fermented "Dessimis" Pinot Grigio.

VIETTI
Piemonte; Castiglione Falletto (CN)
DOC(G)s: Barolo; Barbaresco; Dolcetto d'Alba; Barbera d'Alba; Roero Arneis

A somewhat dizzying range of wines is produced at this classic Langhe estate, which bottled its first wines in the early '60s. Some wines are from estate-owned grapes, such as the top-of-the-line Barolo "Rocche," others from contract growers. If Vietti could be summed up with one word, it would be *consistent*. Year after year, the estate's Barbera d'Asti "Tre Vigne" is a great bottle of wine for the money. Ditto for the Barolos, regardless of cru, and for the floral and flinty Roero Arneis. This is a reliable house making clean and correct wines across the board.

VIGNALTA
Veneto; Terreglia (PD)
DOC(G)s: Colli Euganei
The best-known winery in the up-and-coming Colli Euganei DOC, this Padova-area winery is best known for "Gemola," a chunky, savory red based on cabernet sauvignon and merlot. It has gotten a lot of attention but isn't yet the kind of red you just must have a case of for your cellar. Luckily, it's not expensive, and thus well worth a try.

VIGNAMAGGIO
Toscana; Greve in Chianti (FI)
DOC(G)s: Chianti Classico; Vin Santo
Good Chianti Classico, particularly the "Monna Lisa" Riserva, complemented by some creative super-Tuscans: "Obsession," a meaty blend of cabernet, merlot, and syrah; and "Vignamaggio," based on cabernet franc.

VILLA CAFAGGIO
Toscana; Panzano in Chianti (FI)
DOC(G)s: Chianti Classico
Great-value Chiantis are the trademark of this large Panzano estate, which packs a lot of smoky fruit

flavor into all its wines, whether Riservas or not. A basic *annata* Villa Cafaggio Chianti Classico is an excellent choice for a picnic or pasta dinner, while the Riserva "Solatio Basilica" is a more serious and structured bottling. The "Cortaccio" cabernet has gotten its share of high marks, as has the varietal sangiovese "San Martino." You really can't go wrong here.

VILLA MATILDE

Campania; Cellole (CE)
DOC(G)s: Falerno del Massico
Located on Campania's north coast, where the ancient Romans once cultivated vineyards, this winery produces some great reds from the aglianico grape. Its basic Falerno del Massico DOC Rosso is one example, spicy, rich, and well priced. But the "Vigna Camarato" is the wine to track down; a deep, dark, chocolatey aglianico, a powerful southern red that stands with Campania's best.

VILLA PILLO

Toscana; Gambassi Terme (FI)
An American-owned estate not far from San Gimignano, making varietal wines from international grapes. The style is fruit-driven, some would say Californian. The most noteworthy wine is the syrah, though there's also a merlot, a cabernet sauvignon, and a blend called "Vivaldia."

VILLA RUSSIZ

Friuli; Capriva del Friuli (GO)
DOC(G)s: Collio
This estate produces some of the best whites in Friuli, preferring a lean, firmly structured, assertively aromatic style. The best example of this may be the "Graf de la Tour" Sauvignon, as intense a sauvignon blanc as you're likely to taste. The

tocai, riesling, ribolla, malvasia istriana, pinot grigio, and pinot bianco are all similarly nervous and fine—high-acid whites that are great for food. On the red side, Menotti has gained fame for his "Graf de la Tour" merlot, which in good vintages (like '97) drinks like a fine Pomerols.

VILLA S. ANNA

Toscana; Montepulciano (SI)
DOC(G)s: Chianti Colli Senesi;
   Vino Nobile di Montepulciano
Good and affordable reds priced for everyday drinking.

VILLA SIMONE

Lazio; Monteporzio Catone (RM)
DOC(G)s: Frascati
Most Frascati is cheap and mass-produced, which works to the disadvantage of artisan producers such as Piero Costantini of Villa Simone. His fragrant and well-structured whites would probably be better known if they didn't say "Frascati." Check out the Frascati "Vigneto Filonardi" in particular.

VILLA SPARINA

Piemonte; Gavi (AL)
DOC(G)s: Gavi di Gavi; Dolcetto d'Acqui; Barbera del Monferrato
The Moccagatta family is trying to turn its beautiful property into Gavi's first real "destination" winery, something the zone has sorely lacked. They are in the process of constructing a restaurant/inn on the premises, while continuing to make Gavi in an ever-bolder style. For those who have an image of Gavi as flinty and floral, try Villa Sparina's Gavi di Gavi "Monterotondo," a wine that incorporates some late-harvested cortese to lend it an almost tropical richness. The Gavi di Gavi "La Villa" is cleaner and more

traditional, but still has more depth than most of the Gavi you're likely to come across. On the red side, the Moccagattas enlist consultant Beppe Caviola to make inky-black dolcettos and barberas with loads of sappy black fruit flavors. These wines are fat, fun, and over-the-top, not unlike the winery's front man, Stefano Moccagatta.

VILLANOVA

Friuli; Farra d'Isonzo (GO)
DOC(G)s: Collio; Friuli Isonzo
It isn't mentioned in the same breath as the Friuli "stars," but this estate is a sleeper, always consistent and often excellent. The whites from the "Monte Cucco" line (sauvignon, ribolla, chardonnay) are all bigger and bolder than the average Friulian varietal white, and the white blend "Menj" has great aromas and brisk acidity. Definitely in the top rank of Friulian wineries, and the prices are great.

VINICOLA SAVESE

Puglia; Manduria (TA)
DOC(G)s: Primitivo di Manduria
A primitivo specialist. The "Terrarossa" is plush and affordable.

VISTORTA

Friuli; Sacile (PN)
DOC(G)s: Friuli Grave
An out-of-the-way estate based near Pordenone, focused almost exclusively on the merlot grape. The Vistorta Friuli Grave merlot is considered a benchmark Friulian red, a warm and savory wine that won't evoke California but rather has its own spicy personality.

VITICCIO

Toscana; Greve in Chianti (FI)
DOC(G)s: Chianti Classico
Alessandro Landini's small estate above Greve is unabashedly modern,

liberally blending cabernet and merlot into its Chianti Classico wines to give them a roundness and fruitiness not often found in the Greve area, which is known more for smoky, angular wines. In addition to rich, barrique-aged Chianti, Landini offers "Prunaio," an evocative varietal sangiovese, and "Monile," a super-Tuscan blend.

VIVIANI
VENETO; NEGRAR (VR)
DOC(G)s: Valpolicella; Amarone della Valpolicella; Recioto della Valpolicella
Very good Valpolicellas and Amarones from high-altitude vineyards in Mazzano, toward the northern edge of Valpolicella. The wines are well balanced rather than over-the-top. The Valpolicella Classico Superiore merits special mention, and the Amarone has received its share of praise as well.

VOERZIO, GIANNI
PIEMONTE; LA MORRA (CN)
DOC(G)s: Barolo; Barbera d'Alba; Dolcetto d'Alba; Langhe; Roero Arneis
Gianni Voerzio and his brother, Roberto (see below), parted ways some years ago because Gianni's approach to Barolo is traditional whereas Roberto's is full-bore modern. The Gianni Voerzio wines have a delicacy and refinement that is traditionally associated with the vineyards of La Morra.

VOERZIO, ROBERTO
PIEMONTE; LA MORRA (CN)
DOC(G)s: Barolo; Barbera d'Alba; Dolcetto d'Alba; Langhe
This boutique estate has been at the center of the debate over style in the Barolo zone, with Roberto Voerzio championing the modernist cause, including aging in small French oak

barrels. His cru Barolos are nothing short of decadent; they receive huge scores in the wine press, and are tightly allocated and prohibitively expensive as a result. Without a doubt, though, his cru Barolos—the delicate "La Serra," the fruit-driven "Brunate," and the brooding "Cerequio"—are considered some of the best Barolos to be found. For those who can't afford such high-end pleasures, check out the excellent Dolcetto d'Alba "Priavino" or the Barbera d'Alba "Vigneto Pozzo dell'Annunziata."

VOLPE PASINI
FRIULI; TORREANO DI CIVIDALE (UD)
DOC(G)s: Colli Orientali del Friuli
A big and prolific winery with all the latest technology and a famous consultant, Riccardo Cotarella. The broad range of bottlings includes a line of varietal whites with the designation "Zuc di Volpe," all of which are plumped up by barrel fermentation and aging. The "Zuc di Volpe" Pinot Grigio is one wine that will surely change your thinking on what pinot grigio is supposed to be like.

WALCH, ELENA (CASTEL RINGBERG)
ALTO ADIGE; TERMENO/TRAMIN (BZ)
The bucolic village of Termeno/Tramin, where this striking winery is located, is thought to be the original home of gewürztraminer. Not surprisingly, rich and exotically aromatic gewürztraminer is a specialty at Elena Walch's winery, although she does just about everything well. Check out any of the varietal whites from the "Kastelaz" or "Castel Ringberg" lines: cool, rich pinot grigio, oily and powerful pinot bianco.... The list

goes on, with all of the whites showing great varietal character in a firm, fine package. These wines demonstrate how a wine can be deeply flavorful without being oaky or heavy. There's also a delicious gewürztraminer passito, if you can get your hands on it.

ZACCAGNINI
ABRUZZO; BOLOGNANO (PE)
DOC(G)s: Montepulciano d'Abruzzo; Trebbiano d'Abruzzo
Plummy, earthy, spicy—the Zaccagnini montepulcianos are rich and rustic reds (look for the wine with the "San Clemente" designation). There's also a chardonnay and, of course, Trebbiano d'Abruzzo, but the funky reds are where it's at.

ZARDETTO
VENETO; CONEGLIANO (TV)
DOC(G)s: Prosecco di Conegliano; Colli di Conegliano
A well-known name in prosecco, with fresh, fine sparklers at very reasonable prices.

ZEMMER, PETER
ALTO ADIGE; CORTINA/KURTINIG (BZ)
DOC(G)s: Alto Adige
A solid and attractively priced lineup of Alto Adige varietal, including standards such as pinot bianco and pinot grigio, lagrein, and pinot nero.

ZENATO
VENETO; PESCHIERA DEL GARDA (VR)
Another of Verona's large wine houses, Zenato has an excellent reputation for quality and consistency across a broad range of products. There's excellent white Lugana, as exemplified by the great-value "San Benedetto" bottling; tasty, tangy Valpolicella, as evidenced by the

benchmark "Ripassa"; and fat, flavorful Amarone, especially the "Sergio Zenato Riserva." These are serious wines made on a large scale, easy to find and always reliable.

ZENI, F.ILLI
VENETO; BARDOLINO (VR)
DOC(G)s: Bardolino; Bianco di Custoza; Valpolicella; Amarone della Valpolicella; Soave
An expansive Veneto wine firm hitting all the regional hot buttons—Valpolicella, Bardolino, Soave, etc. Everything is consistent and solidly made at a minimum, and the standouts include the smoky, berried "Vigne Alte" Valpolicella Classico and the Amarone. In general, look for wines with the "Vigne Alte" moniker for a step up from the norm. Bargain prices.

ZENI, ROBERTO
TRENTINO; SAN MICHELE ALL'ADIGE (TN)
DOC(G)s: Trentino
Not to be confused with the Zeni estate of nearby Veneto, this Trentino winery is notable for making excellent wines from just about all of Trentino's unusual native grapes. There's a crisp and aromatic nosiola; plump and peachy müller-thurgau; black currant–scented Teroldego Rotaliano; and a rosy, berried sweet wine from moscato rosa. This is an excellent winery with interesting wines—something a little different, for a change.

ZONIN
VENETO; GAMBELLARA (VI)
DOC(G)s: Gambellara; Valpolicella; Amarone della Valpolicella; Friuli Aquilea

Another of Veneto's huge wine firms, which tends to be much better known for its wine holdings in other regions than for its wines made close to home. Zonin is a many-tentacled beast, with holdings in Piedmont (Castello del Poggio), Tuscany (Castello d'Albola), Friuli (Ca' Bolani), Lombardy (Tenuta Il Bosco), and Sicily (Principe di Butera). Some of its best wines at the moment are being made at Ca' Bolani in Friuli's Aquilea DOC, headlined by a racy sauvignon and a chardonnay-tocai blend called "Opimio." In the Veneto, meanwhile, Zonin makes various DOC wines, most of them decent if not especially memorable. There's also a super-cheap line of varietal wines for supermarkets.

APPENDIX V

Resources

—⟨⟩⟨⟩—

KEY ITALIAN WINE IMPORTERS

Angelini Wines
565 Coleman Street
New London, CT 06320
www.angelini-wine.com

Artisan Wines Inc.
37 King Street
Norwalk, CT 06851

Banfi Vintners
1111 Cedar Swamp Road
Old Brookville, NY 11545

Bedford International
16 Hazel Street
Larchmont, NY 10538

Brown-Forman Corp.
P.O. Box 1080
Louisville, KY 40201
www.brown-forman.com

Casanove-Opici Wine Corp.
One Dupont South, Suite 101
Plainview, NY 11803

Robert Chadderdon Selections
30 Rockefeller Plaza, Suite 4538
New York, NY 10020

Clicquot Inc.
717 Fifth Avenue
New York, NY 10022
www.clicquot.com

Dalla Terra Inc.
21481 Eighth Street East, Suite 20
Sonoma, CA 95476
www.dallaterra.com

Domaine Select Wine Estates
38 West 39th Street, 3rd Floor
New York, NY 10018
www.domaineselect.com

Dufour & Co. Ltd.
P.O. Box 407588
Brookline, MA 02447
www.dufourwines.com

Empson USA Inc.
719 Prince Street
Alexandria, VA 22314
703-684-0900
www.empson.com

Elizabeth Imports
6500 Stapleton Drive, Unit A
Denver, CO 80216

Fruit of the Vine Inc.
161 West 54th Street
New York, NY 10019
www.fovusa.com

John Given Wines
972 Centre Street
Staatsburg, NY 12580

William Grant & Sons, Inc.
1271 Avenue of the Americas
New York, NY 10020

JK Imports
P.O. Box 946
Pasadena, CA 91102
www.wineday.com

Kobrand Corporation
134 East 40th Street
New York, NY 10016
www.kobrand.com

Lauber Imports
24 Columbia Road
Somerville, NJ 08876
www.lauberimports.com

Martin Scott Wines
1981 Marcus Avenue, Suite E117
Lake Success, NY 11042
www.martinscottwines.com

Omniwines LLC
29-16 120th Street
Linden Hill, NY 11354
www.omniwines.com

Palm Bay Imports
434 Underhill Boulevard
Syosset, NY 11791
www.palmbayimports.com

Panebianco LLC
1140 Broadway, Suite 504
New York, NY 10001

Paterno Imports
900 Armour Drive
Lake Bluff, IL 60044
www.paternoimports.com

Premiere Wine Merchants/Remy
  Amerique Inc.
1350 Avenue of the Americas
New York, NY 10019
www.remy-cointreau.com

Douglas Polaner Selections
19 North Moger Avenue
Mount Kisco, NY 10549
www.polanerselections.com

Schieffelin & Somerset Co.
Two Park Avenue
New York, NY 10016

Selected Estates of Europe Ltd.
620 Concord Avenue
Mamoroneck, NY 10543

Michael Skurnik Wines (Mark
  DeGrazia Selections)
575 Underhill Boulevard, Suite 216
Syosset, NY 11791
www.skurnikwines.com

Summa Vitis LLC
20580 Eighth Street East
Sonoma, CA 95476
www.summavitis.com

Tricana Imports
1120 Old Country Road, Suite 207
Plainview, NY 11803

Tri-Vin Imports
One Park Avenue
Mount Vernon, NY 10550

Vias Imports Ltd.
875 Sixth Avenue, Suite 2200
New York, NY 10001
www.viaswine.com

Vignaioli Selection
560 West 43rd Street, Suite 34E
New York, NY 10036
www.vignaioliamerica.com

Vin Divino
1811 West Bryn Mawr
Chicago, IL 60660
www.vindivino.com

Vinifera Imports
205 13th Avenue
Ronkonkoma, NY 11779

Frederick Wildman & Sons, Ltd.
307-311 East 53rd Street
New York, NY 10022
www.frederickwildman.com

Winebow (Leonardo LoCascio
  Selections)
22 Hollywood Avenue, Suite C
Ho-Ho-Kus, NJ
www.winebow.com

Wine Emporium
29 North 11th Street
Brooklyn, NY 11211
www.wineemporiumny.com

Wines We Are
104 Sackett Street
Brooklyn, NY 11231

KEY
ITALIAN
WINE
RETAILERS

New York & New Jersey:

Italian Wine Merchants
108 East 16th Street
New York, NY 10003
Tel: 212-473-2323
Fax: 212-473-1952
www.italianwinemerchant.com

Zachy's
16 East Parkway
Scarsdale, NY 10583
Tel: 800-723-0241 or 914-723-0241
www.zachys.com

Sherry-Lehmann
679 Madison Avenue
New York, NY
Tel: 212-838-7500
www.sherry-lehmann.com

Pop's Wine & Spirits
256 Long Beach Road
Island Park, NY 11558
Tel: 516-431-0025
www.popswine.com

Gary's Wine & Marketplace
100 Morristown Road
Bernardsville, NJ 07924
(Locations also in Madison and
  Livingston, NJ)
Tel: 908-766-6699
www.garyswine.com

Carlo Russo's Wine World
102 Linwood Plaza
Fort Lee, NJ 07024
Tel: 800-946-3276

Northeast:

Cirace's
173 North Street
Boston, MA 02109
Tel: 617-227-3193

Table & Vine
122 North King Street
Northampton, MA 01060
Tel: 800-474-BIGY
www.bigywines.com

Gasparro's
361 Atwells Avenue
Providence, RI 02903
Tel: 401-421-4170

Southeast:

Calvert Woodley
4339 Connecticut Avenue NW
Washington, DC
Tel: 202-966-4400

ABC Fine Wines & Spirits
Multiple locations in Florida
Tel: 305-944-6525

Midwest~West:

Sam's
1720 North Marcey Street
Chicago, IL 60614
Tel: 800-777-9138
www.samswine.com

Brown Derby
2023 South Glenstone
Springfield, MO 65804
Tel: 417-883-4066

California:

Wally's
2107 Westwood Boulevard
Los Angeles, CA 90025
Tel: 310/475-0606
www.wallywine.com

The Wine House
2311 Cotner Avenue
West Los Angeles, CA
Tel: 800-626-WINE
winehse@wavenet.com

K&L
766 Harrison Street
San Francisco, CA
Tel: 415-896-1734

The Wine Club
2110 East McFadden, Suite E
Santa Ana, CA
(locations all over CA)
Tel: 714-835-6485

The Jug Shop
1567 Pacific
San Francisco, CA
Tel: 415-685-2922
www.jugshop.com

ITALIAN GOURMET TRAVEL

Esperienze Italiane
Contact: Shelly Burgess Nicotra or
Tanya Bastianich Manuali
c/o Felidia Ristorante
243 East 58th Street
New York, NY 10022
Tel: 800-480-2426
Fax: 212-935-7687
www.lidiasitaly.com

ONLINE FOOD & WINE RESOURCES

www.lidiasitaly.com
Lidia Bastianich's extensive website
includes a huge downloadable recipe
database.

www.shawguides.com
An all-purpose travel website, covering not only Italy but a range of other countries. Comprehensive information on a wide range of travel packages, including all manner of gourmet travel.

www.peck.it
The website of the legendary Milanese *gastronomia* (specialty food shop). All manner of Italian specialties are available, and most can be shipped direct to the States.

www.it-food
Another excellent specialty foods website for direct ordering.

www.italianmade.com
The website of the Italian Trade Commission. It includes a wealth of information on Italian wines and foods, including technical information about DOC zones.

www.vinitalyonline.com
The website of the VinItaly wine fair, the largest Italian wine exposition in the world, which is held every spring in Verona. The site includes an extensive producer database.

ACKNOWLEDGMENTS

———— ❦ ————

Our sincere and heartfelt thanks go out to the following people, all of whom contributed greatly to this book:

To Lidia Bastianich and Mario Batali, for their inspired recipes and invaluable insights into Italian food, wine, and culture;

To everyone at Clarkson Potter, especially our editor, Chris Pavone, who put it all together, and Pam Krauss, who believed in the book to begin with;

To Douglas Riccardi, Lisa Eaton, Caitlin Daniels Israel, and Marysarah Quinn, for giving the book its look;

To Sergio Esposito, Wayne Young, Dan Latham, Carrie Pillar, and the rest of the staff at Italian Wine Merchants, NYC;

To the many people in our restaurant family who've helped along the way: Mark Coscia; the entire staff at Babbo; Richard Luftig, Fortunato Nicotra, and Shelly Burgess-Nicotra at Felidia; Dave Pasternack and Simon Dean at Esca;

To Tanya Bastianich Manuali, for the details and destinations she provided, and to Richard Lynch, just because;

To Jane Dystel and Miriam Goderich of Jane Dystel Literary Management;

To our friends in Italy for their hospitality and advice, most especially the crew in Friuli: Valter and Maria Grazia Scarbolo, Bruno Vesnaver, Mario Picozzi, Beppe Stradolini, Emilio Del Medico, Roberta DeSabata, Andrea Brunisso, and Bujar Kuqi. There's also the great Maurizio Castelli, who, perhaps more than anyone, has deepened our understanding of winemaking and viticulture. Sincere thanks also to Andrea Carelli, Daniele Cernilli, Francois Dufour, Giulio Colomba, Phil Langford, Giovanna Morganti, Fabrizio Pedrolli, Piero Rotini, Prof. Attilio Scienza, Eugenio Spinozzi, Tommaso Tedeschi and Family, Ursula Thurner, Cesare Turini, Mauro Versio and Family, Paolo Vita, and Faith Heller Willinger. And a special mention must also be made of the late Ignazio Miceli, whose great influence on Italian wine is still felt today;

To the incredible community of Italian winemakers, who have graciously given their time (and wine!) over the past many years. While there are ultimately far too many to list here, special mention should be given to these vintners and industry professionals for their invaluable assistance in the preparation of this book: Piero and Allegra Antinori, Giorgio Badin, Valter Bera, Pio Boffa, Emanuele Bonomi, Sandro Boscaini, Stefano Campatelli, Bruno and Roberta Ceretto, Constantino Charrère, Mario Consorte, Paolo DeMarchi, Marco DeBartoli, Paola DiMauro, Martini DeRosa, Enzo Ercolino, Elda Felluga and the entire Livio Felluga family, Angelo Gaja, Celestino Gaspari, Edi Kante, Ales Kristancic, Nicodemo Librandi, Chiara Lungarotti, Valentino Migliorini, Stefano Moccagatta, Gregory Perrucchi, Francesca Planeta, Stefano Porcinai, Francesco Ricasoli, Teresa Severini, Giancarlo Soverchia, Emanuela and Roberto Stucchi, Aldo Vacca, and Angela Velenosi;

To our friends and colleagues on the American side of the Italian wine trade, who offered all manner of assistance in putting this thing together: Paul Angelini, Michael Belardo, Rolando Ruiz Beramendi, Alessandra Bezzi, Robert Chadderdon, Paolo Domeneghetti, Barbara Edelman, Anthony Giglio, Beth Kane, Jane Kettlewell, Brian Larky, Lars Leicht, Augusto Marchini, Deena Miskiel, Livio Panebianco, Mary Anne Sullivan, Jodi Stern, Margaret Stern, Kathleen Talbert, Tara Q. Thomas, and Lara Zahaba;

To Josh Greene of *Wine & Spirits*, for giving us both a place to write about wine;

To the entire staff of the Italian Trade Commission in New York City for the invaluable resources and assistance they've provided;

To Alessandro Puccinelli, for his evocative photos; Jeffrey Lindenmuth, for the map design; and Marcia Kiesel, for testing all of the recipes;

To our parents and grandparents, for making it possible to do whatever we want to do;

And last but certainly not least, to our wives, Deanna Kristen Bastianich and Josie Peltz, for everything.

Bibliography

Anderson, Burton. *Vino: The Wines and Winemakers of Italy.* Boston: Little Brown & Company, 1980.
———. *The Wine Atlas of Italy and Traveler's Guide to the Vineyards.* London: Mitchell Beazley, 1990.

Bastianich, Lidia. *La Cucina di Lidia.* New York: Doubleday, 1990.
———. *Lidia's Italian Table.* New York: William Morrow, 1998.

Batali, Mario. *Mario Batali's Simple Italian Food.* New York: Clarkson Potter, 1998.

Belfrage, Nicolas. *Barolo to Valpolicella: The Wines of Northern Italy.* London: Faber & Faber, 1999.

Blanchard, Paul. *Blue Guide Southern Italy.* London/New York: Black/Norton, 1996.

Cernilli, Danielle, and Marco Sabellico. *The New Italy: A Complete Guide to Contemporary Italian Wine.* London: Mitchell Beazley, 2000.

Codice Denominazioni di Origine dei Vini 2000 (supplement to *Il Corriere Vinicolo*). Milan: Unione Italiana Vini, 2000.

Fini, Marco. *Sassicaia: The Original Super Tuscan.* Florence: CITAI, 2000.

Fiori, Giacomo, et. al. *Formaggi Italiani.* Turin, Italy: EOS Editrice, 1999.

Gambero Rosso Vini d'Italia 1999. Rome: Gambero Rosso Editore, 1999.

Gambero Rosso Vini d'Italia 2000. Rome: Gambero Rosso Editore, 2000.

Gambero Rosso Vini d'Italia 2001. Rome: Gambero Rosso Editore, 2001.

Garner, Michael, and Paul Merritt. *Barolo, Tar & Roses: A Study of the Wines of Alba.* London: Random Century Group, 1990.

Ginsborg, Paul. *A History of Contemporary Italy: Society and Politics 1943–1988.* London: Penguin Books, 1990.

Guy, Patricia. *Amarone.* Sommacampagna, Italy: Morganti Editore, 1999.

Italy 2000: A Supplement to Decanter Magazine. London: *Decanter* magazine, 2000.

Johnson, Hugh, and James Halliday. *The Vintner's Art: How Great Wines Are Made.* New York: Simon & Schuster, 1992.

Lynch, David. "Lucky 7." *Wine & Spirits* magazine, October 2000.
———. "Some Like it Hot." *Wine & Spirits* magazine, August 2000.

Macadam, Alta. *Blue Guide Northern Italy.* London/New York: Black/Norton, 1997.

Maresca, Tom. "Tuscany's Wild West." *Wine & Spirits* magazine, October 2000.

Mariani, John. *The Dictionary of Italian Food and Drink.* New York: Broadway Books, 1998.

Michelin Italy. Paris: Michelin et Cie, 1998.

Pellucci, Emanuele. *Vino Nobile di Montepulciano.* Fiesole, Italy: Vipsul Edizione, 1998.

Plotkin, Fred. *Italy for the Gourmet Traveler.* New York: Little, Brown, 1996.

Robinson, Jancis, ed. *The Oxford Companion to Wine,* Second Edition. New York: Oxford University Press, 1999.
———. *Vines, Grapes, and Wines.* London: Mitchell Beazley, 1986.

Root, Waverly. *The Food of Italy.* New York: Atheneum, 1971.

Wasserman, Sheldon, and Pauline Wasserman. *Italy's Noble Red Wines.* Piscataway, N.J.: New Century, 1985.

Willinger, Faith Heller. *Eating in Italy.* New York: Hearst, 1989.

Wine Routes in Sardinia. Cagliari, Italy: Consorzio Vini D.O.C. di Sardegna, 1999.

INDEX